ESSAYS IN THE HISTORY OF CANADIAN LAW
VOLUME VIII
IN HONOUR OF R.C.B. RISK

Edited by G. Blaine Baker and Jim Phillips

PATRONS OF THE SOCIETY

Aird & Berlis

Bennett Jones

Blake, Cassels & Graydon

Davies, Ward & Beck

Fasken Campbell Godfrey

Fraser Milner

The Law Foundation of Ontario

McCarthy Tétrault

Osler, Hoskin & Harcourt

Tory Tory DesLauriers & Binnington

Weir & Foulds

BENEFACTORS OF THE SOCIETY

Bastedo Stewart Smith

Kathleen, John, and Stephen Risk

The Society also thanks The Law Society of Upper Canada
for its continuing support.

Essays
in the History of
Canadian Law

VOLUME VIII

IN HONOUR OF R.C.B. RISK

Edited by

G. BLAINE BAKER AND JIM PHILLIPS

Published for The Osgoode Society for Canadian Legal History by
University of Toronto Press
Toronto   Buffalo   London

ISBN 0-8020-4729-7

∞

Printed on acid-free paper

Canadian Cataloguing in Publication Data

Main entry under title:

Essays in the history of Canadian law

Includes bibliographical references.
Partial contents: v. 8. In honour of R.C.B. Risk / edited by G. Blaine Baker
and Jim Phillips.
Vols. 5–8 published for the Osgoode Society for Canadian Legal
History by
University of Toronto Press.
ISBN 0-8020-4729-7 (v. 8)

1. Law – Canada – History and criticism.   I. Flaherty, David H.
II. Osgoode Society.   III. Osgoode Society for Canadian Legal History.

KE394.Z85E87 1981   349.71   C81-095131-2
KF345.E87 1981

University of Toronto Press acknowledges the financial assistance to its
publishing program of the Canada Council for the Arts and the
Ontario Arts Council.

University of Toronto Press acknowledges the financial support for its
publishing activities of the Government of Canada through the
Book Publishing Industry Development Program (BPIDP).

Canadä

Contents

Foreword

THE OSGOODE SOCIETY
FOR CANADIAN LEGAL HISTORY

The purpose of The Osgoode Society for Canadian Legal History is to encourage research and writing in the history of Canadian law. The Society, which was incorporated in 1979 and is registered as a charity, was founded at the initiative of the Honourable R. Roy McMurtry, a former attorney general for Ontario, now chief justice of Ontario, and officials of the Law Society of Upper Canada. Its efforts to stimulate the study of legal history in Canada include a research support program, a graduate student research assistance program, and work in the fields of oral history and legal archives. The Society publishes volumes of interest to the Society's members that contribute to legal-historical scholarship in Canada, including studies of the courts, the judiciary, and the legal profession; biographies; collections of documents; studies in criminology and penology; accounts of significant trials; and work in the social and economic history of the law.

Current directors of The Osgoode Society for Canadian Legal History are Jane Banfield, Tom Bastedo, Brian Bucknall, Archie Campbell, J. Douglas Ewart, Martin Friedland, Charles Harnick, John Honsberger, Kenneth Jarvis, Allen Linden, Virginia MacLean, Wendy Matheson, Colin McKinnon, Roy McMurtry, Brendan O'Brien, Peter Oliver, Paul Reinhardt, Joel Richler, James Spence, Harvey Strosberg, and Richard Tinsley.

The annual report and information about membership may be obtained by writing to The Osgoode Society for Canadian Legal History, Osgoode Hall, 130 Queen Street West, Toronto, Ontario, M5H 2N6.

Collections of essays are usually organized around a particular theme. This book, which represents Canadian legal historians' tribute to Professor

Dick Risk, is, at first glance, something of an exception to that practice. The essays here cover subjects that range from the form of the criminal trial in the eighteenth century to debates over the meaning of property in the nineteenth to lawyer and poet Tom MacInnes's views on the law of Aboriginal title in the early twentieth century. In an important sense, however, there is a theme here, that of recognition of the scholarship and teaching of a pioneer in the field of Canadian legal history, a man who for many years has been the subject's best-known voice and who was, for a time, its only serious practitioner.

After graduating from the University of Toronto Law School (1959), receiving his call to the bar (1961), and attending Harvard Law School for graduate work (1962), Risk joined the Faculty of Law at Toronto in 1962. His first few years as an academic saw him writing principally about real estate law, and in later years he became one of the country's leading administrative law scholars. But it has always been legal history that most engaged and excited him. Risk taught his first course in the area in 1964, and has been teaching at least one a year ever since. His first major publication in the field was in 1973 and he has been publishing regularly ever since; Blaine Baker's review of Risk's work in this volume charts the changes in interest and emphasis that have occurred during that time. On retirement he is continuing his work on the history of constitutional thought in Canada.

We are fortunate that Professors Baker and Phillips have together conceived and carried through this volume in honour of their colleague. They are both very familiar with Risk's teaching and scholarship. Blaine Baker has been a long-time colleague and collaborator, and Jim Phillips describes himself as the University of Toronto Law School's 'other' legal historian. It is not surprising, therefore, that they should have jointly proposed a *festschrift* for Dick Risk, and the Society thanks them both for that idea and for all the work they have done in putting this volume together. It is equally unsurprising that they were able to generate an enthusiastic response from the authors of the essays who make up the volume. That enthusiasm has resulted in these original essays by well-known legal scholars (and one practising lawyer), some of whom were students of Risk. The essays are representative of work on the cutting edge of Canadian legal historical scholarship. Collectively they make an excellent tribute to Professor Risk, one which the Society is delighted to be able to publish.

R. Roy McMurtry
President

Peter N. Oliver
Editor-in-Chief

Acknowledgments

As editors our greatest debt is, of course, to the contributors to this volume. They responded with enthusiasm to our original requests to contribute, produced drafts in a timely fashion, and put up with our suggestions with exemplary patience. It has been a pleasure to work with a group of such committed and conscientious people; the Canadian legal history community may not be large, but it is as collegial as it is possible to be. A number of the papers published here were presented at a conference on Canadian Legal History held at the University of Toronto Law School in May 1998, and we acknowledge the support for that conference given by the University of Toronto Law School, the SSHRC, and The Osgoode Society for Canadian Legal History. Three people deserve particular thanks for making this a better volume than it would otherwise have been. Professors David Bell of the Faculty of Law, University of New Brunswick, and John Weaver of the Department of History, McMaster University, reviewed all of the papers and provided timely and incisive advice. Allyson May's excellent copy-editing was appreciated by all of the authors and we thank her on our own and their behalf. We are, of course, greatly indebted to those who have provided financial assistance to help these essays see the light of day: the Risk family and, if we may be excused the nomenclature, the 'Risk' law firm of Fasken Campbell Godfrey (see page xiii).

Finally, we thank Professor Peter Oliver, not just as one of the contributors but as editor-in-chief of The Osgoode Society. In that role he has consistently and enthusiastically assisted this project and provided much useful criticism and practical support. Publishing with The Osgoode Society means that one also works with Marilyn MacFarlane, whose now legendary efficiency and good humour we have benefited from in equal measure.

G. Blaine Baker
Jim Phillips

Special Acknowledgment

We at Fasken Campbell Godfrey are proud to be a joint sponsor of this tribute to Dick Risk, a pioneer of Canadian legal history. One important reason is that the Risk family has played a significant role in the history of our own firm. In 1980, the Risk Cavan Gardner firm merged its practice into Fasken & Calvin, one of the two firms that merged in 1989 to form Fasken Campbell Godfrey. John Risk, Dick's father, became counsel to the merged firm and Stephen, one of Dick's brothers, became (and still remains) one of our partners. Both John and Stephen have joined with us in this sponsorship.

However, we have other links to Dick Risk. Many of our lawyers studied under him at the University of Toronto Faculty of Law. Our firm historian (and director of our Computer & Technology Law Group), Ian Kyer, first studied Canadian legal history with Risk. In this tribute volume, Ian looks at one chapter of our firm's 136-year history, our incorporation of Gooderham & Worts, in light of Dick's pioneering efforts to explain the how and why of nineteenth-century incorporations.

This volume demonstrates the vigour and health of the discipline of Canadian legal history which Dick Risk inspired and nurtured. As part of the Canadian legal community, we owe him a huge debt and we are happy to help repay some small part of it through this sponsorship.

The Partners of Fasken Campbell Godfrey

Contributors

CONSTANCE BACKHOUSE is professor of law at the University of Western Ontario. She is the author of *Petticoats and Prejudice: Women and Law in Nineteenth-Century Canada* (1991), which was awarded the Willard Hurst Prize in Legal History by the Law and Society Association. Her study of race discrimination in Canadian legal history is forthcoming as *Colour-Coded: A Legal History of Racism in Canada, 1900–1950*.

G. BLAINE BAKER is associate dean and professor of law at McGill University. He has written extensively about the history of Canadian legal thought and Canada's legal professions. He was awarded the Surrency Prize by the American Society for Legal History in 1986.

JAMIE BENIDICKSON teaches at the Faculty of Law, University of Ottawa. His previous publications include *The Temagami Experience: Recreation, Resources, and Aboriginal Rights in the Northern Ontario Wilderness* (1989), *Idleness, Water, and a Canoe: Reflections on Paddling for Pleasure* (1997), and *Environmental Law* (1997).

PAUL CRAVEN is associate professor of social science and a member of the graduate programs in history and sociology, York University. His publications include books and articles on Canadian labour, legal and industrial history, and on historical methods. He is principal investigator on the Master and Servant Project at York University, a comparative study of employment law in the British empire and commonwealth from the mid-sixteenth century to the 1930s.

GEORGINA FELDBERG is associate professor in the Division of Social Sciences and director of the Centre for Health Studies, York University. An historian of science and medicine, she writes on matters pertaining to the use of evidence in formulating health policy.

HAMAR FOSTER is professor and associate dean in the Faculty of Law at the University of Victoria. He has written extensively on Canadian legal history, Aboriginal law, and comparative Canadian and U.S. criminal law. He was editor (with John McLaren) of *Essays in the History of Canadian Law, Volume Six – British Columbia and the Yukon* (1996).

PHILIP GIRARD is professor of law at Dalhousie Law School and editor of the *Dalhousie Law Journal*. He was awarded the Surrency Prize by the American Society for Legal History in 1993 and his doctoral dissertation, 'Patriot Jurist: Beamish Murdoch of Halifax, 1800–1876,' was awarded the John Buller Prize by the Canadian Historical Association, 1999. His research interests lie in comparative law and legal history, with particular reference to Atlantic Canada.

ROBERT W. GORDON is Johnston Professor of Legal History at Yale Law School.

BERNARD J. HIBBITTS is professor and associate dean for Communications and Information Technology in the School of Law, University of Pittsburgh. He has published various articles on law and the history of communication, and is the director of Jurist, an on-line legal education network.

R.W. KOSTAL is associate professor, Faculty of Law, and adjunct professor of History, University of Western Ontario. He is the author of the Ferguson Prize–winning monograph, *Law and English Railway Capitalism, 1825–1875* (1995), and of other articles on nineteenth-century Anglo-American legal history.

C. IAN KYER is a partner with Fasken Campbell Godfrey of Toronto and has a PhD in history. He is co-author, with J. Bickenbach, of *The Fiercest Debate: Cecil A. Wright, the Benchers, and Legal Education in Ontario, 1923–1957* (1987). He is currently engaged in writing the history of Fasken Campbell Godfrey. One part of that history appeared as 'The Transformation of an Establishment Firm: From Beatty Blackstock to Faskens, 1902–1915,' in C. Wilton, ed., *Inside the Law: Canadian Law Firms in Historical Perspective* (1996).

MARGARET E. MCCALLUM is professor at the Faculty of Law, University of New Brunswick, where, among other things, she teaches property. She has published in the areas of married women's property rights, the regulation of employment relations, the welfare state, and Aboriginal land claims.

JOHN MCLAREN is Lansdowne Professor of Law at the University of Victoria. He has published extensively in many areas of Canadian legal history and was the co-editor (with Hamar Foster) of *Essays in the History of Canadian Law, Volume Six – British Columbia and the Yukon* (1996).

PETER OLIVER is professor of history at York University and editor-in-chief of The Osgoode Society. He is the author of *'Terror to Evil-Doers': Prisons and Punishments in Nineteenth-Century Ontario* (1998).

JIM PHILLIPS is professor of law at the University of Toronto, where he is also cross-appointed to the Department of History and Centre of Criminology. He was co-editor (with Philip Girard) of *Essays in the History of Canadian Law, Volume Three – Nova Scotia* (1990) and (with Susan Lewthwaite and Tina Loo) of *Essays in the History of Canadian Law, Volume Five – Crime and Criminal Justice* (1994)

DAVID SUGARMAN is professor of law and head of the Department of Law at Lancaster University. His recent publications include 'Bourgeois Collectivism, Professional Power and the Boundaries of the State: The Private and Public Life of the Law Society, 1825–1914' in the *International Journal of the Legal Profession* (1996); *Law in History: Histories of Law and Society* (editor, 2 vols., 1996); *Property Law, Personhood and Citizenship: A Comparative Social and Cultural History of Property Law and Property Rights* (co-editor with H. Siegrist, 1999). His *Lawyers and Vampires: Cultural Histories of the Legal Professions* (co-editor with Wesley Pue) will be published in 1999.

W. WESLEY PUE is Nemetz Professor of Legal History in the Faculty of Law, University of British Columbia. His major research interests are in the areas of the history of the legal profession and legal education and interdisciplinary legal studies.

ROBERT VIPOND is associate professor and chair of the Department of Political Science, University of Toronto. He has written widely on constitutional issues and for some years taught, with Dick Risk, a course on Canadian constitutional history at the University of Toronto Faculty of Law.

Essays in the History of Canadian Law
Volume VIII

In Honour of R.C.B. Risk

1

Richard C.B. Risk: A Tribute

ROBERT W. GORDON AND DAVID SUGARMAN

I

Dick Risk is arguably the most respected academic authority on Canadian legal history. To appreciate his impact on the field we need only consider what the world of Canadian legal history looked like before Dick Risk transformed it. In Canada, as in England, legal history was a Cinderella subject. Many students, law teachers, and legal practitioners found it dull, technical, and largely irrelevant to the 'real world' and it was not typically taught within law schools in any thoroughgoing fashion. Insofar as it manifested itself within the curriculum, legal history was normally confined within 'Introduction to Law'–type courses. When it did appear as a discrete element, it was usually as lawyers' legal history, largely preoccupied with the 'origins' of legal doctrine, the earliest historical foundations of the common law, and what Pollock termed the 'rugged exclusiveness' that bequeathed the rule of law to half the world, a system at least as influential as the law of the Roman Empire.[1]

The confines of legal history were reinforced by the uneasy relationship between the disciplines of law and history. One example will have to suffice. Sir Geoffrey Elton, the leading historian of Tudor England and its government, insisted in an essay published in the early 1970s: 'I am not a legal historian.'[2] For Elton and other historians, legal history was not 'a branch of real history. Thus his devastating critiques of its deities, such as Holdsworth and Radzinowicz, and his gibes at the flagship of Anglo-

Canadian legal scholarship, the *Law Quarterly Review*: 'an austere journal in which incomprehensible problems so regularly receive incomprehensible solutions.'[3] Elton exhibited an unease with legal questions that was not uncommon among historians in this period. There was a tendency among historians to deride rather than try to understand the thought processes of the law, and the ideas and culture of the legal profession, that are essential to any understanding of the history of law and society.[4] Not surprisingly, perhaps, some legal historians reciprocated Elton's contempt.[5]

Despite these occasional tribal disputes, the disciplines shared much in common, including a mindset that inhibited a serious understanding of law in history: namely, a tendency toward a teleological interpretation of the constitution and, more generally, of English and Canadian history. This emphasized the continuities, coherence, evolution, and expansion of democratic life and the political sphere as part of the triumph of modernity. Historians wrote histories of England and Canada that celebrated parliamentary government, the common law, ordered progress toward democracy, and the avoidance of revolution. They took English and Canadian exceptionalism for granted: it existed, it was good, and it was the historian's task to explain and applaud it. Canadians were assumed to be much like the English, a loyal and valiant people who understood the ties of history, culture, and family and whose behaviour was contrasted with the general lack of good manners that the British associate with people so unfortunate as to be born east of the cliffs of Dover.[6] This, in turn, often sustained a highly introverted, predemocratic conception of nationhood. Under this optic, 'the common law mind,' as Pocock called it,[7] enshrined what have often been portrayed as the quintessentially English qualities: a stubborn individualism that is heroic to the point of eccentricity and a hatred of authoritarianism and bureaucracy, a philosophy that can be summed up in the slogan 'small is beautiful, old is good, English is best.'

Of course there were many notable exceptions to what used to be the dominant tradition, for the idea of lawyers as humanistic scholars has a long and distinguished lineage. But in retrospect what is striking is the relative marginalization until so recently of the broader tradition within legal education and legal history epitomized by Dick Risk, and no more so than when Dick was studying law and when he first began to teach it and publish. If you will pardon the analogy with popular music, Dick Risk began to sing the blues at a time when the legal scholarship of his day resembled the unremittingly white popular music of the early 1950s, such as Guy Mitchell's jolly songs, 'Feet Up, Pat Him on the BOPO' and 'She Wears Red Feathers and a Hooley Hooley Skirt.' In truth, much of the legal scholarship of the 1950s was of the Guy Mitchell variety. It was that incredibly bland period, a sort of white hole, which made not only rock and roll but the very significant changes in the scale, content, and style of Anglo-Canadian legal education and research that have cumulatively contributed to a new perception of law as an academic subject seem in retrospect almost inevitable.

Risk's initial forays into legal history were rooted in first-hand and lengthy experience of legal practice (law was 'in the blood,' in that Dick came from a family of lawyers) and his deep knowledge of and respect for legal doctrine. As a practising lawyer and consultant he experienced the importance of legal *mentalité* and the way in which lawyers compartmentalized their minds. His scholarly interests were further aroused by a sojourn at the Wisconsin Law School and by his encounter with America's premier legal historian of the period, Willard Hurst. There is a sense of revelation about Risk's celebrated essays, published between 1973 to 1977, on law and economy in nineteenth-century Ontario.[8] Though written in the shadow of Hurst, they clearly recognize that Ontario was no Wisconsin. (In any case, nobody but Hurst could write that way!) Appearing in a veritable desert, the Risk quartet of articles on nineteenth-century law demonstrated the importance and potential of a new history of Canadian law and society. This was coupled to a Maitland-like exhortation: that an exhilarating but almost daunting labour was required to reconstitute Canadian legal history.

The theme of a history as yet unwritten is also evident in Dick's 1973 prospectus for a comprehensive program in writing and research in legal history,[9] which announced the birth of a new field of study and provided a map of issues and concerns that might engage the interests of a wider community of scholars. The prospectus was a call to arms, a solicitation of support. Despite its perspicacity, this clarion call appears to have fallen largely on deaf ears. At any rate, for the remainder of the 1970s Risk seems to have retired from the fray. Of course, he had opened up a veritable Pandora's box, one likely to alarm and petrify even the converted. Risk had outgrown the Hurstian paradigm but had found neither a comparable inspiration nor, it seems, a sympathetic and supportive audience for his work.

It was during the early to mid-1980s that Risk started anew. Gradually, alongside the sea change that was occurring in higher education and the human sciences, Risk reformulated the enterprise, inspired, in part, by the new history of ideas and political thought that was beginning to blossom in Canada, as in the work of Carl Berger and A.B. McKillop.[10] Crucially, a platform for his research emerged in the shape of the week-long summer seminars in legal history for Canadian university teachers held in the mid-1980s at the University of Western Ontario, in what once had been a railway magnate's house, under the benign stewardship of Professor David Flaherty. Flaherty was an impresario of Diaghilev-like significance and insight, determinedly committed to dragging Canadian legal history into the second half of the twentieth century. Flaherty and the seminar provided the much-needed oxygen (and deadlines!) that Risk needed. They took the ideas of Canada's premier legal historian seriously. Indeed, many of its participants were there principally to meet with and learn from Risk. Here was a new, young generation of Canadian students, scholars, and practitioners who seemingly shared his passion for law in Canadian history. He had a reputation to live up to, new lectures to write, and there were other lecturers with whom to compete. Risk was a recidivist, returning again and again to participate in the seminars. Along with the good food and wine, the wonderful camaraderie, and outings to Gilbert and Sullivan, Risk appeared over the years with various lecturers including Morton Horwitz, Ted White, Dirk Hartog, John Beattie, Connie Backhouse, and of course, David Flaherty. It was as if the renaissance in Anglo–North American legal history was actually taking place in the seminar halls of Western Ontario. Certainly, it is difficult to underestimate what this experience, along with the increasing support that he received from the Faculty of Law of the University of Toronto, did for Risk's subsequent work and his sense of self-worth. But if we are to truly understand this renaissance, a central role must be afforded to Gail Morrison, whom Dick met and married in this period. Thus it was that in the mid- and late 1980s, a new R.C.B. Risk[11] set off in search of the singular consciousness of the Canadian legal tradition.

II

We first got to know Dick Risk as his colleagues on the staff of 'Camp Flaherty.' Many scholars who have since become central figures in Canadian legal history (and contributors to this volume) passed through the Western seminar and with us listened to Risk's lectures. He was then working through the preliminary versions of his portrait gallery of Canadian legal thinkers. No one who has experienced the fascinating aesthetic and gymnastic spectacle of the Risk expository style can ever forget it. It calls to mind a Chinese calligrapher poised above his rice paper with raised pen, hesitating while he chooses the exact word, then suddenly dive-bombing onto the paper like a heron going after fish. Or to change the metaphor again, Risk in lecturing mode is like a careful hiker crossing a stream of white water, picking his way from rock to rock, pausing every so often to make sure of his route. Dick has thought the whole thing out in advance, of course, but once he's launched you can see him thinking it all through again from the beginning, not sure he was right the first time, not wanting to commit the thought to speech until he's convinced that he's right this time, and he is very exacting in the demands he makes on himself to get it right. The Western seminar was a high and happy time in our intellectual development, owing in large part to Dick's companionship. He enlisted us all in the cause of getting it right, and we struck sparks off one another.

III

In his essay for this volume Blaine Baker has provided a singularly lucid and expert review of the body of Dick Risk's pioneering work on Canadian legal history. Our assignment is more modest, to look at Risk's work from the point of view of complete outsiders to Canadian historiography, whose chief interest in the history of Canadian law lies in how it parallels and varies from British and American developments. Risk is of course an insider, but his interest is similarly comparative in purpose, in trying to describe what is distinctive in the Canadian legal experience. His long and extremely productive career as a legal historian has been largely given to elaborating with ever greater complexity and precision the details of several distinctively Canadian forms of legal consciousness.

Risk's early work, the path-breaking quartet of articles on nineteenth-century law, was, as Blaine Baker's essay points out, written under the influence of the great Wisconsin legal historian, Willard Hurst. As Hurst had done before him for the United States, Risk attempted to bring a whole field into existence by sheer force of will. And like Hurst, when no one responded to the call, he created the field by doing the work himself. (Ultimately, of course, Risk did inspire followers, as this volume amply demonstrates.) The main themes of these first articles were the Hurstian ones of the functional roles of the law in the construction of supporting frameworks for economic enterprise, especially through the law of contract and corporations. Even in this early work, however, Risk showed signs of deviation from or restlessness with the Hurstian model, revealed in his attention to the inner worlds of some of his principal characters, such as Sir John Beverley Robinson and Chancellor William Hume Blake, a

prefiguring of the later Risk's more focused attention on legal consciousness or ideology. Hurst was not uninterested in ideology: for him, the
distinctive contours of American law were produced not by functional
requirements alone, but through the collision of those necessities with a
particular liberal–middle-class–Protestant sensibility, at once utopian and
grasping, individualistic and cooperative, driven by a Promethean hunger
to conquer land and natural resources, divide them up into fee simple
tracts, and speedily convert them into cash. This *mentalité*, as it informed
legal policy, produced at its best the 'release of energy' from quasi-feudal
and mercantilistic restraints and at its worst a 'bastard pragmatism' driven
by short-term calculation and indifferent to the damage to victims and the
environment done by unrestrained business enterprise. Hurst appreciated
the causal importance of *mentalités* but had scant interest in them as an
object of study. In his work the liberal-Protestant mindset looms vastly
over the law but has little specificity and no further history after its
migration to the New World.

A large part of Risk's project, by contrast, has been to describe a distinctive Canadian legal consciousness, to fill in its details and spell out some of
its varieties, and to give it a history. The project falls loosely into three
parts: a history of judicial mindsets, a portrait gallery of legal scholars
(sunken treasures of Canadian legal culture whom Risk has rescued from
obscurity), and a history of constitutional thought. The task of elaborating
a legal consciousness from the clues left behind by these lawyers has
evidently not been an easy one and the reader often senses Risk's frustration with the job of cracking these hard old chestnuts, a breed of men who,
even by Canadian standards, were reticent and taciturn in the extreme, as
well as his relief at coming across a Robinson or Blake or John Willis – or
even a Dalton McCarthy – who gave him something more to work with.

On Canadian judicial mentalities and methods, perhaps the most revealing of Risk's essays and the most interesting to comparative legal
historians is his portrait of Chief Justice Sir William Meredith in his dual
characters as judge and architect of Ontario's workers' compensation
laws. Meredith is a fascinating case study because from Risk's account he
was anything but a colourless conservative who accepted the legal plati-
tudes of his time as conventional wisdom. We know from Risk's essay that
Meredith was extremely dissatisfied with the law of workplace accidents
and the barriers that it placed in the way of compensation; we also know
that although he had a difficult time accepting the idea of shifting compensation off the fault principle and onto compensating the fact of injury, he
eventually did so. So we are dealing with a powerful and not inflexible

judicial mindset, and that is what makes Risk's report so striking. Here was a man who felt tied down by his role as a judge yet drove in extra pegs to tie himself down further, who generally avoided the opportunities the system gave him for discretion and, when he occasionally took them, did so in the driest way imaginable in order to call the least possible attention to his sporadic acts of creativity. The essay is especially illuminating for its contrast of Meredith with Chancellor Blake and an earlier, much freer style of judging, closer to what Karl Llewellyn famously called the 'Grand Style.' For Meredith judging was a search for authority, and 'the search consisted of describing the possible authorities as though he were taking them out of the cupboard in the order in which he found them and holding them up to the light to see if they might fit ... He did not believe that the contents of the cupboard of common law were organized in any rational way or were internally consistent.'[12]

Risk's account of Meredith helps to show what a Protean and elastic term 'legal formalism' can be. Meredith's 'formalism,' plainly, is not in the least like Windscheid's or Langdell's – it is certainly not a concept of law as a unified, comprehensive field of principles with gapless applications. The notion of the judicial role as devoted to the hunt for the right single precedent leaves no space to develop any kind of legal 'science,' empirical, conceptual, or historical. Indeed, Risk implies that Meredith may have put himself to so little trouble to rationalize his opinions and work them up into a coherent jurisprudence or body of doctrinal writing not because he had so much respect for the authority of the common law, but because he had so little. The 'weight' of authority, for Meredith, lay in the numbers: the quantity not the quality of that authority. He frequently mentioned how much he disliked the result he was compelled to by the cases. In construing statutes, Risk tells us, he was happy to have them modify the common law. Yet even when he had to supply the law, to fill gaps and resolve conflicts, he pretended the law was supplied by someone else or by some vague, offstage presence as 'the reason of the thing.'

It is admirable in some ways to see such a lack of ego in a judge, such diffidence about bidding for literary immortality but, as Risk points out, his minimalist approach to judging caused him to shirk some important judicial functions, such as helping to clarify and arrange cases for lawyers and future judges.[13] In statutory interpretation a different and somewhat more adventurous Meredith emerges – in substance if not in style. One would expect the common law Meredith to be a strict textualist or 'plain-meaning' – bound interpreter, but he is actually more sophisticated – a judge with 'an unexpressed understanding of an institutional relationship that required from him respect a and willingness to elaborate and implement the *purpose* of legislation,'[14] to reason from the history and purpose of the statutes and possible consequences of decisions.

Risk's portrait of Meredith and of other judges who exemplified the Canadian style of late-nineteenth-century formalism contrasts sharply in some respects with the American experience, although it parallels that experience in other ways. The main difference is, of course, in the degree of judicial deference – to English case law, to the authority of precedent rather than 'principle' or the demands of 'changed circumstances,' and to legislative supremacy. In the United States, nationalist reaction to colonial domination had propelled the courts into declaring some degree of independence from the English common law, to assume the role of creatively adapting it to the distinct requirements of a dynamic commercial republic. By the 1850s, not only American courts but American political culture at large were developing a generalized suspicion of much legislative activity as captured by 'special interests' and requiring new constitutional controls, enforced by judges, on such legislation. In the United States (as occasionally in other legal cultures as well) when judges speak the language of 'deference' to something outside themselves – the settled law; clear rules; the plain positive commands of statutes, legal instruments, or constitutional texts – the critical observer immediately suspects a shell game is afoot, that a bid for more judicial authority is thinly veiled in the passive display of modesty and restraint. When Canadian judges said they were deferring, however, they seemed to have meant it: if their objectivity was a mask, it was a mask for timidity or arbitrariness rather than a grab for power.

Frustrated (as it seems) by his judicial subjects' reluctance to articulate a theory of their role, much less a self-critical or introspective theory, Risk turned in the late 1980s to the study of academic lawyers. He discovered a remarkable collection of writers who had hitherto been neglected or ignored – notably John Skirving Ewart, A.H.F. Lefroy, John Willis, and, most recently, W.P.M. Kennedy, among others. To some extent he found in them what he had missed in the judges, a willingness to theorize particular fields, to discuss issues of general jurisprudence, and to criticize formulaic wisdom about the nature of law and the judicial role. Risk's essay on Ewart, for example, rescues from obscurity the treatise on *Waiver Distributed*, an impressive feat of turn-of-the-century synthetic jurisprudence, which gathered up fragments of doctrine scattered widely across common law categories and constructed a simplifying scheme that subsumed them all.[15] Ewart also made some illuminating contributions to general jurisprudence in his distinction of two meanings of 'principle': one consisted of generalizations about doctrines, the other involved 'ethical propositions that were not doctrines but ideals, sources of doctrine, or standards for its application,' and which came from sources outside the decisional law.[16]

Risk's most thorough as well as his most affectionate appreciation is of his predecessor as the dean of Canadian administrative law studies, John Willis.[17] Willis was the leading Canadian legal realist, a persistent and ruthless critic of formalist views of the judicial role, especially in statutory interpretation and review of administrative action: he insisted on the inevitably discretionary and political character of judicial decision making and urged that legal doctrine be based on the actual 'facts' of administration and adopt a 'functional approach.' As Risk points out, however, Willis did not go on to specify very clearly what such an approach would entail. In all his appreciative tributes, Risk has a keen eye for the points where his heroes run out of ideas, where analysis is replaced by unsupported assertion or silence. Risk is a patriot, but a critical one. His attitude toward the legal thinkers he has sympathetically reconstructed is like that of a proud and pushy but anxious parent: he takes care to show off every talent and accomplishment of his offspring, but is unsparing in pointing out where they have come up short. It turns out that the Canadian, like the American, legal realists and their English counterparts (such as Laski and Robson) were much better at critique than at constructive theory, and although they talked about how important it was to take a 'functional' and 'sociological' approach to law based on 'the facts of social life as they are,' they actually undertook very little research into such 'facts.'[18] The irony of Risk's story of the aims and limits of Canadian legal realism is that Risk himself has come nearer than any of the major figures he celebrates to fulfilling its programmatic ambitions, especially in his historical work.

Risk's explorations of the development of Canadian legal consciousness also included constitutional thought. This work, especially the essay co-authored with Robert Vipond on 'Rights Talk,'[19] is explicitly comparative: it seeks to describe and explain the emergence of a rights discourse strikingly different from that of the United States. In Canada, rights against the central state were likely to be argued as inhering in the structure of federalism rather than in the natural liberty of individuals and they were primarily to be protected by legislatures rather than courts. Arguments about federalism were thus arguments over which legislatures should have the job of protecting rights and setting limits to their exercise in the public interest. The authors illustrate the point through a series of fascinating case studies, which show Canadian lawyers and politicians constantly reframing disputes about rights into disputes about federalism. They (very tentatively) try to explain these variations in the rights discourses of Canada and the United States by reference to some basic ideological axioms of Canadian constitutional politics – the old fear of executive power left over from memories of Stuart tyranny in Britain,[20] the principle of legislative supremacy, and the relative absence of the threat of popular majorities using their power to redistribute wealth.

'Rights Talk' turns out to be one of those seminal works the suggestiveness of which lies as much in its power to provoke and to open up new questions as in its conclusions. For virtually every feature of constitutional thought that Risk and Vipond identify as characteristically Canadian is characteristically American as well. Americans also have a legacy of suspicion of executive power and a habit of converting arguments over basic issues of rights into issues of federalism (the entire controversy over slavery, for example). Perhaps most surprising of all, given American fondness for indulging in *laissez-faire* political rhetoric, their legal culture is strongly disposed to confirm the authority of legislatures exercising the general police power to promote 'public rights' and the interests of the community in order and collective welfare, at the expense of individual rights where necessary.[21] Similarly, in today's Britain, positioned within a European federation, committed to the devolution of power to a Scottish parliament and a Welsh assembly, to a written bill of rights and other manifestations of a North American 'rights revolution,' the characteristically Canadian is increasingly characteristically British.[22]

Indeed, such founders of Canadian legal culture as Robinson and Blake, as Risk portrays them, resemble nothing so much as their counterparts among leading English and American whigs, who also promoted a hierarchical society bound together by a commonality of interest in progressive improvement underpinned by organic moral and social order, all under the benevolent supervision of leading men of property and the professions. Such strong family resemblances as these do of course have the effect of highlighting the – undeniably real and major – residual differences in the constitutional cultures of Canada, England, and the United States, including the Americans' much greater reliance on judges as policemen of the boundaries of legislative and administrative action and their fiercer and more frequent deployment of libertarian rhetoric. But perhaps they also suggest that the explanations of such differences are more likely to be found in contingent events and political formations – such as the public outcry over waste and corruption in public railway financing in the United States in the 1850s, which led to pressure for more constitutional controls over legislatures and, by extension, an enhanced judicial supervisory role – than in long-term ideological differences between the two societies.

IV

There is perhaps no more fitting tribute to Risk than to say that he has probably taught and inspired more people about Canadian legal history than any other individual. It must be unique for a single person to exercise as much influence on the development of a nation's legal history as he has. The fact that Canadian legal history is flourishing is in no small part due to his teaching, mentoring, and research.

But what now of the history of the Canadian 'legal mind'? In a world of globalization and electronic communication, in which legal advice and information is available from the Web and where professional boundaries are increasingly blurred, the claims of the law to a distinctive mindset appear problematic.[23] Moreover, the enterprise of writing history is itself by no means certain in a world determined to stress the importance of 'useful knowledge.' And then there are those who argue for 'the end of history': historical arguments are unavailable to the present since they are irredeemably context-bound and parochial. The Enlightenment project that sought to create universal justifications for democracy, human rights, toleration, and the rule of law is, according to this view, irretrievably doomed.[24] At this juncture, early retirement seems imminent for all legal historians.

Yet in continuing to analyse and discuss the past, historians perform a vital function. In Gabriel García Márquez's *One Hundred Years of Solitude*,[25] the author described an illness that descends upon the isolated township of Macondo. The main symptom of this illness is loss of memory, which so debilitates the sufferers that they cannot remember the name of individual objects until the silversmith hits on the method of writing the names of each object on it. It then becomes apparent that the use and proper treatment of the object must also be written out, since this too would otherwise be fogotten. Thus, writes García Márquez, the inhabitants of Macondo went on living in a reality that was slipping away, momentarily captured by words, but which would escape irredeemably when they forgot the values of the written letters. In an attempt to arrest this process the patriarch of the town builds a memory machine, a kind of revolving encyclopedia constructed so that the operator could review every morning all the knowledge acquired during his life. This is a powerful image. The possibility of words changing their meaning is ever present; indeed, it is part of the process of political and legal persuasion and argument. The only yardstick we have is what we can draw on from our historical culture. Historians of political and legal thought such as Risk try to keep the civic equivalent of José Arcadio's memory machine in good repair. But we must also use it so that we may never forget the names of the institutions we have created or lose the means to think critically about them.

NOTES

1 F. Pollock, 'English Opportunities in Historical and Comparative Jurisprudence,' in Pollock, *Oxford Lectures and Other Discourses* (London: Macmillan 1890), 47–8.
2 G.R. Elton, 'English Law in the Sixteenth Century: Reform in an Age of Change,' in *Studies in Tudor and Stuart Politics and Government: Volume 3 – Papers and Reviews 1973–1981* (Cambridge: Cambridge University Press 1982), 274.
3 *Times Literary Supplement*, 20 September 1974, 991.
4 See generally C. Holmes, 'G.R. Elton as a Legal Historian,' *Transactions of the Royal Historical Society*, 6th series, 7 (1997), 267–80.
5 For example, S.F.C. Milsom has asserted that the historian and the legal historian are very different, and that the methods of the historian 'do not suit the legal historian.' See, generally, S.F.C. Milsom, 'Pollock and Maitland: A Lawyer's Retrospect,' in J. Hudson, ed., *The History of English Law: Centenary Essays on Pollock and Maitland* (Oxford: Oxford University Press 1996), 243–60.
6 These images of Canada were mobilized by the British press during the Canada-Spanish Fish War of 1995: see D. Herman and D. Cooper, 'Anarchic Armadas, Brussels Bureaucrats, and the Valiant Maple Leaf,' *Legal Studies* 17 (1997), 415–33.
7 See J.G.A. Pocock, *The Ancient Constitution and the Feudal Law: Reissue with Retrospect* (Cambridge: Cambridge University Press 1987). Pocock's scholarship (along with that of Quentin Skinner) played a major role in creating a new history of political thought in the 1970s and 1980s and was a signal influence on Dick Risk's excavation of the Canadian legal mind. See also J.G.A. Pocock, *Politics, Language, and Time: Essays on Political Thought and History* (London: Methuen 1972) and *Virtue, Commerce, and History: Essays on Political Thought and History, Chiefly in the Eighteenth Century* (Cambridge University Press, 1985 and J. Tulley, ed., *Meaning and Context: Quentin Skinner and His Critics* (Cambridge: Polity Press 1988).

8 'The Nineteenth-Century Foundations of the Business Corporation in Ontario,' *University of Toronto Law Journal* 23 (1973), 270–306; 'The Golden Age: The Law About the Market in Nineteenth-Century Ontario,' *University of Toronto Law Journal* 26 (1976), 307–46; 'The Last Golden Age: Property and the Allocation of Losses in Ontario in the Nineteenth Century,' *University of Toronto Law Journal* 27 (1977), 199–239; 'The Law and the Economy in Mid-Nineteenth Century Ontario: A Perspective,' *University of Toronto Law Journal* 27 (1977), 403–38.

9 'A Prospectus for Canadian Legal History,' *Dalhousie Law Journal* 1 (1973), 227–45.

10 See especially C. Berger, *The Sense of Power: Studies in the Idea of Canadian Imperialism, 1867–1914* (Toronto: University of Toronto Press 1970) and A.B. McKillop, *A Disciplined Intelligence: Critical Inquiry and Canadian Thought in the Victorian Era* (Montreal and Kingston: McGill-Queen's University Press 1979).

11 The metamorphosis from 'R.C.B.' to 'Richard' Risk is of much more recent vintage.

12 'Sir William Meredith, C.J.O.: The Search for Authority,' *Dalhousie Law Journal* 7 (1983), 719.

13 Ibid., 723.

14 Ibid., 727 (emphasis added).

15 'John Skirving Ewart: The Legal Thought,' *University of Toronto Law Journal* 37 (1987), 335–57.

16 Ibid., 338.

17 'John Willis – A Tribute,' *Dalhousie Law Journal* 9 (1984), 521–54.

18 See Risk's account of the reformist program of realism and its shortfalls in performance in 'Volume 1 of the Journal: A Tribute and a Belated Review,' *University of Toronto Law Journal* 37 (1987), 193–211.

19 'Rights Talk in Canada in the Late Nineteenth Century: The Good Sense and Right Feeling of the People,' *Law and History Review* 14 (1996), 1–32.

20 Interestingly, Risk and Vipond note that nineteenth-century Canadians perceived the main vice of American government to be not judicial, but executive, dominance. Ibid., 16.

21 For recent work stressing the breadth and legitimacy of public authority in nineteenth- century America, see especially William J. Novak, *The People's Welfare: Law and Regulation in Nineteenth-Century America* (Chapel Hill: University of North Carolina Press 1996) and Harry N. Scheiber, 'Public Rights and the Rule of Law in American Legal History,' *California Law Review* 72 (1984), 217–51.

22 See M. Loughlin, *Legality and Locality: The Role of Law in Central-Local Government Relations* (Oxford: Clarendon Press 1996); I. Loveland, ed., *A Special*

Relationship: American Influences in Public Law in the UK (Oxford: Clarendon Press 1995); and I. Loveland, *Constitutional Law: A Critical Introduction* (London: Butterworths 1996); R. Rawlings, 'The New Model Wales,' *Journal of Law and Society* 25 (1998), 461–509, and the Human Rights Act 1998.

23 See R.E. Susskind, *The Future of Law: Facing the Challenges of Information Technology* (Oxford: University Press 1996); W.T. Murphy, *The Oldest Social Science? Configurations of Law and Modernity* (Oxford: Oxford University Press 1997).

24 See, for example, R. Rorty, *Philosophy and the Mirror of Nature* (Princeton: Princeton University Press 1979).

25 (London: Jonathan Cape 1970).

2

R.C.B. Risk's Canadian Legal History

G. BLAINE BAKER

The Osgoode Society's first academic conference was held in Toronto in the spring of 1980. Convened by David Flaherty, the purposes of that gathering were to take stock of early scholarship in Canadian legal history and to canvass support for the society's projected anthology of essays.[1] At Flaherty's urging, I prepared a presentation for that meeting, 'R.C.B. Risk's Canadian Legal History.' It is surely a mark of Risk's enduring prominence in his field, rather than a badge of my slow learning, that almost twenty years later I am writing another paper on the same subject. I am humbler and more patient than I might then have been, and those changes are positive signs of Risk's personal influence. But the principal difference between then and now is that in 1980 five articles totalling about 150 pages were available for assessment, whereas by the late 1990s the Risk bibliography had grown to more than twenty major articles in the field of Canadian legal history that run, collectively, to some 700 pages.[2] That bibliography also includes eight or ten other substantial papers on contemporary issues that contain important socio-legal material.

Risk's scholarship has attracted periodic published and unpublished accolades. Flaherty, for example, referred in 1981 to Risk's four studies of the role of law in the mid-nineteenth-century Ontarian economy as 'seminal articles.'[3] He also confessed to being 'struck by Risk's sweeping perspective and the perceptiveness of his judgments on a range of legal-economic issues.'[4] John McLaren more recently singled out Risk's prospectus for Canadian legal history as a 'path-breaking and inspirational article.'[5] With regard to Risk's work on the post-Confederation period, Robert Vipond and Georgina Feldberg have drawn attention to that scholarship's 'creative contribution to our understanding of late-nineteenth-century Canadian legal thought' and highlighted 'examples of the way in which Risk's scholarship has enriched the Canadian intellectual community.' Vipond's commentary has special poignancy since he, like five other contributors to this volume, co-taught numerous courses with Risk over the years.[6] Hamar Foster's historiographical summary was simply that 'Risk deserves a goodly share of the credit ... [for transforming] Canadian legal history from professional pastime into academic discipline.'[7]

Private correspondence about Risk's central position in modern Canadian legal historiography is to the same effect. Commenting on Risk's study of the origins of workers' compensation in Ontario, the University of Toronto Press reviewer of manuscripts for the second volume of *Essays in the History of Canadian Law* said the quality of that essay was 'commensurate with Risk's status as the granddaddy of Canadian legal historians.'[8] In the same vein Osgoode Society editor-in-chief Peter Oliver has written of Risk's 'many outstanding contributions as a pioneer of Canadian legal history.'[9] And in Jim Phillips' words, '[Risk] is the best-known historian of Canadian law. He has been not only a leader in the field for almost thirty years, but for a part of that time he was practically the only academic working in that area. He therefore pioneered academic legal history in this country, taught or inspired many others to take an interest in it, and continues to be its most prominent practitioner.'[10]

It bears disclosure, as further acknowledgement of Risk's stature, that all eighteen contributors to this volume participated in the project enthusiastically in spite of tight deadlines. The topical and geographic diversity of their papers, greater than that of any earlier Osgoode Society or other anthology in Canadian legal history, is similarly indicative of Risk's profile. Publication of this collection of essays was also subsidized financially by several private supporters, who were keen to assist celebration of a distinguished academic career that began at the University of Toronto in 1962 and has not strayed from that institution. Indeed, Risk's presence gave that school its institutional role in the recent renaissance of Canadian legal history.

Finally, on the point of Risk's mentoring of younger legal historians, Constance Backhouse has observed that he 'has played a leading and instrumental role in the development of this field of law, and so many of us owe such a great deal of our interest in legal history, and our success in the area, to his support and inspiration.'[11] Margaret McCallum, one of four

of Risk's former students who contributed to this volume, has characterized him as 'a thoughtful, demanding and supportive supervisor' in doctoral studies.[12] Reflecting on his experience in Risk's classroom in light of
his erstwhile instructor's impending retirement, Jamie Benidickson said
that he 'would have thought that students might assert a constitutionally
protected interest in keeping teachers of Risk's calibre in office.'[13] To those
express testimonials, mention must be added of numerous student essays
written for Risk that promptly found their way into print.[14]

   With context provided by these representative scholarly, professional,
and pedagogical assessments, how should one proceed with an initial,
collective appraisal of Risk's published work? Prototypes for such a study
can be found elsewhere.[15] But Risk himself would probably counsel sensitivity to the distinctiveness of each person's scholarship rather than the
expedient borrowing of models suitable to other bodies of writing. Risk's
'A Prospectus for Canadian Legal History' of a quarter-century ago is an
eligible, local organizer for this review essay.[16] Indeed, Flaherty commended
that overview in his own foundational 'Writing Canadian Legal History:
An Introduction' as 'an initial agenda for comprehensive approaches to
Canadian legal history.'[17] Risk's prospectus emphasized the influences of
social values on the law, the impact of legal ideas on the human mind and
social events, and the internal or institutional structures of agencies of the
law such as legislatures, administrative tribunals, courts, and the legal
professions. Building on those complementary standpoints for the study
of legal history, he suggested eight provisional themes for ordering historical inquiry in law: the contribution of the law to the expression of
Canadian identity, metropolitan influences on local institutions, the relationship of law to the facilitation or regulation of economic growth, the
implication of the law in community or distributive initiatives, the impact
of law on individuals, the role of the law in structuring the physical
environment, law and social control, and the relationship of agencies of
government to official law.

   Summarizing Risk's agenda for Canadian legal history helps to reveal
the implausibility of its three grand standpoints and eight subsidiary
themes as organizing categories for his scholarship. While it is possible to
say that one or another of Risk's essays began from a particular standpoint
or addressed a specific theme, none of the twenty-some papers in issue
was exclusive. Each of them ultimately examined a topic from multiple
historical perspectives and contributed to readers' understanding of the
impact of Canadian law on a range of public and private dimensions of
national life. At the least, Risk encouraged his readers to eschew narrow

inquiries and unicausal or instrumental explanations of change over time. Struggle, tension, and reconciliation were recurrent themes in his scholarship, perhaps because those themes repeatedly overlapped with one other, and his subjects were rarely approached from a single interpretive standpoint. Risk's historical world was, more often than not, a complicated place that he approached with nuanced, cautious curiosity. Attempts to use his prospectus for Canadian legal history as an organizing device in historiographic appraisals of his work therefore proved futile.

One can, however, separate Risk's historical scholarship into five loosely ordered categories that represent shifts in his interests, their periodization, and refinements of his methodology. Those clusters of writing had to do, in chronological succession, with private law and the economy, rule-of-law thought and the administrative state, assumptions about judging and legal knowledge, conceptual models for constitutional divisions of power, and the discourse of public and private rights. That scholarship was set in the period between 1840 and 1940, but Risk was most interested in events of the decades straddling the turn of the twentieth century. He also realigned his teaching of contemporary law several times to coincide with shifting historical enthusiasms. Property-related subjects of the 1970s gave way to administrative law and legislative processes in the early 1980s, to be replaced by constitutional law in the late 1980s and 1990s.

Risk's major production of the seventies was an interrelated set of articles on law and economic growth in Canada West during the 'Union period' of 1841 to 1867. Those essays dealt, respectively, with the institutional foundations and practical uses of the corporate form, facilitative (especially contract) law in the marketplace, the role of real property law in the allocation of risks associated with economic development, and the interaction of legislative and judicial law from a unified perspective of legal process and material change.[18] But there was also an earlier paper, sometimes overlooked, that essayed systems for the registration of interests in land and contained a rare discussion of the local origins of nineteenth-century records of titles to land.[19] In any case it was entirely appropriate, in terms of the recognition of an author and the profile of an essay, that the fourth or overview article from that law and the economy series was reproduced by The Osgoode Society in its maiden volume.[20] That appears to have been the only occasion on which the society published a previously published work.

Risk's papers on mid-nineteenth-century Ontario were researched and partly written on sabbatic leave from the University of Toronto's Faculty of Law at the University of Wisconsin Law School. The attraction of that site for him was the late James Willard Hurst, *doyen* of modern Anglo-American legal historians and an important personal mentor to many members of the second and third generations of U.S. scholars active in that field. Risk shared Hurst's conception of socio-legal history writ large, but the intellectual boundaries of his early historical scholarship were not entirely derivative. He deviated from the 'Wisconsin school's' major premise or principal research finding that nineteenth-century American legal ideas, institutions, and agents were committed to facilitating a release of creative human energy.[21] Despite superficial demographic and geographic similarities between Wisconsin and Ontario, Risk's parastatal and business corporations, his special contracts, his property torts, and especially his Ontarian legislative initiatives were tinted with regulatory and distributive shades of meaning. The sovereignty of a local parliament and legal discourse about legislative jurisdiction would later become dominant themes in Risk's constitutional history.[22]

Modestly self-described as a 'technical product,' 'The Nineteenth-Century Foundations of the Business Corporation in Ontario' was a survey of the provincial legislature's provision of various vehicles for incorporation and general patterns in the use of those devices by public utilities and businesses in Canada West. It built on earlier, pan-Canadian work by Eugene Labrie, Earl Palmer, and Bray Hammond, and has since been used as a model for overviews in other British North American jurisdictions, as well as the basis for at least two case studies of nineteenth-century Canadian businesses.[23] The key point is that Risk established, for Canada West, descriptive contours of mid-nineteenth-century company law and practice that are now taken for granted. Written mostly from provincial statute books and Toronto newspapers, that essay showed that general patterns in the use of corporate forms moved from public utilities like transportation enterprises to financial services like banks to manufacturing businesses. Local corporate law thus evolved, simply put, from an aspect of state-building administrative law to a facilitative law of the marketplace. Institutionally, Risk documented a shift from the predominant use of special acts of incorporation, to incorporation under sector-specific general laws in the 1850s, to incorporation by bureaucratic registration in the 1860s. Delegations of state power to artificial juridical people and increasingly streamlined processes for achieving state concessions raised, said Risk, perplexing questions about the relationship of public to private power and the legitimacy of the corporate form. He also provided readers with detailed, charted tallies of incorporations during the relevant period, still the best such description available for any Canadian place or time. Those charts resulted from the deployment of considerable empirical skill, one hallmark of a good historian.

'The Golden Age: The Law about the Market in Nineteenth-Century Ontario' was, as Risk asserted, 'a companion' to the business corporations article. In much the same way that he conceived of incorporation as a facilitative act that empowered enterprises to make unofficial but state-sanctioned law for themselves in the marketplace, Risk characterized economic activity in Canada West as a function of private initiative, 'expressed in three basic forms: agreements between individuals for an exchange, for example, contracts; agreements among individuals to combine to achieve some common purposes, for example, partnerships and corporations; and decisions made by individuals about the use of natural resources, for example, the use of a fee simple or a license to cut timber.'[24] He then focused on contracts, negotiable instruments, and financing vehicles, working from judicial engagement with those devices. That article was therefore Ontario's version of well-known overseas examinations of emerging modern contract law by authors like Morton Horwitz, Patrick Atiyah, and Brian Simpson.[25] It was most akin to traditional, doctrinal history, but frequently transcended that category to resemble mainstream business history with descriptions of local shipping, grading, or financing practices drawn from judicial decisions. It also reads, in some of its passages, like good cultural history with references to English liberalism, the Canadian Loyalist myth, and the Victorian idea of progress.

It is revealing that 'Law about the Market' stands more or less alone twenty years after it was written. Several complementary studies of Ontario's nineteenth-century commercial law and practice have appeared, but they have tended to focus on the work of particular judges and to do so with the entire field of corporate-commercial activity in view.[26] The bulk of what is now known about specific bodies of British North American private law like contracts, especially from a perspective internal to law, was rediscovered and publicized by Risk.

'Property and the Allocation of Losses' was another densely written discussion of legal doctrine and material change that traversed the boundaries between economic, intellectual, and legal history. It was about individuals' power to make legally effective decisions regarding the use of natural resources, and asked how the mid-nineteenth-century Canadian state allocated liability for losses caused by economic activity. When a worm's-eye view of doctrine and decisional law was required to advance that inquiry, Risk was able to move confidently among lawyers' artifacts like strict settlements, prescription, and trespass with the sure-footedness of a modern property lawyer.[27] One key feature of that essay was that its author synthesized linguistic and conceptual disparity into broad categories like the law of agreements (restrictive covenants and licences to use), the law of shared interests (waste and riparian rights), and the law of accidents (nuisance and fault). He also distinguished usefully between the political and demographic challenges of settling a colony that were largely taken up by legislative and executive branches of government and ownership or allocation issues that tended to be judicial prerogatives. Risk punctuated those discussions with tentative generalizations to the effect that 'values, economic structure, and law and legal institutions have usually been consistent' but avoided assigning a causal role in that symmetry to social needs or raw legal ideas.[28] Although he did not use it, and probably would not then have recognized the term, Risk was effectively assigning a 'relatively autonomous role' to law in processes of social change.[29]

The doctrinal sweep of 'Property and the Allocation of Losses' was, however, its most striking feature. Indeed it is noteworthy that, in a country with so much land, comparatively little history of local land law has been written. The best available scholarship has tended to focus on pin-point episodes of law reform,[30] specific political or economic challenges to prevailing conceptions of ownership,[31] or the implication of particular doctrines in the allocation of risks associated with development.[32] In an important sense, often expressly acknowledged, Risk's overview of Ontario's judicially administered property relations made those subsequent, topically modest inquiries possible.

'The Law and the Economy in Mid-Nineteenth-Century Ontario: A Perspective' differed from its sibling essays in that it was a synthetic and integrated account organized around institutions, influences, and personalities.[33] Its subject matter was how diverse agencies of the law conceived of their respective roles in state formation, economic management, and social control and the influence of various legal and nonjuridical factors on the exercise of those roles. The article concluded with two short biographical examinations of those themes, through the persons of Chief Justice John Beverley Robinson and Chancellor William Hume Blake, who were described as 'possible heroes.' But, overall, Risk asserted that Ontario's mid-nineteenth-century courts were

deferential to apparent authority, unwilling to initiate change, and inclined to consider issues in terms of precedents and doctrine ... All these elements combined to make our courts – and our entire legal community – a legal colony [of England], forbidden and eventually unwilling to consider its own destiny openly. The courts in Ontario during [the union] period did not participate in change and innovation, even vicariously as spectators and beneficiaries on the sidelines ... Distinctively Canadian needs and wants that seemed to affect law and require differences [from the English experience] were usually appropriately the subject of legislation.[34]

He went on to link that apparent preference for law-making by parliamentary means to the general triumph of legislative utilitarianism that has been well documented by Canadian political historians of the Union period.[35]

On the more profound question of socio-legal interface, Risk concluded that 'the expression of values through law tended to reinforce them and to contribute to the shaping of values in Ontario. From this perspective, law was a massive means of communication, not simply of legal doctrine, but of ideas.'[36] Risk was effectively emphasizing the role of the law as constitutive of professional and sometimes popular consciousness.[37]

Written before standard, local economic histories had appeared, 'Law and the Economy' made a respectable contribution to the general history of Ontario, primarily by piquing historians' awareness of the potential contribution of legal history to a critical understanding of the mid-nineteenth century. It also became a magnet for competing scholarship that challenged some of Risk's assessments of influences on Canada West's judiciary, aspects of his conclusions about divisions of labour among agencies of the law, and his emphasis on judicial formalism.[38] Indeed, it spawned a cottage industry devoted to biographic depictions of his two potential heroes, especially Robinson.[39] But that public, intellectual engagement did not begin in the immediate wake of Risk's publications of the 1970s. Reception and appreciation of his work took more than half a decade, during which time Risk produced no historical scholarship.[40]

David Flaherty's managerial extroversions into the study of Canadian legal history in the early 1980s may have been a significant factor in Risk's belated recognition as an academic pioneer and his intellectual rejuvenation as an historian. An important colonial American legal historian in his own right, Flaherty can be characterized as the 'mid-wife' of contemporary interest in Canadian legal history.[41] Through early editorial work for The Osgoode Society, operation of an annual summer program at the University of Western Ontario for legal historians (at which Risk invariably taught), informal mentoring of newcomers to the field, and through steady supervision of graduate students like Mary Stokes, Curtis Cole, and Jonathan Swainger, Flaherty attended actively at the birth of Canadian legal history.[42] And he did so with appropriate light on Risk and his scholarship as national markers.

Risk's renewed historical resolve led to the production of a second cluster of topically and chronologically coherent articles in the mid-1980s, which were linked by their author's interest in the post-Confederation regulatory state and its accountability for administrative allocations.[43] Perhaps most significantly, those essays reflected explicit curiosity on the part of their writer about legal ideas and lawyers' culture, concerns that were more latent than patent in his law and the economy scholarship. That refinement of Risk's research orientation was most obvious in his study of the work and thought of Chief Justice William Ralph Meredith which, although not primarily about the administrative state, is eligible to be grouped as a fifth essay in the regulatory cluster because it grew out of his writing on Meredith as a commissioner for the socialization of Ontario's workers' compensation laws.[44] But that shift of attention was also apparent in Risk's evocative tribute to the late John Willis where, for the first time, the historian's main subject was legal scholarship and an academic lawyer's attitudes towards state law.[45] Those two articles therefore anticipated what would become a major preoccupation in Risk's later work on changing scholarly conceptions of public and private rights.[46]

Almost twice the length of Risk's other historical essays, 'This Nuisance of Litigation: The Origins of Workers' Compensation in Ontario' was set in the decades straddling the turn of the twentieth century and assessed Ontario's removal of disputes about workplace injuries from the purview of courts applying tort principles to a novel administrative agency created to administer no-fault compensation from a consolidated revenue fund stocked by employers.[47] More abstractly, Risk's emphasis in that article was 'ideas about law, especially about the content of law and how to think about it, and about legal institutions.'[48] Its well-known international forerunner was Lawrence Friedman and Jack Ladinsky's pan-American survey of similar transitions from *respondeat superior* to the fellow-servant rule to socialized accident compensation, but Risk's study had the added attractions of an interesting law reformer in the person of Meredith and careful attention to the lobbying efforts of employers' organizations like the Canadian Manufacturers' Association and employees' trade journals such as the *Industrial Banner*.[49]

The role of the common law triumvirate of fellow-servant liability, voluntary assumption of risk, and contributory negligence in shifting responsibility for the costs of industrial accidents as between employers and employees during the middle decades of the nineteenth century has been well documented for a broad cross-section of North Atlantic jurisdictions. Risk's brief description of changing paradigms in Ontarian tort law closely followed those accounts of international patterns, except that local doctrinal reforms lagged in time behind them. The important part of the story, which Risk described comprehensively for Wentworth County from 1888 to 1914, was a comparative explosion of workplace litigation in the decades surrounding 1900 and the sharply increasing frequency with which trial courts compromised prevailing negligence principles to find in favour of injured plaintiffs or their next-of-kin. Exhaustive case counting, comparisons among damage awards, and plumbing the depths of judicial decisions led Risk to speculate that diminutions of faith in individual responsibility, equality of bargaining power, and mechanized progress opened the door to judicial sympathy toward the suffering of employees on a case-by-case basis. Unable to predict the frequency or monetary quantum of departures from *laissez-faire* rules that insulated them from tort liability for industrial accidents, employers forged an unholy alliance with their workers in favour of administratively managed, no-fault compensation. The empirical component of 'Nuisance of Litigation' that supported those conclusions was labour intensive and arguably Risk's best demonstration of that methodological talent.

Perhaps most insightful was Risk's conclusion that turn-of-the-twentieth-century lawyers like Commissioner Meredith accommodated parliamentary intrusions into established private law 'by making two compartments [in their minds]. One contained law, which included principle, the common law, and its interstitial legislation. The other included politics, expediency, legislation and the change to [socialized workers'] compensation ... [The gulf between law and politics] probably became deeper and more apparent at this time, perhaps because the massive changes were usually done by legislation and made the lawyers' need for the gulf more pressing.'[50] Risk thus assigned nascent appreciation of the distinction between corrective and distributive justice to his turn-of-the-century Ontarian law reformer, and even attributed to him a recognition that corrective is subservient to distributive justice insofar as there is nothing necessary about the jurisprudential category into which a particular issue is put.

'Nuisance of Litigation' provoked theoretical reflection on its themes by Eric Tucker, detailed studies of the legal resolution of two Ontarian accidents, and preliminary assessments of shifting workplace liability in other Canadian jurisdictions.[51] Its observations about the structural tension in turn-of-the-century lawyers' minds have, as will be seen, been even more provocative of academic engagement.[52]

The second entry in Risk's administrative process scholarship, 'Lawyers, Courts, and the Rise of the Regulatory State,' surveyed tentatively the politics of late-nineteenth- and twentieth-century state regulation of economic activity, especially the constitutional legitimacy of regulatory power.[53] Its subject matter was, admittedly, vast, but that essay was written when companion historical scholarship on the political fact of Canadian regulatory activity was sparse and work on legal accountability for those initiatives was virtually non-existent.[54] Risk was nonetheless able to summarize attitudes toward the administrative state held by lawyers, judges, and the fledgling legal academy revealed by law journal publications, judicial decisions, records of professional organizations and monographic writing, classifying them according to identifiable stages in the emergence of the Canadian welfare state. His periodizations of those developments were the late-nineteenth century, 1900–30, the 1930s, and 1950–80. Similar temporal divisions in academic lawyers' attitudes toward federal division of powers litigation would later be deployed in Risk's constitutional history.

For late-nineteenth-century Canadian lawyers, said Risk, law was the common law, and statutes were narrowly understood as interstitial modifications of decisional law. Those lawyers conceded the state's implication through law in economic change, but its involvement was thought to be facilitative and subsidiary. That understanding was destabilized by a first wave of public, regulatory activity in the period c. 1900 to 1920, when standards for agricultural products, minimum wage laws, municipal land use regulations, occupational licensing requirements, and price and service specifications for transportation enterprises and utilities were imposed. Most important, that era witnessed the creation of the Board of Railway Commissioners, a flagship for other independent Canadian agencies. Risk observed that early-twentieth-century lawyers' 'dominant response to the advent of regulation seems to have been to insulate their thinking from its implications.'[55] He also noted that local courts' embrace of the concept of legislative supremacy tempered their use of rules related to *ultra vires* activity and natural justice to call early agencies to judicial account.

By contrast, rank-and-file lawyers of the 1930s left a prominent paper trail for Risk that was comprised of nothing less than irrational ranting about the emergent administrative state. But their academic colleagues supported those Canadian 'New Deal' developments as vehemently as judges and practising lawyers deplored them. That intriguing ideological schism, said Risk, continued to characterize competing views of tax-based funding, institutional design, distributive goals, and accountability for administrative action during much of the succeeding half-century.

'Rise of the Regulatory State' sowed seeds that germinated in Bernard Hibbitts's work on the early-twentieth-century Boards of Railway Commissioners and Commerce, as well as Kent Roach's examination of the administrative law scholarship of Marshall Gordon, and it nourished Jamie Benidickson's studies of legislative antitrust measures and the Board of Railway Commissioners.[56] It also led Risk into a more or less comprehensive study of the administrative-process scholarship of John Willis, arguably Canada's most influential and apparently its favourite legal academic.

In 'John Willis – A Tribute,' Risk combined admiration for his then-living, historical subject with curiosity about the impact of Willis's legal realism of the inter-war period on the bar's reception of new public authorities.[57] He identified three abiding themes in Willis's writing. A first enthusiasm was for the ability of an expanding state to change the relationship of individuals to their communities. Willis was optimistic that increased legislative and administrative activity would circumscribe market-related, common-law values. A second theme identified by Risk in Willis's scholarship was his insistence that administrative law should be understood as what really happens in government, rather than the application of formal doctrine by courts in retrospective conflict with legislatures or agencies. By that Willis meant that lawyers should study such functions of commissions as their expert elaboration and implementation of social policy and eschew judicial or conceptual approaches to agency action. The accountability of administrative delegates was acknowledged by Willis in what Risk thought was an incomplete way, with the observation that the effectiveness of mechanisms as diverse as publicity, praise of human decency, shame, and other informal controls on state action can be scrutinized alongside the potency of formal controls. A final theme in Willis's scholarship highlighted by Risk was its caustic and iconoclastic scepticism about abstract legal thought. That pervasive doubt was said to have enabled Willis to challenge the prevailing 'lawyers' constitution,' comprised of the rule of law, separation of governmental powers, primacy of state courts, and sharp distinctions between administrative and judicial, political and legal, powers.

Often geographically and intellectually isolated in his day, Willis became a kind of folk hero to later generations of Canadian law teachers, who had not sat in his classrooms but who read his insightful and sometimes shrill representations of fleeting Canadian legal realism like 'Three Approaches to Administrative Law,' 'Statute Interpretation in a Nutshell,' and 'The McRuer Report: Lawyers' Values and Civil Servants' Values.'[58]

That renewed interest in Canadian legal thought about the welfare state notwithstanding, a merely modest volume of research has been undertaken in recent years on the history of Canadian public administration, nonconstitutional public law, and lawyers' understandings of the legitimacy of state action.[59] The priority Risk urged his readers to accord those themes in their own work has not yet been fully achieved.

A third topically or methodologically coherent cluster of Risk's publications was unified by its biographic focus on the thought of selected, late-nineteenth-century Ontarian legal writers and judges. William Ralph Meredith, John Skirving Ewart, and Augustus Henry Fraser Lefroy were chosen as subjects for that exercise in intellectual history.[60] Although not entirely in line with those studies' orientation, a fourth essay that assessed collectively articles published in the 1935 issue of the *University of Toronto Law Journal* could be appended to them.[61] Two later papers that dealt with late-nineteenth-century Canadian constitutional scholarship might also be attached to that group.[62] But they have even more in common with a series of articles that Risk published in the 1990s on post-Confederation Canadian constitutional ideology and will therefore be reserved for later discussion.[63]

It bears repetition that 'Sir William R. Meredith, CJO: The Search for Authority' grew out of Risk's investigation of the introduction in Ontario of tribunal-based, no-fault compensation for victims of industrial accidents.[64] In addition to being the one-man commission delegated responsibility to study liability for workplace injuries and propose legislative reform to the administration by common law courts of tort doctrine, Meredith sat on Ontario's superior courts from 1894 to 1921. During that time, he wrote some 750 reported judgments that provided the primary source material for Risk's study of Meredith's judicial mind. Again, Risk's tolerance for empirical overload was noteworthy.

'William R. Meredith' was researched and written against a background of general conclusions its author had already drawn about Ontario's judiciary in the late nineteenth and early twentieth centuries:

The courts seemed to assume that the common law was composed of rules firmly settled by authority, primarily English authority. It was almost never expressly justified, beyond the justification explicit in its mere existence and the internal authority of courts in a hierarchy. For example, it was almost never justified by invoking science, or by its age, fairness, or utility. The process of making decisions seemed usually to be simply finding facts and applying the rules. If the law was obscure or uncertain, the court simply had to look harder to find it. This process of finding almost never included any reasoning, even to deduce implications from the rules. The judgments contain virtually no discussions of the functions of courts, especially their responsibility for the common law or interpreting statutes, but a basic and pervasive article of faith was apparent: their function was only to apply the law in an impartial way.[65]

In addition to decoding the underlying *mentalité* that enabled judging along those lines to occur, Risk set out to explain in 'William R. Meredith' how his historical subject could so easily have detached himself the from the version of rule-of-law thought depicted in that quotation when he moved from judicial to legislative arenas.

Risk began by noting that Meredith's ideas about the common law and statutes were significantly different from those of Ontario's leading judges half a century earlier. Pre-Confederation members of the local judiciary were said by Risk to have shared a responsibility to settle and declare law and to encourage economic activity. Consideration of distinctive provincial conditions, justifications for judicial results that went beyond conclusory statements of legal doctrine, and a general quality of openness characterized their discharge of those obligations. By contrast,

[Meredith] gave no hint of any belief that his [judicial] work had any public importance. He did not profess or even hope to be making rules for the conduct of a society or to be responsible in any way for the legal order itself ... [Meredith's] finding and applying the common law was essentially a search for authority ... the typical authority he searched for was a single case ... [The] doctrine of strict precedent ... was settled for Meredith, beyond any doubt and beyond any realization that there might be an alternative ... [He] seemed to assume that the common law was composed of single cases ... not principles derived from and tested by them ... He did not believe that the contents of the cupboard of common law were ordered in any rational way or were internally consistent ... [Meredith's] job was to attempt to determine the weight of authority.[66]

Ironically, in view of that conception of judicial responsibility, 'Meredith demonstrated no general tendency to interpret statutes narrowly to preserve common law rights or to restrict the powers of an expanding administrative state ... He seems to have assumed that change in the law should be made by the legislature, not the courts, and that courts had a responsibility to interpret the legislation faithfully and to implement the change it seemed to require.'[67] Expressed bluntly, Meredith's idea of a sovereign Parliament overrode the related concept of the rule of formalistically applied common law. That legal mindset departed significantly from late-nineteenth-century versions of rule-of-law thought well documented for other corners of the North Atlantic world: Meredith does not seem to have regarded substantive common law, the rules of statutory interpretation, or the principles of natural justice as constituting an unentrenched bill of rights against which legislative action was to be measured.[68]

Risk observed that Meredith was often called on to interpret the statutory products of a legislature controlled by groups whose interests he shared. Those values, and his unspoken assumptions about the functions and limits of legal institutions, were mutually supportive. At least one other historian interested in Canadian deference to legislative processes has speculated that that attitude may, in part, have been a result of a venerable reform tradition in Canadian politics that assigned great importance to the achievement in the 1840s of responsible government.[69] Comparative deference to parliamentary processes could also be productively explored through studies of turn-of-the-twentieth-century expansions of voting franchises.

Few biographically oriented assessments of the late-nineteenth- or early-twentieth-century attitudes of English-speaking Canadian judges have been attempted: David Williams's monograph on Lyman Poore Duff and Gordon Bale's work on William Johnstone Ritchie are the only similarly comprehensive studies that come to mind.[70] The historical study of judicial culture has, however, taken recent but firm root in a part of Canada that Risk did not write much about: Quebec.[71]

'John Skirving Ewart: The Legal Thought' was an assessment by Risk of Ewart's legal scholarship of the 1875–1930 period, writing that comprised twenty articles and five book-length publications.[72] It was conceived as a complement to the Meredith essay, since the focus remained common law thought of the late-nineteenth and early-twentieth centuries, but the source materials for study shifted from judicial decisions to a practising lawyer's law journal and monographic writing. Indeed, Risk concentrated on Ewart's estoppel scholarship because 'it is the best part of his legal writing and it is among the best legal scholarship done in Canada between Confederation and the 1920s.'[73] 'John Skirving Ewart' was, in part, a rare Canadian contribution to the international literature on the nineteenth-century treatise-writing tradition.[74] It examined the epistemological basis for that species of legal intelligence and the larger project of professional legitimation that treatise writing represented.

The centrepiece of Ewart's scholarship, *An Exposition of the Principles of Estoppel by Misrepresentation*,[75] was styled by Risk as 'an ambitious synthesis of a neglected and tangled corner of doctrine.'[76] In design, originality, and cosmopolitan outlook that book differed from the majority of contemporary Canadian common law treatises, which were almost uniformly English monographs reproduced locally with footnotes enhanced by Canadian case law and statutes.[77] But the structure and assumptions that animated Ewart's writing on the law of estoppel were consistent with those of leading English and American legal treatises of the late-nineteenth century.

Ewart began with an abstract, ostensibly universal statement of eleven principles that were said to give conceptual clarity and coherence to what Anglo-American courts had done in thousands of estoppel cases. Those principles were set out in less than a page, in near-codal fashion. They were also said to have been distilled, 'scientifically,' by a process of inductive reasoning from the pre-existing confusion of decisional law. Ewart thus embraced the emerging article of jurisprudential faith that each self-contained body of common law was ultimately grounded in a small number of highly abstract, orderly, and comprehensive principles. Properly trained scientists, legal scholars, identified those principles and publicized them in treatise or codal form, and judges applied them through a process of deductive reasoning to the particularized facts of litigious disputes. Ewart was thus said by Risk to have tidied up an autonomous area of law through empirical generalization and to have enabled courts to make the legal future of estoppel a consistent version of its past. Indeed, Ewart anticipated that judicial activity by committing the bulk of his treatise to application of his principles in a range of contexts, all the while defining and classifying social facts to suit legal rules of general application.

Unlike his English and American fellow travellers, Risk observed, Ewart was not so adventurous or foolhardy as to address the entire law of contracts, torts, or property. Ewart regarded estoppel as a small and obscure aspect of tort law. His estoppel scholarship thus most closely resembled the work of an earlier generation of Anglo-American treatise writers, who tended to work on narrow topics like the law of bailments, contingent remainders, or dower. Indeed, Risk set up an implicit comparison in his history of legal ideas scholarship between Ewart's circumscribed approach to systematization, and Lefroy's contemporaneous efforts to produce an all-inclusive treatise on Canadian constitutional law.

Risk's work on Ewart provided a model for Canadian legal history that has been used to good advantage in more recent writing by Philip Girard and Nicholas Kasirer, both of whom have used a book or lecturer as a springboard for provocative inquiries into the history of legal culture.[78] Other enigmatic Canadian legal scholars of the day, such as John Hamilton Grey, Thomas Kennedy Ramsay, and Thomas-Jean-Jacques Loranger, would be suitable subjects for similar treatment.

In 'A.H.F. Lefroy: Common Law Thought in Late-Nineteenth-Century Canada,' Risk set out to 'reconstruct Lefroy's ways of thinking about law, especially his thought about the common law and the constitution through an analysis of his writing.'[79] Among Lefroy's four monographs and twenty-some periodical articles, Risk chose to examine most closely 'Judge-made Law,' 'The Basis of Case Law,' 'Rome and Law,' and 'Jurisprudence' as distillations of his subject's common law ideas. He selected *The Law of Legislative Power in Canada* as a reflection of Lefroy's constitutional thought.[80] Risk observed that Lefroy's private law scholarship 'made little or no impact on his own generation, and remains virtually unknown [even though] his account of lawmaking was ambitious, and the most elaborate and sustained of his generation, in England or Canada.'[81] By contrast, *Legislative Power* quickly became a standard text in Canadian constitutional law and engendered lawyers' preoccupation with the federal-provincial division of powers that was to dominate local public law until the advent of the Charter of Rights and Freedoms in the 1980s.

It was Lefroy's view, said Risk, that relations among Anglo-American individuals were governed exclusively by judicially administered common law. The ideal form of that law was what individuals would have willed for themselves, unconstrained by legislation or custom. Courts, by and large, applied settled common law rules in an objective and apolitical fashion. Their late-nineteenth-century faith in precedent and positivism, as well as their anglophilia, were praised by Lefroy. Risk was, moreover, able to report that all of the examples used in Lefroy's private law scholarship were English cases and all of his secondary references were to British or other European scholarship.

Lefroy's originality shone, however, when he asked whether judges made law and, if so, how they constructed it. He concluded, said Risk, that courts were occasionally obliged to fill gaps in an existing skein of common law, which they did by extrapolating from 'great, basic principles' of justice, humanity, moral obligation, common sense, or public convenience. That may seem a modest insight to late-twentieth-century sensibilities but, from the standpoint of the intellectual desert that was late-nineteenth-century Anglo-Canadian legal thought, Risk was justified in calling that account of law-making ambitious and elaborate.

Lefroy's much better known public law milestone, *Legislative Power*, was constructed around sixty-eight numbered propositions about constitutional interpretation, each a pithy synthesis of case law, followed by commentary.[82] Risk characterized that treatise's author as a typical, late-nineteenth-century Canadian imperialist who valorized legislative supremacy, responsible government, personal freedom, and organic national growth in the context of strong allegiance to the British Empire. Perhaps naturally, therefore, *Legislative Power* featured a blend of the British North America Act's federalism and its incorporation by reference of traditional, British values. Lefroy was said to have made that organic document and its first thirty years of interpretive case law appear necessary, unchanging, and divorced from social or political context: 'The undertaking to synthesize, the faith in meanings embedded in the text, the objectivity of the judicial function, the mutually-exclusive and absolute spheres of power, and the distinctions between law and context and values were all familiar elements of English scholarship in the late nineteenth century [and distinguished Lefroy's text from earlier Canadian constitutional writing that included material on Confederation and the history and structure of government].'[83] Risk was ultimately less interested in what Lefroy did with legal terms of constitutional art like ancillarity, pith and substance, double aspects, paramountcy, or concurrency than he was keen to use his historical subject's publications as a window on the assumptions about judging, knowledge, and cultural nationalism that made late-nineteenth-century common law thought possible. Distinctively Canadian features of that ideology, such as its emphasis on responsible government and protection of individual liberty in parliamentary settings, were highlighted by Risk. But so were characteristics that distinguished Lefroy's generation from its Upper Canadian forerunners, like slavish formalism: 'Lefroy respected his grandfather [Chief Justice Robinson] greatly, but his own writing helped make a gulf that today obscures Robinson from our understanding.'[84] Risk thus identified an as-yet incompletely understood paradigm shift in local conceptions of judicial agency and legal knowledge that seems to have occurred gradually between Confederation and 1900.

'Volume 1 of the Journal: A Tribute and a Belated Review' was a last entry in the cluster of Risk's scholarship that dealt with the history of Canadian legal thought at large.[85] Undertaken by that periodical's editor-in-chief from 1972 to 1987, it was a retrospective assessment of nine essays that appeared in the inaugural volume of the *University of Toronto Law Journal*. It can profitably be read alongside another paper more recently produced by Risk, 'The Many Minds of W.P.M. Kennedy.'[86] The journal in issue was a centrepiece of Dean William Paul McLure Kennedy's 'honour school of law and jurisprudence' at the University of Toronto during the inter-war years, and Kennedy served as its first editor. As such, he solicited for publication the papers studied in 'Volume 1.'

Of the articles available for review, Risk singled out contributions by Caesar Augustus Wright, James Alexander Corry, John Willis, and Vincent Christopher Macdonald for special attention.[87] Those essays were said by Risk to have been faithful to Kennedy's declaration of goals for his journal that its writers study law as more than the doctrinal preserve of lawyers, undertake research of high comparative quality, and that they be excited about changes in the social context of the law, engaged by the need for law reform and its possibilities, and confident of the unique roles of legal scholarship and education in reform. The authors under consideration also shared rejection of late-nineteenth-century attitudes that featured the paramountcy of courts and common law, devotion to the internal coherency and consistency of legal doctrine, faith that rules and syllogistic logic could determine the outcomes of cases, and the sharp separation of law from personal experience. Like his earlier tribute to Willis, Risk's review of the 1935 volume of the *University of Toronto Law Journal* focused on the scholarly output of Canadians who believed that legislatures and administrative agencies were important dimensions of their legal universe, and that law was related to the achievement of social ends identified through immersion in the facts of community life. That focus was also part of Risk's legal nationalism, and an important aspect of his editorial mission for that journal a half-century later.

Risk's identification of sentiments about state law and social engineering embraced by his pioneering journal writers and the professionally unaccredited school of jurisprudence that launched the *University of Toronto Law Journal* led him to brief reflection on Wright: 'within a few years [of his 1949 appointment as Dean of the University of Toronto's Faculty of Law] Wright had erased whatever remained of Kennedy's vision and established his vision of a professional law school.'[88] Viewed from the favourable standpoint from which Wright's role in the mid-twentieth-century's reconstruction of Ontarian legal education has generally been seen by historians, that quip was revisionist.[89] But it was a theme to which Risk returned in 'Minds of W.P.M. Kennedy': '[Kennedy's] vision of legal education is a chastening reminder to contemporary law schools that they were not the first to embrace the interdisciplinary study of law ... [For Kennedy] law must be taught, not in isolation, but together with the other social sciences ... The student in the professional law school, studying the traditional concepts of the lawyer, knew nothing of the social meaning of it all, of its validity as social doctrine ... [Kennedy's] law school, his distinctive accomplishment, has been obscured by Wright's determination to make a different school, one dedicated to training lawyers for practice.'[90] An extended study of Wright's borrowing from Kennedy of the rhetoric, but not the substance, of law in context would be a suitable sequel to 'Volume 1' and 'Minds of W.P.M. Kennedy.'

Comprehensive, belated reviews of law journal publications have not been favoured Canadian vehicles for studying legal culture. But if demonstration of the power of that methodology beyond Risk's work on the first volume of the *University of Toronto Law Journal* were needed, one has only to consider Jean-Guy Belley's treatment of Quebec's *Revue du droit*, or Wilbur Bowker's work on Albertan legal periodicals.[91] A developing literature on legal education in twentieth-century Canada has also provided helpful context for Risk's study of Kennedy insofar as research has begun to move beyond Ontariocentric, professionally driven themes.[92] Like those companion studies, 'Minds of W.P.M. Kennedy' showed there was more variety in pedagogy and academic aspiration outside the mainstream of the Law Society of Upper Canada's Osgoode Hall Law School than received wisdom has allowed. Canadian legal scholarship published between the wars echoed that creativity.

Risk's major production of the 1990s was an interrelated set of five articles on theories about constitutional divisions of power that vied for prevalence during the late- nineteenth and early-twentieth centuries. Those essays had to do, respectively, with a group of cases in which jurisdiction to regulate liquor was disputed, Canadian commentators' reception of the Privy Council's treatment of the federal 'peace order, and good government' power, the jurisdiction of the Supreme Court, the relationship of constitutional scholarship to the turn-of-the-twentieth-century judicial triumph of the provincial rights movement, and with transforming academic approaches to division-of-powers questions between Confederation and the mid-twentieth century.[93] Like their immediate chronological forerunners, those papers dealt with Canadian legal thought in general, but they ultimately turned to focus on constitutional thought in particular. They also displayed a new interest on the part of their author in the intricacies of developing constitutional doctrine. Those articles also differed from their forerunners in that Risk did not regularly remind readers of his legal subject's political and social relevance. Assertions about the common law's mid-nineteenth-century implication in economic growth seem to have required repeated justification, whereas conclusions regarding the role of late-nineteenth-century constitutional doctrine in Canadian political life apparently did not!

'Canadian Courts Under the Influence' was an intricate essay about thirty constitutional challenges in the courts to regulatory actions of municipalities, provinces, and the federal government directed towards liquor, temperance, and prohibition.[94] The real subject matter of those decisions, however, was jurisdiction and sovereignty. In convoluted ebbs and flows of judicial reasoning in provincial appellate courts, the Supreme Court of Canada, and in the Judicial Committee of the Privy Council, British North America Act provincial powers over 'matters of a merely local and private nature' and 'property and civil rights' were pitted against that statute's delegation to the federal government of authority with respect to 'criminal law,' 'trade and commerce,' and 'peace, order and good government.' Fashions in the sources and structure of constitutional argument were shown by Risk to have changed frequently and sometimes radically during his thirty-year period, as did Canadian and English courts' reception of those arguments.

Most of the disputes considered in 'Courts Under the Influence' involved Ontario and the federal government, and many of them were argued on behalf of the province personally by Oliver Mowat, premier and minister of justice for Ontario for much of the last quarter of the nineteenth century. Mowat selected adjudication as a battleground over provincial rights, and he eventually dominated that arena. By 1900 it could be said that the result of Canadian constitutional divisions-of-power litigation was that each province was autonomous and supreme, rather that subordinate, within its sphere of power described by the British North America Act. But Risk went further, by way of conclusion, with insights into the relationship between the judicial success of the provincial rights movement and neoclassical legal liberalism: 'The language of mutually-exclusive spheres of power was united with the language of coordinate legislatures in the rule of law understanding of the constitution, and it was used in the political arena as well as in the courts ... In its basic form that language was the legal structure of nineteenth-century liberalism, and for Canada it became the dominant structure of lawyers' thinking about federalism.'[95] Those conclusions complemented Robert Vipond's observations about the impact of legal liberalism on nonjudicial provincial rights discourse of the late-nineteenth century and apparently opened the door to fruitful collaboration between Vipond and Risk in jointly authored scholarship.[96]

Risk also made provisional observations about his constitutional courts' perception of their own jurisdiction in the liquor cases under consideration. Their self-described function was, abstractly stated, to identify the limits of the power of other agencies of the law. More precisely, said Risk, those courts set out to determine the will of the relevant legislative principal and to assess whether a parliamentary delegate had exceeded its legally described boundaries. That judicial function was, it was said, understood by courts to have been objective, autonomous, and apolitical.

Scholarship in Canadian constitutional history has traditionally been overwhelmingly formalistic and whiggish.[97] That dominant orientation notwithstanding, a handful of writers preceded Risk with respectable spadework on counsel and jurists such as Lord William Watson and Lord Richard Burdon Haldane, and on provincial rights theorists like David Mills.[98] The historical sweep of 'Courts Under the Influence,' and its author's reconstruction of doctrinal detail, justifies the observation that that essay helped move a fledgling field to a higher plane of inquiry. Risk's work on late-nineteenth-century constitutional ideas gave direct impetus to companion studies by several younger researchers closely associated with him.[99] It also provided indirect inspiration to historians like Paul Romney who turned to mining similar constitutional veins in a concerted way.[100]

'The Puzzle of Jurisdiction' amplified 'Courts Under the Influence' to the extent that Risk there scrutinized perceptions by the late-nineteenth-century Supreme Court of Canada and contemporary constitutional critics of that court's jurisdiction.[101] A monographic political history of the court was available to Risk, as were a couple of essay-length polemical studies of its creation.[102] But nowhere in extant secondary literature had anyone asked why the appellate jurisdiction of the Supreme Court was one of the few federal or nationally unifying institutions that survived the late-nineteenth-century's onslaught of provincial rights agitation.

Eight years after it was constitutionally empowered to create a general court of appeal, the federal government did so by conferring comprehensive appellate jurisdiction on a new, pan-Canadian institution with authority not only to hear appeals on matters within Dominion jurisdiction but also to conduct judicial review of provincial legislation and to manage, through appellate action, the application of potentially diverse common law and the interpretation of *intra vires* provincial statutes. Risk observed that, in 1875, theoretical models for provincial autonomy were neither ascendant nor clear. National, common law unity may also then have seemed uncontroversial, owing to the prevailing lawyers' faith in law as a set of general principles that were neither time nor space specific. But why did provincial rights advocates leave the Supreme Court's broad jurisdiction alone after coordinate federalism became a controlling force in courts and legislatures of the 1890s? Risk's answer was that strategists of provincial autonomy like Mills and Mowat selected litigation about federal-provincial divisions of power and the nature of provincial governments as preferred battlefields for alternate conceptions of federalism and deliberately avoided the arena of conflict offered by the Supreme Court's authority to deal with issues within provincial jurisdiction. The latter battleground was effectively abandoned to Prime Minister John Alexander Macdonald's federal forces, without noticeable effect on the turn-of-the-twentieth-century triumph of provincial rights. Attribution of that capacity for forum shopping to Canada's late-nineteenth-century constitutional combatants was a creative and persuasive argument by Risk, and one the closest analogues of which can be found in parallel political history by Vipond.[103]

Like the concluding article in Risk's series on law and the economy in mid-nineteenth-century Ontario, 'Constitutional Scholarship in the Late Nineteenth Century: Making Federalism Work' was a synthetic and integrated overview of its subject, namely Canadian constitutional thought between Confederation and 1900.[104] Ostensibly organized around the textbooks, articles, and lecture notes of eleven writers, the essay had more to say about the struggle for power between the Dominion and the provinces in that era, and about ways of reasoning legally about federalism, than the sources in which it was grounded might on first blush have suggested. Risk described his scholars' construction of a model of 'autonomous Canadian federalism,' the connection between that model's doctrinal substance and late-nineteenth-century legal reasoning at large, and the relationship of the form and substance of constitutional law to political discourse about provincial rights.

Textbook writers Dennis Ambrose O'Sullivan, Jeremiah Travis, T.-J.-J. Loranger, William Henry Pope Clement, and A.H.F. Lefroy; law journal editor Edward Douglas Armour; law teachers Richard Chapman Weldon and David Mills; and political commentators Alpheus Todd and John George Bourinot were taken by Risk as historical subjects.[105] But he insisted their writing could only be understood against the political background of provincial rights manoeuvring. By 1900, said Risk, the legal and political model of autonomous federalism had achieved dominance, an interpretive paradigm based on coordinate governments, independent of one another, each having exclusive and supreme authority in its sphere of power. That model was, in turn, said to have been as closely linked to dominant beliefs regarding legal reasoning in general and to ideas about the proper functions of courts in particular as it was related to constitutional texts or political expediency.

Risk began with the commonplace observation that Confederation's initial subordination of provincial to federal powers was evident in the British North America Act's allocation to the Dominion of power to appoint superior court judges and lieutenants-governor, authority to disallow and reserve provincial legislation, and in the Dominion's ability to create a court of general appeal with comprehensive jurisdiction. Through persistent litigation over seemingly trivial issues like the regulation of taverns, the right to escheats, the appointment of Queen's Counsel, and access to rivers and streams for timber slides, profoundly incompatible models of subordinate and autonomous federalism vied for ascendancy. Treatise writers built a coherent, interpretive model out of provincial gains in the courts, synthesizing that case law from the perspective of shared articles of faith like loyalty to the glories of the British constitution, the urgency to structure federal-provincial struggles in legal form, and the belief that Canada was comprised of autonomous and equal federated governments, exclusive and sharply bounded in character. The resulting scheme of autonomous federalism was conceded by Risk to have been deployed frequently in extralegal settings, but academically minded lawyers were said to have expressed it most powerfully and coherently.

Risk's refinement in 'Constitutional Scholarship' of the connection he made in 'Courts Under the Influence' of provincial rights rhetoric to the prevailing structure of legal thought was, however, that article's signal feature. The dominant form of Anglo-American legal reasoning of the day emphasized the autonomy and equality of juridical persons, sharp conceptual divisions between public and private realms, near-deification of courts and common law, and an understanding of legal relations as contractual exchanges between spheres of power separated by bright lines. In that view of the sources and legitimacy of provincial rights, Dominion legislative intrusions into provincial spheres of power were primarily affronts to the integrity of neoclassical legal liberalism rather than mere violations of the British North America Act. Again, Risk emphasized the capacity of the law to structure political and professional consciousness.

On the issue of who gained and lost, materially, from the triumph in the courts of the provincial rights movement, Risk was direct: 'nothing in what the [treatise]-writers said, nothing in what they perceived the stakes of their work to be, and nothing of substance in their immediate relations suggests that they had any sense that the stakes were anything but federalism.'[106] Interests like those of corporations seeking to be free from regulation and that welcomed delegation of regulatory power to provincial legislatures they could successfully lobby, or corporations that applauded sharp divisions of constitutional power which themselves offered to frustrate effective regulation, were said by Risk to have been irrelevant to his treatise writers and lecturers. He thus characterized Canada's late-nineteenth-century constitutionalization of the common law as an extension of legal and political power. That conclusion contrasts with a significant current of opinion in Canadian history to the effect that provincial governments had real and immediate economic motives for judicial expansion of their sovereignty.[107]

'The Scholars and the Constitution: Models of Canadian Federalism' was an as-yet unpublished sequel to 'Constitutional Scholarship' that dealt briefly with the late nineteenth century's scholarly construction of autonomous Canadian federalism and then moved forward in time to reconstruct the 'model of a nation' that prevailed in academic commentary on division-of-powers issues during the first four decades of this century and the 'model of balance' that emerged between the Second World War and 1970.[108] Seven scholars' visions of federalism were assessed for those three periods, yielding the conclusion that successive legal models of federal-provincial relations were shaped by entanglements of the dominant mode of Anglo-Canadian legal thought with controlling currents of national life in each era.

By the first decades of the twentieth century, said Risk, concern about the nature of Canadian federalism had been displaced by interest in the division of federal and provincial powers. Constitutional adjudication in the Privy Council had, by then, made the Dominion government's powers a pale image of what had been contemplated in the Confederation debates and recorded in the British North America Act. W.P.M. Kennedy, Francis Reginald Scott, and V.C. Macdonald protested aggressively in Canadian law journals of the 1920s and 1930s that the Privy Council's legalistic emasculation of the federal government had pre-empted construction of the strong and expansive central government they thought necessary to attack economic depression with social welfare initiatives. Canada was said by those scholars to have been condemned by that court to constitutional paralysis by exclusion from division-of-powers adjudication of information about the context in which Confederation originally materialized. Social engineering and legal functionalism thus merged in those academic efforts to call the Privy Council's provincial rights jurisprudence into question and promote the expansion of a national government with constitutional powers appropriate to a modern regulatory state. The general inattentiveness of the Privy Council and Canada's practising bar to scholarship was said by Risk to have consigned those writers' model of a nation to legal and political impotence.

Following the Second World War, academic lawyers like Bora Laskin carried forward ideas prevalent in the 1930s about the need for a powerful federal government and about the Privy Council's betrayal of that requirement as well as the goals of Confederation articulated in the British North America Act. For those proponents of what Risk called the model of balance, the meanings of words were indefinite and judges were obliged to make choices on the basis of social problems or factual nuance. Reasonable equilibrium between centralization and provincial autonomy was called for, with a fulcrum located in interpretive case law rather than constitutional texts. Risk characterized nontextual balancing of extralegal considerations as a tamed scholarly version of ferment associated with the inter-war years, and noted that it sometimes muffled social issues with doctrinal analysis. Expressed positively, the model of balance trimmed realism's political edges and featured scholars skilled in the workings of legal processes and the institutional implementation of social preferences. It was said by Risk to have corresponded to the modern practice of cooperative federalism and to have come to dominate constitutional scholarship and adjudication during the 1960s and '70s.

Risk thus periodized academic approaches to Canadian divisions of constitutional power litigation comprehensively. Documenting the entanglement of currents in national life with fashions in legal thought was more or less original, but Risk was otherwise able to build on earlier work by contemporary constitutional scholars.[109] He also challenged implicitly, as he did in his work on Willis, Kennedy, and the rise of the Canadian regulatory state, the received wisdom among Canadian legal historians that the nineteenth century should be sorted out before the present one is addressed. Not least because it is nearly over, the twentieth century is eminently eligible for historical scrutiny.[110]

A fifth and, for present purposes, final cluster of Risk's scholarship was a pair of mid-1990s articles that assayed late-nineteenth-century Canadian conceptions of civil and political rights, and the discourse related to those rights, in a range of forums.[111] It is convenient to merge review of 'Blake and Liberty' into consideration of 'Rights Talk in Canada in the Late-Nineteenth Century: The Good Sense and Right Feeling of the People,' since the former paper was a path-breaker for the latter, more ambitious one. Risk and Vipond developed their themes through assessment of seven late-nineteenth-century episodes in Canadian political life, namely the debate about federal disallowance of Ontario's Rivers and Streams Act, prohibition of sales of alcohol, Sunday closing laws, regulation of factory conditions and railway rates, official languages in the Northwest, and the controversy over religion in Manitoba's schools. The common denominator in those causes célèbres was that debates that began as arguments about individual rights ended as claims for the autonomy of provincial legislatures. Mainstream Canadian politicians and lawyers of the day were therefore labelled by Risk and Vipond, cryptically, as protectors of 'constitutional liberty.' Individual rights, in every case, were limited by the needs of the community expressed in legislative form.

The large questions posed by Risk and his co-author of their historical subjects were how they understood where to draw the line between personal liberty and state power, and who should draw that line. Late-nineteenth-century Canadians were reported to have thought that civil and political liberties were at once mutually reinforcing and mutually limiting and that legislatures rather than courts had primary responsibility for determining limits on private rights. Explanations offered by Risk and Vipond for that local persistence of Britain's late-eighteenth-century whig constitution were historically given allegiance to the supremacy of parliament, fear of executive power, continuing celebration of the colonial achievement of responsible government, the absence of any real threat of legislative redistribution of entitlements, and the triumph of provincial rights or autonomous federalism.

'Rights Talk' concluded with the observations that late-nineteenth-century Canadian courts played a limited role in determining private rights or declaring the values of the new nation, and that when they were active they tended to prefer legislative policy to vested common law rights. Individual entitlements were thus said to have been comparatively unimportant in posing or resolving public issues between Confederation and 1900. The rhetorical power of assertions about provincial autonomy, grounded as they were in legal liberalism's deification of sovereign power within rigidly bounded spheres, was also said to have obviated the need for substantive argument about whether federal or provincial governments could best advance the Commonwealth's interests.

It was appropriate for 'Rights Talk' to have been published in the American *Law and History Review*, not only because it was written with extensive references to secondary sources on late-nineteenth-century U.S. constitutional thought, but also because its conclusions about the relationship of public to private rights by leading contemporary Canadian scholars, politicians, and lawyers should be provocative of international debate about competing conceptions of those rights. That kind of engagement has typically characterized the reception extended to other Canadian articles in that journal.[112] Indeed the *Law and History Review*'s editorial board has recently grown to include Canadian scholars such as Constance Backhouse, Jean-Marie Fecteau, Douglas Hay, John McLaren, Wesley Pue, and Brian Young. It is a sign of the subtlety and confidence of increasing numbers of Canadian legal historians that they are aspiring, as Flaherty originally urged, 'to be comparative at all levels.'[113]

In stark contrast with the situation that prevailed in 1980, when the first version of 'R.C.B. Risk's Canadian Legal History' was written, the field in which Risk pioneered and led for the last quarter-century is diverse, healthy, and growing.[114] Historical work on criminal justice,[115] law and social diversity,[116] Aboriginal rights,[117] and the legal professions[118] merit particular attention since, due to the topical orientation of Risk's scholarship, there have been few opportunities to allude to that writing elsewhere in this review essay. The Osgoode Society is currently planning publication of its thirty-sixth book, whereas in 1980 it was organizing its inaugural volume, and Canadian researchers have begun to make important contributions to the modern legal history of neighbouring jurisdictions.[119] Much work nonetheless remains to be done, and there has, admittedly, been unevenness of quality and ambition in some of that which has been undertaken. But cause for celebration by the expanding community of Canadian legal historians there clearly is. In that connection, Backhouse's representative observation about Risk's instrumental role in those developments and his support and inspiration to others bears recall.[120]

Recognition should also be accorded to early and regular contributions to Canadian legal history by John Brierley,[121] Wilbur Bowker,[122] Dale Gibson,[123] Murray Greenwood,[124] Louis Knafla, [125] André Morel,[126] and Graham Parker.[127] But it is unlikely that any of those scholars would deny the singular and sustained character of Risk's attention to historical themes over an extended period of time. Flaherty's observation that, depending on how it is done, legal history can be closely aligned with cultural, social, political, or economic history also merits recollection.[128] Most of Risk's work has had to do with legal thought and is therefore best understood as species of intellectual history. Observations about that scholarship made in this review essay compare favourably with injunctions for cultural history that can be found in leading surveys of that field.[129] In that regard, special attention and praise is warranted for 'Law and the Economy,'

'Nuisance of Litigation,' 'Courts Under the Influence,' 'Constitutional Scholarship,' and 'Rights Talk.'[130] Those articles ultimately speak to a vibrant body of local literature that has taken various strands in the history of Canadian ideas as its subject matter.[131] Interdisciplinary dialogue has not always been as voluble as Risk might have hoped, and Canadian historians of diverse stripe could justifiably be motivated by friendship and loyalty to him to promise to do more on that front.

A similarly notable feature of Risk's work is that he was ultimately looking for national history, as opposed to a composite of provincial accounts pasted together. That aspiration was most evident in his constitutional history. But it was also latent in his studies of Canada West, where there was talk of themes and ideas that transcend local knowledge, rather than emphasis on provincial history in an Ontariocentric mode. Risk's work on provincial terrain was, more often than not, on the 'grain of sand' basis. He was unrepresentative of Canadian legal historians in that respect, since the general character of recent historiography has been regionalist. That prevailing local knowledge paradigm has not only handicapped Canada, it has also impaired its present-day legal historians. Risk's discreet role as a national scholar, and his implicit pan-Canadianism, therefore deserve plaudits.

Consistent with the scholarly genre that prevailed in Canadian law schools during the last half of the twentieth century, all of Risk's historical work was published in article form. In the result, regrettably few reviews that touch on his scholarship exist. Risk's contribution therefore cannot be readily understood or assessed through that medium. The present essay is thus offered as a partial and tentative effort to fill that gap, with the hope that it will be received as a first but not last word on its subject and that it will promote evolving, collective reflection on how his work fits into larger historiographical currents.

When the editors of this volume approached Risk in the fall of 1996 to seek his blessing for the *festschrift* that has now taken shape they were told that he was not actually retiring from the academy, that he had not really been a legal historian, and that he had not done anything particularly noteworthy. In the wake of that bashful shrug, it has been difficult to formulate a suitable ending for this essay. Eventually, a couple of leaves were selected from Risk's book, such that two of his conclusions became mine: 'Canadians do not easily believe that one of us has been outstanding, not only within our community but beyond, but that is my claim and my tribute.'[132] *Deo volente*, Dick Risk will continue to make those kinds of contributions into the next millenium. It was gratifying, in that regard, that he presented 'W.P.M. Kennedy's Canadian Constitutional Thought' and chaired a panel on 'Professional History' at the May 1998 Canadian Legal History Conference held in Toronto in his honour!

NOTES

For their comments on an earlier version of this paper, I thank Nicholas Kasirer, Peter Oliver, and Jim Phillips.

1 See D.H. Flaherty, ed., *Essays in the History of Canadian Law*, 2 vols. (Toronto: The Osgoode Society for Canadian Legal History 1981 and 1983).
2 See 'R.C.B. Risk Bibliography' in this volume.
3 D.H. Flaherty, 'Writing Canadian Legal History: An Introduction' in Flaherty, *Essays*, 1:3 at 8.
4 Ibid. at 9.
5 J. McLaren 'Race and the Criminal Justice System in British Columbia, 1892–1920: Constructing Chinese Crimes,' in this volume, describing R.C.B. Risk 'A Prospectus for Canadian Legal History,' *Dalhousie Law Journal* 1 (1973), 227.
6 R. Vipond and G. Feldberg, 'The Law of Evolution and the Evolution of the Law: Mills, Darwin, and Late-Nineteenth-Century Legal Thought,' in this volume. Compare notes 22, 46, 60, and 63, infra. The other participating 'team teachers' were Constance Backhouse, Blaine Baker, Robert Gordon, Jim Phillips, and David Sugarman.
7 H. Foster, 'A Romance of the Lost: The Role of Tom MacInnes in the History of the British Columbia Indian Land Question,' in this volume.
8 M.L. Friedland to P.N. Oliver, 12 November 1982, assessing R.C.B. Risk, 'This Nuisance of Litigation: The Origins of Workers' Compensation in Ontario,' in Flaherty, *Essays*, 2:418. Compare B. Adams, 'Review,' *Ontario History* 75 (1983), 436 at 436, where the 'preeminence among legal historians in Canada' of that paper's author was discussed; D.J. Guth, 'Review,' *University of British Columbia Law Review* 18 (1984), 407 at 410, where that essay was described as 'masterful'; J.P.S. McLaren, 'Review,' *Canadian Bar Review* 62 (1984), 707 at 711, where it was called 'excellent'; and R.K. Osgood, 'Review,' *Law and History Review* 2 (1984), 161 at 164, where it was labelled 'distinguished.' See also D. Kettler, 'Review,' *Journal of Canadian Studies* 19, no. 3 (1984), 150 at 159–62.
9 P.N. Oliver to G.B. Baker, 29 May 1997.
10 J. Phillips to S.T.B. Risk, 11 March 1997.
11 C. Backhouse to J. Phillips, 14 January 1997.
12 M.E. McCallum, 'The Sacred Rights of Property: Title, Entitlement, and the

Land Question in Nineteenth-Century Prince Edward Island,' in this volume. The other participating Risk alumni(ae) were Jamie Benidickson, Bernard Hibbitts, and Ian Kyer.

13 J. Benidickson to G.B. Baker, 13 November 1996.

14 See, e.g., J. Benidickson, 'Private Rights and Public Purposes in the Lakes, Rivers, and Streams of Ontario 1870–1930,' in Flaherty, *Essays*, 2:365; B.J. Hibbitts, 'A Change of Mind: The Supreme Court and the Board of Railway Commissioners, 1903–1929,' *University of Toronto Law Journal* 41 (1991), 60; B.J. Hibbitts, 'A Bridle for Leviathan: The Supreme Court and the Board of Commerce,' *Ottawa Law Review* 21 (1989), 65; W. Lahey, 'Constitutional Adjudication, Provincial Rights, and the Structure of Legal Thought in Late Nineteenth-Century New Brunswick,' *University of New Brunswick Law Journal* 39 (1990), 185; R. Yalden, '*Unité et différence*: The Structure of Legal Thought in Late Nineteenth-Century Quebec,' *University of Toronto Faculty of Law Review* 46 (1988), 365; D.J. McMahon, 'Law and Public Authority: Sir John Beverley Robinson and the Purposes of the Criminal Law,' *University of Toronto Faculty of Law Review* 46 (1988), 390; C. Stychin, 'Formalism, Liberalism, Federalism: David Mills and the Rule of Law Vision in Canada,' *University of Toronto Faculty of Law Review* 46 (1988), 201; R. Gold, 'Sir Lyman Duff and the Fork in the Road,' *University of Toronto Faculty of Law Review* 46 (1988), 424; and K. Roach, 'The Administrative Law Scholarship of D.M. Gordon,' *McGill Law Journal* 34 (1989), 1.

15 See, e.g., D.H. Flaherty, 'An Approach to American History: Willard Hurst as Legal Historian,' *American Journal of Legal History* 14 (1970), 222; H.N. Scheiber, 'At the Borderland of Law and Economic History: The Contributions of Willard Hurst,' *American Historical Review* 75 (1970), 744; and R.W. Gordon, 'J. Willard Hurst and the Common Law Tradition in American Legal Historiography,' *Law and Society Review* 10 (1975), 9.

16 Risk, 'Prospectus.' See also R.C.B. Risk, 'New Directions for Legal History,' in D. and R. Gagan, eds., *New Directions for the Study of Ontario's Past* (Hamilton, Ont.: McMaster University 1988), 117 esp. 120–6.

17 Flaherty, 'Writing Canadian Legal History,' at 8.

18 R.C.B. Risk, 'The Nineteenth-Century Foundations of the Business Corporation in Ontario,' *University of Toronto Law Journal* 23 (1973), 270; 'The Golden Age: The Law about the Market in Nineteenth-Century Ontario,' *University of Toronto Law Journal* 26 (1976), 307; 'The Last Golden Age: Property and the Allocation of Losses in Ontario in the Nineteenth Century,' *University of Toronto Law Journal* 27 (1977), 199; and 'The Law and the Economy in Mid-Nineteenth Century Ontario: A Perspective,' *University of Toronto Law Journal* 27 (1977), 403.

19 R.C.B. Risk, 'The Records of Title to Land: A Plea for Reform,' *University of*

Toronto Law Journal 21 (1971), 465. See also E. Kolish, 'Le conseil législatif et les bureaux d'enregistrement (1836),' *Revue d'histoire de l'Amérique français* 35 (1981), 217.

20 R.C.B. Risk, 'The Law and the Economy in Mid-Nineteenth-Century Ontario: A Perspective,' in Flaherty *Essays* 1:88. Compare A.W.B. Simpson, 'Review,' *Western Ontario Law Review* 21 (1983), 195 at 195, where that essay's author was described as 'a leading pioneer'; H.R.S. Ryan, 'Review,' *Queen's Law Journal* 8 (1982), 309 at 313, where that paper was called 'admirable'; B. Young, 'Review,' *McGill Law Journal* 29 (1983), 212 at 213, where it was labelled 'measured,' 'thoughtful,' and 'probing'; L.A. Knafla, 'Review,' *American Journal of Legal History* 27 (1983), 389 at 391, where it was said to be 'analytical legal history at its best'; P. Schabas, 'Review,' *University of Toronto Faculty of Law Review* 41 (1983), 74 at 75, where it was designated 'a classic.' See also B.D. Bucknall, 'Review,' *Ontario History* 74 (1982), 243 at 243; D. Hay, 'Review,' *Canadian Historical Review* 46 (1983), 583 at 584; and D. Kettler, 'Review,' *Journal of Canadian Studies* 18(1) (1983), 136 at 136.

21 The leading expression of that historic and historiographic ideology is J.W. Hurst, *Law and the Conditions of Freedom in the Nineteenth Century United States* (Madison: University of Wisconsin Press 1956). It has been brought forward in contemporary monographs like T.A. Freyer, *Forums of Order: The Federal Courts and Business in American History* (Greenwich, Conn.: JAI Press 1979); L.M. Friedman, *A History of American Law* (New York: Simon and Schuster 1985); and H. Hovenkamp *Enterprise and American Law, 1836–1937* (Cambridge: Harvard University Press 1991).

22 See, e.g., R.C.B. Risk and R. Vipond, 'Rights Talk in Canada in the Late Nineteenth Century: The Good Sense and Right Feeling of the People,' *Law and History Review* 14 (1996), 1; R.C.B. Risk, 'Canadian Courts Under the Influence,' *University of Toronto Law Journal* 40 (1990), 687; and R.C.B. Risk, 'Constitutional Scholarship in the Late-Nineteenth Century: Making Federalism Work,' *University of Toronto Law Journal* 46 (1996), 427.

23 See F.E. Labrie and E.E. Palmer, 'The Pre-Confederation History of Corporations in Canada,' in J.S. Ziegel, ed., *Studies in Canadian Company Law* (Toronto: Butterworths 1967), 1:33; B. Hammond, *Banks and Politics in America from the Revolution to the Civil War* (Princeton: Princeton University Press 1957), 631–70. See also J.-M. Fecteau, 'Les petites républiques: les compagnies et la mise en place du droit corporatif moderne au Québec au milieu du 19e siècle,' *Histoire sociale/Social History* 25 (1992), 35; B.A.M. Patton, 'From State Action to Private Profit: the Emergence of the Business Corporation in Nova Scotia, 1796–1883,' *Nova Scotia Historical Review* 16 (1996), 21; B. Young, *In Its Corporate Capacity: The Seminary of Montreal as a Business Institution, 1816–1876*

(Montreal and Kingston: McGill-Queen's University Press 1986); and C.I. Kyer, 'Gooderham & Worts: A Case Study in Business Organization in Nineteenth-Century Ontario,' in this volume.

24 Risk, 'Law About the Market,' at 308.

25 Compare M.J. Horwitz, *The Transformation of American Law, 1780 to 1860* (Cambridge, Mass.: Harvard University Press 1977), 160–210; P.S. Atiyah, *The Rise and Fall of Freedom of Contract* (Oxford: Clarendon Press 1979), 398–505; and A.W.B. Simpson, 'Innovation in Nineteenth Century Contract Law,' *Law Quarterly Review* 91 (1975), 247.

26 See, e.g., B.J. Hibbitts, 'Progress and Principle: The Legal Thought of Sir John Beverley Robinson,' *McGill Law Journal* 34 (1989), 454; P.D. George and P. Sworden, 'The Courts and the Development of Trade in Upper Canada, 1830–1860,' *Business History Review* 60 (1986), 258; and W.N.T. Wylie, 'Instruments of Commerce and Authority: The Civil Courts in Upper Canada 1789–1812,' in Flaherty, *Essays*, 2:3. But see J. Webber, 'Labour and the Law,' in P. Craven, ed., *Labouring Lives: Work and Workers in Nineteenth-Century Ontario* (Toronto: University of Toronto Press 1995), 171 and D. McCalla *Planting the Province: The Economic History of Upper Canada, 1784–1870* (Toronto: University of Toronto Press 1993).

27 Compare R.C.B. Risk, 'Condominiums and Canada,' *University of Toronto Law Journal* 18 (1968), 1; B.J. Reiter and R.C.B. Risk *Real Estate Law* (Toronto: Emond, Montgomery 1979); and Risk, 'Records of Title.'

28 Risk, 'Property and the Allocation of Losses,' at 236.

29 See generally R.W. Gordon, 'Historicism in Legal Scholarship,' *Yale Law Journal* 90 (1981), 1017.

30 See, e.g., McCallum, 'Sacred Rights of Property'; T. Johnson, 'In a Manner of Speaking: Towards a Reconstitution of Property in Mid-Nineteenth Century Quebec,' *McGill Law Journal* 32 (1987), 636; and J.E.C. Brierley, 'The Co-existence of Legal Systems in Quebec: Free and Common Soccage in Canada's *pays de droit civil*,' *Cahiers de droit* 20 (1979), 277.

31 See, e.g., L. Chambers *Married Women and Property Law in Victorian Ontario* (Toronto: The Osgoode Society for Canadian Legal History 1997); P. Girard, 'Married Women's Property, Chancery Abolition, and Insolvency Law: Law Reform in Nova Scotia 1820–1867,' in P. Girard and J. Phillips, eds., *Essays in the History of Canadian Law: Nova Scotia* (Toronto: The Osgoode Society for Canadian Legal History 1990), 80; and J.C. Weaver, 'While Equity Slumbered: Creditor Advantage, a Capitalist Market, and Upper Canada's Missing Court,' *Osgoode Hall Law Journal* 28 (1990), 871.

32 See, e.g., J. Nedelsky, 'Judicial Conservatism in an Age of Innovation: Comparative Perspectives on Canadian Nuisance Law 1880–1930,' in Flaherty

Essays, 1:281; J.P.S. McLaren, 'The Tribulations of Antoine Ratté: A Case
Study of the Environmental Regulation of the Canadian Lumbering Industry
in the Nineteenth Century,' *University of New Brunswick Law Journal* 33 (1984),
203; and D.N. Dewees and M. Halewood, 'The Efficiency of the Common
Law: Sulphur Dioxide Emissions in Sudbury,' *University of Toronto Law Journal* 42 (1992), 1.
33 Risk, 'Law and the Economy.'
34 Ibid., at 438, 424.
35 Compare B. Young, *The Politics of Codification: The Lower Canadian Civil Code
of 1866* (Montreal and Kingston: McGill-Queen's University Press 1994); A.
Greer and I. Radforth, eds., *Colonial Leviathan: State Formation in Mid-
Nineteenth-Century Canada* (Toronto: University of Toronto Press 1992); and
J.M.S. Careless, *The Union of the Canadas: The Growth of Canadian Institutions
1841–1857* (Toronto: McClelland & Stewart 1967).
36 Risk, 'Law and the Economy,' at 422.
37 See generally R.W. Gordon, 'Critical Legal Histories,' *Stanford Law Review* 36
(1984), 57, esp. 100–16.
38 See, e.g., P. Romney, *Mr. Attorney: The Attorney General for Ontario in Court,
Cabinet, and Legislature 1791–1899* (Toronto: The Osgoode Society for Canadian Legal History 1986); G.B. Baker, 'The Reconstitution of Upper Canadian
Legal Thought in the Late-Victorian Empire,' *Law and History Review* 3 (1985),
219; and J.D. Howes, 'Property, God and Nature in the Thought of Sir John
Beverley Robinson,' *McGill Law Journal* 30 (1984), 365.
39 See, e.g., Hibbitts, 'Progress and Principal'; McMahon, 'Law and Public Au-
thority'; Howes, 'Property, God and Nature'; and P. Brode, *Sir John Beverley
Robinson: Bone and Sinew of the Compact* (Toronto: The Osgoode Society for
Canadian Legal History 1984). See also J.D. Blackwell, 'William Hume Blake
and the Judicature Acts of 1849: The Process of Legal Reform at Mid-Century
in Upper Canada,' in Flaherty, *Essays* 1:132; D. Swainson, 'William Hume
Blake,' in F.G. Halpenny and J. Hamelin, eds., *Dictionary of Canadian Biography*
(Toronto: University of Toronto Press 1976), 9:55.
40 The only thing he published during that period was R.C.B. Risk, 'A Long, Sad
Story: Siting Transmission Lines in Ontario,' *University of Toronto Law Journal*
31 (1981), 27.
41 See, e.g., D.H. Flaherty, 'An Introduction to Early American Legal History,' in
D.H. Flaherty, ed., *Essays in the History of Early American Law* (Chapel Hill:
University of North Carolina Press 1969), 3; 'Law and the Enforcement of
Morals in Early America,' in D. Fleming and B. Bailyn, eds., *Law in American
History* (Boston: Little, Brown 1971), 95; *Privacy in Colonial New England*
(Charlottesville: University of Virginia Press 1972); 'Crime and Social Control

in Provincial Massachusetts,' *Historical Journal* 14 (1981), 339; and 'Criminal Practice in Provincial Massachusetts,' in Colonial Society of Massachusetts, ed., *Law in Colonial Massachusetts 1630–1800* (Boston: Colonial Society of Massachusetts 1984), 191.

42 See generally D.G. Bell, 'The Birth of Canadian Legal History,' *University of New Brunswick Law Journal* 33 (1984), 312; B. Wright, 'Towards a New Canadian Legal History,' *Osgoode Hall Law Journal* 22 (1984), 349; and B. Young, 'Law in the Round,' *Acadiensis* 16 (1986), 155; see also V. Masciotra, 'Quebec Legal Historiography, 1760–1900,' *McGill Law Journal* 32 (1987), 712.

43 Risk, 'Nuisance of Litigation'; R.C.B. Risk, 'The Beginnings of Regulation,' in E.G. Baldwin, ed., *The Cambridge Lectures: Selected Papers Based upon Lectures Delivered at the Conference of the Canadian Institute for Advanced Legal Studies* (Toronto: Butterworths 1983), 252; 'Lawyers, Courts, and the Rise of the Regulatory State,' *Dalhousie Law Journal* 9 (1984), 31; and 'John Willis – A Tribute,' *Dalhousie Law Journal* 9 (1984), 521.

44 R.C.B. Risk, 'Sir William R. Meredith CJO: The Search for Authority,' *Dalhousie Law Journal* 7 (1983), 713.

45 Risk, 'John Willis.'

46 See, e.g., R.C.B. Risk, 'A.H.F. Lefroy: Common Law Thought in Late Nineteenth-Century Canada,' *University of Toronto Law Journal* 41 (1991), 307; 'Blake and Liberty,' in J. Ajzenstat, ed., *Canadian Constitutionalism, 1791–1991* (Ottawa: Canadian Study of Parliament Group 1992), 195; and 'The Scholars and the Constitution: POGG and the Privy Council,' *Manitoba Law Journal* 23 (1996), 496.

47 Risk, 'Nuisance of Litigation.'

48 Ibid., at 419.

49 Compare L.M. Friedman and J. Ladinsky, 'Social Change and the Law of Industrial Accidents,' *Columbia Law Review* 67 (1967), 50. See also P.W.J. Bartrip and S.B. Burman, *The Wounded Soldiers of Industry: Industrial Compensation Policy, 1833–1897* (Oxford: Oxford University Press 1982).

50 Risk, 'Nuisance of Litigation,' at 475.

51 See E. Tucker, 'The Law of Employers' Liability in Ontario 1861–1900: The Search for a Theory,' *Osgoode Hall Law Journal* 22 (1984), 213; R.W. Kostal, 'Legal Justice, Social Justice: An Incursion into the Social History of Work-Related Accident Law in Ontario, 1860–86,' *Law and History Review* 6 (1988), 1; P. Craven, 'The Meaning of Misadventure: The Baptiste Creek Railway Disaster of 1854 and its Aftermath,' in R. Hall, et al., eds., *Patterns of the Past: Interpreting Ontario's History* (Toronto: Dundurn Press 1988), 108; J.A. Dickinson, 'La législation et les travailleurs québecois, 1894–1914,' *Relations industrielles* 41 (1986), 357; and D. Pothier, 'Workers' Compensation: The

Historical Compromise Revisited,' *Dalhousie Law Journal* 7 (1983), 309. See also
E. Tucker, *Administering Danger: The Law and Politics of Occupational Health and
Safety Regulation in Ontario 1850–1914* (Toronto: University of Toronto Press
1990).

52 See notes 69, 71, 91, 96, 100, and 103, infra.

53 Risk, 'Rise of the Regulatory State.' See also Risk, 'Beginnings of Regulation.'

54 Compare J.E. Hodgetts, *Pioneer Public Service: An Administrative History of the
United Canadas* (Toronto: University of Toronto Press 1955); R.B. Splane, *Social
Welfare in Ontario, 1791–1893* (Toronto: University of Toronto Press 1965); and
H.V. Nelles, *The Politics of Development: Forests, Mines and Hydro-Electric Power
in Ontario, 1849–1941* (Toronto: University of Toronto Press 1974).

55 Risk, 'Rise of the Regulatory State,' at 39.

56 See Hibbitts, 'Change of Mind'; Hibbitts, 'Bridle for Leviathan'; Roach, 'Administrative Law Scholarship'; J. Benidickson, 'The Combines Problem in
Canadian Legal Thought, 1867–1920,' *University of Toronto Law Journal* 43
(1993), 799; and J. Benidickson, 'The Canadian Board of Railway Commissioners: Regulation, Policy and Legal Process at the Turn-of-the-Century,' *McGill
Law Journal* 36 (1991), 1222.

57 Risk, 'John Willis.' See also R.C.B. Risk, 'In Memoriam: John Willis,' *University
of Toronto Law Journal* 47 (1997), 301.

58 J. Willis, 'Three Approaches to Administrative Law: The Judicial, the Concep-
tual, and the Functional,' *University of Toronto Law Journal* 1 (1935), 53; 'Statute
Interpretation in a Nutshell,' *Canadian Bar Review* 16 (1938), 1; and 'The
McRuer Report: Lawyers' Values and Civil Servants' Values,' *University of
Toronto Law Journal* 18 (1968), 351.

59 See, e.g., J. Benidickson, 'Ontario Water Quality, Public Health and the Law,
1880–1930,' in this volume; Tucker, *Administering Danger*; J.E. Hodgetts, *From
Arm's Length to Hands-On: The Formative Years of Ontario's Public Service, 1867–
1940* (Toronto: University of Toronto Press 1995); P. Baskerville, 'Transportation, Social Change, and State Formation, Upper Canada, 1841–1864,' in Greer
and Radforth, *Colonial Leviathan*, at 230; J. Nedelsky, 'From Private Property
to Public Resource: The Emergence of Administrative Control of Water in
Nova Scotia,' in Girard and Phillips, *Essays*, at 326; K. Cruikshank, *Close Ties:
Railways, Government, and the Board of Railway Commissioners, 1851–1933*
(Montreal and Kingston: McGill-Queen's University Press 1991); J. Webber,
'Living Wage and Living Profit: Wage Determination by Conciliation Boards
under the Industrial Disputes Investigation Act, 1907–1925,' in W.W. Pue and
B. Wright, eds., *Canadian Perspectives on Law and Society: Issues in Legal History*
(Ottawa: Carleton University Press 1988), 207; M.E. McCallum, 'Assistance to
Veterans and their Dependants: Steps on the Way to the Administrative State,

1914–1929,' in ibid., at 157; P.M. Sibenik, 'Points of Departure: Urban Relief in Alberta, 1930–1937,' in L.A. Knafla, ed., *Law and Justice in a New Land: Essays in Western Canadian Legal History* (Toronto: Carswell 1986), 313; J. Webber, 'The Malaise of Compulsory Conciliation: Strike Prevention in Canada During World War II,' *Labour/Le travail* 15 (1995), 57.

60 Risk, 'William R. Meredith'; 'John Skirving Ewart: The Legal Thought,' *University of Toronto Law Journal* 37 (1987), 335; and 'A.H.F. Lefroy.'

61 R.C.B. Risk, 'Volume 1 of the Journal: A Tribute and a Belated Review,' *University of Toronto Law Journal* 37 (1987), 193.

62 Risk, 'Scholars and the Constitution'; 'Constitutional Scholarship.'

63 Risk, 'Courts Under the Influence,' 'Blake and Liberty'; Risk and Vipond, 'Rights Talk'; R.C.B. Risk, 'The Puzzle of Jurisdiction,' *South Carolina Law Review* 46 (1995), 703; Risk, 'Scholars and the Constitution.'

64 Risk, 'William R. Meredith.'

65 Risk, 'Nuisance of Litigation,' at 449.

66 Risk, 'William R. Meredith,' at 716, 717–18.

67 Ibid., at 732, 737.

68 Compare D. Sugarman, 'The Legal Boundaries of Liberty: Dicey, Liberalism and Legal Science,' *Modern Law Review* 46 (1983), 102; R. Gordon, 'Legal Thought and Legal Practice in the Age of American Enterprise,' in G.L. Geison, ed., *Professions and Professional Ideologies in America* (Chapel Hill: University of North Carolina Press 1983), 70; and M.J. Horwitz *The Transformation of American Law, 1870–1960: The Crisis of Legal Orthodoxy* (Oxford: Oxford University Press 1992), 9–31.

69 Compare P. Romney, 'From Constitutionalism to Legalism: Trial by Jury, Responsible Government, and the Rule of Law in the Canadian Political Culture,' *Law and History Review* 7 (1989), 121 and 'From the Rule of Law to Responsible Government: Ontario Political Culture and the Origins of Statism,' *Canadian Historical Association Papers* (1988), 86. See also Risk and Vipond, 'Rights Talk.'

70 See D.R. Williams *Duff: A Life in the Law* (Toronto: The Osgoode Society for Canadian Legal History 1984); G. Bale, *Chief Justice William Johnstone Ritchie: Responsible Government and Judicial Review* (Ottawa: Carleton University Press 1991).

71 See, e.g., D. Howes, 'From Polyjurality to Monojurality: The Transformation of Quebec Law, 1875–1929,' *McGill Law Journal* 32 (1987), 523; G.-G. Tremblay, 'La pensée constitutionnelle du juge Pierre-Basile Mignault,' *Cahiers de droit* 34 (1993), 257; and J.-G. Castel, 'Le juge Mignault: défenseur de l'integrité du droit civil québécois,' *Canadian Bar Review* 53 (1975), 544.

72 Risk, 'John Skirving Ewart.'

73 Ibid., at 336.
74 Compare D. Sugarman, 'Legal Theory, the Common Law Mind, and the Making of the Textbook Tradition,' in W. Twining, ed., *Legal Theory and Common Law* (Oxford: Basil Blackwell 1986), 26; A.W.B. Simpson, 'The Rise and Fall of the Legal Treatise: Legal Principles and the Forms of Legal Literature,' *University of Chicago Law Review* 48 (1981), 632; R.W. Gordon, 'Review [of C.M. Cook *The American Codification Movement. A Study of Antebellum Legal Reform* (Westport, Conn.: Greenwood Press 1981)] *Vanderbilt Law Review* 36 (1983), 431.
75 (Chicago: John Skirving Ewart 1900).
76 Risk, 'John Skirving Ewart,' at 347.
77 See generally Baker, 'Reconstitution,' at 233–70.
78 See, e.g., P. Girard, 'Themes and Variations in Early Canadian Legal Culture: Beamish Murdock and his *Epitome of the Laws of Nova-Scotia*,' *Law and History Review* 11 (1993), 101 and N. Kasirer, '*Apostolat Juridique*: Teaching Everyday Law in the Life of Marie Lacoste Gérin-Lajoie (1867–1945),' *Osgoode Hall Law Journal* 30 (1992), 427. See also G.B. Baker, 'Interstate Choice of Law and Early-American Constitutional Nationalism,' *McGill Law Journal* 38 (1993), 454.
79 Risk, 'A.H.F. Lefroy,' at 308.
80 A.H.F. Lefroy, 'Judge-made Law,' *Law Quarterly Review* 20 (1904), 399; 'The Basis of Case-Law,' *Law Quarterly Review* 22 (1906), 293; 'Rome and Law,' *Harvard Law Review* 20 (1907), 606; 'Jurisprudence,' *Law Quarterly Review* 27 (1911), 180; and *The Law of Legislative Power in Canada* (Toronto: Toronto Law Book and Publishing 1897).
81 Risk, 'A.H.F. Lefroy,' at 316.
82 Compare F.P. Walton, *Scope and Interpretation of the Civil Code of Lower Canada* (Montreal: Wilson and Lafleur 1907), which was organized around twelve rules for the interpretation of the quasi-constitutional document that provided that book's subject matter.
83 Risk, 'A.H.F. Lefroy,' at 329–30.
84 Ibid., at 309.
85 Risk, 'Volume 1.'
86 R.C.B. Risk, 'The Many Minds of W.P.M. Kennedy,' *University of Toronto Law Journal* 48 (1998), 353.
87 C.A. Wright, 'The American Law Institute's Restatement of Contracts and Agency,' *University of Toronto Law Journal* 1 (1935), 17; J.A. Corry, 'Administrative Law and the Interpretation of Statutes,' ibid. at 286; Willis, 'Three Approaches'; V.C. Macdonald, 'Judicial Interpretation of the Canadian Constitution,' *University of Toronto Law Journal* 1 (1935), 260.
88 Risk, 'Volume 1,' at 196.

89 Compare C.I. Kyer and J.E. Bickenbach, *The Fiercest Debate: Cecil A. Wright, the Benchers, and Legal Education in Ontario 1923–1957* (Toronto: The Osgoode Society for Canadian Legal History 1987); J.P.S. McLaren, 'The History of Legal Education in Common Law Canada,' in R.J. Matas and D.J. McCawley, eds., *Legal Education in Canada* (Montreal: Federated Law Societies of Canada 1987), 111; and B.D. Bucknall, T.C.H. Baldwin, and J.D. Lakin, 'Pedants, Practitioners and Prophets: Legal Education at Osgoode Hall to 1957,' *Osgoode Hall Law Journal* 6 (1968), 137.

90 Risk, 'Minds of W.P.M. Kennedy,' at 367, 372, and 386.

91 See J.-G. Belley, 'Une croisade intégriste chez les avocats du Québec: *La Revue du droit* (1922–1939),' *Cahiers de droit* 34 (1993), 183 and W.F. Bowker, 'Extrajudicial Writing: The *Alberta Law Quarterly* and the *Alberta Law Review*,' *Alberta Law Review* 18 (1980), 458. See also B.J. Hibbitts, '"Our Arctic Brethren": Canadian Law and Lawyers as Portrayed in American Legal Periodicals, 1829–1911,' in this volume; M. MacLaren, 'A History of the *University of Toronto Faculty of Law Review*,' *University of Toronto Faculty of Law Review* 55 (1997), 375; and S. Normand, 'Profil des périodiques juridiques québécois au XIXe siècle,' *Cahiers de droit* 34 (1993), 153.

92 See, e.g., W.W. Pue, '"The Disquisitions of Learned Judges": Making Manitoba Lawyers, 1885–1931,' in this volume; W.W. Pue, *Law School: The Story of Legal Education in British Columbia* (Vancouver: University of British Columbia Faculty of Law 1995); Kasirer, '*Apostolat Juridiqué*'; D.G. Bell, *Legal Education in New Brunswick: A History* (Fredericton: University of New Brunswick 1992), 116–208; S. Normand, 'Tradition et modernité à la Faculté de droit de l'Université Laval de 1945 à 1965,' *Cahiers de droit* 33 (1992), 141; R.A. Macdonald, 'The National Law Programme at McGill: Origins, Establishment, Prospects,' *Dalhousie Law Journal* 13 (1990), 211; and D. Stanley, 'Richard Chapman Weldon, 1849–1925: Fact, Fiction and Enigma,' *Dalhousie Law Journal* 12 (1989), 539.

93 Risk, 'Courts Under the Influence'; 'Scholars and the Constitution'; 'Puzzle of Jurisdiction'; 'Constitutional Scholarship'; and 'The Scholars and the Constitution: Models of Canadian Federalism,' (unpublished ms).

94 Risk, 'Courts Under the Influence.' See also R.C.B. Risk, 'Constitutional Thought in the Late Nineteenth Century,' *Manitoba Law Journal* 20 (1991), 196.

95 Risk, 'Courts Under the Influence,' at 736–7. See also Risk, 'Scholars and the Constitution,' where similar themes were teased out of judicial interpretation of the federal 'peace, order, and good government' power.

96 Compare R.C. Vipond, *Liberty and Community: Canadian Federalism and the Failure of the Constitution* (Albany: State University of New York Press 1991). See also Risk and Vipond, 'Rights Talk.'

97 See generally P.H. Russell, 'Overcoming Legal Formalism: The Treatment of the Constitution, the Courts and Judicial Behaviour in Canadian Political Science,' *Canadian Journal of Law and Society* 1 (1986), 5 and M. Gold, 'Constitutional Scholarship in Canada,' *Osgoode Hall Law School* 23 (1985), 495.

98 See, e.g., F.M. Greenwood, 'Lord Watson, Institutional Self-Interest, and the Decentralization of Canadian Federalism in the 1890s,' *University of British Columbia Law Review* 9 (1974), 244; S. Wexler, 'The Urge to Idealize: Viscount Haldane and the Constitution of Canada,' *McGill Law Journal* 29 (1984), 608; A.C. Cairns, 'The Judicial Committee and its Critics,' *Canadian Journal of Political Science* 4 (1971), 301; and F.M. Greenwood, 'David Mills and Coordinate Federalism, 1867–1903,' *Western Ontario Law Review* 16 (1977), 93.

99 See, e.g., Lahey, 'Constitutional Adjudication'; Yalden, *'Unité et différence'*; Stychin, 'Formalism, Liberalism, Federalism.'

100 See, e.g., P. Romney, 'The Nature and Scope of Provincial Autonomy: Oliver Mowat, the Quebec Resolutions and the Construction of the British North America Act,' *Canadian Journal of Political Science* 25 (1992), 3; P. Romney, 'Why Lord Watson was Right,' in Ajzenstat, *Canadian Constitutionalism*, at 177; and P. Romney, 'From Railway Construction to Constitutional Construction: John Wellington Gwynne's National Dream,' *Manitoba Law Journal* 20 (1991), 91.

101 Risk, 'Puzzle of Jurisdiction.'

102 See J.G. Snell and F. Vaughan, *The Supreme Court of Canada: History of the Institution* (Toronto: The Osgoode Society for Canadian Legal History 1985); F. MacKinnon, 'The Establishment of the Supreme Court of Canada,' *Canadian Historical Review* 27 (1946), 285; and F.H. Underhill, 'Edward Blake, the Supreme Court Act and the Appeal to the Privy Council,' *Canadian Historical Review* 19 (1938), 245.

103 See, e.g., R.C. Vipond, 'Alternative Pasts: Legal Liberalism and the Demise of the Disallowance Power,' *University of New Brunswick Law Journal* 39 (1990), 126 and 'David Mills,' in R. Cook and J. Hamelin, eds., *Dictionary of Canadian Biography* (Toronto: University of Toronto Press 1994), 13:707.

104 Risk, 'Constitutional Scholarship.' Compare Risk, 'Law and the Economy.'

105 See, e.g., D.A. O'Sullivan, *A Manual of Government in Canada, or The Principles and Institutions of our Federal and Provincial Constitutions* (Toronto: J.C. Stuart 1879); J.D. Travis, *A Law Treatise on the Constitutional Powers of Parliament and of the Local Legislatures Under the British North America Act, 1867* (St. John, N.B.: Sun Publishing 1884); T.-J.-J. Loranger, *Letters Upon the Interpretation of the Federal Constitution* (Quebec: Morning Chronicle 1883); W.H.P. Clement, *The Law of the Canadian Constitution* (Toronto: Carswell 1892); Lefroy, *Legisla-*

tive Power; A. Todd, *Parliamentary Government in the British Colonies* (Boston: Little, Brown 1880); J.G. Bourinot, *A Manual of the Constitutional History of Canada from the Earliest Period to the Year 1888* (Montreal: Dawson Bros. 1888); and J.G. Bourinot, *Federal Government in Canada* (Baltimore: Johns Hopkins University 1889).

106 Risk, 'Constitutional Scholarship,' at 449.

107 Compare C. Armstrong and H.V. Nelles, 'Private Property in Peril: Ontario Businessmen and the Federal System, 1898–1911,' in G. Porter and R.D. Cuff, eds., *Enterprise and National Development: Essays in Canadian Business and Economic History* (Toronto: Samuel Stevens Hakkert 1973), 20; P. Gillis, 'Big Business and the Origins of the Conservative Reform Movement in Ottawa, 1890–1912,' *Journal of Canadian Studies* 15 no. 1 (1980), 93; and C. Armstrong, *The Politics of Federalism: Ontario's Relations with the Federal Government, 1867–1942* (Toronto: University of Toronto Press 1981).

108 Risk, 'Scholars and the Constitution.'

109 Compare P.J. Monahan, 'At Doctrine's Twilight: The Structure of Canadian Federalism,' *University of Toronto Law Journal* 34 (1984), 47; K. Swinton, *The Supreme Court and Canadian Federalism* (Toronto: Carswell 1990); and B. Ryder, 'The Demise and Rise of the Classical Paradigm in Canadian Federalism: Promoting Autonomy for the Provinces and First Nations,' *McGill Law Journal* 36 (1991), 308.

110 Compare W. Kaplan, *Bad Judgment: The Case of Mr. Justice Leo A. Landreville* (Toronto: The Osgoode Society for Canadian Legal History 1996); C. Wilton, ed., *Inside the Law: Canadian Law Firms in Historical Perspective* (Toronto: The Osgoode Society for Canadian Legal History 1996); J. Benidickson, 'From Empire Ontario to California North: Law and Legal Institutions in Twentieth Century Ontario,' *Manitoba Law Journal* 23 (1995), 620.

111 Risk, 'Blake and Liberty'; Risk, 'Rights Talk.'

112 Compare Baker, 'Reconstitution'; Kostal, 'Legal Justice, Social Justice'; C.B. Backhouse, 'Married Women's Property Law in Nineteenth-Century Canada,' *Law and History Review* 6 (1988), 211; Romney, 'From Constitutionalism to Legalism'; Girard, 'Themes and Variations in Early Canadian Legal Culture'; M.M.P. Stokes, 'Petitions to the Legislative Assembly of Ontario from Local Governments, 1867–1877: A Case Study in Legislative Participation,' *Law and History Review* 11 (1993), 145; E. Tucker, 'The Faces of Coercion: The Legal Regulation of Labour Conflict in Ontario, 1880–1889,' *Law and History Review* 11 (1993), 277; and C. Backhouse, 'The White Women's Labor Laws: Anti-Chinese Racism in Early Twentieth-Century Canada,' *Law and History Review* 14 (1996), 315.

113 Flaherty, 'Writing Canadian Legal History,' at 10.

114 See generally J. Phillips, 'Recent Publications in Canadian Legal History,'
     Canadian Historical Review 78 (1997), 236; J. Benidickson, 'Survey of Canadian
     Legal History in the '90s,' *Ottawa Law Review* 28 (1997), 433; and J. Phillips,
     'Crime and Punishment in the Dominion of the North: Canada From New
     France to the Present,' in C. Emsley and L.A. Knafla, eds., *Crime Histories and
     Histories of Crime* (Westport, Conn.: Greenwood Press 1996), 163.
115 See, e.g., P.N. Oliver, *'Terror to Evil-Doers,' Prisons and Punishments in Nine-
     teenth-Century Ontario* (Toronto: University of Toronto Press for The
     Osgoode Society for Canadian Legal History 1998); F.M. Greenwood and B.
     Wright, eds., *State Trials: Law, Politics and Security Measures, 1608–1837* (To-
     ronto: The Osgoode Society for Canadian Legal History 1996); J.C. Weaver,
     *Crimes, Constables and Courts: Order and Transgression in a Canadian City,
     1816–1970* (Montreal and Kingston: McGill-Queen's University Press 1995);
     and J.-M. Fecteau *Un nouvel ordre des choses: la pauvreté, le crime et l'état au
     Québec, de la fin du XVIIIe siècle à 1840* (Outremont, Que.: VLB 1989).
116 See, e.g., C. Backhouse, *Petticoats and Prejudice: Women and Law in Nineteenth-
     Century Canada* (Toronto: The Osgoode Society for Canadian Legal History
     1991); J.W. St. G. Walker, *Race, Rights and the Law in the Supreme Court of
     Canada* (Toronto: The Osgoode Society for Canadian Legal History 1997);
     and S.G. Drummond, *Incorporating the Familiar: An Investigation into Legal
     Sensibilities in Nunavik* (Montreal and Kingston: McGill-Queen's University
     Press 1997).
117 See, e.g., S. Harring, *White Man's Law: Native People in Nineteenth Century
     Canadian Jurisprudence* (Toronto: The Osgoode Society for Canadian Legal
     History 1998); T.M. Loo, *Making Law, Order, and Authority in British Colum-
     bia, 1821–1871* (Toronto: University of Toronto Press 1994); and K. McNeil,
     Common Law Aboriginal Title (Oxford: Clarendon Press 1989).
118 See, e.g., C. Moore, *The Law Society of Upper Canada and Ontario's Lawyers,
     1797–1997* (Toronto: University of Toronto Press 1997); R.D. Gidney and
     W.P.J. Millar, *Professional Gentlemen: The Professions in Nineteenth-Century
     Ontario* (Toronto: University of Toronto Press 1994); and G. Gallichan, *Livres
     et politiques au Bas Canada: 1791–1849* (Sillery, Que.: Septentrion 1991).
119 See, e.g., D. Hay, *et al.*, eds., *Albion's Fatal Tree: Crime and Society in Eight-
     eenth-Century England* (New York: Pantheon 1975); H.W. Arthurs, *Without
     the Law: Administrative Justice and Legal Pluralism in Nineteenth-Century Eng-
     land* (Toronto: University of Toronto Press 1985); J.M. Beattie, *Crime and the
     Courts in England, 1660–1800* (Princeton: Princeton University Press 1986);
     R.W. Kostal, *Law and English Railway Capitalism, 1825–1875* (Oxford:
     Clarendon Press 1994); S.M. Waddams, *Law, Politics and the Church of Eng-
     land: The Career of Stephen Lushington, 1782–1873* (Cambridge: Cambridge

University Press 1992); and B. Boissery, *A Deep Sense of Wrong: The Treason Trials and Transportation to New South Wales of Lower Canadian Rebels After the 1838 Rebellion* (Toronto: The Osgoode Society for Canadian Legal History 1995).

120 C. Backhouse to J. Phillips, 14 January 1997.

121 See, e.g., J.E.C. Brierley, 'Quebec's Civil Law Codification Viewed and Reviewed,' *McGill Law Journal* 14 (1968), 521; J.E.C. Brierley, 'Quebec's common laws (*droits communs*): How Many are There?' in E. Caparros, ed., *Mélanges Louis-Philippe Pigeon* (Montreal: Wilson et Lafleur 1989), 109; and J.E.C. Brierley and R.A. Macdonald, 'Nature, Scope, and Techniques of the Civil Law,' in J.E.C. Brierley and R.A. Macdonald, eds., *Quebec Civil Law: An Introduction to Quebec Private Law* (Toronto: Emond, Montgomery 1993), 5.

122 See, e.g., M.M. Bowker, ed., *A Consolidation of 50 Years of Legal Writing of Wilbur F. Bowker* (Edmonton: University of Alberta Press 1989).

123 See, e.g., D. and L. Gibson, *Substantial Justice: Law and Lawyers in Manitoba 1670–1970* (Winnipeg: Peguis Publishers 1972); D. Gibson, *Attorney for the Frontier: Enos Stutsman* (Winnipeg: University of Manitoba Press 1983); and D. Gibson, 'Company Justice: Origins of Legal Institutions in Pre-Confederation Manitoba,' *Manitoba Law Journal* 23 (1996), 247.

124 See, e.g., Greenwood, 'Lord Watson'; *Legacies of Fear: Law and Politics in Quebec in the Era of the French Revolution* (Toronto: The Osgoode Society for Canadian Legal History 1993); and 'Lower Canada (Quebec): Transformation of Civil Law, from Higher Morality to Autonomous Will, 1774–1866,' *Manitoba Law Journal* 23 (1996), 132.

125 See, e.g., L.A. Knafla and T.L. Chapman, 'Criminal Justice in Canada: A Comparative Study of the Maritimes and Lower Canada 1760–1812,' *Osgoode Hall Law Journal* 21 (1983), 245; L.A. Knafla, 'From Oral to Written Memory: The Common Law Tradition in Western Canada,' in Knafla, *Law and Justice*, at 31; and L.A. Knafla, 'Richard Bonfire Bennett: The Legal Practice of a Prairie Corporate Lawyer, 1898 to 1913,' in C. Wilton, ed., *Beyond the Law: Lawyers and Business in Canada, 1830 to 1930* (Toronto: The Osgoode Society for Canadian Legal History 1990), 320.

126 See, e.g., A. Morel, *Les limites de la liberté testamentaire dans le droit civil de la Province de Québec* (Paris: L.G.D.J. 1960); A. Morel, 'La codification devant l'opinion publique de l'époque,' in J. Boucher et A. Morel, eds., *Le droit dans la vie familiale: Livre centenaire du code civil* (Montreal: Presses de l'Université de Montréal 1970), 27; and A. Morel, 'La réception du droit criminel anglais au Québec (1760–1892),' *Revue juridique thémis* 13 (1978), 449.

127 See, e.g., G. Parker, 'The Masochism of the Legal Historian,' *University of Toronto Law Journal* 24 (1974), 279; G. Parker, 'The Origins of the Canadian

Criminal Code,' in Flaherty, *Essays*, 1:249; and G. Parker, 'Canadian Legal Culture,' in Knafla, *Law and Justice*, at 3.

128 Flaherty, 'Writing Canadian Legal History,' 4.

129 Compare W.W. Fisher, 'Texts and Contexts: The Application to American Legal History of the Methodologies of Intellectual History' *Stanford Law Review* 49 (1997), 1065; M. Ermath, 'Mindful Matters: The Empire's New Codes and the Plight of Modern European Intellectual History,' *Journal of Modern History* 57 (1985), 506; and J.G.A. Pocock, 'Introduction: The State of the Art,' in J.G.A. Pocock, ed., *Virtue, Commerce, and History: Essays on Political Thought and History, Chiefly in the Eighteenth Century* (Cambridge: Cambridge University Press 1985), 1.

130 Risk, 'Law and the Economy,' 'Nuisance of Litigation,' 'Courts Under the Influence,' 'Constitutional Scholarship'; Risk and Vipond, 'Rights Talk.'

131 See, e.g., M. Gauvreau and N. Christie, *A Full-Orbed Christianity: The Protestant Churches and Social Welfare in Canada, 1900–1940* (Montreal and Kingston: McGill-Queen's University Press 1996); M. Valverde, *The Age of Light, Soap, and Water: Moral Reform in English Canada, 1885–1925* (Toronto: McClelland & Stewart 1991); W. Westfall, *Two Worlds: The Protestant Culture of Nineteenth-Century Ontario* (Montreal and Kingston: McGill-Queen's University Press 1989); F. Roy, *Progrès, harmonie, liberté: le liberalisme des milieux d'affaires francophones de Montréal au tournant du siècle* (Montreal: Boréal 1988); S.E. Zeller, *Inventing Canada: Early Victorian Science and the Idea of a Transcontinental Nation* (Toronto: University of Toronto Press 1987); D. Owram, *The Government Generation: Canadian Intellectuals and the State, 1900–1945* (Toronto: University of Toronto Press 1986); R. Cook, *The Regenerators: Social Criticism in Late Victorian English Canada* (Toronto: University of Toronto Press 1985); L. Armour and E. Trott, *The Faces of Reason: An Essay on Philosophy and Culture in English Canada 1850–1950* (Waterloo, Ont.: Wilfrid Laurier University Press 1981); A.B. McKillop, *A Disciplined Intelligence: Critical Inquiry and Canadian Thought in the Victorian Era* (Montreal and Kingston: McGill-Queen's University Press 1979); and C. Berger, *The Sense of Power: Studies in the Ideas of Canadian Imperialism, 1867–1914* (Toronto: University of Toronto Press 1970).

132 Risk, 'John Willis,' at 550, 521.

3

'Your Conscience Will Be Your Own Punishment':The Racially Motivated Murder of Gus Ninham, Ontario, 1902

CONSTANCE BACKHOUSE

Shortly before midnight on 21 June 1902, Gustus 'Gus' Ninham, a forty-one-year-old Aboriginal man, was brutally beaten to death by a group of drunken, white, working-class men. The murder took place several miles south of the outskirts of London, Ontario, near Sharkey's Hotel on Pipe Line Road (now Springbank Drive) where the white men had been drinking and carousing late into the evening.

The murder of Gus Ninham, together with the resulting coroner's inquest, preliminary inquiry, and criminal trial, offers a particularly salient window into the history of racism in central Canada at the turn of the century. Although Canadian legal historians are now beginning to subject issues of race to serious scrutiny, there are as yet few detailed studies of racially motivated violence from Canada's past. While some historical writing has begun to examine mob violence directed against Jewish, Asian, and African-Canadian communities during the first half of the twentieth century, very little research has been published that explores racially motivated violence between whites and Aboriginal peoples.[1]

A clear-cut example of a racially motivated crime, the murder of Gus Ninham provides an opportunity to redress this omission. The ensuing legal proceedings permit a detailed dissection of the sensitive nature of race relations between Aboriginal and white communities in south-western Ontario and the complex interplay between race, class, and masculinity. The role played by the press adds another fundamental element to this inquiry and invites analysis of how newspapers have reflected and shaped perceptions of the legal process in the past. This was a cross-race murder that not only gripped the individuals, families, and friends directly involved but also captivated public attention for four full months. The substance and tone of the local press coverage is remarkably revealing of the attitudes that prevailed toward Aboriginal and white, working-class communities at the time.

Gus Ninham was a member of the Onyota'a:ka Nation, also known as the 'Oneida' of the Six Nations Confederacy.[2] He was a descendant of the group of Onyota'a:ka forced off their ancestral lands in New York in the wake of the American War of Independence. Many resettled in Wisconsin, but about four hundred migrated to Delaware Township in Middlesex County between 1840 and 1845, where they formed the nucleus of what came to be known as the 'Oneida on the Thames.' The overriding motivation of the group that settled in south-western Ontario was to establish a new community where they could maintain their language, religion, and culture separate from white people. Initially, the Onyota'a:ka outnumbered the whites in Delaware Township, and for the first twenty years there was little direct contact between the Onyota'a:ka and their white neighbours. Both communities tended to designate the other as racially distinct and inferior.[3]

By the last quarter of the nineteenth century, however, the insularity that had characterized the two communities began to disintegrate. As subsistence farming gave way to commercial crop production, there were pressures on some members of both the Onyota'a:ka and white populations to seek day labouring jobs. The young white men and women from the rural farms migrated to growing urban centres, such as London, whose population increased from 5,000 in 1851 to 39,000 by 1901. The Onyota'a:ka hired themselves out as agricultural labourers to the remaining white farmers.[4]

Onyota'a:ka society was subjected to increasing stress from economic dislocation and acculturating pressures from missionaries, teachers, and Indian agents. Two years before Gus Ninham's murder, however, there had been concerted efforts to re-enforce traditional culture, marked in part by the establishment of a Longhouse, the emergence of the Handsome Lake religion, and efforts to reclaim Onyota'a:ka linguistic heritage. Some have characterized the first years of the twentieth century as a 'period of renaissance' for the Onyota'a:ka.[5]

NEWS OF THE MURDER

The first word the citizens of London had of the murder was the headline blazoned across the top of the London *Free Press* on Monday morning,

23 June 1902: 'Gus Ninham ... Murdered ... Indian Berry Picker Victim of Foul Play – Attack Unprovoked.' The paper described the murder as 'foul' and 'brutal,' reporting that Ninham had been felled by a fist or a stone, repeatedly kicked or jumped on when prostrate, then carelessly dragged from where he fell in the dust on the road across the ditch to a fence. One reporter noted indignantly that the murderers 'had not [even] taken the trouble to carry the probably dying man.' No arrests had been made, but the newspapers advised that the men who committed the assault were 'white,' that the attack had ensued after the culprits directed a 'running tirade' of racial abuse toward Ninham, and that local constables were hot on the trail of the men involved.[6] The other local newspaper, the London *Advertiser*, covered the murder with equal interest.[7] The virtually identical coverage from the two rival papers, which rarely dealt with the same material, suggests a remarkable unanimity of opinion regarding Gus Ninham's death and provides one of the most accurate surviving gauges with which to measure the response of the white community to the racially motivated murder.[8]

In bizarre juxtaposition, both newspapers situated the brutal attack in a landscape described in vocabulary worthy of a travelogue brochure:

The terrible deed occurred at one of the prettiest spots in the whole of magnificent Middlesex. About are luxuriant fruit farms. The eye takes in on one hand the water-works hill; on the other is Woodland Cemetery. At the foot of the sideroad may be seen through the trees the River Thames flowing peacefully by ... The night was beautifully moonlight ... It is a place inviting calm and repose. (London *Free Press*)[9]

The scene of the murder is well known to the people of London ... only sixty paces from the Pipe Line road, one of the most used thoroughfares in the county of Middlesex. [...] The country in the immediate neighbourhood of Woodbank, which is the post office name of the corner where Sharkey's hotel is, is strikingly beautiful ... A spring of pure water flows continually by the side of the hotel ... [F]rom the hotel itself a view can be obtained, of rice fields and woodlands, of the winding Thames and heavily-forested hills, that is unexcelled in this portion of Ontario. (London *Advertiser*)[10]

Londoners were fond of extolling the praises of their city and its environs. They were proud of having founded a settlement at the picturesque forks of the Thames River, of having supplanted forest with a bustling urban centre of finance, manufacturing, and trade. The city self-consciously displayed its affluence through proper Victorian accoutrements: great public edifices, well-groomed parks and lawns, magnificent churches, and costly private homes. Yet the surrounding countryside retained a lingering fascination for the citizens of progress. It was as if the 'mellow June moon, looking down upon the neighbourhood of Sharkey's hotel ... [amidst] the peaceful natural beauties of the surroundings' accentuated the heinousness of the crime.[11]

The attention to physical detail that marks the description of the murder scene also punctuated the reporters' sketches of the deceased. The London *Advertiser* pronounced the murdered man 'of splendid physique ... a fine specimen of manhood ... a clear six feet high, and muscularly built,'[12] while the London *Free Press* informed its readers that the deceased was 'very fleet of foot and an athlete.' He was 'splendidly developed,' particularly in height and upper body dimensions: 'Standing six feet in his stockings, he was broad of shoulder, with powerful chest.'[13] The reporters seem to have wished to draw a parallel between the verdant, fertile countryside and the virile, muscular body of the deceased. The tragic demise of Gus Ninham, the 'splendid' 'Oneida brave,' somehow accentuated the importance of reflecting upon the flora and fauna of the countryside itself.[14]

Apart from their almost prurient accounts of Gus Ninham's physique, the newspapers also disclosed more salient details about the deceased man's family and status in the community. Gus Ninham was the son of Elijah Ninham, a former county constable appointed by the Royal Canadian Mounted Police to keep the peace on the 'reserve,' and an 'aged mother [living] in Wisconsin.'[15] The newspapers reported that Gus had lived on the Onyota'a:ka reserve, was married, and that his grieving wife was lying seriously ill back home.[16] Gus Ninham had two sons, Zachariah and Elijah, aged fifteen and thirteen respectively, both of whom were overcome with sorrow on learning of their father's death.[17] He was also survived by a sister and a brother, Alf Ninham, who was a 'famous sprinter.'[18] Another well-known relative, Gus Ninham's uncle Martin, was acknowledged throughout both the Onyota'a:ka and white communities as 'Doctor' Ninham and widely acclaimed for his expertise in 'Indian remedies' and herbal medicine.[19] Gus Ninham was a first cousin to John Ninham, a hereditary chief of the Onyota'a:ka on the Thames.[20] Both Chief John Ninham and Elijah Ninham, Gus's father, were highly respected leaders among the Onyota'a:ka, known for their skill in resolving property and family disputes between members of the community.[21]

Under the caption 'An Inoffensive Indian,' the *Free Press* noted that Gus

Ninham's death was 'deeply deplored by the Oneida tribe,' and that 'the dead man had many friends among his own people.' The reporters seem to have had some difficulty eliciting direct information about Ninham from his Onyota'a:ka friends and relatives, who were depicted as 'very stoical' and 'very quiet all day Sunday,' reputedly engaged in serious discussions amongst themselves about the murder.[22] Great sadness had spread through the Onyota'a:ka community at the news, and a number of theories were circulating about Gus Ninham's death.[23] There was some fear that the Onyota'a:ka would not cooperate in the criminal investigation, with the detectives assigned to the case advising that 'they expect[ed] some difficulty in securing a complete statement, owing to the reticence of the Indians and their disinclination to talk.' There were consequently few press interviews with any of the Onyota'a:ka as to Gus Ninham's reputation and character. But the London *Advertiser* did cite the comments of his white employer, a more 'ready informant.' Charles Wesley Baker Jr, the owner of a fruit farm near Pipe Line Road about a third of a mile from Sharkey's Hotel, described Ninham as 'a quiet sort of a fellow' and 'a good worker.' Baker added that he had 'never heard of him getting into any rows,' and that he was 'good to his wife and family.'[24]

Baker's strawberry crop had ripened one week earlier, and Gus Ninham had been one of thirty-five Onyota'a:ka men, women, and children employed to harvest the fruit. The First Nations fruit pickers were housed in the hay lofts of the large barns at the rear of Baker's property.[25] The *Free Press* described the situation, for the benefit of its urban readers, in patronizing prose: 'The Indians are particularly clever in gathering the luscious fruit. With their nimble fingers they fill the berry boxes before noon with comparative ease. They are controlled without much trouble, and are always on hand, because they sleep in the barns and outbuildings on the farm. Besides, it is difficult to obtain whites who are content to pick berries for a living.'[26]

Gus Ninham's dead body was initially transported to one of Baker's barns and subsequently removed, under orders from the detectives, to 'Ferguson's undertaking warerooms.' A 'curious crowd' thronged the morgue later that day, hoping to 'catch a glimpse of the dead man.'[27] Since an inquest was scheduled to inquire into the circumstances surrounding the death, two white male physicians were appointed to conduct a post mortem examination of the body. Then the remains were turned over to the Onyota'a:ka community. Their customs required the laying out of the dead at home for a wake that lasted several days and nights. During the mourning period, normal activities were postponed so that people could congregate in the home of the deceased to eulogize the dead, recount his accomplishments, mourn his passing, pray for the safe journey of his spirit, and organize a 'tenth day feast' to send the spirit on its way.[28] Undoubtedly ignorant of the Onyota'a:ka customs, the press advised that 'the body of [the] deceased will be taken to Oneida, near Munceytown, for burial. "Gus" Ninham will sleep with his fathers in the little cemetery of the redmen.'[29]

THE ARREST OF THE SUSPECT

On Wednesday, 25 June 1902, a mere four days after the murder, the papers announced the arrest of the main suspect, John Colin McArthur. The accused was a twenty-eight-year-old, red-haired white man, who resided on a farm on Wharncliffe Road just outside the city limits in Westminster township. In the midst of a neighbourhood peopled by small farmers, gardeners, labourers and pedlars, the McArthur property had originally been farmed by John's father, the late Alexander McArthur. After Alexander's death, John, his widowed mother Catherine, and his two other brothers, Alexander Jr (aged thirty) and Albert (aged twenty-six) continued to cultivate wheat, prune small orchard plots, and raise some cattle, hogs, and horses. It was the youngest brother, Albert, who seems to have inherited the status of head of the family. Despite his youth, Albert was listed along with his mother as the freeholder of the land in the local directory.[30] The younger brother may have been the more responsible of the three boys. Certainly, John's reputation suggests that there was good reason to pass over him. According to the press, John McArthur was a 'well known character about town,' recognized for his signature 'black Fedora' hat and said to be 'fond of a fight,' a 'hard drinker,' and 'a dangerous man when in his cups.' He had been 'in trouble with the local police more than once' and had had at least one former scuffle with a police constable. McArthur had also been charged previously in connection with the 'brutal beating' of a young man from north of the city, ostensibly for stealing his whip. The warden who booked McArthur into the London Jail listed his country of birth as 'Canada,' his religion as 'Presbyterian,' his race as 'white,' his marital status as 'single,' his education as 'elementary,' and his 'habits' as 'intemperate.' The reporters eagerly seized on the opportunity to sketch a provocative portrait of the arrested man. In language similar to that used to describe the deceased, McArthur was described as 'a man of magnificent physique,' a 'strapping fellow,' 'massively built' and of 'unusual proportions,' a 'very powerful man, standing six feet six inches, and weighing 230 pounds.' Indeed, he was pronounced 'even bigger than the dead Indian.'[31]

It seems as if the press were treating the affair as a sporting match, expecting readers to be avid for the exact measurements of the contestants, their records as prizefighters, and the predictions of the odds-makers. Unquestionably a cavalier and disparaging way to report on a murder, the perspective seems to have framed the racial and class backgrounds of the deceased and his alleged killer, reflecting stereotypical assumptions about the physical attributes and pugilistic prowess of both subordinate groups. The press irreverently capitalized on the reputation of the Onyota'a:ka, who were famed throughout south-western Ontario for the many skilled athletes among their community. 'Given a fair chance, [Ninham] should have made a great fight for his life,' wagered the *Free Press*. One reporter even unearthed details about a cousin of Gus Ninham's, said to be 'an athlete of no mean powers,' who 'was famous as a fighter of the rough-and-tumble variety.' The papers contained detailed descriptions of one of the celebrated matches Gus's 'dusky' cousin had won at an Elgin county fall fair. The Ninham family was represented to be solidly behind Gus. 'His uncle said that with a fair chance [Gus Ninham] would have given any man a stiff fight,' offered the London *Advertiser*.[32]

Having sized up the support of the Onyota'a:ka community for their candidate, although not without some difficulty, given the reluctance of the First Nations community to speak to the press, the reporters took care to foster some balancing sentiment for his white opponent. Noting that John McArthur's mother and son were 'much respected,' the London *Free Press* intoned: 'Intense sympathy will be felt for them on all hands, for they are esteemed by many.'[33]

That the race dimensions of the fight were evident to all is underscored by one reporter who quoted Rudyard Kipling:

> But there is neither east nor west,
>   nor border, nor breed, nor birth
> When two strong men stand face to face,
>   though they come from the ends of the earth.

The same reporter reminded readers that Gus Ninham was 'not the first of his family to meet a violent death at the hands of a member of the supposedly more civilized dominant race in Canada.'[34] Gus's uncle, 'Doctor' Martin Ninham, had been murdered by a pair of white male ruffians some years earlier. This murder, too, had overtones of a grudge match. Martin

Ninham's assailant was a young, white prizefighter, embittered by his recent drubbing at the hands of Ninham's son in a scheduled match at the Elgin county fall fair. Setting upon Martin Ninham and his son as they were shopping for supplies in St Thomas, the white avenger had mistakenly killed the elder Doctor Ninham instead of his son.[35]

THE INQUEST PROCEEDS

It was the 'more civilized dominant race' that took full and exclusive charge of the legal inquiry into the circumstances of Gus Ninham's death. The nine-day inquest began on Friday evening, 27 June 1902. Coroner Robert Ferguson, a thirty-four-year-old, white London physician who ran a general medical practice from his Wortley Road residence, presided over the forty-seven witnesses called to testify in the matter. The office of the coroner was an English legal institution that had been transplanted to Canada. Coroners were appointed to investigate situations of violent or apparently unnatural death; charged with determining the cause of death, they swore in a panel of local male jurors to hear evidence from medical and other witnesses. Hearings were usually less formal and the testimony more candid than would be offered in court. Findings were forwarded to the Crown attorney, and where there was evidence of foul play formal criminal charges would ensue.[36]

At the commencement of the inquest, 'several hundred spectators' packed into the small chamber and 'strained their ears to catch every word of the evidence.' In keeping with its self-defined role as colour commentator at an event akin to a boxing match, the press took great pains to relay the appearance and mood of the contestants. John McArthur 'appeared cheerful and collected,' without the 'slightest sign of discomposure,' the London *Advertiser* disclosed. Although he 'scanned keenly the dark faces of the Indian witnesses,' he seemed 'in good spirits' and was observed 'conversing with his lawyer unconcernedly.' The *Free Press* expanded enthusiastically on its description of the 'young giant': '[McArthur stood] 6 foot 6 of splendid physical manhood ... He maintained a calm if not cheerful countenance and frequently his features relaxed into a smile as one or other of the Indian witnesses made a funny "break" in telling their stories in their imperfect English. His huge and not unhandsome bulk, seated just behind his counsel, formed the most striking figure in the room ...'[37]

The imbalance in the contest is starkly apparent here. Not only was one of the chief protagonists, Gus Ninham, missing from the courthouse proceedings, but those who served as witnesses on his behalf were all

Aboriginal, and the testimony of Aboriginal people had long been regarded with some suspicion.[38] The usage of Aboriginal language loomed large over the inquest. During the hearing, the newspapers made no fewer than nine comments, many in disparaging terms, about the Onyota'a:ka witnesses who insisted upon giving their testimony in the Onyota'a:ka language through the services of a First Nations interpreter.[39] The London *Advertiser* complained that one young Onyota'a:ka man, Jacob Doxtater, 'disclaimed all knowledge of the English language' and 'stood like a Sphinx till the services of Mrs. Antone, an intelligent Oneida interpreter were secured.'[40]

Indeed, facility with English seems to produce an uncanny fit in the newspapers' assessment of intellectual prowess. The *Free Press* pronounced Cornelius Antoine, 'a somewhat bright [Indian] boy, who spoke English very well and seemed anxious to tell all he knew about the murder,' while the unilingual Jacob Doxtater, a 'brave of sixteen years,' was labelled 'decidedly dull.' The apparently incredulous reporter advised that Doxtater had 'led the Crown Attorney to believe that he could not speak a word of English and it was only with difficulty that his evidence was dragged out of him with the assistance of Mrs. Antoine [sic], an intelligent Indian woman, who was acting as interpreter.' With gratuitous finality, the *Free Press* added that Doxtater was 'very unkempt in his appearance, even for a red man.'[41] When another Onyota'a:ka witness, Joshua Nichols, disclaimed knowledge of English, John McArthur's white defence lawyer, John F. Faulds, expressed the opinion that 'the Indians could all talk English, as he had lived near them.' He accused the First Nations witnesses of deliberately conspiring 'to evade the giving of evidence in the English language.'[42]

This was an era in which whites who professed expertise over First Nations matters had concluded, with virtual unanimity, that Aboriginal languages should be rooted out and destroyed. The 'more civilized dominant race' had decided that First Nations communities required assimilation into the European social order. A report commissioned by the federal government in 1879 had recommended that First Nations children be removed from their homes to be educated in residential and boarding schools, away from all Aboriginal influences, where attendance, dress, behaviour, and language could be carefully monitored. By 1900, out of an estimated total First Nations population of 20,000 between the ages of six and fifteen, 3,285 children were enrolled in twenty-two industrial and thirty-nine boarding schools, and another 6,349 in 226 day schools. Many were subjected to physical punishment for speaking their own languages, even when they knew no English.[43]

There were several small Methodist and Anglican schools operating within the Onyota'a:ka community. Although Onyota'a:ka teachers staffed two of the three schools for some period of time, all teaching was done in English, and the curriculum centred on manual arts with a stress on 'discipline and order.' Students who wished to go beyond the primary grades were shipped off to residential schools such as the Mohawk Institute at Brantford and the Mount Elgin Industrial Institution across the Thames River at Delaware. The latter was derogatorily known as 'the Mush Hole' by former students, due to the 'mushlike' character of most meals. There the girls studied cooking, sewing, cleaning, mending, and quilting, while the boys learned carpentry, care of livestock, and farming skills. Harsh corporal punishment was the order of the day. At the Mount Elgin Industrial Institution, the young Onyota'a:ka were forced to accept complete acculturation: 'The children were forbidden to speak their Indian [sic] languages: punctuality, a balanced diet, and tidy housekeeping were emphasized along with religion and the "three R's." The children went to school for half of the day, and they worked on the school farm and performed housekeeping chores during the other half.'[44]

Some within the First Nations successfully resisted this drive toward assimilation. Unwilling to abandon their spiritual, political, and cultural traditions, they strove to maintain their linguistic inheritances. The Onyota'a:ka, in particular, struggled to preserve their language, viewing it as essential to Longhouse traditions and the political foundations of First Nations sovereignty. That so many of the Onyota'a:ka witnesses spoke their own language during the inquiry into Gus Ninham's death is indicative not of ignorance or evasiveness but of pride in Onyota'a:ka traditions and insistence that the distinctive Onyota'a:ka culture and language be recognized and accommodated by the white legal system.[45]

Efforts to bully the Onyota'a:ka witnesses into speaking English were not the only intimidatory tactics facing the Aboriginal participants. There had apparently been even more blatant efforts to threaten the witnesses. One day after the murder the press released a report that John Charles, the man expected to be the key Onyota'a:ka witness in the trial, had been subjected to an attempt at evidence tampering. 'Word reached the county detectives that Charles had been visited Sunday night by strange men, who warned him to keep his mouth shut,' advised the London *Free Press*.[46]

John Charles was a fifty-one-year-old resident of the Onyota'a:ka reserve, employed on a sugar beet farm in Glanworth in Westminster township. He had travelled to Baker's strawberry farm on Saturday, 21 June the day of the murder, to spend the weekend with friends, and had been the only other Onyota'a:ka present when Gus Ninham was fatally assaulted. Despite the threats directed against him, Charles took the stand first at the inquest. He gave an eyewitness account of the beating Gus Ninham had suffered and provided an unequivocal identification of John McArthur as Ninham's assailant, calling out, 'That's the man,' as McArthur was led into the courthouse.[47]

John Charles recounted how he had met Gus Ninham and Ninham's two sons at Springbank Park on the night of the murder, to take in the vaudeville show at the Pavilion. Theatre, band concerts, and fireworks displays had been drawing large crowds in Springbank Park since 1897, when the London Street railway company began offering public entertainment as a promotional device to entice Londoners to ride its newly constructed streetcar line between London and Springbank Park. When the show ended shortly after 10:00 p.m., the Ninham boys left by streetcar. Gus Ninham and John Charles departed separately on foot, intending to walk back to Baker's farm. Their route on Pipe Line Road took them past Sharkey's Hotel around midnight, where they decided to stop for a drink of water. A nearby spring fed into a tapped pipe at the side of the road near the hotel verandah. The two Onyota'a:ka men walked over to the tap, then noticed six or eight white men on the verandah. The tallest called out 'with an oath' and ordered Gus Ninham and John Charles away.[48]

John Charles explained that he stepped back quietly at this point. This was not the first time he had encountered John McArthur's erratic behaviour. Some two years earlier, McArthur and one of his white friends, James Glover, had launched a vicious fist attack on the Onyota'a:ka man, lacerating Charles's ear. But Charles revealed nothing of the earlier altercation at the inquest that day; he stated merely that he had chosen not to antagonize McArthur in front of Sharkey's Hotel on the night of the murder.[49] Gus Ninham, however, refused to be intimidated. 'Hello John,' said Ninham, who apparently recognized the white man as John McArthur. 'Hello, Ninham; what are you doing here?' was the reply. 'I want a drink,' responded Ninham. 'You can't get a drink,' was the retort. 'You damn Indians had better get out of here.' Gus Ninham stood his ground, and the tall white man jumped off the verandah shouting, 'Damn you, I'll make you go,' as he shoved the Onyota'a:ka man backwards. Ninham's reply was direct and to the point: 'I don't think I'll go any further. I ain't going to be shoved by anybody; I'm not doing anything and am on the King's highway.'

The white man continued to swear at Gus Ninham and began shoving and pushing him over the course of some fifty or sixty yards. Then he struck Ninham with his right fist and knocked him on the grass. Ninham apparently gave no provocation and made no attempt to strike back. The white man took his boots to Ninham, repeatedly kicking the prostrate man while Ninham protested, 'Hold on, John,' three or four times. The kicking continued well after Ninham stopped speaking. Charles identified McArthur without hesitation as the white assailant, stating that prior to the altercation McArthur had walked up to Charles shouting 'You damned Indian get out of here,' and stuck his face 'within ten inches of my face' making it fully visible in the bright moonlight.[50]

When McArthur finally stopped kicking Ninham, John Charles fled away from the hotel 'as fast as he could' and soon overtook four Onyota'a:ka men driving home in a buggy. Levi Doxtater, Jonas Cooper, David Williams, and Cornelius Antoine turned the buggy around and raced back to the spot where Gus Ninham had last been seen. They told the inquest that they found Ninham's body lying in the dirt, his coat 'drawn up to under his arm pits,' his hat 'lying about 8 or 10 feet from his feet.' They had just climbed down to examine the body when they saw two 'good sized' men jump up from beside the fence near the body and run off through the field. The Onyota'a:ka gave chase but failed to apprehend the fleeing suspects and were unable to identify them. They explained that white men were milling about the verandah and inside Sharkey's Hotel during the chase. One of the fugitives who ran through the field apparently returned to the hotel for shelter. Levi Doxtater told the inquest he pursued the fugitives no further, and that he did not 'did not think it safe' to report Ninham's death 'to any one at the hotel.'[51]

Five other Onyota'a:ka youths, Joshua Nichols, Augustus Doxtater, Jacob Doxtater, Jacob Ireland, and John Elijah, recounted how they had passed by Sharkey's Hotel just prior to the murder that night, and stopped to pump up one of their bicycle wheels. There they had been harassed by a tall white man with 'reddish hair,' who leaped down from the hotel verandah and jumped on one of the bicycles. 'Don't you break my wheel,' exclaimed Joshua Nichols. 'Who in hell wants to break your wheel?' replied the white man, who then drove off with it. When he returned ten minutes later, he was restrained by several of the other white men present, who told him, 'Don't touch the boys. They are going home.' One of the white men brought out a 'parcel' containing a bottle of liquor and handed it to the Onyota'a:ka boys, apparently as a conciliatory gesture. The tall man then imperiously ordered the Onyota'a:ka to 'go right straight home.' Two of the Onyota'a:ka youths were able to make positive identification of John McArthur as the 'big white man' who had harassed them.[52] At least one of these young men was also subjected to intimidation for giving this evidence, his horse and buggy chased out of town by white supporters of John McArthur.[53]

The First Nations testimony stands in stark contrast to the evidence of the white witnesses. Hugh Sharkey Jr, the proprietor of the hotel, claimed he had closed down the hotel bar well before the murder, about 11:30 p.m. that night, after which not a single light was left on in the building. He admitted that McArthur, a long-time acquaintance of his, had been at the bar earlier, but insisted that the accused man had left nearly an hour before closing. Questioned closely on cross-examination whether 'these Indians are all mistaken, then, who said there was a light in the bar room,' Sharkey Jr replied vehemently: 'They are mistaken, and it was the worst lie ever heard ... between God and man.' Sharkey Jr swore that although there had been a few 'Indians' around the hotel at dusk, he had seen none, dead or alive, thereafter.

Hugh Sharkey's testimony was systematically corroborated by no fewer than thirteen white men, all of whom claimed to have been at the hotel that evening. The hotel, famous as one of the toughest hang-outs around, seems to have been something of an after-hours club for hard-drinking, roustabout labourers. One after another, teamsters, railway employees, cigar makers, carpet layers, barrel makers, factory hands, brickyard workers, barbers, and tinsmiths took the stand under subpoena to recount their recollections of the night in question. All duly testified that John McArthur, if he had been there at all, had left well before the hotel closed. All carefully held to the story that they had 'seen no Indians,' 'seen no one running across the field,' and 'heard no trouble.'[54]

William McBride, a brickyard worker who resided on Johnston Street in south London, was one of those suspected of taking to flight across the field. He testified that he saw John McArthur leave Sharkey's Hotel around 10:30 p.m., driving a horse-drawn, covered Gladstone rig. McBride claimed he had left the hotel himself shortly after 11 p.m., and insisted that 'he saw no Indians.' Under cross-examination, McBride got quite confused about the time, contradicting himself and finally admitting he could not reconcile conflicting statements about the time of departure from Sharkey's.[55] Jeanette (Nettie) McBride, the wife of William McBride, testified next in an endeavour to provide her husband with a sound alibi. She told the inquest that her husband had returned home from Sharkey's Hotel around midnight, in 'sober' condition. She denied having met with McArthur after the murder to reconcile the stories, but the London *Advertiser* reported that, throughout her testimony '[Mrs McBride] showed signs of great nervousness.'[56]

The press was quite free with its assessment of the credibility of various witnesses. William Quick, a labourer who lived on Bruce Street, proved to be an 'excitable and hesitant' witness, who 'made anything but a favourable impression' according to the *Advertiser*. Quick was another of the men suspected of direct involvement in the fatal assault. He too insisted that McArthur had left the hotel around 10:30 p.m., and he had followed shortly thereafter. He was so quick to swear he did 'not see any Indians that night' that the coroner had to caution him 'not to get excited' and 'to listen to the attorney's question before answering it.' Quick denied having boasted he was within five feet of Ninham when the deceased was knocked down, and denied being one of the men who fled across the field that night. He protested vigorously that he had not crossed the border to Michigan to avoid giving evidence, insisting that he was merely visiting a brother-in-law in Marine City for a few days after the murder.[57]

At least two of the white witnesses were caught in outright falsehoods. Albert Abel, a carpet layer who lived with his father on Pipe Line Road, conceded his story conflicted with the alibi he had concocted for detectives earlier. Another of the key suspects, Abel first claimed he arrived home as early as 8:30 p.m. on the night of the murder, but this, he later acknowledged, was a 'wilful lie.' Queried about the reason for the lie, Abel admitted that 'he did not think [the detectives] had any business to ask him such questions.'[58] James 'Brasil' Fox, a cigar maker who lived with his mother on William Street, also admitted lying to the police, adding he was 'drunk at the time and so was liable to say anything.' He was 'always liable to lie to the police,' Fox added for good measure. There was also evidence from a London livery employee regarding one of their Gladstone rigs and dark stallions, hired out on the evening of 21 June and returned to the stable later that evening. The records from the livery orderbook had apparently been tampered with, for they showed 10:30 p.m. as the time the rig was brought back, a time well in advance of the actual return.[59]

John F. Faulds, McArthur's defence counsel, must have been concerned about his client's position, given the weaknesses inherent in the testimony of McArthur's friends. Faulds was well known within the London legal community for his large plaintiff's practice, in which he represented scores of injured individuals seeking compensation for their damages. An astute and eloquent barrister, known as a 'ready and effective jury lawyer,' Faulds had other strategies held in reserve.[60]

Mid-way through the inquest, Faulds set up an entirely distinct line of argument. Faulds called two teenage white girls to testify they had observed a scuffle in front of a downtown London hotel around 7:30 p.m. on the night of Gus Ninham's murder. Alice and Beatrice Cox claimed to have been standing in front of the Grand Central Hotel at King and Ridout Streets, when they observed 'two Indians' rush out of the hotel fighting. About a dozen white men followed them out, and one of them separated the fighters, delivering a 'hard blow' to the 'tall Indian's nose,' which sent him staggering up against the wall. Although the girls were not able to identify anyone else in the fracas, they asserted that the 'tall Indian' was Gus Ninham. They claimed to know Ninham because they had worked with him previously picking strawberries at Baker's farm. Cross-examination revealed that the two girls had not made the positive identification until well after they arrived home, where they lived on Pipe Line Road with their parents, Mr and Mrs Thomas Cox. And then their identification had been rather hazy: '[They] thought they knew the tall Indian, and that it was Gus Ninham.' On the stand, however, there was no hesitation or uncertainty. Furthermore, the Cox girls insisted that 'no one had been talking to [them] about [their] evidence.' In statements very damaging to Gus Ninham, the girls testified that during the scuffle Ninham had a jackknife in his hand that glinted in the sunlight, and that the two Aboriginals 'appeared to be drunk.'[61]

This evidence cast a discrediting shadow over Gus Ninham's character, suggesting that he was a drinker, that he was prone to fighting, and that he was a violent sort of man. There were rumours circulating that although the girls could not identify the First Nations man they ostensibly saw fighting with Ninham, McArthur's defence lawyer would claim it was none other than John Charles. Indeed, there was some speculation that if McArthur's alibi did not hold up in court, the defence would insinuate that John Charles was the guilty party and had murdered Gus Ninham himself and blamed McArthur out of spite.[62] Some observers, however, were apparently sceptical about the veracity of the two girls' statements, and several additional witnesses were called in rebuttal. Charles Thomas, the bartender at the Grand Central Hotel, testified that he 'saw no trouble between any Indians or white man' the night of 21 June, and that 'he heard of no fight at the hotel.' Edward Patton, who boarded upstairs at the Grand Central, explained that he had been confined to his room all day and evening on 21 June with a sprained foot. He certainly had not seen or heard of 'any row between Indians,' he asserted.[63]

Just as the press had seen fit to castigate the Onyota'a:ka witnesses, so it took considerable liberties with the working-class whites. John Clark, a cigar maker from Saunby Street in London West, was roundly criticized for having 'interlarded his evidence with slangy utterances.' The newspaper editors laced their coverage of the evidence of the white men with captions such as 'searching after women,' 'a wilful lie,' and 'flippant and slangy.' Complaints about the use of slang suggest a distinct class bias, but 'flippancy' appears to have been a sound characterization of the bearing displayed by some of the white men.[64]

John Glover, the man who had attacked John Charles along with John McArthur several years earlier, was one of the brickyard workers who lived about a half mile southwest of Sharkey's Hotel. He admitted at the inquest that Ninham's death had occasioned much speculation and rumour as well as 'some joking on the subject' among the workmen at William McBride's brickyard.[65] When the Crown attorney demanded of one white witness, 'Can't you open your mouth without lying?' the reply was a short and succinct 'No.'[66] James 'Brasil' Fox gratuitously and cheerfully offered the comment that he 'was pretty drunk that evening [21 June].' Questioned by the coroner about his sobriety in the witness box, Fox replied: 'Yes, I'm sober now. I've had three or four drinks.' Even the lawyers took a devil-may-care attitude. The *Advertiser* reported the following jovial exchange: 'Did you kill the Indian?' asked defence counsel Faulds, 'with a smile.' 'No,' answered a nonchalant William Quick, 'also smiling.'[67]

The Crown attorney who directed the inquest, James Magee KC, was clearly upset over the behaviour and testimony of the white men. Magee was a fifty-four-year-old white lawyer who had been born in Liverpool, England, and immigrated to London, Ontario in 1856. Called to the bar in 1867, he had practised continuously in London, where he developed a reputation as a hard-working, courteous barrister, one of the finest legal orators in the county. He would receive a judicial appointment to the High Court of Ontario in 1904, two years after this case. A letter Magee wrote at the time of the inquest reveals his disgust: 'All these Indians saw white men round the Hotel and spoke to them, and yet not a white man was to be found who saw any Indians there after 8 p.m. The Hotel is one of the toughest and no reliance can be placed on the oaths of most of the crowd ... They have made up their minds to get MacArthur off – though it is notorious that he is guilty ...'[68]

The medical testimony also played a central role in the hearing. London physicians Dr William Ebenezer Waugh and Dr Charles F. Neu reported that their post mortem findings established without doubt that Gus Ninham had been brutally assaulted. The body was badly torn up, with three bruises to the upper back of the head caused by three separate blows, a bruise to the left cheek bone, a wound on the right elbow, a broken leg, and four fractured ribs, severed right through the cartilage. 'It was impossible to say how many blows were delivered on the body to cause the fractures found,' they concluded. The cause of death was identified as 'stoppage of the heart, due to the shock of the injuries received and the accompanying excitement.' 'If a man was knocked down and kicked as witnesses say Gus Ninham was, would it be sufficient to cause his death?' asked Crown attorney Magee. 'It would,' replied Dr Neu, one of London's leading medical experts in pathology.[69]

The most startling medical finding, however, relates to Gus Ninham's heart. The heart was 'hypertrophied and dilated, [diseased] and enlarged to about twice its normal size.' John Faulds seized eagerly on this point, with the following series of questions to Dr Neu:

Q. Would a man with a healthy heart and with his organs in normal condition have survived these injuries?
A. Yes, he would.
Q. A moderate blow would be sufficient to cause death in Ninham's case?
A. It might be.
Q. Would you have been surprised if Ninham had been found dead with no marks of violence upon his body?
A. No. I don't think I would have been.

Crown attorney Magee was quick to try to recover ground here. His questions to Dr Neu concerned Ninham's expectation of life:

Q. How long would Ninham have lived, anyway, with his heart in that condition, if he had not been injured?
A. I can scarcely give a definite answer. Without meeting with violence, Ninham might have lived for years, or might have dropped dead any minute.[70]

Another key strategy for McArthur's defence was to discredit the Onyota'a:ka witnesses with endless questions about alcohol consumption. Faulds cross-examined John Charles extensively as to his drinking activity on the day of the murder. Charles admitted that he 'drank some' earlier in the afternoon, and that the effects of the alcohol made him 'feel good.' Charles Wesley Baker testified that 'John Charles smelt strongly of liquor' when he returned to the barn after the murder later that night, and that Gus Ninham 'drank frequently, especially on pay days.' Charles admitted on cross-examination that 'he thought Ninham had been drinking' prior to arriving at Springbank Park, although 'Ninham was able to walk without staggering.' At least three of the Onyota'a:ka boys apparently took a drink out of the bottle from the parcel they were given at Sharkey's Hotel. Baker complained that nearly 'all of the Indians ... were the worse of liquor.' Even Levi Doxtater and Cornelius Antoine, who had not been drinking at all, were grilled extensively on their patterns of alcohol consumption.[71]

The press took up the same theme, portraying Ninham as 'fond of liquor' and the murder as 'undoubtedly the end of a day's carousal in which [Ninham] was joined by others of his tribe.' The London *Advertiser* interviewed William Collins, proprietor of the Collins' House tavern at York and Talbot, who advised that he 'knew Ninham well.' 'Indians Had Been Drinking,' 'Indian Was Dead Drunk' blazoned the headlines. None of this accords very well with the medical evidence, which reported 'no indications of alcohol in the contents of [Ninham's] stomach.'[72] But it played into the stereotypical assumptions linking First Nations people with liquor and violence.

From the earliest days of Aboriginal and white contact, alcohol was used as a central component of barter and exchange to grease the wheels of the profitable trade in furs. The introduction of alcoholism into North America played a devastating role in dislocating the social fabric of First Nations communities.[73] Provincial governments responded with a series of statutes to outlaw the sale of alcohol to Aboriginal peoples, enacted in 1777 in Quebec, 1801 in Ontario, 1829 in Nova Scotia, 1854 in British Columbia, and 1882 in Newfoundland.[74] When the federal government obtained constitutional jurisdiction over 'Indians' after Confederation, it enacted a host of prohibitions as well.[75] It was unlawful to 'sell, barter, supply or give' intoxicants to 'any Indian or non-treaty Indian.' It was also unlawful for 'Indians' to have intoxicants on their person, or to be found with intoxicants in their 'house, tent, wigwam or place of abode.'[76]

The legal enactments were both paternalistic and punitive in nature, many of them authorizing constables to arrest intoxicated First Nations individuals 'without process of law,' detain them in prison until they were 'sober,' and then levy substantial jail terms and fines.[77] Such draconian measures ignored the efforts of many Aboriginal communities to assert control over their own alcohol problems in more supportive and rehabilitative ways. The religious revival inspired by the Code of Handsome Lake, which spread widely throughout Iroquois communities in Canada and the United States, used spiritual efforts to root out the abuse of alcohol, for example. The approach of the legislators, however, was to lay criminal charges and imprison thousands of Aboriginal people. This mistook alcoholism as the primary problem and distracted attention away from the theft of land and cultural disruption that spawned the alcoholism in the first place. Such measures also re-enforced the damaging stereotypical belief that all 'Indians' abused alcohol.[78]

Hugh Sharkey Jr, testified that he was not alarmed when he first heard that Gus Ninham was dead, because he merely 'supposed that the Indian was dead drunk.' The Crown attorney responded sarcastically, 'Calling up the coroner for a dead drunk Indian, eh? You must call up the coroner pretty often if you do it every time.'[79] Indeed, Sharkey, whose only recollections of 'Indians' around the hotel had been confined to seeing a few at dusk, volunteered that the group he had seen 'were drunk when I first noticed them on the road.' He stressed to the London *Advertiser* that he entirely disapproved of Indians drinking liquor: 'I was told that they were drinking whisky from a bottle, so I went out and told them to go away because it would look as if I had sold the liquor to them. One of them said they were not drinking, but they moved away. I have never sold liquor to any Indian. I would not even sell them cigars, because I didn't want them to hang around here. I know the law on this matter and I've kept it.'[80]

The obvious disapproval inspired by First Nations use of liquor seems somewhat at odds with the treatment of the alcohol consumption on the part of whites. The scene of the murder was, after all, a tavern reputedly frequented by hard-drinking white labourers. The accused man, John McArthur, had apparently been out drinking at a series of bars on the day of the murder, starting around 4:00 p.m. at Boswell House, progressing to Collins' Hotel, and winding up the evening at Sharkey's. Hugh Sharkey Jr, so haughtily adamant about refusing to serve liquor to Aboriginals, bestirred the courtroom crowd to gales of laughter over his reticence to answer questions about his hours of operation. 'I refuse to testify for fear of incriminating myself,' he announced when asked whether he had breached the law by selling liquor after lawful closing time. One of his customers, James Dean, let the cat out of the bag when he testified that Sharkey Jr often insisted that after-hours drinkers leave 'by the side door,' for 'the inspector might be along.'[81]

Hugh Sharkey Sr, known as 'Old Man Sharkey,' who admitted to spending considerable time at his son's tavern, nearly brought the house down with his description of the habits of the drinking set at Sharkey's Hotel: 'They stopped to water their horses ... and to water their horses,' he announced 'amid a laugh from the crowd.' Sharkey Sr was indubitably 'an entertaining witness' pronounced the London *Advertiser*. At least three of the labourers who had been drinking at Sharkey's Hotel that night 'amused the spectators and jury' with their 'frank confessions' that they were 'pretty drunk.' They admitted to drinking a bottle of liquor in the rig on the way to Sharkey's Hotel, with one testifying he was 'too drunk to know much about the trip' and another claiming 'he was under the influence of liquor and knew practically nothing of the return journey.' Yet another claimed that the police constables who pumped him for information about the crime 'bought him a drink' during the questioning and 'bought him another drink' when they served him with a subpoena. The last was recounted by both newspapers without further comment.[82]

Neither the crowd observing the proceedings nor the press seemed concerned about the excessive consumption of liquor by the white men who testified. Hard drinking was a well-established component of white, working-class culture. But the temperance movement was in full swing in Ontario at the turn of the century, and its impact was having a discernible effect upon the middle-class jurors who officiated at the coroner's inquest. The coroner's jury obviously wished to wash its hands of the unsavoury crowd of hooligans who habituated Sharkey's Hotel bar. It urged that Sharkey's liquor licence be cancelled and pronounced the hotel 'a menace to the sobriety and morals of the community.'[83]

Initially sympathetic to the victim, the press quickly submerged its rhetoric of compassion. Possibly swayed by the theatrics of the inquest, the reporters filed stories that were fundamentally disrespectful of the solemn matter at hand, the murder of Gus Ninham. Attributing something of a 'heavyweight prize fight' atmosphere to the proceedings, reporters jocularly assessed the demonstrative crowd for size, enthusiasm, and lust for the kill. The venue was portrayed as a sort of gladiator's arena, and the contenders were evaluated for their capacity to exhilarate and sway the fans. There was endless commentary on the 'good sized crowd of spectators' drawn to witness the spectacle. The reporters were at pains to try to evoke some of the flavour of the moment for their readers: 'The usual large crowd was present ... every seat being occupied and the doors and aisles blocked.' 'The crowd was packed into the small chamber, where the air soon became foul and heavy.' 'It was somewhat boisterous, in parts unsavory, and none too kindly a crowd that occupied the back benches.'[84]

Although the papers did not trouble to describe the racial composition of the crowd, the noisiest section was clearly rooting for McArthur, who was cast as something of the 'neighbourhood champion.' Whenever McArthur's lawyer rose to make an objection, there were spontaneous shouts of 'hear, hear' from the approving and partisan crowd, which broke into wild, uproarious applause. The *Free Press* noted that the Crown attorney made some sparring remarks about 'bar room adherents' sympathy,' and the coroner, acting the part of referee, warned all present to keep to the rules. McArthur was clearly the crowd-pleasing favourite, with his devoted and impetuous entourage creating a great melee milling about the hall.[85]

On 16 July 1902, the inquest drew to a close and after two hours of deliberations, the fourteen men of the coroners' jury brought down their decision. On the matter of Gus Ninham's murder, their finding was unequivocal. He 'came to his death ... [from an] assault committed by John McArthur.' Defence counsel Faulds had clearly lost this round, despite his best efforts to impugn the character of the Aboriginal witnesses and capitalize on stereotypical beliefs about 'Indians' and alcohol. Whether Faulds scored any points with the white jurors by adopting this strategy will never be known. Whatever they may have thought of Gus Ninham and his community, they appear to have been even less impressed with the unruly crowd stepping up to attest on behalf of John McArthur. Summing up the impact of the defence witnesses on the inquest, the Crown attorney noted succinctly: 'the coroner's jury simply did not believe them.' This lesson would not be lost on John Faulds at a later stage in the proceedings. By the time of the trial, he seems to have deduced that the case would have to stand or fall on his ability to poke deeper holes in the prosecution's evidence, rather than depend upon McArthur's cronies for support.

As for the identification of McArthur as the man responsible, the Crown attorney retained no doubts: 'McArthur is a powerful fellow ... who could not be mistaken for any one else in the county.' The *Advertiser* offered its alternate assessment, in the best post-bout tradition. 'The verdict will be something of a surprise to those who have been following the evidence,' it advised, since 'it was expected that the violent treatment received by Ninham would be ascribed to unknown persons rather than to the prisoner, or other persons.' Clearly hungering for another round, the press complained that 'it was thought that the coroner's jury would leave to another body the responsibility of connecting any individual's name with the killing of the Indian.'[86]

The actual legal determination of guilt was not the province of the coroner's inquest. Its role was only to provide a public forum for an inquiry into the circumstances surrounding suspicious death. Where the evidence warranted, it was entirely proper for a coroner's jury to issue findings linking a murder to a named individual, as had been done here, but then it was up to the legal authorities to set the criminal process in motion to ascertain responsibility in a judicial forum. The next step came in the form of the preliminary inquiry before justice of the peace John B. Smyth, which began on Wednesday, 23 July 1902. John McArthur stood charged with murder and duly entered a plea of not guilty.

THE CRIMINAL TRIAL

At the preliminary inquiry, eighteen witnesses covered much the same ground as at the inquest. Only the medical evidence produced some new turns. Dr Waugh, one of the founders of the Faculty of Medicine at the University of Western Ontario, was questioned extensively about the implications of Ninham's diseased heart. He told the court:

The heart was [diseased] and enlarged to twice its normal size. A man with a heart in that condition might drop dead at any time, but under the most favourable condition might live for twenty years. The injuries to the head such as we found would produce a certain amount of shock and this shock might be sufficient to stop the heart. The cause of death was the stoppage of the heart.

A heart in that condition might stop acting without any exciting cause, I mean that would be possible. If Ninham had been a healthy man he might have recovered from any of his injuries that we found.

While much of this is a repetition of the evidence from the inquest, Dr Waugh was now much more precise about Ninham's expectation of life. He estimated a longevity of up to twenty years under the most favourable conditions.

Defence counsel John Faulds was anxious to score some points in return. His cross-examination of Dr Waugh elicited the following: 'The injuries on the head might possibly have been received some time before death. Excessive drinking would put a severe strain on [a diseased] heart and might have produced death without violence.' Faulds's tactics were directed towards planting a seed of doubt, insinuating that Ninham might have dropped dead spontaneously from complications due to heart disease. And the reference to alcoholism was clearly designed to capitalize on all of the stereotypical assumptions and speculations that had congealed around Ninham and his Onyota'a:ka community, despite the lack of any definitive evidence yet tendered regarding Ninham's consumption of alcohol on the day in question. On the whole, however, the testimony of the Onyota'a:ka witnesses as to McArthur's actions on the evening of the murder was more than sufficient to meet the threshold of evidence required to set the case down for a murder trial at the fall assizes in September.[87]

Judge William Lount presided over the opening of the assizes on 15 September 1902. Born at Holland Landing in Upper Canada in 1840, Lount received his education at the University of Toronto. He was called to the bar of Upper Canada in 1863 and first took up legal practice in Barrie before moving to Toronto. Highly regarded as a prominent criminal lawyer, Lount combined practice with political pursuits, serving as the Liberal member of the Ontario Legislature representing North Simcoe between 1867 and 1872. From Toronto, he was elected federally to the House of Commons in 1896, where he represented the riding of Toronto Centre until 1897. Lount had been appointed to the Ontario High Court of Justice just one year prior to the McArthur trial in 1901. His judicial career was fated to be short: he would die suddenly in 1903.[88]

Roger Conger Clute, KC, dubbed by the press as a lawyer with 'a heart as well as a mind,' was brought in from the Toronto Crown attorney's office to prosecute. Born in 1842 'of United Empire Loyalist stock' near Picton, Ontario, Roger Clute practised law in Belleville from 1873, moving his practice to Toronto the year of Gus Ninham's murder. Clute was frequently asked to prosecute capital cases for the Crown. Highly regarded within the profession, in 1900 he was also appointed to serve on the Royal Commission into Chinese and Japanese Immigration, and in 1904 he would be named vice-president of the Toronto Bar Association. Roger Clute would be appointed to the Ontario High Court (Exchequer Division) in 1905 and elevated to the Ontario Court of Appeal in 1913.[89]

Thirteen men were empanelled to sit on the grand jury, which was assigned to screen the cases to ensure there was sufficient evidence upon which to proceed.[90] Clute presented the key points for the Crown's case, with Mary Lyons acting as interpreter for the Onyota'a:ka witnesses. In his charge to the grand jury, Judge Lount took considerable care to draw distinctions between murder, 'the highest crime in the calendar' punishable by death, and manslaughter, a lesser offence. 'If Ninham came to his death from the effects of kicks or blows from McArthur,' Lount advised, 'the assault was wilful, malicious and unlawful' and it would amount to murder. Whether McArthur intended to kill Ninham was irrelevant, so long as he intended to administer bodily harm likely to cause death and death ensued. As for the evidence of Ninham's diseased heart, Lount counselled the jury that this was also irrelevant if the assault had accelerated the Onyota'a:ka man's death:

[I]f the assault shortened the term of Ninham's life, if he might reasonably have been expected to live for a longer term even with his diseased heart, if he had not been assaulted, [the grand jury would have to] find it murder.

If there was disease of the heart and the blows created a shock from which the Indian died, then it would be in law an acceleration of death. In such case the blows would be the primary cause of death, because in such case death would not have occurred but for the blows.[91]

In contrast, if the grand jury found Gus Ninham's death was 'due to his diseased heart, then it did not come under the crime of murder,' and the jurors should recommend proceeding under the charge of 'manslaughter.' Manslaughter was a lesser form of homicide, punishable not by death but by a maximum term of life in prison. It applied to cases where the Crown was unable to prove the requisite degree of intent or recklessness, or where the court concluded that the defence of provocation diminished the legal responsibility for the death.[92]

Cautioned by Judge Lount to be 'careful,' 'painstaking,' and 'expeditious,' the grand jury returned its finding the next afternoon. Its recommendation was to proceed under the reduced charge of manslaughter.[93] The decision to downgrade the charge appears, at least on its face, to be anomalous and somewhat at odds with the evidence. There was no legal basis for concluding that John McArthur had acted under provocation. All Gus Ninham had done was to insist on his right to take a drink of water from the spring-fed pipe at the side of a public road. Furthermore, the Crown was well positioned to prove that the kicks and blows McArthur inflicted upon Gus Ninham were intended to cause grievous bodily harm. Where the victim subsequently expired, that was sufficient to justify holding McArthur to the full charge of murder. There was no need to prove that John McArthur intended death to result from the beating. As for the complicating factor of the diseased heart, in order to reduce the charge to manslaughter the grand jury would have had to believe that Gus Ninham's death was caused by a spontaneous heart attack, unrelated to the physical beating or to the emotional shock concurrent upon the beating.[94]

But Judge Lount had taken great care to emphasize the seriousness of the murder charge, and it may be that the grand jurors were taken aback by the capital penalty, preferring to let the trial go forward on the lesser charge. Did they conclude that the murder of a man who had only a limited time left to live did not warrant hanging? Were they influenced to reduce the charge because of Ninham's Aboriginal racial status? Were they motivated by a reluctance to place a white man in jeopardy of his life for the murder of an 'Indian?' The precise reasons for the grand jurors' verdict will always remain a subject for speculation.

The newspaper reporters, who had been temporarily sidelined with coverage of the other trials that session, were quick to return with their best ringside commentary. The London *Free Press* remained fixated upon McArthur's powerful physical presence:

The prisoner's magnificent bulk was never more noticeable than on this occasion. He was neatly attired in a stylish suit of some dark material and looked to have fared very well, despite the confinement of prison life. He had himself well in hand, and betrayed no emotion, either before or after the jury had announced that they thought there was sufficient ground for him to be placed on trial on the grave charge of manslaughter.

'McArthur, stand up,' commanded the clerk of the court. ... 'Are you guilty or not guilty?' 'Not guilty,' replied McArthur in firm, full tones.

The trusty prizefighter was clearly ready for the match. His athletic prowess was implicitly being assessed against that of the deceased, whose absence ought to have struck the reporters as something of a loss to the competition. The *Free Press* could not resist a reference to 'the splendidly-proportioned body of the dead Indian' that had been laid to 'stiffen upon the rude boards' of the barn floor where it had been removed after the murder. The London *Advertiser* seemed somewhat disappointed that the reduction in charge had lowered the stakes: 'The fact that the grand jury had brought in a true bill for manslaughter against the prisoner ... has robbed the case of some of the intense interest which it would have otherwise possessed, as now only the prisoner's liberty is in jeopardy and not his life.'[95]

The trial jury was empanelled on 18 September 1902, a process that took half an hour to complete with both lawyers scrimmaging over the final selections. Faulds challenged a number of elderly men, who were removed. Presumably the defence lawyer was concerned that older jurors would be less likely to sympathize with the excesses in lifestyle of his younger client. Motivated by the opposite concern, Clute challenged a series of young men on behalf of the Crown; they were similarly unseated. Finally twelve men were found who were satisfactory to both sides. All but one were farmers from towns and rural areas just outside of London; the other was a mechanic from Westminster township. None came from Onyota'a:ka on the Thames.[96]

The omission of First Nations men from the jury was in part a factor of the legal prerequisites for jury duty. The Ontario Jurors' Act set out minimum property qualifications that would have precluded most Aboriginal and many white working-class individuals as well. A potential juror had to own assets 'in his own right' or through his wife worth no less than $600 in cities or $400 in rural areas. Few First Nations individuals held land under private title in fee simple. The communal property conditions that governed many First Nations communities would have disentitled even the relatively well-to-do. Further barriers would present themselves in 1909, when the act was amended to require jurors to be 'British subjects by birth or naturalization.'[97]

The question of First Nations citizenship was fairly complex, since many Aboriginal nations (including the Onyota'a:ka, along with the other members of the Six Nations Confederacy of the League of the Iroquois) took the position that they were 'allies' of the British monarch, not 'subjects.' The hallmark of citizenship, the right to vote, was also denied 'Indians' federally until 1960, with the exception of a brief interlude between 1885 and 1898. The Province of British Columbia barred 'Indians' from voting until 1949, Manitoba barred them until 1952, Ontario until 1954, Saskatchewan until 1960, Prince Edward Island and New Brunswick until 1963, Alberta until 1965, and Quebec until 1969.[98]

The absence of Onyota'a:ka jurors seems to have been so commonplace as to have gone unremarked by all the participants and observers at John McArthur's trial. However, the racial overtones of the case were very apparent to Crown attorney Clute, who opened his preliminary address by stressing the equality of First Nations individuals before the law. 'An Indian's life was of as much value in the eyes of the law as that of any other citizen,' he reminded the jury. The very statement indicates that the Crown attorney was aware that some in the courtroom might be rather doubtful. Clute did not go further and emphasize the racialized nature of the crime itself, where a white man was charged with bludgeoning to death a First Nations man because of his race. Clute did not exhort the jury to consider racialized murder a more heinous crime than murder that was not motivated by discrimination. He scanned the courtroom, the audience, the judge, and the members of the jury, and resolved to argue more defensively that the law should not focus on Gus Ninham's race, but treat him as any murder victim deserved to be treated.

The racial implications of the trial were not lost on the press, where coverage seemed fixated upon distinctions between the Onyota'a:ka and whites. The London *Free Press* described the Onyota'a:ka witnesses in starkly racial terms: 'In the history of this important and interesting case, yesterday will be called Indian Day, for the principal witnesses examined during the day were Indians, compatriots of the man whose life was taken on the night of June 21 last, and for whose death the prisoner stands

charged. In all, ten of the red-skinned descendants of the original Americans were put on the stand to tell what they knew of the circumstances of,
or appertaining to, the tragic death of Gus Ninham.' The juxtaposition of
the 'red-skinned descendants of the original Americans' with the awe-
some might of a British courtroom inspired the reporters to grandiose
eloquence: 'It is a grim, a sad story that is being unfolded, yet now and
then comes a flash of humor or of wit to relieve the tension, though
expressions alike of sadness or of joy are allowed no vent under the
rigorous if necessary formality of a British court of law. A dignified and
able judge, keenly-fighting counsel, an interesting story of life and death at
stake, the liberty of a man well known and with many friends, the case is
one of the most interesting of lesser actions in the history of Middlesex in
recent years.'

Although all of the Onyota'a:ka witnesses were depicted as 'picturesque,' John Charles was sketched in flagrantly stereotypical terms. The
press observed 'no change' in his 'dark-visaged face' as he stood rigidly in
the witness box, grasping the rails 'with both hands,' his eyes wandering
'from the floor to the Crown prosecutor's face,' and then fixing 'upon
some friend in the crowd outside the rails.' The *Free Press* portrayed his
evidence as 'told in the emotionless, phlegmatic, almost sullen, manner
that has characterized this Indian since he was first called upon to relate
his version of the tragic event.' 'In husky, emotionless voice, he made his
recital and with outstretched arm accused John McArthur of being the
slayer of his friend.'[99]

Cross-examination by defence counsel Faulds was so rigorous that the
reporters compared it to torture 'on the rack.' Faulds seized upon any
inconsistencies he could find between the evidence Charles had given in
previous proceedings and his statements at the trial. Asked what McArthur
had shouted to the two Onyota'a:ka men who stopped to drink at the
spring, Charles had originally testified the white man called out: 'You
damn Indians had better get out of here.' Now he claimed McArthur had
said 'You black Indians, you need to get straight out of here.' Grilled on the
incongruity, Charles simply could not explain why he had not recited the
reference to 'black Indian' earlier. Faulds charged Charles with making
several statements to the police and to other Onyota'a:ka 'to the effect that
he did not know Ninham's assailant and that he did not see the kick
delivered.' Charles denied this. Questioned repeatedly about his alcohol
consumption on the day of the murder, Charles conceded that he 'had
taken probably ten or twelve glasses of beer,' but had drunk 'nothing after
six o'clock.' He was, however, 'feeling the effects of the liquor' that Satur-

day night. As for Gus Ninham, Charles stuck to his position that his friend 'had no liquor whilst in Charles's company,' but admitted 'Gus had been drinking during the day' and 'his speech was thick,' although 'it did not affect his walk.'[100]

Saving the most biting remarks for his climax, Faulds demanded of Charles why he had not tried to come to Ninham's aid during the attack. Charles tried to explain that he was 'afraid to go to Ninham's defense, afraid to go back to the hotel, and afraid to yell for help.' 'Then do you know you are a coward?' thundered Faulds. 'I know I am,' answered Charles quietly. This from a man who had courageously insisted upon testifying despite documented threats to his safety from strange men who had come under cover of darkness to terrorize Charles in his home at Onyota'a:ka on the Thames.[101]

John Charles's fortitude held but little sway, however, in comparison to the medical evidence led at trial. The same two London physicians who had conducted the post mortem again took the stand. Their testimony regarding Gus Ninham's heart disease seems to be something of an embellishment of their earlier statements. At the inquest, Drs Waugh and Neu had noted that Gus Ninham's diseased heart was swollen to 'about twice' its normal size. At the preliminary inquiry, there was no further reference to 'about'; Dr Waugh testified that the heart was 'enlarged to twice its normal size.' By the time of trial, the heart seems to have taken on a life of its own. Dr Neu now claimed that the 'heart was found to be more than twice the normal size.' 'It weighed over thirty ounces,' pronounced Dr Waugh, 'nearly two and a half times the normal weight.' Indeed, he swore, 'It was the largest heart that I ever saw in my practice; [I] never saw such a large heart as Ninham's.' Much of this is in keeping, of course, with the larger-than-life image of Gus Ninham. A man renowned for his 'splendid physique' and 'powerful chest' might, understandably, have body parts significantly out of proportion to normal dimensions. Even in disease and death, he was portrayed as extraordinary. But the physicians' tendency to aggrandize their findings had a seriously detrimental impact upon the case.[102]

Dr Neu testified that 'Ninham might have died at any moment, so serious was the condition of his heart.' Gone is any reference to a potential life expectancy of up to twenty years under favourable conditions. 'If there had been no injuries on the body at all, you would not have been surprised at his sudden death?' queried Faulds. 'Not with his heart in that condition,' replied Dr Neu. Even more problematic is the doctors' commentary on the dangers of heart disease. 'To people afflicted with heart disease, the advice is given to refrain from drinking, from excitement, and from violent exercise. Any of these things might cause death at any moment to a person with a weak heart,' cautioned Dr Neu.[103]

This gratuitous admonition presented dizzying opportunities for McArthur's defence. Much could now be made of the rumours that Gus Ninham had been engaged in a fight at the Grand Central Hotel earlier on the evening of the murder. His refusal to back off when John McArthur accosted him verbally could now be viewed as a reckless and foolhardy joust with death. Even Ninham's decision to walk home from Springbank Park rather than take the streetcar, with all the strenuous exercise this entailed, presented possibilities. And there was always the issue of alcohol consumption. In earlier proceedings, Ninham's employer had testified that Gus Ninham 'drank frequently, especially on pay days.' John Charles had told the inquest that he had not seen Ninham drink at all on the day of the murder, although he admitted on cross-examination that 'he thought Ninham had been drinking' prior to arriving at Springbank Park. At trial, Charles had been pressed beyond speculation to admit that there were some visible signs that Gus Ninham had some alcohol on the day of the murder. Defence counsel Faulds wasted little time in getting Dr Neu to stress that 'heavy drinking during the day would have affected Ninham.' Gone is any reference to the tell-tale absence of alcohol in the contents of Ninham's stomach.[104]

The climax came when Dr Neu took the position that 'any undue excitement, excessive drinking, fear, fright or a blow might bring on the fatal issue.' What is more, 'nor could he say to which of these he attributed Ninham's death.' 'No human tongue could do so,' insisted Dr Neu. In the earlier proceedings the doctors had identified the cause of death as 'stoppage of the heart, due to the shock of the injuries received and the accompanying excitement.'[105] By the time of trial, there is some obvious slippage in the linkage between the heart failure and the injuries. Now the doctors state that 'the immediate cause of Ninham's death was heart failure' and that 'the heart stopped as a result of shock.' Questioned as to 'what kind of shock' had produced this, Dr Neu is much more equivocal than he had been earlier: 'It might have been from injuries received *or* the accompanying excitement. One or both of these might have been the cause.' The injuries from the assault are no longer central to the diagnosis.[106]

It is difficult to know what to make of the shifting medical testimony. There is no indication that Drs Neu and Waugh had done any further autopsy examinations that might have caused them to alter their original opinions. Nor is there much in their backgrounds that might lead one to speculate as to their motives. Dr Neu's considerable intellectual talents had brought him from relatively obscure origins to substantial international prominence in the field of pathology. Born to German immigrant parents in Delhi, Ontario in 1866, Charles Neu worked as a 'cheese-maker' for eight years before enrolling at the University of Western Ontario. Capturing the gold medal there in 1894, Dr Neu interned at the London General Hospital and then went on to study pathology in Germany, Austria, and England. Returning to London in 1898, he was appointed pathologist at the Victoria Hospital, and in 1902 he became a professor of pathology at Western. In 1903, he would leave London to take up the prestigious position of professor of neuropathy at the University of Indiana and pathologist at the Indiana State Hospital for the Insane, eventually acquiring a significant reputation in the field of nerve disorders, brain tumours, and other neurological topics.[107]

Dr William Waugh was born to Scottish parents in London Township, Ontario in 1850. He studied at the Komoka Academy, apprenticed with Dr Alexander Anderson in London, and obtained a medical degree from McGill University in 1872, where he was awarded a prize in dissection. After Dr Anderson's death in 1873, Dr Waugh took over his medical practice at 374 Dundas Street. Upon the founding of the University of Western Ontario School of Medicine in 1882, Waugh was elected chair of anatomy, and in 1886 he assumed the chair of principles and practice of surgery. A 'quiet and determined man,' Dr Waugh was also somewhat eccentric. In later years, students described him as driven by punctuality, a man in perpetual motion. He would ride in his horse and carriage out to the medical school every day at exactly 7:45 a.m., commencing his lecture as he breezed through the doors at 8:00 a.m., well underway before he reached the desk and not stopping for breath until he uttered the closing words as he strode out at 9:00 a.m. 'He was never known to be late, he did not use a note, and his knowledge of his subject was thorough and encylopaedic,' they recollected. So intent was Dr Waugh that he once completed an evening address in the dark, after an electricity interruption cut the power, without missing a beat. Waugh's intellectual reach sometimes exceeded his practical expertise. One former student, Edwin Seaborn, described it thus: Dr Waugh 'lectured most acceptably to the students, never failing to cover the whole of his field, but in the many years that the author has known him he has never seen or heard of his having performed any operation.'[108]

What accounts for the transformation in the pivotal medical testimony? It seems unlikely that the doctors' evidence had been tampered with by the threats of ruffians, such as the scoundrels who had tried to intimidate the Onyota'a:ka witnesses. Was it the case that by the time of trial the two doctors had legitimately come to revise their earlier opinions? Had they come to believe that their former testimony linking the assault with the heart failure more directly was incorrect? Had they had further discussions between themselves or with other members of the medical profession on the matter? If so, they did not openly admit to it. They seem oblivious to the shifting nature of their diagnosis, and showed no inclination to explain their departure from previous positions.

It also seems unlikely that the physicians would have tempered their views out of a sense of sympathy with the throngs of McArthur partisans who followed the legal proceedings of their compatriot with such zeal. The doctors' professional and class status militated against any identification with the crowd who cheered on John McArthur. They might have been slightly more compassionate toward the individual accused. Did they decide that it was safer to hedge their testimony given the seriousness of the life imprisonment sentence facing John McArthur? Their evidence had begun to shift between the inquest, a proceeding designed to focus on the cause of death rather than criminal responsibility, and the preliminary inquiry, where the accused was faced with an actual charge. At the trial, where the greatest backtracking of testimony occurred, the fate of the man in the dock may have been foremost in their minds.

Or were their views altered by the forcefulness of the questions posed by McArthur's defence counsel? Did Gus Ninham's precarious hold on life become magnified in their minds as they listened to the various ruminations and theories advanced by John Faulds? To the outside observer, it appears almost as if the medical evidence underwent a gradual evolution that curiously seemed to mirror McArthur's defence strategy. If so, was this an innocent response, a matter of two physicians simply succumbing to the forcefulness of Faulds's questioning? Or did the doctors more deliberately begin to tailor their evidence to fit the loopholes in the law of causation as they understood more clearly the nature of the testimony that defence counsel Faulds required for an acquittal? It is possible that the medical witnesses may also have been affected in some way by the newspaper hoopla that surrounded the proceedings. Were they simply caught up in the public attention that greeted their every pronouncement about the growing girth of Gus Ninham's heart? Did the size of Gus Ninham's heart swell with the inflated press columns that recounted the testimony? From the surviving documentation, it is also impossible to know whether the doctors' racial heritage and perspectives might have influenced their assessment of this racialized trial, either consciously or unconsciously.

The Crown had been concerned about the testimony of Waugh and Neu from the outset. Correspondence between James Magee, who handled the earlier proceedings for the Crown, and Roger Clute, who took over at the trial, suggests that the two agonized over whether they should try to obtain 'additional expert medical testimony.' They did not do so. Whether other physicians could have pointed out the inconsistencies in the medical evidence and whether these inconsistencies would have carried the day remains unclear. The newspaper reporters were already speculating that Faulds had handled the case brilliantly, and that McArthur's chances were 'considered as very favorable.' The upshot of the medical testimony was that Crown attorney Roger Clute simply threw up his hands in despair. John McArthur's defence would not be called upon to establish an alibi for the prisoner and there would be no need for any concocted insinuations that John Charles had murdered his friend Gus Ninham. The whole matter would stand or fall on Ninham's heart disease. As Dr Waugh left the stand, Clute declared that he no longer intended to call the rest of the fifty witnesses he had subpoenaed earlier. 'His case was complete,' he announced, and approached the bench to consult with Judge Lount.[109]

The suspense was almost palpable. The ever-vigilant reporters rendered John McArthur in terms that portrayed the accused man as coiled and poised to spring. 'The massively-built prisoner' sat immobile, 'still and quiet,' intently 'watchful,' the focus of everyone's attention 'in the guarded dock at the centre of the court room.' The tension increased with each passing minute that the Crown attorney and the judge communed in low tones. Five minutes of complete stillness enveloped the courtroom. Then Judge Lount issued his ruling. 'Having considered the evidence of Dr. Neu and Dr. Waugh,' Judge Lount explained that he no longer thought it 'proper' to submit the case to the jury. The prisoner would be discharged: 'If Charles's story is true, a most brutal and cruel assault was made on the deceased, but evidence of mere brutality and cruelty does not make a case for the Crown unless the prosecution brings home the fact that death was caused by reason of that assault. You would have to find affirmatively that he did cause death. You ought not to be allowed to speculate or imagine or come to conclusion merely on speculation.'[110]

Causation is undeniably one of the critical matters standing in the way of conviction in this case. The jurors would have to conclude beyond a reasonable doubt that John McArthur's actions had triggered Gus Ninham's heart failure. But the doctors had testified that the blows Ninham received *might* have provoked the heart attack. They had also pinpointed excitement, fear, or fright as potential triggers. There was nothing to stop the jury from concluding that the repeated racial threats issued by McArthur prior to the physical attack created sufficient apprehension in Gus Ninham's mind to bring on heart failure. This would have been more than enough to identify McArthur as the legal cause of Ninham's death. The only factor that lay completely outside McArthur's zone of responsibility was the issue of alcohol. And here the jury would have had to conclude that it was alcohol alone that induced the heart failure, a finding that would seem at odds with the uncontradicted evidence that Gus Ninham was not intoxicated and had not been drinking for hours prior to the events in question.

Instead, Judge Lount seems to have become sidetracked by the testimony concerning the enlarged dimensions of Gus Ninham's heart: 'The evidence of both doctors is that Ninham was a man having a very serious heart trouble. He had an abnormally large heart. Dr Waugh says it was the largest heart he ever saw. Heart disease may cause a man's death at any time from the effects of fright, fear, excitement or drink, or from the effects of blows or assaults on the person. I do not think I should speculate as to what caused Ninham's death.'[111] Gus Ninham was undeniably a man at risk of heart attack. But Judge Lount seems to have forgotten the rule of law he had cited to the grand jury only three days earlier. Criminal actors were not to be exonerated simply because their victims might have died from natural causes at some time in the near future. In tort law, the doctrine is known as the 'thin skull' plaintiff. If you injure an individual with a thin skull, whose injuries are unforeseeably greater than you might reasonably have anticipated, you are liable for the full damages caused. You take your victim as you found him or her. In criminal law, the rule is described as 'acceleration of death.' The Criminal Code provided that 'every one who, by any act or omission, causes the death of another kills that person, although the effect of the bodily injury caused to such other person be merely to accelerate his death while labouring under some disorder or disease arising from some other cause.[112] Crown attorney Roger Clute had told the jury as much when he opened the case the day before: 'Anyone who accelerates the death of another, even by a few minutes, is guilty of killing.' If McArthur's threats and blows had shortened the term of Gus Ninham's life, he was criminally responsible for the death.[113]

Yet Judge Lount honed in on Ninham's alcohol consumption, stressing that 'the evidence shows that he had been drinking that afternoon or evening.' Emphasizing the vagaries in the doctors' conclusions regarding cause of death, Lount continued: 'The medical evidence shows that, whether he died from excitement then affected, or whether from a combination of liquor and excitement, he might have died from the excitement only. Thus, Ninham might have died from excitement or from a blow. And as it might have been either, you are left in the region of conjecture as to the cause. It would not be right to ask you to arrive at a conclusion as to the cause of Ninham's death when even the medical men are unable to speak definitely on that point.'[114] Judge Lount seems to have washed his hands of the argument that John McArthur's racial bullying might have created the 'excitement' that provoked the heart failure. He also seems to have forgotten that jurors were often called upon to render decisions based on contradictory evidence. One of the fundamental principles of Canadian law dictates that 'judges shall decide questions of law, and juries questions of fact.'[115] The division of responsibilities can, however, become blurred on occasion. Judges are expected to make an initial determination of whether sufficient evidence has been adduced which – if believed by the jury – would prove that the accused committed the crime charged. Where there is no evidence, it is up to the judge to direct the jury to acquit the prisoner. Where there is evidence on material questions of fact, the truth or falsity of the evidence is entirely a matter for the jury's determination.[116]

This case sits right on the borderline, but Judge Lount expressed no hesitation in intervening to prevent the jurors from weighing the testimony and deciding the question for themselves. Summing up with the statement that 'I could not myself as a juror or as a judge conscientiously say he died by reason of blows inflicted by the prisoner,' Judge Lount insisted that 'human life is too valuable to be taken away by conjecture.' Perhaps he had forgotten for the moment that John McArthur was on trial for manslaughter and not facing the death penalty for the offence of murder. In the final result, the judge instructed the jury that the proper course was to direct a verdict of 'not guilty.'[117]

CONCLUSION

The murder of Gus Ninham was a starkly devastating tragedy for his family, friends, and community. For legal historians who scrutinize the past to learn more about the foundations upon which our criminal justice system is rooted, it also offers a rare opportunity to reflect upon the impact of issues of race, class, and masculinity in the context of a dramatic and highly publicized series of legal proceedings. The tensions between the

Onyota'a:ka community nestled on the Thames River in Delaware Township and the white male working-class youth from nearby London and its
surrounding rural environs are vividly portrayed in the skirmishes that
marred relations between the two groups and resulted in Gus Ninham's
demise.

The fate of the man accused of Ninham's murder rested upon four
distinct legal proceedings. As John McArthur's culpability was subjected
to assessment at each of these different stages, a gradual pattern of back-
sliding emerges. The context in which this slippage took place was replete
with racial discrimination directed against Aboriginal peoples in education, employment, social relations, and law.[118] Given the prevailing
racism, so evident in the nature and tone of the press commentary on the
case, some sceptics might be forgiven for wondering how it was that John
McArthur was ever arrested in the first place.

Yet the initial press outcry and the formal trappings of the rule of law
seem to have necessitated the launch of a criminal investigation when Gus
Ninham's body was first discovered in the dirt on the road beside Sharkey's
Hotel. The momentum carried the process forward through the early
stages of inquiry, when the prospect of serious retribution toward Ninham's
assailant was still speculative and distant in time. As the criminal proceeding moved into its final, more serious phase, energies seemed to flag and
witnesses to falter.

The first legal proceeding, the coroner's inquest, resulted in the most
serious verdict against the accused man. The white male jurors of the
inquest pronounced Gus Ninham's death to be the direct result of 'an
assault committed by John McArthur.' The verdict seems to reflect the
jurors' distaste for the cavalier testimony and unsavoury lifestyles of
McArthur's lower-class cohorts, who collectively produced alibis and
excuses that struck even the press as absurd. The verdict may also reflect
the nature of the forum in which it was delivered: inquests do not order
people to be hanged or sent to prison for life. The second legal proceeding,
the preliminary inquiry, pushed the case against John McArthur forward
on charges of murder. Although the medical witnesses were already
starting to retreat from their initial testimony about the cause of death, the
justice of the peace determined that given the low threshold of proof
demanded in a preliminary inquiry the murder charge should go on to
trial.

It was the third stage of the proceeding, before the grand jury at the fall
assizes, that ought to have registered the first signal of prosecutorial
alarm. When the thirteen white, male grand jurors recommended pro-

ceeding against McArthur on the reduced charge of manslaughter, they took the first step toward dismantling the Crown's case. The fourth stage, the actual trial before the petit jury at the assizes, never ran the gamut to completion. After listening to the blistering cross-examination of John Charles and the latest version of the medical evidence, Crown attorney Clute chose to cut the trial off in mid-course. Then Judge Lount took the matter out of the jury's hands and issued a directed verdict of not guilty. Had the case gone forward it is possible that the twelve white, male jurors would have reached the same verdict.

In the final result, there were many who influenced the outcome of the criminal justice process. The coroner's jurors, the grand jurors, the Aboriginal and white men who gave testimony, the doctors who conducted the post mortem, the lawyers who questioned them, the coroner, the justice of the peace, the Ontario High Court judge, and the newspaper reporters all placed their mark upon the legal system's response to Gus Ninham's death. In the contest between the Onyota'a:ka and the unruly sector of London's white working class, the latter ultimately proved to be triumphant. To the extent that the legal proceeding into Gus Ninham's death is indicative of the prevailing views in south-western Ontario at the turn of the century, the attribute of whiteness seems undeniably to have been a source of empowerment that could help to override working-class disadvantages.

'Sensational,' 'unexpected,' and 'surprising' were the epigraphs with which the newspapers heralded the final twist in the criminal proceedings. The press had feasted upon the proceeding at all four stages, mirroring and actively contributing to the racial and class-based perspectives that tainted the case. Now the reporters seem to have become somewhat petulant that the match was called before the bout had gone the regulatory full rounds. Not so John McArthur, the 'stalwart young man' awaiting the verdict in the corner of the ring. After eighty-eight days in jail, he was now free to go. McArthur was quickly surrounded by his well-wishing fans, but before he was actually discharged, Judge Lount admonished the released man at length. Speaking solemnly, he cautioned McArthur: 'I do not know if John Charles's story is true. No one but you knows that ... [I] express the hope that it was not true that [you were] guilty of so brutal and cruel a crime [...] If the evidence of John Charles is true, and you are the man who struck Ninham – for there was no one else there – then you are guilty of a higher crime than the one upon which you stood indicted. Your conscience will be your own punishment if that is the case.' Judge Lount closed with an 'earnest' warning to the freed man 'to avoid evil associations and wrong tendencies.' McArthur should 'endeavour to live an honorable, straightforward life,' using his 'strength and talents as God intended them to be used.' It is almost as if the judge were admitting he suspected John McArthur to be, in truth, the murderer.

Whether pangs of conscience ever did befall John McArthur seems unlikely. Certainly his supporters, friends, and relatives were in no mood for sombre reflection. As McArthur stepped down from the dock, he was immediately encircled by a lusty throng. Hoisted high above his exhilarated fans, he was 'followed up Dundas Street by a large crowd of sympathizers,' 'the centre of a group of congratulatory friends.'[119]

NOTES

I am indebted to Jessica Hill, Caroline Doxtator, and Kelly Riley of the Onyota'a:ka Administration Office; Mercy Doxtator of the Onyota'a:ka Language Centre; Debra Doxtator, Harvey Antone, Hazel K. Cornelius, Olive Elm, Clifford Cornelius, Angus Abram, Myrtle Ninham, Mabel Smith, Thomas A. Doxtator, Gerry Ninham, Dorothy Ireland, Flora Doxtator, and Dorothy Williams of the Onyota'a:ka Nation; Sheila Staats of the Woodland Cultural Centre; Sharon Fleming, Judy Kuramoto and John Choles at the Archives of Ontario; Ann Marie Langlois of the Archives of the Law Society of Upper Canada; Mary Velaitis and Glen Curnoe of the London Room of the London Public Library; and Marianne Welch of the Law Library at the University of Western Ontario. I am also grateful to the following individuals for their research assistance: Christy Bressette, Anna Feltracco, Kevin Misak, Alexandra Hartmann, Anne Eichenberg, Jennifer Hall, Signa Daum Shanks, and Debbie Rollier. Funding from the Law Foundation of Ontario and the Social Sciences and Humanities Research Council of Canada is gratefully acknowledged.

1 The historical literature that examines the imposition of Anglo-Canadian criminal law upon Aboriginal communities does touch upon a number of interracial murders that began shortly after European contact with the First Nations. Although these could arguably be classified as racially motivated crimes, the cases constitute a distinct category deserving of separate treatment. Some scholars have described interracial criminal cases in their writing, although few have focused explicitly on the question of whether the violence itself was racially motivated. See, for example, Sarah Carter, 'Categories and Terrains of Exclusion: Constructing the "Indian Woman" in the Early Settlement Era in Western Canada,' *Great Plains Quarterly* 13 (Summer 1993),

147 at 156–7. Carter explores the trial of William 'Jumbo' Fisk, a young white man charged in Calgary in 1889 with the brutal murder of a Cree woman identified only as 'Rosalie,' who was reputed to be a prostitute. Fisk was initially acquitted, but convicted of manslaughter upon retrial. Carter notes that during the second trial the issue of race was specifically addressed, although in terms that seem to suggest an effort to overcome stereotypical assumptions about the inferiority of non-white victims. Judge Charles Rouleau instructed the jury: '[F]orget the woman's race ... [I]t made no difference whether Rosalie was white or black, an Indian or a negro. In the eyes of the law, every British subject is equal.' Due to petitions from many influential whites, Fisk's sentence was reduced from life to fourteen years in prison.

2 For sources on the Oneida, see Eileen M. Antone, *The History of the Oneida of the Thames Move to Canada* (Brantford: Woodland Cultural Centre 1990); Eileen M. Antone, 'The Educational History of the Onyota'a:ka Nation of the Thames,' *Ontario History* 85, no. 4 (December 1993), 309–20; Jack Campisi, 'Ethnic Identity and Boundary Maintenance in Three Oneida Communities' (PhD thesis, State University of New York, Albany, 1974); Jack Campisi and Laurence M. Hauptman, eds., *The Oneida Indian Experience: Two Perspectives* (Syracuse, N.Y.: Syracuse University Press 1988); Jack Campisi, 'New York–Oneida Treaty of 1795: A Finding of Fact,' *American Indian Law Review* 4 (Summer 1976), 71–82; Catherine Hinckle Ricciardelli, 'Kinship Systems of the Oneida Indians' (PhD dissertation, University of Pennsylvania 1966); Alex F. Ricciardelli, 'The Adoption of White Agriculture by the Oneida Indians,' *Ethnohistory* 10, no. 4 (Fall 1963), 309–28; Andrea Green, 'Land, Leadership, and Conflict: The Six Nations' Early Years on the Grand River' (MA thesis, University of Western Ontario 1984), at 49–51; Thomas S. Abler, 'The Kansas Connection: The Seneca Nation and the Iroquois Confederacy Council,' in Michael K. Foster et al., *Extending the Rafters* (Albany: State University of New York Press 1984), 81 at 84; Olive Patricia Dickason, *Canada's First Nations: A History of Founding Peoples from Earliest Times* (Toronto: McClelland & Stewart 1992), at 224; Cara E. Richards, *The Oneida People* (Phoenix: Indian Tribal Series 1974); Barbara Graymont, *The Iroquois in the American Revolution* (Syracuse, N.Y.: Syracuse University Press 1972); G. Elmore Reaman, *The Trail of the Iroquois Indians* (London: Frederick Muller 1967), at 52–5; and Jill Duvall, *The Oneida* (Chicago: Children's Press 1991), at 4–5.

3 On the desire of the Onyota'a:ka to maintain their political, religious, and cultural traditions, see Campisi, 'Three Oneida Communities,' at 270, 458–9 and Ricciardelli, 'Kinship Systems of the Oneida Indians,' at 407. On the social distance between whites and Onyota'a:ka, see Wayne Paddon, 'Steam and Petticoats' 1840–1890 (London: Murray Kelly 1977), at 94–5.

4 For London population figures, see Frederick H. Armstrong, *The Forest City: An Illustrated History of London, Canada* (London: Windsor 1986), at 327.
5 Campisi and Hauptman eds., *The Oneida Indian Experience*, at 97–100.
6 23 June 1902, 4.
7 23 June 1902, 1–2.
8 On the starkly different coverage in events and issues by the two rival newspapers, see Frederick H. Armstrong, 'Obscenity in Victorian London,' in Guy St-Denis, ed., *Simcoe's Choice: Celebrating London's Bicentennial, 1793–1993* (Toronto: Dundurn 1992), 175 at 177, who notes that the 'difference in coverage is not unusual for these two papers; one sometimes wonders if they are writing about the same city.'
9 23 June 1902, 4.
10 23 June 1902, 1.
11 Paddon, '*Steam and Petticoats*,' at 284–6; Armstrong, *The Forest City*, chaps. 1–5; London *Free Press*, 19 September 1902, 6.
12 23 June 1902, 2 and 6.
13 24 June 1902, 6.
14 London *Free Press*, 23 June 1902, 4; 24 June 1902, 6.
15 London *Free Press*, 24 June 1902, 6; London *Advertiser*, 19 September 1902, 2. Ricciardelli, 'Kinship Systems of the Oneida Indians,' notes at 334–49 that Oneidas born before 1900 all had First Nations' birth names, chosen by close clan relatives, as well as 'English given names.' I have been unable to trace Gustus Ninham's Onyota'a:ka name. Campisi, 'Three Oneida Communities,' notes at 268 that the paid position of Oneida constable, an appointee of the Royal Canadian Mounted Police, was commonly held for many years by the same individual. Gus Ninham's mother's name was Mary Bread.
16 London *Advertiser*, 23 June 1902, 2; London *Free Press*, 24 June 1902, 6. According to Gus Ninham's granddaughters, his wife (Jennie Parkest Ninham) was not ill before or after her husband died. They speculate that the reporters may have hoped their depiction of his ailing wife would create greater interest in the case. Notes of research assistant, Christy Bressette, 'Interview with Flora Doxtator and Dorothy Ireland,' Onyota'a:ka Territory, 5 and 31 May 1995.
17 London *Free Press*, 24 June 1902, 6. Gus Ninham's granddaughters recollect that Zach was twelve and Elijah thirteen at their father's death. Bressette, 'Interview with Flora Doxtator and Dorothy Ireland.' Myrtle Ninham recollects there was a difference of about four years between the two sons, with Elijah about eleven years old. Notes of research assistant, Christy Bressette, 'Interview with Myrtle Ninham,' Onyota'a:ka Territory, 8 May 1995.

18 London *Free Press*, 24 June 1902, 6. Gus Ninham's parents apparently had five children: Gustus, John, Louisa, Jennie and Alfred; see 1905 Oneida Band List. Gus Ninham's granddaughters are less certain of the sibling line, explaining that they had never been told of 'an auntie' and the Alf Ninham who was alive at the time of the murder may have been from a different family. Bressette, 'Interview with Flora Doxtator and Dorothy Ireland.'

19 London *Advertiser*, 25 June 1902, 8: 'what with his personal popularity and the efficacy of his medicines, ['Dr' Ninham] was a welcome visitor at [fairs and similar gatherings] throughout Western Ontario.'

20 London *Advertiser*, 23 June 1902, 1. There is reference to John Ninham in the Oneida Chiefs' Council Minute Books, 1904–1914, 3 September 1912 (quoted in Ricciardelli, 'Kinship Systems of the Oneida Indians,' at 253), which record that 'The honorable Chief John Ninham [a pine chief] has this day declared to offer his resignation as chief of the Oneida council ...' Campisi, 'Three Oneida Communities,' notes at 461 that during this period the Onyota'a:ka on the Thames had nine hereditary sachems, each with an alternate and each representing one of three clans. All chiefs were appointed and removed by clan mothers. Ricciardelli notes at 238 that the chiefs had four major duties: 1) to give advice; 2) to maintain peace; 3) to preserve tradition; and 4) to dispense welfare aid from their own resources as well as from band resources.

21 Campisi, 'Three Oneida Communities,' notes at 269 the appointment of the two men, along with Chief Louis Scannado, to investigate, conciliate, and adjudicate disputes, citing 'Letter, Thomas Gordon, Indian Agent, to Secretary General of Indian Affairs, 11 October 1889.' Ricciardelli, 'Adoption of White Agriculture,' notes at 318–19 that the Onyota'a:ka community was governed by a hereditary chiefs' council until 1934, when an elective system was instituted. The chiefs' council served in the capacity of peacemaking and arbitration, settling domestic quarrels, land inheritance disputes, land boundary differences, supervising the construction of roads and bridges, impounding stray livestock, and surveying land: 'Indian agents during the 19th century lived 10–20 miles distant from the Oneidas and do not appear to have, in practice, subordinated the chiefs' authority. People in the present-day community say that the Indian Act ... was ignored by the chiefs and that the Department representatives themselves applied the regulations of the Act only casually during the 19th century.'

22 London *Free Press*, 24 June 1902, 6; London *Advertiser*, 23 June 1902, 2.

23 Thomas Doxtator, an Onyota'a:ka Elder born in 1913, recalls that his cousin, Evan John, who was born twenty years earlier, told him that 'all the people in the settlement were pretty sad at what happened ... They felt really bad about it.' See Notes of research assistant, Christy Bressette, 'Interview with Thomas

Doxtator,' Onyota'a:ka Territory, 8 May 1995. According to oral history
accounts of the murder, there were at least three theories about Gus Ninham's
death. Some believed he had been deliberately murdered by two white
brothers, whom he had 'licked' previously in a fight. Bressette, 'Interview
with Thomas Doxtator.' Others believed that he was murdered by Adam
Beck, one of London's 'most celebrated citizens,' and the founder of the
Ontario Hydro-Electric Commission, who would be elected mayor of the city
in 1902. A drunken Beck had allegedly been throwing stones at First Nations'
men and hit Gus on the head. According to this version, Beck had 'enough
money to cover his tracks by paying off people,' and financial payments were
made to a number of individuals, with Gus Ninham's widow being provided
with a horse and buggy by an anonymous donor. See Notes of research
assistant, Christy Bressette, 'Interview with Harvey Antone, Clifford
Cornelius, Mercy Doxtator, Hazel Cornelius, Gerry Ninham, Verlin
Cornelius, and Olive Elm,' Onyota'a:ka Territory, 15 May 1995. The third
theory is that Gus Ninham was actually murdered by fellow Aboriginals.
Bressette, 'Interview with Flora Doxtator and Dorothy Ireland.' Gus
Ninham's granddaughters indicate that their father, Zach Ninham, 'won-
dered all his life' who killed his father. Bressette, 'Interview with Flora
Doxtator and Dorothy Ireland.'

24 London *Advertiser*, 23 June 1902, 2 and 6.

25 London *Advertiser*, 23 June 1902, 1.

26 23 June 1902, 4.

27 London *Advertiser*, 23 June 1902, 1 and 2; London *Free Press*, 23 June 1902, 4;
24 June 1902, 6.

28 The death and mourning rituals practised at the Onyota'a:ka on the Thames
during this period constituted a variation upon original traditions, which
required a more concerted and lengthy period of mourning, culminating with
a 'Tenth-day Feast' at which the property of the deceased was distributed. See
Campisi, 'Three Oneida Communities,' at 56–7, 282–3; Ricciardelli, 'Kinship
Systems of the Oneida Indians,' at 357–77. Gus Ninham's granddaughters
recall somewhat differently that their grandfather's body was found propped
up by a tree in Springbank Park and was transported to the Onyota'a:ka
community where it 'was traditionally entombed' and preparations completed for a 'nine day feast.' See Bressette, 'Interview with Flora Doxtator and
Dorothy Ireland.'

29 London *Free Press*, 24 June 1902, 6.

30 There are a variety of spellings used to identify John McArthur in the press
clippings and legal records. He is variously called 'John' and 'Jack,' and his
last name is spelt 'McArthur,' 'MacArthur,' 'Macarthur,' and 'M'Arthur.'

Alexander McArthur Sr died in 1883 at the age of 46. Woodland Cemetery Burial Register, 12 May 1883, Row 20 Section 4, London and Middlesex County Branch, Ontario Genealogical Society. The McArthur farm is shown on the West Wharncliffe Concession, Lots 2, 3, and 4, consisting of 182 acres, assessed at a value of $10,000. All three brothers, John, Alex, and Albert, are listed as farmers. *Assessment Roll for the Municipality of Westminster* 1899, numbers 1730, 1731, 1732, and 1733, 73; *City of London Directory 1902* Westminster, at 529.

31 London *Free Press*, 19 September 1902, 6; 24 June 1902, 6; 25 June 1902, 4; London *Advertiser*, 25 June 1902, 8; Jail Register, London Jail, Achives of Ontario (AO) RG20, Series F-21, v. 7, 88. The jail register stipulates his age as '35' but this would appear to be in error.

32 London *Free Press*, 24 June 1902, 6; London *Advertiser*, 19 September 1902, 2; 23 June 1902, 2. Paddon, *'Steam and Petticoats'* describes the historical fascination that First Nations athletes, and those of the Onyota'a:ka in particular, inspired throughout southwestern Ontario at 198, 225–6.

33 London *Free Press*, 25 June 1902, 4.

34 London *Advertiser*, 19 September 1902, 2.

35 Martin Ninham's son, unnamed in the press accounts, had defeated Harry Fitzsimmons, his white opponent, at a prizefight at an Elgin county fall fair. Attempting to avenge his loss with a surprise attack upon Martin Ninham's son, Fitzsimmons killed the father in error. Some years afterward, Fitzsimmons was arrested in Minnesota, extradited to Canada, convicted of manslaughter, and sentenced to ten years in prison. London *Advertiser*, 19 September 1902, 2.

36 The inquest was heard on 27 and 30 June, 3, 7, 9, 11, 12, 15. and 16 July, with several of the sessions concluding only after midnight. London *Free Press*, 17 July 1902, 6. The Archives of Ontario retain no records from this inquest. For biographical details about Robert Ferguson (1858–1927), who obtained a medical degree from the University of Western Ontario in 1890 and joined the faculty of medicine in 1896, see Murray L. Barr, *A Century of Medicine at Western* (London: University of Western Ontario 1977), at 170, 187. On inquests generally, see William Fuller Ayles Boys, *A Practical Treatise on the Office and Duties of Coroners in Ontario and the other Provinces and Territories of Canada and in the Colony of Newfoundland* (Toronto 1893).

37 London *Advertiser*, 28 June 1902, 5; 1 July 1902, 6; 4 July 1902, 8; London *Free Press*, 28 June 1902, 9.

38 On the uneasy response of Canadian legal authorities to the reception of Aboriginal evidence generally, see Constance Backhouse, 'They are a People Unacquainted with Subordination'; First Nations' Sovereignty Claims: *Sero* v.

Gault, Ontario 1921, in Constance Backhouse, *Colour-Coded: A Legal History of Racism in Canada, 1900–1950* (Toronto: University of Toronto Press for The Osgoode Society, 1999).

39 See, for example, London *Advertiser*, 1 July 1902, 6; 4 July 1902, 8; 8 July 1902, 2; London *Free Press*, 1 July 1902, 1; 8 July 1902, 2.

40 1 July 1902, 6. The name of the interpreter also appears as Mrs 'Antoine.'

41 London *Free Press*, 1 July 1902, 1. The paper also notes that Doxtater 'was evidently afraid when he took the witness stand and faced the crowd of spectators.'

42 London *Advertiser*, 8 July 1902, 2.

43 Antone, 'Educational History of the Onyota'a:ka Nation'; Suzanne Fournier and Ernie Crey, *Stolen From our Embrace: The Abduction of First Nations Children and the Restoration of Aboriginal Communities* (Vancouver: Douglas & McIntyre 1997); Jean Barman, Yvonne Hebert, and Don McCaskill, *Indian Education in Canada: Vol. I, The Legacy* (Vancouver: UBC Press 1986), at 1–22; E. Brian Titley, *A Narrow Vision: Duncan Campbell Scott and the Administration of Indian Affairs in Canada* (Vancouver: UBC Press 1986), at 6, 15, 75–93; J.R. Miller, *Shingwauk's Vision: A History of Native Residential Schools* (Toronto: University of Toronto Press 1996), at 204; Robert A. Williams Jr, 'The Algebra of Federal Indian Law: The Hard Trail of Decolonizing and Americanizing the White Man's Indian Jurisprudence,' *Wisconsin Law Review* (1986), 219–99.

44 Antone, 'Educational History of the Onyota'a:ka Nation'; Campisi, 'Three Oneida Communities,' at 296–7; Paddon, 'Steam and Petticoats,' at 198; Ricciardelli, 'Adoption of White Agriculture,' at 317; Bressette, 'Interview with Flora Doxtator and Dorothy Ireland.' Ricciardelli, 'Kinship Systems of the Oneida Indians,' notes at 35 that the Mount Elgin Industrial Institution was established by the Methodist Church in the late 1840s. Intended to be 'an industrial and trade school providing advanced training to capable children,' in reality 'most children who went there were orphans, came from disorganized homes, or were delinquents.' Ricciardelli notes that 'the children sometimes reacted strongly to the routine, discipline and food,' but that 'in spite of this, many children who attended Mt. Elgin became leaders in the religious, economic and political life of the community.' See also Miller, *Shingwauk's Vision*, at 84–6; Jennifer Pettit, 'From Longhouse to Schoolhouse: The Mohawk Institute 1834–1970' (MA thesis, Department of History, University of Western Ontario 1993).

45 Floyd Lounsbury, 'Recollections of the Works Progress Administration's Oneida Language and Folklore Project, 1938–41'; Orville Clark, Clifford Abbott, Amos Christjohn, and Marie Hinton, 'Recollections of the Oneida Language Revival, 1972–85'; Rosalie M. Robertson, 'Oneida Educational

Planning'; William A. Gollnick, 'Educational Development for the Oneida Reservation,' in Campisi and Hauptman, eds., *The Oneida Indian Experience,* at 131, 139–44, 157–76, and 177–81 respectively; Campisi, 'Three Oneida Communities,' at 206–7. Ricciardelli, 'Kinship Systems of the Oneida Indians,' notes at 44 that for the first half of the twentieth century, most Onyota'a:ka spoke their own language at home, and that an interpreter was used during services at the Methodist Church at least until the First World War. Patricia Monture-Angus, *Thunder in My Soul: A Mohawk Woman Speaks* (Halifax: Fernwood Publishing 1995), notes at 32: 'The process of language ... is definitional (or perhaps more accurately, re-definitional) and structural. I do not believe that First Nations people use English words in the same way as people who do not share our culture with us.' At 264 she adds: 'Those with the privilege of having [their language] reflect their cultural reality do not see the contradictions that arise for us who are continually forced to negotiate, converse and discuss in a second and foreign language.'

46 London *Free Press,* 24 June 1902, 6.
47 London *Free Press,* 25 June 1902, 4; 28 June 1902, 9; London *Advertiser,* 28 June 1902, 5.
48 London *Free Press,* 28 June 1902, 9; London *Advertiser,* 28 June 1902, 5; Paddon, 'Steam and Petticoats,' at 120–1.
49 Reference to the earlier altercation can be found in the handwritten notes made by the Crown attorney, filed in Middlesex County Court Records, Crown Attorney and Crown Prosecutor Criminal Court Records 1902, Rex vs. MacArthur, University of Western Ontario Library, Regional Room, Box 558.
50 London *Free Press,* 28 June 1902, 9; London *Advertiser,* 28 June 1902, 5.
51 London *Advertiser,* 28 June 1902, 5; 1 July 1902, 6. Levi Doxtater's name is spelled 'Doxtator,' 'Dockstater,' and 'Dockstader'; Cornelius Antoine's name is also spelled 'Antone.'
52 London *Free Press,* 1 July 1902, 1; 4 July 1902, 6; 8 July 1902, 2; London *Advertiser,* 4 July 1902, 8; 8 July 1902, 2. Joshua is also spelled 'Nickles.'
53 Harvey Antone recounts that John Elijah, who later became known as Old Man John, talked with him 'about the way he was treated' when he appeared as a witness. After testifying, John Elijah rode home with his son-in-law in a horse and buggy. 'He was lucky to come home and eat by 11:30 p.m. or 12:00 a.m. and they would chase him with his horse and buggy,' explained Harvey Antone. Bressette, 'Interview with Harvey Antone, Clifford Cornelius, Mercy Doxtator, Hazel Cornelius, Gerry Ninham, Verlin Cornelius and Olive Elm.'
54 London *Free Press,* 4 July 1902, 6; 8 July 1902, 2; 10 July 1902, 4 and 6; 12 July 1902, 6; 14 July 1902, 6; 16 July 1902, 6; London *Advertiser,* 4 July 1902, 8;

8 July 1902, 2; 10 July 1902, 8; 12 July 1902, 1; 14 July 1902, 8; 16 July 1902, 8.

55 London *Advertiser*, 4 July 1902, 8; London *Free Press*, 4 July 1902, 6. The suspicion is recorded in correspondence of James Magee to R.C. Clute, KC, 4 September 1902: Middlesex County Court Records, Crown Attorney and Crown Prosecutor Criminal Court Records 1902, Rex vs. MacArthur, University of Western Ontario Library, Regional Room, Box 558.

56 London *Advertiser*, 10 July 1902, 8; London *Free Press*, 10 July 1902, 6.

57 London *Advertiser*, 16 July 1902, 8; London *Free Press*, 16 July 1902, 6; Correspondence of James Magee to R.C. Clute, KC, 4 September 1902.

58 London *Free Press*, 8 July 1902, 2; London *Advertiser*, 8 July 1902, 2; Correspondence of James Magee to R.C. Clute, KC, 4 September 1902.

59 London *Free Press*, 14 July 1902, 8; London *Advertiser*, 14 July 1902, 6; 16 July 1902, 8.

60 *London and Its Men of Affairs* (London: Advertiser Job Printing Company, c. 1915), at 189, 194.

61 London *Free Press*, 10 July 1902, 4 and 6; 16 July 1902, 6; London *Advertiser*, 10 July 1902, 8; 16 July 1902, 8.

62 Reference to these rumours is found in rough notes written by R.C. Clute, KC, the prosecuting Crown Attorney, 4 September 1902: Middlesex County Court Records, Box 558.

63 London *Advertiser*, 14 July 1902, 8; London *Free Press*, 14 July 1902, 6.

64 London *Advertiser*, 8 July 1902, 2; 16 July 1902, 8; London *Free Press*, 10 July 1902, 4 and 6.

65 London *Advertiser*, 14 July 1902, 8.

66 London *Free Press*, 10 July 1902, 4. The witness was Hugh Sharkey Sr, father of the proprietor of Sharkey's Hotel.

67 London *Advertiser*, 14 July 1902, 6; 16 July 1902, 8; London *Free Press*, 14 July 1902, 8.

68 Correspondence of James Magee to R.C. Clute, KC, 4 September 1902. James Magee's law firm, Magee, McKillop & Murphy, had a large solicitors' practice with several influential English clients. Known as an expert in Chancery practice, Magee also held a part-time posting as Crown attorney and clerk of the peace. He would be appointed a judge of the Chancery Division of the Ontario High Court of Justice in 1904 and later to the Ontario Court of Appeal. *London and Its Men of Affairs*, at 183–4, 189, 198; *History of the County of Middlesex, Canada* (Toronto and London: Goodspeed 1889), at 1073; *City of London Directory, 1902*, at 23, 386; London *Advertiser*, 28 March 1930, 1.

69 London *Free Press*, 12 July 1902, 6; London *Advertiser*, 12 July 1902, 1. Dr Neu's name is also spelled 'New.' Dr Neu served as the pathologist at the Victoria Hospital and professor of pathology at the University of Western

Ontario. Barr, *Century of Medicine*, at 193.

70 London *Free Press*, 12 July 1902, 6; London *Advertiser*, 12 July 1902, 1.

71 'Depositions' in the preliminary inquiry, Middlesex County Court Records, Crown Attorney and Crown Prosecutor Criminal Court Records 1902, Rex vs. MacArthur, University of Western Ontario Library, Regional Room, Box 558; London *Free Press*, 28 June 1902, 9; 1 July 1902, 1; London *Advertiser*, 23 June 1902, 2; 28 June 1902, 5; 1 July 1902, 6.

72 London *Advertiser*, 23 June 1902, 1 and 2; 1 July 1902, 6; London *Free Press*, 23 June 1902, 4; 8 July 1902, 2. The London *Advertiser*, 12 July 1902, 1 reports that 'there were no indications of alcohol in the contents of the stomach. Had there been much present it would have been noticeable.' The London *Free Press*, 12 July 1902, 6, notes that the post mortem found 'no traces of alcohol' in Ninham's stomach. Rather confusedly, the report adds that 'there might have been a very little there.'

73 Jan Noel, *Canada Dry: Temperance Crusades Before Confederation* (Toronto: University of Toronto Press 1995), at 183, 187–90; Robert A. Campbell, *Demon Rum or Easy Money: Government Control of Liquor in British Columbia From Prohibition to Privatization* (Ottawa: Carleton University Press 1991), at 9; Peter C. Mancall, *Deadly Medicine: Indians and Alcohol in Early America* (Ithaca, N.Y.: Cornell University Press 1995); Edwin M. Lemert, *Alcohol and the Northwest Coast Indians* (Berkeley: University of California Press 1954); J.F. Mosher, 'Liquor Legislation and Native Americans: History and Perspective' (Berkeley, University of California, Boalt Hall School of Law, May 1975); Anastasia Shkilnyk, *A Poison Stronger than Love: The Destruction of an Ojibwa Community* (New Haven, Conn.: Yale University Press 1985); Arthur Ray, *Indians in the Fur Trade* (Toronto: University of Toronto Press 1974); Sidney L. Haring, *Crow Dog's Case: American Indian Sovereignty, Tribal Law, and United States Law in the Nineteenth Century* (New York: Cambridge University Press 1994), at 163, 278.

74 The first legislative prohibition appeared in Quebec in 1777: 17 Geo. III, c. 7 (reprinted in RSLC 1845 at 572); see also RSUC 1792–1840; CSLC 1861, c. 14, s. 1–3. Other jurisdictions began by prohibiting liquor sales to specific Aboriginal groups (see the 1801 statute in RSUC 1792–1840, c. 8) and then legislating more broadly (see the 1840 statute in RSUC 1792–1840, c. 13.) Additional statutes passed in the geographic area that came to be known as Ontario include: S. Prov. C. 1850, c. 74, s. 6–7; CSC 1859, c. 9, s. 3–4; S. Prov. C. 1860, c. 38, s. 2. Nova Scotia's legislation includes SNS 1829, c. 29, s. 1–3; RSNS 1864, c. 19, s. 30; RSNS 1884, c. 75, s. 46. British Columbia prohibitions are contained in 'An Act Prohibiting the Gift or Sale of Intoxicating Liquours to Indians,' Colony of Vancouver Island, Passed by Council 3 Aug. 1854;

'Proclamation,' Colony of British Columbia, 6 Sept. 1858; Colony of Vancouver Island, 1860, No. 16, s. 2–3; Colony of British Columbia, 1865, No. 16; Colony of British Columbia, 1867, No. 28 (reprinted in Laws of British Columbia 1871, No. 85); CSBC 1877, c. 87; SBC 1900, c. 18, ss. 2(g) and (h), 37; SBC 1902, c. 40, s. 2; SBC 1910, c. 30, ss. 65(c), 75(i); RSBC 1911, c. 170. s. 349(f); RSBC 1911, c. 142; SBC 1912, c. 20, s. 5; SBC 1913, c. 40, s. 8; SBC 1921 (First Session), c. 30, s. 36; RSBC 1924, c. 146, s. 41; SBC 1926–27, c. 38, s. 11; RSBC 1936, c. 160, s. 43; SBC 1947, c. 53, s. 16; RSBC 1948, c. 192. In Newfoundland, see S.Nfld. 1882, c. 8, s. 6. After the turn of the century, other jurisdictions followed suit. Prairie province enactments include SM 1928, c. 31, s. 38(1)(e); SS 1909, c. 38, s. 12; SA 1927, c. 35, s. 5. The Northwest Territories prohibited liquor sales to Indians and Eskimos: Ord. NWT 1948, c. 23, s. 15(1)(e), 26–8. Prince Edward Island prohibited 'Indians' from voting on prohibition: SPEI 1929, c. 15, s. 6.

75 SC 1868, c. 42, s. 9, 12–13; SC 1869, c. 6, s. 3; SC 1874, c. 21, s. 1; SC 1876, c. 18, ss. 27, 68, 79–85; SC 1880, c. 28, s. 90; SC 1882, c. 30, s. 5; RSC 1886, c. 43, ss. 94–105; SC 1887, c. 33, s. 10; SC 1888, c. 22, s. 4; SC 1890, c. 29, s. 8; SC 1894, c. 32, s. 6–7; RSC 1906, c. 81, ss. 135–46; SC 1919–20, c. 50, s. 4; RSC 1927, c. 98; SC 1930, c. 25, ss. 13–14; SC 1936, c. 20, ss. 6–12; SC 1951, c. 29, ss. 93–102.

76 SC 1888, c. 22, s. 4; RSC 1886, c. 43, s. 96.

77 See for example, SC 1874, c. 21, s. 1; SC 1880, c. 28, s. 90; Ord. NWT 1948, c. 23, ss. 26–28. Some statutes barred 'Indians' from holding liquor licences; see, for example, SBC 1910, c. 30, s. 65. Others made it a criminal offence for 'Indians' to enter the premises of government liquor stores; see, for example, RSBC 1936, c. 160, s. 43.

78 Mimi Ajzenstadt and Brian Burtch, 'The Idea of Alcoholism: Changing Perceptions of Alcoholism and Treatment in British Columbia, 1870–1988,' *Health and Canadian Society* 2, no. 1 (1994–95), 9–34; Mimi Ajzenstadt and Brian E. Burtch, 'Medicalization and Regulation of Alcohol and Alcoholism: The Professions and Disciplinary Measures,' *International Journal of Law and Psychiatry* 13 (1990), 127–47; Haring, *Crow Dog's Case*, at 163, 278; Arthur Ray, *Indians in the Fur Trade* (Toronto: University of Toronto Press 1974). On the anti-alcohol proselytization of the Code of Handsome Lake, see Edmund Wilson, *Apologies to the Iroquois* (Syracuse: Syracuse University Press 1992).

79 London *Advertiser*, 8 July 1902, 2; London *Free Press*, 8 July 1902, 2.

80 London *Advertiser*, 23 June 1902, 2. Mrs Sharkey, Hugh's wife, added her own support for this policy, advising the London *Free Press*, that they 'did not allow Indians about the hotel,' and 'would not permit the sale of even a cigar to the redmen'; 23 June 1902, 4.

81 'Depositions' in the preliminary inquiry, Middlesex County Court Records,

Box 558; London *Advertiser*, 8 July 1902, 2; 10 July 1902, 8; 16 July 1902, 8; London *Free Press*, 8 July 1902, 2.

82 London *Advertiser*, 10 July 1902, 8; 14 July 1902, 8. The London *Free Press*, reports something slightly different, noting that Sharkey Sr testified the drinkers 'came to water their horses and —— to water themselves if it's lawful hours to do it.' 10 July 1902, 4; 14 July 1902, 6.

83 London *Advertiser*, 17 July 1902, 8; London *Free Press*, 17 July 1902, 6. The occupations of the coroner's jurymen include positions such as county constable, grain buyer, auctioneer, vinegar manufacturer, journalist, clerk, street watering inspector, shoemaker, and sewing machinist. On the increase of beer consumption among urban labourers in Ontario at the turn of the century, see M. Graeme Decarie, 'Something Old, Something New ... Aspects of Prohibitionism in Ontario in the 1890s,' in Donald Swainson, ed., *Oliver Mowat's Ontario* (Toronto: University of Toronto Press 1972), 154–71. On the rise and impact of the temperance movement, see Sharon Anne Cook, *'Through Sunshine and Shadow': The Woman's Christian Temperance Union, Evangelism, and Reform in Ontario, 1874–1930* (Montreal and Kingston: McGill-Queen's University Press 1995); Cheryl Krasnick Warsh, ed., *Drink in Canada: Historical Essays* (Montreal and Kingston: McGill-Queen's University Press 1993), and, in an earlier period, Noel, *Canada Dry*.

84 London *Advertiser*, 28 June 1902, 5; 1 July 1902, 6; 4 July 1902, 8; 10 July 1902, 8; London *Free Press*, 19 September 1902, 6.

85 London *Free Press*, 8 July 1902, 2; London *Advertiser*, 12 July 1902, 1.

86 Correspondence of James Magee to R.C. Clute, KC, 4 September 1902; London *Advertiser*, 17 July 1902, 8; London *Free Press*, 17 July 1902, 6.

87 'Deposition,' 25 July 1902, 'Depositions' and 'Statement of Accused,' 29 July 1902, in the preliminary inquiry, Middlesex County Court Records, Box 558.

88 AO RG22–464, Introductory Notes to the 'Benchbooks of William Lount,' 1901–1902; W.A. McKay, *Macmillan Dictionary of Canadian Biography* (Toronto: Macmillan 1978), at 475.

89 Henry James Morgan, ed., *The Canadian Men and Women of the Time*, 2nd ed. (Toronto: Briggs 1912), at 242. The newspaper accounts erroneously refer to 'Robert' Clute, but there is no 'Robert Clute' registered on the rolls of the Law Society of Upper Canada at this time, only 'Roger Conger Clute.' I am indebted to Ann-Marie Langlois of the Law Society of Upper Canada Archives for locating this information. Clute's parents were Richard R. Clute and Hannah Wright. He was Presbyterian by religion, and Liberal in politics, standing unsuccessfully for federal election for the district of West Hastings in 1891. His Toronto law firm was Clute, Macdonald, Macintosh and Hay. Clute also served on an 1899 Royal Commission regarding miners and mine owners in British Columbia. His biographical entry notes that he 'imposed a

fine of $10,000 upon the Central Supply Association for conspiracy in December 1905' and 'declined to receive a congratulatory address from the bar on his appointment to the bench.' The 'man with a heart' quotation is attributed by Morgan to the Toronto *Telegram*, in 1898. For further reference to Clute's prosecutorial talent, see Carolyn Strange and Tina Loo, 'Spectacular Justice: The Circus on Trial, and the Trial as Circus, Picton, 1903,' *Canadian Historical Review* 77, no. 2 (June 1996), 159–84.

90 London *Free Press*, 16 September 1902, 6. Clarke, *Treatise on Criminal Law*, describes at 592 the process of the grand jury: 'The evidence offered to a Grand Jury is evidence of accusation only. It is to be given and heard in secret according to the oath administered. The accused has no right to appear before, or be heard by, the Grand Jury either for the purpose of examining his accuser or of offering exculpatory evidence [...] A reasonable conclusion only is required, the rest is for the jury on the trial. They must have reasonable evidence of the *corpus delicti*, and that the accused is the guilty person. The intent laid or charged against the accused should clearly appear, either expressly or by necessary implication, from the circumstances.'

91 London *Free Press*, 16 September 1902, 6. 'The Criminal Code, 1892,' SC 1892, c. 29, defines murder as follows:

s. 227. Culpable homicide is murder in each of the following cases:
(a) If the offender means to cause the death of the person killed;
(b) If the offender means to cause to the person killed any bodily injury which is known to the offender to be likely to cause death, and is reckless whether death ensues or not;

...

s. 231. Every one who commits murder is guilty of an indictable offence and shall, on conviction thereof, be sentenced to death.

92 London *Advertiser*, 17 September 1902, 8. 'The Criminal Code, 1892,' SC 1892, c. 29 provides:

s. 229.1. Culpable homicide, which would otherwise be murder, may be reduced to manslaughter if the person who causes death does so in the heat of passion caused by sudden provocation.
2. Any wrongful act or insult, of such a nature as to be sufficient to deprive an ordinary person of the power of self-control, may be provocation if the offender acts upon it on the sudden, and before there has been time for his passion to cool.
3. Whether or not any particular wrongful act or insult amounts to provocation, and whether or not the person provoked was actually deprived of the power of self-control by the provocation which he received, shall be questions of fact. No one shall be held to give provocation to another by doing that

which he had a legal right to do, or by doing anything which the offender incited him to do in order to provide the offender with an excuse for killing or doing bodily harm to any person.

...

s. 236. Every one who commits manslaughter is guilty of an indictable offence, and liable to imprisonment for life.

93 London *Advertiser*, 17 September 1902, 8.
94 Burbidge, *Digest of the Criminal Law of Canada*, outlines at 216–19 the common law doctrines upon which the Code is based:

Manslaughter is unlawful homicide without malice aforethought. Murder is unlawful homicide with malice aforethought. Malice aforethought means any one or more of the following states of mind preceding or co-existing with the act or omission by which death is caused, and it may exist where that act is unpremeditated.

(a) An intention to cause the death of, or grievous bodily harm to, any person, whether such person is the person actually killed or not;

(b) Knowledge that the act which causes death will probably cause the death of, or grievous bodily harm to, some person, whether such person is the person actually killed or not, although such knowledge is accompanied by indifference whether death or grievous bodily harm is caused or not, or by a wish that it may not be caused ...

Illustrations:

1. A. knowing that B. is suffering from disease of the heart, and intending to kill B., gives B. a slight push, and thereby kills B. A. commits murder.

2. A. in the last illustration pushes B. unlawfully, but without knowledge of the state or health or intention to kill him, or do him grievous bodily harm. A. commits manslaughter. If A. laid his hand gently on B. to attract his attention, and by doing so startled and killed him, A.'s act would be no offence at all.

...

4. A. waylays B., intending to beat, but not intending to kill him or do him grievous bodily harm. A. beats B. and does kill him. This is manslaughter at least, and may be murder if the beating were so violent as to be likely, according to common knowledge, to cause death.

95 London *Free Press*, 17 September 1902, 6; 19 September 1902, 6.
96 London *Advertiser*, 18 September 1902, 5; 'Petit Jury Panel for the Superior Courts, No. 2 and 2a, County of Middlesex,' Middlesex County Court Records, Box 558.

97 RSO 1897, c. 61 s. 3. SO 1909, c. 34, s. 3 also introduces the adjective 'male,'
which was only implicit in the previous legislation. Women are permitted to
serve on juries in Ontario by SO 1951, c. 41. However, the provisions regarding citizenship and property qualifications continue in force until 1972: see
RSO 1914, c. 64; RSO 1927, c. 96; RSO 1937, c. 108, RSO 1950, c. 191; RSO 1960,
c. 199; RSO 1970, c. 230. SO 1972, c. 112 substitutes the following prerequisites
in s. 2: 'Subject to section 44, and unless exempted or disqualified, every
person in the possession of his or her natural faculties and not infirm or
decrepit, who is resident in a county or district and whose name is entered on
the last revised polling list prepared under, *The Municipal Elections Act, 1972*
of electors for the election of members of the council of a municipality in the
county or district or of a school board in territory without municipal organization, is qualified and liable to serve as a juror on grand and petit juries in
the Supreme Court and in all courts of civil or criminal jurisdiction in the
county or district.' SO 1973, c. 81 substitutes yet another formula in s. 2:
'Subject to sections 3 and 5, every person who,

(a) resides in Ontario;
(b) is a Canadian citizen or other British subject; and
(c) in the year preceding the year for which the jury is selected had attained
the age of eighteen years or more and had not attained the age of sixty-
nine years or more, is eligible and liable to serve as a juror on grand and
petit juries in the Supreme Court and in all courts of civil or criminal
jurisdiction in the county in which he resides.'
The 1973 statute also enacts the first provisions expressly directed towards First Nations communities. Section 11(9) provides: 'In the selecting
of persons for entry in the jurors' book in a county or district in which an
Indian reserve is situate, the sheriff shall perform in respect of the reserve
the duties the Director of Assessment would have under subsections 1, 2,
3, 4, 5 and 8 if the reserve were a municipality and, for the purpose, the
sheriff may obtain the names of the inhabitants of the reserve from any
record available.' This new provision seems to have meant the inclusion
of First Nations individuals for jury duty for the first time. See London
Free Press, 4 April 1974, 48, which notes that the first 'Indians' ever
empanelled for jury duty in the province were four individuals from the
Six Nations reserve, selected in Brant County court in 1974.

98 For further details, see Backhouse, 'They Are a People Unacquainted with
Subordination,' in Backhouse, *Colour-Coded* (1999).
99 London *Free Press*, 19 September 1902, 6.

100 AO RG22–464-1-6, Judge Lount's Judge's Notebook, Common Pleas Circuit Book, June 1902–October 1902, 223, 18 September 1902; London *Advertiser*, 18 September 1902, 5, 19 September 1902, 6; London *Free Press*, 19 September 1902, 6.
101 London *Advertiser*, 18 September 1902, 5.
102 London *Advertiser*, 12 July 1902, 1; 19 September 1902, 1; London *Free Press*, 12 July 1902, 6; 20 September 1902, 6; 'Deposition,' 25 July 1902, in the preliminary inquiry, Middlesex County Court Records, Box 558.
103 London *Free Press*, 20 September 1902, 6; London *Advertiser*, 19 September 1902, 1.
104 'Depositions,' in the preliminary inquiry, Middlesex County Court Records, Box 558; London *Advertiser*, 23 June 1902, 2; 28 June 1902, 5; 19 September 1902, 1 and 6; London *Free Press*, 29 June 1902, 9; 1 July 1902, 1; 19 September 1902, 6.
105 For the inquest testimony in which the physicians used the exact phrase specified, see London *Free Press*, 12 July 1902, 6; London *Advertiser*, 12 July 1902, 1. At the preliminary inquiry, Dr. Waugh testified: 'The injuries to the head such as we found would produce a certain amount of shock and this shock might be sufficient to stop the heart. The cause of death was the stoppage of the heart &c. We found no other cause, excepting injuries to the head.' 'Deposition,' 25 July 1902, in the preliminary inquiry, Middlesex County Court Records, Box 558; London *Free Press*, 20 September 1902, 6.
106 London *Free Press*, 20 September 1902, 6, emphasis added. The London *Advertiser*, 19 September 1902, 1, reports: 'The immediate cause of Ninham's death was heart failure. The heart stopped as a result of shock. The shock might have been from injuries received or from excitement.'
107 Barr, *Century of Medicine*, at 169, 193.
108 Dr Waugh would become an emeritus professor and bursar in 1913 and receive an honourary degree from the University of Western Ontario in 1919. Barr, *Century of Medicine*, at 88, 110–11, 454, 620; N.C. James, 'The Western University,' in *London and Middlesex Historical Society Transactions, 1911–12* (London: The Society 1913), at 42–3; Edwin Seaborn, *The March of Medicine in Western Ontario* (Toronto: Ryerson 1944), at 338–47; obit., London *Free Press*, 26 May 1936.
109 Correspondence of James Magee to R.C. Clute, KC, 4 September 1902; London *Advertiser*, 19 September 1902, 1; London *Free Press*, 20 September 1902, 6.
110 London *Free Press*, 19 September 1902, 6; 20 September 1902, 6.
111 London *Free Press*, 20 September 1902, 6.
112 'The Criminal Code, 1892,' SC 1892, c. 29, s. 224 is a codification of earlier common law doctrine, which is described in Clarke, *Treatise on Criminal Law*, at 246: 'If a man has a disease which, in all likelihood, would terminate his

life in a short time, and another gives him a wound or hurt which hastens his death, this will constitute murder, for to accelerate the death of a person is sufficient. [Arch. Cr. Pldg. 625; *R. v. Martin*, 5 C. & P. 130.]' See also Burbidge, *Digest of the Criminal Law*, at 212–13:

A person is deemed to have committed homicide, although his act is not the immediate or not the sole cause of death in the following cases –

...

If by any act he hastens the death of a person suffering under any disease or injury which apart from such act would have caused death.
Illustration: A. strikes B., who is at the time so ill that she could not possibly have lived more than six weeks if she had not been struck. B. dies earlier than she would otherwise have died in consequence. A. has killed B. [1 Hale 428; *R. v. Fletcher*, 1 Russ. Cr. 703.]

See also William Oldnall Russell, *A Treatise on Crimes and Misdemeanors*, 5th American, from the 3rd London ed. (Philadelphia: Johnson 1845), at 505; Seymour F. Harris, *Principles of the Criminal Law* (London: Stevens and Haynes 1877), at 157; and James Fitzjames Stephen, *A Digest of the Criminal Law* (London: Macmillan 1894), at 178–9.

113 London *Advertiser*, 18 September 1902, 5; London *Free Press*, 19 September 1902, 6.

114 London *Free Press*, 20 September 1902, 6.

115 Clarke, *Treatise on Criminal Law*, at 598.

116 The proper procedure for directed verdicts would be outlined in *R. v. Roubichaud* (1950), 98 CCC 86 (NBCA); *Fraser v. R.* (1936), 66 CCC 240 (SCC). *R. v. Comba* (1938), 70 CCC 205 (SCC) propounded a lower threshold: 'the learned trial judge ought, on the application made by counsel for the prisoner at the close of the evidence for the Crown, to have told the jury that in view of the dubious nature of the evidence, it would be unsafe to find the prisoner guilty and to have directed them to return a verdict of acquittal accordingly.' The case dealt with evidence that was entirely circumstantial and the 'dubious' terminology was directly linked to the special rules of evidence relating to circumstantial proof.

117 London *Free Press*, 20 September 1902, 6. Criminal texts attest to the complexity of the rules of causation in murder and manslaughter trials. Although insisting that one could be convicted of murder for merely accelerating the death of a man already sick with disease, Russell, *Treatise on Crimes*, notes at 505: 'See Johnson's case, 1 Lewin, 164, where on an indictment for manslaughter in causing a death by a blow on the stomach, on a surgeon stating that a blow on the stomach in this state of things, arising from passion and intoxication, was calculated to occasion death, but not so if the

party was sober. Hullock, B., is said to have directed an acquittal, saying, "that where the death was occasioned partly by a blow, and partly by a predisposing circumstance, it was impossible so to apportion the operations of the several causes as to be able to say with certainty that the death was immediately occasioned by any one of them in particular." This ruling is questioned in Roscoe's Cr. Evid. 647, and as it should seem with very good reason, as it is contrary to the other authorities on this point.' Russell also reports the case of *R. v. Fletcher*, Gloucester Spring Assizes 1841: 'So where a husband was indicted for the manslaughter of his wife by accelerating her death by blows, and it appeared that she was at the time in so bad a state of health that she could not possibly have lived more than a month or six weeks under any circumstances; Coleridge, J. told the jury that if a person inflicted an injury upon a person labouring under a mortal disease, which caused that person to die sooner than he otherwise would have done, he was liable to be found guilty of manslaughter, and the question for them was, whether the death of the wife was caused by the disease under which she was labouring, or whether it was hastened by the ill usage of the prisoner.' In *Fletcher*, Russell notes that the jury acquitted, 'the evidence of the surgeon leaving it doubtful whether the death did not arise purely from natural causes.' This commentary suggests that despite the rhetoric regarding criminal responsibility for the acceleration of death, in practice equivocal medical evidence could prompt a jury to acquit.

118 For a more detailed assessment of the legal underpinnings of race discrimination see Backhouse, *Colour-Coded*, forthcoming.

119 London *Free Press*, 20 September 1902, 6; London *Advertiser*, 19 September 1902, 1. John McArthur's widowed mother died in 1904 at the age of 65: Woodland Cemetery Burial Register, 1 March 1904; London *Free Press*, 1 March 1904. Entries in the *London City Directories* show that John McArthur left the farm in 1906. By 1911, his brothers were no longer living on the farm either, and Alex appears to be working as a labourer at Labatt's in London. In 1925, John C. McArthur reappears in the London directory as living in London at 92 Askin. No occupation is indicated, which may suggest he was unemployed. Alex A. McArthur, employed at the CNR, takes over the listing in 1927. John McArthur's obituary appears in the London *Free Press* on 11 June 1929, listing his residence as still at 92 Askin Street. The Woodland Cemetery Burial Register, 12 June 1929, lists John Colin MacArthur's age at death as fifty-four and his occupation as 'returned soldier,' which seems to suggest that his civilian employment history remained scanty and unworthy of classification. I am indebted to Glen Curnoe of the London Room of the London Public Library for assistance in locating these details.

4

Ontario Water Quality, Public Health, and the Law, 1880–1930

JAMIE BENIDICKSON

INTRODUCTION

In 1882 a select committee of the Ontario legislature found that in three-quarters of the eighty municipalities that responded to its inquiries the water supply was being polluted by privies. Remedial efforts were virtually non-existent and disease was widespread. Legislators concluded that locally designated administrative officials were 'too subject to local influences to act efficiently' and called for a provincially appointed agency.[1] Thus, in response to the apparent inability of individuals or the disinclination of local officials to address such public health problems as sewage and contaminated water supplies, a provincewide solution was elaborated in the form of a Provincial Board of Health (PBH).[2]

This essay examines legal dimensions of water quality protection during the period from c. 1882, when Ontario established a Provincial Board of Health, to c. 1930, when the board was dissolved and replaced by the rapidly evolving departmental structures of central public administration.[3] The PBH and the local medical officials responsible to it campaigned persistently to accomplish their water quality objectives within a complex legal framework grounded in the common law of nuisance. Although it offered gratifying successes, the law was equally a source of frustration. Legislation facilitated the work of the PBH – indeed, it was the formal source of the board's authority – but it simultaneously constrained that authority within broader norms. Efforts to reshape the legal framework became one important element of the PBH's agenda. The overall legal framework for water quality emerged from the interaction of these public and private mechanisms applied in relation to a series of challenges in which public health officials often figured prominently.

It is possible to discern at least three perspectives on the legal dimensions of the early public health regime and its relationship to Ontario water quality. To some, the legal and administrative controversies detailed here seem never to have occurred, with the result that, in their view, environmental protection – a good thing – originated only in the late twentieth century. While others acknowledge the efforts of public health officials, those efforts have sometimes been discredited or questioned as intrusive and perhaps illegitimate intervention by social regulators seeking to impose their own values on other sectors of the community. Measures taken were essentially those of contol and their underlying objectives have been associated with the moral preferences and self-interest of middle-class and professional busybodies. From yet another perspective, the public health enterprise appears genuine in its ambitions, but ultimately ineffectual in the face of industrial forces that undermined its potential while other contemporaries remained oblivious to pressing needs, disregarding or underestimating the threat of pollution.

This essay focuses on a sequence of public health challenges and their relationship to the legal regime, beginning with privies and sewerage systems, followed by municipal waste treatment facilities and the eventual need to safeguard drinking water supplies directly through such means as filtration. Concluding comments address the three perspectives previously noted: the existence, legitimacy, and effectiveness of the public health response to water quality problems in late-nineteenth- and early-twentieth-century Ontario.[4]

THE PRIVY PROBLEM

The privy pit constituted a formidable challenge to health in late-nineteenth-century Ontario communities. In the transitional process that saw open countryside gradually absorbed within urban boundaries, animal wastes and manure also became pressing concerns for 'town folk.' Sewers and the crude drainage systems introduced to transport household wastes in a somewhat diluted form away from their point of origin frequently produced difficulties of their own. Contamination from privies, cess pools, and – in several of the larger municipalities – from sewage outfall pipes was significant and worrisome. In Toronto, as the 'modern conveniences" of water closets and drainage took hold, increasing pollution of the harbour was apparent. 'The water front of the whole city ... becomes a source of unpleasantness and of danger to the public health ... [A]s the water supply pipe from the lake is laid on the bottom of the bay leaks may at any time contaminate with sewage the city water.'[5]

Common law actions, generally alleging nuisance or an interference with riparian rights, provided recourse against some of the more obvious threats to water quality. In *Park v. White*, privy pits on premises adjacent to the plaintiff's property were recognized as a nuisance. In addition to paying nine dollars in proven damages, the defendants were required to fill in the privies or otherwise remove the nuisance.[6] In a later action, Justice Middleton issued an injunction against the Town of Cobourg, whose sewers discharged untreated human waste into a waterway known as Factory Creek that flowed through the grounds of plaintiff hotel owners.[7] On the other hand, a private litigant's attempt to encourage the London Lunatic Asylum to abate a sewage nuisance in the vicinity of the Thames River foundered on the court's unwillingness to produce an order appearing to depend for its implementation on an unauthorized expenditure by the commissioner of public works of some $30,000.[8] Vice-Chancellor Blake remarked that the commissioner's duty 'is to manage his department as well as that can be accomplished, using the means which the Legislature places at his disposal; but beyond that he is not bound to go.'[9] Chancellor Spragge, who was firmly persuaded that a 'very serious character' of nuisance existed, nonetheless accepted the thrust of Blake's position. He found it hard to imagine the expenditure of so considerable a sum essentially for the purpose of shifting the nuisance from one location to another by extending the asylum's drain to the Thames River itself. The only potential benefit, Spragge remarked, would be to transform 'a gross private nuisance, to a gross public nuisance,' with the result that the commissioner of public works would be authorized to abate it without obtaining prior legislative approval for the specific expenditure.[10]

The Provincial Board noted such cases as well as interesting local prosecutions and reported encouragingly in 1884 that 'the reading of the law has been so clear that verdicts against offenders have been obtained and remedies have been effected.'[11] Several local boards claimed great success in eliminating privy nuisances and in controlling cess pools and other forms of contamination. But any sense of satisfaction and accomplishment must have been short-lived. The need for ongoing legal proceedings to deal with waves of individual offenders was common in certain communities. Moreover, the London Asylum case hints strongly at the broader public or communitywide implications of concentrated urban populations and the special problem of imposing standards on public institutions and facilities, or in cases of public rather than private injury. In this context there was a need for systematic administrative responses.

The PBH repeatedly endeavoured to persuade local councils to act systematically and methodically to deal with the sewage of expanding municipalities. 'The day is past for box drains, and drains pretending to be sewers, which in more than one town and village in Canada have been found to run up-hill, as also for the filthy collections which too commonly exist in our backyards.'[12] Citing Toronto (where civic officials had allocated a mere $500 to the local board of health, which had responsibilities for sanitary conditions affecting nearly 100,000 people) as an egregious example of municipal penny-pinching, the PBH lamented the limitations of municipal funding.[13]

The inventory of problems to be addressed included an array of nuisances, defined initially in legislation with reference to common law principles as 'anything which is injurious to health, or which is materially offensive to the senses, or which interferes with the enjoyment of life and property.'[14] However, the statistical record suggests that local boards of health generally left remedial activity to those most directly affected, relying heavily upon inspections, educational measures, and warning notices to secure abatement measures without going to court. In Toronto, in 1889, 6,000 complaints gave rise to 18,000 visits by eight sanitary police officials, leading to 1,400 notices and 5,500 post-notice inspections. Of 234 prosecutions initiated, 170 were withdrawn on the grounds that the necessary work had been done. Two thousand privies were cleaned, 113 were repaired, and 143 were closed.[15] In 1893, the year of the *Park v. White* litigation, there were 3,473 privy pit complaints. Two thousand three hundred and sixty-nine were abated on notice; 473 were abated on prosecution, and in 222 cases officials concluded that the complaints were unfounded.[16] In the following year, on the basis of 1,474 complaints about privy pits, only ninety proceedings were instituted in police court.[17]

For their part provincial public health professionals (despite their early enthusiasm) soon grew sceptical of the legal process. It seemed excruciatingly difficult to establish at trial 'not only whether this or that condition is *injurious to the public health*, but whether it is *materially offensive to the senses*, or interferes with the *enjoyment of life and property*.' The board lacked confidence in the capacity of the jury to reach decisions that would be considered appropriate from the perspective of its own expertise. 'To make the question of whether a man with senses rendered obtuse is or is not nauseated by a smell a criterion of the existence or absence of a nuisance is as crude as was trial by fire in old Saxon times, since the guilt or innocence of the accused was tested by his power to endure pain.'[18] The Toronto situation was sufficiently difficult to resolve on a case-by-case basis that local officials resorted to a by-law prohibition as a more comprehensive response to privy pits.[19] Other Ontario communities endeavoured to address local problems of pollution in the late nineteenth and early twentieth centuries as population expansion and industrial development placed increasing pressure on water quality.[20]

The problems of pollution, including sewage contamination, were by no means confined to urban centres. Small, transient, but nonetheless densely populated lumber and mining camps in the north presented special difficulties, and it was reportedly common for the summer residents of the Muskoka district to 'draw their water from the same bay or locality into which the closets drained, and the kitchen slops ultimately found their way.' Two doctors investigating the situation urged cottage owners to initiate 'some system to prevent the pollution which is of so widespread a character.'[21] This was an important but not unique call for preventive measures, suggesting the desirability of avoiding sewage nuisances rather than trying to abate them after the fact.

SEWAGE REMOVAL, DUMPING, AND DRAINAGE

Sewage systems represented one approach to nuisance prevention. And indeed, municipalities around the province shifted to collective systems of sewage removal, eventually adding treatment and management procedures. The transition, however, did not bring an end to public health concerns or to judicial proceedings, for the legal actions that had once been contemplated in relation to individual polluters were increasingly redirected against public institutions: the municipal operators of sewage removal and waste treatment facilities.

A charge of criminal nuisance against the Town of Walkerville for polluting the Detroit River where it flows from Lake St Clair to Lake Erie between Ontario's Essex County and Michigan led to an indictment on 12 April 1893.[22] The consequence of Walkerville's sewerage program, according to the grand jury, was that the waters, having been polluted with refuse, were 'corrupted, fouled, offensive and unhealthy to the great damage and common nuisance' of residents nearby and other users. Within a few months, The Queen v. Walkerville was settled according to a detailed covenant worked out between Walkerville and the water commissioners of Windsor concerning the installation of a new water intake pipe for the joint use of the two municipalities.[23]

A similar controversy erupted elsewhere, when, in 1908, the Township of Guelph, having lost patience with the City of Guelph's inattention to contamination of the River Speed, resorted to measures under the Public Health Act to have the nuisance abated through the construction of a filtration bed.[24] The local Board of Health notified the city of the proposed course of action and remained wholly dissatisfied with the municipal claim that any basis for complaint could be eliminated by the simple expedient of installing a new septic tank. The local police magistrate expressed hesitation about hearing the matter, arguing that such a complaint was more properly the subject of an indictment under the direction of the attorney general or a judge at the assizes. However, the county Crown attorney appeared anxious to proceed, hoping by either means to get the critical testimony of the provincial health inspector onto the record. This, in his view, would 'ventilate' the complaints sufficiently to induce the city to initiate a more appropriate and effective response.[25]

Toronto was not immune from pollution controversies arising from local drainage practices. In the aftermath of various 'improvements,' the condition of Ashbridge's Bay gave rise to numerous but largely fruitless legal proceedings. The cause of the complaints was graphically described in a court judgment: 'Sewage and manure and refuse from the cattle byres, where some 3,000 head of cattle were kept and fed upon 'slops' from Gooderham and Worts Distillery, were discharged into the marsh.'[26] Justice Middleton indicated delicately that the resulting condition 'can be understood by perusing the reports of the health officers put in as exhibits.'[27] In 1892, the situation, referred to judicially as 'an incipient pestilence,' provoked the Ashbridge's Bay Property Owners Association to threaten litigation and the PBH to recommend abatement measures including dredging, channelling, and alternative disposal of animal refuse.[28] Gooderham and Worts took remedial measures, but the City of Toronto, with litigation pending against it, was unsuccessful in its efforts to open a channel between Ashbridge's Bay and Toronto Bay to flush the marsh.[29]

The unsanitary condition of Ashbridge's Bay was the subject of a negligence claim (possibly a test case) on the part of a resident whose children had experienced severe illness as a consequence, he alleged, of the contaminated state of the marsh. Irregularities associated with the premature dispersal of the jury threatened to undermine the integrity of the deliberations, but the bottom line reassured the city: 'the jury find that the illness was not caused by any nuisance created by the defendants.'[30]

After construction – first of a railroad switching station and then of city sewers – interfered with navigation in Keating channel on the lower Don River, Richard Schofield experienced repeated setbacks in a frustrating effort to maintain water access to his boat works. Schofield complained to Dr Hastings, Toronto's medical health officer, about 'the rotten conditions of the water front around our premises, due to putrid matter coming from the sewers' that formed two breakwaters on either side of Schofield's land. The sewers, Schofield protested to no avail, 'effectually prevent this matter from circulating and it all lodges in and around our wharves and sheds with the result that half of our employees are laid up at the present time.'[31] An elaborate riparian claim against the city and the Toronto Harbour commissioners was dismissed, largely on the basis that Keating's channel was an artificial 'cut.' Schofield, therefore, owned no lands abutting navigable water and had accordingly never been a riparian owner. [32]

In 1913 Schofield joined other Toronto residents to launch proceedings against the city over the deteriorating condition of Ashbridge's Bay.[33] On the advice of W.E. Raney, KC, the Schofield group applied for leave to bring common nuisance charges under the Criminal Code[34] against the Corporation of the City of Toronto; specifically, they sought the court's permission to proceed by way of indictment rather than on the basis of a summary trial before a police magistrate. This choice of procedure was necessary, Raney insisted, because the Criminal Code made no provision for summary conviction of corporations in cases of criminal common nuisance, although it did so explicitly in relation to other offences for which summary proceedings were established as a procedural alternative.[35]

What had seemed to Raney an inescapable conclusion failed to impress Chief Justice Meredith. In insisting that the matter could only enter the judicial stream via the police court, Meredith asserted the traditional virtues of criminal procedure, which requires a thorough preliminary investigation of indictable offences to ensure that the facts are properly brought to light. He would not alter the ordinary pattern of proceeding in the absence of some compelling reason to do so: 'There is no royal road for anyone; every one must take the common road up to this Court.'[36] As examples from numerous Ontario communities demonstrated, the common road up to court was beset with obstacles and hard on the feet of those who trod it in the hope of safeguarding water quality or controlling sewage nuisances.

An important alternative to private litigation at common law, with its procedural and financial pitfalls, or to formal criminal prosecutions, where technical and evidentiary requirements might prove insurmountable, was regulatory action against those suspected of violating public welfare norms. This option was recognized in the legislative and regulatory codes of a rapidly developing administrative state. The PBH welcomed a series of legislative measures bolstering the formal authority of health officials in their campaign against pollution of public water resources.[37] In 1906, a sternly worded prohibition appeared: 'No garbage, excreta, manure, vegetable or animal matter or filth shall be discharged into or be deposited in any of the lakes, rivers, streams or other waters in Ontario, or on the shores or banks thereof.'[38] In a significant revision of the Public Health Act, officials were empowered to develop regulations for the purpose of preventing pollution in the province's lakes, rivers, streams, and other inland waters.[39] Perhaps most significantly, for purposes of the act, nuisance was redefined as 'any condition ... which is or may become injurious to health or prevent or hinder in any manner the suppression of disease.'[40] Regulatory and approval powers with respect to municipal water and sewage systems were included in the fortified arsenal of public health measures. The public health regime also included a model municipal by-law providing avenues of recourse against problems brought to the attention of officials through the complaints process or identified through systematic inspection procedures.

The practical and symbolic significance of all these measures would be publicly tested. For example, the Village of Weston employed the model Public Health Act by-law to prohibit placing or unloading any car containing manure on any portion of railway premises in the community. Charges were laid against a number of defendants for unloading manure from a railway car to a wagon for subsequent removal. The case for the prosecution was that '[t]he removal of manure is itself a matter prejudicial to public health as the effect of the tossing and pitching the manure from the car to the waggons might set loose disease germs or noxious matter.'[41] Justice Rose rejected defence arguments about the need to show actual harm to public health and that the by-law meant unloading to leave on the railway premises. He concluded that the actions of the defendants indeed fell within the scope of the prohibition on unloading manure and accepted the public health argument advanced by the prosecution.[42] In this instance, a wide reading of the Weston by-law supported enforcement efforts, but regulatory officials continued to face obstacles.

The experience of Sault Ste Marie provides some indication of the challenges. Several years after a severe typhoid outbreak in the rapidly developing northern industrial community, public health officials actively campaigned against unsanitary situations.[43] In 1912, for example, several local businesses and individuals were charged with failing to maintain a proper cover on a receptacle for manure.[44] In addition, the Sault Ste Marie Coal and Wood Company and the New Ontario Dock and Coal Company were charged with dumping manure into the St Mary's River, contrary to the broadly worded prohibition of 1906.

In the midst of an outbreak of diphtheria, local public health officials complained about enforcement difficulties. As reported by Dr A.S. McCaig, medical helath officer at the Sault, 'In two cases where we had offenders up for dumping manure into the river we could not get a conviction from the Magistrate although both parties pleaded guilty.'[45] The complaint progressed up the hierarchy to the desk of the provincial chief officer of health, and then crossed over to the attorney general's department before finding its way back down to the district Crown attorney, who claimed personally to 'know nothing of these prosecutions under the *Health Act* as same are usually attended to by the City Solicitor.'[46] However, the Crown attorney identified a police magistrate, a lawyer named Andrew Elliot, as a source for a full account of the situation.

Elliot explained that neither defendant had actually pleaded guilty. In one case, a water pipe used for fire protection purposes ran out to the end of a very long dock. The magistrate accepted the defendant's evidence that 'this pipe was boxed in and must be protected from frost' and that 'it was absolutely necessary to pack the box around the pipe with manure.' In the second case, also prosecuted by the city solicitor, the magistrate – at the prosecution's suggestion – inspected the defendant's premises and neighbouring properties, regrettably in the absence of counsel for the defendant. This procedural mishap had the unfortunate legal consequence of rendering a conviction impossible to sustain.

On the same day that Elliot sat down to deal with the inquiry initiated by health officials he had to face up to more public criticisms. In relation to critical coverage by the *Sault Star* of his decisions in another set of pollution prosecutions, Elliot referred to the police court records to provide a detailed history of the proceedings, including the apparent reluctance of the sanitary inspector to respond in open court to a defendant's testimony. As a consequence, one case was dismissed and charges against three other companies were withdrawn when the defendants demonstrated, following a brief adjournment, that they had complied fully with the relevant regulations.

When cases relating to unsanitary conditions under the Publich Health Act reached the police court, as they seemingly did with some frequency, it was Elliot's practice, apparently approved of by the Crown attorney, to grant adjournments to permit defendants to remedy the situation. Upon receiving satisfactory assurance that the offence would not be repeated, Elliot would dismiss the charges. He concluded that this well-established practice was the basis of 'the insinuation that there was no conviction upon a plea of guilty.' In a further effort to diminish any adverse effect that the *Sault Star* coverage of his performance might have on the deputy attorney general's assessment of him, Elliot accused local health officials of having demonstrated a 'ludicrous desire for notoriety.' He referred to the newspaper's coverage of Board of Health meetings as having reached the point where the paper was known locally as the 'Bulletin of the Chairman of the Board of Health.' Perhaps these rather dismissive remarks are an indication that health officials were pursuing their mandate with some diligence. Elliot's observations may have been largely defensive posturing, but they do suggest lack of enthusiasm for the entire apparatus of local health protection measures on the part of a minor legal official with significant influence over the utility of prosecutions as a mechanism for effecting environmental improvements.

Other incidents more positively indicate the potential of a determined environmental and public health bureaucracy to achieve its objectives given the support of the judiciary and the legislature. In 1914, Dr John W.S. McCullough put Ontario residents on notice that anyone contravening the Public Health Act's pollution provisions would be 'prosecuted to the full extent of the law.' In 1922, Deputy Attorney General Edward Bayly received a delegation of Milton area farmers. They protested that pollution of Sixteen Mile Creek by the town and certain local industries had harmed their cattle but appeared to fall outside the scope of the public health regime. The local Crown attorney, having been instructed to consider indictments for nuisance, corresponded with the parties who were subject to complaints. One company reported that it had recently installed a filtering system in response to the recommendations of public health officials, while the other denied that its waste water was in any way harmful, adding for good measure that 'the little frogs and fishes thrive in the stream immediately below our disposal plant, which of itself would possibly upset any contention that we were polluting the creek.' Bayly, who had accumulated a good deal of experience with similar views, asked the Crown attorney to invite the company 'to take this a little more seriously.' At this point, however, the matter temporarily came to rest while the board sought an enlargement of its jurisdiction.[47]

The fact that W.E. Raney, the man who had attempted to prosecute Schofield's complaints against the City of Toronto, had become attorney

general in the United Farmers of Ontario administration, no doubt facilitated the passage of legislation enhancing the powers of the PBH in the
interests of agrarian water users. Amendments to the Public Health Act in
1923 authorized the PBH to make inquiries on behalf of riparian proprietors concerning 'polluting material of any kind' that interfered with their
ordinary water uses and to report on remedial measures 'in respect to any
alleged injury or invasion of right as it may deem just.'[48]

Very shortly after the passage of this legislation the board made such an
inquiry in the Milton area and reported with recommendations on remedial measures. Not long after that, on the application of one of the farmers
affected by pollution of the creek, the Ontario courts declared the PBH's
report and recommendations to be fully enforceable. Justice Orde took the
opportunity to remark: 'The discharge of waste materials into public
streams is not to be encouraged.'[49] Nice words, of course, but the PBH was
actually more anxious to learn how actively it could discourage such
discharges.

An opportunity to test the strengths of administrative authority under
the revised statutory nuisance provisions arose in 1918, when the Waterloo Board of Health sought to enforce a local abatement order against a trio
of offenders: the City of Kitchener, a business provocatively operating as
the Riverside Garbage Disposal Company, and a land owner, Campbell,
who gave his name to the case.[50] When these three parties disregarded the
Waterloo board's order of abatement and removal concerning garbage
from Kitchener that had been deposited by Riverside near a creek on
Campbell's property draining into the Grand River, local officials called
upon the PBH to investigate. The latter confirmed the presence of ashes,
metal and enamel wear, and kitchen wastes, as well as decomposing
animal and vegetable material along the creek bank. The board declared
the situation a 'most insanitary one, a serious nuisance, and extremely
dangerous to the public.'[51]

The local Waterloo board then applied to the Supreme Court of Ontario
for an order to remove and abate the nuisance pursuant to a provision
authorizing a judge to make such an order 'upon the report of the Provincial Board or upon such further evidence as he may deem meet.' In
upholding a court order issued against Kitchener, Campbell, and Riverside, the court of appeal was unanimous in declining to open up the
question of the existence of a nuisance. 'The Act,' stated Chief Justice
Mulock, 'confers jurisdiction upon the Provincial Board of Health to determine that question, and there is no jurisdiction in the Court to try that
question of fact.'[52] Subsequent decisions followed the *Waterloo* holding in

this respect, although under a strict reading of the legislation the chief officer of health, an official otherwise empowered to perform the duties of the board between meetings, was not permitted to exercise the PBH's power in relation to nuisances.[53]

MUNICIPAL SEWAGE TREATMENT, HEALTH OFFICIALS, AND THE COURTS

Municipal sewage collection and treatment facilities represented the next generation of domestic waste technology. The innovations may have reduced conflicts between immediate neighbours, but larger concerns about environmental and public health risks immediately emerged. The new municipal sewage treatment operations received a good deal of attention from public health officials who had supervisory responsibilities; several facilities eventually became the subject of litigation.

Shortly after the First World War, only about one in three of Ontario's 284 organized cities, towns, and villages had sewerage facilities.[54] Frederick A. Dallyn, sanitary engineer for the PBH, believed the time was right for the province to suggest to the municipalities means of handling sewage as well as for improving their water supply. Dallyn insisted that smaller municipalities were 'keenly concerned' about the situation but as they lacked local engineers, no steps were being taken to assess the practicality of remedial alternatives.

Assuming that some initiative was taken, Dallyn outlined further issues to be considered. Would the PBH be content to discuss generalities and ultimately to generate a little business for consulting engineers, or would it wish to furnish each municipality with a plan and a general cost estimate, either at no charge or on the basis of some formula for cost recovery? Given some provincial support, Dallyn argued that the engineering department might (without waiting for civic initiatives) collaborate with local health officers to campaign for improved sewers, treatment facilities, the extension of water systems, and purification processes – especially in the smaller municipalities.

As an example of the difficulties that had to be overcome, the provincial sanitary engineer outlined the situation at Kincardine, on Lake Huron's eastern shore, where the mayor was anxious to instal sewerage facilities.[55] As Dallyn explained, 'their desire is to sewer one little section of the town and drain the same into a septic tank, allowing the effluent to discharge directly into the river.' On a recent visit he had observed 'very little flow of water in the river and in some places it was practically dry.' In such circumstances, almost no dilution occurred during the summer months. Accordingly, Dallyn cautioned against permitting the town to discharge untreated effluent and against a partial or patchwork solution. As the provincial sanitary engineer explained, a previous attempt to implement a comprehensive scheme had foundered: 'unfortunately the by-law was defeated by the rate-payers principally owing to the fact that they had not consulted the provincial board of health.'

The provincial sanitary engineer sought permission to visit England to evaluate and possibly to order a recently patented centrifuge for demonstration purposes.[56] The technology was intended to 'change the present methods in dewatering sewage sludge so that the material can be handled without a nuisance.' The provincial sanitary engineer thought that such a machine (estimated to cost $3,900 for a large model or $2,000 for a smaller one of the same type) could also be applied to waste from canneries and wool-scouring plants, where existing solutions were prohibitively expensive. Although he actively encouraged municipalities to take appropriate measures and offered advice, the provincial sanitary engineer seems not to have had a great deal of formal authority to impose any specific measures on unwilling local governments.

Nevertheless, having previously addressed the privy problem, health officials campaigned for improvements in municipal sewage and water systems. Litigation was not central to the official strategy, but the evidence, opinions, and support of health authorities were often crucial to the efforts of other parties to defend water quality in court. In addition, the PBH had to defend its jurisdiction against attacks.

Ashbridge's Bay and the Courts

In 1908, after years of debate, Toronto approved construction of an interceptor sewer system to transport sewage for treatment in settling tanks at Ashbridge's Bay.[57] Construction of the sewer system and a treatment plant on Morley Avenue soon got underway. Completion of the undertaking in 1913 was generally hailed as a major advance, but plans for the sewage treatment plant had been under attack from east-end residents from the outset. Complaints from residents and deputations to city officials produced expressions of sympathy and triggered municipal investigations into the plant's operation, but they failed to bring about improvements.

City residents who had been adversely affected by the construction and operation of the new facility embarked on legal action. Samuel E. Fieldhouse, a food, confectionary, and ice cream merchant, had the misfortune to carry on business from premises just opposite the lakeshore location of the Morley Avenue sewage disposal plant. He was one of those who had petitioned civic officials to remedy the situation, but when minor modifications failed to produce satisfactory improvement Fieldhouse took civil action against the city in November 1915, alleging nuisance and negligence in the construction and operation of the plant.[58] He specifically charged that 'the said nuisance and pollution of waters is dangerous to public health,' that it had destroyed his business, and that it had rendered it 'unbearable' to live on the premises. Fieldhouse, claiming special damages, also sought an abatement order against the city and an injunction to bring the nuisance to an end.[59]

The city denied the claim, arguing that care had been taken in the construction of the works, and that their operation represented a statutory duty which it was obligated to perform. Municipal officials also asserted, somewhat problematically as it later emerged, that plans had been approved by the PBH.[60]

Despite Toronto's formal denial of legal responsibility, the Fieldhouse claim was amply supported by municipal documentation. Certain municipal officials acknowledged the existence of the nuisance, and the municipal board of control went so far as to investigate possible claims against the experts from New York and Birmingham who had advised on the Morley Avenue plant. That specific inquiry produced a sobering response from Toronto's commissioner of works, who concluded 'that the advice of the experts, relative to sludge disposal was not followed, and the condition they foresaw if sludge were deposited contiguous to the premises, has eventuated.'[61]

Moreover, whatever approval that provincial health officials might once have expressed for the city's plans had evaporated. A provincial health inspector (after effectively conducting a raid on the plant) unhesitatingly asserted that the complaints were 'well founded, as the pollution of the atmosphere by this plant cannot help but be a nuisance and menace to the health of the nearby residents who are compelled to breathe it.' For good measure, he added, 'Undoubtedly some different method of treating and disposing of the sludge is required and should be insisted upon without unnecessary delay.'[62]

Civic inquiries about means to eliminate the problem identified a solution with estimated costs of approximately six million dollars. There was little enthusiasm to proceed with such costly remedial action, especially in wartime, and the city was of the opinion that there was actually no adverse impact on the drinking water supply. A universal 'do nothing' argument also emerged in the form of the proposition that even if the six million dollars were to be spent, 'new discoveries or experiments in treatment might soon render the whole plant out of date.'[63]

Having at least engaged the city's attention, Fieldhouse moved elsewhere in Toronto, though he retained an interest in the proceedings that continued to bear his name. Given his removal from the immediate vicinity, as well as some uncertainty concerning the entitlement of a private plaintiff to an injunction rather than mere damages, in the summer of 1916 Fieldhouse invited Ontario's attorney general to join the proceedings as co-plaintiff. After looking into the matter 'pretty thoroughly' Deputy Attorney General Edward Bayly concluded that this was a 'reasonably proper' situation for the attorney general to be added. He recommended that consent be given to add the attorney general if the applicants undertook to assume responsibilities for all costs incurred.

When the matter came before the master in the form of Fieldhouse's application to add the attorney general as a party plaintiff, the Master 'seemed indisposed' to follow a precedent along these lines and almost dismissed the motion.[64] Eventually, two individuals working or living near the city's sewage disposal system were joined as plaintiffs, but by the time the matter came before Chief Justice Mulock for trial in December 1917 they too had been forced to move away.

The 'Big Odor' case, as the Toronto *Daily Star* labelled the proceedings, was a *cause célèbre*. One hundred and fifty witnesses were assembled while 'blueprints without end festooned the judicial desk.' Mulock took an active part in the trial, reportedly, at one point, offering the city his services as a sanitary engineer on the principle that anyone could do a better job.[65] On another occasion he rebuked counsel for the city with the observation: 'This can't be tolerated; you are emptying more faecal matter into the lake than you originally contemplated.'[66]

Mulock identified two sources of offensive odours: concentrated sewage (sludge) that was allowed to settle on a nineteen-acre disposal site and effluent drained off through a defective and inadequate outfall pipe and a storm overflow line to Ashbridge's Bay. In response to the city's defence that the sewage treatment facility had been authorized, the chief justice explained: 'They have statutory authority to establish a sewage plant, but no authority to create a nuisance by its operation; and inability to operate it without causing a nuisance does not, in my opinion, furnish an excuse for their creating a nuisance.' He continued: 'While I am of the opinion that the operation of the plant causes a nuisance, and the absence of negligence would not furnish a defence, I think the facts show that the nuisance is traceable largely, if not entirely, to negligence.'[67]

The trial result was precisely what Fieldhouse had sought and what the city had feared: in addition to two thousand dollars' damages for Fieldhouse, the plaintiffs secured an injunction prohibiting the city from operating the plant so as to cause a public nuisance and an abatement order requiring remedial action by 1 May 1918. When the city appealed the negligence finding and reasserted statutory authority as a defence, the Ontario Court of Appeal confirmed the trial judgment. Toronto's long-standing failure to repair the deficient outfall pipe was clear evidence of negligence. In addition, members of the court carefully reviewed the requirements of the defence of statutory authority in the context of munici-pal construction of sewage facilities under the approval of the PBH and concluded that the defence was not available to the city. Toronto had neither passed a by-law to authorize the installation of the Morley Avenue sewage plant nor obtained approval from the board for the facility it established. There had been by-laws, of course, though nothing intro-duced in evidence indicated by-law approval for construction. Signifi-cantly, although some plans submitted to the PBH received acceptance in 1908, important modifications were made in the actual implementation of the sewage facility as completed in 1913.

The Public Health Act required municipalities contemplating the con-struction or extension of a sewage system to seek approval from the PBH. In turn, the PBH was charged with reporting as to whether the proposed work was 'calculated to meet the sanitary requirements of the inhabitants of the municipality and as to whether such sewer or system of sewerage is likely to prove prejudicial to the health of the inhabitants of the municipal-ity or of any other inhabitants liable to be affected thereby.' The PBH could require amendments, impose terms and conditions 'in the public interest,' and modify such conditions from time to time.[68]

It is clear that Toronto municipal expenditures on sewage facilities and water treatment increased substantially in the early decades of the cen-tury,[69] but it is somewhat more problematic to link specific remedial action with the Fieldhouse litigation.[70] In fact, while a decision on the appeal was pending, the city attempted unsuccessfully to settle the action and an official attributed the difficulty to 'the uncompromising attitude of the plaintiff.'[71] At the same time, that is, before the unfavourable appeal decision, Toronto council decided to petition for provincial legislation that would retroactively authorize the operation of the sewage treatment facilities. A few months later, civic officials experienced second thoughts and the application was reconsidered.[72] However, as of 30 April 1921, a master reviewing Fieldhouse's entitlement to damages from the date of the trial to the date of abatement fixed the amount at $3,820, noting that that long-awaited date had not yet arrived.

WATER SUPPLY AND TREATMENT

More or less at the same time that they moved to address privy contamination through closures and to eliminate sewage pollution with treatment, municipalities intervened actively to ensure the supply of clean water to their inhabitants. New technology, in terms of filtering, sedimentation, and the addition of chemicals, was utilized to safeguard water quality. Once again, however, legal proceedings in which the influence and authority of public health regulators was tested were required because more than a few communities resisted the expense.

In the nation's capital, a singularly unhealthy set of circumstances had threatened water quality for years. The Ottawa River was mistakenly, perhaps perversely, presumed to be pure, and civic officials declined to spend funds to clean out a public well on Stewart Street in which a dog had drowned. Recognition of the linkage between health and contaminated water supplies was slow in coming.[73] By 1913, a consultant's report recommended that Ottawa draw its water from Thirty-one Mile Lake, Pemichangaw Lake, and Long Lake in Quebec's Gatineau Hills. Provincial and federal statutes were enacted to facilitate the project, and one municipal council eagerly passed a by-law to fund the new waterworks. Irate ratepayers succeeded in having that by-law quashed[74] and a virtually identical successor, which the city claimed it had been compelled to enact by order of the province's chief officer of health, met the same fate. Justice Lennox found the consultants' study insufficiently developed in terms of planning detail to receive PBH approval, but he reflected generously on the potential scope of the board's authority. Assuming the proper steps were followed, and notwithstanding the protests of 'any majority' of citizens, Lennox concluded that the chief officer of health 'has the power to compel a small community like Ottawa to assume a burden of $8,000,000 or for that matter, of $13,000,000 or more.' He admitted that 'this is a long step from government of the people by the people,' but concluded nevertheless that 'in view of the criminal negligence of some municipalities, it cannot be said that the provisions of the Public Health Act are too arbitrary or drastic in this regard.'[75]

In 1914, following the election of a new city council, Ottawa ratepayers formally expressed their continued preference for water drawn from the Ottawa River – an industrial thoroughfare for the lumber trade of the nineteenth century[76] – and filtered locally over the more costly scheme to deliver uncontaminated water from Quebec. But when the actual plans for the less costly pumping, filtration, and chlorination of river water reached the PBH under a statutory reference, that body unanimously refused to approve the scheme.

The PBH observed that the Ottawa River was 'beyond any question, a polluted source of supply at all points in the vicinity of the city of Ottawa.' Accordingly, the board concluded that it would not be consistent with its duty to the citizens of Ottawa or to visitors to the national capital to 'countenance the use of water which, after mechanical filtration, constantly requires chlorination, when a pure and adequate supply, requiring no treatment whatever, may be readily procured.'

Ottawa's incoming civic administration took exception to the board's conduct and applied successfully for an order of mandamus to compel the PBH to address its responsibilities in relation to the river scheme. Although Justice Middleton agreed that the PBH had exceeded its authority, he offered an assessment of its status that again reflected importance if it did not confer power: the board, he observed, is not 'a mere emanation of the Crown' but rather a body created to discharge 'important administrative and quasi-judicial functions.'[77]

This particular skirmish was not an isolated incident, a one-time-only regulatory clash between local politicians concerned with the practical realities of municipal finance and a remote provincial agency intent on imposing abstract and artificially high standards. The need to address drinking water quality in the nation's capital had been pressing for half a decade, and it had been particularly acute since the deaths in 1911 and 1912 of 174 people in successive typhoid epidemics. With the outbreaks of disease attributed to pollution from the untreated sewage of the community of Hintonberg flowing down Cave Creek to Nepean Bay, where it entered the city's faulty supply pipe, the situation was urgent. Nevertheless the PBH found itself struggling to impose a high quality but capital-intensive plan against the resistance of local politicians who baulked at the cost when compared with the alternative of filtering and chemically treating water from the Ottawa River. At a point when the PBH once more seemed close to succeeding, a reassessment of the city's water volume requirements for fire-fighting purposes conclusively removed the Gatineau lakes plan from contention.[78]

Ottawa's resistance to sanitary expenditures was certainly not unique. When a 1917 investigation of water quality at Kingsville on Lake Erie some twenty miles east of the Detroit River produced evidence of 'gross pollution' traceable to town sewage and industrial contamination, provincial public health officials recommended remedial measures. The chief officer of health advised the town clerk that chlorination and filtration were needed on the intake side, as well as sanitary sewers and some basic sewage treatment measures. To avoid misunderstanding, he explained that the order was made pursuant to the Public Health Act. Provincial officials continued to follow up with Kingsville representatives, including the local health officer who had actually endeavoured to have the order rescinded. This produced a concession to the effect that the chlorination requirement might be waived if the town proceeded with filtration. After further inspections, and following additional pressure from the provincial level, Kingsville installed filtration facilities and secured PBH approval for its water supply system in 1922. At the same time, however, the board's sanitary engineering division continued to urge chlorination in case the filtration system should fail.

The Kingsville story is known because some years later such a mishap did occur. When the intake pipe deteriorated and town officials introduced an unauthorized drainage ditch, typhoid struck Kingsville. Among nearly fifty victims of the disease at least one elderly resident died, and her husband successfully sued the town. By the time of trial, very soon after the first reported cases, provincial public health officials had implemented chlorination and a permanent facility was in place shortly thereafter.[79]

CONCLUSION

Various commentators have questioned the existence, legitimacy, and effectiveness of an earlier generation of Ontarians' regulatory efforts to protect water quality. Each of these lines of criticism invites some concluding observations.

Insofar as the existence of a regulatory effort is concerned, ample evidence exists of turn-of-the-century attempts to safeguard water quality through inspections, controls, approvals, dissemination of standard practices, and so on.[80] The PBH had an expert staff that supported its approval powers, and a regime of prohibitions was used to promote abatement. It is thus somewhat misleading to imagine – as observers sometimes do today – that our's is virtually the first generation to fight pollution systematically.[81]

Amongst those who have acknowledged earlier concerns with pollution, there is an inclination to regard the common law – despite certain doctrinal limitations – as the most formidable previously existing defence of the environment.[82] This assessment must be associated with a few high-profile cases, for the record casts considerable doubt on the proposition that the primary defenders of the environment were individual litigants with private interests to protect under the common law. There is certainly nothing new about regulatory measures to address environmental problems, water quality in particular, in Ontario. The precise objectives may have varied from one time period to another, but official measures to prevent, to control, and indeed to remedy pollution are long-standing.

The legitimacy of public health activities has also been called into question on the grounds, it appears, that certain public health issues camouflaged a social reform agenda and that the application of standards often discriminated against immigrant and other minorities. The proposition has been floated that the extension of the public health regime into the realm of environmental protection was religiously motivated, entangled in some enterprise of nation building and class-based social purification. The slum, runs one formulation of the argument, was not only an economic or public health problem but 'an *essentially* moral category' whose population posed a danger that was 'simultaneously sanitary and moral.'[83] Dr Charles Hastings, a Toronto medical health officer, is implicated in this provocative conflation of scientific and moral categories. The appearance of many dirty outhouses in the photographs accompanying the text of his report on Toronto slums is said to reflect the 'ascription of moral deviance to physical objects.' Hastings was on record to the effect that 'rear' and outhouses constituted 'a danger to public morals, and ... an offence against public decency' and that 'criminals and moral lepers are born in the atmosphere of physical and moral rottenness pervading the slums of large cities.'[84] A prominent recent account asserts in relation to turn-of-the-century reform efforts that religious and secular reformers regarded social and moral reform as inseparable elements of an 'ambitious project to transform Canadian society.' Clean water and milk were championed, it is suggested, for their contribution to the enterprise of inducing working-class mothers to raise their children as Christian Canadians.[85] A London, Ontario temperance advocate contributed to the discourse with the claim that her home town enjoyed an 'abundant supply of pure, sparkling water – water that leaves no excuse for drinking anything else.'[86]

Whatever the merits of the overall thesis, these colourful examples may overextend its foundations. Thus, it is worth recalling that a vigorous public health campaign was underway well in advance of the arrival of immigrant groups considered to be its target, and that it was waged in cottage country against hotel operators and an established, 'respectable,' summering population. When sometimes inadequate municipal sewage treatment facilities replaced the outhouse, state institutions were also vigorously prodded to respond to new realities. And a good many explanations might be offered for defensive remarks about the quality of London's water supply, beginning with the PBH's observation that 'the negligence of the public authorities in respect to the pollution of the River Thames by raw sewage is, in our opinion, deserving of the severest condemnation ... The ... pouring of the raw sewage into the River Thames in our opinion amounts to criminal negligence.'[87] If immigrant communities were 'targeted' with sanitary measures it is worth recalling that officials of their countries of origin often paraded through Ontario (and other North American jurisdictions) in an attempt to find out how the same sanitary advances could be implemented. Dr Hastings aside, it is important to note the acknowledgment that there were, in fact, public health and sanitation problems, and the possibility that such concerns might well establish legitimate motivation for a very extensive institutional response.

Having described the existence of a formidable public health regime, and having argued that significant elements of its operation may be seen as genuinely directed toward something of a communitywide public interest, the extent to which the regime was effective, at least in terms of improving water quality must be addressed. Against what standard might the performance of the emerging regulatory regime for water quality, as it has been described here, be measured? From the persistence of legislative reform of the Public Health Act, one might surmise that contemporary observers were not convinced that the courts were effectively controlling pollution through common law nuisance or riparian claims, however principled and well intentioned they might have been.[88] Common law 'victories,' *Fieldhouse*, for example, did not necessarily produce remedial responses, and may actually have represented rather short-term advances in comparison with the determined problem-solving approach of physicians, engineers, and others dealing with community health. A footnote to *Fieldhouse* in the form of a 1929 letter from the Toronto city solicitor to a local law firm that had borrowed the brief and pleadings confirms the modest pace of change: 'As far as I can see, these papers were never returned. As we have now some similar actions pending, I trust you will be good enough to return this brief and other papers which I lent you ...'[89]

Public health officials sometimes sought abatement rather than penalties and generally considered themselves successful when a problem was satisfactorily addressed prior to conviction. Negotiated progress falling somewhat short of perfection was reasonably preferred to a litigated standstill outside the closed gates of paradise. Thus levels of prosecution and conviction were not really benchmarks of progress either. An entirely different set of indicators interested public health officials, municipal leaders, and presumably also the residents of Ontario: was the water and sewerage infrastructure being built, were typhoid and comparable epidemics under control, was the water safe to drink? By these measures significant advances were made even as another set of problems was set to emerge through industrial discharges to the new underground water systems.

The evolution of the legal framework of the public health regime for water quality and the reaction of lawyers to it merit a final observation. Those outside the community of legal professionals, in this case public health officials, saw the legal framework as a necessary but hardly sufficient element in their campaign to safeguard water quality. The common law of nuisance underpinned their framework, but repeated frustrations led to a continuing series of reforms. Those reforms transferred power to officials, and the question therefore arises as to how this situation was perceived. Although various – often minor – legal officials generated obstacles to successful prosecutions in the interests of legal form and procedural safeguards, senior legal officers do not appear to have obstructed public interest environmental litigation in the early twentieth century, even if they were reluctant to undertake it directly or to assume the costs. During the period examined here it is hard to make the case that the courts were hostile to administrative intervention either for the purpose of preserving judicial turf or to constrain officials in their efforts to promote public health.

NOTES

I wish to acknowledge with thanks the research assistance of Barry Ditto and Bill Wade and the financial support of The Osgoode Society.

1 J.E. Hodgetts, *From Arm's Length to Hands-On: The Formative Years of Ontario's Public Service, 1867–1940* (Toronto: University of Toronto Press for the Ontario Historical Studies Series 1995), 20–1.

2 45 Vict., c. 29 (1882).
3 For general background on the development of provincial institutions during this period see Hodgetts, *From Arm's Length to Hands-On*. An Act for the Establishment of the Department of Health, SO 1924, c. 69. The Public Health Act, 17 Geo. V, c. 73 (1927).
4 For a comparable argument based on the U.S. experience see William J. Novak, *The People's Welfare: Law and Regulation in Nineteenth-Century America* (Chapel Hill and London: University of North Carolina Press 1996), chap. 6.
5 Ontario Provincial Board of Health [hereinafter PBH], *Annual Report, 1884*, 28.
6 *Park v. White* (1893), 23 OR 611.
7 *Crowther v. Cobourg*, [1912] 1 DLR 40 (Ont. HC).
8 *Hiscock v. Lander* (1876), 24 Grant's Upper Canada Chancery Reports 250.
9 Ibid., 270.
10 Ibid., 272.
11 *PBH, Annual Report, 1884*, 15, 22, 26.
12 Ibid., 21.
13 Ibid., 14.
14 Ibid., 22.
15 PBH, *Annual Report, 1889*, 23, 25.
16 PBH, *Annual Report, 1893*, 100e.
17 PBH, *Annual Report, 1894*, 115–16.
18 PBH, *Annual Report, 1884*, 22.
19 Heather A. MacDougall, 'The Genesis of Public Health Reform in Toronto, 1869–1890,' *Urban History Review* 10 (1982), 1 at 6. Similar measures were implemented in other communities, Kingston, for example.
20 John S. Hagopian, 'Would the Benefits Trickle Down? An Examination of the Paris, Ontario, Waterworks Campaign of 1882,' *Ontario History* 87 (June 1995), 129–53. Comparable developments were occurring in the United States around the turn of the century. See Martin Melosi, ed., *Pollution and Reform in American Cities, 1870–1930* (Austin and London: University of Texas Press 1980).
21 Chas. A. Hodgetts, MD, and John A. Amyot, MD, 'Report on the Sanitary Conditions of the Muskoka and Kawartha Districts,' in PBH, *Sanitary Reports 1904*, 142–50.
22 The April indictment date preceded by less than three months the proclamation of the Criminal Code, 1 July 1893. See Desmond H. Brown, *The Genesis of the Canadian Criminal Code of 1892* (Toronto: University of Toronto Press for The Osgoode Society for Canadian Legal History, 1989) 145.
23 Archives of Ontario [hereinafter AO] RG22-392, Criminal Assize Indictments, Town of Walkerville, 1893.

24 See RSO 1897, c. 248, s. 73. Details of the Guelph situation may be found in PBH, *Annual Report, 1908*, 47.

25 AO, Attorney General's Records, RG4-32 (1908), no. 1538.

26 *Merritt v. City of Toronto* (1911), 23 OLR 365 at 371.

27 Ibid.

28 *Rickey v. City of Toronto, Schofield Holden Machine Co. v. City of Toronto* (1914), 30 OLR 523.

29 Gene Desfor, 'Planning Urban Waterfront Industrial Districts: Toronto's Ashbridge's Bay, 1889–1910,' *Urban History Review* 17 (1988), 83.

30 *Coleman v. City of Toronto* (1893), 23 OR 345 at 346.

31 City of Toronto Legal Records Office, Schofield File, Schofield to Hastings, 7 July 1911.

32 *Rickey v. City of Toronto.*

33 *Re Schofield and City of Toronto* (1913), 22 CCC 93.

34 Section 222 created the indictable offence of committing 'any common nuisance which endangers the lives, safety or health of the public, or which occasions injury to the person of any individual.'

35 *Re Schofield and City of Toronto* at 94.

36 Ibid., 95.

37 See PBH, *Annual Report, 1906*, 8, 111, 161 for expressions of the board's interest in legislative reform.

38 Charges were laid under the Public Health Act, 2 Geo. V, c. 58, s. 91. The prohibition was introduced to Ontario law by the Statute Law Amendment Act, 1906, 6 Edw. VII. SO c. 19, assented to 14 May 1906.

39 SO 1912, c. 58, s. 8(o).

40 SO 1912, c. 58, s. 73.

41 *R. v. Redmond, R. v. Ryan, R. v. Burk* (1893), 24 OR 331 at 332.

42 Ibid., 334.

43 Discussion of the early typhoid experience (including recommendations of the grand jury) can be found in PBH, *Annual Report, 1906*, 192–200.

44 Charges were laid against McMillan Bros., R.M. McMeekin, Seal Ireland, and Thomas Irwin.

45 AO, Attorney General's Records, RG4-32 (1912), no. 1676, Dr J.W.S. McCullough, 'Memorandum for Attorney General,' 5 December 1912.

46 Ibid., Moses McFadden (district Crown attorney) to J.R. Cartwright (deputy attorney general), 21 December 1912.

47 PAO, RG4-32 (1922), no. 2369.

48 The Public Health Amendment Act, SO 1923, c. 52, s. 4, amending s. 90 of the Public Health Act, RSO 1914, c. 218.

49 *Re Sixteen Mile Creek*, [1924] OWN 498 at 499.

50 *Re Waterloo Local Board of Health* (Campbell's Case) (1918), 44 OLR 338.
51 Ibid., 346.
52 Ibid., 348.
53 *Leather v. Doolittle* (1927), 62 OLR 162 (CA).
54 AO, F.A. Dallyn to McCullough, 2 August 1919. Dallyn may have been relying on data from Leo G. Denis, *Water Works and Sewerage Systems of Canada* (Ottawa 1916), a compilation prepared for the Committee on Waters and Water-Powers of the Commission of Conservation.
55 Ibid., 17 June 1919.
56 Ibid., 18 December 1919.
57 Desfor, 'Planning Urban Waterfront Industrial Districts,' at 88; R.E. Riendeau, 'Servicing the Modern City, 1900–1930,' in Victor L. Russell, ed., *Forging a Consensus: Historical Essays on Toronto* (Toronto: University of Toronto Press 1984), 162, 177. At the same time, Toronto constructed a water filtration plant.
58 Files on the Fieldhouse litigation are located in the Archives of Ontario and in the City of Toronto Legal Records Office.
59 AO, Fieldhouse File, 'Statement of Claim.'
60 Ibid., 'Statement of Defence.'
61 Ibid., Commissioner of Works to Mayor Hocken and the Board of Control, 16 June 1914.
62 Ibid., R.M. Bell, Provincial Inspector of Health, to PBH, 'Report re Nuisance Main Sewage Works, Toronto,' 14 May 1915.
63 Ibid. Commissioner of Works and Medical Officer of Health to Mayor Church and Board of Control, 21 July 1916; 'Memorandum for the Honourable the Attorney General,' 5 December 1916.
64 Ibid. In 1914 the attorney general also agreed to proceed in an injunction application against Coniagas for air pollution in Thorold. In light of agreeing to stand as plaintiff, the attorney general felt it was inappropriate to prefer an indictment and insisted on 'the usual understanding that the parties interested enter into a guarantee that they will protect him in respect of all costs.' See AO RG4-32 (1914), no. 69, E. Bayly to the attorney general, 6 January 1914, and accompanying correspondence. See also *Cairns v. Canadian Refining and Smelting Company*, 5 OWN 423 (1 December 1913) and 6 OWN 562 (June 15 1914).
65 Toronto *Daily Star*, 14 December 1920, 20.
66 Toronto *Daily Star*, 12 December 1917, 17.
67 *Fieldhouse v. Toronto* (1918), 43 OLR 491 at 494.
68 RSO 1914, c. 218, s. 94.
69 Riendeau, 'Servicing the Modern City,' 160.
70 Philip Anisman, who reviewed the Fieldhouse case some twenty years ago,

found that 'No information is available as to what steps were taken to correct the operations of the plant.' See Anisman, 'Water Pollution Control in Ontario,' *Ottawa Law Review* 5 (1972), 342 at 344, note 18.
71 City of Toronto, Fieldhouse File, William Johnston, city solicitor, to Mayor Church and the Board of Control, 18 July 1918.
72 Ibid., Toronto City Council, Minutes, 1919 vol. 1, 27 January 1919 and 24 February 1919.
73 John H. Taylor, 'Fire, Disease and Water in Ottawa: an Introduction,' *Urban History Review* 8 (1979), 7.
74 *Clarey v. City of Ottawa* (1913), 5 OWN 340.
75 *Clarey v. City of Ottawa* (1914), 25 OWR 615 at 616.
76 John S.P. McLaren, 'The Tribulations of Antoine Ratte: A Case Study of the Environmental Regulation of the Canadian Lumber Industry in the Nineteenth Century,' *University of New Brunswick Law Review* 33 (1984), 203.
77 *Re City of Ottawa and Provincial Board of Health* (1914), 33 OLR 1.
78 Chris Warfe, 'The Search for Pure Water in Ottawa: 1910–1915,' *Urban History Review* (1979), 90.
79 *Campbell v. Kingsville*, [1929] 4 DLR 772. See also *Re Public Utilities Commission of Thorold and the Town of Thorold* (1927), 60 OLR 429.
80 For discussion of one major pollution question viewed as environmental rather than a public health matter and pursued by federal authorities on the basis of their constitutional interest in fisheries, see J.S.P. McLaren, 'The Tribulations of Antoine Ratte,' *University of New Brunswick Law Journal*, 33 (1984), 203–59. Interestingly, sawdust pollution was also on the agenda of the public health officials of Ontario almost as soon as the Provincial Board of Health came into existence. See PBH, *Annual Report, 1884*, 26–8, 29.
81 Kernaghan Webb, *Pollution Control in Canada: The Regulatory Approach in the 1980s* (Ottawa: Law Reform Commission of Canada 1988) at 11–13 acknowledges some earlier regimes but assesses them as 'hopelessly simplistic' and 'only sporadically enforced.' With reference to a shift from blanket prohibitions to control regimes between the 1950s and the 1970s he observes at 14: 'this shift represented the first indication of government coming to grips with environmental protection in Canada.'
82 Ted Schrecker, 'Of Invisible Beasts and the Public Interest: Environmental Cases and the Judicial System,' in Robert Boardman, ed., *Canadian Environmental Policy: Ecosystems, Politics and Process* (Toronto: Oxford University Press 1992), 83–108; Elizabeth Brubaker, *Property Rights in the Defence of Nature* (Toronto: Earthscan Canada 1995). A.W. Bryant, 'An Analysis of the Ontario Water Resources Act,' in P.S. Elder, ed., *Environmental Management and Public Participation* (Toronto: CELRF 1975), 162 is an exception.

83 Mariana Valverde, *The Age of Light, Soap, and Water: Moral Reform in English Canada, 1885–1925* (Toronto: McClelland & Stewart 1991), 132.
84 Ibid., 133.
85 Ibid., 47.
86 Ibid., 23.
87 PBH, *Annual Report, 1905*, Drs Hodgetts and Amyot, 'Second Report on the Outbreak of Enteric Fever in London,' 149.
88 Jennifer Nedelsky, 'Judicial Conservatism in an Age of Innovation: Comparative Perspectives on Canadian Nuisance Law 1880–1930,' in David H. Flaherty, ed., *Essays in the History of Canadian Law* (Toronto: The Osgoode Society 1981) 1:281.
89 City of Toronto, Fieldhouse File, 18 February 1929, city solicitor to MacMurchy and Spence.

5

'The Modern Spirit of the Law': Blake, Mowat, and the Breaches of Contract Act, 1877

PAUL CRAVEN

There were on the Statute books of several of the Provinces – Quebec, Ontario, and Prince Edward Island – certain labour laws framed upon the antiquated models in England, in which breaches of contracts of service were made criminal offences punishable by fine and imprisonment. The modern spirit of the law was not to treat such offences as criminal, but to deal with them, as in point of fact they were, as civil matters.

Edward Blake, House of Commons, 7 March 1877

The Breaches of Contract Act, 1877[1] purported to repeal certain pre-Confederation enactments prescribing fines or imprisonment for workers who quit their jobs or disobeyed their employers, declaring instead that it was 'just' to treat infringements of the employment bargain 'like other breaches of contract, as civil wrongs, and not as crimes.' At the same time, the statute created new offences, characterized in the preamble as 'wilful and malicious breaches of contract, involving danger to persons or property, or grave public inconvenience.' The Breaches of Contract Act has been understood as a legislative landmark in Canadian labour history, whereby the old punishments for simple breaches of the employment contract in the provincial master and servant acts were finally abolished.[2] But this impression is wrong. Instead, section 1 only confirmed that ordinary breaches of the employment contract fell squarely within the provincial jurisdiction. For all its posturing, Blake's 'modern spirit of the law' placed provincial rights above labour rights and political expediency above both of them.

The present chapter is located in the no-man's-land between labour history and constitutional law. This is less a disputed territory than a mutually despised barren. Historians of the constitution attach no particular significance to the Breaches of Contract Act; labour historians, who encounter the law chiefly in its immediate impact on trade unions and working people, are little concerned with questions of doctrine and jurisdiction. Both schools are perhaps somewhat inclined to accept the law's symbolic claims at face value. Nevertheless, this chapter, which illustrates how provincial and federal politicians could manipulate the division of powers to deflect embarrassment, co-opt criticism, and avoid decisive action, reaches some conclusions of interest to both labour and constitutional history. It shows that the constitutional fragmentation of Canadian labour legislation, which is usually traced to the Law Lords' decision in *Snider* (1925),[3] was really instituted a half-century earlier, and by Canadian politicians rather than imperial judges. For labour historians, this means that national generalizations cannot be drawn from the Ontario experience, and that much remains to be learned about the impact of employment law on working people and labour relations in other provinces, even after 1877. For constitutional lawyers, it is at least another reminder that much of the meaning of the British North America Act, 1867 was the product not of statesmanlike argument or principled judicial deliberation, but of bureaucratic friction and covert political collaboration in the years following Confederation.

The Breaches of Contract Act (in particular its preamble and first section) was the product of three distinct vectors whose paths crossed in the early weeks of 1877. After a brief overview of Blake's act, this chapter examines each of these in turn: the history of friction over the allocation of colonial legislation between the Dominion and the provinces; the Ontario labour movement's campaign for statute reform; and the Mackenzie government's sensitivity to charges that it had mishandled the recent Grand Trunk strike. Then it considers their intersection as illuminated (and obscured) by the parliamentary debate. The chapter concludes with a brief examination of the act's consequences for employment law in Ontario, Quebec, and Prince Edward Island – the three provinces whose colonial legislation it specifically addressed – as well as in other Canadian jurisdictions.

THE BREACHES OF CONTRACT ACT

The full title of Blake's bill was An Act to repeal certain laws making Breaches of Contract of Service criminal, and to provide for the punishment of certain Breaches of Contract. In its final form,[4] it consisted of a preamble and eight numbered sections. Only part of the preamble and section 1 of the body dealt with the existing master and servant legislation. Sections 2 through 7 defined the new crimes and provided for their enforcement. Section 8 supplied the act's short title.

The first part of the preamble recited that '... breaches of contract, whether of service, or otherwise, are in general civil wrongs only, and not criminal in their nature; and it is just that breaches of contract of service should in general be treated like other breaches of contract, as civil wrongs, and not as crimes; and that the law should be amended accordingly ...' To the extent that this policy was actually accomplished by the legislation, its implementation was set out in section 1.[5] This provision purported to repeal certain parts of certain sections of certain pre-Confederation statutes of Upper and Lower Canada[6] and Prince Edward Island.[7] (I say 'purported' because the act could only repeal these provisions to the extent that they fell within the Dominion jurisdiction. As will be seen below, this was very much in issue.) The Upper Canada act was the most recent, dating in its original form from 1847; the Breaches of Contract Act referred to the version in the 1859 consolidation.[8] The Lower Canada statute dated back directly to 1836, when the legislature adopted rules to govern relations of master and servant outside the main towns, and indirectly to 1802, when justices of the peace in the judicial districts of Quebec, Montreal, and Trois Rivières were empowered to regulate employment contracts.[9] Prince Edward Island's Servants' Act was passed in 1833 to redress the insufficiency of that province's original employment legislation, which dated from 1795.[10]

The three colonial statutes punished workers' breaches of the employment contract.[11] In Ontario, workers could be fined up to twenty dollars, or jailed for up to one month, if they failed to commence work for which they had contracted, left before their contracts ended, refused to obey their employers' lawful commands, neglected their work, or damaged their employers' property.[12] In Quebec, the same punishments applied to workers who quit without proper notice or engaged in any of a lengthy list of employment offences: '... ill behaviour, refractory conduct, or idleness or of deserting from his service or duties, or of absenting himself by day or night without leave, from his said service, or from the house or residence of his employer, or who refuses or neglects to perform his just duties, or to obey the lawful commands which may be given him by his master or mistress, or who is guilty of dissipating his master's or mistress' property or effects, or of any unlawful act that may affect the interest of his master or mistress ...'[13] Workers in Prince Edward Island faced loss of wages and a month's imprisonment for a similar catalogue of offences.

Having disposed of these old crimes by section 1, Blake proceeded to make some new ones. Section 2 made it an offence, punishable by a fine of up to one hundred dollars or three months' imprisonment 'wilfully and maliciously' to break any contract, 'knowing or having reasonable cause to believe that the probable consequences ... will be to endanger human life, or to cause serious bodily injury, or to expose valuable property ... to destruction or serious injury,' or (as provided by subsections 2 and 3) with the effect of depriving a municipality of water or gas, or delaying or preventing the running of trains.[14] This effectively amended the Criminal Law Amendment Act, which had accompanied Macdonald's Trade Union Act in 1872, and which the Mackenzie government had recently revised to meet trade union criticism.[15] While the crimes it announced were new ones (modelled on sections 4 and 5 of the English Conspiracy and Protection of Property Act, 1875[16]), using the criminal law to regulate railway labour relations was already a Canadian tradition.[17]

CONSTITUTIONAL CONSIDERATIONS

With Confederation, much of the legislation of the former colonies became *ultra vires* their provincial successors. Both levels of government set about identifying and resolving the problems that this caused. In 1868 Macdonald appointed Gustavus Wicksteed and Hewitt Bernard as public service commissioners to unify the Canadian criminal law.[18] An Ontario commission carried out an extensive consolidation and revision of that province's statutes between 1874 and 1877.[19] The codification of Lower Canada's civil law, adopted in 1866, was an integral part of the statutory foundation of Confederation.[20]

The master and servant legislation was a good candidate for jurisdictional uncertainty.[21] In defining the terms of contracts of employment and making them enforceable by such means as actions for unpaid wages, it seemed to fall within the provincial sphere of property and civil rights.[22] But to the extent that it made various other breaches of contract – such as desertion or disobedience on the worker's part or cruel mistreatment on the part of the employer – punishable upon conviction by fines or imprisonment, it was more like criminal legislation and therefore arguably within the federal jurisdiction. Moreover, while the diversity of provisions in the various provincial master and servant acts was acceptable and indeed expected in the civil aspect, in the criminal aspect it offended the principle of uniformity in the criminal law under the federal constitution.

Nevertheless, the mere fact that a pre-Confederation statute imposed punishments like fines or imprisonment did not remove it automatically into the Dominion sphere by the application of section 91(27) of the British North America Act, 1867. By section 92(15), the provinces were given exclusive jurisdiction over 'the imposition of punishment by fine, penalty, or imprisonment for enforcing any law of the province made in relation to any matter coming within any of the classes of subjects' reserved to them.[23] Two other sections provided additional potential complications. Section 129 continued the laws of the pre-Confederation colonies 'as if the Union had not been made,' subject to subsequent repeal by whichever level of government possessed the requisite jurisdiction. By section 94, the Dominion Parliament had an unrestricted power to legislate for uniformity in the laws relating to property and civil rights in the common law provinces, with the proviso that such legislation should have no effect in a province until adopted by the local legislature.

Distinguishing between crimes and breaches of provincial law occasioned a good deal of friction between federal justice ministers and provincial attorneys general in the first decade of Confederation. A good illustration is the continuing disagreement over the use of the term 'offence' to describe a breach of a provincial statute. In 1873 Macdonald complained that this usage was 'inexpedient' because '[t]he word, offence, in legal parlance seems to imply a breach of the criminal law, and when not expressly declared to be treason or felony, may be considered as synonymous with misdemeanor.'[24] Four years later Blake called the attention of the Ontario government to the appearance of the term in the new provincial liquor act: 'The objections to the use of this word in describing a violation of a provincial law were pointed out on previous occasions.'[25] Mowat rebutted, arguing that 'offence' was a 'convenient and proper term to employ in speaking of a violation of provincial law,' and noting that it was used in that sense in Dominion legislation as well as in municipal by-laws, which included 'many offences which are not crimes in any recognized sense; not to speak of the somewhat limited sense that the expression "criminal law" has in *The British North America Act, 1867*.'[26] Much the same dispute was waged over other statutory terms, for example, 'misdemeanor.'[27] The problem, as the Ontario consolidation commissioners pointed out in their 1875–6 report, was that many statutes dealing with subjects entirely within the competence of the provincial legislatures contained provisions for their 'effectual execution' which thereby 'trenched' on the Dominion jurisdiction over the criminal law.[28]

The constitutionality of the provincial master and servant acts was not put directly in issue before 1877. In 1875, however, Blake threatened disallowance of a closely related statute and secured the repeal of the offending provisions. Ontario's Apprentices and Minors Act, originally adopted in 1851, regulated indentures of apprenticeship and contracts with under-age employees. In 1874 Mowat tried to amend it so that any incorporated charity could apprentice its wards without requiring a private act. The measure, which enjoyed the 'entire approval' of the Opposition leader, passed the Ontario legislature within a few days and received royal assent.[29] Mowat's amendments were unobjectionable. In framing the bill, however, he had incorporated the unaltered text of the pre-Confederation statute.[30] Several sections, copied verbatim from the version in the 1859 consolidation, supplied punishments for breaches of the employment contract. In particular, sections 17 and 18 contained provisions very like those in the master and servant acts of Ontario and other provinces.[31] In November 1875, a few days before the year permitted for federal disallowance ran out, Blake reported that sections 17 and 18 'appear to trench upon the criminal law, most, if not all of the Acts to be dealt with by a magistrate, being criminal.'[32] This was only one among several recent Ontario statutes to come under attack. Mowat, clearly embarrassed, told the Assembly: 'So many difficulties of this nature were continually arising that many were of opinion that they were caused by the mode of diction in the British North America Act ...'[33] He rushed an omnibus bill through the legislature: among other amendments to statutes of the previous session it repealed sections 17 and 18 of the apprentices act.[34]

The fate of the Apprentices and Minors Act in 1874–5 is interesting for several reasons. It demonstrates that before late 1875 Mowat did not consider provisions like those in sections 17 and 18 to be *ultra vires* the province. It suggests that the Dominion department of justice was content to leave pre-Confederation statutes to their operation under section 129 of the British North America Act, at least until they were re-enacted by the provincial legislature. It also makes it clear that Blake's objection was to the words of the act rather than the punishment of notionally civil infractions. What the two sections had in common was their use of the term 'conviction.' Section 20 of the apprentices act, which authorized justices to imprison apprentices for failing to make satisfaction to their masters for neglect of duty, was allowed to stand: it did not use the term 'conviction.'[35] The chief mischiefs of section 17 eventually found their way into the Criminal Code, 1892,[36] while those of section 18 more closely resembled the merely civil breaches in the 1877 act. The threatened disallowance and consequent repeal of sections 17 and 18 is also interesting because, unlike the corresponding provisions of the Ontario master and servant act, there was no trade union pressure on either level of government to soften the apprenticeship law. On the contrary, at its 1873 founding convention, the Canadian Labor Union (CLU) – which, with the Toronto Trades Assembly, was to lead the campaign against fines and imprisonment for breaches of the employment contract – had called for 'the enactment of a more stringent Apprenticeship Law, so as to secure to the master the service of the youths whom he undertakes to instruct for a reasonable length of time, so that such apprentice may be turned upon the world a finished workman, and therefore a credit to the country at large.'[37]

LABOUR REFORM

While trade unions had existed for half a century and more in the Canadas, a labour movement with a program of statute reform was barely five years old in 1877. Economic recession and political opportunism had combined to reshape workplace and community struggles for shorter hours into a program of legislative lobbying in 1872.[38] Parliamentary activity reproduced its own agenda: for several years after the triumph of the Trade Unions Act, 1872 the movement laboured to secure the repeal of the worst features of the Criminal Law Amendment Act that accompanied it. The focus of the handful of activists in the Toronto Trades Assembly and the southern-Ontario-based Canadian Labor Union was on removing legal barriers to organization and collective action. It was notorious that Ontario's master and servant act had been used by the Toronto newspaper publishers to undermine the typographers' strike in 1872, and other city employers had since turned the lesson to their advantage in similar circumstances. Moreover, the Toronto activists were keenly aware of developments in the British trade union movement, including the successful campaign against the master and servant acts that resulted in the passage of the Employers and Workmen Act, 1875.[39] It was therefore inevitable that repeal of the offensive provisions in the Ontario statute should form part of labour's platform.

The first tentative sallies against the master and servant legislation came in 1874. In the spring of that year, the Toronto Trades Assembly called on its constituent unions to pass resolutions 'asking for the repeal of the Criminal Law Amendment Act and amendment of the Masters and Servants Act.'[40] When the Canadian Labor Union met at Ottawa in August, it adopted a committee report dealing with the master and servant act among other legislation; the details have not survived.[41] The pressure mounted with the culmination of the British campaign. At its St Catharines congress in 1875, the CLU denounced the master and servant act as 'a piece of class legislation of the most despicable character' and called for its members to lobby the provincial legislature so that it could be 'brought into line with the English act of 1875.'[42] The following year, buoyed by its success in having the Criminal Law Amendment Act revised, the CLU instructed its executive to press for 'the repeal of all criminal clauses' in the master and servant act.[43] In September 1876 a deputation of four Toronto labour leaders waited on Mowat to present their 'principal objection' – that the act 'allowed an employer to prosecute an employee who broke his contract, and get him sent to jail for a month, or fined; while if the employer broke his contract, the employee could only recover in a civil court' – as well as several lesser difficulties in the act's 'practical working.' Mowat promised 'to consider the points submitted before the law was consolidated.'[44]

It is noteworthy that in the fall of 1876, less than a year after the Apprentices and Minors Act fiasco, Mowat raised no concern that 'the repeal of all criminal clauses' in the master and servant act might be beyond the capacity of the provincial legislature. The statute consolidation commission was nearing the end of its work. To avoid further embarrassment, Mowat was now corresponding closely with Blake to ensure that any infringements on federal jurisdiction were resolved silently as the new statute book was being prepared.[45] The master and servant legislation did not appear in the volume of pre-Confederation statutes 'still in force in Ontario, and which are supposed to relate to matters not within the jurisdiction of the provincial legislature,' published by the provincial government in 1876.[46] Nevertheless, when Ottawa MLA Daniel O'Donoghue, labour's principal spokesman in the provincial legislature, rose on 7 February 1877 to ask whether the government would introduce amendments to the master and servant act, Mowat replied that he was 'doubtful' whether the changes sought were within the provincial jurisdiction: 'This and a number of other such questions could only be finally settled by the Supreme Court.'[47]

RAILWAY STRIKE

For five days, from 29 December 1876 until 3 January 1877, the Brotherhood of Locomotive Engineers brought the Grand Trunk Railway system west of Montreal to a halt.[48] Alongside the declared hostilities between the country's largest private corporation and its workers, an almost equally public diplomatic battle raged between the railway's chief executive, Joseph Hickson, and the prime minister, Alexander Mackenzie, over the deployment of troops to keep the line open. Hickson maintained that the Grand Trunk's preparations for a strike were sufficient to keep the trains running and the mails moving so long as law and order were preserved along the line; Mackenzie insisted that the municipal authorities, not the federal government, had the power to call out the local militia.[49] Throughout Ontario, the tide of public sympathy ran against the widely despised railway corporation. '[E]ven persons of some position and intelligence,' wrote one official observer, 'openly expressed opinions in approval of the actions taken by the engineers.'[50] This factor no doubt weighed heavily on the minds of local politicians in the midst of municipal election campaigns. That militia expenses would be charged to local ratepayers was no less a concern. Most railway towns saw no need to summon military aid. At Belleville, the chief exception, the local militia was criticized for being thoroughly disorganized and ill-equipped.

No sooner was the strike over than Hickson and his allies in business and politics sought to lay the blame for the whole affair at the government's door. On 3 January Hickson wrote Mackenzie that the government's refusal to order in the troops had forced him to 'compromise with the mutinous men who were openly violating the law in various parts of the country': 'The terms which have been made with the men I do not consider by any means satisfactory, and law and order, and that discipline necessary amongst the staff of a great railway company, in order to secure the maximum of safety to the public using the railway, have received a rude shock by the proceedings of the last few days, for which I hope I may be pardoned saying, it seems to me the Government of the country is responsible.'[51] A few days later, Montreal's city council debated a resolution deploring 'that under our existing laws the entire trade of the country may at any time during the winter months be paralyzed' and calling on the federal government 'to take such steps as may be needed to prevent a recurrence ...'[52] The Toronto Board of Trade took up the chorus, insisting that 'all the powers of Government should have been promptly exercised for the suppression of riot and outrage.'[53]

The new parliamentary session was to begin in February. Mackenzie and Blake were acutely aware that the government would be called to account for its alleged mismananagement of the strike. On 6 January, Blake drafted a memorandum for cabinet, drawing its attention to the view then current in the opposition press, that either the existing laws were insufficient to maintain law and order or they had not been brought properly into operation. Acting on his recommendation, the government agreed to solicit reports from the officers of militia and, through the Ontario government, the municipal authorities, so as to be prepared to meet the anticipated criticisms.[54] Mackenzie wanted to reply publicly and at once to the Montreal resolution and to Hickson's charge that the government was 'responsible' for the rail stoppage. Blake dissuaded him, urging delay until the enquiry was complete and disputing the 'propriety' of attacking Hickson directly: 'The session is now very near, and it seems to me the more dignified course would be to cause the letter of the [Montreal] Council to be acknowledged ... with the answer that the subject was already engaging the attention of the government, and to reserve our defence for Parliament.'[55]

In the mean time, Blake prepared to legislate. He made a thirty-seven-page abstract of the existing statutory provisions relevant to the strike.[56] On 1 February he advised Hickson's deputy,[57] Grand Trunk traffic manager Lewis Seargent, that he was 'considering whether any amendment should be made in the law with reference to persons under contract with Railway Companies,' and asking for information about 'the present mode of hiring train employees.'[58] On 12 February he sent 'a further draft of the Bill for amending the law relating to protection of Life and Property' to G.W. Wicksteed, the parliamentary law clerk.[59] It seems clear, then, that Blake not only contemplated but had actually drafted legislation (based, so the title suggests, on the English Conspiracy and Protection of Property Act, 1875) even before Mowat declared that amendments to the master and servant act might be *ultra vires* Ontario. It seems a reasonable and economical hypothesis that Blake's draft consisted of sections 2 through 8 of what was to become the Breaches of Contract Act, 1877.

Blake had one further worry as the session began. He knew that the Opposition would be certain to call for production of the documents that had passed between the government and the Grand Trunk during the strike. One letter in particular could be a great embarrassment. On 2 January, Mackenzie had written to Hickson reiterating that the federal government had no power to call out the volunteer militia and explaining the steps he had taken to have the Ontario government instruct the municipalities on how to requisition troops. In assuring Hickson of his government's impotence, Mackenzie made an ill-considered and indiscreet attack on the striking workers. 'I entertain the strongest possible desire to aid you in resisting the monstrous usurpations of the engine-drivers,' he told Hickson at one point in the letter and, at another, assured him (quite without foundation) 'that the entire public sympathy is with the Company and against the strikers.' On the very eve of a settlement, the prime minister went so far as to counsel against one: 'The conduct of these men seems to every one to be infamous, and I trust it will not be necessary for the Company to make any arrangements at all with persons who have acted so badly.'[60]

On 15 February the Ontario government transmitted the reports it had requested from crown attorneys in the various counties affected by the strike. This concluded the cabinet investigation; it was now time for the government to launch its 'defence.' When Blake reviewed 'the information which we ought to bring down,' he asked Mackenzie to consider whether in tabling correspondence in Parliament, the 2 January letter to Hickson 'might be fairly omitted without your being liable to the suggestion of having suppressed it.' Blake warned that 'some of its expressions will be received with very great disfavour by the Trades Union people generally ... I dread lest it may afterwards be produced with still more damaging effect.'[61] Blake went further, revising Mackenzie's memorandum transmitting the various documents, to exclude the offending letter.[62] The original memorandum (dated 1 February) was in these terms: 'The Undersigned transmits herewith for the information of Council copies of the official correspondence with the Grand Trunk Railway Company and the Attorney-General of the Province of Ontario, relating to the strike of the Engine drivers on the Grand Trunk Railway in the months of December and January last.' As revised by Blake, it read: 'The Undersigned transmits herewith for the information of Council copies of certain official Telegrams relating to the strike on the Grand Trunk Railway between the 30th of December and the second day of January last.' The 2 January communication was a letter, not a telegram.

Parliament opened on 8 February, just one day after Mowat told the Ontario legislature that he doubted its jurisdiction to amend the master and servant act. On 15 February, three days after Blake sent his 'further draft' of a protection of property bill to the parliamentary law clerk, O'Donoghue introduced a bill to amend the master and servant act into the Ontario legislature. It contained four short clauses. Verbal contracts of employment, formerly binding for up to a year, would now be limited to no more than a month. The anticrimping provision would be repealed. No one would be sent to jail for non-payment of a fine; instead, a distress warrant would issue. Finally, the section empowering justices to act wherever the offender was found was to be amended so that it applied to employers as well as to employees.[63] O'Donoghue had apparently accepted Mowat's opinion that the most desired reform, the repeal of the workers' offences in section 4, might be beyond the power of the legislature. He took a 'deputation of working men,' evidently the CLU parliamentary committee, to meet Mowat the following evening. Arguing that the government had power to deal with his amendments, O'Donoghue went on to point out: 'As the law at present stood, the servant could be imprisoned for breach of contract but not the employer. The working classes wanted the offence to be made a civil one.' Mowat responded that 'any thing that had been made a crime by the late Province of Canada the government could not declare not a crime. The Dominion Government alone could deal with that matter.' To this, Alf Jury, the tailors' union activist, replied 'that he had no doubt the working man could get justice from Mr. Blake.'[64] On 24 February, once Jury had reported the committee's progress,[65] printers' union activist J.S. Williams appealed to Blake on behalf of the Toronto Trades Assembly. Blake replied on 6 March: 'The subject of the Criminal law as applied to breaches of contract has for some time engaged my attention, and it is my hope to be able within a few days to propose some legislation in the matter.'[66]

The Trades Assembly appeal could hardly have been better timed. On 22 February the government's role in the Grand Trunk strike had been broached in the federal Parliament for the first time, when Senator Read moved in the upper house for a committee 'to inquire into the causes of the detention of the Mails on the Grand Trunk Railway, during the last week of December, 1876, and the first week in January, 1877 ...'[67] Read's motion was probably not planted by the ministry,[68] but the exchange in Question Period on 1 March surely was:[69]

Mr. SCRIVER asked whether, in view of the difficulties recently occurring between the Grand Trunk Railway Company and the Locomotive Engineers in their employ and the great injury to the public interest arising therefrom, it was the intention of the Government at the present Session to introduce any legislation having for its end the prevention of similar evils in future.

Mr. BLAKE: This very important subject has been under the consideration of the Government. I cannot see that there is any hope of preventing the evil by legislation; but it is in expectation to propose to the House some measure which may have for its end the prevention of some of the evils, or at any rate which would tend to their mitigation.

A week later, Mackenzie moved pre-emptively to table a bundle of 'papers relating to the late strike on the Grand Trunk Railway Company.'[70] This evidently caught the Opposition unawares: on 12 March Tupper moved, on behalf of Macdonald, 'for copies of all Orders in Council relating to the late strike on the Grand Trunk Railway Company, and of all correspondence with the Ontario Government and with the officials of the Grand Trunk Railway Company on the subject ...' Tupper withdrew the motion on Blake's assurance that 'all the information in the possession of the Government was contained in a recent return.' Mackenzie's 2 January letter to Hickson was not in the return.

MASTER AND SERVANT IN PARLIAMENT

Blake introduced his breaches of contract bill on 7 March, the same day that Mackenzie tabled the strike correspondence.[71] Debate in the Commons was fairly extensive, taking up sixty-three columns (or partial columns) in the published report. The greater part of the discussion focused on the proposal to punish 'wilful and malicious breaches of contract' as crimes, and in particular on the experience of the Grand Trunk strike. These topics were spoken to in forty-seven of the Hansard columns, three-quarters of the total. Nevertheless, there was substantial discussion of the first clause, the repeal of the pre-Confederation provisions, which was addressed in twenty-three columns, more than a third of the report.[72] Our concern here is with the debate about the first clause.

In introducing the topic, Blake sketched out two somewhat incompatible themes.[73] First, he stressed that the law making ordinary breaches of contract criminal was outdated. It was 'ancient,' based on 'antiquated models,' rejected by the 'modern spirit of the law.' Second, he pointed out that it was uncertain whether the pre-Confederation master and servant acts were criminal statutes, and therefore *ultra vires* the provinces. On the one hand, Quebec had 'assumed to repeal' some of the pre-Confederation provisions; on the other hand, 'the Bill introduced for the same purpose in Ontario was rejected, owing to the view that it was beyond the power of the Local Legislature ...' Here, the object was not so much to impose the modern spirit of the law as to make it clear that there was no bar to new provincial legislation: 'The matter was somewhat of a mixed character, but no harm could be done by repealing the laws so that the local Legislatures might feel at liberty to make provision to dispose of those complicated and somewhat difficult questions which arose between masters and servants.' By stating both themes Blake attempted to occupy the high ground, conveniently staked out by the mother of parliaments in the Employers and Workmen Act, 1875, without infringing on provincial rights. The Parliament of the Dominion might declare the modern spirit in principle, but it would be left to the provinces whether to embrace it in practice.

Blake's approach enabled him to circumvent all arguments for and against penalizing ordinary breaches of contract. One member argued that 'servants were indifferent to being condemned to pay a certain sum of money, and it was only by having the summary means of punishing by imprisonment, as he believed they could do under the local law, they were able to compel the fulfilment of engagements.'[74] Another complained that woods workers 'often deserted their employment, and it seemed to him that, unless there was some way other than that of punishing such persons by a fine, as proposed in the Act, employers were exposed to serious loss.'[75] A third expressed himself 'quite willing that every man in the country should have the best right to labour and enter into contracts, yet he denied the right of workmen to co-operate and combine, and could quite understand why such an act should be made a crime.'[76] Blake was not required to answer any of these objections directly. Instead, he recited again his two themes. 'In times past' such acts were crimes, but now that 'the last vestige' had been 'swept from the English Statute-book,' the 'true principle' was recognized: ordinary breaches of contract were civil matters. But if they were civil matters, then they came within provincial jurisdiction and the provinces should be free to do what they liked with them:

It was competent for these Legislatures to punish breaches of civil contracts, although not as crimes. He had before him local laws providing for two years' imprisonment for breaches of a civil law. If any Local Legislature proposed, at this time, to pass a law providing for breaches of contracts of service, without peculiar circumstances connected with them, being punished by imprisonment, it had the power to do so. This Bill did not, as it could not profess to, affect any right possessed by Local Legislatures, or any Act of such Legislatures.
Mr. Palmer: It repeals them.
Mr. Blake: No. It only repealed so much of the Acts of the old Provincial Legislatures before Confederation, as dealt with the Criminal Law, which law belonged to this Parliament. These were not repealable by the Local Legislatures. This was the principle of the Bill.[77]

To make the point still more clear, Blake accepted Macdonald's amendment to the first clause, restricting repeal to those parts of the named statutes 'making the violation of any provisions of any of the said sections a crime.' He also agreed to put off the repeal to 1 May 1878, to 'give an opportunity to the Legislatures of Ontario, Quebec, and Prince Edward Island to make whatever local laws they pleased to provide for the repression of those breaches of contracts now punished as crimes in these Provinces,' and to insert section 1(2) to confirm the Quebec provincial legislation that had 'assumed to repeal' parts of the pre-Confederation statute.[78]

Nevertheless, Blake continued to maintain that '[t]he policy of the Government was to remove the stigma of crime from breaches of contract of service, which were not attended with peculiar circumstances.'[79] The act meant that ordinary breaches were not crimes, but there was nothing to prevent the provinces from jailing workers who broke their contracts. It is hardly a wonder that some participants in the debate – and historians who succeeded them – were confused. At one point in what must have been an exhausting day, Blake himself mixed up his terms:

Mr. Masson: The result – the punishment is the same. In one case you give a man two months' imprisonment, and say he is not a criminal; and in another you give him two months and say he is a criminal. Where is the difference?
Mr Blake said he was not called upon to determine what would be the policy of the Local Legislatures in framing the laws which they had the power to enact. He had merely pointed out that *it was competent for a Local Legislature to make a certain act a crime after this House had removed it from the category of crimes under the Dominion law.* It was not for this House to discuss whether a Local Legislature would make simple breaches of personal contracts a crime or not.[80]

It would be possible, perhaps, to take Blake at his word and conclude that the Mackenzie government had done all it could, within the confines of the British North America Act, to uphold 'the modern spirit of the law,' were it not for three considerations.

First, in one significant area of undisputed federal jurisdiction over the enforcement of private employment contracts – merchant shipping – the government showed no intention of repealing imprisonment for ordinary breaches of contract. This was not an oversight. Asked during the debate whether his bill 'would in any way interfere with engagements between masters and seamen,' Blake responded that this was not his intention, 'but, if it was found that the Bill did effect [sic] these relations, a clause could be easily introduced preventing any such application.'[81] In fact, Canadian merchant seamen were to remain liable to imprisonment for absenteeism, desertion, work refusal, and other ordinary breaches well into the twentieth century.[82]

Second, Blake had declared the government's policy to be that ordinary breaches of contract were purely civil matters. Yet what this meant oscillated during the debate between two poles. On the high ground of policy, it meant that they were not to be punished by fine or imprisonment. In the swampier terrain of practice, it meant that they were to be governed by provincial law, which might mean – indeed, as we shall see, already meant – the imposition of penalties even more severe that those in the pre-Confederation statutes. Yet leaving it to the provinces in this way was not the only option open to the federal government. It might have taken the additional step (under section 94 of the British North America Act) of enacting a model provision, at least for the common law provinces. The model was readily available in the English Employers and Workmen Act, 1875 which gave courts of summary jurisdiction a limited power to award civil damages in disputes between employers and workers (including apprentices).[83]

Third, Blake confined the government's implementation of its newfound policy to the narrowest possible constitutional difficulty, the reconciliation of pre-Confederation legislation with the division of powers under the British North America Act. Compared with the sweeping declaration in the preamble, the list of specific sections of a handful of colonial statutes in section 1 of the act seems positively niggling, and all the more so after the incorporation of Macdonald's coy amendment. Similar provisions in other provincial legislation – including the Quebec enactment mentioned in section 1(2) and legislation in the newly created Province of Manitoba – remained untouched. Indeed, if the true policy of the act was to remove doubts that ordinary breaches of employment contracts fell within the provincial jurisdiction, it had the effect of confirming existing provincial acts punishing workers for breach of contract. Had the act's true intent been to relieve workers of jail and fines for breach of contract, so far as that lay within the power of the federal government, the net of section 1 would surely have been cast more widely.

Section 1 of the Breaches of Contract Act, 1877 was effective only to the extent that the pre-Confederation statutes were *ultra vires* the provinces. The federal justice department had not objected to provincial legislation establishing fines and imprisonment for ordinary breaches of contract, as in the Quebec and Manitoba statutes mentioned above.[84] Blake assured

Parliament that the government had no intention of interfering with the Quebec enactment.[85] In Ontario, the question had been raised not by Blake, but by Mowat, who had pressed the issue even though O'Donoghue's bill dealt with issues that were clearly within the provincial competence.[86] On more than one occasion during the debate, Blake hinted that section 1 might not be strictly necessary. The jurisdictional question was 'of a mixed character' but 'no harm could be done' by the (purported) repeal.[87] There was 'considerable divergence of opinion' between the governments of Quebec and Ontario as to whether repeal was *ultra vires* the provinces.[88] Perhaps Mowat merely found it more convenient to serve the ball to Blake than to repeal the penal provisions or risk alienating the unions. But Blake volleyed: the ball was now back in the provincial court.

The rest is speculation. Mowat had written privately to Blake on 30 December 1876 that the statute revision commissioners had completed their work of deciding 'as to the inclusion of certain Canadian laws' in the revised statutes. Mowat's letter has not survived, but Blake's reply, written immediately following the Grand Trunk strike, offers a glimpse of its contents. Mowat apparently suggested a reference to the Supreme Court to resolve outstanding questions; compare this to his comment on first reading of O'Donoghue's bill on 7 February, that 'this, and a number of other such questions, could only be finally settled by the Supreme Court.' Blake concluded his reply by assuring Mowat that 'every effort will be made on our part to settle in the most convenient mode any difficulties which may arise.'[89] Without access to Mowat's outgoing correspondence or the minutes of the statute revision commission, it is impossible to know exactly when the question of the master and servant act first arose, or whether Mowat raised it with Blake before the 1877 session commenced.[90] It remains a tantalizing possibility that the first clause of the Breaches of Contract Act, 1877 represented Blake's effort to make a convenient settlement of one of the Ontario premier's difficulties. If so, the convenience was assuredly mutual. Certainly Blake made the most of it: during the debate on the new crimes arising out of the Grand Trunk strike he was able to assure the House that he had heard from 'the great body of operatives who were considerably interested in any measure which affected a branch of the working classes' that they believed his bill to be 'based on just and equitable principles.'[91]

Dick Risk has shown that provincial autonomy within the provincial sphere was a natural corollary of Blake's idea of political liberty. As Blake put it in an 1886 election speech about the disallowance of Ontario legislation, 'I care not whether the Act is just or unjust, whether it is right or wrong, whether it is good or bad, whether it is robbery or not. I inquire as to this only, is it a law passed by the Local Legislature, within the exclusive competence of that Legislature, and not substantially affecting Dominion interests?'[92] From a constitutional rights point of view, the Breaches of Contract Act was consistent with this approach. But if we concede that, we might pursue another of Risk's insights, that Blake was never 'pushed to make a firm, clear choice between autonomy and liberty in a situation where provincial legislation was a vital restriction of liberty.'[93] By insisting on the right of the provinces to be wrong, Blake left it open for the local legislatures to reject the 'modern spirit' and continue to imprison workers for breach of contract. If Blake 'did not face many difficult choices about the strength of individual rights,'[94] the story of the Breaches of Contract Act suggests that this was partly due to his adroitness in evading them.

PROVINCIAL RESPONSE

The labour movement greeted Blake's measure with guarded optimism. The Toronto Trades Assembly regretted the new crimes, but nevertheless lauded the act as 'a great boon to the working classes of Canada, as it *tends* to place employer and employee on the footing of equality before the law in reference to such breaches.'[95] In August 1877, at the sadly diminished Canadian Labor Union's final convention, J.S. Williams moved: 'That this Congress recognizes the liberal spirit in which the Bill, recently passed, bearing upon breaches of contract, was framed, making such breaches of contract in general civil wrongs only; and thereby meeting the objections that have been urged against the unfair clauses of the Masters and Servants Act; and further, that this Congress endorses such Bill; and still further, that this Congress maintain vigilant watchfulness upon the actions of the Legislature on this question through its Parliamentary Committee.' Williams' resolution, which passed without discussion, suggests that the labour movement understood the true policy of Blake's bill – that the field was clear for provincial action.

The CLU's interest was limited to Ontario, but it would have taken more than 'vigilant watchfulness' to discern legislative action there. True to form, Mowat buried repeal of the penal provisions in the 1877 statute revision. The legislature was given no opportunity to debate a bill to amend the master and servant act. The repeal was carried out by publishing a new masters and servants act in the Revised Statutes, 1877, and reporting in a schedule to the whole revision that the entire pre-Confederation act was thereby repealed and replaced.[96] The new act was produced by consolidating the 1859 version with amending statutes passed in 1865 and 1873, then removing the sections named in the Breaches of Contract Act.[97] Sections 4, 5, 9, and 10 were simply dropped from the statute. Section 8, providing how fines were to be paid, was also dropped; there were no fines provided for in the revised act. Sections 7 and 11 were silently altered by removing the references to offences.[98] The rest of the matter remained unchanged.[99] In the result, Ontario had an extraordinarily liberal master and servant act, which now provided remedies for workers against breach of contract by the employer but no remedies for employers against workers' breaches. A short-lived amendment in 1901 (repealed 1904) made desertion by an employee who had not worked out an advance punishable by fine or imprisonment.[100] Otherwise, Ontario remained a worker's paradise, wherein a benevolent Master and Servant Act provided for summary recovery of small amounts of unpaid wages, until the 1990 statute revision, when the province's first social democratic government renamed it the Employers and Employees Act.[101]

Quebec was the only province to have 'assumed to repeal' pre-Confederation master and servant offences before the passage of the Breaches of Contract Act. During the 1877 debate, Quebec members expressed the concern of the province's bar that Blake's bill would trench on provincial rights. To meet these objections, Blake agreed to the addition of section 1(2), which confirmed the provincial legislation by removing any doubt that the Quebec statute of 1870 was *intra vires*. However, the 1870 act imposed a more stringent penalty for breaches of the employment contract than the pre-Confederation statute that it (and Blake's act) repealed. Where the old act provided for a twenty dollar fine, thirty days' imprisonment, or both, the new one increased the maximum prison term to two months for the same contraventions.[102] This provision remained in force until 1881, when the sole penalty became a twenty dollar fine, with two months jail in default of payment.[103] This penalty remained unchanged until 1949.[104] Moreover, the statutes mentioned applied only to masters and servants in the 'country parts.' In incorporated towns and cities employment contracts could be regulated by municipal by-laws. In Montreal, to take the leading example, a series of by-laws dating back to 1802 provided mandatory jail sentences for ordinary breaches of the employment contract. As I have shown elsewhere, these by-laws were used against workers (other than seamen) more frequently after 1877 than before, and did not fade into desuetude until the mid-1920s.[105]

The fate of the Prince Edward Island statute is something of a mystery. The province had joined Confederation in 1873 and in 1877 was still actively negotiating the reconciliation of its criminal law with that of Canada.[106] The only reported case to have cited the 1833 Servants' Act dates from 1857.[107] One might be forgiven for assuming that the statute, if not expressly repealed, had effectively expired after the Breaches of Contract Act, 1877, if not before. In 1906, however, the Labour Gazette's review of Canadian master and servant law stated that it was still in force, and it was listed in the periodic consolidations issued by the federal Department of Labour in 1915, 1920, 1937, and 1948.[108] The Servants' Act was finally repealed by chapter 2 of the province's first post-Confederation statute revision, in 1951. More research is required to determine whether it was used at all in the interim.

In other jurisdictions, and for other classes of workers, fines and imprisonment for ordinary breaches of contract remained common despite the preamble to the 1877 Dominion act. A survey of the 1915 Department of Labour consolidation will show how far the modern spirit of the law had progressed a generation after the Breaches of Contract Act. Seamen on Dominion government vessels and on any ship registered in any province remained liable to imprisonment and forfeiture of wages for desertion, absence from duty, and other breaches.[109] Workers could be fined or jailed for absence or disobedience in Prince Edward Island, Manitoba, Alberta, and the Yukon,[110] as could voyageurs and fishermen in Quebec.[111] Apprentices could be jailed for absence or disobedience in Prince Edward Island, Nova Scotia, New Brunswick, Ontario, Manitoba, British Columbia, and the Yukon,[112] and fined in Quebec.[113] Many of these punishments were not finally abolished until after the Second World War.

SUMMARY AND CONCLUSION

The Breaches of Contract Act was not intended to abolish fines and imprisonment for ordinary breaches of the employment contract, nor did it have that effect. The Mackenzie government's main purpose was to legislate against railway strikes in the 1877 session. The celebrated preamble and first section were inserted to secure labour activists' support for the new measures for the protection of property and to ward off criticism of the government's role in the Grand Trunk strike. The effect of section 1, as Blake intended and understood, was to confirm the provincial jurisdiction over employment contracts. It resolved a constitutional conundrum, particularly as it affected the Ontario statute revision. While the silent repeal of the penal provisions in Ontario's pre-Confederation Master and Servant Act was a substantial gain for workers in that province, it had no notice-

able effect on employment law elsewhere in the country. Fines and imprisonment for simple breaches of employment contracts remained available
in several provinces, and in the Dominion employment jurisdiction, well
into the twentieth century. Moreover, the Blake Act was neither a necessary nor a sufficient condition for the Ontario repeal. Despite the brave
promises of its preable, the true policy of the Dominion Act was not to
place employers and workers on a footing of legal equality, but to leave the
provinces to their own devices while seeming to be doing something to
keep the trains on time.

NOTES

This essay draws in part on materials collected for the Master & Servant Project
at York University, with the support of the Social Sciences and Humanities
Research Council of Canada. I am grateful to Seann McAleese for additional
research assistance and to Douglas Hay, Gregory Kealey, Jeremy Webber, the
editors of this volume, and the anonymous assessors for their helpful comments.

1 (Can.) 40 Vict., c. 35 (1877).
2 For labour and legal historians' accounts of the legislation and its significance
  see, among others, R.H. Coats, 'The Labour Movement in Canada,' in Adam
  Shortt and Arthur G. Doughty, eds., Canada and Its Provinces: Volume IX
  (Toronto 1914), 299; Bernard Ostry, 'Conservatives, Liberals, and Labour in
  the 1870's,' Canadian Historical Review 41 (1960), 126–7; Desmond Morton,
  'Taking on the Grand Trunk: The Locomotive Engineers' Strike of 1876–7,'
  Labour/Le travailleur 2 (1977), 32; H. Clare Pentland (Paul Phillips, ed.), Labour
  and Capital in Canada, 1650–1860 (Toronto 1981), 21n154; Gregory S. Kealey,
  Toronto Workers Respond to Industrial Capitalism, 1867–92 (Toronto 1980), 149–
  53; Paul Craven, 'The Law of Master and Servant in Mid-Nineteenth-Century
  Ontario,' in David H. Flaherty, ed., Essays in the History of Canadian Law:
  Volume I (Toronto 1981), 199; Eric Tucker, '"That Indefinite Area of Toleration": Criminal Conspiracy and Trade Unions in Ontario, 1837–77,' Labour/Le
  travail 27 (1991), 50; and Jeremy Webber, 'Labour and the Law,' in Paul
  Craven, ed., Labouring Lives: Work and Workers in Nineteenth-Century Ontario
  (Toronto 1995), 171.
3 Toronto Electric Commissioners v. Snider, [1925] 2 DLR 5. Thus one authoritative text has it that 'In 1925, the Judicial Committee of the Privy Council
  changed the course of Canadian labour law ... From that moment on, the
  future of Canadian labour law rested primarily in the provincial domain.'

G.W. Adams, *Canadian Labour Law: A Comprehensive Text* (Aurora 1985), 9.

4 The bill was amended during the legislative process. The original text seems to have perished in the parliamentary fire of 1916.

5 '1. All those parts of sections four, five, seven, nine, ten and eleven of the Act chapter seventy-five of the Consolidated Statutes for Upper Canada, intituled, *"An Act respecting Master and Servant,"* and all those parts of sections five and seven of the Act chapter twenty-seven, of the Consolidated Statutes for Lower Canada, intituled, *"An Act respecting Masters and Servants in the Country Parts,"* (as amended by the Act of the legislature of the late Province of Canada, twenty-ninth and thirtieth Victoria, chapter thirty-four, intituled, *"An Act to amend chapter twenty-seven of the Consolidated Statutes for Lower Canada, respecting Masters and Servants in the Country Parts,"*) and all those parts of section three of the Act of the legislature of the Province of Prince Edward Island, second William the Fourth, chapter twenty-six, intituled, *"An Act for repealing an Act of the thirty-fifty year of the reign of King George the Third, intituled 'An Act for regulating Servants,' and for substituting other provisions in lieu thereof,"* which make a violation of any of the provisions of any of the said acts criminal, shall be and stand repealed from and after the first day of May in the year of Our Lord one thousand eight hundred and seventy-eight. (2). All those parts of sections two and three of the said chapter twenty-seven of the Consolidated Statutes for Lower Canada, as amended as aforesaid, which make a violation of any of the provisions of either of the said sections criminal, and which sections have been repealed by an act of the Legislature of Quebec, thirty-third Victoria, chapter twenty, intituled, *"An Act further to amend chapter twenty-seven of the Consolidated Statutes for Lower Canada respecting Masters and Servants in the country parts"* are hereby repealed.'

6 Although the Canadas were joined in legislative union from 1840 until Confederation, many enactments were made to apply to only one or the other of its former components. For the sake of clarity, and consistently with the legal descriptions in the pre-Confederation consolidated statutes, I refer to them here as Upper and Lower Canada: compare British North America Act, 1867, s. 6.

7 For the history of master and servant legislation and its enforcement in Nova Scotia, Quebec, and Ontario, see Paul Craven, 'Masters, Servants and Magistrates in British North America,' in Paul Craven and Douglas Hay, eds., *Master and Servant in Britain and the Empire: Uses of the Law* (forthcoming).

8 For the Ontario master and servant legislation, see also Craven, 'The Law of Master and Servant,' and Webber, 'Labour and the Law.'

9 The 1836 rules were based on those adopted at Montreal. Craven, 'Masters, Servants and Magistrates.'

10 Paul Craven, 'Master & Servant Legislation of Atlantic Canada in Imperial
Context,' paper presented to Atlantic Law & History Workshop II, Dalhousie
Law School, Halifax, March 1995.

11 Other offences were defined in these Acts and made subject to fines or
imprisonment. Some of these are noticed below.

12 Section 4 of the Upper Canada act described the offences; s. 7 empowered
justices of the peace to punish them; s. 9 quantified the punishments; s. 10
provided for imprisonment for non-payment of fines; s. 11 gave jurisdiction to
justices residing wherever the offenders were found. Section 5, also listed in
the Breaches of Contract Act, was an anticrimping provision.

13 The amendments in (Lower Canada), 29 & 30 Vict. c. 34 included a new entry
in the catalogue: 'refuses or neglects to enter the service of his master at the
time agreed upon' (s. 2). Section 5 of the CSLC, c. 27, listed in s. 1 of the
Breaches of Contract Act, gave justices of the peace jurisdiction to enforce the
statute.

14 Corporations – municipal, business, and railway – were made subject by s. 3
of the act to a 'penalty' of up to $100 if their breaches of contract threatened
water or gas supplies or kept the trains from running on time.

15 Section 5 of the Breaches of Contract Act, 1877 provided that 'All offences
against the second section of this Act shall be prosecuted as provided by the
Act thirty-fifth Victoria, chapter thirty-one, intituled *"An Act to amend the
Criminal Law relating to Violence, Threats and Molestation,"* as amended by the
Act thirty-ninth Victoria, chapter thirty-seven, intituled *"An Act to amend the
Criminal Law relating to Violence, Threats and Molestation."'* On the politics of
the 1876 amendment, see Ostry, 'Conservatives, Liberals, and Labour,' 122–5
and Kealey, *Toronto Workers*, 142–50. For contrasting views of the significance
of the 1872 statutes, see Paul Craven, 'Workers' Conspiracies in Toronto,
1854–72,' *Labour/Le travail* 14 (1984), 49–70, Tucker, '"That Indefinite Area of
Toleration,"' and Webber, 'Labour and the Law.'

16 (U.K.) 38 & 39 Vict., c. 86 (1875).

17 Paul Craven, 'Law and Railway Accidents, 1850–80,' in Wesley Pue and Barry
Wright, eds., *Proceedings of the Carleton Conference on Law and History* (Ottawa
1987), 47–56; Paul Craven, 'The Meaning of Misadventure: The Baptiste Creek
Railway Disaster of 1854 and its Aftermath,' in Roger Hall et al., eds., *Patterns
of the Past: Interpreting Ontario's History* (Toronto 1988), 108–29.

18 Susan W.S. Binnie, 'Explorations in the Use of Criminal Law in Canada, 1867–
1892' (PhD thesis, Carleton University 1991), 139ff.

19 The Ontario commissioners reported the progress of their work in (Ontario),
Sessional Papers 38 Vict. (1874), no. 26; 39 Vict. (1875–6), no. 37; 40 Vict. (1877),
no. 20; and 41 Vict. (1878), no. 21. See also C.R.W. Biggar, *Sir Oliver Mowat: A*

Biographical Sketch (Toronto 1905), I:248ff; Paul Romney, *Mr Attorney: The Attorney General for Ontario in Court, Cabinet and Legislature, 1791–1899* (Toronto 1986), 282ff; and A. Margaret Evans, *Sir Oliver Mowat* (Toronto 1992), 187ff.

20 Brian Young, *The Politics of Codification: The Lower Canadian Civil Code of 1866* (Toronto 1994); see also John W. Cairns, 'Employment in the *Civil Code of Lower Canada*: Tradition and Political Economy in Legal Classification and Reform,' *McGill Law Journal* 32 (1987), 673–711.

21 For example, the Upper Canada statute provided that claims for wages proceeded by way of summons, while prosecutions for desertion proceeded by way of arrest.

22 In 1862 the *Upper Canada Law Journal* (8:278), had expressed the view that the action for wages under the Upper Canada statute was 'more in the nature of a civil than a criminal proceeding.'

23 'When, under the limited authority conferred upon them, provincial legislatures impose a fine or a penalty or imprisonment for a disobedience of a provincial law, they do not thereby create the criminal offence involved in such disobedience. Disobedience of a statute is a crime under the common law; it is a crime under the general criminal law of the country; ... So that, if the limited authority given to provincial legislatures by the B.N.A. Act were not in existence at all, or, if, though in existence, it were not exercised, a contravention of a provincial statute would be punishable under the general criminal law, controlled by the Dominion Parliament; ...' – James Crankshaw, *The Criminal Code of Canada* (Montreal 1894), 779.

24 W.E. Hodgins, comp., *Correspondence, Reports of the Ministers of Justice, and Orders in Council upon the subject of Dominion and Provincial Legislation 1867–1895* (Ottawa 1896), 103ff.

25 Hodgins, *Correspondence*, 151. The same objection was taken to legislation by other provinces: see, for example, Blake's strictures on P.E.I. statutes, ibid. 1180, 1182.

26 Hodgins, *Correspondence*, 157.

27 Examples from several provinces will be found in Hodgins, *Correspondence*. The difficulty of talking about breaches of statute without employing one of the disputed words is pointed up, ironically, in the complaint of federal Deputy Minister of Justice H. Bernard about the Manitoba act incorporating the City of Winnipeg, that 'constituting an offence a misdemeanor is a branch of criminal law, and, therefore, not within the legal competence of the legislature of Manitoba,' (786). The province was not to call an offence a misdemeanour, but neither was it to call it an offence.

28 In their third (1877), report, the commissioners explained that they had tried

to avoid the jurisdictional conflict by substituting specific punishments for the common provision that a breach be punishable as a misdemeanour.

29 (Ont.), 38 Vict., c. 19.

30 In introducing the bill, Mowat explained that he 'intended to introduce these [new] clauses in such a manner that they could be incorporated in the present law.' Toronto, *Globe*, 17 November 1874.

31 '17. Any Justice of the Peace or Police Magistrate, on complaint made before him on oath by an Apprentice against his Master for refusing necessary provisions, or for misusage, cruelty or ill-treatment, may cause the Master to appear before him to answer the complaint, and shall thereupon, hear and determine the complaint, and on conviction may levy on the offender a fine not exceeding twenty dollars, and issue a warrant of distress to collect the same, and the costs, and in default of satisfaction of the distress, may direct the offender to be imprisoned in any common gaol for a term not exceeding one month, unless the fine and costs be sooner paid. C.S.U.C. c. 76, s. 9. 18. Any Justice, or Police Magistrate, may also, on complaint of a Master against an Apprentice for refusing to obey his commands, or for waste or damage to property, or for any other improper conduct, cause the Apprentice to appear before him, and shall hear and determine the complaint, and on conviction, order the Apprentice to be imprisoned in a common gaol or house of correction for a term not exceeding one month. C.S.U.C., c. 76, s. 10.'

32 Hodgins, *Correspondence*, 143.

33 Ontario Archives (hereafter AO), Newspaper Hansard, 8 December 1875.

34 (Ont.), 39 Vict., 1st session, 3rd parliament, Bill no. 98, s. 3; for Blake's approval of these amendments see Hodgins, *Correspondence*, 144.

35 I am obliged to Douglas Hay for this observation. A broadly similar provision was preserved in the English Employers and Workmen Act, 1875.

36 55 & 56 Vict., c. 29, Title V, ss. 211 and 217.

37 Leslie E. Wismer, comp., *Canadian Labor Union Proceedings*, 1873–77 (Ottawa 1951), 27.

38 John Battye, 'The Nine-Hour Pioneers: The Genesis of the Canadian Labour Movement,' *Labour/Le travailleur* 4 (1979), 25–56.

39 (U.K.), 38 & 39 Vict., c. 90 (1875).

40 Toronto Trades Assembly and Toronto Trades and Labour Council *Minutes*, *1871–1887* (Ottawa 1979), [microfilm of typewritten transcription], 128 (31 March 1874).

41 Wismer, *Canadian Labor Union*, 37, 39ff.

42 Ibid., 45ff, 49.

43 Ibid., 72; see also 64, 69, 71.

44 Toronto, *Globe*, 4 September 1876.

45 Blake Letter Books, vol. 9, Blake to Mowat, 4 January 1877; Blake to Mowat, 8 January 1877.

46 Ontario, *Statutes of the Province of Canada and Dominion of Canada Comprising those Portions of the Consolidated Statutes of Canada and Upper Canada, and of the Statutes of the Province of Canada still in force in Ontario* ... (Toronto 1876).

47 Newspaper Hansard, 7 February 1877.

48 Morton, 'Taking on the Grand Trunk,' Shirley Ann Ayer, 'The Locomotive Engineers' Strike on the Grand Trunk Railway in 1876–1877' (MA thesis, McGill University 1961).

49 Their exchange of telegrams is published in Canada, *Sessional Papers*, 40 Vict. (1877), no. 55, 'Correspondence respecting disturbance on the line of the Grand Trunk Railway of Canada, 1st January 1877, Military Districts Nos. 1, 2 and 3, Sarnia and Belleville; Also, disturbance on the line of Grand Trunk Railway of Canada, 1st January 1877, Military Districts Nos. 2 and 3, Belleville and Sarnia' [henceforth, G.T.R. Corr.], 26–30; for correspondence missing from this report, see below.

50 Report of W.A. Reeve, county crown attorney (Lennox & Addington), in G.T.R. Corr. 45.

51 G.T.R. Corr. 30.

52 Montreal, *Witness*, 9 January 1877.

53 Toronto, *Globe*, 17 January 1877.

54 'Copy of a Report of a Committee of the Hon. the Privy Council ...,' with letters of transmittal and the official response of the Ontario government, in OA RG8-1-1 (provincial secretary general correspondence), #61/77, docket dated 11 January 1877. Mowat issued a circular letter to county Crown attorneys for the requested reports; these were not transmitted to Ottawa until 15 February.

55 Mackenzie Papers (General Correspondence), 1657ff, Blake to Mackenzie, 17 January 1877.

56 Blake Letter Books, vol. 9, 217–53 (10 January 1877).

57 Hickson left for England on 19 January and did not return until early April, after the breaches of contract bill had passed the Commons. Montreal, *Witness*, 19 January 1877, 6 April 1877.

58 Blake Letter Books, vol. 9, 570.

59 Ibid., 583.

60 Mackenzie Papers (General Correspondence), 1492–4, Mackenzie to Hickson (copy), 2 January 1877.

61 Blake Letter Books, v. 9, 665 (Blake to Mackenzie 19 February 1877).

62 Mackenzie Papers (General Correspondence), 1521. Written at the top of the paper is 'Rewrite as corrected and send over.'

63 (Ont.), 40 Vict. (1877), 2nd session, 3rd parliament, Bill no. 117.
64 Toronto, *Globe*, 19 February 1877. O'Donoghue subsequently withdrew his bill, after Mowat told the legislature that 'there was a question of jurisdiction involved in the Bill which was still doubtful. He hoped it would be withdrawn for the present.' Toronto, *Globe*, 26 February 1877.
65 T.T.A., *Minutes*, 21 February 1877; see also Wismer, *Canadian Labor Union*, 80.
66 Blake Letter Books, vol. 9, 826; Williams read the letter to the trades assembly meeting on 7 March.
67 Canada, Senate, *Journals*, vol. 11 (1877). Debate on this resolution was postponed from day to day until 22 March, when the order was discharged.
68 Grand Trunk solicitor John Bell wrote Blake to dissociate the railway company from Read's motion, which suggests that it was viewed as a hostile one. Blake Letter Books, vol. 9, 771 (Blake to Bell, 28 February 1877).
69 Julius Scriver was 'an ardent supporter of Mr. Mackenzie throughout his administration.' Henry James Morgan, *The Canadian Men and Women of the Time: A Hand-book of Canadian Biography* (Toronto 1898), 924.
70 These were published as Sessional Paper No. 55: for the full title see note 49 above.
71 The bill received second reading on 20 March and was amended in committee on 27 March. It passed the Commons on 29 March and the Senate on 17 April, receiving royal assent on 28 April.
72 This is obviously a crude measure. Both topics were addressed in some columns, and there were a few columns in which neither topic appeared. For a different view of the debate, see Kealey, *Toronto Workers*, 151ff.
73 This paragraph draws on Blake's speech in Canada, House of Commons, *Debates* (1877), 524f.
74 *Debates*, 856 (Brooks).
75 *Debates*, 868ff (White).
76 *Debates*, 1010 (Palmer).
77 *Debates*, 1011.
78 *Debates*, 1010ff.
79 *Debates*, 1011.
80 *Debates*, 1014 (emphasis added).
81 *Debates*, 1011.
82 The English Employers and Workmen Act, 1875 did not apply to seamen.
83 Blake cited the English act to justify the breaches of contract bill at several points in the debate.
84 These and other penal statutes are discussed further below.
85 *Debates*, 855.

86 The clause repealing s. 5 (the anti-crimping provision), which was subsequently listed in s. 1 of Blake's act, may have been the exception, but it was not specifically referred to in the interview with Mowat.

87 *Debates*, 524.

88 *Debates*, 1011.

89 Blake Letter Books, vol. 9 Blake to Mowat, 4 January 1877.

90 The minutes are mentioned by Biggar, *Mowat*, I:250. Neither they nor the correspondence seem to have survived.

91 *Debates*, 1017.

92 As quoted by R.C.B. Risk, 'Blake and Liberty,' in J. Ajzenstat, ed., *Canadian Constitutionalism* (Ottawa 1993), 205.

93 Ibid., 209.

94 Ibid., 206.

95 In the manuscript copy of this resolution sent by the Trades Assembly to Blake, the word *tends* was heavily underscored. AO, Blake Papers, General Political Correspondence, D.A. Macneil to Blake, 19 April 1877. Compare, *T.T.A. Minutes*, 17 April 1877.

96 The new act was RSO 1877, Title X, Part 4, c. 133.

97 The amending statutes were (Ont.), 29 Vict., c. 33 (1865), providing for disputes arising after the term of the contract, 36 Vict., c. 24 (1873), providing for extraprovincial contracts, and 36 Vict. c. 25 (1873), providing for profit-sharing agreements.

98 The change to s. 11 was consistent with one of O'Donoghue's proposed amendments. One reference to punishment of offences remained in the act, probably by oversight: in s. 13 (appeals) of both the 1859 consolidation and the 1877 revision it was provided, *inter alia*, that, 'the Court appealed to shall order and adjudge the offender to be punished according to the conviction ...'

99 The *Revised Statutes* printed part of s. 12 of the 1859 consolidation, providing remedies for ill-treatment of servants, in 'bourgeois type,' indicating that there remained some doubt as to whether the provision was *intra vires* the province. See, in this regard, Blake's 4 January 1877 letter to Mowat, suggesting that doubtful statutes be included 'verbatim et literatim' but with an indication of their doubtful status.

100 (Ont.), 1 Edw. VII, c. 12 (1901), s. 14, repealed by (Ont.), 4 Edw. VII, c. 10 (1904), s. 38.

101 RSO 1990, c. E.12.

102 (Que.), 33 Vict., c. 20 (1870), ss. 2, 3.

103 (Que.), 44 & 45 Vict., c. 15.

104 SQ 1949, c. 69.

105 Craven, 'Masters, Servants and Magistrates.'
106 National Archives, RG13 Department of Justice Central Registry Files A1,
vol. 456, file 77/236.
107 *Brenan v. McIsaac*, Peters 112 (Chancery).
108 Canada, Department of Labour, *Labour Gazette* (July 1906), 54, 57; *Labour Legislation in Canada* for these years.
109 RSC 1906, c. 111, s. 9; 1907, c. 46 s. 1.
110 SPEI 1833, c. 26, s. 3; RSM 1913, c. 124, ss. 11, 12; SA 1904, c. 3, s. 2; *Yukon Consolidated Ordinances*, 1914, c. 62, s. 2.
111 RSQ 1909, cc. 7430, 7431, 7432.
112 SPEI 1845, c. 14, s. 8; RSNS, 1900, c. 117, s. 12; RSO 1914, c. 147, s. 18(2); RSM 1913, c. 124, s. 9; RSBC 1911, c. 107, s. 28; *Yukon Consolidated Ordinances*, 1914, c. 62, s. 2.
113 RSQ 1909, cc. 7418, 7419, 7423(2).

6

A Romance of the Lost: The Role of Tom MacInnes in the History of the British Columbia Indian Land Question

HAMAR FOSTER

No Indian in Canada has ever recognized the sovereignty of any Colonial, Provincial or Dominion Government – whenever his primitive rights to his lands are threatened, he appeals direct to the King, or to the Governor or other officer whom he understands to be the King's personal representative.

T.R.E. McInnes, 1909[1]

INTRODUCTION

It is a pleasure to contribute to a volume honouring someone who has done so much to transform Canadian legal history from professional pastime into academic discipline. Not of course that the former is of no account – it is – but the latter moves the study of the past beyond anecdote and professional loyalty toward the placing of law and legal culture in a wider context.[1] Dick Risk deserves a goodly share of the credit for accomplishing this transformation, and for doing it in the spirit of the Shakespearean injunction to be as lawyers are: strive mightily, but eat and drink as friends. Anyone who has attended academic conferences or read review articles knows that there are disciplines that might profit from this homely bit of advice.

The topic of this chapter – a remarkable and largely ignored legal opinion on Indian title provided to the Dominion government in 1909 – is really the Canadian constitution, a subject of more than passing interest to Dick.[2] In fact, the chapter deals with what Dr Brian Slattery has aptly called the 'hidden constitution,' that is, the unique and, until recently, largely unexplored legal position of Canada's Aboriginal peoples.[3] More precisely, it focuses on an aspect of that position that used to receive much more attention than it does today: the special relationship between Aboriginal people and the imperial Crown.[4]

That relationship, obviously, has eroded with time: whatever its role in the past, the imperial Crown has withdrawn politically and legally from its obligations to Canada's Aboriginal peoples. Imperial statutes dealing with the 'Indian Territories' were repealed in the nineteenth century;[5] Canada's status as a self-governing Dominion was affirmed in 1931;[6] appeals to the Judicial Committee of the Privy Council were abolished in 1949;[7] and the constitution was 'patriated' in 1982, terminating the authority of the imperial Parliament in Canada.[8] An interesting and early example of this trend relates to Clause 13 of British Columbia's Terms of Union, which provides that disagreements between the Dominion and provincial governments over Indian land may be submitted to the secretary of state for the colonies. When Ottawa and British Columbia were preparing to confirm by statute in the 1920s that they had agreed to a 'final' resolution of their dispute over reserve lands, the Allied Indian Tribes of British Columbia were concerned that the proposed legislation was intended to terminate imperial authority, and specifically the authority of the secretary of state, in such matters.[9]

Thus, although today it is still possible to emphasize the importance of imperial law to Aboriginal title, arguments in support of any degree of continuing imperial authority are unlikely to be successful.[10] The disappearance of this aspect of the matter may be gleaned from the fact that, in a seminal article written for the *Canadian Bar Review* in Canada's centennial year – the stated purpose of which was 'to examine the constitutional base upon which Canadian "Indian law" rests' – no mention is made of any special relationship with the imperial Crown.[11]

Nonetheless, the British Crown remains important to many Aboriginal elders today and, as the epigraph for this chapter suggests, less than a century ago it was at the centre of the struggle for Aboriginal title in British Columbia. Indeed, for the lawyers who involved themselves in the 'British Columbia Indian land question' in the years between the turn of the century and 1927, when Parliament criminalized such involvement if it took place without Ottawa's prior approval, the imperial connection was virtually all that mattered.[12]

Thus in 1909 a lawyer retained by Ottawa – a man who, like Deputy Superintendent of Indian Affairs Duncan Campbell Scott (1913–32), was a published poet – invoked this connection when he advised the minister of the interior that Indian title is a form of ownership.[13] Thomas Robert Edward McInnes also concluded that there was unextinguished Indian title in British Columbia quite apart from existing Indian reserves. To get around British Columbia's refusal to permit a judicial reference on the question, he recommended that Ottawa, in its capacity as 'trustee and guardian of the Indians whose rights are being invaded by white settlers,' bring an action of ejectment against Crown grantees in the Skeena region of the province.[14] The Skeena, of course, is where the Gitxsan, or the 'People of the Ksan River' live; seventy-five years later they and their neighbours, the Wet'suwet'en, would begin a lawsuit known as *Delgamuukw v. The Queen*.[15] The 1927 law accounts for much of this delay. But how can the lack of judicial involvement until then be explained?

THE B.C. INDIAN LAND QUESTION, 1849–1927

In June of 1874 a settler named Dods wrote to the provincial government from his homestead at Cowichan on Vancouver Island. His situation was not an unusual one. Although Aboriginal title to the land at Cowichan had not been extinguished, Dods had settled in that area with government approval and was now unhappy about what he saw as trespassing Indians. He was also unhappy about the failure of Dr Israel Wood Powell, the Dominion superintendent of Indian affairs, to do anything about it. 'Everyone says, "sure what the devil is the good of a Government that can't put a few siwashes off a man's land,"' Dods complained to the provincial attorney general. '[Y]ou must make the Indians respect your power,' he concluded, because they 'have a hundred times more respect for a gunboat than all the talk in creation.'[16]

Dods's attitude, however justified it may have seemed to him and to his neighbours at the time, neatly sums up why the B.C. Indian land question – as the controversy was already called in Dods's day – has proved so intractable. From the gunboats of the colonial and early provincial eras to the constitutional conferences of the 1980s, successive colonial and provincial governments consistently denied that the claims of British Columbia's Aboriginal peoples to their traditional territories had any legal validity.[17]

In fact, from the mid-1860s until 1938 British Columbia not only refused to acknowledge the law of Aboriginal title but clashed with Ottawa and Aboriginal people over both the size of Indian reserves and whether the province retained a residual interest in them.[18] As a result, with one exception no treaties were made in the province after the 1850s and a great deal of time, money, and energy was spent in Dominion-provincial haggling.[19] A decade or so after Dods's complaint, the problem was obvious even to two British travelogue writers who had spent time in the Kootenays: '[M]any places there are which *have* been owned and lived on by Indians in a perfectly regular manner, and we believe that the Government has paid very little attention to facts of this kind, but treating all the land as Crown land, has in many instances sold such plots to white settlers. They have given the Indians, it is true, certain reserves, but these often inadequate in amount, and selected without much regard to the feelings of the allottees as to position or quality.'[20]

Disagreement between Ottawa and the province over how much land should be transferred to the Dominion in trust as Indian reserves began the year after British Columbia joined Canada in 1871. Legally, it centred upon the proper interpretation of Clause 13 of the Terms of Union, which obliged the province to transfer land to Ottawa in trust as Indian reserves and, as we have seen, provided for disputes to be settled by the imperial authorities.[21] On the ground, of course, the problem was simpler to state but much more challenging to resolve. British Columbia has a relatively small amount of arable and pastoral land, virtually all of which is within the traditional territories of various Indian tribes. Aboriginal people were becoming increasingly aware of how important such land was to their future welfare in the new economy and knew that, for both settler and Indian to prosper, it had to be shared on an equitable basis. The problem was that most settlers thought it 'a novel idea that the Indians should have a full share of the natural gifts of their own country.'[22]

When the two governments finally agreed in 1876 to establish a joint commission to allot reserves, the province argued that it retained a 'reversionary interest' in such reserves.[23] Relations over this issue became so sour that in 1908 Premier Richard McBride effectively put a stop to the reserve allotment process.[24] In 1912 McBride and J.A.J. McKenna for the Dominion reached another agreement: Ottawa said it would take the question of Aboriginal title off the table if British Columbia would abandon its claim to a reversionary interest in the reserves. So another commission was established to 'adjust' the reserves, and it concluded that the province's position respecting its alleged reversionary interest had made it impossible for Ottawa to discharge its constitutional responsibilities. Although the issues of reserve size and the province's reversion were eventually resolved (more or less), the 1928 edition of a leading British textbook on colonial government in the Empire continued to refer to the 'difficulty' that was being 'experienced in inducing the province to conform to the standard of generosity of the Dominion.'[25]

Even more troublesome in the long run, however, was the much more fundamental question of Aboriginal title. As early as 1875, Télésphore Fournier, the Dominion minister of justice, advised Ottawa that British Columbia's failure to extinguish the Indian title meant that the province's public lands were probably subject to an interest 'other than that of the province.'[26] Fournier's advice resulted in the disallowance of the province's consolidated land statute. But this was only temporary. Other considerations prevailed and, just as they would do again in 1912, the two governments set aside the issue of Aboriginal title and agreed instead to set up the joint reserve commission referred to above.[27] The nature of the compromise was perhaps best expressed in 1877, in instructions from the Dominion minister of the interior, David Mills, to the superintendent of Indian affairs for British Columbia (who was a Dominion official). Mills stated: 'Indian rights to soil in British Columbia have never been extinguished. Should any difficulty occur, steps will be taken to maintain the Indian claims to all the country where rights have not been extinguished by treaty. Don't desire to raise the question at present but Local Government must instruct Commissioners to make reserves so large as to completely satisfy Indians.'[28] This passage not only summarizes the problem; it anticipates the history of the century that followed. Indian title is acknowledged, as is the apparent need to extinguish it prior to settlement, but the issue is postponed in the hope that generous reserve allotments will make it go away. When the allotments turn out to be less than generous and the problem does not go away Ottawa is faced with a province that will not cooperate in any attempt to take what Mills called steps 'to maintain the Indian claims to ... country where rights have not been extinguished by treaty.'

In the 1920s the chief inspector of Indian agencies in British Columbia confirmed that the federal government's acquiescence had been a serious mistake. W.E. Ditchburn was by then a veteran of a number of attempts to resolve the land question, all of which foundered primarily (but not exclusively) on British Columbia's intransigence. '[O]ne of the outstanding features of this question which is to be regretted,' he told Deputy Superintendent of Indian Affairs Duncan Campbell Scott, was that Ottawa had not maintained 'its disallowance of the B.C. laws affecting Crown lands until some provision had been made for the cession of the Indian title.'[29] Viewed from this perspective, the policy decisions of the 1870s lead, in a straight line, to the Supreme Court of Canada's pronouncements on Aboriginal title in *Delgamuukw v. The Queen* in 1997.[30] However, for those who lived this history the line was anything but straight.

The years between the late 1870s and the First World War saw, among other things, numerous Aboriginal delegations to Victoria, Ottawa, and even London; the appointment of a royal commission to investigate the discontent and violence associated with Indian land and self-government issues on the north coast; increasing tension between British Columbia and Ottawa over the size of Indian reserves and the problem of which government was legally entitled to the proceeds of the sale of reserve lands; the appointment of yet another royal commission (McKenna-McBride) to deal with these issues; and the emergence of tribal[31] and intertribal[32] organizations formed to pursue land claims. In 1913 the Nisga'a presented their famous petition to the imperial Crown, and when the McKenna-McBride Commission completed its report in 1916, the Allied Indian Tribes of British Columbia was established. This body took the land claims issue to Parliament in 1927.[33]

It is important to note two significant changes in how Aboriginal people pressed their claims at this time. The first is that a small number of educated Aboriginal men began to emerge as spokespersons, replacing the missionaries who had often performed this function in the nineteenth century, and who were the target of government criticism as a result.[34] Arguably, the turning point occurred when Peter Kelly, a Haida chosen by his people to represent them at a meeting in Victoria in 1911, opposed the signing of a petition to the provincial government because it had been drafted by missionary C.M. Tate. Kelly believed that petitions drafted by the clergy, begging for grace and understanding, had in the past been singularly ineffective, not least because the government knew that most of the Aboriginal delegates to such meetings could not read. He thought that such petitions should be replaced by demands, formulated politely by Indians themselves, for legal rights.[35] However, the clergy continued to involve themselves in land claims, partly through organizations such as the newly formed 'Friends of the Indians' and the Moral and Social Reform Council of Canada. Indeed, Kelly himself became a Methodist minister not long after his rise to prominence in 1911.

The second important change in this period is the decision to seek counsel from lawyers instead of missionaries. It is at about this time, in 1908 and 1909, that men such as J.M. Clarke in Toronto and Arthur E. O'Meara (who was both a lawyer and a missionary) in British Columbia begin to advise the Nisga'a, the Friends of the Indians, and eventually the

Interior and Allied Tribes.[36] Predictably, both the Dominion and the provincial governments were soon describing lawyers, and especially O'Meara, in terms they had previously reserved for 'meddling' missionaries.[37] The Dominion and provincial governments, of course, had never lacked legal advice; both Fournier and Mills were lawyers, and the department of justice had a few more, besides.[38] The appearance of lawyers on the Indian side was a new and clearly unwelcome development, and it may have influenced Ottawa's decision in 1909 to commission a detailed report on the Indian title question.

But it was Aboriginal discontent with British Columbia's intransigent position on title that got the ball rolling. In 1904, for example, two interior chiefs, after failing to secure an audience with King Edward VII, put their grievances before Pope Leo XIII. Then in 1906 a group of interior and Coast Salish tribes submitted a petition to the imperial Crown and sent a delegation to London consisting of three chiefs, the most prominent of whom was Joe Capilano of the Squamish. King Edward met with them, and more petitions followed.[39]

Two of these petitions were presented to Prime Minister Laurier in 1908 by a delegation of 'chiefs' whose visit was prompted by the construction of the Grand Trunk Pacific Railway in the north of the province.[40] For present purposes, this grievance is of particular significance because three of these delegates were Gitksan, who eighty years later would be plaintiffs in *Delgamuukw*, and they travelled to Ottawa because they were concerned that land grants in their traditional territories on the Skeena River violated their title.[41] This in turn led Prime Minister Laurier to consider whether it was time for the courts to consider the B.C. Indian land question. His resolve may have been further influenced in March of 1909 when lawyers Clark and O'Meara travelled to London on behalf of the Cowichan people on Vancouver Island and presented yet another petition, this time one for a treaty based on the requirements of the Royal Proclamation of 1763.[42]

ENTER TOM MACINNES

A month later, the Hon. Frank Oliver, Dominion minister of the interior and superintendent general of Indian affairs, retained lawyer T.R.E. McInnes – whose *nom de plume* was Tom MacInnes – 'to investigate and report upon the nature and present status of the Indian Title to certain lands known as "Indian Lands" in Canada, with special reference to British Columbia.'[43] The text of MacInnes's report provides strong evidence that Ottawa's decision to commission it was prompted by the troubles in the northern part of the province. He accuses the government of British Columbia of 'an attempt to dispossess the Skeena Indians from the lands occupied by them from time immemorial' and, as we have seen, proposes that legal action be taken to prevent this.[44] MacInnes also notes that, only three weeks earlier, Premier Richard McBride was reported in the Montreal *Star* as stating, in reference to protests over land grants in the Skeena, that 'it would be madness to think of conceding the Indians' demands.' It was, said the premier, 'too late to discuss the equity of dispossessing the red man in America.'[45]

It is interesting that the Indian title report was not the only task MacInnes undertook for the Dominion government at this time. As *The Canadian Who's Who* put it in 1936, he 'executed a few confidential comns. under instrs. of Sir Wilfrid Laurier and the Hon. Frank Oliver, 1907–1911,'[46] notably the drafting of the narcotics and immigration legislation associated with the cabinet responsibilities of W.L. Mackenzie King. These facts are almost invariably mentioned in most standard sources and in MacInnes's obituary notices.[47] But the same sources make no mention of MacInnes's report on Indian title.[48] It is true that in 1913 the report surfaced briefly in the House of Commons, but it was not printed and MacInnes was not named.[49] Indeed, except for Forrest E. La Violette, who refers to MacInnes in his 1961 book on the Protestant ethic and Aboriginal culture in British Columbia, no one has regarded the report worthy of academic attention: it seems to have sunk almost without a trace.[50]

The author of this elusive document was Thomas Robert Edward McInnes (who will be referred to as Tom MacInnes from now on). MacInnes was born in 1867 in Dresden, Ontario, a town which for years had been a haven for escaped slaves.[51] The family's decision to settle in Dresden is interesting, given that MacInnes's father had been a surgeon on the southern side in the American Civil War. They did not stay long, however. Thomas Robert McInnes (1840–1904) completed his medical training in Chicago and involved himself in municipal politics in Dresden, but then decided that it was time to go west. He took his family to New Westminster, British Columbia, in 1874, where he practised both medicine and politics, becoming a member of Parliament in 1878 and a senator in 1881.[52] Young Thomas went to school in British Columbia and then attended the University of Toronto and Osgoode Hall. In 1889 he was admitted as a student-at-law by the Law Society of Upper Canada and articled to Ira Standish, esq. Four years later he successfully completed the British Columbia bar examination after articling with Hezekiah George Hall.[53] Once called to the bar, he practised law in Nanaimo on Vancouver Island with his younger brother, William Wallace Burns McInnes.

Before continuing the son's life story, however, it is necessary to say a little more about McInnes the father, not so much because he looms larger in the history of British Columbia than his son (which he does), but because the careers of the two men came to be connected. McInnes Sr was appointed lieutenant-governor of British Columbia in 1897 and promptly made his son Tom his official secretary. The elder McInnes is known to posterity for having the most controversial term of office conceivable for what is normally a largely ceremonial position. The details are beyond the scope of the present chapter, but suffice it to say that he is probably the only lieutenant-governor to endure having every member of the legislature (save one) get up and leave when he began to read the speech from the throne. In 1900 McInnes was dismissed from office; only one other Canadian lieutenant-governor has suffered that fate.[54] Tom MacInnes later maintained 'emphatically' that the real reasons for his father's dismissal were two: Prime Minister Laurier's hostility to Joseph Martin, the man his father chose to form a government during a legislative crisis, and the opposition of big business.[55]

It was during these years that Tom MacInnes seems to have developed a certain distrust for most provincial politicians. Between 1898 and 1903 British Columbia had six premiers, and when Lieutenant-Governor McInnes selected Martin he was on his third in two years. He had dismissed the first, Premier John Herbert Turner, in August of 1898 when Turner refused to resign after having lost his majority in the July election.[56] A controversy of sorts developed over the role of the lieutenant-governor's two sons in all this, and on 28 August Tom MacInnes wrote a lengthy letter to the editor refuting the allegations made against him. It was published under the heading, 'Now the Secretary: What Mr. T.R.E. McInnes Says of His Reported Suggestions to the Premier. He Does Not Forget an Old Prosecution and Writes Quite Bitterly.'[57]

The prosecution referred to had taken place during Premier Turner's term of office, when the McInnes brothers were in practice in Nanaimo. In his letter to the editor, MacInnes described it as an attempt by the Turner administration 'to wreak its political malice on me ... with special case, special assize, special Crown prosecutor, and very special evidence ...'[58] He provides no details – presumably most readers would have known them – but it appears that, by engaging in a rather creative attempt to bring certain irregularities in the police and local magistracy to public attention, the brothers ended up being charged at the spring assizes in 1895 with compounding a *qui tam* action.[59] The jury took only ten minutes to acquit, and the experience did not prevent William Wallace Burns McInnes being appointed a county court judge in 1909. But Justice George Anthony

Walkem, who presided at the trial, was critical of both defence and prosecution, remarking somewhat oddly that he 'regretted ... that some of Nanaimo's dirty linen should have been washed in court' rather than 'left at home.'[60]

Both the prosecution and MacInnes's use of it years later seem typical: he had a capacity for controversy and was willing to assert strong opinions.[61] These qualities are apparent both in his 1909 report on Indian title and in a short poem over his signature in the autograph album of the Vagabond Club, an association of writers and artists that flourished in Vancouver between 1914 and 1928. 'I would rather go down with those I love,' he wrote, '[t]han float among those I hate!'[62]

Although Tom MacInnes's relations with provincial politicians were stormy, his brother, who is usually referred to as W.W.B. McInnes, became provincial secretary and minister of education in Premier Edward Gawler Prior's administration (1902–3) before his appointment to the bench. For Tom, however, government work seemed to come only from Ottawa. This may have been because, notwithstanding his father's dismissal by Laurier, his brother – who had been elected MP for Nanaimo in 1896 – was a Laurier 'protégé.'[63] Whatever the reason, Tom MacInnes was appointed secretary to the Bering Sea Claims Commission in 1896–7, and then spent some time in the Yukon with a special police and customs force set up by Ottawa. After two years as his father's secretary during the latter's term as lieutenant-governor, MacInnes accepted the post of secretary to the B.C. Salmon Fisheries Commission. In 1907 he acted for Chinese who had lost property in the race riots in Vancouver that year and apparently wrote a 'secret' report on the riots for the Dominion government.[64] As we have seen, he then carried out a number of tasks at the request of the Dominion until the defeat of the Laurier government in 1911.[65]

In 1908, at the age of forty, MacInnes published his first volume of poetry, A Romance of the Lost. More were to follow: In Amber Lands (1910), Rhymes of a Rounder (1913), Roundabout Rhymes (1923), Complete Poems (1923), and High Low Along (1934). When Rhymes of a Rounder was republished in the 1930s, MacInnes was guest of honour at the annual meeting of the League of Western Writers, whose bulletin described him as 'one of the foremost of living Canadian poets.' MacInnes and Wilson MacDonald, it went on, were the only two who 'dared to be original.' Rhymes of a Rounder included an excerpt from an earlier review by the Toronto Globe critic describing MacInnes as 'a poet of considerable power and daring ... bolder than [Robert] Service.' When Prof. E.K. Brown wrote an assessment of Canadian poetry in 1935 he singled out MacInnes's Rhymes of a Rounder as one of three collections that represented 'the most solid gains of the year.'[66] And according to (Sir) Charles G.D. Roberts, even Bliss Carmen thought highly of MacInnes.[67] We may smile at such assessments now, but they speak to his position in the 'Canlit' of his day.

Between 1916 and 1927 MacInnes was in China for much of the time, and this proved to be a bitter experience. Discussions with Sun Yat Sen led to 'a concession to modernize transportation in Canton' and, after raising Chinese capital for the project, he tore down the ancient city wall and widened boulevards for a bus system.[68] MacInnes was by this time the only foreign director of the Kwontung Tramway Company, a position he held from 1919 until 1924, and he had a high opinion of some of the Asian capitalists who were his partners in the project. But China was hardly a stable nation in the 1920s, and civil war forced his return to Canada. One of his poems strikingly evokes a time in which he nearly died during this period, but it was the missed opportunity that plagued him.[69] As he put it, the scheme for running streetcars in Canton was conceived in the autumn of 1916 after 'several talks with Sun Yat Sen at his guarded residence on Rue Vallon' in Shanghai. 'My scheme was sober, compared to the ones he was nursing, and it came to flower in spite of obstacles and my ignorance, and promised gorgeously. But I had no fruit of it.' Control, he said, was seized by 'Bolsheviks and blackguards.'[70] This experience also seems to have changed MacInnes's attitude towards Asia. Soon the man who had acted for the Chinese victims of the Vancouver riots was writing articles 'in which he played on existing prejudices against Orientals living in the province.'[71] These were collected and published in 1927 as the *Oriental Occupation of British Columbia*.[72]

From then on MacInnes seems to have spent a great deal of time propagating his antisocialist views, which were no doubt fortified by his Chinese adventure. For example, in a letter to the newspapers in 1936 he complained about a 'weepy' article by Harold Winch, a provincial MLA and CCF party member.[73] The article was about the hanging of convicted murderer Earl Dunbar at Oakalla Prison, and to MacInnes it was part of 'a deliberate campaign in progress by revolutionary elements in Canada to play up the violent criminal as purely a product of the present social system.'[74] Dunbar had been the 'wheel man' in an armed robbery and his defence was duress, that is, he told the court that the others had threatened to kill him if he did not help. He took no part in the robbery itself (he stayed in the car), but someone was killed and Dunbar was convicted and hanged. Years later, the law facilitating this result changed, and not in the direction advocated by MacInnes.[75]

In 1937 trade unionist Burt Showler sued MacInnes for libel because he had stated in one of his regular radio broadcasts on radio station CKMO that Showler had cooperated 'with strike leaders in the United States in an effort to bring about a strike of all teamsters here.' A year later, MacInnes was 'banned from the air' for his antilabour broadcasts but reinstated when he threatened the CBC with a lawsuit. During this period he was also involved with the Nationalist League of Canada. According to that party's basic principles, Canada required only one government and one national bank, one national system of insurance and one police force; money should 'no longer be a commodity,' that is, an end should be 'put within Canada [to] making money by lending money as a private business'; and there should be only five provinces, each administered by an appointed governor and a small, provincially elected council.[76] In short, MacInnes was a complex and, like most of us, not always an entirely consistent human being.

Other than his opposition to usury, there seems to be little in all this to account for the conclusions that he reached in his 1909 report on Indian title. However, the *Oriental Occupation of British Columbia* was not MacInnes's only book of prose. He also wrote *The Teaching of the Old Boy* (1927), a translation and interpretation of the philosophy of Lao-Tse, and *Chinook Days* (1926), dealing with stories and memories of provincial history and Aboriginal culture and life. A self-described animist, he wrote in his sixties that '[s]cientists who confine their work to the basement are apt to become soused with what they find there, and going on then entirely by dead reckoning they report the world deader and deader the farther they go ... Since childhood I have been vaguely aware of another quality of life in certain places through the wilderness ... in parts of Canada, where fortunately men can never find it worthwhile to settle and work.'[77] Perhaps this attitude, coupled with an attachment to the monarchy and his obvious preference for the Dominion as opposed to the provincial government, provides some insight into the frame of mind he brought to the task he undertook in April 1909.

Some literary assessments of MacInnes also confirm that, poetically as well as politically, he marched to a different drum. For example, one critic wrote that it was evident that MacInnes's 'philosophy of life runs counter to that usually accepted by Canadians,' and that, as a consequence, his importance had been underestimated.[78] The author of the introduction to *High Low Along* also liked MacInnes's verses, and in the following passage probably says as much about the nation in which the poet lived as he does about the poet: 'MacInnes appears to be inordinately opinionated. He is

openly sceptical regarding accepted conclusions of both science and religion. He goes so far as to ridicule belief in unalterable natural laws. Such
an attitude is not approved in Canada, where the reading public adheres
to the best standards of the Nineteenth Century in such things, and is not,
in any case, inclined to take seriously from a Canadian writer what has not
first been endorsed abroad.'[79] But the 'reading public' never got to see
what may have been MacInnes's only written work that did contain views
that had, after a fashion, already been endorsed abroad. His report on
Indian title relied heavily on British policy, the Royal Proclamation of
1763, and what the Supreme Court of the United States had said about
Indian title a century earlier.[80] Nonetheless, successive governments of
British Columbia still did not take such title seriously – or perhaps they
did, and consequently strove assiduously to keep the issue from the
courts.

MACINNES'S REPORT ON INDIAN TITLE IN CANADA

The report MacInnes submitted to the minister of the interior on 20 August
1909 is divided into four parts:

1. The General Title recognized;
2. The Title Recognized by the English;
3. The Title Recognized by British Columbia; and,
4. The True Nature of the Indian Title.

However, he proves unable to keep the argument so neatly confined; as a
result, topics appear and reappear, only to be deferred and then taken up
once again. Although the present account more or less follows the order in
the document, it will group the topics a little differently and focus only on
those details that illustrate MacInnes's main theses.

Throughout the report, MacInnes's primary emphasis is on the control-
ling authority of the imperial Crown and imperial law, on the need for
Aboriginal consent to land surrenders, and on what he conceives to be the
illegal and dishonest behaviour of settler governments – particularly in
British Columbia. Noting that the corporate seal of the Corporation of
Massachusetts was 'the figure of an Indian, erect, naked, a bow in one
hand, an arrow in the other, with these words, – "Come over and help us,"'
MacInnes sourly observed that what the colonists did instead was 'come
over and help themselves.'[81] With respect to the legal situation, he is even
more emphatic: '[N]o declaration or act of the Dominion Government, or

of any Provincial Government, nor of both acting conjointly, can *without the express consent of the Indians concerned and of the Imperial Government,* derogate from the Indian Title or appropriate the reversionary interest in Indian lands.'[82] The remainder of the report is devoted to constructing a historical narrative and the legal argument based on this narrative. For reasons of space, both can only be outlined, relatively uncritically.

British Imperial Policy

MacInnes began by asserting that, by way of contrast with Mexico and Peru, the Aboriginal peoples of North America 'were never dispossessed of their lands by any European Government.'[83] Instead, land was taken by purchase or treaty. The English met 'the sachems of the Five Nations and assumed the "Covenant Chain" of the Dutch which was, and has remained, so far as the Five Nations (now the Six Nations) are concerned, unbroken ever since.'[84] Citing the U.S. Supreme Court decisions in *Worcester v. Georgia* and *Mitchell et al. v. United States,* MacInnes concluded that, 'whether it was the souls or the skins of the Indians which most concerned the Europeans,' there was no dispossession of the former '*vi et armis.*'[85]

When he embarked upon his examination of English practice MacInnes made a distinction that animates the remainder of the report. From the beginning of the eighteenth century, he maintained, Europeans, insofar as the tribes were concerned, separated into two groups: 'the European colonists, who tended more and more to become unfriendly, and the European sovereigns, governments, soldiers and merchants, who continued friendly and disposed to uphold the rights of the Indians as against the interests of the colonists.'[86] As time went on,

the needs and fears and land hunger of the colonists ... made them jealous of and antagonistic to Indian rights and privileges, and officially and unofficially, through such powers of local government as were gradually accorded to them by the King they began a policy of ignoring or belittling the Indian Title, and they became more insistent in pursuit of this policy as they became numerically stronger. A century later a repetition of this policy was begun by whites in British Columbia. The Indians on the other hand at no time made, and to this day will not make, an appeal to a colonial, provincial or federal government in Canada as the sovereign power from whom they ask recognition of their title. Their appeal has always been made, and from British Columbia is now being made, direct to the King.[87]

MacInnes then asserted, correctly, that the archives are full of documents –

despatches, royal instructions, military communications, etc. – that confirm the imperial policy of recognizing title 'from motives of natural justice, religion, trade, good politics and general necessity.' But these documents also confirm a 'gradual divergence of interest between the mother-country and the colonies in regard thereto.'[88]

Now, he lamented, 'we are apt to forget or overlook ... the circumstances existing at the time when we entered into an obligation – when a promise was given for a promise – between ourselves and the Indians.' Citing as a recent example the remarks of Premier McBride about what MacInnes refered to as British Columbia's 'attempt to dispossess the Skeena Indians' from their lands,[89] he concluded that colonial and provincial governments, 'presuming to act in the name of the King, have insidiously evaded and made that promise of little or no effect, and this is particularly true of the Government of British Columbia after the Imperial Government entrusted it with carrying out the Imperial policy towards the Indians begun under the regime of Sir James Douglas.'[90]

MacInnes cited extract after extract from books and archival records to show that the Indians were 'recognized and treated with' as separate nations; that they were regarded first as allies, 'by degrees assuming the status of subjects with rights and privileges distinct from ordinary colonial subjects'; that, whether regarded as allies or subjects, 'the King gave instructions to respect the Indian Title to lands occupied by them'; and that when France ceded Canada to Britain the French King 'stipulated that his Indian allies should be maintained in quiet possession of their lands the same as his French Canadian subjects' – a stipulation that was 'agreed to by the English King.'[91] Unfortunately, he said, these policies lasted only so long as 'restraint' was imposed by England. In Massachusetts and elsewhere, colonists 'had the advantage of constantly arriving reinforcements, weapons and wealth.' Moreover, they were 'as calculating, treacherous and cruel towards the Indian nations as any of the Indians were ever shown to be toward each other or toward the Colonists.'[92] MacInnes then referred to the complaint of Vancouver Island settler Dods, quoted above.[93]

When he came to the Royal Proclamation of 1763, MacInnes anticipated the Supreme Court of Canada by more than sixty years by insisting that it be viewed as a document 'recognizing and confirming – not creating as some have supposed – the Indian Title.'[94] He noted that it was referred to with approval by the U.S. Supreme Court and asserted that in the leading case of *Campbell v. Hall* Lord Mansfield interpreted it as having statutory force in Canada.[95] MacInnes then addressed issues specific to British Columbia.

British Columbia

The section dealing with British Columbia is without a doubt the most interesting in the report, because it anticipates not only the legal developments of the late twentieth century but the historical scholarship of recent years as well. MacInnes began by stating unequivocally that, after the retirement of Governor Douglas, 'there was an official colonial policy pursued in British Columbia which apparently was designed to lower the nature of the Indian Title till it should be regarded as a mere charity – till the Indians should be held to be in no better position than tenants on sufferance of Crown Lands subject to colonial regulations as regards cutting timber and working mines thereon – having at best 'squatter rights' and no more.'[96] And who, according to MacInnes, was the architect of this policy? More than sixty years before Robin Fisher's damning *BC Studies* portrait of the province's first lieutenant-governor, MacInnes pointed his finger squarely at Joseph William Trutch.[97]

However, before proceeding to make his case against Trutch he dealt with the legal basis of Indian title in British Columbia, and he started by providing another clue as to why Ottawa retained him. Only ten months earlier, in November of 1908, the B.C. government had referred 'certain questions' relating to Indian lands to the Full Court of the province.[98] Ottawa would not take part, preferring that any reference be made directly to the Supreme Court of Canada; as a result, the province's case went nowhere.[99] But British Columbia's lawyers filed submissions with the court which MacInnes had seen, and these included a copy of Edward Blake's argument in *St. Catherine's Milling and Lumber Company v. The Queen*, a case the B.C. government relied on heavily.[100]

One might have thought that MacInnes rather than British Columbia would seek comfort from *St. Catherine's*, because in it the Judicial Committee of the Privy Council states that if lands within a province are subject to Indian title they may not be exploited as 'a source of revenue' until that title is extinguished.[101] However, British Columbia was citing the decision to support its argument that whenever reserve land was surrendered the underlying title of the province (British Columbia's 'reversionary interest') was perfected, and, possibly because the province had embraced the decision in this fashion, a crucial distinction between the facts of *St. Catherine's* and the situation in British Columbia was ignored.

Indian reserves, properly so called, were not the issue in *St. Catherine's* – Indian title was.[102] In *St. Catherine's*, the Indian title to lands determined to be within Ontario had been extinguished by treaty, and the issue was which government controls those lands and their resources, Ottawa or Ontario? The answer was Ontario. In British Columbia, however, the Indian title had *not* been extinguished; and, according to the Privy Council, this meant that the province could *not* use the land 'as a source of revenue.'[103] *St. Catherine's*, therefore, may have been of some tactical use to British Columbia on the reserve question because it held that the underlying title was provincial, but, assuming that the lack of treaties west of the Rockies means that there was (and is) unextinguished Indian title there, the decision stands squarely in the way of any local attempt to settle or exploit lands subject to that title. Hence the B.C. government's stoutly maintained position that, uniquely, there was no such title in their province, and its grimly determined efforts to ensure that this position would never be exposed to the scrutiny of the courts.[104]

But MacInnes – like many others before and since – did not focus on this aspect of *St. Catherine's*. Instead, he proceeded, in some detail, to argue that the grant of Vancouver Island to the Hudson's Bay Company in 1849, although complete on its face, 'could not affect the rights of those already in possession ... as aboriginal occupants' or as occupants whose claim was based on a discovery 'made before the memory of man.'[105] He then cited what are now well-known colonial despatches to establish the same principle for mainland British Columbia and provided a noteworthy interpretation of Governor Douglas's Land Ordinance of 14 February 1859, which provided that all the lands in the new colony belonged 'to the Crown in fee.' This ordinance would become one of the foundations of British Columbia's legal argument that there was no Aboriginal title in the province. Indeed, from the *Calder* case in the 1960s to the trial in *Delgamuukw* in the late 1980s, British Columbia argued that this and other colonial laws extinguished all such title prior to Confederation.

MacInnes's position, however, was that the Crown *grants* land in fee, it does not hold *ungranted* land in fee; fee, in other words, describes a heritable tenement, and the Crown is never a tenant.[106] He therefore argued that Douglas could not have meant that all the land belonged to the Crown in fee, pointing out that there was clearly a great deal of land – for example, lands reserved by the Royal Proclamation and lands purchased by the Hudson's Bay Company from the Indians – that did not fit this description. What Douglas did mean, said MacInnes, may be gleaned from the course of his administration and the legal principles that bound him, and these reveal two things. The first is that, by proclaiming that the Crown owned all land in fee, Douglas 'could have only meant to proclaim the common law doctrine that the Crown is the Lord Paramount of all the lands in the Kingdom.'[107] In other words, in order to secure 'the protection of the Crown for the Indians against improvident sale to the Colonists,' Douglas was asserting that only the Crown could make grants of land, and therefore that 'the right of escheat or reversionary interest was in the Crown.' This is of course pretty much the doctrine that has been most succinctly laid out in the late twentieth century by the High Court of Australia in *Mabo v. Queensland [No. 2]*.[108]

Even more interesting is the second conclusion that MacInnes drew from the evidence. Citing in support the letter that Douglas wrote to the secretary of state for the colonies when he sent him a copy of the Land Ordinance, MacInnes argued that the 'whole of Governor Douglas' administration and instructions to his subordinates proves beyond question that he distinguished between Crown lands and Indian Lands. He knew personally the great areas unoccupied by any tribe of Indians. And he knew personally the small areas occupied by the several Indian tribes. And recognizing things as they were he took the Indians' word for it as to what constituted the limits of their several territories, and fixed their limits accordingly.'[109] In short, Douglas appears to have taken the view that the Indians were entitled to their villages, fields, hunting grounds, and favourite fishing spots, even perhaps to other areas they thought necessary to support themselves in the new economy. He also appears to have thought – although MacInnes does not say this – that, so long as the Indians themselves set the boundaries of such lands, no formal treaty process was necessary.

What, then, did MacInnes make of the imperial government's apparent refusal in 1861 to provide funds for the purpose of extinguishing the Indian title to lands designated by the Indians as theirs, but which the colony wanted for settlement? Here the argument becomes more complex. The colonial legislature had formally recognized the Indian title and petitioned the imperial government for help in extinguishing it. Douglas sent this petition to the secretary of state for the colonies, asking for money for this purpose. According to MacInnes the legislature had to do this, because the underlying title, or reversion, was in the imperial Crown, and the colony 'had not the power of itself to extinguish [the Indian] title.' The colony, to be sure, had full authority over lands that were not subject to the circumscribed Indian title described above, that is, to unoccupied lands unclaimed by any tribe, but not to public lands 'to which an Indian title adhered.'[110] Thus although the Duke of Newcastle in his well-known reply to Douglas gave the go-ahead to extinguishment and indeed 'earnestly recommended' that this be done, it was, to MacInnes, 'reasonable enough' for the imperial government to refuse 'to make the Colony a present of the Indian Title or of its reversionary interest in the Indian lands.' The colony did not take Newcastle's advice and did not extinguish the title. Moreover, said MacInnes, it *has not done so to this day.*' He therefore asked 'by what occult process' could the provincial government 'have acquired *for nothing* the Indian Title and reversionary interest which it now [in 1909] claims, and which the Colonial Government acknowledged it did not possess ...'? The answer, he concluded, 'is a mystery.'[111]

Another mystery has been why, after Confederation, there was no formal conveyance to Ottawa of the lands set aside as Indian reserves.[112] According to MacInnes, when British Columbia transferred the Railway Belt to Ottawa pursuant to Article 11 of the Terms of Union, 1871, it did so formally, by Crown grant. But the land set aside by the reserve commissioners as Indian reserves had not been conveyed in this way. The obvious speculation is that the province made no formal conveyance so it could retain control of the land while it bargained with Ottawa, and in the late twentieth century some courts have decided, surprisingly, that this disreputable tactic (assuming that is what it was) was effective.[113] MacInnes, as we might expect by now, had another explanation.

According to him, no conveyance was made of these lands because they were not Crown lands; at least, they were not lands owned by the Crown in the right of the province, which British Columbia 'had inherited from the preceding Colonial Government.' Quite the contrary. Whether they had been adequately defined or not, these lands were, in MacInnes's view 'in a class by themselves.' They were 'Indian Lands and Indian Settlements within the meaning and wording of the Proclamation of 1763.'[114] As such, they could not be the subject of a provincial grant. Once it was determined that particular lands were Indian lands, all the province 'could properly do was to signify its acquiescence in the action of the [Reserve] Commissioners.' On occasion the province did this by order in council, 'such as that of the 20th April 1878 [regarding reserves in the Electoral District of Yale], ... sometimes it did this by letter.'[115] The point, said MacInnes, is that the agreement setting up the reserve commission was a 'mere matter of arrangement' between the province and Ottawa for expediting the allotment process, 'to which agreement neither the Indians nor the Imperial Government were parties, or ever gave assent.'[116]

This view is interesting on two counts. In the nineteenth century Ottawa and British Columbia appear to have been genuinely uncertain about how the reserve transfer should take place. In 1879 Reserve Commissioner Gilbert Malcolm Sproat had been concerned about this, and Ottawa told him that patents should be issued. When this was not done, Ottawa informed Superintendent Powell in 1881 to treat allotted reserves 'as formally held in trust by [the Dominion Government] for the Indians' anyway.[117] Seven years later the two governments sent delegates, one of whom was Provincial Secretary John Robson, to a meeting in Ottawa to attempt to resolve this and a number of other issues. It appears that the delegates agreed that no formal grants or letters patent were necessary, but it is unclear whether they thought an order-in-council was required.[118] Today, however, British Columbia has taken the position that, until the reserves were formally conveyed by order-in-council in 1938, they were not 'lands reserved for the Indians' under federal jurisdiction.[119]

Secondly, MacInnes's position on this question is noteworthy because of his description of Indian reserves as being 'in a class by themselves' and therefore outside normal conveyancing rules. In 1912, the Supreme Court of British Columbia had to determine in *Gosnell v. Minister of Lands (B.C.) and A.G. (Canada)* whether the failure of the province to 'gazette' its Indian reserves as required by statute meant that, legally, they were not Indian reserves. In the 1990s some judges have drawn the somewhat startling conclusion that this was indeed the case.[120] Chief Justice Hunter, however, ruled that no formal transfer or conveyance was necessary 'to effectually segregate these lands.' Reserve allotments were transactions 'altogether outside the regular course which is provided for in the local statutes.'[121] Had the chief justice, one wonders, read MacInnes's opinion?

The report goes on to address another debate that has plagued British Columbia in the 1990s. The precise definition of Aboriginal title has always been uncertain, with some writers suggesting that it is a form of ownership and others regarding it as a lesser interest. Treaties, however, have always distinguished between Indian title on the one hand and rights to hunt and fish on the other, usually extinguishing the former but preserving the latter as treaty rights. This distinction alone suggests a wider meaning for title. Yet some critics of the B.C. treaty process that was established in 1993 argue that negotiations have gone way beyond what Aboriginal people are entitled to on the basis of court rulings, contending that these rulings establish that Aboriginal title amounts to little more than an non-exclusive right to hunt and fish, etc. on unoccupied lands.[122] This view has now been definitively rejected by the Supreme Court of Canada in *Delgamuukw*, but the fact that it took so long to kill is compelling evidence of the persistence of the settler mentality.

In 1909, MacInnes concluded that Indian title is indeed a form of ownership, and in so doing he used the submissions of Edward Blake in the *St.*

Catherine's case as a foil. Blake is a frequent target of MacInnes in his report, and he criticized him here for arguing that Indian title is no more than 'a right or easement to hunt and fish.' Using Blake's own report of the submissions before the Privy Council to argue the contrary, MacInnes pointed out that on Vancouver Island Governor Douglas 'bought title to large areas subject to an easement by which Indians were to be "at liberty to hunt over the unoccupied land and carry on their fisheries as formerly." That is to say after the Indians sold a part of their land to ... Douglas, they retained in the lands thus surrendered the full right and title which Mr. Blake would have us believe was all they had in the first place – a right to hunt and fish ...'[123] Obviously if this were true, the Hudson's Bay Company 'paid out its good money for nothing.' But it is not true, said MacInnes, who then made the interesting suggestion that Indian title, 'if not a fee simple, was at the least, a fee tail in each tribe.'[124] Citing the fact that Indians were allies of the King who had 'faithfully' answered his call to military service on many occasions, MacInnes concluded that nothing had happened since the eighteenth century to change the nature of this essentially 'feudal' tenure. The estate is 'one of freehold ... unlimited as to duration, and passed by inheritance.'[125]

The report then documented the activities of the chief commissioner of lands and works in the 1860s, Joseph William Trutch, in particular the decision by Trutch and Colonial Secretary W.A.G. Young to reduce the size of reserves laid out by royal engineers in the lower Fraser and Kamloops regions of the colony. Denying that Governor Douglas had ever issued any written instructions that Indians were entitled to as much land as they wished, Trutch and Young accused the engineers of having misunderstood the verbal instructions Douglas may have given them. Trutch then proceeded to reduce these reserves in size.[126]

Today, anyone who cares to read the *Papers Connected with the Indian Land Question 1850–1875*, which were not easily accessible until about ten years ago, can see that Trutch's version is false.[127] Written instructions by Douglas did exist, and Trutch must have known this. In 1909, MacInnes went to the archives and proved these charges, accusing Trutch of 'deliberately misinforming' the Indians when he told them that the engineers had no authority to lay out as much land as they had. MacInnes also uncovered a letter by Douglas himself, written years after his retirement, confirming that the men who had originally laid out the reserves had correctly understood him.[128] The tenor of MacInnes's views may be gleaned from a passage in which he began by saying Douglas's letter made it unnecessary for him to 'characterize the statements and conduct' of Trutch and other officials 'who encroached on the Indian rights after the regime of Governor Douglas.' But he did so anyway. The letter, he said, 'fully vindicates' the men who had laid out the reserves. They were soldiers, 'and as such, accustomed to execute their instructions exactly as they received them from their superior officer.' Douglas's letter proved that this is what they had done when allotting reserves. It also proved that 'when Sir Joseph Trutch repudiated their official acts and materially reduced the Indian reserves defined by them, he robbed the Indians of their land.'[129]

The Nature of Indian Title

In the last part of his report MacInnes made the statement that appears at the beginning of this chapter. But he acknowledged that the 'ordinary Canadian citizen of today' is unaware of the law and history he had outlined, and that it therefore 'comes rather as a surprise to be told that the Indians have or claim to have any inherent title to land in Canada. They are prone to look upon Indians as undesirable and incapable public charges whom the Government is unable to deport to another country as in the case of undesirable immigrants, and consequently rounds them up and confines them in limited remote districts where they will not be a nuisance to the whites.' Even the 'ordinary lawyer looks askance at the Indian title,' said MacInnes, because it does not fit very well with what he has been taught about land tenure.[130] Once again, his prime example of this sort of thinking is Edward Blake, counsel for Ontario in the *St. Catherine's* case.

Blake did not like the 'mystery and magic' of Indian title; he therefore characterized it as much less than ownership, stressing its inalienability to anyone other than the Crown. So MacInnes made the obvious point: although today alienability is associated with ownership, in earlier times owners were people 'whose right to maintain or recover possession was secured by law,' even though their power of disposition might be limited.[131] He then noted that in the eighteenth century settlers in Upper Canada held title by certificates of occupation, and 'were not always free to alienate such land.' Moreover, he says, we should not ask when title passed from the sovereign to the Indian, as Justice Taschereau did when the *St. Catherine's* case was before the Supreme Court of Canada, but rather, when did it pass from the Indian to the sovereign?[132] Of this sort of European pretension, which began in the sixteenth century, he said: 'It was a great age for making claims. The Pope claimed to be the disposer of the Kingdoms of this world, but ... he was not. The King of England claimed to be the King of France, but he was not. The King of France claimed to be the ruler of "the western extremity of Asia" because Jacques Cartier had discovered Hochelaga; but he was not. The rulers of those days were good claimers, but they could not make their claims good.'[133]

MacInnes then reproduced portions of the argument in the Privy Council in which everyone acknowledged that, although terrible things have been done 'in the name of Christianity in taking possession of land,' the doctrine that the law is what pleases the strong had never been the law of England. Yet when Blake doubted that 'the Indian conceived of having any title to his land' and argued that such title is whatever the sovereign, rather than the courts, chooses to say it is, there was no real dissent.[134] This silence clearly irritated MacInnes, who cited examples from B.C. records that show a clear appreciation of title (although he displayed some ignorance of the nature of land tenure on the coast). He also took exception to Blake's assertion that a 'gentle pressure has always been put upon the Indian' to sell his land, 'to which pressure he has always yielded.' The King, said MacInnes, had never done this, 'however much the Colonial or Provincial Governments are disposed to do so.'[135]

After stressing that, where they have not been 'utterly discouraged by whites' Aboriginal people often proved adept at agriculture and stock-raising, he assailed Blake yet again for his definition of Indian title as a mere easement to hunt and fish. Blake, he said, 'would have us believe that hunting and fishing was the only use of land known to the Indian, that he was a mere vagrant hunter living from hand to mouth on the game he found.' History, said MacInnes, 'proves this notion to be false.' It therefore 'cannot now be honorably or logically contended' that all the King meant when he promised that Aboriginal lands would be protected and that the tribes would be maintained in possession was an easement to hunt and fish.[136]

Why this obsession with Blake? Because counsel before the Full Court of British Columbia in November 1908 had relied so heavily on Blake's submissions in the *St. Catherine's* case. It irked MacInnes that 'many of Mr. Blake's inaccurate statements' to the Privy Council, which appeared to 'have gone unchallenged by learned counsel for the Dominion Government,' had been presented to the B.C. court as having some sort of authority.[137] To MacInnes, the most likely reason for this omission was that although there were four interested parties, only Ottawa and Ontario were really before the court, and they were concerned only with their own interests. For MacInnes, the only way to 'settle the questions raised by the Government of British Columbia last November' in an authoritative way was to include the other two parties: the imperial government and the

Indians.[138] Otherwise an unfair decision would result.[139] He stated that 'the interests of the Indians and of the Dominion Government might not always be one – the trustee might have an adverse interest.' To avoid this possibility, he concluded, the Indians should have their own lawyer, 'solely upholding their claims and unconcerned with mere questions of advantage as between the Dominion and Provincial Government.' Of course this is what, eighteen years later, Parliament decided specifically to prohibit.[140]

Finally, MacInnes addressed what he conceived to be the heart of Blake's position, which is that in the end it was policy, not law, 'which induced the English to make the representations which they did to the Indians ... and to enter into treaties with them.' Of course, he said, but to suggest that this means they can be repudiated is 'monstrous.' All such agreements are a matter of policy, 'but that never justifies repudiation when the policy is no longer felt to be imperative or pressing. It was policy which induced the British Government to grant to the French Canadians the right to their own laws, religion and language. But who would now attempt to justify repudiation of those rights because the policy – the pressing necessity – which led in the first place to their being granted, has now abated? It is conceivable that the French Canadian population in comparison with the general population of Canada will, a century from now, be small. Yet their rights will be as sacred then as now.'[141]

Blake, he argued, was of the view that the words of obligation in the Royal Proclamation and the treaties were 'swelling words,' put in to 'please the Indians' but without real legal effect. When the Earl of Selbourne said, 'There is no magic in the word "treaty" of course,' Blake replied: 'No; it is simply a bargain [and] the language ... is rather the language of bounty and good will.' 'How much more honest,' retorted MacInnes, 'and in accord with fundamental principles of law' is the meaning accorded to Indian treaties by the Supreme Court of the United States. To this end he quoted Chief Justice Marshall's view that the words 'treaty' and 'nation' are 'words of our own language, selected in our diplomatic and legislative proceedings by ourselves, and having each a definite and well understood meaning.' Marshall noted that both the British and the Americans had applied these terms 'to the Indians, as [they had] applied them to the other nations of the earth. They are applied to all in the same sense.'[142]

MacInnes concluded his report by referring once again to the province's abortive attempt to refer the question of its reversionary interest to the B.C. courts, and affirming that any such interest in Indian lands in British Columbia 'has never been parted with by the Imperial Government.'

Therefore, he said, the 'Indians today are technically correct in making appeal direct to the King ... whenever they think their title is being infringed [by the province], or ... their trustee, the Dominion Government, is not properly protecting their interests and title.'[143] Then, as we have seen, he recommended that Ottawa take advantage of the protests on the Skeena to bring all the parties before the courts.

CLAIM JUMPERS

In order to put the essence of MacInnes's report on Indian title in accessible form, I have done so relatively uncritically. Obviously, his legal reasoning and historical knowledge are not without their flaws, and some of his opinions are no less imbued with the prejudices of his day than Blake's. But, all in all, his report is a remarkable document. Not only did he search out and analyse sources hitherto largely ignored (notably the 1875 *Papers Connected with the Indian Land Question*), he also brought to the task considerable legal ability and a willingness to follow premises through to their obvious – and, for some, uncomfortable – conclusions. Moreover, he clearly enjoyed doing so. His report is therefore an unusual, perhaps even a unique, combination of man and topic that, whatever its merits, has been largely vindicated by events. It also underlines the importance of the imperial connection at the time, and serves to remind us that we should be slow to condemn Aboriginal groups and their lawyers for placing so much reliance on the Royal Proclamation of 1763 and appeals to the King. After all, the Laurier government took steps to launch the very action of ejectment that MacInnes had recommended.

But the lawsuit never came to pass. It appears that Ottawa tried to induce British Columbia to agree to a reference to the Supreme Court of Canada that would specifically include the issue of Aboriginal title. At first this was successful. The deputy minister of justice and British Columbia's deputy attorney general agreed on a list of ten questions, the first three of which concerned the Indian title. But at the eleventh hour Premier McBride, who only two years earlier had approved an attempt to refer Indian land issues to the Full Court in British Columbia, refused his consent.[144] One cannot know, but perhaps by then he had realized that the case for Indian title was legally much stronger than he had previously thought.

It was only after McBride stymied the reference that Ottawa began to implement McInnes's advice. The Indian Act was amended to provide in section 37A for an action at the suit of His Majesty where the 'possession of any lands ... claimed to be reserved for the Indians ... is withheld.' The action was to be in the Exchequer Court, instituted by information of the attorney general of Canada 'upon the instructions of the Superintendent General of Indian Affairs.'[145] The suit would be brought against a Crown grantee in the Skeena, who would produce his grant in defence; this would raise the question of the validity of the grant and whether the land was subject to Indian title.

But Laurier decided to call a general election on the issue of free trade with the United States, and when he lost and left office the lawsuit contemplated by section 37A left with him. Sir Robert Borden's Conservative government, and the Liberal and Conservative ones that followed them, struggled with the B.C. Indian land question but never again came close to the sort of unilateral action contemplated by MacInnes, and they became increasingly frustrated by what they believed was the advice being given to organizations such as the Allied Indian Tribes of British Columbia by lawyers. In 1927 Parliament put a stop to the lawyers, who from then until 1951 could not be paid to pursue an Indian claim against government without written government consent.[146] At about the same time, a parliamentary committee concluded that the claims of the Allied Tribes that there was unextinguished Indian title in British Columbia were unfounded. But a parliamentary committee is not a court, and the land question did not go away. Fifteen years after the legislative restriction on lawyers was lifted, the *Calder* case began to work its way through the judicial system, and in 1984 *Delgamuukw*, a case from the Skeena and thereabouts, began a similar journey.

Perhaps an editorial in the Prince Rupert *News* in April 1911 says it best. Reacting to Laurier's initiative and McBride's intransigence (which they attributed in part to the fact that Indians did not vote), the editors applauded the former's decision to find a way into court, whether British Columbia consented or not. McBride's refusal to cooperate and his 'insulting references' to groups supporting the Indians, they wrote, 'tell their own tale.' Citing the Royal Proclamation of 1763, the editorial concluded that to 'refuse to recognize the title conferred in the historic papers, and to refuse to allow a court of justice to decide the question is not an honorable attitude for a guardian government to take. It is a policy worthy only of a set of claim jumpers ... Sir Wilfrid Laurier's efforts to have the whole matter submitted to the courts will commend themselves to every lover of justice in Canada.'[147] One imagines that, if he read this, Tom MacInnes would have been pleased.

After submitting his report MacInnes, as we have seen, went on to other adventures and disappointments. One writer described him as a man who 'took the joys that life brought and the bludgeonings, too and did not complain.'[148] His son Loftus maintained MacInnes's link to both literature and Indian affairs by marrying the daughter of poet Archibald Lampman and by going to work for the Indian department, where he made a successful career.[149] By 1934 Loftus was chief clerk and, ironically, was writing very critically of lawyers who involved themselves in Indian matters, making dark allegations even against one T.G. Norris, KC, whom he accused of 'encouraging Indians to resist the department' for improper motives.[150] One suspects that to Loftus MacInnes, there was no 'proper' motive for resisting the department. But he may not have been entirely wrong about Norris, who appears to have been more in tune with the views expressed by Tom MacInnes in 1909. When, years later, Norris became a member of the British Columbia Court of Appeal he wrote a separate, concurring judgment in the first B.C. case to hold that provincial hunting laws were subject to Indian treaty rights. *R. v. White and Bob* not only persuaded the Nisga'a to take their land question to the courts; it began a chain of litigation that culminated in December of 1997 with *Delgamuukw*.[151]

MacInnes appears not to have involved himself in Indian law after 1909. When he died on 12 February 1951 at the age of eighty-four he was survived by Loftus, who by then was secretary of the Indian affairs department; his brother, W.W.B. McInnes; and a grandson. His wife, the former Laura Hostetter, had predeceased him by several years. The obituaries detail his careers as author, lawyer, poet, radio broadcaster, civil servant, and Oriental entrepreneur; they even speak of his work on narcotics and immigration law for the Laurier government. But they say nothing of the *Report on the Indian Title*, and little of the man himself. For that, one has to go to the literary critics.[152] As E.K. Brown put it when MacInnes was still alive, he was 'one of the few Canadian poets who have something unusual to say and who say it with an unusual accent.'[153] Alfred Myrick Pound of Vancouver agreed, but was less sympathetic. 'MacInnes,' he said, 'assumes the irritating pose of pretending that he does not care a whit for contemporary opinion in Canada or abroad; that he writes for an audience which will only begin to assemble fifty years hence.'[154] That audience may now be ready to see what MacInnes the lawyer, if not MacInnes the poet, had to say.

NOTES

I want to express my appreciation to two students, Lynda Cassels and Carole Aippersbach, who at various times over the past few years did research for me in connection with this project; to the staff at the Provincial Archives [BCARS] and the National Archives [NAC]; to George Brandak of the Special Collections Division at the University of British Columbia's Library [UBC, SC]; to Ann Carroll at the Vancouver City Archives [VCA]; to Nikki Shaw of the Oweekeno First Nation, who provided me with a typescript copy of the legal opinion that is the subject of this essay; and finally, to editors Jim Phillips and Blaine Baker and the anonymous reviewers for their helpful editorial comments.

1 See John McLaren and Hamar Foster, 'Hard Choices and Sharp Edges: The Legal History of British Columbia and the Yukon,' in Hamar Foster and John McLaren, eds., *Essays in the History of Canadian Law, Vol. VI: British Columbia and the Yukon* (Toronto: University of Toronto Press for the Osgoode Society for Canadian Legal History 1995), 3 at 4.
2 See, for example, Richard Risk, 'The Scholars and the Canadian Constitution,' *Manitoba Law Journal* 23 (1996), 496.
3 'The Hidden Constitution: Aboriginal Rights in Canada,' *American Journal of Comparative Law*, 32 (1984), 361. See also 'Understanding Aboriginal Rights,' *Canadian Bar Review* 66 (1987), 727 and 'The Independence of Canada,' *Supreme Court Law Review* 5 (1983), 369.
4 In 1991 this comparative neglect was thrown into sharp relief by an exchange between Slattery and Dr Bruce Clark, a lawyer whose views have received a certain amount of publicity lately: see Brian Slattery, 'Bringing the Constitution Home' and Bruce Clark, 'Constitutional Alternatives: In Defence of the Imperial Model,' in Andrea P. Morrison, ed., *Justice for Natives: Searching for Common Ground* (Montreal and Kingston: McGill-Queen's University Press 1997).
5 For example, the Canada Jurisdiction Act of 1803, which described what is now British Columbia as being within the Indian Territories, was repealed by (U.K.) 35 & 36 Vict., c. 63 (1872). See Hamar Foster, 'Forgotten Arguments: Aboriginal Title and Sovereignty in Canada Jurisdiction Act Cases,' *Manitoba Law Journal* 21 (1992), 343–89.
6 Statute of Westminster (U.K.), 22 Geo. V, c. 4 (1931). However, for theoretical and domestic political reasons (the latter being a concern that French and English could never agree on amending the constitution without provoking a crisis), the imperial Parliament retained legislative authority. For detail, see Peter Hogg, *Canada Act 1982 Annotated* (Toronto: Carswell 1982), at 6–7.
7 SC 1949, c. 37, s. 3. The authority of Canada to take this step was confirmed in *Reference Re Bill 9 of 1939*, [1940] SCR 49 and *A.G. Ontario v. A.G. Canada*, [1947] AC 127.
8 Canada Act, 1982, enacting the Constitution Act, 1982.

9 Petition of the Allied Indian Tribes to the Senate of Canada, 9 June 1920, protesting the second reading of Bill 13 (NAC, RG10, Series C-II-3, vol. 11,047,
File 33/General, Part 6). The petitioners added that '[o]f course we do not
concede that the Parliament of Canada has power by this or any other Bill to
do so.' The McKenna–McBride Agreement of 1912, which had been reached
only because Ottawa agreed not to raise the Indian title issue, had proposed a
'final adjustment' of the dispute between the two governments over Indian
lands. Bill 13 was the Dominion statute authorizing the implementation of
this agreement. See text accompanying notes 25 and 33, infra.

10 See the decision of the English Court of Appeal in *Re The Queen v. The
Secretary of State for Foreign and Commonwealth Affairs, ex parte the Indian
Association of Alberta, Union of New Brunswick Indians, Union of Nova Scotian
Indians*, [1981] 4 CNLR 86. In a 'Note from the Appeal Committee of the
House of Lords,' [1982] 3 CNLR 195, Lord Diplock (for the court) denied leave
to appeal and stated that 'it simply is not arguable that any obligations of the
Crown in respect of the Indian peoples of Canada are still the responsibility of
Her Majesty's government in the United Kingdom ... [I]t is the Canadian
courts ... that alone have jurisdiction to determine what those obligations are.'

11 Kenneth Lysyk, 'The Unique Constitutional Position of the Canadian Indian,'
Canadian Bar Review 45 (1967), 513. The author does note at 516, however, that
a finding that unextinguished Aboriginal title exists in British Columbia
would 'suggest a broader ambit of federal authority in relation to "lands
reserved for the Indians" [pursuant to s. 91(24) of the BNA Act] than is
generally conceded' – a conclusion recently confirmed by the Supreme Court
of Canada in *Delgamuukw v. The Queen* (1997), 153 DLR (4th) 193.

12 SC, 1926–7, c. 32, s. 6 enacted s. 149A, which became s. 141 in the 1927
consolidation, RSC 1927, c. 98.

13 On Scott, see E. Brian Titley, *A Narrow Vision. Duncan Campbell Scott and the
Administration of Indian Affairs in Canada* (Vancouver: UBC Press 1986),
chapter 2 of which deals with Scott's literary career. See also Melvin H. Dagg,
'Scott and the Indians,' *The Humanities Association Bulletin* 23, no. 4 (1972), 3–
11; E.K. Brown, 'Duncan Campbell Scott: A Memoir,' in David Staines, ed.,
E.K. Brown. Responses and Evaluations (Toronto: McClelland & Stewart 1977);
Gerald Lynch, 'An Endless Flow: D.C. Scott's Indian Poems,' *Studies in
Canadian Literature* 7, no. 1 (1982), 27–54; Lyle P. Weis, 'D.C. Scott's View of
History and the Indians,' *Canadian Literature* (1986), 27–40; James Morrison,
'The Poet and the Indians,' *The Beaver* 68, no. 4 (1988), 4–16; Stan Dragland,
Floating Voice: Duncan Campbell Scott and the Literature of Treaty 9 (Concord:
Anansi 1994); and Nicole McLelland, 'Policy Poetry, Aboriginal People: The
Administrative and Poetic Writing of Duncan Campbell Scott' (MA essay,

Department of English, University of Victoria 1996) to whom I am indebted
for some of the preceding references. Further sources may be found in
Titley.

14 T.R.E. MacInnes, *Report on the Indian Title in Canada with special reference to
British Columbia*, 20 August 1909 [*Report*], at 96. For citation, see note 43, infra.

15 *Delgamuukw*, supra note 11.

16 Letter from A. Dods dated 11 June 1874, reproduced in *Papers Connected with
the Indian Land Question 1850–1875* (Victoria: Richard Wolfenden 1875), at 133.
'Siwash' in the Chinook jargon meant 'Indian,' but it became a derogatory
term that, as an adjective, meant 'no good.' The reference to gunboats is not
fanciful: they were used often on the coast between 1850 and the 1880s to
intimidate and occasionally to level Indian villages the authorities believed
were sheltering persons they sought. See generally Barry Gough, *Gunboat
Frontier: British Maritime Authority and Northwest Coast Indians, 1846–1890*
(Vancouver: UBC Press 1984).

17 Up until the early 1860s Governor James Douglas and even the colonial
legislature on Vancouver Island appeared to acknowledge the need to
extinguish the Indian title before the land could be settled, but even before
Douglas retired in 1863 this attitude was changing.

18 I have discussed these issues elsewhere, most recently in 'Letting Go the
Bone: The Idea of Indian Title in British Columbia, 1849–1927,' in Foster and
McLaren, ed., *Essays ... Volume VI* at 28–86, and in a two-article series entitled
'Roadblocks and Legal History, Part I: Do Forgotten Cases Make Good Law?'
and 'Roadblocks and Legal History, Part II: Aboriginal Title and s. 91(24),' *The
Advocate* 54 (1996), 355–66 and 531–41. The government of British Columbia
did not acknowledge that Aboriginal title was an enforceable legal right until
1991.

19 The exception is Treaty 8, made in 1899 with the primarily Athapaskan
peoples of northern Alberta and the southern Northwest Territories, etc.
Because these groups included bands in northeastern British Columbia, treaty
was made with them, as well. But the B.C. government took no part.

20 J.A. Lees and W.J. Clutterbuck, *1887: A Ramble in British Columbia* (London:
Longmans, Green, and Co. 1892), at 2–3, 200 (emphasis in original). Lees and
Clutterbuck, however, were hardly opposed to settlement. As they put it, they
had come to the Kootenay Valley 'to test its capabilities as a home for ...
public-school and university young men who, in this overcrowded old
England of ours, every year find themselves more *de trop*. What are they and
their wives, the English country girls to do? The Girton and Newnham young
ladies are of course a sufficiency unto themselves ... but what of the not
unimportant majority?'

21 The secretary of state for the colonies was never called upon to do so. But see text accompanying note 9, supra.

22 Reserve Commissioner Gilbert Malcolm Sproat to David Mills, Dominion minister of the interior, 27 October 1877, NAC, RG10, vol. 3656, file 9063.

23 It is important to note that the province agreed to the commission only after Ottawa had disallowed B.C.'s Crown Lands Act on the ground that it did nothing to acknowledge unextinguished Indian title. Although Ottawa then set aside the issue of Indian title and allowed B.C.'s land laws to operate, Edward Blake, the minister of justice, stated that 'there remains a serious question as to whether the [Crown Lands] Act is within the competence of the provincial legislature ...' See *Journal of the House of Commons, Vol. 64 (1926–27), Appendix No.2: Special Committees of the Senate and House of Commons ... To Inquire Into the Claims of the Allied Indian Tribes of British Columbia ... Proceedings, Report and the Evidence* [1927 Report], Appendix B at 44 and text accompanying notes 26–28, infra.

24 The triggering event was a dispute over which government received the benefit of the surrender of a large portion of a reserve near Prince Rupert: see note 41, infra.

25 Keith, *Responsible Government in the Dominions*, 2nd ed. (Oxford: Oxford University Press, 1928), vol. 1 at 786.

26 See Fournier and H. Bernard, 19 January 1875, reproduced in the 1927 Report at 39ff.

27 See text accompanying note 23, supra.

28 Mills to Dr Israel Wood Powell, 2 August 1877. Quoted in Wilson Duff, *The Indian History of British Columbia, Vol. I: The Impact of the White Man* (Victoria: Anthropology in British Columbia Memoir No. 5 1965), at 67. Duff says this is a letter, but it reads more like a telegram. A day later, Mills told Reserve Commissioner Sproat that '[i]n order that the question [of title] may not be raised, and war avoided, it is of the utmost consequence that the [Reserve] Commissioners ... should make [reservations] as ample as to avoid the necessity, if possible, or raising the question.' Quoted in Barry S. Cottam, 'Indian Title as a "Celestial Institution": David Mills and the *St. Catherine's Milling Case*,' in Kerry Abel and Jean Friesen, eds., *Aboriginal Resource Use in Canada: Historical and Legal Perspectives* (Winnipeg: University of Manitoba Press 1991), 247 at 252.

29 Ditchburn to Scott, 8 December 1925, NAC, RG10, vol. 3820, file 59, 335, part 3A. Only a few years earlier Ditchburn had been more optimistic, predicting a settlement in the summer of 1923. He noted that the minister had told the Allied Tribes that Ottawa was 'prepared to concede the fact that the Indians had a case and that if it reached the Privy Council the decision, *no doubt*,

would be in the Indians' favour ...' Ditchburn had even drawn up a plan for a new treaty process: see Ditchburn to Scott, 28 November 1922 and Ditchburn to the Indian agent at New Westminster, 5 March 1923, NAC, RG10, series C-II-3, vol. 11047, file 33/ general, part 6 and part 7 (emphasis added).

30 Supra, note 11.

31 For example, the Nisga'a Land Committee. Although this organization may have existed in the nineteenth century, it was put on a formal footing in 1907.

32 For example, the Indian Rights Association (c.1909) and the Interior Tribes of British Columbia (c.1909). For more detail see R.M. Galois, 'The Indian Rights Association, Native Protest Activity and the "Land Question" in British Columbia, 1903–1916,' *Native Studies Review* 8, no. 2 (1992), 1–34; Peter Campbell, '"Not as a White Man, Not as a Sojourner." James A. Teit and the Fight for Native Rights in British Columbia, 1884–1922,' *left history* 2 (1994), 37–57; and Wendy Wickwire, 'We Shall Drink From the Stream and So Shall You: James A. Teit and Native Resistance in British Columbia, 1908–1922,' *Canadian Historical Review* 79(2) (1998), 199–236.

33 See Paul Tennant, *Aboriginal People and Politic: The Indian Land Question in British Columbia, 1849–1989* (Vancouver: UBC Press 1990), chaps. 4–7; Galois, 'The Indian Rights Association'; and Darcy Anne Mitchell, 'The Allied Indian Tribes of British Columbia: A Study in Pressure Group Behaviour' (MA thesis, University of British Columbia, 1977).

34 The government seemed to regard most Methodists as agitators, and Attorney General A.E.B. Davie even spoke of prosecuting William Duncan, the CMS missionary at Metlakatla, for treason – or at least sedition: see Patricia Roy, 'Law and Order in British Columbia in the 1880s: Images and realities,' in R.C. MacLeod, ed., *Swords and Ploughshares: War and Agriculture in Western Canada* (Edmonton: University of Alberta Press 1993), 55 at 63.

35 Taped interview by the author with the late Reg Kelly, son of Peter Kelly, 14 November 1995. See also John Morley, *Roar of the Breakers: A Biography of Peter Kelly* (Toronto: Ryerson Press 1967), at 75–7.

36 On O'Meara see E. Palmer Patterson II, 'Arthur E. O'Meara, Friend of the Indians,' *Pacific Northwest Quarterly* 58, no. 2 (1967), at 90–9.

37 I have addressed the issue of the role of lawyers in the land question at this time in 'We Are Not O'Meara's Children: Law, Lawyers and the Aboriginal Campaign for Indian Title in British Columbia, 1871–1927,' a paper presented to the Thirteenth British Legal History Conference at Cambridge University in July of 1997. It is currently being revised for publication.

38 See text accompanying notes 26 and 28, supra.

39 Galois, 'The Indian Rights Association,' at 6–7.

40 Ibid., at 8.

41 Another issue for Ottawa was British Columbia's claim that it should receive the benefit of the surrender of reserve lands near the proposed terminal of the railway at Prince Rupert, and Premier McBride's decision to suspend the operation of the reserve commission. See note 24, supra, and accompanying text.

42 Galois, 'The Indian Rights Association,' at 8.

43 This is from the first paragraph of MacInnes's *Report*, which is dated 20 August 1909. A copy is in the National Library of Canada, catalogued as COP.CA.CI.205. What appears to be the original, bound in leather and containing extra appendices, is in the National Archives of Canada at NAC, RG10, series B-8, vol. 11208, file 1. These versions are 117 pages in length, and are titled 'D.I.A. Report on the Indian Title in Canada with special reference to British Columbia. By T.R.E. McInnes, B.A., Barrister-at-Law.'

Two points. First, the spelling of MacInnes's name varies because, although the family name was 'McInnes,' he changed the spelling to 'MacInnes' and used 'Tom' rather than 'T.R.E.' as a pen name when he began to publish poetry. Second, for the purposes of this essay I have used a typescript copy of the report that is more compressed, running to only 96 pages (exclusive of any appendices). My page references will therefore be slightly different from page references to the original and to the copy in the National Library.

44 See text accompanying note 14, supra.

45 *Report*, at 15–16, quoting the Montreal *Star*, 31 July 1909. McBride went on to say, in a passage as remarkable for its bad law as its veiled threat, that when the Indians 'accepted the white man's machinery, for the policing and general direction of the country, they tacitly confessed themselves conquered. Surely we do not have to go to war and injure a helpless people to technically perfect a title to any part of Canada.' However, the sovereign cannot, by an act of state such as war, take property from people already declared to be subjects of the Crown. See Kent McNeil, *Common Law Aboriginal Title* (Oxford: Clarendon Press 1989) at, *inter alia*, 160, 163–4 and 246, and authorities cited therein.

46 *The Canadian Who's Who* (London: Arthur Leonard Tunnell 1936).

47 See, e.g., the entries in the *Oxford Companion to Canadian History and Literature* (Oxford: Oxford University Press, 1967) at 489 and the *MacMillan Dictionary of Canadian Biography*, 4th ed. (Toronto: MacMillan 1978), at 517, and the obituary in the Vancouver *Sun*, 12 February 1951.

48 The government may have regarded it as privileged, both as a solicitor-client communication and as an attorney's work product (because it was prepared with respect to contemplated litigation).

49 See 'Letting Go the Bone,' at 51–2 and 8on. The report was, however, recorded as House of Commons *Sessional Paper No. 47* (1914).

50 Forrest E. La Violette, *The Struggle for Survival: Indian Cultures and the Protestant Ethic in British Columbia* (Toronto: University of Toronto Press, 1961) at 101–2, 104, 109, 118, 120, 121, 127, and 128. Patterson ('Arthur E. O'Meara, Friend of the Indians,' at 90, 91) relies upon La Violette for a quotation from MacInnes's report, but is under the mistaken impression that he was an 'official in the Indian administration.' It seems likely that Patterson is confusing him with MacInnes's son, Loftus (as to whom see text accompanying notes 149–51, infra).

51 Including, apparently, two of the leading characters upon whose experiences Harriet Beecher Stowe's *Uncle Tom's Cabin* was based. (When MacInnes's brother died in 1954, the Vancouver *Sun* reported on 5 August that, as a child, the deceased had 'sat many times on the knee of the Rev. Josiah Hanson, the original Uncle Tom.') There are a number of sources for this biographical information and most of that which follows. These include an interview with MacInnes in July of 1941 that is preserved in *Early Vancouver*, vol. 6 (1945), VCA at 116; material in the second edition of *Rhymes of a Rounder* (North Vancouver City: The Review Presses 1931); and various standard sources, e.g., the entry on MacInnes's father in the *Canadian Who was Who, 1875–1933: A Standard Dictionary of Canadian Biography* (Toronto: Times Canada Press 1934), at 343–6, which states that the son of 'Uncle Tom,' whom Eliza carried over the ice floes while being pursued by bloodhounds, later became a member of the Ontario bar. After the Second World War Dresden found itself at the centre of a highly publicized controversy concerning the treatment of its black community, a controversy that included a number of anti-discrimination prosecutions: see, *inter alia*, J. Walker, *'Race,' Rights and the Law in the Supreme Court of Canada: Historical Case Studies* (Toronto: Wilfrid Laurier University Press and The Osgoode Society for Canadian Legal History 1997), 173, 176.

52 The *Oxford Companion to Canadian History and Literature* states that the family came west in 1881, but this is not correct. MacInnes recalled in 1941 that in July of 1876 his father had dug a bullet out of 'Portuguese Joe,' a Gastown resident of Aboriginal ancestry; Joe may not have been a model citizen, because his father subsequently decided 'he should have let the blackguard die' (*Early Vancouver* at 116). Gastown would, in the 1880s, become Vancouver.

53 BCARS, Add. Mss 948, vol. 64, file 370.

54 An account of may be found in any standard work, but for a detailed examination see John Tupper Saywell, 'The McInnes Incident in B.C., 1897–1900' (MA thesis, University of British Columbia 1950). The other lieutenant-governor to lose his job was Luc Letellier de Saint-Just in Québec, who was dismissed by Macdonald in 1879.

55 Joseph ('Fighting Joe') Martin had a remarkably varied and incendiary political career in dominion, British Columbia, Manitoba, and even British politics. Laurier had favoured Clifford Sifton over Martin for the interior ministry and was not alone in holding a low opinion of him. As for big business, Martin had indicated that he would, as premier, cancel the coal concessions at Crow's Nest Pass. According to Tom MacInnes, Senators George A. Cox and Robert Jaffrey, both of whom were directors of the Crow's Nest Pass Coal Co., had said they would have his father's 'scalp' if he called on Martin to form a government: see the *Canadian Who Was Who, 1875–1933* and Tom MacInnes's reminiscences in D.A. McGregor's 1955 column ('From an Angle on the Square') in the Vancouver *Province* (n.d., VCA, News Clippings).

56 Judith Antonik Bennett and Frederike Verspoor, *British Columbia Executive Council Appointments 1871–1986* (Victoria: BC Legislative Library 1989), at 26.

57 Victoria *Colonist*, 28 August 1898. For a brief account of the public dispute between Turner and Tom MacInnes, see Margaret A. Ormsby, *British Columbia: A History* (Vancouver: Macmillan 1958) at 319.

58 Victoria *Colonist*, 28 August 1898. Elsewhere in the paper the editors are quite critical of MacInnes's decision to contribute publicly to the debate.

59 Where a statute provided a penalty for doing or omitting to do a particular act, anyone could bring a suit known as a *qui tam* action on the state's behalf, as well as his own, to enforce the penalty. Part of this penalty would go to the plaintiff or informer as a reward. To compound an action is to agree, for valuable consideration, not to prosecute.

The prosecution of the McInnes brothers is reported in the Victoria *Colonist*, 30 May 1895. They had brought an action, on behalf of clients who claimed to have been persecuted by police and made to pay exorbitant fines, against the local magistrate for failing to make quarterly returns of fines. It seems this was done instead of taking the more difficult route of charging a conspiracy by the police and the magistrate to injure the clients. When the magistrate came to the McInnes's law office to see what the suit was about, he was apparently more inclined to pay $500 to their clients rather than have the allegations against him examined in court. Hence the charge against the McInnes brothers for compounding the case.

60 Victoria *Colonist*, 30 May 1895.

61 Although, according to Alfred Myrick Pound, a member of the Vancouver literary circle who wrote about such matters in the local newspapers, in later years he became 'taciturn.' See 'Tom MacInnes,' Pound Papers, UBC, SC, box 1, file 6 (n.d., although probably written in 1926 or 1927).

62 'The Vagabond's Album,' Pound Papers, UBC, SC, box 4, file 2. Robert Gore of the Special Collections Division of the UBC Library, writing of the Vaga-

bond Club in 1978, quotes a 1967 letter by former member A.C. Cummings that described the club as an 'outlet for whatever small talents we possessed in a city in which the buying and selling of real estate was the preoccupation of the majority of the inhabitants' (Vagabond Club records, UBC, SC).

63 Vancouver *Sun*, 5 August 1954. This obituary article on 'Billy' McInnes states that 'it was his silver-tongued oratory in the Commons that attracted the attention of Sir Wilfrid Laurier ...'

64 Vancouver *Province*, 12 February 1951.

65 See text accompanying note 46, supra.

66 E.K. Brown, 'Canadian Poetry 1935–1949' in Staines, *E.K. Brown*, at 145. In the same year Duncan Campbell Scott published *The Green Cloister*.

67 *Rhymes of a Rounder*, at 9, 10 and 12.

68 Vancouver *Province*, 12 February 1951; *Oxford Companion to Canadian History and Literature*, at 489.

69 The poem is 'The Old Man's Milk Bowl,' in *Rhymes of a Rounder*.

70 *Rhymes of a Rounder*, at 101–2.

71 *Oxford Companion to Canadian History and Literature*, at 489.

72 *Oriental Occupation of British Columbia* (Vancouver: Sun Publishing 1927). In this work MacInnes states that when he was retained to work on immigration (see text accompanying note 46, supra) he was 'much in need at the time of the small fee allowed for drafting the act ...'

73 Winch subsequently became the CCF leader in British Columbia, and almost became premier in 1952.

74 Vancouver *Province*, 11 December 1936.

75 *R. v. Dunbar*, 67 CCC 20 (SCC) is a familiar case to generations of law students because in it the Supreme Court of Canada held that, even if Dunbar may have taken part in the robbery only to save his life, this was irrelevant to whether he had an intention in common with the others to commit robbery. The Supreme Court of Canada has since changed its mind twice on this question, but today duress can be a defence to a murder charge if, like Dunbar, you are not the actual perpetrator: see *R. v. Pacquette* (1976), 30 CCC (2d) 417 and *R. v. Hibbert* (1995), 99 CCC (3d) 193.

76 From unidentified clippings in the VCA file, supra, note 55, dated 26 January 1937; 14, 18, and 19 April 1938; 20 October 1938; and 8 July 1939. MacInnes felt that, because Nazi supporters were calling themselves nationalists, the name of the Nationalist League should be changed to the 'New Democracy Party.'

77 *Rhymes of a Rounder*, at 104–5, 107.

78 V.B. Rhodenizer, PhD, in *Handbook of Canadian Literature* (1931), quoted in the introduction to *High Low Along* (Vancouver: Clark & Stuart 1934), at 9.

Rhodenizer added that in 'both fantastic romance and Epicurean philosophy MacInnes holds a unique position in Canadian poetry.'

79 John M. Elson, a lecturer in journalism and writing at the University of Toronto, in his introduction to *High Low Along* at 7. MacInnes's scepticism about religion is evident in his 1909 report on Indian title, in which he not only condemns the colonists' treatment of the Indians but 'their nauseous habit of doing it all in the name of God' (*Report* at 19).

80 MacInnes relied in particular upon *Worcester v. Georgia*, 31 U.S. (6 Pet.) 515 (1831) and *Mitchell et al. v. United States*, 34 U.S. (9 Pet.) 711 (1835).

81 *Report*, at 4.

82 Ibid., at 2 (emphasis added). The reference to joint action is to 'the 5th article of the Agreement between the Dominion and British Columbia Governments of 1876, whereby it is declared that any land taken from an Indian Reserve by reason of decrease in the number of Indians thereon shall revert to the Province.' David Mills was of the same opinion, telling Parliament in 1880 that Indian title was 'protected by law, and that protection is not abrogated or taken away by' the agreement made between Ottawa and British Columbia in 1876 to allot reserves rather than make treaties to extinguish title. *House of Commons Debates*, 1880, vol. 2 at 1633.

83 Ibid., at 3.

84 Ibid., at 6.

85 Ibid., at 7. For citations to the U.S. cases see note 80, supra.

86 Ibid., at 13.

87 Ibid. The latter reference is to the delegations to King Edward VII described in the text accompanying note 39, supra.

88 Ibid., at 14.

89 See text accompanying note 45, supra.

90 *Report*, at 15.

91 Ibid., at 16, and see *R. v. Sioui*, [1990] 3 CNLR 127 (SCC). The extracts continue until p. 33. At p. 34 MacInnes asserts that the reason Indians are 'sometimes referred to as Allies and sometimes as subjects' is their 'dual status.' They are 'nationally independent as among themselves, not independent as regards their national dealings with foreigners.'

92 *Report*, at 17–18.

93 See text accompanying note 16, supra.

94 *Report*, at 28. The Supreme Court did not specifically adopt this interpretation of the royal proclamation until its decision in *Calder v. A.G.B.C.* (1973), 34 DLR (3d) 145.

95 Ibid. *Campbell v. Hall* is most accessibly reported at (1774), 98 ER 848 and [1558–1774] All ER 252 (KB).

96 *Report*, at 35. The 'settler mentality' MacInnes describes proved resilient. As late as 1971 one of the justices of the Court of Appeal in British Columbia who heard the *Calder* appeal wrote that the effect of colonial land legislation was that the Indians 'became in law trespassers on and liable to actions of ejectment from lands in the Colony other than those set aside as reserves.' See (1971), 13 DLR (3d) 64 at 94. Although in the Supreme Court of Canada Hall J. described this statement as embodying a 'proposition which reason itself repudiates' (*Calder v. A.G.B.C.*, at 217), versions of it can be found in the popular media even today.

97 Robin Fisher, 'Joseph William Trutch and Indian Land Policy,' *BC Studies* 12 (1971–72), 3–33. For MacInnes's discussion of Trutch, see text accompanying notes 126–9, infra.

98 *Report*, at 36. See *Re Indian Land*, 19 November 1908, BCARS, GR 1727 (Benchbooks), vols. 504 and 525.

99 Deputy Minister of Justice E.L. Newcombe explained in an undated memorandum to the prime minister that the court in British Columbia ultimately refused to hear the reference, possibly because the Dominion chose not to attend and because the reference seems to have been artificially confined to the question of reserve lands. So in 1910 he and his provincial counterpart, H.A. Maclean, came up with ten questions for the Supreme Court of Canada dealing with Indian land issues in British Columbia, including Indian title – which Newcombe clearly regarded as crucial. See NA, RG10, vol. 3820, file 59,335, part 3A. For Premier McBride's response to this initiative, see text accompanying note 144, infra.

100 (1888) 14 AC 46. The *St. Catherine's* case is discussed in detail by S. Barry Cottam and Anthony J. Hall in their essays in Kerry Abel and Jean Friesen, eds., *Aboriginal Resource Use in Canada. Historical and Legal Aspects* (Winnipeg: University of Manitoba Press 1991) at 247 and 267.

101 *St. Catherine's* at 59. More precisely, their Lordships said that federal jurisdiction over Indian lands 'is not in the least degree inconsistent with the right of the province to a beneficial interest in these lands, available to them as a source of revenue *whenever the estate of the Crown is disencumbered of the Indian title*' (emphasis added).

102 Even the members of the parliamentary committee that looked into the claims of the Allied Indian Tribes of British Columbia did not seem to grasp this. See Hamar Foster, 'How not to draft Legislation: Indian Land Claims, Government Intransigence and how Premier Walkem nearly sold the farm in 11874,' *The Advocate* 46 (1988), 411 at 416–17.

103 I have dealt with this point in more detail in 'Roadblocks and Legal History, part II: Aboriginal Title and s. 91(24),' at 536 and 540–1.

104 The attempted reference to the Full Court in 1908 is probably not an exception: it appears to have been restricted to the issue of the provincial
reversionary interest rather than Indian title per se. Perhaps Ottawa would
not take part because it was concerned that a B.C. court might be too
sympathetic to a B.C. point of view?

105 *Report*, at 37, quoting from *Worcester v. Georgia*. Since MacInnes wrote this,
colonial office records have been unearthed establishing that this was the
understanding of that office as well, that is, that the company was obliged to
extinguish the Indian title. See 'Letting Go the Bone,' at 40, 75n.

106 The government of British Columbia was still having this sort of drafting
problem in the 1870s. When the B.C. Crown Lands Act, 1874 was being
considered by Ottawa (see text accompanying note 26, supra), Télésphore
Fournier, the minister of justice, pointed out that the act defined Crown
lands as meaning 'all lands of this province held by the Crown in free and
common socage.' But of course this meant that 'Her Majesty is tenant by
freehold,' and Fournier therefore wondered, tongue-in-cheek no doubt,
whether the province was conceding that the Crown was tenant of the
Indian tribes. See 'How not to draft Legislation.'

107 *Report*, at 41.

108 Ibid., at 43–4. *Mabo v. Queensland [No.2]* is reported at (1992), 175 CLR 1.

109 Ibid., at 42.

110 Ibid., at 44.

111 Ibid., at 46 (emphasis in original).

112 At least, not until Order-in-Council 1036 in 1938, the validity of which has
been suspect for some time: see 'Roadblocks and Legal History, part II:
Aboriginal Title and s. 91(24).' But MacInnes was writing long before 1938.

113 See 'Roadblocks and Legal History, Part I: Do Forgotten Cases Make Good
Law?' at 358 and *Moses v. R. in right of Canada*, [1979] 5 WWR 100 (BCCA);
Dunstan v. Hell's Gate Enterprises et al., [1986] 3 CNLR 47 (BCSC), reversed on
other grounds at 20 BCLR (2d) 29; and *Wewayakum Indian Band v. Canada and
Wewayakai Indian Band* (1996), 99 FTR 1 (formerly *Roberts et al. v. The Queen et
al; Dick et al. v. The Queen*). However, in *B.C. (A.G.) v. Mt. Currie Indian Band*
(1991), 54 BCLR (2d) 156 (CA) at 176, the court of appeal weakened the
authority of these cases by stating that their own previous decision in *Moses*
was decided *per incuriam*. *Delgamuukw*, arguably, destroys the authority of
such decisions altogether.

114 *Report*, at 47–8. And, he goes on, within the class of land purchased by treaty
in the early 1850s, within the class contemplated by the 1861 petition, etc.

115 Ibid., at 48. This passage avoids the issue of whether the province could
refuse to accept the findings of the reserve commissioners. MacInnes seems

to think it could, but he probably also thought that, should this occur, the dispute would be referred to the secretary of state for the colonies (see text accompanying note 9, supra).

116 Ibid., at 49 and see the views of David Mills, supra, note 82.

117 'Summary of Government Correspondence re form of conveyance from Provincial Government to Dominion Government of Indian Reserves in British Columbia,' NA, RG10, vol. 3780, file 39, 675–1, part I.

118 Unsigned memorandum dated 16 February 1906, citing a note by Dominion delegate Thomas Smith that the issue was 'settled' and that no patents were necessary. The author states that Ottawa 'was evidently of the opinion at that time that when the lands for the Indians were set apart for them in this way they were secured to them as fully as if a patent had been issued therefore' (NA, RG10, vol. 3820, file 59, 335, part 2).

119 See note 113, supra, and accompanying text. *Delgamuukw* would appear to have put an end to this argument, at least insofar as reserves carved out of Aboriginal title lands are concerned.

120 See, for example, *B.C. (A.G.) v. Mt. Currie Indian Band* and *Wewayakum Indian Band v. Canada and Wewayakai Indian Band.*

121 *Gosnell v. Min. of Lands (B.C.) and A.G. (Canada)*, SCC. Case File 3238 (1912), the subject of 'Roadblocks and Legal History, Part I: Do Forgotten Cases Make Good Law?' The chief justice concluded that the reserves in question had been 'segregated under the Terms of Union' and were 'well reserved without any formal notice in the Gazette.'

122 See, for example, Melvin H. Smith, *Our Home or Native Land? What Government Aboriginal Policy Is Doing to Canada* (Victoria, B.C.: Melvin H. Smith 1995).

123 *Report*, at 50. Blake's account of the Privy Council hearing in *St. Catherine's* (reproduced in the report at 50–1 and 91) indicates that Lord Watson, speaking of the Treaty of Fort Stanwick in 1768, said that it proceeded 'on the express assumption that the Indians have absolute rights over the land in question.' Blake's response to Lord Watson was that certain expressions in the treaty were simply 'swelling words' that meant little.

124 Ibid., at 51. For the view that Aboriginal title is more like a fee simple, see McNeil, *Common Law Aboriginal Title.*

125 Ibid., at 80 and 85, where MacInnes lists the conflicts beginning in 1775, 1812, and 1837 as ones in which Indians 'answered the King's call.' He also states, contrary to much popular mythology, that they 'remained faithful to the King' during the Northwest rebellion in 1885, and that they had offered their services in the Boer War.

126 Oddly, MacInnes does misread one document, and in Trutch's favour. He

says that Trutch advised Governor Seymour to buy back land originally reserved to the Indians; in fact, Trutch considered this option but recommended that the government 'disavow absolutely' the engineers' authority and start again. The Indians, he said, 'have really no right to the lands they claim ...' Trutch to Governor Seymour, 28 August 1867, in *Papers Connected with the Indian Land Question 1850–1875* at 42.

127 *Supra*, note 16 at 41–6. On the accessibility of these documents in the past see Tennant, *Aboriginal People and Politics*, at 47–9.

128 *Report*, at 65. Douglas's letter is reproduced in Fisher, 'Joseph William Trulch,' at 17–18, and is now well known.

129 *Report*, at 65–6. The men in question were Colonel Moody, Sergeant McColl, and Sapper Turnbull.

130 Ibid., at 70–1.

131 Ibid., at 71, quoting from Williams on *Real Property*.

132 'Always bearing in mind,' he adds, 'that the Indians were not one people any more than Europeans are one people.' Ibid., at 72, referring to the report at (1887), 13 SCR 577.

133 Ibid., at 73.

134 Ibid., at 74–6. As Lord Watson put it, a 'pretext has never been wanted for taking land.'

135 Ibid., at 78.

136 Ibid., at 88. Again, a proposition now clearly confirmed in *Delgamuukw*.

137 For the abortive 1908 reference, see notes 98–100, supra, and accompanying text. MacInnes is referring to counsel for the Dominion in *St. Catherines*; Ottawa was unrepresented in 1908.

138 *Report*, at 89. MacInnes does not appear to have regarded the appellant lumber company as a true party because its interests were the same as Ottawa's.

139 Ibid. Lord Watson himself acknowledged that the Dominion might pay the Indians much less for their title than what it would receive by reselling the land to settlers. That, in a nutshell, was the dominant approach to colonization at the time. See W.K. Hastings, 'The Wakefield Colonization Plan and Constitutional Development in South Australia, Canada and New Zealand,' *The Journal of Legal History* 11 (1990), 279–99.

140 Ibid.

141 Ibid., at 90–1.

142 Ibid., at 92, quoting Chief Justice Marshall in *Worcester v. Georgia*.

143 Ibid., at 96. It is noteworthy that this is also the advice that lawyer Arthur E. O'Meara would soon give the Nisga'a, who tried for years to take their case directly to the Privy Council in England.

144 See note 99, supra.

145 SC 1910, c. 28, s. 1, enacting s. 37A. The act was amended again in 1911, apparently because there were concerns this was not clear enough. See SC 1911, c. 14, s. 4. Note also that, although it referred to withholding possession of lands 'reserved for the Indians,' Ottawa sought to apply this to land outside designated Indian reserves.

146 SC, 1926–7, c. 32.

147 'A Daniel Comes to Judgment,' *Prince Rupert News*, 29 (?) April 1911.

148 D.A. McGregor, 'From an Angle on the Square,' Vancouver *Province*, 15 February 1951. McGregor quotes in support the following lines from a poem MacInnes wrote in his old age:

> Meagre indeed my circumstance
> Troubles increase while days grow less;
> Yet still with an air of nonchalance
> Roving I go to the green of Romance,
> And thumb my nose at Soberness.

149 E.K. Brown, 'Duncan Campbell Scott: A Memoir,' in Staines, *E.K. Brown*, at 141. Scott was a close friend of Lampman's, a great admirer of his poetry, and 'unofficial custodian of Lampman's works and fame.' Brown suggests that Scott was pleased that this duty would eventually be carried out by Loftus MacInnes, Lampman's son in law and for twenty years Scott's 'own associate in the department of Indian Affairs.'

150 T.R.L. MacInnes to Dr McGill, 18 December 1934, NA, RG10, vol. 3780, file 39,675, part 2, at 5–6. Presumably the 1927 law was being interpreted as applying only to land claims, not to routine legal matters that did not involve soliciting funds on a large scale.

151 *R. v. White and Bob* (1964), 50 DLR (2d) 613 (BCCA), affirmed in (1965), 52 DLR (2d) 481 (SCC).

152 See text accompanying notes 78–79, supra.

153 Staines, *E.K. Brown*, at 146.

154 'Tom MacInnes,' Pound Papers (c. 1927). Pound concluded that such an attitude was 'not the way to win support these days.'

7

Taking Litigation Seriously: The Market Wharf Controversy at Halifax, 1785–1820

PHILIP GIRARD

In addressing the topic of judicial salaries in a speech to the Nova Scotia House of Assembly in the spring of 1830, the young lawyer Beamish Murdoch observed that 'he could speak feelingly, as he had all that he was worth in the world, at one time depending upon [the judges'] decision.'[1] He did not need to elaborate. Provincial society was still small enough that most of the men in the chamber would have known instantly that he was referring to a *cause célèbre* in the provincial Court of Chancery involving a valuable wharf property, which had ended a decade earlier. This epic struggle had pitted Murdoch and his maternal Beamish kin against the three Cochran brothers, wealthy Halifax merchants who had dominated Nova Scotian society for decades. The Cochrans had pursued the dispute to the foot of the throne, but to no avail. His Majesty in Council affirmed the Nova Scotia Chancery decree, which returned title to the wharf to the Beamish family some thirty years after the Cochrans had wrested it from them. In examining the long and tortuous course of this litigation I hope to glean some insight into the nature of civil justice in colonial Nova Scotia.

By 'civil justice' I mean the entire process of civil (i.e., noncriminal) litigation. A study of civil justice would try to answer some of the following questions. Why did litigants begin legal action? Why did some settle or discontinue their actions while others pursued them to final decision? Did people use the civil law for purposes other than the ostensible ones: to harass others, or to vindicate their reputations, for example? What kinds of patterns, if any, can be discerned from the use of the civil law by particular groups of plaintiffs against particular groups of defendants in particular courts for particular categories of legal wrongs? In short, what was the meaning of 'going to law' for the participants, and what can that tell us about the nature of the legal order and the legal culture of the day?

It might be thought that such questions would be better answered in the context of a quantitative study, where patterns can be identified more easily. By definition, there is no pattern in an individual case study. There are problems with the quantitative approach, however, which have recently been stated by Peter Hoffer: 'Behind the aggregate data of litigation rates are individual stories, and each represents a decision to invest time, money, and effort in a lawsuit. In human terms, the cases were ... major personal events, invested with hope and fear ... The proper study of lawsuits begins with the litigants themselves, with the motivations of real men and women in the past. [What is required] is a thick description of the context of individual cases ... an exhaustive search of prior legal controversies, family relationships, position in community, and the like.'[2] Hoffer does not recommend abandoning quantitative studies, merely that they be sensitive to the kinds of factors that only the intensive study of particular cases can reveal.

The exceptionally full documentation of the Market Wharf litigation provides an opportunity to put colonial justice under the historian's microscope.[3] Studies of individual instances of civil litigation have been put to a number of purposes in the last twenty years by legal and social historians in the common law world. They focus, broadly speaking, on one of three themes, although there is often some overlap among them: the law, the litigants, and the litigation. Scholars who focus on the law have created a distinct genre of legal history: the study of `leading cases.'[4] Such studies derive their interest from the fact that the cases under review are still considered authoritative in modern jurisprudence. Leading case studies are based on a tension between 'what the "great" cases ha[ve] come to mean after having been processed by doctrinaire legal scholars and used by generations of barristers ... and what [they] meant to the parties involved in them.'[5] These efforts at reconstruction by the historian sometimes prove deconstructive for the modern lawyer, since they suggest that the afterlife of a 'leading case' often has little to do with the case itself or its reasoning, but depends on other historical circumstances.

The remaining types of case study explore litigation that never achieved authoritative status within the world of legal precedent. Those that focus on the litigants examine litigation dossiers because they provide evidence of the actions and attitudes of the people of a bygone era. This evidence is particularly valuable where it provides a window on the world of those whose voices are muted in the historical record: the poor, the working classes, women, children, and members of ethnic and racial minorities.[6] The litigation itself is usually of less interest than what it reveals about the life experiences of the litigants outside the world of the courtroom.

Finally, there are studies that focus on the process of litigation. These explore changes within adjectival law and curial institutions, the use and abuse of litigation,[7] and the attitudes of litigants toward litigation itself and toward the law in general.[8] The meaning of the particular dispute, and of dispute resolution in general, is a principal concern. This study of the Market Wharf litigation falls mainly in the third category. *Beamish et al. v. Cochran et al.* contributed nothing to the substantive law, and the lives of the litigants outside the courtroom are not of particular interest here. It is rather the course of the litigation itself and the attitudes of the litigants that will be the primary focus.

THE CONTEXT OF THE DISPUTE, 1751–1785

It goes without saying that the existence of wharves is crucial to the functioning of any port city. In the Halifax of the 1750s, summoned into existence by imperial fiat for purely strategic reasons, wharves were in short supply. The government was prepared to construct some facilities for naval purposes, but others were needed for commercial purposes. The governor and council moved quickly to license the construction of a number of wharves along the waterfront, and on 1 July 1751 one John Grant was empowered to construct a wharf opposite George Street. He did so, and added a house to the premises as well. His heirs sold part of the property to merchant Charles Mason for £60 in 1756, and Mason died in 1763, leaving a widow and two young daughters, Margaret and Amelia. By will he left all his realty to his widow, but on her remarriage to his daughters equally. It is Amelia, born in 1755, who will be of particular interest, as she would become the grandmother of Beamish Murdoch and a key figure in the eventual litigation over the wharf.[9]

The widow Mason and her two young daughters continued to inhabit the house on the wharf until Mrs Mason remarried in 1764. Her second husband, victualler Frederick Ott, eventually acquired a number of properties in and around the town of Halifax, including the other part of the wharf formerly owned by John Grant, which now came to be called Ott's Wharf.[10] Having no children of his own, Ott treated his stepdaughters as his own kin.

In 1770 fifteen-year-old Amelia Mason married an Anglo-Irish merchant, Thomas Beamish, who had come to Halifax from Cork a few years before. Thomas and Amelia occupied the wharf with their growing family, and in 1780 Thomas bought out the half-share of Amelia's sister in the part of the wharf that the two women owned as devisees of Charles Mason. The other part, which had been purchased by Frederick Ott, was left by him in his will to all his stepgrandchildren, born and to be born, in equal shares, with the parents to hold the shares of their children in trust until the age of majority. Ott left all his other landholdings subject to the same trust. Thomas and Amelia took possession of all these properties at Ott's death in 1783, none of their children having reached the age of majority. Margaret's only child having died young, Thomas and Amelia's children were the only beneficiaries of the Ott estate.

Ott's Wharf was the jewel in the crown of the Ott real estate empire. It occupied a central location on the Halifax waterfront, just north of the imperial government's wharves, and just south of the site that would become the terminus for the Dartmouth ferry in the 1790s. The main fish market was held next door, and the town produce market was located just across Lower Water Street. Westward from the wharf, up George Street, the land rose sharply to the spot where the fortifications known as the Citadel were constantly being built and rebuilt. By 1805 labourers on the wharf could look up George Street and see Halifax's Town Clock, the Duke of Kent's parting gift to a population he believed to be insufficiently punctual. In good times the wharf was a thriving business, its warehouses and retail premises providing rental income to supplement the wharfage fees its owners were entitled to charge. Over the period 1787–1815 the wharf produced about £340 gross income annually, but only a little over £100 net. The 'normal' net income was probably closer to £200 per annum, as a hurricane in 1798 virtually destroyed the wharf and necessitated large sums for its reconstruction. The Beamish family retained the wharf until 1874, when they sold it for $53,200.

In planning how to distribute his estate after his death, Ott presumably bypassed his stepdaughters because he believed he had advantaged them sufficiently during his own lifetime; possibly too he feared that his property might be seized for the future debts of his sons-in-law.[11] He imposed two conditions on his devise, one precedent and one subsequent. His grandchildren were required to take the name of Ott at the age of majority in order for their share to vest in possession. Such a clause was an echo of the 'name and arms' clause sometimes found in English wills, whereby a childless testator would provide for the continuation of his name by a form of testamentary adoption, at a time when adoption was not recognized in law. All the grandchildren were scrupulous about adding the name Ott to their own family name. Thus Beamish Murdoch's mother was known as Elizabeth Ott Beamish before her marriage and Elizabeth Ott Murdoch afterwards. The second condition was less benign, although common enough at the time. Perhaps concerned that his generosity to his step-grandchildren might foster a spirit of unwonted independence, Ott provided that any granddaughter who married without her parents' consent would lose her share.[12]

At Frederick Ott's death, then, Thomas Beamish came into possession of the entire wharf property, both the 'Mason portion' and the 'Ott portion,' though by three different titles: as trustee for his children of the Ott portion, and, with regard to the Mason portion, by the *jus mariti* with respect to Amelia's personal half-share[13] and as owner only with respect to the half-share which he had bought from his sister-in-law. Hence Thomas was free to use only the latter interest as security for his debts, which unfortunately began to mount just as Ott died. With the end of the war in 1783, reduced British spending, a fall in commodity prices from inflated wartime levels, and the sudden appearance of a whole troop of competitors in the form of the Loyalists gave a sharp shock to the Halifax mercantile community. Thomas Beamish was overwhelmed by this challenge, which was accompanied by growing domestic responsibilities: Amelia would bear fourteen children by 1792, eight of whom survived to adulthood.

Beamish's countrymen, the northern Irish-born Thomas, William and James Cochran, were his principal financiers. They had advanced him at least £1,100 by 1784, when the solvency of the Beamishes began to be a concern. The Cochrans then began to demand security for the sums that they had advanced. Thomas and Amelia could mortgage their own interests in the Mason portion of the wharf, but they had been given no power under Frederick Ott's will to sell or mortgage their children's interests in the Ott portion or in Ott's other lands. In England such deficiencies were sometimes rectified by a private act of Parliament — indeed, much parliamentary time in the eighteenth century was spent fine-tuning family settlements. Thomas Beamish duly explored this route, appearing with counsel before the House of Assembly on 10 November 1784 in support of 'A Bill to enable Thomas Beamish to sell Real Estate of Frederick Ott.' The bill was amended and passed, but failed in the council and did not become law. The Beamishes edged closer to the precipice.[14]

THE FIRST CHANCERY DECREE AND ITS AFTERMATH, 1785–1802

The legislative door having closed, the Beamishes tried the last door open to them — the judicial.[15] In February 1785 an application was made to Chancery to remove the executors named in Ott's will, John Loader and James Stephens, to confirm Thomas and Amelia as sole trustees and to give them power to sell or mortgage any of the properties in the Ott estate.[16] Normally, if a trust instrument fails to equip trustees with a power of sale or mortgage, a court has no jurisdiction to add such powers contrary to the wishes of the settlor or testator. There were (and are) some exceptions to this rule, however, and the Beamishes tried to bring their case within one of them.

The bill of complaint filed by Thomas and Amelia alleged that Ott was incapacitated and had been neglecting his property for years before his death, and that much of it was now in need of substantial repair. The Beamishes justified their request for powers of sale and mortgage on what is now known in the law of trusts as the salvage or emergency jurisdiction.[17] The court granted the Beamishes a wide power to deal with the lands: they could sell or mortgage such part of the Ott estate's lands as they saw fit, 'for the purpose of raising money for the Repairs and Improvements of the Remainder.' The effect of such conveyances was stated to be 'sufficient in Law to create to such purchasers ... an Estate in Fee Simple forever. And such Deeds ... shall stand free and unimpeached by the defendants ... or by the children of the plaintiffs ... or by any other person or persons whatsoever.' The final decree issued on 31 March 1785, the cause having been heard by Governor John Parr sitting as Chancellor, assisted by Richard Bulkeley, Master of the Rolls, and Foster Hutchinson, Master in Chancery.

Armed with this decree, the Beamishes then began a mad scramble to keep creditors from the door. They mortgaged the wharf and some other Ott properties to the Cochrans in August and November, and mortgaged the wharf again for £233 to Thomas Craine, a Jamaican merchant, in December 1785. They sold outright a number of properties in the 'North Suburbs' of the town, including one to the newly arrived Loyalist and Attorney General Sampson Salter Blowers.

It was all to no avail. In Trinity Term 1786 Peter McNab and London merchant Brook Watson recovered judgments for some £900 against Thomas Beamish, and subsequently had him committed to the common jail at Halifax. In May 1787 McNab consented to Beamish's release only on his paying £200 down on his debt plus making over title to a Water Street property near the wharf. At the same time the Cochrans administered the *coup de grâce*: by deed dated 21 April 1787 the Beamishes unconditionally sold Ott's wharf to the Cochrans for a consideration expressed to be £1,400. The Cochrans then took the precaution of having a confirmatory Crown grant issued to themselves, as there had been some confusion about the exact nature of the interest created by Crown grants for wharf purposes in the past.[18] When the Cochrans took possession the Beamishes moved to Cole Harbour, a small fishing village five miles east of Halifax, where one of Ott's properties had survived the shipwreck of the Beamish fortunes. A few properties elsewhere had also survived unscathed, so the Beamishes were not destitute, but undoubtedly their prospects were much reduced.

By 1792 Thomas Beamish was, in the words of the ballad, 'a broken man on a Halifax pier.' He appears to have abandoned Halifax and his family about this time, leaving Amelia in a difficult position. She was now thirty-seven years old and responsible for nine children, all under the age of majority and the youngest but a few months old. Aided by the revenues produced by the remaining properties from the Ott estate, as well as a few properties that she owned in her own right, Amelia managed to support her family. Thomas's absence at least meant that she could control these lands without any interference from him, and indeed she did not hesitate to describe herself as a widow in a deed of 1801.[19]

After assuring her family's survival, Amelia's ultimate goal was to recover the Ott properties that had been left to her children. She harboured an acute sense of grievance against the Cochrans, whom she alleged to have procured the 1787 deed by duress when Thomas was in debtors' prison. Amelia nourished this sense of grievance among her offspring, but a decade would pass before her older children were in any position to assist her in launching legal action to contest the Cochrans' ownership of the wharf. Her eldest son Frederick came of age about 1794, but he became a mariner and spent much time at sea until he settled at Blandford, Lunenburg County, about 1800. The next and only other surviving son, Thomas, came of age about 1801. In October 1799 Amelia acquired two sons-in-law who, through the common law doctrine of *jus mariti*, had a clear pecuniary incentive to assist Amelia in her mission. Elizabeth Ott Beamish married merchant Andrew Murdoch of Halifax, while her sister Margaret married merchant Thomas Akins (Aikins) of Liverpool. Both men assisted their new relations in preparing for litigation.

THE DISPUTE ERUPTS, 1802–1816

By 1801 the Beamishes were prepared to go on the offensive. Thomas Cochran, the patriarch, had just died, so they named as defendants only his younger brothers James and William as surviving partners. It is hard to avoid the inference that the Beamishes were waiting for Thomas's death to bring their action. He was, after all, a member of the Council, on which the chief justice also sat. The latter would likely be involved in the Supreme Court action which the Beamishes wished to launch, and might well be asked to assist the lieutenant-governor, sitting as Chancellor, if there were further proceedings in Chancery.

An action in ejectment in the Supreme Court was the usual way of trying title at common law. The eight surviving Beamish children (plus the husbands of two of the daughters) duly brought this action, but Amelia was not a party to it. No doubt they anticipated the Cochrans' next move, which was to apply to the Chancellor for an injunction preventing the Beamishes from proceeding with their suit at law until the Cochrans' bill of complaint against them could be heard. Filed on 3 February 1802, the bill rehearsed the sequence of events outlined above. The Cochrans' position was that all the money advanced to the Beamishes was used either to repair the wharf, which was in a ruinous condition at Frederick Ott's death, or to improve Ott's property at Cole Harbour; the mortgages securing those amounts were thus valid exercises of the power conferred by the Chancery decree of March 1785. When the Beamishes fell behind on those mortgages, the Cochrans were within their rights in taking the wharf in full settlement by the deed of April 1787, and they were protected by the 1785 decree from the claims of the Beamish children or anyone else. The injunction issued as a matter of course a month later.

It took the Beamishes over two years to file their answer, which was dated 7 April 1804 and filed 15 August 1804. No doubt the delay is explicable both by ongoing financial difficulties and by the personal tragedies that intervened. Amelia's daughter Elizabeth Ott Murdoch, alive in April 1803, is described as 'lately dead' in the answer a year later, while her husband Andrew was imprisoned for debt in June 1803. Thomas Akins, meanwhile, bought out the interest of the adult Beamishes in one of the Ott estate properties in dispute (not the wharf) for £100, probably in order to help finance the lawsuit.[20]

In their answer the Beamishes differed with the Cochrans on some crucial matters of fact and alleged other facts not mentioned by the complainants. They denied that the wharf was in a decayed state at Frederick Ott's death. Ott, they alleged, was an industrious man who took care of his property, and the annual income of his estate was £750, which was adequate to support him and keep his property in repair. The Cochrans induced Thomas and Amelia Beamish to apply for the Chancery decree of

1785, which was 'procured by the Interest and Influence of the said Complainants ... for the express and only purpose of enabling them to apply the property of the Defendants to the payment of a Debt the said Complainants ... considered to be otherwise desperate.' Thomas, they said, was 'well known to the [Cochrans] to be unfortunate by lapses in Trade,' and the Cochrans took advantage of him when imprisoned in 1787 to procure the deed to the wharf. Thomas and Amelia only agreed to sign in order to secure his liberation and because they were assured that the deed would not affect their children's rights. In addition, Thomas by this point was 'totally unfit to manage his own concerns,' an ambiguous reference which nonetheless fits with his unexplained departure a few years later.[21]

The answer of the Beamishes raised three distinct legal arguments, only the first of which depended on the court believing their story about the real purposes to which the money was put. If the mortgages were granted to the Cochrans only to secure Thomas and Amelia's personal debts and not in connection with repairing estate property, arguably they were not within the scope of the 1785 decree. If the Cochrans knew these facts to be true, then they would not be able to enforce the mortgages in equity or to rely on the deed of 1787 as a 'settlement' of those mortgages. Even the confirmatory Crown grant was invalid on this reasoning: obtained on the basis of wilfully incomplete information, it should be set aside.

Alternatively, Chancery had a broad jurisdiction in the eighteenth century to relieve the vulnerable from the consequences of imprudent transactions. In addition to the description of Thomas's difficult state, the Beamishes' answer painted Amelia Ott Beamish as a struggling but vulnerable figure, worn down by the oppressive action of the Cochrans. She 'did use every argument she was capable of and even Tears to dissuade the said Complainants ... from their unjustifiable Attempt upon the Property of her Children.' Further, she admonished 'that if she lived to see her children grow up, she would inform them of the aforesaid circumstances, and do every thing in her power to defeat the unjust Intentions of the said Complainants, and that although her children were Infants borne down by poverty, distress and the unfeeling proceedings of the Complainants, she entertained the Hope the day would come, when Justice should be rendered them, and their Property, thus unjustly wrested from them, restored.' This kind of heartfelt appeal was permissible only in Chancery and would never be encountered in the more formulaic pleadings of the common law courts. It is precisely the more verbose Chancery pleadings that are so useful to the modern historian, though productive of much of the delay lamented by contemporaries.

Finally, the Beamishes invoked, albeit elliptically, the argument that the deed of 1787, although an absolute conveyance on its face, was intended by the parties to be only a mortgage. This equitable doctrine, epitomized in the maxim, 'once a mortgage, always a mortgage,' dated back to the mid-seventeenth century at least, and is occasionally invoked even today.[22] Acceptance of this argument would mean that the Beamishes could get back the wharf once they had acquitted their debts to the Cochrans, with interest.

What exactly was the Cochrans' 'Interest and Influence' of which the Beamishes complained? The three brothers had arrived from the north of Ireland with their father Joseph c. 1765, about the same time as Thomas Beamish. They arrived in the province early enough to benefit from large grants (26,750 acres in Amherst Township alone), and between property speculation and a large mercantile business in Halifax amassed a considerable fortune in a relatively brief period of time. The three brothers, but especially Thomas, became part of an Irish clique that dominated provincial life until the coming of the Loyalists and afterwards. Thomas Cochran sat in the House of Assembly for Liverpool Township from 1775 until 1785, when he was elevated to the Council.[23] His younger brother William then sat for Halifax Township from 1785 to 1816. In the years just before the Loyalist arrival, the province was effectively ruled by the Irish-born 'duumvirate' composed of Chief Justice Bryan Finucane (1778–1785) and the Hon. Richard Bulkeley, Master of the Rolls and provincial secretary. Finucane championed the interests of the Irish merchants and was substantially indebted to Thomas Cochran, for whom he lobbied hard for a Council seat. Governor Parr, also an Irishman, has been portrayed as something of a pawn in the hands of Finucane and Bulkeley.[24]

At the time that Thomas and Amelia Beamish sought the Chancery decree of 1785, Thomas Cochran was Speaker of the Assembly. He would be named to the Council three months after the decree. Parr as Chancellor was advised by Bulkeley and Foster Hutchinson, a former Massachusetts judge who had come to Halifax in 1776.[25] Chief Justice Finucane did not formally attend the hearing, as Supreme Court judges were sometimes requested to do, but Parr admitted that he normally sought Finucane's advice on matters of law.[26]

A number of other factors support the Beamishes' allegation that the decree was procured at the instance of the Cochrans for their own purposes rather than instigated by Thomas and Amelia. Counsel for Thomas and Amelia were the Crown law officers, Attorney General Sampson Salter Blowers and Solicitor General Richard John Uniacke, acting in their private capacities. Uniacke was definitely associated with the Cochran-Finucane-Bulkeley clique at this time. He was the protégé of Finucane, who had arranged for his appointment as solicitor general in 1781. Moreover, Uniacke had acted for the Cochrans in other matters since at least 1783, and later served as counsel to the Cochrans during their Chancery suit against the Beamishes. His actions would not have been seen as embodying a conflict of interest by contemporary standards, but it is clear that his primary role in this matter was to protect the interests of the Cochrans rather than the Beamishes.

The 1785 proceeding, an action by the Beamishes against the executors named in Ott's will, Loader and Stephens, was adversarial in form only. The answer of John Loader was made by 'Thomas Cochran, the said Defendant's Agent and friend,' and filed with the consent of Uniacke. There was in substance no dispute at all: the 'complaint' was really just an opportunity to bring the matter before the court to vary the terms of the trust, ultimately to the Cochrans' benefit. Even granting that the salvage jurisdiction was exercised more freely in the eighteenth century than later, the responsibility of the Court of Chancery was to protect the interests of the infant beneficiaries, Thomas and Amelia's children. The decree, however, imposed no effective constraints on the parents' ability to sell their children's property and no mechanism to ensure that any money secured by such sales would be used for the authorized purposes. For example, the court might have directed a Master in Chancery to carry out a periodic account of the proceeds of any sales of the trust property. Without such constraints it was entirely predictable that the Ott estate properties would be disposed of for the parents' benefit, not the children's.

The argument made by the Beamish children in 1804, that the 1785 decree was part of a plot orchestrated by the Cochrans to secure the Ott properties for the payment of the parents' debts, is quite plausible. Thomas and Amelia were not totally innocent in this affair, since they were desperate to get at their children's property in order to solve the family's financial problems. Nonetheless, they were being guided through the maze of Chancery by someone whose interests were directly in conflict with their own, arguably with the knowledge and acquiescence of the judges concerned. Worse yet, the judges who were supposed to look after the property of infants with particular solicitude failed entirely in their duty, arguably because they were overly concerned to protect the interests of the powerful Cochrans.

On the basis of their answer to the Cochrans' petition, counsel for the Beamishes, the prominent Loyalist lawyer Simon Bradstreet Robie, moved that the injunction be dissolved, thus allowing the ejectment action in the Supreme Court to proceed. Lieutenant-governor Sir John Wentworth, acting as Chancellor, ordered on 14 August 1804 that the injunction be dissolved unless cause were shown to the contrary within twenty-one days. Uniacke filed an appearance on 5 September stating that he wished to oppose the order for dissolution, but no date for a hearing was set. For unknown reasons, the proceeding remained paralysed for the next seven years. On the face of it, the injunction should have been dissolved when the terms of the order of 14 August were not met. Yet this did not happen, as the Beamishes were asking anew in 1811 that the injunction be dissolved.

There are a number of possible explanations for this long hiatus. It may be that the parties began settlement negotiations that dragged on longer than expected. Certainly the Beamish clan, who now resided at Blandford and Liverpool as well as Halifax, were an unwieldy group for purposes of client consultation. Andrew Murdoch's protracted stay in debtors' prison, until some time in 1808, probably complicated matters. Margaret Ott Akins died in 1809, her death a tragic echo of her sister's six years earlier. Both Elizabeth and Margaret died not long after giving birth to their first-born sons, Beamish Murdoch and Thomas Beamish Akins, each of whom in turn was taken in by his grandmother Amelia. Each boy inherited his mother's interest in the Ott estate, subject to his father's entitlement to it for life, pursuant to the common law doctrine of curtesy.

Another complication was the fact that Lieutenant Governor Wentworth was succeeded by Sir George Prevost in 1808. When Prevost came out to Nova Scotia, he was accompanied by his private secretary Samuel Hood George, who was none other than Thomas Cochran's grandson. Prevost promoted his protégé to the post of provincial secretary as soon as it became vacant. Samuel Hood was the son of Sir Rupert George, who was on very good terms with Prevost, and Margaret Cochran, Cochran's eldest daughter.[27] It may be that the Beamishes despaired of a fair hearing before a Chancellor who was on such terms of intimacy with the Cochran family, and preferred to wait for Prevost's departure.

Whatever the reasons, the delay could only be of benefit to the Cochrans. As they were the parties in possession and the parties who had commenced the Chancery suit, they were essentially in control. However, in spite of their intimacy with the Prevost regime, things had changed since those halcyon days in the 1780s when the Cochrans ruled the province. The Loyalist influx had rearranged the political situation, and the Loyalists had seen their efforts for recognition crowned with success in the appointment of John Wentworth as lieutenant-governor in 1792 and Sampson Salter Blowers as chief justice in 1797. The Cochrans remained on reasonably good terms with the emergent Loyalist political hierarchy, but their principal power base had been in the pre-Loyalist population, and their 'Interest and Influence' were slowly diminishing, if by no means gone.

If the Loyalists were successful in exerting their influence politically, they were also having a marked impact on the bar and the judiciary, an impact that would be felt in the Cochran-Beamish litigation. Finucane's death in 1785 had left the judiciary in some disarray, and the pre-Loyalist bar, aside from a few leading lights such as Uniacke, was relatively undistinguished. An influx of the cream of the pre-Revolutionary New England bars in the 1780s changed the situation dramatically. The most obvious fallout of this change was the 'judges' affair' of 1787–8, which pitted the newly arrived Loyalist lawyers against the somewhat hapless judges who remained on the Supreme Court after the demise of Chief Justice Finucane.

Provincial history has tended to emphasize the political aspects of the struggles between Loyalists and pre-Loyalists in Nova Scotia. Yet there were positive aspects to the arrival of the Loyalist lawyers. While they certainly fought for their share of patronage, they also breathed new life into the bar and insisted upon more exacting standards of professional competence. In selecting one of these lawyers, Simon Bradstreet Robie, as their counsel, the pre-Loyalist Beamishes paid tribute to the reputation of the Loyalist bar and shrewdly acknowledged their strong position in the new judicial and political order of the province.

The change was perhaps even more noticeable in the judiciary than in the bar. After the death of Finucane, Governor Parr pleaded with London to send him a worthy successor from England. Parr has been criticized for not recommending a Loyalist for the post, but in view of the strained relations between Loyalist and pre-Loyalist at this point in provincial history, it would have been impossible for a candidate from either 'camp' to fulfil the role adequately.[28] Under the circumstances the appointment of a candidate from England with close ties to neither group was probably the wisest course if the office of chief justice was to preserve any claim to impartiality. Thomas Andrew Strange, although young and untried, ultimately rose to the challenge.[29] By the time he left the province in 1796 he had enhanced the image of the Supreme Court and taken steps to improve standards at the bar, most notably by donating his collection of law books to serve as the nucleus of a barristers' library.

Strange provided the bridge to the appointment of Sampson Salter Blowers as the first Loyalist chief justice. Blowers, a scion of the pre-

Revolutionary Massachusetts bar, was a good choice. Extremely competent and authoritative, he seemed able to rise above the bickering between Loyalist and pre-Loyalist, and was seen as administering justice fairly according to law. His role in the Beamish litigation was decisive.

In 1811 the Beamishes attempted to revive the case by asking anew that the injunction, preventing them from continuing their ejectment suit, be dissolved. The complainants responded with a petition to make the injunction permanent, and it was Blowers who endorsed the petition 'A day should be given for hearing the petition.' Yet once again nothing happened, such that the Beamishes petitioned to have the bill dismissed for want of prosecution in December 1814. Finally, a year later, Lieutenant-Governor Sherbrooke, assisted by Blowers, heard counsel on both sides on the substance of the complaint. Sherbrooke ruled that three Halifax merchants should act as commissioners to audit the accounts of the Beamish Wharf since 1785, and that the injunction be dissolved. The commissioners moved much more speedily than anyone ever had before in this lawsuit; appointed on 27 November 1815, they filed their report on 10 January 1816.

In effect, the Beamishes had already won, even though counsel presented further arguments in February, and the final decretal order did not issue until 26 April 1816. Given the politically sensitive nature of the allegations, it was not surprising that the order was embellished with only the briefest of reasons. The court accepted the third of the arguments advanced by the Beamishes, which imputed no actual wrongdoing to the Cochrans. Although the deed of 1785 to the Cochrans was absolute on its face, stated the court, in equity it was intended to function at most as a lien or mortgage. The auditors found that the Cochrans had spent £6,454 repairing the wharf and building premises thereon over the period 1787–1815, while receiving £9,603 in rentals over that period, leaving a surplus of £3,149 to the credit of the Beamishes. Against that the Cochrans had to be credited with the £3,950 they had advanced to Thomas and Amelia by way of loan (with interest), leaving a balance owing to the Cochrans of £802. On payment of this sum by the Beamishes, the court ordered the Cochrans to reconvey the wharf. Receivers were appointed to manage the property pending the final reconveyance, or, as it turned out, in case of an appeal.

THE APPEAL TO THE KING IN COUNCIL, 1816–1820

The Cochran brothers were determined to resist. Within three days they gave notice that they would launch an appeal. Appeals from the Atlantic colonies to the King in Council at this period were not common, but nor were they unknown. During the years that the Cochrans' appeal was underway, several other petitions to the King in Council from the Atlantic colonies were dealt with: another one from Nova Scotia, two from Prince Edward Island, and five from Newfoundland. That the Cochrans chose to appeal probably attests more to the symbolic affront to their power and status and a concern with familial reputation than to the value of the property as such. James and William Cochran were two childless old men, aged seventy-five and sixty-five, by 1816, but they had the honour of their nieces and nephews, Thomas's progeny, to uphold.[30]

Once again, matters seemed to drag. The Cochrans filed the bond for £500 required as security for costs on the appeal on 17 January 1817, but on 5 May 1818 the Beamishes sought enforcement of the Chancery decree and forfeiture of the bond on the basis that the appeal had not been prosecuted. William Cochran replied via Uniacke that he could not get copies of the whole file made until January 1817, but that they had immediately been sent off at that time, and that his London counsel had been instructed to bring on the matter as soon as possible. This sounds plausible, as the order-in-council referring the appeal to the committee for hearing appeals from the plantations was dated 13 August 1817. In view of the steps taken by the appellants, Lord Dalhousie, now lieutenant-governor, noted that he could not allow the Chancery decree to be enforced 'until the decision [of the King in Council] be known.'

The identity of the Cochrans' counsel shows just how seriously they took the appeal. Sir Samuel Romilly, the political radical and noted criminal law reformer, was at the zenith of his political and legal career in the second decade of the nineteenth century. Solicitor general in the Ministry of All the Talents in 1806–7, he was rumoured to be next in line for the post of Lord Chancellor if the whigs managed to resume office. He was undoubtedly the best-known and most successful Chancery practitioner of the day, with an income reputed to be £16,000 a year. His clients included the Prince of Wales, the Duke of Kent, Sir Walter Scott, Lady Byron, and numerous scions of the English aristocracy. Romilly was on excellent terms with Lord Eldon, Lord Chancellor from 1801 to 1827, in spite of the wide divergence of their political views.[31]

Appeals to the King in Council from colonial courts did not yet go to that body so familiar to students of Canadian constitutional law, the Judicial Committee of the Privy Council. The Judicial Committee was established by statute in 1833, part of the wide-ranging Wilhelmine and Victorian reforms to the administration of justice in England.[32] From 1696 to 1833, appeals from the plantations were heard by a standing committee of the whole council, often called the appeals committee. It was to sit with a quorum of three, and was thus differently constituted for each cause. Any councillor might attend and there was no requirement that any of those present be judges or legally trained, though some legal men usually sat on each appeal. The lack of any degree of specialization in colonial laws and of any formal distinction between the council's colonial and domestic functions meant that the system was increasingly seen as unsatisfactory.[33] Lord Brougham, a future Lord Chancellor and severe critic of the pre-1833 system, claimed that he had witnessed property 'worth thirty thousand pounds sterling per annum, disposed of in a few minutes ... by the learned members of the Privy Council who reversed a sentence pronounced by all the [colonial] judges upon no less than nineteen days of anxious discussion.'[34]

The next delay in the proceedings was the fault of no one. Distraught at the death of his beloved wife Anne, Sir Samuel Romilly slit his throat three days later, on 1 November 1818. New counsel had to be instructed, which again retarded the cause. Back in Halifax, William Cochran was left to carry on alone when his brother James died in 1819. The appeal was finally heard on 11 May 1820, by a panel of three highly eminent judges: Sir William Scott, Sir William Grant, and Sir John Nicholl.[35] It is not known who replaced Sir Samuel Romilly or who represented the Beamishes; the order of council merely states that counsel were heard on both sides.[36] Did Beamish Murdoch's erstwhile principal, Crofton Uniacke, now studying at Lincoln's Inn, attend the hearing? No doubt he acted as liaison with London counsel on behalf of his father, who continued to represent the Cochrans in Halifax.

Four years to conclude the appeal may seem unduly long, but *Cochran v. Beamish* in fact did much better than most cases heard by the Privy Council during this period. Between 1814 and 1826 517 appeals were lodged, but only one-quarter had been heard by early 1828; another quarter were abandoned or dismissed for want of prosecution, and half remained undisposed of.[37] Given this dreadful record and the change in counsel, a four-year delay hardly seems a source of complaint.

On 29 May the committee's decision was read before the Privy Council, who humbly advised His Majesty that the decree of the Nova Scotia Court of Chancery should be affirmed. Had Romilly survived, his unparalleled standing as a Chancery lawyer might have persuaded the committee that the Cochrans were in the right. As it was, the members of council sitting around the table had other matters on their mind. The nation had been in a state of ferment since the massacre at Peterloo the previous summer, and in February a plot to overthrow the government ('the Cato Street conspiracy') had been uncovered. The kingdom was now rife with rumours of the impending return from the continent of Queen Caroline, the long-estranged wife of the new king, George IV having succeeded his father on the latter's death on 29 January 1820. The rumours were true: Caroline arrived in England on 5 June, and the ensuing attempt by the King to divorce her and deprive her of her title made her – improbably – the focus of a popular movement that threatened briefly to become insurrectionary. Under these circumstances, it is unlikely that council members were unduly concerned about the fate of a wharf in far off Nova Scotia.

Although he could not have known of the result, William Cochran died the day after the committee dismissed the appeal. To Beamish Murdoch, the coincidence was a fitting one. In the precedent-cum-commonplace book he kept during the years 1814–21, he made the following solemn inscription: 'June 1st 1820. Wm Cochran is dead – died 3 days ago in the Country. Thus ends the Trio.'[38] The death of the last of the Cochran brothers coincided, precisely and poetically, with the utter failure of their attempt to crush the Beamish family.

It may be that 'the better-informed counsel and judges in the colonies had little respect for Conciliar decisions' as legal precedents at this time,[39] but the order in the Market Wharf case was implemented in Nova Scotia as if it constituted Holy Writ. The news of the decision took six weeks or so to reach Halifax. On 24 July 1820 the Beamishes petitioned to enforce the decree, expressing for the first time a hint of impatience. They prayed for an early day to hear the petition, 'as the Cause has been pending upwards of eighteen years, to the great loss and injury of your Petitioners.'[40] The court ordered the same day that the receivers appointed in 1816 account for the rents received, and that the Beamishes show that they had complied with the terms of the 1816 decree as affirmed, i.e., that they could tender the amount of £802 determined to be owing the Cochrans. With interest since 1816, this sum now amounted to a round £1,000.

The final capitulation came in a declaration dated 16 October 1820. Representatives of the Cochran estate stated that, having been required by the Chancery decree to 'yield up and deliver the peaceable and quiet possession of the Land and Premises described in the Bill commonly called the Market Wharf or Cochran's Wharf,' and to deliver up all relevant title documents in their possession, they now did so on receipt of £1,000 from the Beamishes. For their part, the Beamishes obtained the money by mortgaging the premises to merchant Samuel Muirhead. Even before the final cession, Beamish Murdoch was busy writing to various parties in possession of lands formerly part of the Ott estate, which had been sold by Thomas and Amelia under the authority of the Chancery decree of 1785. Brandishing the Privy Council's order confirming the rights of the Beamishes, Murdoch sought to convince these parties to give up without a fight, and offered compensation for any improvements made during the period of their possession.[41] In fact, the Beamishes had taken a number of ejectment actions in the Supreme Court against parties who had bought lands on the strength of the 1785 Chancery decree and had been successful in many of them. Only the Cochrans and one other party seem to have resisted by means of a Chancery suit.[42]

JUSTICE DELAYED – BUT NOT DENIED

The significance of the Market Wharf litigation may be assessed on a number of levels: the biographical, the institutional, and the legal-cultural. On the biographical plane, the victory was a defining moment in the life of the young Beamish Murdoch. Without the material security provided by the confirmation of his inheritance, he might still have become a lawyer. But it is unlikely that he could have pursued his aspirations to contribute to the political, legal, and cultural leadership of his society. The victory had an ideological impact, too, confirming for Murdoch his faith in the perfection of the Nova Scotia constitution. For all his support of political reform in the 1825–35 decade, Murdoch had a basic faith in provincial institutions, which meant that he was unlikely to follow those who wanted more significant change.[43] That faith was based on an intense personal experience of the law, which he did not hesitate to proclaim publicly. In dedicating his *Epitome of the Laws of Nova-Scotia* to the nonagenarian Sampson Salter Blowers, Murdoch wrote of his respect for the chief justice's 'public services, high judicial qualities, and inflexible integrity, which are interwoven with the author's earliest recollections.'[44]

At the institutional level, the litigation provides important evidence of changes over time in the Court of Chancery. The experience of Thomas and Amelia Beamish in the 1780s illustrates the dangers inherent in the old Governor-as-Chancellor model that prevailed in the Maritime provinces and the Caribbean. For routine matters the model might well suffice, but in cases where powerful friends of the governor were involved, it was hard to dispel perceptions that their 'Interest and Influence' might secure a favourable Chancery decision. It is not so much that there might have been bribery or active bias on the part of the governor or his advisers, but that it would be easy enough to base one's action on the assumption that what was good for the Cochrans, or other powerful litigants, was good for the province.

Critiques of Chancery's political bias and its lack of common law safeguards were also heard in Prince Edward Island at the end of the eighteenth century. The agent of a proprietor lamented in 1798 that 'neither life nor property are safe under the present government of Governor Fanning and the Chief Justice's family ... [I]f it should so happen that a jury, more inclined to do justice than our Chief Justice, should give a verdict to one obnoxious to the [government] party, the case is immediately hung up in Chancery, the Governor being Chancellor, where the known partiality, and great expense of the court frighten them from justice.'[45] In Nova Scotia the rather freewheeling attitude of the governor can also be seen in Governor Parr's *ex cathedra* adoption of the Irish form of foreclosure and sale in 1783–4, when the English form of foreclosure had been used invariably for the previous thirty years. This new remedy offered fewer protections for the borrower than the traditional English foreclosure, and was adopted without a scintilla of legislative authority. The Chancery courts of the Maritime provinces in the eighteenth century are in fact reminiscent of the English Chancery of the seventeenth century, when critiques of the court as an illegitimate arm of royal government reached their apogee.

By the second decade of the nineteenth century the 'Interest and Influence' of great magnates, while by no means extinct, seems much reduced. Lord Dalhousie was keen to professionalize the Court of Chancery, and would have appointed Blowers Master of the Rolls if London had permitted it.[46] The appointment of a legally trained Master of the Rolls to preside in Chancery in place of the governor and prevent the kinds of delays experienced in the Market Wharf litigation was made soon after, in 1825. The post went, appropriately enough, to the Beamishes' lawyer, Simon Bradstreet Robie. Much of the credit for any improvement in the administration of civil justice between 1785 and 1815 must go to Blowers and to the highly professionalized Loyalist bar.

The decisive intervention of Chancery in this matter also cautions us about making generalizations based on experiences in the common law courts alone. The administration of the common law in the colonial period often appears as a harsh and rigorous exercise in which possessive individualism enjoyed free rein. Yet it was tempered in some instances, as in the Market Wharf case, by equitable doctrines. The law appears Janus-faced, committed to uphold both the rigour of the common law of contract and conveyancing and the flexibility that allowed the clear terms of a duly executed deed of sale to be interpreted as a mere security arrangement.

W.R. Cornish has suggested that between the common law's 'severely individualistic view of freedom and sanctity of contract' and equity's 'protective jurisdiction of conscience ... a peculiar balance was reached which depended on the structure of institutions.'[47] John Weaver has recently drawn attention to the importance of the equitable jurisdiction in the context of early Upper Canadian mortgage law, prior to the introduction of that province's Court of Chancery in 1837.[48] We see this 'peculiar balance' in action in the Market Wharf case, where the judges were compelled to take into account values other than those of possessive individualism.

An important caveat about this 'peculiar balance' must be registered, and that is its confinement to cases dealing with property and debtor-creditor matters. It is possible to find a broad social consensus that while the law should provide for the strict enforcement of contracts and property transactions, it should also provide an 'escape route' through equitable doctrines in particular cases of hardship or rough dealing. Where employment contracts were concerned, however, no such balance was evident. Equity had little involvement with such contracts, and the harshness of the common law remained unmitigated until late Victorian legislation began to constrain the power of capital to some extent. In the field of employment law, the discrepancy between 'legal justice' and 'social justice' remained wide throughout the nineteenth century.

In terms of methodology, the Market Wharf litigation suggests the potential that lies largely untapped in the hundreds of files in Chancery archieves. Although this case is unusual both in the fulness of its documentation and in the time it took to conclude, there are many others with ample written records. For legal, social, and economic historians, the Chancery archives contain a wealth of quantitative and qualitative data on mortgage transactions in particular, which always formed the major part of Chancery's caseload.

In order to assess the wider meaning of the Market Wharf litigation for the legal culture of British North America, we must return to some of the questions posed at the beginning of this chapter. What did this litigation mean to the participants? Why were they so tenacious? Why did they not settle? Here we must speculate to some extent, since the parties did not leave any private papers in which they explained their motivation. It seems clear that something other than mere money was at stake here. On both sides matters of honour and reputation were involved. The Beamishes were alleging that the Cochrans, one of the most highly placed families in the entire province, had acted oppressively and unjustly. What could the Cochrans do but resist? The Beamishes' allegations were tantamount to saying that the Cochrans were not 'fit and proper persons' to hold high office. They had to seek the authoritative determination of a tribunal, the highest in the land if necessary, in order to uphold their family name. The Cochrans could easily have afforded to give up the wharf or to make a financial settlement to end the litigation. But to have settled or resorted to some more informal means of resolution would have left the insult unaddressed.

For their part, the Beamishes felt their honour was also at stake. Their father had been imposed upon, advantage had been taken while he was in a vulnerable state. Perhaps the Beamishes even blamed the Cochrans for Thomas's disappearance. Even worse, however, was the Cochrans' seeming attempt to deprive the entire Beamish family of their rightful place in Halifax society. Amelia Beamish stated to the court that the Cochrans had assured them that the deed of 1787 would not affect their children's interests, and she believed that they had either misled her and her husband or gone back on their word. In Amelia's world-view, *restitutio in integrum* by the Cochrans was the only acceptable outcome.

The honour-related aspects of this litigation make it easier to understand why the parties did not settle, and why they were prepared to tolerate such lengthy delays. Each side wanted some authoritative ruling on what it perceived to be an unacceptable insult. Very astutely the court provided something for everyone: the Beamishes regained their property, but there was no finding of colourable behaviour by the Cochrans. Both parties could interpret the ruling in a manner favourable to their fundamental interests. Closure was well and truly effected.

Were rich and powerful litigants like the Cochrans subject to any effective constraint, it may be asked, if the Beamishes were required to follow them to the foot of the throne to achieve it? Would not most litigants in such a position have given up or run out of resources long before the Beamishes did? Even at the nadir of their troubles, the Beamishes still belonged to a relatively advantaged stratum of provincial society; they could rely on some financial assistance from their extended family and continued to employ one of the best lawyers in the province. While it is true that many litigants would not have been able to 'stay the course,' it is nonetheless of interest that the Beamishes did so. They clearly would not have persevered if they had believed that their position was hopeless. Equally clearly, they had faith in the impartiality of a provincial judiciary that had many ties of kinship, affinity, and office with the Cochrans.

The point of the story for the Beamish family, and very likely for contemporaries, was that ultimately the Cochrans' power was constrained by law and was seen to be so constrained. 'Equity will not suffer a wrong to go without a remedy' was in this case no hollow boast, when a settled possession of thirty years' duration might be overturned to right what was determined to be an historic wrong. Cases such as this, which by definition must be rare, are nonetheless potent symbols of equality before the law. In a small jurisdiction such as Nova Scotia, governed by a tiny mercantile and office-holding élite with which all the judges were tightly connected by bonds of kinship and intermarriage, achieving even the appearance of equality before the law was no mean feat.

Members of a society judge its legitimacy and that of its government in large part on the perceived efficacy and fairness of its dispute resolution mechanisms. Much of the literature on dispute resolution in colonial New England has been concerned to understand whether seemingly high litigation rates were an index of health or disease. There is a persuasive argument that high litigation rates indicate a basic satisfaction with the service on offer. If litigants were not satisfied, they would evade the formal system, possibly in favour of alternatives less productive of closure and social peace. A near contemporary of Murdoch, Nathaniel Whitworth White, was struck by the seeming paradox of high litigation rates and relative social harmony during his apprenticeship at Annapolis Royal. 'There is ... scarcely an individual that is not in the course of the year either Plaintiff or Defendant,' he reported to his father in 1815. 'And the beauty of it is they do it with such perfect good humor that like the spatting of two Attornies, their disputes cease and entire cordiality prevails the instant the suit is decided. In truth they are ... like man and wife, occasional jarrings among them [being] indispensably necessary to cement social union and render it still stronger.'[49]

This observation does not sit well with the assumptions often held about the nature of the civil justice dispensed under the family compacts of British North America. With its 'dismayingly irrational' structures, its seemingly impenetrable technicalities and long delays, and its unattractive displays of bias and nepotism in the appointment process, it is easy to think of colonial justice as a kind of joke. Yet the parties to the Market Wharf litigation, and the residents of Annapolis County, clearly did not regard it so. For them it was deadly serious and essentially legitimate.

NOTES

An earlier version of this paper was presented at the University of Toronto Legal History Seminar, where Dick Risk educated me about some of the intricacies of mortgage law. I would like to thank the editors of this volume, the anonymous assessors, and Barry Cahill for their comments and suggestions.

1 *Novascotian* (Halifax), 18 March 1830
2 Peter C. Hoffer, 'Honor and the Roots of American Litigiousness,' *American Journal of Legal History* 33 (1989), 295–319 at 301
3 'Colonial justice' should not be taken as coextensive with the domain of the formal court system. A rich variety of methods of 'alternative' dispute resolution existed in British North America and these deserve investigation in their own right; see generally D.G. Bell, 'A Perspective on Legal Pluralism in 19th Century New Brunswick,' *University of New Brunswick Law Journal* 37 (1988), 86–93. The shadowy and unsystematic documentary record of such processes poses particular challenges for those wishing to study them.
4 E.g., A.W.B. Simpson, *Leading Cases in the Common Law* (Oxford: Clarendon Press 1995). The genre is reviewed in W.E. Brett Code, 'The Salt Men of Goderich in Ontario's Court of Chancery: *Ontario Salt* v. *Merchants Salt Co.* and the Judicial Enforcement of Combinations,' *McGill Law Journal* 38 (1993), 517–68 at 519, note 5.
5 Code, 'The Salt Men,' at 519, note 5.
6 See, for example, Constance Backhouse, *Petticoats and Prejudice: Women and Law in Nineteenth Century Canada* (Toronto: The Osgoode Society for Canadian Legal History); James W. St. G. Walker, *'Race,' Rights and the Law in the Supreme Court of Canada* (Toronto: The Osgoode Society for Canadian Legal History 1997); and Philip Girard, 'Church, Children, Migration and Money: Three Tales of Child Custody in Nova Scotia,' in Hilary Thompson, ed., *The Child in Atlantic Literature and Culture* (Guelph: Children's Press 1995).
7 Julian Gwyn, 'Capitalists, Merchants and Manufacturers in Early Nova Scotia, 1769–1791: The Tangled Affairs of John Avery, James Creighton, John Albro and Joseph Fairbanks,' in Margaret Conrad, ed., *Intimate Relations: Family and Community in Planter Nova Scotia, 1759–1800* (Fredericton: Acadiensis Press 1995); and Ernest A. Clarke and Jim Phillips, '"The Course of Law cannot be Stopped": The Aftermath of the Cumberland Rebellion in the Civil Courts of Nova Scotia, 1778–1808,' *Dalhousie Law Journal* 21 (1998), 440–74.
8 For particularly good examples, see Rande Kostal, 'Legal Justice, Social Justice: An Incursion into the Social History of Work-Related Accident Law in Ontario, 1860–86,' *Law and History Review* 6 (1988), 1–24, and the case studies presented by Tina Loo in *Making Law, Order, and Authority in British Columbia, 1821–1871* (Toronto: University of Toronto Press 1994).
9 All information about the dispute comes from the case file in the Court of Chancery fonds at Nova Scotia Archives and Records Management (hereafter

NSARM, formerly the Public Archives of Nova Scotia), RG 36, box 24, no. 138, unless otherwise stated. The accuracy of most of the information has been confirmed by cross-checking newspaper records, genealogies, and land records in the registry of deeds.

10 During the course of the dispute the Cochrans invariably called the wharf 'Cochran's Wharf,' while the Beamishes invariably called it 'Beamish's Wharf.' It was also known as the 'Market Wharf,' which is the title used here, unless the context demands otherwise.

11 This interpretation is supported by comparing Ott's 1780 will with his 1774 will, which the later will revoked (see Halifax County Court of Probate, no. O23). In 1774 Ott had left all his property to his daughters, subject only to a life interest in favour of his widow. The gift to the daughters contained no clause reserving it to their separate use, free from their husband's control. Had this will remained unrevoked, the assets of the Ott estate would likely have disappeared into the hands of Thomas and Amelia's creditors.

12 Will of Frederick Ott, 1 June 1780, Halifax County Court of Probate, no. O22. The will may be read at one point as imposing this condition on all the grandchildren, regardless of sex, but at another point it is only females who are mentioned.

13 Upon marriage, the common law dictated that Amelia's share came under the control of her husband for their joint lives. He could not dispose of it without her consent, however, and if she outlived him, as happened, she would regain full power to deal with it on her own.

14 *Journals and Proceedings of the House of Assembly of Nova Scotia*, vol. 6 (1783–84), 67, 69. Cochran was the Speaker of the House during this session, but came down from the chair so that he could speak to the merits of the bill. The reasons for the ultimate failure of the bill are unclear.

15 An earlier impediment had arisen in that the executors named in Frederick Ott's will no longer resided in Nova Scotia and declined to act. In view of their absence, the Court of Probate appointed Thomas Beamish as administrator with the will annexed of the estate of Frederick Ott, by order dated 30 September 1783.

16 The original Chancery file, *Thomas and Amelia Beamish* v. *John Loader and James Stephens*, is found at NSARM, RG 36A, box 13, no. 65.

The governor of Nova Scotia was empowered in his 1749 instructions to exercise jurisdiction in equity with the advice of his council. In 1764 the court was reconstituted to comprise the governor as president, assisted by three Masters in Chancery. There is now a considerable modern literature on the origins and evolution of the Nova Scotia Court of Chancery, in addition to Charles J. Townshend's, *History of the Court of Chancery in Nova Scotia* (To-

ronto: Carswell 1900). See Barry Cahill, *'Bleak House* Revisited: The Records
and Papers of the Court of Chancery of Nova Scotia, 1751–1855,' *Archivaria* 29
(1989–90), 149–67, and 'From Imperium To Colony: Reinventing a Metropolitan Legal Institution in Late Eighteenth-Century Nova Scotia,' in D.W. Nichol
et al., eds. *Transatlantic Crossings: Eighteenth-Century Explorations* (St John's:
Memorial University of Newfoundland 1995); Jim Cruickshank, 'The Chancery Court of Nova Scotia: Jurisdiction and Procedure, 1751–1855,' *Dalhousie
Journal of Legal Studies* 1 (1992), 27–48; and Philip Girard, 'Married Women's
Property, Chancery Abolition and Insolvency Law: Law Reform in Nova
Scotia, 1820–1867,' in Philip Girard and Jim Phillips, eds., *Essays in the History
of Canadian Law, Vol. III, Nova Scotia* (Toronto: The Osgoode Society for
Canadian Legal History 1990). For a comparative perspective see Elizabeth
Brown, 'Equitable Jurisdiction and the Court of Chancery in Upper Canada,'
Osgoode Hall Law Journal 21 (1983), 275–314.

17 Jill E. Martin, *Hanbury and Martin's Modern Equity*, 14th ed. (London: Sweet &
Maxwell 1993), at 601–2. By the later nineteenth century the jurisdiction was
very sparingly exercised (see *In re Jackson* (1882), 21 ChD 786), but in the
eighteenth century it seems to have been employed more freely, especially in
cases involving the property of infants. *Inwood* v. *Twyne* (1762), 1 Amb. 417,
27 ER 279; John David Chambers, *A Practical Treatise on the Jurisdiction of the
High Court of Chancery over the Persons and Property of Infants* (London:
Saunders & Benning 1842), at 538.

18 Halifax Registry of Deeds, RG 47, vol. 24, p. 309 (deed from Beamish to
McNab, 22 May 1787, reciting Beamish 'now' in jail); RG 47, vol. 26, p. 199
(deed from Thomas and Amelia Beamish to Cochrans, 21 April 1787).

19 NSARM, Halifax Registry of Deeds, RG 47, vol. 35, p. 607, deed from Amelia
Beamish to William Sabatier and Foster Hutchinson, 29 May 1801. In theory
the common law did not allow a married woman's legal identity to revive
upon the mere absence, as opposed to the death, of her husband, but colonial
attitudes seem to have been fairly relaxed on this point. The absence of proof
of Thomas Beamish's death was never raised in any of the subsequent legal
proceedings, in spite of the fact that his children reported in 1804 that they
did not know whether he was alive or dead.

20 Halifax Registry of Deeds, RG 47, vol. 35, p. 607, deed from Frederick Ott
Beamish et al. to Thomas Akins, 19 April 1803.

21 It is not clear whether the respondents meant that Beamish was mentally
incompetent or simply a poor businessman.

22 Joseph A. Roach, *The Canadian Law of Mortgages of Land* (Toronto: Butterworths 1993), at 59–61. On the origins of the doctrine, see David Sugarman
and Ronnie Warrington, 'Land law, citizenship, and the invention of 'English-

ness.' The strange world of the equity of redemption,' in John Brewer and Susan Staves, eds., *Early Modern Conceptions of Property* (London: Routledge 1995). This argument was also raised, although generally not with success, in a number of cases in Upper Canada, including one that went to the Privy Council in 1855. R.C.B. Risk, 'The Golden Age: The Law about the Market in Nineteenth-Century Ontario,' *University of Toronto Law Journal* 26 (1976), 307–46 at 330–1.

23 For an example of the kind of influence that Cochran exercised as an Assemblyman, see Brian Cuthbertson, *Johnny Bluenose at the Polls: Epic Nova Scotian Election Battles, 1758–1848* (Halifax: Formac 1994), at 176–7.

24 This interpretation follows that of Barry Cahill, '"Fide et fortitudine vivo": The Career of Chief Justice Bryan Finucane,' Nova Scotia Historical Society, *Collections* 42 (1986), 153–69.

25 Bulkeley had been named Master of the Rolls, a sort of deputy judge in Chancery, in 1782, at which time Hutchinson had replaced him as Master in Chancery, which was more of an administrative post. Cahill, 'Imperium to Colony,' at 15–18.

26 Cahill, 'Finucane,' at 163.

27 Samuel Hood George died prematurely in 1813 and was succeeded as provincial secretary by his brother Rupert Denis, who remained an important figure in the province until the achievement of responsible government, when he retired to England. Letters by Samuel Hood George in the George Fonds at NSARM, MG 1, vol. 2160, reveal the closeness of the ties between the George family and Prevost.

28 Neil MacKinnon, *This Unfriendly Soil: The Loyalist Experience in Nova Scotia, 1783–1791* (Montreal and Kingston: McGill-Queen's University Press 1986), 127. In fact, Parr did recommend the Loyalist Blowers for the post when it fell vacant again a year later (see note 29), but Strange had been appointed before his letter reached London; see CO 217/61/173 PRO (mfm at NSARM), cited in Barry Cahill, 'Henry Dundas' Plan for Reforming the Judicature of British North America, 1792,' *University of New Brunswick Law Journal* 39 (1990), 281–307, note 22.

29 Strange was preceded as chief justice by another Englishman, the Hon. Jeremy Pemberton, but he remained in the province for less than a year (1788–9), and departed for reasons of health.

30 The progress of appeals to the King in Council can be traced through the annual Privy Council Registers at the Public Record Office, London, where they are classified under PC 2. The volumes relevant for this appeal begin with vol. 198 (1816); each subsequent year is numbered consecutively. Petitioners were obliged to submit to the committee a printed record includ-

ing the entire proceedings in the courts below as well as the arguments of counsel, and these are still held by the office of the Judicial Committee of the Privy Council in Downing Street, where they can be consulted with the permission of the registrar. Unfortunately, the only gap in the last two centuries covers the decade 1815–25, so that the record submitted by the Cochrans does not survive.

31 Patrick Medd, *Romilly: A Life of Sir Samuel Romilly, Lawyer and Reformer* (London: Collins 1968).

32 3 & 4 Wm IV, c. 41.

33 Joseph Henry Smith, *Appeals to the Privy Council from the American Plantations* (New York: Columbia University Press 1950), at 323–8.

34 Hansard, *Debates* H.C. 2nd Ser. XVIII, 7 February 1828, 155, as quoted in David B. Swinfen, *Imperial Appeal: The Debate on the Appeal to the Privy Council, 1833–1986* (Manchester University Press 1987), at 6. Lord Brougham was the one of the few barristers with any regular practice on colonial appeals, according to William Burge, *Observations on the Supreme Appellate Jurisdiction of Great Britain* (London 1841), 14.

35 Sir William Scott (1745–1836), was judge of the London Consistory Court and of the High Court of Admiralty and was created Baron Stowell in 1821. Sir William Grant's presence was highly prized on colonial appeals. He had been attorney general of Quebec, was familiar with a variety of legal systems, and took a keen interest in colonial law. Howell, *The Judicial Committee of the Privy Council*, at 10–11. Sir John Nicholl (1759–1838), a distinguished civilian lawyer, was President of Doctors' Commons and Dean of the Arches, a member of Parliament and subsequently judge of the High Court of Admiralty.

36 RG 36, box 41, file 138, doc. 44a, copy of Order of Council affirming original decree, 29 May 1820.

37 Swinfen, *Imperial Appeal*, at 5–6.

38 This manuscript volume, entitled 'Forms of the Supreme Court,' is held in the Rare Books Collection of the Sir James Dunn Law Library at Dalhousie University.

39 Howell, *Judicial Committee of the Privy Council*, at 9.

40 Thomas Ott Beamish and Beamish Murdoch signed the petition on their own behalf and on behalf of the other defendants, marking the first time that Murdoch had taken an active role in the proceeding. He had completed his articles with Uniacke in November 1819 and was waiting to reach the age of majority so that he could be admitted as an attorney, a necessary stage before finally being called as a barrister.

41 In 'Forms of the Supreme Court,' there is a draft letter on this matter to the heirs of one John Charles Rudolf dated 9 September 1820, with reference to a

parcel of land in Lunenburg (facing p. 145), and an undated fragment of a
similar letter to one John Bolman, Esq. at p. 146.

42 *Thomas Goudge* v. *Thomas Akins et al.*, RG 39A, box 27, no. 154. The Beamishes
had obtained an order of ejectment against Goudge in 1804, and he filed his
bill of complaint 29 July 1804. There is no indication that Goudge was
successful, so presumably the Beamishes were left to exercise their rights at
law. It is not clear why these ejectment suits should have been successful at
law. The rights of the Beamishes depending on an equitable doctrine, any
subsequent purchasers of the legal estate should have taken free of an earlier
equitable interest provided they had no notice of it.

43 Murdoch's career is explored in Philip Girard, 'Themes and Variations in
Early Canadian Legal Culture: Beamish Murdoch and his *Epitome of the Laws
of Nova-Scotia*,' *Law and History Review* 11 (1993), 101–44 and in the author's
doctoral dissertation, 'Patriot Jurist: Beamish Murdoch of Halifax, 1800–1876,'
(PhD dissertation, Dalhousie University 1998), from which this study is
drawn.

44 4 vols. (Halifax: Joseph Howe 1832–3), I:iii.

45 Cited in H.T. Holman, 'The Early History of the Court of Chancery on Prince
Edward Island,' (unpublished ms. 1981), at 35.

46 Cahill, 'Imperium to Colony,' at 19.

47 W.R. Cornish and G. de N. Clark, *Law and Society in England 1750–1950*
(London: Sweet & Maxwell 1989), at 202.

48 John C. Weaver, 'While Equity Slumbered: Creditor Advantage, A Capitalist
Land Market, and Upper Canada's Missing Court,' *Osgoode Hall Law Journal*
28 (1990), 871–914 at 910–12.

49 Nathaniel Whitworth White to Gideon White, 23 November 1815, White
Papers, MG 1, vol. 953, no. 1023.

8

'Our Arctic Brethren': Canadian Law and Lawyers as Portrayed in American Legal Periodicals, 1829–1911

BERNARD J. HIBBITTS

Canadians are very good – perhaps too good – at intellectually 'burying their grandfathers.' Dick Risk has described how Alfred Henry Fraser Lefroy did so to Chief Justice John Beverley Robinson.[1] He has similarly demonstrated how, in a less familial but no less substantial sense, Chief Justice William Ralph Meredith performed that role for Chancellor William Hume Blake.[2] In doing all this he has greatly enriched our understanding of mid-nineteenth-century Canadian legal culture. Here I do not wish to bury Risk; rather, on the occasion of his retirement, I seek to follow in his footsteps and undertake the kind of invaluable excavation work that has so marked his writings. Imitation may be flattery, but it is also praise, and my project is to draw back the curtain of contemporary American disregard of Canadian legal affairs to 'excavate' a period in which the American legal community, sometimes for good and occasionally for ill, took much greater note of Canadian law and lawyers than it now does.

Between 1829 and 1911 a number of influential American attorneys evinced a considerable interest in the lives and business of their Canadian counterparts.[3] That interest can be traced through the articles and other commentary that appeared in nineteenth- and early twentieth-century American legal periodicals. While those writings were principally illustrative of contemporary American legal culture, they also throw light on Canadian developments of the time.

It should be emphasized that this chapter is principally an unearthing of the ways in which American legal periodicals viewed and portrayed Canadian law and lawyers. It does go beyond that project to offer some explanations for the extent and nature of the American interest and why that interest changed over time. But my conclusions are both speculative and modest, necessarily so at this stage. Before definitive statements can be made about cross-fertilisation between jurisdictions or legal pluralism or harmonization other building blocks will be necessary.

The chapter opens with an examination of the operation of American legal periodicals in the nineteenth and early twentieth centuries. Subsequent sections review the principal themes of American journals' coverage of Canadian legal affairs, dividing that topic into three periods: 1829–79, 1880–95, and 1896–1911. Within each section I speculate about the conclusions that can be drawn from the extent and nature of the coverage. The chapter concludes with suggestions about its overall significance.

THE HISTORY AND OPERATION OF AMERICAN LEGAL PERIODICALS, 1808–1911

The first American periodical dedicated exclusively to legal matters was the Philadelphia-based *American Law Journal*, whose nine-year life began in 1808.[4] Prior to that date – and for some time after it – Americans published articles on law and legal affairs in what would now be called 'literary' magazines: most notably the *North American Review*, the *Southern Literary Messenger*, the *United States Magazine and Democratic Review*, and the *New England Magazine*. Insofar as those journals were read and frequently edited by lawyers (acting in their capacity as leading members of America's post-Revolutionary intellectual elite), they became a natural outlet for legal scholarship and related commentary.[5]

As the volume of American law and the size of the U.S. legal profession grew in the early decades of the nineteenth century, American lawyers' interests increasingly diverged from those of the educated public at large. It became practical and even convenient for American attorneys to strike out on their own with journals devoted to their concerns, publications that would be better at bringing them 'the literature of the bar, especially its biographical and statistical material, questions of legal reform, chit-chat, gossip, and enlivening anecdote.'[6] In the antebellum period between the Revolutionary and Civil Wars, the *American Law Journal* was joined and ultimately succeeded in those tasks by, among other organs, the *American Jurist* (Boston), the *Monthly Law Reporter* (Boston), the *United States Law*

Intelligencer and Review (Philadelphia), and the *Western Law Journal* (Cincinnati). Largely because of high costs to publishers, poor or irregular financial support from subscribers, and burn-out on the part of editors, most of those antebellum law journals were short-lived: of forty-eight established before 1860, only two survived after that date.[7] In the years following the Civil War, a new generation of legal periodicals appeared that fared considerably better than their predecessors. The *Albany Law Review* and the Boston- and later Saint Louis-based *American Law Review* rapidly became leading professional organs. Eventually, they were joined by the *Central Law Journal* (also based in Saint Louis) and the *Chicago Legal News.* In the 1880s and 1890s, as printing costs dropped due to technological improvements, a wide variety of state bar journals appeared, as did the first student-run law reviews at Columbia, Harvard, Yale, and Iowa universities.[8]

Until the early years of the twentieth century, most American legal periodicals (including student-edited law journals) looked rather different from modern academic 'law reviews.' Like their late-twentieth-century counterparts, they contained legal articles and reviews of new law books. But unlike what one ordinarily sees in the contemporary *Harvard Law Review*, the *Yale Law Journal*, or the *University of Pittsburgh Law Review*, they also reprinted legal judgments (in full or as digests), frequently reported professional 'news,' and even carried editorials on important legal and political issues. The publication of judgments in early American legal periodicals was encouraged by the increasing importance of case law as judicial authority in nineteenth-century Anglo-American jurisprudence. It was, moreover, rendered feasible by the cost advantage that journal publishers enjoyed over official reporters, combined with the speed and regularity with which the journals could disseminate judgments. In reporting the latest professional news (and sometimes gossip), early American legal periodicals performed a further function that was soon shared and ultimately taken over by legal newspapers whose coverage was more overtly local. In the meantime, journal coverage of legal news helped to promote a stronger sense of identity, community, and power among members of the nineteenth and early twentieth-century American bar.[9] Editorial writing was, in part, an extension of early legal periodicals' self-assumed journalistic responsibilities. Not incidentally, such pieces gave the editors of early American law journals an opportunity to become consequential players in the events and trends they were reporting.

Editors (along with their professional contacts) frequently served as authors of the editorials, articles, and book reviews that appeared in their journals, but the same cannot be said of their cases or their news. Those materials were often secured with the assistance of other people, usually by individual correspondence and exchanges. To a considerable extent, early American legal periodicals relied on letters from their readers to tell them what was going on in the wider legal world.[10] Judging from the frequency with which journals made offhand references to individual informants, many subscribers were willing voluntarily to assume the burden of informing journal editors of local events, personalities, and developments that might interest readers. Sometimes information would come in the form of a personal letter, a clipping from the press, or in a copy of a local law report. More formally, after a variety of legal journals appeared, the editors of individual journals followed what appears to have been a practice common among general periodical publishers in the United States, namely that of sending extra copies of their law reviews to each other free of charge. The idea was that the sending journal would get publicity, and the receiving journal would acquire news. Sometimes the receiving journal would simply review the journal issue sent to it (usually with praise, and perhaps with an endorsement saying that the other publication 'deserves support'). Sometimes it would reprint an article from the sender, usually with attribution. Sometimes the receiving journal would simply report a story, acknowledging the source in passing ('The *Albany Law Journal* says that ...'). On occasion, American law journals took advantage of the exchange system to take issue with one another's editorial positions in what was usually a gentlemanly dispute over the niceties of legal etiquette or law reform.[11]

That heavy reliance on correspondence and exchanges enabled but did not require American law journals to report on Canadian legal affairs during the nineteenth and early twentieth centuries. In a number of instances, American lawyers – especially in border regions – sent law journal editors news or clippings of important Canadian legal cases or events about which they had heard or in which they had been involved. Eventually, Canadian subscribers to American legal periodicals did likewise, sometimes after overt solicitation by an American editor.[12] After Canadian law journals began to be established in the 1850s, the Canadian legal press participated in the exchange system that was already operating in the United States. The resulting cross-border traffic in legal periodicals proved important not only because it regularly brought Canadian affairs to the attention of American editors and readers, but also because it enabled editors of Canadian legal periodicals to see – and reply to – what Americans were saying about Canada.

GETTING ACQUAINTED:
AMERICAN LEGAL PERIODICALS DISCOVER CANADA, 1829–1879

The first American legal periodicals did not carry news of Canadian law or lawyers. In retrospect, this is unsurprising. The early journals were experimental publications that could not easily have risked carrying information on 'colonial' legal affairs that would have been of only incidental interest to most of their readers. Moreover, American journal editors working in the first half of the nineteenth century lacked convenient sources of information on Canadian law and lawyers. There were, for example, no Canadian legal periodicals on which to draw by exchange. Finally, the earliest American legal periodicals were not published in areas of the United States with particularly strong social or economic connections to Canada, the existence of which might have encouraged attention to Canadian matters. The *American Law Journal*, for instance, was published in Philadelphia, as was the *United States Law Intelligencer and Review*. The *Carolina Law Repository* was published in Raleigh, North Carolina, and the *United States Law Journal* was published in New York City.

In 1829, however, a reprint of an 1827 Lower Canadian criminal decision appeared in one of the first issues of the *American Jurist*.[13] The *Jurist* was published in Boston, a city with considerable international commerce and strong social ties to two British North American colonies, Nova Scotia and New Brunswick. One of its readers apparently subscribed or otherwise had access to the Montreal *Gazette* daily newspaper, which had reprinted the decision shortly after it was pronounced. It is interesting that the case was considered to be news despite being two years old when it was republished (indicating both the paucity of current information on Canadian affairs and the slow speed at which professional intelligence travelled at that time). The decision to republish was doubtless based on the ongoing relevance to Americans of the subject matter of the Canadian case, namely extradition of criminals to the United States (in that instance, one Joseph Fisher, accused of stealing bank notes in Vermont). It was probably also not immaterial that the presiding judge, Justice James Reid, had expressed willingness to consider relevant American case law before rendering his decision and had discussed rulings by Chancellor James Kent of New York and Judge John Tilghman of Pennsylvania.[14]

Extradition issues ultimately took up a significant portion of the space that American legal periodicals devoted to Canadian legal affairs in their first fifty years of Canadian coverage.[15] One of the most famous extradition cases was the *Anderson* decision of 1860, in which the 1842 *Ashburton*

Treaty between the United States and Great Britain was invoked to obtain the extradition of John Anderson, a runaway slave who had killed a would-be slave catcher in Missouri and afterwards found his way to Upper Canada.[16] That case was accorded article-length treatment in the *Monthly Law Reporter*,[17] it was also the subject of extended reporting in the regular American press.[18] The *Reporter* and other American legal periodicals kept close track of subsequent Canadian developments in that area. In 1864, for instance, the *Reporter* reviewed a pamphlet reprinting the decision of the New Brunswick Supreme Court in the similarly well-known *Chesapeake* case, in which that court had refused to authorize extradition to the United States of Confederate agents who had seized and brought to Nova Scotia an American steamer bound from New York to Portland, Maine. The *Reporter* registered its regret over the decision: '... we think it might reasonably have been expected that [the Court] ... would have reached a different conclusion ... [T]he practical result [, however,] may only be an increase of a somewhat undesirable class of inhabitants of the province by a quasi compulsory emigration from the United States, in which case our regrets ought to be proportionately mitigated.'[19] The following year, 1865, the *Reporter* reprinted the Upper Canadian Court of Queen's Bench decision in *Re: Asher Warner* regarding the extradition of a prisoner who had been arrested for forgery in Cleveland, Ohio and escaped to Canada.[20] Appearing with the Crown in that case was H.B. Brown, U.S. District Attorney for the Eastern District of Michigan. It was Brown who provided the *Monthly Law Reporter* with its copy of the judgment. In 1865 the same journal reported the decision in *Re. Bennet G. Burley*, which involved the extradition of the Confederate agent Burley to the United States to answer charges of theft and piracy for taking over an American steamboat on Lake Michigan and subsequently diverting it to the Canadian shore.[21] In 1867, the new *American Law Review* reported on the extradition of the forger Ernest Sureau Lamirande from Canada to France, reprinting in that process a judgment by Justice Lewis Thomas Drummond of the Lower Canadian bench.[22] Three years later, the *Albany Law Review* reprinted an Ontario decision regarding the alleged forger Richard Caldwell, in which it was held that the *Ashburton Treaty* permitted extradition even when formal charges had not been laid against an individual in the United States.[23]

Extradition judgments did not, however, monopolize early American coverage of Canadian jurisprudence. Between 1829 and 1879 American legal periodicals were also interested in Canadian maritime and commercial cases, new Canadian law reports, Canadian statutory changes affecting usury, juries and intellectual property, and stories related to the development, personalities, and professional standards of the Canadian bench and bar.

Like extradition, these interests were driven not so much by their importance in Canada or to Canadians, as they were piqued by their significance to America and Americans. In the early to mid-nineteenth century, Canadian maritime and commercial law cases were of growing concern to American attorneys who worked on behalf of the increasing number of American merchants doing business with Canadian companies. The *Monthly Law Reporter*, which had taken the lead in reprinting Canadian extradition judgments, was again the most assiduous in collecting Canadian cases in those fields, although decisions of interest to American maritime and commercial lawyers also appeared sporadically in the Cincinnati-based *Weekly Law Gazette* and the *American Law Review*.[24] Notably, the *Reporter's* selections included two Quebec decisions on the English Merchant Shipping Act and a Nova Scotian ruling on the disposition of the steamer *Chesapeake* after it had been abandoned by its hijackers.[25] Most of the reprinted decisions were run without attribution, but the editors of the *Reporter* took at least one Lower Canadian maritime case from the Boston *Daily Advertiser* newspaper. The *Reporter* also acknowledged that it had taken the *Chesapeake* judgment from a corrected copy of the decision sent by the presiding judge, Justice Alexander Stuart, to Benjamin Gray of the Boston bar, who had sent it on to the *Reporter's* office.[26]

Canadian law reports received most of their attention in American legal periodicals prior to 1865, at a time when the publication or arrival of a volume of reports in the United States itself was still considered a sufficiently remarkable event to warrant a comprehensive review of its contents (witness the contemporary reviews of law reports not only in legal periodicals but also in the *North American Review*). American periodical editors were especially attracted to the study of Canadian reports by the fact that Canadian and American judges faced many of the same issues, by the willingness of Canadian judges to cite American authorities, and by the consequent Canadian inclination (as far as American reviewers were concerned) to resolve many legal issues in the same fashion as did Americans. Even more importantly, perhaps, American editors and reviewers were animated by a lingering conviction that foreign and American precedents (however superficially different they might have appeared) shared a core of principle that made them relevant to one another.

In 1862, the *Monthly Law Reporter's* reviewer mentioned each of those points in his appraisal of two new volumes of John Campbell Allen's *New*

Brunswick Reports. He declared that he had been 'struck not merely by the general similarity of legislation, but more especially by the uniformity of decisions between the courts of the province and the adjoining state, and with the identity of the subject matters to which they relate.' As for authority, he found that 'the decisions of the Queen's Bench, or of the highest courts of the several States, are alike cited ... and [it may thus been seen that] the courts on each side of the line dividing democracy from royalty, bow with equal deference to Blackstone and Kent as the great masters of the common law; and to Mitford and Story as authoritative expositors of the liberal doctrines of equity jurisprudence.'[27] Ultimately, he decided that 'the differences between the reports of Allen of New Brunswick and Allen of Massachusetts [Charles Allen, the law reporter of that state from 1861 to 1867], are not so much in matters of law as in matters of form.'[28]

American concerns and convictions similarly motivated U.S. reports of Canadian statutory changes and even animated American reports of professional news from the Canadian bar. Usury, the unanimity of jury decisions, and the appropriateness of jury trials were leading legal issues in early to mid-nineteenth-century America, and the editors of American law journals repeatedly picked up on Canadian developments to guide what might be done in the United States.[29] In 1858, for instance, the editors of the *Weekly Law Gazette* reported approvingly on new Canadian legislation that voided the previous limit of 6 per cent interest on loans and allowed all parties (except banks) to set any limit they pleased.[30] The same year, they noted that recent statutes in Nova Scotia and New Brunswick had established that civil juries composed of nine persons could hand down verdicts so long as seven jurymen were in agreement. The *Gazette* observed that this was not only a new but a 'sensible' plan.[31] Still interested in the issue in 1870, the *Albany Law Journal* endorsed an unspecified Canadian act that dispensed with juries in criminal law cases at the request of the accused.[32] Later in the 1870s, American legal journals became interested in Canadian 'intellectual and industrial property' statutes that stood to affect American inventors and authors. In 1872, the *American Law Review* reprinted a lengthy description of the Canadian patent law that had originally been written for the *Maryland Law Reporter*, and in 1875 the *Albany Law Journal* praised the Canadian Copyright Act of 1868, extending protection to individuals who were not British subjects, as 'a most generous concession to the demands of authors of all nationalities.'[33]

Most of the professional news and gossip reported from Canada had an American angle. In 1840, for instance, the *American Jurist* reprinted the

Quebec *Gazette*'s obituary of Lower Canadian Solicitor General Andrew Stuart, who was familiar to American lawyers for his pamphlets on North American boundary disputes between the United States and Great Britain.[34] Eight years later, the *Monthly Law Reporter* ran the Montreal *Herald*'s obituary for James Reid, chief justice of the Lower Canadian Court of Queen's Bench. In a footnote to that obituary, referring to the quality of Reid's judgments, the editors of the *Reporter* drew attention to the *American Jurist*'s 1829 republication of the *Fisher* extradition case.[35] In 1878, the *Albany Law Journal* noted the promotions of John Hawkins Hagerty to Ontario's Court of Queen's Bench and Adam Wilson to the chief justiceship of that province's Court of Common Pleas. Both judges would have been familiar to American readers due to their involvement in important extradition and commercial decisions previously reported in the American legal press.[36]

Particular personalities aside, the organization and quality of the Canadian bench and bar were of interest to American observers who were concerned about their own professional circumstances. In 1872 and 1873, for example, the *American Law Review* and the *Albany Law Journal* commented on problems with the Quebec bench that had originally been raised in the Montreal-based *Revue critique de legislation and de jurisprudence du Canada*. The *American Law Review* observed that, in respect of judicial appointments being treated as political perquisites, Quebec was 'as badly off as we are in the United States.' As for the *Revue*'s proposed solution – vesting powers of judicial appointment jointly in the government, the bar, and the bench – the *Review* warned that that strategy would only work so long as the bar 'could be improved by a rigid exclusion of uneducated men.'[37] It acknowledged, however, that the ability of bar admittees was perhaps more of a problem in the United States than in Canada. The *Albany Law Journal* offered its condolences to Canadians and expressed its hope that 'sturdy and pure reformers such as [the author of the *Revue* article] should be quickly elevated to the bench.' At the same time, it did not share the *American Law Review*'s optimism about the quality of the Canadian bar. Quoting the *Revue*'s contention that men could be admitted to legal practice in Quebec 'who might, perhaps, have graced a shoemaker's bench, but who simply disgrace a learned profession,' it agreed that the Canadian minister of justice had a Herculean labour to perform in cleaning up the unprofessional mess.[38] Two years later, in 1874, the *American Law Review* took considerable satisfaction in the eventual success of the Quebec bar's protests against its corrupt and inefficient provincial judiciary. Speaking of several judicial reappointments that had resulted from those protests, the editors of the *Review* held the episode up as an example and an inspiration for its readership: '... the bar may congratulate itself on the success of their public spirit and unity and energy of action. This whole transaction furnishes an argument for the organization of the bar into associations to provide for the common defence, and promote the general welfare.'[39]

The fact of American interest in Canadian legal affairs did not, however, ensure equal U.S. coverage of all Canadian regions. Between 1829 and 1879, a statistically disproportionate amount of attention was paid to Lower Canadian/Quebec laws and lawyers as opposed to legal developments in Nova Scotia, New Brunswick, or Upper Canada/Ontario. In part, that slant may have been due to the prominence of Montreal in mid-nineteenth-century American commerce. It probably also reflected the limitations of the exchange system that, while giving the editors of contemporary American legal periodicals access to several Canadian law journals published out of Montreal, provided only a couple from Toronto and none from the Maritimes (where no legal journals were printed).[40] In some instances, the editors of American periodicals revealed how little they knew of law in those other areas by the naivety of their questions.[41] Thus, the *American Jurist*'s groping 1838 inquiry, made after reviewing a volume of Lower Canadian cases (from 1834!): '[a]re there any Upper Canadian or Nova Scotian reports?'[42]

The fact that most Americans found Canadian legal developments interesting did not, moreover, prevent some Americans from criticizing Canada or Canadians, or treating them with condescension. On several occasions in the first fifty years of coverage, American legal editors and their correspondents wrote as though they saw Canada – or British North America – as something of a political, social, or legal backwater. In 1844, for instance, a reviewer in the *Monthly Law Reporter* began his assessment of an 1843 volume of David Shank Kerr's *New Brunswick Reports* by triumphantly proclaiming that 'the paper, the type, the opinions of the court, the labors of the reporter, all bear the stamp of an *English colony*. The most hasty glance suffices to satisfy the mind, that this volume is neither the ripened product of Westminister Hall, or of the press in London, nor again can it be confounded with the multitudinous reports, the offspring and spawn of the jurisprudence of the United States' (emphasis in original). To make matters worse, the reviewer admitted that the New Brunswick volume surpassed one that he had previously perused from Newfoundland, 'a collection of cases as rough and shaggy as one of the dogs of the Island ...'[43]

What did Canadians think of this coverage? For the early period, it is difficult to answer this question. From the 1850s onwards, exchanges exposed the editors of Canadian law journals to what some of their American counterparts were reporting about Canada. For instance, in the 1850s and early 1860s, the editors of the *Upper Canada Law Journal* were obviously familiar with such contemporaries as the *Monthly Law Reporter*, the *Pittsburgh Legal Journal*, the *Philadelphia Legal Intelligencer*, the *Weekly Law Gazette*, and even the Richmond-based *Quarterly Law Journal*.[44] In addition to reprinting articles and cases from those and other American sources, the *Upper Canada Law Journal* occasionally turned the tables by commenting on American legal affairs.[45] There is, nonetheless, virtually nothing in its pages by way of reaction or response to American reports on Canadian law or lawyers. After 1867, the editors of the *Canada Law Journal* were similarly aware of their American analogues, but through 1879 they too ignored the latters' Canadian coverage. Perhaps that coverage was too intermittent to draw much attention to itself, or perhaps even at that stage editors of the Canadian legal journals were more interested in what metropolitan English journals were saying about them and about Canadian affairs.[46] Whatever its basis, Canadian editorial silence proved temporary.

Between 1829 and 1879 American legal periodicals slowly 'got acquainted' with Canada, as Canadian case reports and law journals fed into established U.S. systems for the exchange of legal literature. Coverage tended to favour Lower Canada/Quebec, perhaps because Montreal was a leading centre for law-book publishing, and was spurred by three kinds of interests. Mutual concern about issues like extradition and the legal resolution of commercial disputes was a prime motivating factor; U.S. coverage of Canadian commercial law is particularly revealing insofar as it was expressly justified by faith that local laws were based on super-eminent principles, observation that Canadian and American courts dealt with similar commercial problems, and by pride in Canadian courts' routine reliance on U.S. precedents. A second area of shared, cross-border ground was law reform projects on topics like criminal procedure and intellectual property. A final formative factor in early American periodical coverage of Canadian law was an emerging U.S. culture of professionalism that found solidarity with Canadian concerns about disseminating legal knowledge and monitoring judicial behaviour. The ethic that underlay American law review editors' early interest in Canada thus involved learning from another North American jurisdiction's engagement with challenges that were perceived to be shared.

It would, perhaps obviously, be illuminating to compare those law reviews' portrayal of Canadian law and lawyers during the period from

1829 to 1879 with their coverage of other jurisdictions. But that study is beyond the scope of this chapter and the comparative insights it might offer await further research.

LOOKING NORTHWARD:
CONTINENTALISM AND THE LAW JOURNALS, 1880–1895

Between 1880 and 1895, the volume of American coverage of Canadian legal affairs increased dramatically. More American legal journals carried articles on Canadian law and lawyers. At the same time, the journals that had covered Canada in the earlier period expanded their coverage significantly to the point where, for a few years at least, one journal – the *American Law Review* – carried Canadian legal news in virtually every issue.

What prompted this increase in coverage? In part, the rise in the number of American legal periodicals running articles on Canadian law and lawyers was a function of a general expansion of the American legal publishing industry in the 1880s and early 1890s. Reduced paper and printing costs stimulated the growth of journals that previously could not have operated at a profit. The origins of the *Criminal Law Magazine, Case and Comment*, the *Green Bag*, state bar journals like the *Kansas Bar Journal* and the *Michigan Bar Journal*, and early university law reviews such as the *Harvard Law Review* and the *Yale Law Journal* can all be traced to that period. As more journals began publishing, the number of articles on Canadian law increased.

More fundamentally, however, the growth of American interest in Canadian legal matters (especially on the part of periodicals like the *American Law Review* that had already been carrying Canadian news) may plausibly be attributed to three factors: Americans' desire to consolidate their international Anglo-Saxon links at a time of profound change in the ethnic make-up of the American population; growing American interest in the annexation of Canada; and the impact of emigré Canadians on the United States and of Canadian-born (and sometimes Canadian-trained) lawyers on the American legal profession.

In the 1880s and 1890s, the shape of America's population was shifting. Waves of immigrants from continental Europe – especially the south and east – brought new ways and novel values to what had previously been an English-oriented country. Many established groups in the United States – including the professional bar – feared for the future.[47] In that context, the bar's leading members began to emphasize America's ties to England and its Anglo-Saxon heritage. They became noticeably fascinated – some might say fixated – by English law and lawyers.[48] That new interest in England and English legal traditions incidentally drew Americans' attention to the laws and legal affairs of England's overseas dominions and possessions – including, in particular, Canada.[49] Canada was, after all, the strongest North American embodiment of America's Anglo-Saxon past. In his 1885 address to Convocation at Dalhousie University in Halifax, Nova Scotia, the aging American jurist David Dudley Field emphasized bonds of English heredity and history that bound Canadians and Americans together, and in turn bound both cultures to England: 'The same current flows in my veins that flows in yours, the triple stream, Anglo-Saxon-Celtic ... My mother tongue is the same that your mothers taught you, the mother tongue of Shakespeare and Milton, of Addison and Burke ... Our laws are from the same sources, however far we may retrace them ... We have continued as you to cite the decisions of Mansfield and Eldon and their successors. The divergencies have been so slight, compared with the whole body, that like the mountains of the moon, they are lost to the distant eye.'[50] The attraction of 'Anglo-Saxonism' to many Americans helped fuel a loose political movement in some parts of the United States that favoured outright annexation of Canada. Annexation was hardly a new idea but, in the 1880s, it attained urgency in some quarters because of changing demographic circumstances in the United States.[51] What better way to ensure a continuing Anglo-Saxon orientation than to absorb the mostly English population of a former English colony that had not yet been (in the words of the distinctly annexationist *American Law Review*) 'swamped by the rag-tag-and-bob-tail of all Europe'?[52] Americans could extend their resource base and satisfy their imperial aspirations in the process of continental expansion. Canadians would not much mind, given what they already shared with Americans, and what they surely stood to gain.[53] The possibility of annexation encouraged the editors of American legal journals writing in the 1880s and early 1890s to increase their Canadian coverage on the premise that Canada would soon be under American jurisdiction.[54] They were, in a sense, betting on a continental future.

A third likely reason for increased American interest in Canadian legal affairs in the 1880s and early 1890s has to do with population shifts within North America itself, especially Canadian out-migration to the United States. In the late nineteenth century, facing increasingly dismal economic conditions at home, a large number of Canadians pulled up stakes and sought their fortunes south of the border.[55] The *American Law Review* commented in 1883 that 'Canada is like a breeding ground of migratory

arctic birds.'[56] Canadian emigrants included not only farmers and crafts-
men, but also trained professionals such as lawyers and recently graduated law students.[57] Despite the ability of many of those individuals to
blend into the existing population, their impact on the United States was
not altogether lost on Americans: 'these emigres are among our very best
citizens. One of them, whom we now have in mind, came to this country
seven years ago, the happy possessor of three things: a barrister's education, a hope for the future, and a plentiful lack of the wherewith. He is now
achieving distinction as a legal author, while his classmates in Canada are
still sighing for briefs. Another emigre from the maritime provinces lives
within a stone's throw of where we now write. He has been for many years
a prominent figure in our public affairs, and has filled the office of Senator
of the United States. He might possibly have reached that of justice of the
peace in Nova Scotia.'[58] Is it any wonder American legal journals ran an
increasing number of articles and editorials on the legal affairs of a country
with whose people they were becoming so personally familiar?

Between 1880 and 1895, the editors of American legal periodicals continued to select their topics on the basis of relevance to American readers.
That is not to say, however, that the substance of American coverage of
Canadian law and lawyers remained the same. New features were added,
and others were cut. American law journals began, for instance, to run
articles on Canadian law and lawyers expressly written for them by Canadian authors.[59] At least in the short term, those practices increased the
'depth' of American coverage of Canada and introduced an explicitly
Canadian perspective to American journal readers. American legal periodicals also began to carry more reviews of Canadian law books. Some of
those books – like Alfred Henry Marsh's *History of the Court of Chancery*
and Malcolm Graeme Cameron's *Treatise on the Law of Dower* – were truly
noteworthy.[60] Robert Vashon Rogers' chatty *Law of the Road* was rather
more notorious.[61] Virtually all of them were recommended to American
readers. At the same time, the journals eliminated their reviews of specific
volumes of Canadian law reports, despite their continued attention to the
publication of individual volumes of American cases. Some Canadian
judgments were still publicized but, after 1880, few of those cases appeared in other than digest form.[62] In one instance, an American journal
(the *American Law Review*) took another one (the *Chicago Legal News*) to task
for publishing cases from Quebec that were of limited use to Americans
because they were based on the Civil Code of Lower Canada and not on
the English common law.[63]

The few Canadian decisions that attracted American comment tended to deal with questions of constitutional and criminal law. A rapidly developing body of Canadian constitutional jurisprudence was of interest to American editors because most of them perceived the British North America Act to be broadly similar to the American founding document. Canadian and English decisions on that act prompted American law journals to compare and contrast the particulars of Canadian and American constitutional experiences.[64] Notably, differences between the two constitutional systems were not always interpreted in Americans' favour. The *American Law Review* expressed the hope at one point that annexation of Canada would provide an opportunity for American constitutional change along Canadian lines, with the national government being given precedence over new states or provinces.[65] American coverage of Canadian criminal trials was more overtly critical, concentrating on what American authors considered to be deficiencies in Canadian criminal procedure (and even in Canadian political judgment). The 1885 trial of Métis rebel leader Louis Riel drew the harshest commentary. The *American Law Review* observed gravely that 'the trial of a person charged with treason, before two justices of the peace and a jury of six men is, so far, an unheard of thing in our history ... Such a trial and conviction could not take place anywhere in the United States.'[66] The *Albany Law Journal* submitted that regardless of the trial's outcome, 'the [Canadian] government will do a very unnecessary and foolish thing if it hangs Riel. Our government did not hang a single rebel [referring to the Civil War], and it was the best thing it never did.'[67]

Criminal matters also dominated American discussions of changes to Canadian statutory law between 1880 and 1895. Calls for an extended extradition treaty binding Canada appeared frequently in the American legal press in the mid- to late 1880s.[68] At one point, the *American Law Review* praised the author of an article in the *Canada Law Journal* for arguing against the doctrine that 'a nation ought to make itself a cesspool for the escaped criminal filth of other nations.'[69] The introduction of the so-called Weldon Extradition Bill to the Canadian Parliament in 1889 was met with considerable enthusiasm: the *Review* took the extraordinary step of reprinting that bill in full.[70] In the early 1890s, American attention shifted to the new Canadian Criminal Code.[71] That legislation was, American commentators agreed, an achievement for codification, but it was not altogether unprecedented, given earlier American attempts in the same area.[72] Declared the *Albany Law Journal*, '[i]f the Canadians have any thing better, at least they have nothing older, and if better, it is merely because they had ours to improve upon.'[73]

Through the early 1890s, editors of American law journals maintained and even increased their earlier interest in professional news from the Canadian bench and bar. The journals carried more articles and reports on the lives and deaths of leading Canadian lawyers and judges, and seemed (from their choice of features) particularly interested in the careers of such Canadian lawyer-statesmen as Sir John A. Macdonald, Sir John Abbott, and Sir John Thompson.[74] Reading that material in the late 1990s, one gets the impression that it was offered for didactic as much as descriptive purposes. Thus, in reporting the death of prominent Toronto lawyer James Bethune in 1885, the *Central Law Journal* praised his memory, his manners, and his 'broad-minded and liberal' thinking. Comparing him to John Dillon in the United States, the *Journal* concluded that 'such a man is an ornament to the legal profession in any country and at any period.'[75]

In assessing the general condition of the Canadian legal community, editors of the American legal press continued to be struck by what they regarded as a similarity in challenges facing bench and bar on both sides of the border. They repeatedly used Canadian experiences to make points about needed reforms in the United States. In 1881, for instance, the *Albany Law Journal* drew its American readers' attention to an article in the Montreal *Star* newspaper, where it was argued that 'with printed evidence and a well-prepared factum there can possibly be no necessity' for long speeches in the courts. The *Star* had praised the 'one-hour' time limit imposed on counsel in the New York Court of Appeals.[76] In 1883, the *American Law Review* observed that 'our Canadian neighbors are having the same trouble of arrears in appellate court work which afflicts Missouri and many other States of the Union,' and described expedients recently recommended in the Montreal *Legal News*.[77] Also in 1883, the editors of the *Review* told their readers that 'America is not the only country in which they are troubled with over-legislation. Canada is afflicted by it.'[78] The *Review* went on to reprint an article from the Montreal *Law Times* [sic, the *Legal News*] complaining about that practice – an article that condemned, as symptomatic of the problem, certain statutory recommendations made by a committee of the New York legislature. In 1891, the *Albany Law Journal* endorsed the comments of a writer in the *Canadian Law Times* who had suggested in the Canadian context that the growing bulk of published case law could be brought under control by a better headnote and digest system, to which the *Journal* appended a call for the elimination of cumbersome counsels' briefs from law reports.[79] Shortly thereafter, the *Michigan Law Journal* took the occasion of a complaint in the Winnipeg *Western Law Times* concerning the scarcity of published Manitoba case law to comment that in the United States, 'the multiplicity of reports is actually becoming embarrassing to the practitioner, and instead of complaining about the scarcity, the bar is endeavoring to conceive of some plan to relieve lawyers from the increasing volume of state reports.'[80]

American concern about professional issues affecting the Canadian bench and bar led naturally to interest in Canadian legal education. Again, Canadian experiences were indirectly brought to bear on an American debate. Between 1880 and 1895, American legal journals spent a good deal of space discussing the virtues and vices, methods and mechanisms, of 'modern' legal education. Was law school to be preferred over traditional apprenticeship? Was formal legal education to be based on cases or lectures? Was it to be narrowly vocational, or broadly academic? Editors of the periodicals occasionally used Canadian developments to promote their own domestic agendas. In that context, it is interesting that they paid so much heed to the opening and operation of Dalhousie University's Faculty of Law in Halifax, Nova Scotia.[81]

As the first modern law school in common law Canada, Dalhousie was perhaps bound to draw more than its share of American attention. Initial American reaction to that school was positive. Discussing that institution and its professoriate in 1884, the *American Law Review* even suggested that Dalhousie was a suitable destination for American students: 'there is no reason in the nature of things why the elements of a good legal education should not be well acquired by an American student in such a school.'[82] In 1885, the editors went further, declaring that 'if we had a boy ambitious to go to a law school, we should send him there in preference to any law school we know of.' Those repeated recommendations were partly based on judgments about the similarity of Canadian and American law and the tasks of law schools: '[t]he systems of common law and equity are the same in both countries; and the most that a law school can do, or profess to do, is to indoctrinate students in the leading principles of jurisprudence.'[83] Underneath those factors were more 'political' considerations: 'if any one portion of Canada is more nearly American than the rest, it is what is termed the "Maritime Provinces." There is more sympathy with American ideas in Nova Scotia, and less in Ontario, than in any other portion of the Dominion ... Much of the American spirit underlies the foundation of [this] promising law school ...'[84] By 1893, however, the *Review*'s enthusiasm for Dalhousie had cooled, perhaps in tandem with waning annexationist fervor. 'This law school,' the editors suggested, 'is, to some extent, wedded to obsolete methods of education.' In an age when the volume of law was growing so quickly, demanding the full-time attention of practitioner and student alike, the editors felt that Dalhousie's emphasis on the 'collateral and ornamental knowledge' of Greek, French, or German language and literature did her professional pretensions a disservice.[85]

The increase in American coverage of Canadian legal affairs between 1880 and 1895 did not mean an evening out of regional bias in reporting. Most American legal articles or editorials dealt with Canadian questions arising federally, or in Ontario, Quebec, and Manitoba. Even considering what was said about Dalhousie, American coverage of legal developments in Nova Scotia and New Brunswick was sporadic, and coverage of Prince Edward Island and Newfoundland was all but non-existant.[86] Extensive coverage of Manitoban material in particular suggests that the distribution of American attention in this period remained a product of the exchange system, which still limited American editors to publications from a few Canadian regions.[87] They did, however, occasionally receive copies or clippings from general circulation newspapers elsewhere in the Dominion.[88]

Similarly, increased American interest in Canadian legal affairs did not mean the end of American condescension or criticism. On the contrary, in the shadow of annexation American condescension toward Canadians and criticism of Canada increased. That increase is paradoxical, since both practices led Americans to denigrate – and in the process, alienate – the very nation the United States supposedly wanted to absorb.

Many of the condescending comments that appeared in the American legal press were harmless. Canadian weather was one popular focus of American derision. In the 1880s, the *American Law Review* variously referred to the Montreal *Legal News* as 'our Arctic jurist' and 'our Arctic contemporary,' while it labelled Canadian legal journals in general 'our Arctic brethren.'[89] The *Albany Law Journal* jocularly concluded that Canadians would make better lawyers than Americans 'in regard to controversies concerning the chief commercial products of that country, such as ice, codfish, beaver, seals (those with legs), blubber … etc. So as to certain forms of conveyances – sledges, for instance.'[90] From time to time, such comments coloured more positive praise of Canadians and their works. In 1884, the *American Law Journal* declared that Rogers' *Law of the Road* was 'brim full of wit and merriment as are the ice crystals of that gelid clime.'[91] In 1885, in a similar state of mind, that *Journal* welcomed the *Manitoba Law Journal* to the ranks of North American legal periodicals, referring to it as 'this sterling little monthly from the ice-bound regions of the frozen north.'[92]

Other observations were more overtly offensive. The inauguration of the *Manitoba Law Journal*, for instance, induced an unabashedly jingoistic comment from the *American Law Review*: '[a] new venture comes to us from the future state of Manitoba, which we still courteously allow the Canadians to call a Province.'[93] In 1885, a number of editorial writers in the American legal press made it clear that they believed Americans – by virtue of their power and privileges – had a paternalistic duty toward Canadians, especially those who had recently gone to the United States. The *Albany Law Journal*, paraphrasing a somewhat ungenerous remark by Dr Johnson about the Scots, opined at one point that 'much may be done with a Canadian, if he is caught young.'[94] The *American Law Review* agreed, and held up Ontarian-turned-Missourian J.D. Lawson as an example.[95] On another occasion, referring to the deferential language of a petition for the appointment of a judge sent to the Crown by the Council of the Bar of Quebec, it provocatively declared that 'there are slavish sounds enough in this petition to excite hot indignation in the breast of any man who considers himself free, and who dares to think independently.'[96]

Twice between 1880 and 1895 American editorial treatment of Canada and Canadian affairs took on a downright ugly tone. In 1883, in the wake of a controversy concerning a visit to the United States (and not Canada) by John Duke Coleridge, Lord Chief Justice of England, the editors of the *American Law Review* sternly lectured the Canadian bar for having made an unseemly (not to mention unsuccessful) fuss about their loyalty to the Crown:

is it not time for intelligent Canadians to stop talking in the above strain? The chief trouble with them is that they are still provinces, and the silliest thing they do is keep up the twaddle about loyalty to Her Majesty. What has such loyalty done for them? They are the tail end of an Empire; they are destitute of distinction in arts, in literature, in agriculture, in manufactures, and in mechanical inventions. They turned the cold shoulder to our ancestors in the war of the Revolution; their country was the basis of an invasion to [sic] our country in the war of 1812; and they have reaped their reward for it. We have grown as a nation, and they have languished as provinces. Halifax is two days nearer Europe than Boston. It has a harbor in which the merchant marine of Europe could ride in safety; but it contains less than one-tenth the population of Boston, and is built of wooden houses that are rotting to the ground. They have a Vice-Regal court, with its dudism and low necked dresses. They also have a few hereditary titles. Their courts are modelled in close imitation of the present English system, and they have justices who would regard it almost a contempt of court to have an American law book read to them ... There is really no hope for their young men; for every good place in their vast mercantile houses and in their educational and civil service is filled by young nincompoops imported from England ... The talk of loyalty on the part of such a people is childish. If they are loyal, why do they not abolish their protective tariff and set up a titled aristocracy with the concomitants of the law of primogeniture and an established church? If they intend to set themselves up in the family of nations, the quicker they cut the umbilical cord the better.[97]

Running underneath that commentary was the unstated conviction that the only thing that lay in the way of successful annexation of Canada by the United States was the imperial tie.

Four years later, the editors of the *Review* hinted ominously that if outstanding disagreements between Canada and the United States (in particular, the fisheries dispute) were not resolved, the United States might absorb Canada by force, the protestations of England notwithstanding. The editors emphasized their 'friendly feeling' for Canadians, declared how 'unkind' it was to speak of such things, but nonetheless stated that 'a war ... could have but one result: a political union between Canada and the United States. The American people have long since outgrown the habit of doing things by halves. They would end this question as they ended the slavery question, by cutting up the cause of the controversy root and branch. In short, they would overrun and annex Canada. Such a war would not be permitted to end in any other way, and England could not prevent it from ending in that way.'[98]

Increased interest by American legal journals in Canadian law between 1880 and 1895 did not go unnoticed in Canada. Self-consciously breaking their previous silence, the editors of Canadian law journals were frequently critical of statements made by their American counterparts.[99] The Montreal *Legal News*, for instance, called the *American Law Review*'s 1883 diatribe against Canada a 'strange portrait': 'once upon a time extraordinary presentments of Canada and Canadian affairs were not uncommon in American journals, but we were under the impression that they were becoming things of the past.'[100] Putting not too fine a point on the episode, the *Legal News* suggested that the American writer, 'if he ever visited Canada, must have fallen into the hands of a Canadian Mark Twain and been very badly stuffed.'[101] The *Canadian Law Times* called the same diatribe 'mental filth,' and wryly suggested that its publication in an American organ proved that 'England is not the only country in which nincompoops originate, nor is Canada the only country which imports them.'[102] For its part, the *Canada Law Journal* labelled the *Review*'s editorials 'periodic ravings,' and observed impatiently that 'it is quite unnecessary to be perpetually saying how much the Eagle wants to clasp the Beaver to its bosom. We know that already. The difficulty is that we do not want to be clasped.'[103]

Other American comments drew similarly resentful responses. When, in 1884 and 1885, the *American Law Review* trumpeted the achievements of Canadian legal emigrés in the United States, the *Legal News* made the provocative (if not altogether serious) suggestion that those were gentlemen 'whose continued presence here would have proved rather embarrassing to themselves and have subjected them to possibly prolonged deprivation of liberty.'[104] Underneath even that light-hearted riposte, however, was a palpable Canadian weariness with the tone and content of American editorials. In 1884, the editor of the Montreal *Legal News* had tried to shame the American legal journals into civility by observing that 'our neighbours are great enough now to be able to dispense with unjust depreciation of Canada...'[105] In 1891, the editor of the *Western Law Times* complained of the editor of the *Albany Law Review* (to whom the former grandiloquently, if mockingly, referred as 'He of Albany') that 'whenever he refers to this country he ... makes some gay and "chipper" reference to the climate or food of the inhabitants.'[106] There is little evidence to suggest that such strategies of shame or complaint had an impact on the editorial policies of contemporary American legal periodicals, but they must have helped Canadian legal journal editors retain their self-respect in the face of a political and cultural continentalism they sought to resist.

In sum, American nativism, annexationism, and immigration patterns were underlying themes in expanding U.S. law journal coverage of Canadian law and lawyers between 1880 and 1895. The geographic focus of that coverage remained central Canada, but the character of American legal reporting of Canadian affairs changed in several key respects. Original contributions by Canadian authors were solicited and published, Canadian legal treatises were reviewed analytically (rather than merely noticed), and the degree of engagement with Canadian legal affairs (whether laudatory or critical) intensified noticably. Express and detailed exchanges with the editors of Canadian law journal also became commonplace. Those changes in the character of American portrayals of late-nineteenth-century Canadian law and lawyers were partly attributable to American editors' domestic legal agendas. A reorientation of their interest in bench-and-bar issues to feature Canadian lawyer-statesmen and model law schools is one example of the deployment of Canadian material in service of professional didacticism. Another case in point would be American law journal editors' commendation of Canadian criminal law reforms and division of federal powers jurisprudence as useful examples for U.S. lawmakers. But the overwhelming theme in American coverage was imperialistic continentalism.

CANADA AS CURIOSITY:

DECLINING AMERICAN COVERAGE, 1896–1911

In the third and final period of this survey, American law journals lost most of their earlier interest in Canadian legal affairs. Leading publications like the *American Law Review* and the *Albany Law Journal* cut back their Canadian coverage dramatically. Instead of running Canadian legal news almost once an issue, the *Review* ran it barely once a year, limiting the length of that coverage as well. A newer national legal periodical titled the *American Lawyer* followed the doings of the Canadian bar in some detail for a while but discontinued that practice after 1901. The multiplying state bar journals dropped Canadian material altogether. Among university-based law reviews, the *Harvard Law Review* ceased its previous practice of taking (or at least reporting) Canadian exchanges. Canadian material that remained in the *Law Review*'s pages appeared principally in brief book reviews.[107]

What had happened? To some extent, the circumstances that had given rise to an increase in American coverage of Canadian law and lawyers between 1880 and 1895 had simply changed. In the first place, the continuing flow of central and southern European immigrants into the United States had made the promotion of Anglo-Saxon solidarity more important than ever in certain quarters of the American bar. In that context, American lawyers chose to stress explicit connections with England over the general association of the United States with the British Empire.[108] That narrowing of focus was especially convenient because it allowed Americans to overlook a Canada that was rapidly becoming the preferred destination of the 'stalwart peasant in a sheepskin coat' so prized by Clifford Sifton, minister of immigration in Prime Minister Wilfrid Laurier's new cabinet. Secondly, American annexation was, by that stage, seen on both sides of the Canada–U.S. border as an idea whose time had passed. Many Americans remained convinced that annexation would someday happen, but in the short term it was, as the *Green Bag* put it, a mere 'ghost.' Looking back on the idea in 1896, the editor of the *Bag* made the previously ignored point that annexation might have caused Americans more problems than it would have solved: '[w]e have plenty of trouble here with our own mixed population, without desiring to add a mixed English and French country; and lawyers especially would not welcome courts carried on in the French language.'[109] American imperialism had, moreover, been mollified by exotic colonial adventures against a weak Spain in Cuba and the Philippines – the attractions of the 'frozen wastes' of a British-defended Canada paled in comparison. With Canadian-American union having become increasingly unlikely, there was less incentive for American legal periodicals to carry extensive coverage of Canadian affairs. Third, the tide of out-migration from Canada that had previously drawn some Canadians to American attention slackened significantly as the Canadian economy improved after 1896.[110] As American legal editors came into contact with fewer Canadian emigrés working in business or at the bar, they apparently became less curious about Canadian legal issues.

In addition to those limiting factors, the late 1890s and early 1900s found American lawyers and jurists awash in a sea of domestically produced law reports and legal treatises. The complaint of 'too many books' was hardly new, but it reached a crescendo at the turn of the century.[111] Declining printing and paper costs, rapid geographic expansion and elaboration of the American political and judicial structure, and the quick growth of the West Publishing Company had resulted in the release of an unprecedented number of legal (not to mention general) hornbooks, treatises, and periodicals.[112] In late 1895, the *Virginia Law Register* was already reporting that one year's case law amounted to more than 60,000 pages, meaning, as the editor put it, that a lawyer who wished to keep abreast of the new law would, if he were not to work Sundays or holidays, have to read 200 pages a day, all year.[113] In 1896, the editor of the *Green Bag* opined that it was 'a positive misfortune to the legal profession to have so many reports and text-books ... In the days of few books there was better and more certain law, and there were better lawyers.'[114] American attorneys simply could not keep up. In trying to read and absorb the professionally acceptable minimum, they necessarily took less of an interest in non-American legal sources and even looked askance at material from outside their own state jurisdictions. The role of local legal publishers in that emerging isolationism deserves a detailed study of its own.

In particular, the editors of contemporary American law journals stopped trying to keep up with Canadian legal affairs. They could no longer afford to do the requisite reading, and they could not be at all sure that their readers – with so many demands on their reading time – would bother to study Canadian legal news even if it were provided to them. The editors of American legal journals must also have recognized that the contents of Canadian law journals from which they derived most of their Canadian news were becoming less interesting from an American perspective. There was less Canadian coverage of American law and lawyers (apart perhaps from American Bar Association news), and there were fewer substantive Canadian references to American cases. Those changes may have had something to do with an increase in domestic legal literature in Canada and even with Canadian despair over the mounting pile of American law reports, but they were primarily a function of Canada's late-nineteenth- and early twentieth-century turn towards the lodestar of imperial law and precedent. Canadian lawyers increasingly wanted and felt they needed to hear about England and English law, but not about American law or lawyers.[115]

In this environment of altered material and political circumstances, the system of exchanges between Canadian and American legal periodicals began to break down. The *Harvard Law Review*'s apparent termination of its Canadian exchanges is a case in point. Judging from the *Green Bag*'s regular 'Index to Periodicals' feature, that review continued to receive Canadian journals through 1911, but after 1904 it too evinced little interest in the articles they contained.[116] The subscriber-based correspondence system on which the American legal journals had depended for information about Canadian legal developments began to disintegrate at the same time. Perhaps Canadian lawyers who had contributed to it were too busy themselves to continue that voluntary practice. Alternatively, they may have discovered that their Canadian submissions were less welcome, leading them to stop writing and even to cancel their subscriptions, thereby starving American periodicals of private Canadian sources.[117] The number of Canadian lawyers advertising in the *American Lawyer* (presumably a subset of that journal's Canadian subscribers) also declined significantly after 1899. Disengagement was clearly in progress.

American coverage of Canadian legal affairs did not, however, terminate overnight in 1896. Some Canadian issues continued to draw significant American attention, at least for a while. Constitutional law was one such attraction. On at least two occasions, American legal editors indulged their interest in the British North America Act by printing lengthy articles or addresses on that subject written by Canadians. In 1896, the *American Law Review* ran Edward Meek's 'Federal Government, and the Distribution of Power in the Canadian Federal System.'[118] In 1899, the *American Lawyer* published an address by Michigan Law School–educated Canadian Minister of Justice David Mills on 'Comparative Constitutional Law of Canada and the United States.'[119] Perhaps as a result of reading works like those articles, American legal editors' own appreciation of Canadian constitutional niceties became more sophisticated in this last period. In

1899, the *American Law Review* published a lengthy and obviously studied book review of A.H.F. Lefroy's constitutional treatise, *Legislative Power in Canada*, made even more interesting by the reviewer's suggestion that Canadian constitutional history – with its tradition of provincial approval of constitutional development – might harbour lessons for America's governance of its new overseas possessions.[120] The same year, the *American Law Review* launched its own Canadian constitutional argument, objecting to projected British Columbia legislation precluding foreign miners from taking up and working mining claims in the province. The editors of the *Review* suggested that such a law was beyond the powers of the British Columbia legislature, perhaps because of its international implications.[121] The argument may not have been particularly good, but the fact that it was made is nonetheless noteworthy. In 1901, perhaps prodded by a Canadian correspondent, the editor of the *American Lawyer* chastised an unnamed American contemporary for misconstruing the basic elements of Canadian constitutional structure: '[i]n the United States,' the *Lawyer* emphasized, 'the definite specified powers are given to the Federal authority, and all remaining powers are in the individual States; but in Canada the provinces have limited and specific powers of legislation, while the residue of the power is reserved to the Federal parliament.'[122]

The *American Law Review*'s musings on the constitutionality of the British Columbia mining bill were related to a more general American interest in Canadian mining law that developed in this period. It bears recollection that 1896 marked the start of the Klondike Gold Rush, and that mining and minerals thereafter assumed new prominence in the North American legal mind. American journals watched Canadian management of the Rush with a critical eye: even before the *Review* took the British Columbia legislature to task, the *Albany Law Journal* had questioned the justice of Canadian governmental decisions to extract royalties and registration fees ('blood-money tax') from miners.[123] When Canadian books finally appeared that discussed or laid out the body of statutory and case law that had developed around the Klondike mining industry, American legal periodicals were predictably quick to draw them to the attention of their readers. In 1898, for example, the *Harvard Law Review* reviewed William David McPherson and John Murray Clark's *The Law of Mines in Canada;* in 1903, the *Albany Law Journal* similarly surveyed Justice Archer Martin's *Reports of Mining Cases Decided by the Courts of British Columbia.*[124]

Somewhat like the Klondike itself, American coverage of the Canadian legal professions between 1896 and 1911 might be described as 'boom and bust.' In the late 1890s, the formation of an initially successful Canadian

266 BERNARD J. HIBBITTS

Bar Association precipitated a flurry of interest in it on the part of American journal editors.[125] They apparently saw that event as the Canadian manifestation of a professional movement that had already swept the United States.[126] The *American Lawyer* nonetheless took the occasion to observe, pedantically, that 'in addition to being the medium of elevating the legal profession and securing needed law reforms, the bar associations are beneficial in many other ways, all having in view one purpose – resulting good for a common whole.'[127] When that story petered out after a few reports on the annual meetings, the *American Lawyer* was left alone to monitor bar news from various provinces.[128] A number of enterprising Canadians managed to place biographical pieces on leading Canadian legal personalities in the *Green Bag*, but those entries stopped after about 1906.[129] Substantial American-authored coverage of Canadian legal education virtually ceased after the *American Law Review* ran an editorial wistfully noting that Dalhousie's law school, 'which ... we have on several occasions commended,' no longer had any American students, although 'in former years there were several.'[130]

In the context of decreasing coverage of serious Canadian legal affairs, the occasional humorous tales about Canada or Canadian law that American legal journals had traditionally printed began to stand out. For example, the *Green Bag* told the story, supposedly obtained from a 'Canadian barrister,' of a semi-literate farmer who declared that 'if I can't have a holographic will, I'll blamed die intestine!'; on another occasion, it reported the antics of a Nova Scotian lawyer who carried his necktie in his pocket because the law said he had to wear one, but it did not say where he had to wear it.[131] The subtext of those and other stories – for all their lighthearted innocence – was not encouraging for Canadians. Canada, it appeared, did not really matter. Indeed, Canada could be held up before the American bar as something to be ridiculed. To a greater extent than ever before, that country had become a curiosity.

One might think that such treatment would have encouraged increased Canadian sniping at American legal journals, but that is not what happened. From 1896 onwards, American reporting of Canadian legal affairs – serious or comical – no longer registered much with Canadians. In early 1897, the editor of the *Canada Law Journal* did take his counterpart at the *Green Bag* to task for various 'ribald jests at the expense of the Canadian people,' and later that year he told the editor of the *Albany Law Journal* to keep to himself his opinions of Canadian attempts to supervise Klondike miners.[132] After those exchanges, however, Canadian journal editors largely ignored the American legal press. Perhaps Canadians believed that, with the forces of continentalism largely spent, they could afford to turn the other cheek. Or perhaps, with continentalism disappearing from the agenda, Canadians no longer perceived American editorial comments as so obviously obnoxious that they demanded replies. In either event, the incipient Canadian-American editorial 'dialogue' that had developed between 1880 and 1895 collapsed during the late 1890s.

The years between 1896 and 1911 thus witnessed a gradual disengagement from Canadian matters by American law journal editors. That disengagement is rendered somewhat enigmatic by its placement against the background of the continuing metropolitan role of Montreal for New England and New York, the expansion of north-south trading links, and the increased technological ease with which ideas could be communicated intracontinentally. These factors suggest that more rather than less legal cross-pollination between Canada and the United States should have been the order of the days straddling the turn of the twentieth century.

The redirection of U.S. imperialism to its Spanish-speaking neighbours and a marked decrease in Canadian out-migration to the United States may have helped to dull continentalist forces that formerly found representation in frequent and varied portrayals of Canadian law and lawyers in American legal periodicals. The turn-of-the-century's proliferation of state laws, lawyers, and legal literature is an even better causal candidate for that diminution in Canadian coverage. Maintenance of a global or even continental perspective must have been significantly handicapped by the state-centrism, legal positivism, and profit-oriented legal publishing that underlay that proliferation. Hyperbolically, one might say that those forces combined to beat back outward-looking federalist gains in American legal culture that had been won three generations earlier.[133]

CONCLUSION

It is fitting that this investigation of American portrayals of Canadian law and lawyers should terminate in 1911. Not only is that conclusion justifiable from an internal perspective, it is also serendipitous insofar as 1911 was the year in which Canadians rejected a proposed reciprocity treaty with the United States. This denial of a closer economic bond summed up and symbolized the mutual disengagement that had already been reflected in the steadily declining coverage of Canadian affairs in American legal periodicals after 1896.

The selection of 1911 as a *terminus ad quem* leaves a relatively well-defined corpus of American legal reporting on Canadian law and lawyers covering a critical eighty-year period in the histories of American and Canadian law. That corpus is a mixture of fact and fancy, bluster and blunder, commendation and condescension. Portrayals of Canadian law and lawyers that survive in the yellowed pages of nineteenth- and early twentieth-century American legal journals reveal – from an unusual, and perhaps unusually revealing perspective – much about the attitudes, values, preferences, and prejudices that prevailed in important quarters of the American legal community. But, as was mentioned at the outset of this study, they also tell modern readers something significant about Canadian legal culture. Collectively, American law journal coverage of Canadian affairs reminds us that our North American grandfathers were different, in some ways more eclectic and perhaps more interesting, than their offspring.

Nineteenth-century eclecticism may not distinguish North American lawyers significantly from their British, continental European, or English colonial contemporaries. Indeed, there is a substantial modern literature that has begun to describe the last century's legal pantheism and to relate its demise to factors like the consolidation of nation states, the imperial use of discretely metropolitan law for empire-building purposes, the triumph of legal positivism, and the proliferation of locally oriented legal publishers.[134] The rate at which those studies in intellectual history are appearing should soon enable patterns in North American legal cross-fertilization to be measured and explained with greater reference to larger international trends.

NOTES

1 See R.C.B. Risk, 'A.H.F Lefroy: Common Law Thought in Late Nineteenth Century Canada: On Burying One's Grandfather,' *University of Toronto Law Journal* 41 (1991) 307.
2 See R.C.B. Risk, 'Sir William Meredith C.J.O.: The Search for Authority,' *Dalhousie Law Journal* 7 (1983) 713.
3 For purposes of this paper, 'Canada' designates not only Canada in the post-1867 national sense, but (as necessary) 'British North America' so as to include British Columbia, Upper and Lower Canada, Nova Scotia, New Brunswick, Prince Edward Island, and Newfoundland prior to Confederation.
4 Publication was 'suspended' in 1817.
5 On lawyers as subscribers, contributors, and editors of early nineteenth-century American literary periodicals, see generally R.A. Ferguson, *Law and*

Letters in American Culture (Cambridge, Mass.: Harvard University Press 1984), 71. See also R.W. Gordon, 'Lawyers as the American Aristocracy,' *Stanford Law Review* 20 (1985), 1.

6 'American Legal Periodicals,' *Albany Law Journal* 2 (1870), 445 at 445.

7 See generally E.C. Surrency, *A History of American Law Publishing* (New York: Oceana Publications 1990), 190. Compare D. Daintree, 'The Legal Periodical: A Study in the Commerce of Information (1761–1875)' (MLS dissertation, University of Sheffield 1975).

8 See generally M.I. Swygert and J.W. Bruce, 'The Historical Origins, Founding and Early Development of Student-Edited Law Reviews,' *Hastings Law Journal* 36 (1985), 739.

9 'After 1800, ... [l]awyers looked to legal magazines as well as to other activities to maintain professional cohesion and power.' R. Stevens, *Law School: Legal Education in America from the 1850s to the 1980s* (Chapel Hill: University of North Carolina Press 1983), 8.

10 In the inaugural issue of the *American Law Review*, for instance, the editors called on their 'professional brethren throughout the Union' to write to them about 'judicial appointments, deaths of leading lawyers, important decisions, legislative changes, interesting trials, or other legal news.' 'Summary of Events,' *American Law Review* 1 (1866), 206.

11 See especially notes 95, 96, infra, and accompanying text.

12 As early as 1868, the *Philadelphia Legal Intelligencer* formally congratulated itself on a quarter-century of existence by claiming subscribers in, inter alia, 'the dominion of Canada.' 'Book Notices,' *American Law Review* 2 (1867), 178. See also the following notice that regularly ran at the beginning of the *American Lawyer*'s 'Canadian Notes' section in the late 1890s and early 1900s: 'Canadian attornies [sic] are requested to send notices of change of address, organization and dissolution of partnerships, etc. for insertion.'

13 See 'Fugitives from Justice,' *American Jurist* 1 (1829), 297.

14 'We are happy to have the opinions of enlightened men upon a question of this kind laid before us, particularly from a country with which our communications are so frequent and our interests mutual.' 'Fugitives,' at 304. The cases cited were *Matter of Washburn* 4 Johns CH. 4 106 (1819), and *Commonwealth v. Deacon*, 10 Serg. & Raw. 125 (1823).

15 On the early history of Canadian extradition to the United States, see generally D. and L. Gibson, 'Railroading the Train Robbers: Extradition in the Shadow of Annexation,' in D. Gibson and W.W. Pue, eds., *Glimpses of Canadian Legal History* (Winnipeg: University of Manitoba Faculty of Law 1991), 71; A.L. Murray, 'The Extradition of Fugitive Slaves from Canada: A Re-evaluation,' *Canadian Historical Review* 43 (1962), 298; R.J. Zorn, 'Criminal

Extradition Menaces the Canadian Haven for Fugitive Slaves, 1841–1861,'
Canadian Historical Review 37 (1957), 284.

16 See generally P. Brode, *The Odyssey of John Anderson* (Toronto: The Osgoode
Society for Canadian Legal History, 1989).

17 See 'The Anderson Case,' *Monthly Law Reporter* 23 (1860–61), 641.

18 See generally Brode, *Odyssey* at 51–3.

19 'The Chesapeake,' *Monthly Law Reporter* 26 (1863–64), 472, at 474–5.

20 See 'In re Asher Warner,' *Monthly Law Reporter* 27 (1864–65), 45.

21 See 'In re Bennet G. Burley,' *Monthly Law Reporter* 27 (1864–65), 92.

22 See 'Extradition Lamirande,' *American Law Review* 1 (1866), 406; 'The Extradition of Lamirande,' *American Law Review* 1 (1866), 757.

23 See 'The Extradition Treaty in Canada,' *Albany Law Journal* 2 (1870), 361.

24 See, e.g., 'Insurance,' *Weekly Law Gazette* 4 (1859), 135; 'Admiralty-Collision,'
American Law Review 11 (1876), 399.

25 See 'The Inga,' *Monthly Law Reporter* 18 (1855–56), 285; 'The Varuna,' *Monthly
Law Reporter* 18 (1855–56), 437; 'The Case of the Chesapeake,' *Monthly Law
Reporter* 26 (1863–64), 271.

26 The *Weekly Law Gazette* routinely credited the *Lower Canada Jurist* and the
Upper Canada Law Journal for its Canadian decisions. See, e.g., 'Service on
Wife of Prisoner,' *Weekly Law Gazette* 2 (1858), 296; 'Insurance,' *Weekly Law
Gazette* 4 (1859), 185; 'By-Law,' *Weekly Law Gazette* 4 (1859), 211.

27 'Reports of Cases Argued and Determined in the Supreme Court of New
Brunswick,' *Monthly Law Reporter* 24 (1861–62), 447–8. For example, '[t]he
temperence reform, with its attendant Maine law and its accompanying
litigation, is hardly less a topic of discussion in the province than in the State
where this legislation had its origin. Similar questions are raised as in Maine
and Massachusetts and usually attended with similar results to the litigants.'
Compare 'Reports of Cases Adjudged in the Supreme Court of the Province
of New Brunswick, Commencing in Hilary Term, 1835,' *American Jurist* 20
(1838), 246, at 247–8: 'we are happy to discover that no royal scruples in the
minds of the judges deter them from raising freely, as precedents, the general
understanding of the legislatures and courts in the former North American
colonies; and the opinions of the most distinguished American jurists of the
present day ...'

28 Compare the *American Jurist*'s 1838 review of an earlier volume of New
Brunswick reports, explaining that 'the moral elements of legal decisions,
constituting the soul of universal jurisprudence, are the same in all countries.'
Ibid. at 248.

29 On the usury debate, see, e.g., 'Usury Laws,' *American Jurist* 6 (1831), 282;
'Usury and the Usury Laws,' *North American Review* 36 (1834), 68; 'On the

Usury Law,' *American Jurist* 17 (1837), 331. On juries, see, e.g., 'Trial by Jury,' *American Jurist* 1 (1829), 274; 'Trial by Jury,' *U.S. Magazine and Democratic Review* 6 (1839), 463; 'Trial by Jury,' *Monthly Law Reporter* 2 (1850), 426; 'Jury Trial,' *Southern Literary Messenger* 16 (1850), 380; 'Have Juries a Right to Decide the Law in Criminal Cases?' *Monthly Law Reporter* 5 (1852); 'Trial by Jury,' *Monthly Law Reporter* 12 (1860), 365.

30 See 'New Usury Law in Canada,' *Weekly Law Gazette* 2 (1858), 174. Compare 'An Act to amend the Law of this Province regulating the Rate of Interest,' SC 1858, c. 85.

31 'Unanimity of Juries,' *Weekly Law Gazette* 2 (1858), 303. Compare 'An Act relating to Jurors,' SNB 1855, c. 24; 'Of Juries,' RSNS 1859, c. 136.

32 'Current Topics,' *Albany Law Journal* 1 (1870), 158. The statute in issue was apparently An Act respecting Procedure in Criminal Cases, and other matters relating to Criminal Law, SC 1869, c. 29.

33 'Patent Law,' *American Law Review* 7 (1872–73), 189; 'Current Topics,' *Albany Law Journal* 11 (1875), 133. Compare 'An Act respecting Copyright,' SC 1868, c. 54 and An Act respecting Patents of Invention, SC 1869, c. 11.

34 See 'The Late Andrew Stuart, Esq.,' *American Jurist* 23 (1840), 248. Compare A. Stuart, *Notes upon the South Western Boundary Line of the British Provinces of Lower Canada and New Brunswick and the United States of America* (Quebec: Cary 1830); A. Stuart, *Succinct Account of the Treaties and Negotiations between Great Britain and the United States of America Relating to the Boundary between the British Possessions of Lower Canada and New Brunswick, in North America, and the United States of America* (London: Thoms 1838).

35 See 'Obituary Notices,' *Monthly Law Reporter* (1847–48), 526.

36 Hagarty had presided in the *Warner* case and had been involved in the *Burley* decision. His judgment in *Smith v. Roe* (on an agency question) had been republished in the *Monthly Law Reporter* 27 (1864–65), 287. Wilson had ruled in the *Caldwell* case, and his decision in *White v. Baker* (on the ability of a bearer of a promissory note issued in the United States to refuse payment of the note in Canadian currency) had been reprinted in *Monthly Law Reporter* 27 (1864–65), 284.

37 'Book Notices,' *American Law Review* 6 (1871–72), 564. See generally J. Swainger, 'A Bench in Disarray: The Quebec Judiciary and the Federal Department of Justice, 1867–1878,' *Cahiers de droit* 34 (1993), 59.

38 'Current Topics,' *Albany Law Review* 7 (1873), 164.

39 'Court of Appeals – Resolutions of the Bar,' *American Law Review* 8 (1873–74), 787.

40 *Lower Canada Jurist*; *Lower Canada Law Journal*; *Revue Critique*; Montreal *Legal News*; and *Upper Canada Law Journal*, later succeeded by the *Canada Law*

Journal. The *Local Courts and Municipal Gazette* was also published in Toronto,
but it was largely made up of selections from the *Upper Canada Law Journal.*
41 The importance of the exchange system to patterns of American coverage,
even in this first period, is reflected in the increase in the number of articles
on Upper Canadian legal developments that appeared in American journals
after the *Upper Canada Law Journal* commenced publication in 1855.
42 'Reports of Cases Argued and Determined in the Courts of King's Bench and
in the Provincial Court of Appeals of Lower Canada,' *American Jurist* 20
(1838), 217. In 1838, the answer to that question would have been 'yes' for
Upper Canada and 'no' for Nova Scotia.
43 'Reports of Cases Argued and Determined in the Supreme Court of New
Brunswick,' *Law Reporter* 6 (1844), 186. Presumably, the Newfoundland
reporter in issue was R.E. Wakeham, *Select Cases* (St. John's, Nfld.: J.W.
Withers 1829).
44 See, e.g., *Upper Canada Law Journal* 4 (1858), 169, 218; 'Warnings,' *Upper
Canada Law Journal* 6 (1860), 221; *Upper Canada Law Journal* 5 (1859), 264; and
Upper Canada Law Journal 3 (1857), 192.
45 See, e.g., 'Law in the United States,' *Upper Canada Law Journal* 4 (1858), 32–3
(reprinting American newspaper articles); *Upper Canada Law Journal* 5 (1859),
282 (reprinting a case from the *Pittsburgh Law Journal*); *Upper Canada Law
Journal* 9 (1863), 145 (reprinting an article from the *Monthly Law Reporter*);
Upper Canada Law Journal 10 (1864), 164 (reprinting an article from the
Philadelphia Legal Intelligencer); *Upper Canada Law Journal* 4 (1858), 125; and
Upper Canada Law Journal 10 (1864), 88.
46 See, e.g., 'U.C. Law Journal in England,' *Upper Canada Law Journal* 5 (1859), 55.
47 See generally J. Higham, *Strangers in the Land: Patterns of American Nativism,
1860–1925* (New York: Atheneum 1981), 12–67.
48 See generally R.A. Cosgrove, *Our Lady the Common Law: An Anglo-American
Legal Community, 1870–1930* (New York: New York University Press 1987), 6–
24, 59–94.
49 For a short while during that period, Americans – judging by digests that
appeared in the *Central Law Journal* – were also interested in legal cases and
news from Australia, New Zealand, India, and South Africa.
50 'David Dudley Field's Address,' *American Law Review* 19 (1885), 616 at 617.
51 On annexationism in the nineteenth century, see generally D.F. Warner, *The
Idea of Continental Union: Agitation for the Annexation of Canada to the United
States, 1849–1893* (Lexington: University of Kentucky Press 1960).
52 'Sir John A. Macdonald,' *American Law Review* 25 (1891), 647, at 649. See also
'Colonial Lawyers Practising in England,' *American Law Review* 18 (1884), 848:
'[t]he conservative influence of Canada in American politics would be very

salutary.' Americans of this period never gave much thought to the implications of absorbing Canada's significant French-speaking population.

53 '[T]he highest offices within the gift of the republic would be opened to Canadians; Americans would delight to honor themselves by making such a statesman as Sir John A. Macdonald their President.' 'Colonial Lawyers' at 849.

54 In 1893, the editor of the *Albany Law Journal* appended this interesting (if perhaps tongue-in-cheek) note to a Canadian-written article on Quebec case law: '[i]n view of the possibility of annexation, boys in the kindergartens of the United States who intend to practice before the Supreme Court at Washington might do well to make a speciality of the ecclesiastical law and lore of Quebec.' R.V.R [R.V. Rogers], 'Some Quebec Cases,' *Albany Law Journal* 47 (1893), 425 at 426.

55 In 1870 there were more than 490,000 Canadian-born individuals living in the United States. By 1890 that figure had risen to almost 1,000,000, representing some 20 per cent of the Canadian population. See R.K. Vedder and L.E. Gallaway, 'Settlement Patterns of Canadian Emigrants to the United States, 1850–1960,' *Canadian Journal of Economics* 3 (1970), 476 at 477. For an extended discussion of Canadian emigration to the United States in the period under consideration, see generally M.L. Hansen and J.B. Brebner, *The Mingling of the Canadian and American Peoples* (New Haven: Yale University Press 1940), 1:182–218.

56 'Notes,' *American Law Review* 17 (1883), 781 at 782.

57 'There seems to be a tendency of late among many young men in Canada to settle in the State of New York, with a view to practising the legal profession ...' 'Correspondence,' *Canada Law Journal* 21 (1885), 62.

58 'Notes,' *American Law Review* 17 (1883), 991 at 992.The individual referred to in the first part of that quotation was probably John Davidson Lawson who, after completing his legal education in Toronto, went to the United States where he became editor of the *Central Law Journal* (1877–81), and the *American Law Review*, as well as dean of the University of Missouri Law School. In 1891, the editors of the *American Law Review* scolded Ontario lawyers for not giving Lawson the recognition he deserved in the province of his birth. See 'The Reception and Banquet at Osgoode Hall,' *American Law Review* 25 (1891), 262.

59 See, e.g., R.L. Weatherbe, 'Codification,' *American Law Review* 20 (1886), 245; A.H. Marsh, 'The Canadian Fisheries Question,' *American Law Review* 21 (1887), 369; R. Cassels, 'The Supreme Court of Canada,' *Green Bag* 2 (1890), 241; D.B. Read, 'The Law School of Osgoode Hall, Toronto,' *Green Bag* 3 (1891), 265; E. Meek, 'Some Observations on the Constitution of the Dominion of Canada,' *American Law Review* 29 (1895), 32.

60 Reviewed at *Green Bag* 2 (1890), 416; *Harvard Law Review* 4 (1890–91), 145; *American Law Review* 17 (1883), 440.

61 Reviewed at *American Law Journal* 1 (1884), 120. Judging by repeated American references to his work, Rogers, who lived in Kingston, Ontario, was the most popular Canadian legal writer of the day in the United States. Most of his books and articles were on arcane or humorous aspects of the law, however, and he contributed little to profound American understanding of Canadian jurisprudence.

62 In part, that result was forced by the discontinuance of full case reprints in the major Canadian law journals on which most American legal periodicals depended for their Canadian material. In 1887, for instance, the editors of the *American Law Review* complained that 'we do not get the decisions of the Canadian appellate courts in any of our legal exchanges, except in the form of abstracts.' 'A Threatened Invasion of Canada,' *American Law Review* 21 (1887), 789. Digests of Canadian cases were a regular feature of the *Central Law Journal* in the early 1880s, thanks perhaps to Lawson's efforts (as editor in the late 1870s) to include more abstracts of Canadian case law. See, e.g., *Central Law Journal* 19 (1884), 57, 58, 77, 135, 155, 256, 278, 317, and 417. Their virtual absence from American periodical literature after 1885 does not, however, appear to have reflected a judgment on the part of American legal editors that Canadian case law had become irrelevant. In 1889, for instance, Seymour Thompson, one of the editors of the *American Law Review*, wrote a letter to the editors of the *Canada Law Journal* declaring that 'more attention to Canadian decisions by our own judges and lawyers would result in an improvement of our own jurisprudence.' 'The Central Bank Case,' *Canada Law Journal* 25 (1889), 392.

63 'The law journals are, we think, too much in the habit of publishing judicial decisions merely because they are out of the way and novel.' 'Notes,' *American Law Review* 17 (1883), 255.

64 See, e.g., 'The Manitoba Exemption Law,' *Central Law Journal* 21 (1885), 22; 'Canadian Constitutional Law,' *Harvard Law Review* 8 (1894–95), 497.

65 'Our Prospective Union with Canada: Revision of the Constitution,' *American Law Review* 26 (1892), 405.

66 'Riel's Case,' *American Law Review* 19 (1885), 929 at 930. Compare 'Points in the Riel Case,' *Central Law Journal* 19 (1885), 373 at 374: '[w]hat would an American lawyer think of trying a citizen for the crimes of murder and treason before a court composed of two justices of the peace and six men, without any indictment by a grand jury, but upon a mere "change" ... ? ... Our courts ... would probably hold that the "process of law" invoked in this case is not "due."'

67 'Current Topics,' *Albany Law Journal* 32 (1885), 381.
68 'It is quite exasperating to a large part of the community that a criminal ... may escape by crossing into Canada, and may live there in open luxury, almost within sight and hearing of those whom he has defrauded, and laugh at the laws.' 'Current Topics,' *Albany Law Journal* 29 (1884), 461.
69 'A Canadian View of Extradition,' *American Law Review* 22 (1888), 272.
70 See 'The New Canadian Extradition Act,' *American Law Review* 23 (1889), 809. Compare 'An Act to extend the provisions of the Extradition Act,' SC 1889, c. 36.
71 See, e.g., 'Canada Criminal Code,' *Criminal Law Magazine* 14 (1892), 938. Compare 'An Act respecting the Criminal Law,' SC 1892, c. 29.
72 The *American Law Review* concluded that it was 'a work entitled to very great praise, and one which ought to command the attention of legislators in the United States.' 'The Canada Criminal Code,' *American Law Review* 27 (1893), 66.
73 'Current Topics,' *Albany Law Journal* 46 (1892–93), 362 at 363. See also 'The Canada Criminal Code': '[i]t is ... a great mistake to think that this is the first and only criminal code possessed by any branch of the English-speaking race. On the contrary, many of the American states have such codes ...'
74 See, e.g., 'John Godfrey Spragge,' *American Law Review* 18 (1884), 514; *Columbia Jurist* 2 (1885–86), 12 [Norman Ritchie]; 'Sir William Johnston Ritchie,' *Green Bag* 4 (1892), 500; *Albany Law Review* 48 (1893), 363; [Justice George King of the Supreme Court of Canada, who was identified as 'a graduate of the Wesleyan University, Connecticut']; 'Sir John A. Macdonald,' *American Law Review* 25 (1891), 646; J.A. Chisholm, 'The Late Right Hon. Sir John A. Macdonald,' *Green Bag* 3 (1891), 395; 'The Late Hon. Sir John Abbott, KCMG,' *Green Bag* 5 (1893), 537; 'Sir John Thompson,' *Green Bag* 3 (1891), 105; 'The Late Rt. Hon. Sir John Thompson,' *Green Bag* 7 (1895), 99; 'Sir John S.D. Thompson,' *American Law Review* 29 (1895), 112.
75 In 1887 New York attorney Nathaniel Moak told the editors of the *Albany Law Journal* that Bethune was 'the ablest lawyer he ever knew.' *Albany Law Journal* 36 (1887), 62.
76 'Notes,' *Albany Law Journal* 24 (1881), 40. In a footnote for their readers, the editors of the *Albany Law Journal* indicated that the time limit was, in fact, two hours.
77 See 'Notes,' *American Law Review* 17 (1883), 964.
78 'Notes,' *American Law Review* 17 (1883), 589 at 590.
79 See 'Current Topics,' *Albany Law Journal* 44 (1891), 141.
80 *Michigan Law Journal* 1 (1892), 368.
81 Discussions of other Canadian law schools were not absent from American

legal literature of this period, but they were infrequent and (apart from David Breckenridge Read's Canadian-written article on Toronto's Osgoode Hall, supra note 59) comparatively short. See, e.g., 'Osgoode Hall,' *Intercollegiate Law Journal* 1 (1891–92), 113; 'More About Our Law Schools,' *American Law Review* 27 (1893), 745 at 746 [Osgoode Hall]; 'More About Law Schools,' *American Law Review* 27 (1893), 891 at 892; [King's College Law School in Fredericton, New Brunswick, now operated by the University of New Brunswick]; 'Law Schools,' *American Lawyer* 3 (1895), 495 [Osgoode Hall]; *American Lawyer* 3 (1895), 175 [McGill].

82 'A New Law School,' *American Law Review* 18 (1884), 285 at 286.

83 'The Dalhousie University Law School,' *American Law Review* 19 (1885), 108 at 109.

84 Ibid. at 109. Did the editors of the *Review* know that Richard Chapman Weldon, the founding dean of Dalhousie, had paid tribute to the Harvard Law School in his inaugural address or that, before the school was established, three of its prospective instructors – John Thompson, Robert Sedgwick and Wallace Graham – had visited Boston and New York for the express purpose of learning from American experiences? See generally J. Willis, *A History of Dalhousie Law School* (Toronto: University of Toronto Press 1979), 31–2.

85 'More About Our Law School,' *American Law Review* 27 (1893), 745 at 748.

86 In 1892, however, the *Green Bag* ran the obituary of a Prince Edward Island probate judge, Charles Young, who was the younger brother of Sir William Young, chief justice of Nova Scotia. See *Green Bag* 4 (1892), 245.

87 See, e.g., 'Arguing v. Wrangling,' *Central Law Journal* 19 (1884), 258; 'Railway Carriers or Warehousemen,' *Kentucky Law Journal* 2 (1885–86), 99; 'Summary Conviction–Certiorari,' *Criminal Law Magazine* 8 (1886), 631; 'Criminal Code–Right of Reply–Joint Trial,' *Criminal Law Magazine* 16 (1894), 75. In this period, the ranks of Canadian legal periodicals were swelled by the inauguration of the *Manitoba Law Journal* and (after its demise) the *Western Law Times*, both published in Winnipeg.

88 In 1885, for instance, the *American Law Journal* indicated that the source of one of its stories was 'a Nova Scotia paper, the *Halifax Record*.' 'Circumstantial Evidence,' *American Law Journal* 2 (1885), 185.

89 'Notes,' *American Law Review* 17 (1883), 991 at 992; 'A Different Picture,' *American Law Review* 18 (1884), 105, 133.

90 'Current Topics,' *Albany Law Journal* 36 (1887–88), 62.

91 'Book Notices,' *American Law Journal* 1 (1884), 120.

92 'Book Notices,' *American Law Journal* 2 (1884–85), 250.

93 'Manitoba Law Journal,' *American Law Review* 18 (1885), 270. For a similar comment, see 'Manitoba Law Journal,' *American Law Review* 18 (1885), 474.

94 'Current Topics,' *Albany Law Journal* 29 (1884), 342.

95 See 'A Canadian Caught Young,' *American Law Review* 18 (1884), 459.

96 'Royal Favor,' *American Law Review* 18 (1884), 460.

97 'Notes,' *American Law Review* 17 (1883), 781–2.

98 'A Kettle of Fish,' *American Law Review* 21 (1887), 446 at 447. Compare Marsh, 'Canadian Fisheries.'

99 See, e.g., 'Editorial Notes,' *Canada Law Journal* 16 (1880), 154: 'Correspondence,' *American Law Review* 19 (1885), 938; 'Correspondence,' *American Law Review* 20 (1886), 762.

100 'A Strange Portrait,' *Legal News* 6 (1884), 337. See also (in a slightly different context) 'The American Law Review on Canada,' *Canadian Law Times* 4 (1894), 526 at 527: '[t]he *Review* is ... under the impression, apparently, that Canada is composed of four provinces, and that the best places in Canada are filled by Englishmen foisted upon the Canadians by imperial influence.'

101 'Strange Portrait,' at 338.

102 'The American The Law Review on Canada,' *Canadian Law Times* 3 (1883), 534. Earlier the same year, the editor of the *Law Times* had rebuked the *Central Law Journal* for carrying certain 'supercilious' comments on such Canadian legal practices as the wearing of robes, especially as 'it owes its early growth and immense circulation to a Canadian [John Lawson].' 'Professional Attire,' *Canadian Law Times* 3 (1883), 333 at 334.

103 'Editorial Notices,' *Canada Law Journal* 21 (1885), 1.

104 *Legal News* 8 (1885), 112.

105 'That Strange Portrait,' 7 *Legal News* (1884), 33.

106 'He of Albany,' *Western Law Times* 2 (1891), 53 at 55.

107 See, e.g., *Harvard Law Review* 12 (1898–99), 286, reviewing E. Lafleur, *The Conflict of Laws in the Province of Quebec*; *Harvard Law Review* 16 (1902–3), 464, reviewing J. Bicknell and A.J. Knapple, *Practical Statutes, Being a Collection of Statutes of Practical Utility in Force in Ontario*.

108 On 'Anglo-Saxonism,' among members of the American bar in the late 1890s and early 1900s, see generally Cosgrove, *Our Lady* at 59–94.

109 '[A]t some future day they [i.e., the Canadians] will inevitably gravitate to us.' I. Browne, 'Canadian Notions,' *Green Bag* 8 (1896), 503 at 504.

110 Indeed, it could be said that the tide of immigration turned in that period, as many Americans moved north to the still relatively unpopulated Canadian prairies. See Hansen and Brebner, *Mingling*, at 218–43.

111 See, e.g., 'Law Reports,' *Southern Literary Messenger* 14 (1848), 255.

112 Declining printing costs were such that the number of general periodicals published in the United States increased from 3,300 in 1885 to about 6,000 in 1905. See generally F.L. Mott, *A History of American Magazines, 1885–1905* (Cambridge, Mass.: Harvard University Press 1957), 11.

113 'Law Reporting,' *Virginia Law Register* 1 (1895), 309.

114 'Current Topics,' *Green Bag* 8 (1896), 83. As early as 1888, the editors of the *American Law Review* had excused the already developing decline in American citation of English cases on the grounds that 'our own appellate courts are supplying us with sources of law in superabundant quantities.' 'Canadian Law,' *American Law Review* 22 (1888), 934 at 935. In 1897, a correspondent of the *University Law Review* suggested that 'the jurisprudence of the American states would be vastly improved if each volume of the State Reports outside of the limits of the jurisdiction in which it was issued, is used for a bonfire on the celebration of the next Fourth of July.' 'Precedents,' *University Law Review* 3 (1897), 197.

115 See generally G.B. Baker, 'The Reconstitution of Upper Canadian Legal Thought in the Late Victorian Empire,' *Law and History Review* 3 (1985), 219. In 1899, the *American Law Review* took impish delight in documenting one excess of that Canadian turn: 'some of the Canadians have gone so far in copying British statutes, as to copy a corrective act, although the Canadian statute did not contain the mistake which the subsequently adopted British statute was passed to correct.' 'Copying Foreign Statutes,' *American Law Review* 33 (1899), 96.

116 In the early 1900s, the editors of the *Green Bag* frequently summarized leading articles in American law journals or reprinted appropriate paragraphs to whet potential readers' appetites, but that type of promotional treatment was hardly ever accorded a paper reported to have appeared in a Canadian law journal.

117 The *American Lawyer*, for instance, discontinued its regular 'Canadian Notes' section in January of 1902, despite its previous success in getting Canadian subscribers to contribute information and news.

118 See *American Law Review* 30 (1896), 203.

119 See *American Lawyer* 7 (1899), 190.

120 'It might be well for our legislators in imposing imperial government on distant provinces to bear this important qualification in mind, even though they be legislating over hordes of semi-civilized orientalists who have not been in the habit of reading newspapers or wearing clothes.' 'Lefroy on Legislative Power in Canada,' *American Law Review* 33 (1899), 151 at 152.

121 See 'Legislation to Bar American Miners from British Columbia,' *American Law Review* 33 (1899), 124. Compare 'An Act to amend the Placer Mining Act,' SBC 1899, c. 50.

122 'Canadian Notes,' *American Lawyer* 9 (1901), 294.

123 See 'Current Topics,' *Albany Law Journal* 55 (1897), 109. Compare 'An Act relating to Gold and other Minerals excepting Coal,' SBC 1896, c. 34.

124 See *Albany Law Review* 12 (1898–99), 289; *Albany Law Review* 65 (1903–4), 193.

Although the reviewer did not make mention of it, cases included in Martin's volume drew heavily on American case law. Compare J.M. MacIntyre, 'The Use of American Cases in Canadian Courts,' *University of British Columbia Law Review* 2 (1964–66), 478 at 484.

125 That ultimately abortive organization should not be confused with the present institution of the same name, founded in 1914.

126 See, e.g., 'A Canadian Bar Association,' *Case and Comment* 3, no. 3 (1896), 9; 'The Canadian Bar Association,' *American Lawyer* 4 (1896), 498; 'Current Topics?' *Albany Law Review* 54 (1896–97), 243. The connection between the Canadian and American bar association movements was explicitly acknowledged by the Canadian Bar Association's first president in 1897: '[t]he renown of [a recent meeting of the American Bar Association], and the example given, there can be no doubt, contributed a good deal to determine the initiative taken up by the leading lawyers of Canada of inviting the members of all the [provincial] bars to a general convention in Montreal.' 'Address of Hon. J.E. Robidoux,' *American Lawyer* 5 (1897), 481.

127 *American Lawyer* 4 (1896), 435.

128 See, e.g., 'Address of Hon. J.E. Robidoux'; 'Canadian Bar Association,' *American Law Review* 32 (1898), 757; 'Canadian Notes,' *American Lawyer* 9 (1901), 183, 293, 488, 582. But see supra note 117 on the 1902 discontinuance of that feature.

129 See, e.g., R.D. McGibbon, QC, 'Sir Melbourne Tait,' *Green Bag* 9 (1897), 417; W. Clayton, 'Hon. Sir Oliver Mowat, G.C.M.G.,' *Green Bag* 10 (1898), 1; C. Morse, 'Charles Fitzpatrick,' *Green Bag* 16 (1904), 509; R.V. Rogers, K.C., 'Christopher Robinson Q.C.,' *Green Bag* 18 (1906), 1. In 1909, however, a number of Canadians (including, most notably, Henri Taschereau, chief justice of Quebec's Court of King's Bench) were featured in the *Green Bag's* necrology columns. See, e.g., *Green Bag* 21 (1909), 314, 367, 370, and 661.

130 'About the Law Schools,' *American Law Review* 31 (1897), 760. But see the Canadian-written piece by N.W. Hoyles [principal of Osgoode Hall], 'Legal Education in Canada,' *American Law School Review* (1902), 6. A thirteen-line report on other developments at Osgoode Hall can be found in *American Law School Review* 3 (1911), 48.

131 *Green Bag* 11 (1899), 37; *Green Bag* 14 (1902), 47. See also *Green Bag* 11 (1899), 533 [a letter written by a Scotsman in Pictou, Nova Scotia]; *Green Bag* 13 (1901), 600 [unusual cases heard in Upper Canada by Chief Justice William Henry Draper]; *Green Bag* 15 (1903), 247 [a 'Halifax, N.S.' jury]; *Green Bag* 16 (1904), 43 [the 'shenanigans' of an Ontario barrister of Irish extraction]. That so many humorous or curious stories about Canada appeared in the *Green Bag* cannot be entirely surprising, in light of that journal's original claim to

be 'A Useless But Entertaining Magazine for Lawyers.' See also *Albany Law Journal* 54 (1896), 426; *Albany Law Journal* 55 (1897), 14.

132 'Causerie,' *Canada Law Journal* 33 (1897), 20. The offending article seems to have been 'Canadian Notions' that, in addition to containing the material quoted in the text, ungenerously compared Canada to one of Lord George Gordon Byron's maidens of dubious morality. See also 'Causerie,' *Canada Law Journal* 33 (1897), 553. The *Albany Law Journal*'s reply to that riposte can be found in 55 (1897), 237.

133 See generally R.K. Newmeyer, *Supreme Court Justice Joseph Story: Statesman of the Old Republic* (Chapel Hill: University of North Carolina Press 1985); G.E. White, *The Marshall Court and Cultural Change, 1815–1835* (Oxford: Oxford University Press 1991); and T.A. Freyer, *Forums of Order: The Federal Courts and Business in American History* (Greenwich, Conn.: JAI Press 1979).

134 Compare M. Reimann, 'Continental Imports: The Influence of European Law and Jurisprudence in the United States,' *Revue d'histoire de droit* 64 (1996), 391; A. Rodger, 'Scottish Advocates in the Nineteenth Century: The German Connection,' *Law Quarterly Review* 110 (1994), 563; M.H. Hoeflich, 'Transatlantic Friendships and the German Influence on American Law in the First Half of the Nineteenth Century,' *American Journal of Comparative Law* 35 (1987), 599; C.P. Rodgers, 'Continental Literature and the Development of the Common Law by the King's Bench,' in V. Piergiovanni, ed., *The Courts and the Development of Commercial Law* (Berlin: Dunker and Humblot 1987), 161; D.R. Coquillette, 'Justinian in Braintree: John Adams, Civilian Learning, and Legal Education,' in Colonial Society of Massachusetts, ed., *Law in Colonial Massachusetts* (Boston: Colonial Society of Massachusetts 1984), 359; A.W.B. Simpson, 'Innovation in Nineteenth Century Contract Law,' *Law Quarterly Review* 91 (1975), 247.

9

Conservative Insurrection: Great Strikes and Deep Law in Cleveland, Ohio, and London, Ontario, 1898–1899

R.W. KOSTAL

'Cars assailed, men attacked, police struggled with, tracks torn up, and shots fired, until at last street fights and mob movements became frequent and the city was invested with militia.'

Theodore Dreiser, *Sister Carrie* (1900)

In the summer of 1899 the street railway workers of London, Ontario and Cleveland, Ohio were engaged in prolonged, popularly supported, and frequently violent labour conflicts. This chapter provides a comparative social and legal history of these 'great' strikes,[1] describing the collision of an archetypal Gilded Age business tycoon with two well-organized workforces and their communities. It also has a less conventional aim. To examine how the legal systems of Ontario and Ohio shaped the contours and outcomes of the conflicts.

A number of factors make the London and Cleveland street railway strikes of 1899 a promising case study in comparative historical analysis. Not only did they occur simultaneously and in the same industry, but against the labour policies of one man: Cleveland street railway magnate Henry A. Everett.[2] The strikes exemplified two significant trends in late-nineteenth-century North American economic and labour history. On one hand, they were about the consolidation of an empire of street and interurban railway franchises in the American mid-west and Canada. On the other, they were about the struggle of low-skilled workers[3] to resist new regimes of labour organization and discipline.

Henry Everett saw the labour unrest of 1899 as a kind of corporate Waterloo. The Amalgamated Association of Street Railway Employees (AASRE), an affiliate of the American Federation of Labor (AFL), was pressing hard to organize a bi-national network of locals. In line with the AFL's commitments to 'pure and simple' unionism, the AASRE's primary goal was to achieve binding collective agreements with street railway companies. Everett (with other dominant figures of his industry)[4] viewed the revival of independent unionism, 'pure and simple' or otherwise, as a grave threat to the autonomy and profitability of his enterprise.[5] As Everett himself commented in 1898: 'A fellow runs his own business, or else he don't.'[6]

The Cleveland and London strikes of 1899 shared a number of other salient characteristics. In both cities the timing, strategy, and tactics of the strikes were carefully planned by local and (more experienced) central office union men. Strikes were declared only when the unions were confident of fervent public support. At the same time, alliances were forged between the unions and prominent voluntary organizations, clergymen, politicians, newspapermen, and, not least of all, lawyers.

The close collaboration of AASRE union executives and lawyers was not incidental. In both cities, it was anticipated that law would impinge on the strike and its supporters in a variety of ways. In both cities, too, the main objective of the strikes was of an overtly legal character: to use the law of contract to constrain Everett's power to dictate changes to the terms and conditions of street railway work.

The labour history of North America unfolded in societies saturated by lawyers and law.[7] In recent years American and Canadian labour historians have begun to come to grips with this fact. Their work makes bold assertions about the impact of judge-made law (particularly injunctions)[8] and legal ideology[9] in the history of labour relations in the United States and Canada. It also makes claims, if more tentative ones, about the comparative impact of law and legal ideas on labour relations in the respective countries. These claims will be examined and tested against a substantial body of integrated, cross-national evidence in the final section of this chapter.

The body of this essay is comprised of four analytical narratives. These sections reconstruct the preconditions, key events, and causal mainsprings of the London and Cleveland strikes. The chapter concludes by defending three lines of interpretation. The first concerns the remarkable similarity of the relevant American and Canadian law in 1899.[10] For the purposes of securing a street railway franchise, implementing labour policies, organizing a union, or prosecuting or breaking a strike, the border between Canada and the United States was practically non-existent. The second line of interpretation concerns strike-breaking in late-nineteenth-century Ontario and Ohio. In London and (more surprisingly) Cleveland, local police, courts, and government proved unwilling or unable to respond decisively to popular violence. The ambivalence of local officials, and the crudeness of their coercive arsenal, afforded strike supporters the space needed to paralyse Everett's business. As late as 1899, the legal and physical machinery of strike-breaking remained tentative and inefficient. The third – 'conservative insurrection' – hypothesis concerns the goals and ideological character of the strikers and their allied communities. These strikes were essentially reactive in character, made, and widely supported, to defend long-standing conditions of employment. If there was a genuinely radical force at work in the great strikes of 1899, it was Henry Everett and his "modern" labour and organizational practices. For the strikers, the conflict was less about impugning law than implementing it. Their principal aim – in both London and Cleveland – was to channel class antagonism into interclass contractualism, to constrain the arbitrary power of employers by recourse to law. Toward this end union executives shunned radical ideologues and hired seasoned lawyers. In both London and Cleveland their plan, their hope, was to defend the interests of street railway workers within the legal framework of liberal capitalism.

STREET RAILWAY CAPITAL AND LABOUR, 1890–1899

In 1899 Cleveland was one of the world's most important centres of heavy and light industrial production.[11] Its sprawling oil-refining, chemical, steel, and machine-making industries had attracted an ethnically and religiously diverse population of some 380,000, a sizeable proportion of which was foreign born. Some 25,000 skilled, and thousands more semi-skilled, workers belonged to more than a hundred different labour unions.[12] Manual outnumbered nonmanual workers by eleven to one.[13] The city sustained five English-language daily newspapers and an array of foreign language periodicals. Cleveland had a police force of some 350 full-time constables. London, Ontario, although the fourth largest city of the most populous Canadian province, was a small, lightly industrialized city of fewer than 40,000 souls.[14] Overwhelmingly British in descent and Protestant in religion, Londoners toiled on railways, in artisanal trades, food processing, and in a variety of small manufactures. A larger proportion of London homes was owned by waged workers than in any other city in Canada.[15] In 1899 London was provincial and notoriously tranquil.[16] It had a police force of fewer than forty constables and staff.

Turn-of-the-century London had a vigorous trade union movement. In the 1880s the city's skilled and unskilled workers had enthusiastically embraced the Knights of Labor.[17] In 1899, a decade after the decline of the Knights, London still boasted some forty craft and railway unions, and total union membership of over three thousand men.[18] The city's waged workers supported a monthly labour newspaper (the *Industrial Banner*), a District Trades and Labour Council, and a Labour Hall. Union men and union activities were closely linked to local, church, fraternal, and recreational organizations.[19] London was fertile soil for a new union cause.

By the mid-1870s both London and Cleveland had extensive horse-drawn street railway systems. By 1892, the City of Cleveland had granted electric railway franchises to a number of independent companies,[20] and in 1893 four of these companies merged to form the Cleveland Electric (known as the 'Big Consolidated' or 'Big Con') Railway Company.[21] The Big Con employed some nine hundred full-time motormen and conductors to operate more than four hundred cars over 130 miles of track. In January 1899, after two years of corporate manoeuvring, Everett (and co-investors) became the largest stockholder. He also assumed the office of company president.[22]

In the early 1890s London's street railway system was unelectrified, locally owned, and profitable. Its owners were reluctant to surrender franchise rights.[23] In 1895, municipal politicians brokered a deal[24] between London Street Railway (LSR) shareholders and Henry Everett's syndicate.[25] The Cleveland company agreed to electrify and operate London's streetcar system in exchange for the remaining thirty years of the LSR's franchise monopoly. Local investors would hold minority interests (and directorships) in the new company. When it was completed in 1896, the electrified – and now foreign-controlled – LSR provided regular employment for 95 to 110 men.[26]

In London as elsewhere, electrification transformed the economics of street railway commerce.[27] Electrified street railway corporations were highly capitalized and often highly leveraged to banks and stockholders. Profit margins, on the other hand, were squeezed between rising costs and tight public regulation of fares.[28] The companies depended on large and steady cash flows to operate the lines, retire debt, pay dividends, and attract more capital for more railways. The prevailing trend in the industry was toward local and regional corporate consolidation.

By 1899, Everett (together with his largest co-investor, E.W. Moore)[29] had acquired controlling or partial interest in sixteen street and interurban railways.[30] The Everett-Moore syndicate also controlled some thirty telephone exchanges.[31] As individual units, most of these concerns were profitable, some extremely so.[32] Everett-Moore was also committed to a number of ambitious expansion plans. Their goal was to create an integrated street and interurban railway empire in the upper mid-west and Canada.[33] The labour conflict experienced by the syndicate in 1899, not coincidentally perhaps, unfolded at a time of rapid expansion and financial vulnerability.[34]

Electrification also changed the rhythm of street railway work.[35] Restricted for decades by the physical limitations of horses, streetcar schedules were liberated by the tireless power of the electric motor. More passengers could be carried more often, and at much greater speed. Unable to increase fares, late-nineteenth-century streetcar corporations had to find other ways to increase profit margins. Technical and organizational innovation was one way, higher labour productivity was another.[36]

In the street railway business, technical and managerial innovation moved in lock-step. The costs and mechanical advantages associated with electrification prompted street railway companies to experiment with more systematic, time conscious, and 'scientific' techniques of operation and labour management.[37] In most cases, these experiments involved a transformation of timetables, shifts, and labour discipline.[38] Streetcar schedules were changed to increase the regularity and speed of the service. The 'swing shift' or ('split run') became a common scheduling practice.[39] In addition, the companies promulgated new and more elaborate codes or 'rule books' of employee procedure, deportment, and conduct.[40]

Henry Everett was a strong proponent of 'modern' ideas about electric streetcar operation and management. He was determined to make a profit by sweeping aside inefficient and paternalistic labour practices. First in London and then in Cleveland Everett swiftly introduced new timetables and rule books, and new superintendents, supervisors, and 'spotters' to enforce them. The rule books minutely described the duties and decorum expected of his men. They also stipulated the prompt dismissal of employees for a wide range of misdemeanours. Men were to be fired for drunkenness and absenteeism, but also for wearing soiled uniforms, talking to passengers or co-workers while on streetcars, and for failing to maintain tight running schedules.

Before the autumn of 1898, the streetcar men of London had shown little interest in unions.[41] Everett's labour policies, coupled with the exertions of union organizers from Detroit, changed this situation. In mid-October, thirty-five LSR men met at the house of co-worker Michael Delisle (an American and AASRE organizer) and agreed to form a union.[42] On 23 October 1898, with the aid and encouragement of Rezin Orr, treasurer and senior organizer of the AASRE, eighty-five of (then) ninety-two full-time streetcar men voted to apply for an AASRE charter.[43] Executive officers were elected, Delisle and another American AASRE organizer, Jordan Pickell, among them. When LSR officials got wind of these developments, Delisle and Pickell were fired on the pretext of their being non-residents.[44] On 25 October Division 97 of the AASRE, supported by all but eight of the LSR's waged employees, declared a strike.[45] Union recognition and the reinstatement of Delisle and Pickell were added to its list of demands.

The strike of 1898 ended two weeks later with a compromise agreement. In a fourteen-clause contract,[46] the company agreed to a fixed nine-hour working day for regular men.[47] Delisle and Pickell were reinstated. The contract provided that the men had 'full liberty to affiliate with any lawful association or club,' but did not recognize the union's right to a closed shop.[48] The men gave up their most contentious demands. November, after all, was a bad month to ask the riding public to support a long streetcar strike. The push for major concessions on unionism would have to wait for another day. That day came within a year.

Two months after the conclusion of the November 1898 strike in London, Henry Everett became majority stockholder and president of Cleveland's Big Con street railway system.[49] The new boss, a pastor later observed, 'had some well-defined ideas of how he would run the road and "better" the service.'[50] For Big Con employees this meant 'faster time, more trips, and a cessation of the customary rests.'[51] It also involved more (and more aggressive) supervision by company 'spotters.' Everett's policies quickly damaged morale among the Big Con's 900 employees. They also exacerbated the safety hazard presented by street railway operation. In the winter of 1899 there was a rash of fatal accidents, many involving children. Under public pressure, the district attorney and Cleveland police began to crack down. Fourteen street railway men were arrested and charged with breaching Cleveland's speed ordinances.[52] More seriously, a number of drivers were charged with manslaughter.[53] At the same time, the Big Con began to discharge motormen who failed to meet the new streetcar timetables. On 22 and 23 March 1899, fifteen men were fired without a hearing.[54]

Cleveland's street railway workers had shown little general enthusiasm for 'united action' until Henry Everett took control of the Big Con in

1898.[55] The dismissals of March 1899 galvanized the pro-union cause. A number of clandestine organizational meetings were held after 25 March. Rezin Orr, the AASRE's chief organizer, attended all or most of these sessions. On 27 March more than half of the Big Con's employees voted to form Division 106 of the AASRE;[56] in early April, the union drive was spurred when another driver was charged with manslaughter.[57] By May of 1899, the executive of Division 106 boasted (exaggerating only a little)[58] that 95 per cent of the Big Con's employees had joined the streetcar union.

No significant legal barriers had stood in the way of the formation of streetcar unions either in Ontario or Ohio in 1899. In Ontario, workers were free to form an association or 'union' for the purposes of collective bargaining and federal legislation protected unions from the common law of criminal conspiracy.[59] In Ohio, unions could be formed for the purpose of collective bargaining.[60] While in both jurisdictions the streetcar unions were entitled to attempt to negotiate a collective agreement, Henry Everett was not obligated to cooperate.

APRIL–JUNE 1899: 'A PEOPLE'S STRIKE'

In the spring of 1899, conflict between Everett's bosses and his Cleveland employees was more frequent and more intense. Everett had hired a new superintendent, H.M. Douglass, to enforce the Big Con's timetable and rule book even more stringently than before.[61] Despite mounting evidence that his new timetables compelled motormen to breach Cleveland's speed ordinances (to the peril of pedestrians), Everett did not order a slowdown. In April, a number of Big Con employees were suspended for petty breaches of company rules. Then a conductor with six years service was fired for having engaged in conversation with his motorman during work.[62] When a request for reinstatement was summarily dismissed, the union men began to discuss the advisability of a strike.

In London, meanwhile, similar trouble was on the boil. Union leaders were harassed by unfavourable shifts and schedules. Prospective employees were carefully screened for union sympathies. The company continued to dole out work to a growing list of non-union 'spare' men.[63] 'There is hardly a clause in the old agreement that has not been violated,' a union leader claimed in May.[64] The London men were fed up and ready to fight.

In early May 1899, two days before the expiry of the November 1898 agreement, the executive of Division 97 presented the LSR with a list of demands, formal recognition of their union and a closed shop prominent among them. The union also demanded binding arbitration of dismissals, scheduling changes, and a raise in pay. By mid-May 1899, a majority of London's street railway men were ready to strike for these concessions. On 22 May 1899, in a secret ballot, the union men voted (nearly unanimously)[65] to 'place their case in the hands of the citizens of London' and declare a strike. Two weeks later, some 850 of the Big Con's 900 men walked off the job.

There is a conspicuous sameness about the strike preparations of the Cleveland and London street railway unions. Both groups understood that it would not be easy to persuade Everett to relent on union recognition. They understood that victory would be the product only of careful timing, planning, and shrewdly constructed and executed propaganda. Faced with these challenges, in both cities local union leadership accepted the tutelage of the vastly more experienced officials of the AASRE.[66]

From 1898 onward Henry Everett and his subalterns repeatedly claimed that the street railway unions were organized and directed by 'paid labour agitators.'[67] This charge was well-founded. AASRE leaders W.D. Mahon and Rezin Orr had been fundamentally important, in overt and covert ways, to the formation of street railway unions in London and Cleveland. They sent organizers Delisle and Pickell to work for the LSR.[68] Although their efforts in Cleveland are less well documented, both Mahon and Orr had been frequent visitors to the meetings of the incipient Cleveland union. Once organized, the AASRE provided moral, financial, and organizational support to both of their new divisions. They were also instrumental in the decision of both divisions to go on strike.[69]

Local streetcar unionists relied heavily on the human and organizational resources of the AASRE. They also moved quickly to retain the services of lawyers. In Cleveland, the union hired two attorneys, D.B. Carpenter (also a city councilman) and Dan Reynolds.[70] Throughout the spring and summer of 1899, Carpenter and Reynolds acted as the union's spokesmen, strategists, and negotiators. One or the other man attended virtually all of the union's general and executive meetings. The constancy of their presence and the zeal of their advocacy strongly suggest that theirs was more than a mercenary relationship with the union. Carpenter and Reynolds appear to have identified closely with the union cause. Along with local and central union officials, the two lawyers were the third arm of the union's executive leadership.[71]

In London, the streetcar union retained lawyer (and former mayor) H.T. Essery to perform a similar range of roles. Essery had negotiated the language of the November 1898 contract and was present at almost all subsequent negotiations between union, LSR, and city during the strike of

1899. Essery lent expertise and experience on matters of law and negotiation strategy. He also made numerous appearances in court (far more than his counterparts in Cleveland) on behalf of union men charged with strike-related criminal offences. Inside, but especially outside the courts, Essery's knowledge, respectability, and prestige were clearly important assets to the new union. Both in London and Cleveland, streetcar union lawyers were opposed by highly experienced lawyers on retainer to Everett.[72] The streetcar strikes of 1899 were not accidental events. They were anticipated and planned for by sophisticated men on both sides.

Every move made by the respective union leaderships was calculated to transform the private conflicts of comparatively small numbers of specialized workers into popular cause, into what a sympathetic London newspaper called a 'people's strike.'[73] 'The success of the street railway men,' the pro-labour *Cleveland Citizen* observed, 'depends on the sympathy of the waged working element, which constitutes three fourths of our populace.'[74] The threat of a broadly supported streetcar boycott would be the union's main source of leverage in a clash with the Big Con.

The creation and preservation of the conditions for a successful streetcar boycott was no small order. The people of London and Cleveland would be asked to accept considerable hardship. A robust sense of common interest and willing self-sacrifice was absolutely vital to union success. And while the street railway men of London and Cleveland were led by the same cadre of American union activists, their propaganda was finely attuned to the similarities and differences between Londoners and Clevelanders.

The people of both cities shared an aversion to walking long distances to work, shop, and leisure, especially in bad weather.[75] (In the north street railway strikes almost invariably were fought in the spring and summer.) They shared a mistrust, even contempt, for street railway companies. The LSR and Big Con were routinely denounced for fare-gouging, monopolism, corruption of city officials,[76] and for the alarming frequency of running-down accidents.[77] Finally, large numbers of London and Cleveland's labouring people also shared the perception that unions and collective bargaining were necessary and legitimate features of the modern workplace.[78] This they made manifest the moment the streetcar strikes commenced.

The London strike began the afternoon of 22 May 1899. The union men were cheered as they returned the LSR's cars to their storage barns. The first major union rally was organized for 25 May. A mile-long procession of strikers, bands, and the city's many craft unions (a 'monster parade ...

one of the largest ever witnessed in this city' the *London Advertiser* claimed), marched to the Opera House.[79] Even the rabidly anti-union *London Free Press* admitted that streets along the route were jammed with thousands of cheering 'sympathisers.'[80] Men, women, and children wore badges proclaiming 'No Surrender'[81] and 'Again We Walk.' After the street railway men had passed through the Opera House door, the theatre filled beyond its 1,500 person capacity. There the audience heard a series of speeches that will be analysed after a brief account of the first days of the Cleveland strike.

In late May 1899, the Cleveland union executive delivered a 'schedule of grievances' to company officials. Leading the list was the company's new code of conduct. This was followed by a plea for the company to obey the city's speed ordinance.[82] Swing shifts were also listed as a major source of disgruntlement.[83] The list ended with demands for union recognition, collective bargaining, and a collective agreement that would establish a closed shop and the binding arbitration of dismissals.

The tension between union and company became even more aggravated in early June, when an angry mob attacked the driver of a streetcar which, minutes before, had 'motored to death' a young boy.[84] On 8 June yet another driver was charged with manslaughter for a previous fatal accident.[85] These events hardened resolve among union men.[86] Sensing an opportunity to demonstrate the coincidence of public and union interest, the union executive publically asserted that the Big Con's timetable policy was to blame for the fatal mishaps.[87] A number of newspapers adopted the same position. On 9 June, for instance, the *Cleveland World* wrote of the 'unfairness' of prosecuting motormen who had been compelled to drive at unsafe speeds.[88] Concerned perhaps by the changing tide of public opinion, Everett announced his decision to reduce speed.[89]

On 10 June the union convened a general meeting. The men voted to strike at four the next morning. Some 865 of the Big Con's 900 employees pledged to stay off the job. By 5:30 a.m., replacement workers already had been assembled to take their places.[90] At 9:30 a.m., the first riot commenced.

By the time the Cleveland men stopped work, the London strike, and the propaganda campaign associated with it, had been waged for more than two weeks. In May and June of 1899 it was plausibly claimed that the union enjoyed the support of '90 per cent' of Londoners.[91] On the first day of the strike, a 'mass of earnest, jostling humanity' (so the *Advertiser* reported), turned out to demonstrate, encourage, and listen. In subsequent days a succession of rallies and benefits, even the *Free Press* acknowledged, consistently attracted crowds of 1,500–2,000, sizeable fractions of London's adult population.[92]

This 'irresistible pressure of a moral boycott,' as the *Advertiser* called it,[93] was the union's most powerful ally. Large numbers of Londoners attended rallies, formed pickets, risked arrest, and gave up a useful public service in support of the strikers. These people clearly believed in the cause. Newspaper accounts of public demonstrations and orations provide some intriguing clues as to the content of this belief.

When, on 23 May, the day after the strike was called, a mile-long parade of London's unionists marched to the Opera House rally, the dense crowds they passed heard 'Rule Britannia' played over and over again. From the early moments of the strike, consciously and reflexively, the propaganda of the strikers successfully exploited two complementary themes: the righteous 'Canadian-Britishness' of the union cause, the perfidious and alien 'American monopolism' of Everett's.

During the streetcar strike of November 1898, union leaders had described the cause of the LSR men as a 'struggle for the rights to which they are entitled under the British Constitution.'[94] At the Opera House rally six months later, lawyer and ex-mayor of London, E.T. Essery, described how 'men under the [the Union Jack] should see that they receive the same rights as Yankee workmen.'[95] At a rally a few days later, J.T. Marks, president of London's Trades and Labour Council and self-avowed socialist,[96] invoked the same theme. 'The people had come,' Marks proclaimed, 'to fight the battle of Canadian citizens ... as against a company of largely American capitalists whose owner would never shoulder a gun to defend this land.'[97] The meeting concluded with a mass pledge of 'undivided sympathy and support' for those fighting for 'their rights as men and British subjects.'[98] It was the rare strike speech that did not exploit this theme.

The editorials of London's pro-strike newspapers were of the same kind. The *Industrial Banner* repeatedly trumpeted that Londoners would 'never allow a Yankee millionaire to crush down Canadian labour.' The 'alien Everett and his trust,' the *Banner* vowed, 'will never strangle British liberty.'[99] The local Liberal paper, the *London Advertiser* (daily circulation: 6,000) described the strikers as a handful of men acting 'in defence of our rights and manhood to exercise the privileges of British subjects ... The whole question at issue is, shall Canadians have the right to belong to a lawful association, or shall they stand as mere individuals, to be crushed by a soulless corporation?'[100]

Everett was harshly criticized, not because he was a capitalist, but for having imported an 'un-British' *style* of capitalism. 'Every working man in the city,' the *Industrial Banner* asserted in November 1899, 'looks upon [the streetcar union] battle as his own affair.'[101] Everett was 'a notorious monopolist, an alien without any interest in London except to draw dividends ... to degrade Canadian labour.' The working men of London, the *Advertiser* asserted, '[have] as much right to combine for mutual protection as the capitalists of the U.S. have a right to exploit public franchises in Canada.'[102] As an academic observer generalized: '[I]n this age of great combinations of capital, people have come to see that ... unions of labour should likewise come into being. The present strike is primarily for the existence of the union and protection of the unionist, and in the second place for another slight increase of pay.'[103] Pro-unionists demonized Henry Everett as a Yankee monopoly-capitalist, a foreigner resolved to use his economic power to subvert the customary rights of 'Canadian labour.' This was astutely crafted and, by all evidence, effective rhetoric.

The nationalism and nostalgia of pro-union propaganda resonated beyond London's working-class neighbourhoods. This was a 'just' and 'respectable' strike, one that quickly received the blessing, literally and figuratively, of much of London's middle-class leadership. The cause of the unionists was not only the cause of waged workers and artisans, but conspicuously of a number of notable clergymen, politicians, newspapermen, businessmen,[104] and at least one lawyer. In its coverage of the Opera House rally of 22 May, the *London Advertiser* noted that while 'wage-earners predominated' among the two thousand people crowded in the hall, the audience was observably 'representative.' It was noted that '[s]everal alderman and prominent business men occupied seats on the platform.'[105] A large number of women were present. The rally was chaired by a Presbyterian minister, the Rev. Thomas Wilson. (A number of other clergymen would, in time, publicly support the strikers.) Lawyer and ex-mayor E.T. Essery spoke at this and nearly every subsequent union rally. London's street railway unionists attracted support from a range of middle-class patrons.

Less inclined to attend rallies or listen to speeches,[106] Cleveland's strike supporters were more willing to confront the enemy on the streets. From the first moments of the 1899 strike, large numbers of blue-collar Clevelanders spoiled for a fight. In Cleveland the strike was only hours old when angry crowds bloodied the first strike-breaker. Here there was visceral enmity, an eagerness for violent confrontation not immediately evident in London. Cleveland was a big city, one experienced of bitter confrontations between working people and large corporate employers. The strike seemed instantly to become a matter of settling a grudge held collectively by waged workers against 'great aggregations of private capital.'[107] As a reporter from *Harper's* commented some weeks later: 'The union sentiment prevails in labouring circles. The alleged wrongs of the union employees ... fell on the ears of a public already well-disposed to sympathise.'[108]

Cleveland's striking streetcar men generated popular support without the propaganda advantage of a foreign employer. Henry Everett might be demonized as a 'heartless plutocrat,' but only as an *American* heartless plutocrat. The AASRE's strategy in Cleveland was to cultivate the predisposition of waged Clevelanders to see the street railway strike as a key moment in the struggle for collective bargaining with business syndicates and trusts. Its job was made easier when 'respectable' voices also expressed this understanding of the conflict. 'On one side,' a local Presbyterian minister observed of the strike, 'is a combination of money, and it refuses to recognise a similar combination of labor.'[109]

Violent affrays with Everett's strike-breakers, and with the police assigned to protect them, began on the first day of the strike, 10 June. In a half-dozen neighbourhoods, Big Con streetcars were met by hooting, hissing, egg- and then brick-throwing crowds.[110] Although the union had not made a direct appeal for physical support on the streets, crowds (even the anti-union papers conceded)[111] numbering in the thousands gathered simultaneously in four or five locations. Without having to organize formal picket lines, the union men were able to obstruct Everett's attempts to continue operating his cars. On 11 June the size and tempestuousness of crowds had begun to escalate dangerously. In what the *Plain Dealer* described as 'wild scenes of disorder and violence,' crowds obstructed tracks, cut trolley lines, and submitted cars and motormen to a barrage of missiles. The active, even violent, support of thousands of people rapidly overwhelmed local government's capacity to keep the peace.

Six weeks after the walkout began, the police had arrested some six hundred people for strike-related crimes. Only three arrests were of members of the streetcar union.[112] This was a 'people's' strike. The fight on the streets had arisen spontaneously, and mainly involved strangers to the streetcar union. As one experienced union organizer contended: '[T]here never was a strike in this city before in which outsiders took such an active part ... The strikers themselves had, in fact, little or nothing to do. Their fellow citizens did it all.'[113]

Although pro-union street crowds appear to have been made up primarily of young, employed, working-class white men, they 'included people from all walks of life.'[114] A *Cleveland Press* report of 12 June provided this account: 'One of the strange sights downtown was to see the manner in which the crowd sympathised with the strikers. Whenever men managed to stop or delay a car, the crowd set up a yell. The windows of the huge blocks ... were black with humanity [including] clerks and business-men. Some of them joined in the enthusiasm. One woman on a bicycle rode beside a Euclid Avenue motor yelling like a Sioux Indian and derisively calling "Scab!". Other women on the street cheered the men who interfered with the cars.'[115] The newspaper sources teem with reports of the 'deep interest' and zealous participation of women[116] in pro-strike demonstrations. The *Plain Dealer* reported that, in the first days of the strike 'time and time again women climbed into cars and persuaded men to leave.'[117]

On at least one occasion during the first week of the strike, 'several hundred [Euclid Avenue] shop-girls' greeted a passing streetcar with a 'fusillade of missiles, bottles and stones.'[118] 'The girls were most bitter in the expression of their hostile sentiments,' the same reporter noted.[119] They were not alone in these sentiments. The size and violence of strike crowds steadily escalated after 10 June. Crowds engaged both in the 'moral suasion' and physical intimidation of strike-breakers.[120] In many instances, strike sympathizers were able calmly to persuade Big Con men to quit their work. (Some of the first cohort of replacements had been misled by Big Con recruiters and wanted no part of strike-breaking.)[121] When the Big Con began to employ more experienced and sturdy strike-breakers, however, moral suasion frequently gave way to physical coercion.[122]

Although the Cleveland strike executive organized a number of public rallies, and at least one parade, these were sideshows. The real action was on the city's main thoroughfares. Virtually every day between 12 and 22 June 1899 crowds of Clevelanders, sometimes eight thousand strong,[123] mounted exuberant assaults on Big Con cars, car barns, and motormen. (These became menacing enough that the Big Con, reassuringly or not, promised to pay the medical bills of strike-breakers.)[124] Replacement motormen were issued pistols.

On 16 June 'tremendous crowds' congregated in at least three parts of the city. Rocks were thrown, Big Con track and switches were torn up, scab motormen were threatened and, in more than one instance, pulled from their cars and beaten.[125] The following day a group of some four thousand people – rallied by bugle calls – made repeated attacks on Big Con cars and men. On 20 June, crowds estimated at five and even eight thousand strong repeated similar attacks in two parts of the city.[126] Local authorities were losing control of the city.

JUNE–JULY 1899: 'STAYERS'

Thus far we have been mainly concerned with the actions and motives of London and Cleveland's street railway men and their supporters. By the end of June 1899, both groups had formed unions affiliated with the AASRE. Both groups were advised and (to an unclear degree) financed by the central office of their union.[127] Even more critically, the striking union men of London and Cleveland had secured the zealous support of majorities of their fellow citizens.[128] Both unions were determined to stay out until they had a contract that included union recognition, collective bargaining, binding arbitration of dismissals, and the closed shop.

None of these developments took Henry Everett by surprise. In fact, so provocative and so uncompromising were his labour policies in London and Cleveland that it is a fair surmise that the strikes were deliberately fomented. Everett's strike-fighting strategy boiled down to three unsubtle tactics: 1) to apply maximum psychological and financial pressure against the rebellious men; 2) to operate his systems with scab labour protected by public and private police forces; and 3) to pressure government officials to use the physical compulsion necessary to vindicate his commercial and property rights. Everett's principal aim was to break the unions, and he believed it was his legal and moral right to do so.

Predictably enough, the touchstones of Everett's view of the business world were liberty of property, commerce, and contract. Everett believed that it was the indivisible right of owners to manage their enterprises as they saw fit and to hire whom they saw fit. Union activity was tolerated only so far as it did not threaten these tenets. Time and again Everett proclaimed that he had 'no objection to any organization [a trade union, for instance] dedicated to the improvement of the men.'[129] The prospect of having to relinquish even the smallest degree of managerial control over his business, however, was unacceptable: '[To] be dictated to by a lot of outsiders,' he once stated, 'is the worst sort of despotism.'[130] 'The one who pays the piper should call the tune, and it is for this principle that the streetcar is contending,' a Big Con circular explained.[131] Everett viewed the closed shop as corrosive of the liberty of capital and labour. A man who is required to join a union to work, he told the *Cleveland Press* during the strike, '[cannot] say his soul is his own.'[132] In Everett's view, then, his position was not merely a self-serving defence of property, but a public-spirited defence of free labour.

Everett's first priority was to hire and protect replacements. In London, imported strike-breakers had been put on the job within a week of the strike call. In Cleveland Everett was even more forward looking. Two days before the Cleveland union struck, the Big Con was 'preparing for a great strike.'[133] Already the company had sent business agents to at least five major cities to recruit an 'army' of replacement workers.[134] It also hired private detectives, including (it was alleged)[135] those infamous shock troops of Gilded Age labour disputes, Pinkerton men.[136] Supplemented by officers from the Field agency of Chicago[137] and Watts of Buffalo,[138] the detectives were hired to guard the Big Con's men and property and to infiltrate the union.[139]

On the second day of the Cleveland strike, Everett issued an ultimatum. The union men were to return to their jobs or lose them to imported labour. Everett reaffirmed his 'absolute refusal' either to recognize the union or to submit this issue to the state board of arbitration.[140] 'There are some features of the [union's] proposal,' Everett stated, 'that the company will never agree to.'[141] Everett was resolved to put the union men to a stern test of nerve.

More definitively than in Ontario,[142] the law of Ohio also afforded Everett another course: to apply to a state or federal court for a labour injunction. In the days immediately prior to the union walkout, Cleveland reporters noted, various members of the Big Con's law firm, Kline, Tolles, Carr and Goff, were frequent visitors to the company's head office. (The firm had also prepared the company's statement to the men circulated on 8 June.)[143] It was rumoured that, in the event of a strike, the Big Con would instruct Kline, Tolles to apply for a 'blanket' injunction (enjoining any activity of any person that might inhibit the street railway company's operations) in federal court. When the strike commenced on 10 June, a Big Con attorney called on the U.S. attorney Dodge. He contended that a federal injunction was required to ensure the free flow of mail carried on Big Con streetcars.[144] This overture was not warmly received. Dodge indicated his unwillingness to support an injunction until the strikers 'showed a disposition to interfere with the mails.'[145] It was made clear that there would be no injunction on demand in the federal court.

On 11 June, Big Con lawyers approached Judge T.K. Dissette of the Ohio Court of Common Pleas about the prospect of a blanket injunction. These overtures were also tersely rebuffed. 'Blanket injunctions,' Judge Dissette was quoted as stating, 'are unjust, and this branch of the Common Pleas will not issue any.'[146] If he were to issue an injunction, the judge added, it would be against specific strikers 'about to commit some act of violence.'[147] This meeting foreclosed the prospect of an early injunctive attack on the strike.

Although the subject of injunctive relief would be discussed again, the first principle of Everett's strike-fighting strategy, both in Cleveland and London, was self-help, not judicial intervention. As we have seen, his primary interest was in the recruitment and (by a combined force of private and public police) protection of a replacement labour force. In both cities, the first wave of recruits gradually was replaced by harder, more seasoned, and better paid strike-breakers.[148] By the end of July 1899, some six hundred men were employed by the Big Con as replacement motormen and conductors. Two hundred more were employed as private security.[149] In London, some hundred men were imported to operate the LSR during daylight hours. Just as in Cleveland, Everett's London security force was led by men from Pinkertons. Tough, strike-experienced,[150] well-paid,[151] and armed,[152] these men could not be talked or scared out of town.

In late May, the *London Free Press* remarked on the 'peaceful condition' of the city in wake of the strike; on 17 June the same paper described the strike as 'proceeding quietly.'[153] On 26 June the *Advertiser* alluded to the 'orderliness that has marked the city.' The calm was notable, the editorial stated, because of the 'strong undercurrent of feeling.'[154] In London, the general peace was disturbed only by verbal abuse, threats, some stone and egg throwing, and the occasional fistfight. As the strike and summer wore on, however, calm began to give way to escalating violence.

On 1 July, London's Dominion Day celebration was organized as a union rally as well. The crowd of thousands, the *Free Press* glumly conceded, was clear evidence that 'the strikers [still] have the sympathy of the great percentage of Londoners.'[155] This was to be one of the last peaceful public gatherings for some time. In subsequent days, groups of angry men gathered at central intersections. Rocks and bricks were hurled at scab motormen. Arrests, not only of rowdy youths, but of 'respectable married men,' became more frequent.[156] Then, on the afternoon and evening of Saturday, 8 July 1899, London experienced its most serious public unrest of the late nineteenth century.

In the early afternoon, large crowds began to gather downtown and in the predominately working class east end of London.[157] At noon it was rumoured (falsely) that some fifteen non-union motormen were preparing to join the strikers. When two streetcars returned early to the car barns, then suddenly re-emerged to commence new runs, the disappointed crowd became enraged. Stones were thrown, the first by a woman. In the course of the afternoon, non-union drivers and private detectives were menaced, some stoned, by groups of angry bystanders. On at least three occasions, motormen and detectives brandished revolvers. The sight of guns incited the crowd, now swelled to around 2,500 persons, to still greater disorder. Arrests by police prompted yet more violence. During the early evening, a number of streetcars were stopped by mobs, their drivers surrounded. When the crowds closed in, terrified motormen fired shots in the air and fled. Abandoned streetcars were attacked, ransacked, and burned.

For the remainder of the evening of 8 July, crowds in the downtown and eastern areas of London continued to obstruct streetcars, run off their drivers, and attack the abandoned equipment. LSR lawyer C.H. Ivey, along with company director T.H. Smallman, approached the county's sheriff and pressed him, unsuccessfully, to read the Riot Act.[158] Meanwhile, beleaguered London Mayor John Wilson stood on a wagon and implored citizens to return to their homes. Remarkably enough, the appeal met with some success.[159] Wilson's pledges to prevent strike-breakers from carrying pistols, and his further assurance that Everett's company would eventually take back all the unionist men, convinced many to disperse. But Wilson's pleas did not sway everyone. At 9:30 in the evening, a large crowd in the downtown area attacked and destroyed six more streetcars.

Alarmed by the size and belligerence of the crowds, and under pressure of 'repeated threats of heavy damage suits' by Everett's lawyers,[160] the mayor consulted Crown Attorney James Magee. On Magee's advice, and in the face of a 'shower of stones,' Wilson stood before the crowd and read the Riot Act.[161] When police were unable to disperse the remaining crowd, Wilson met senior County Court Judge William Elliott and, sometime before midnight, called out the military. In the first hour of Sunday morning thirty-two red-coated soldiers, 'bayonets glistening beneath the electric lamps,' chased the last two hundred persons from the streets.[162]

Although the riots of 8 July were the most serious within living memory, probably the most serious in the history of the city, they ended without a fatality. Some twenty-five people had suffered (minor) injuries. As many as seventeen of the LSR's cars had been damaged, some irreparably, and some dozen store windows had been smashed.[163] The police made forty arrests.[164] Many hundreds of people, many of them 'eminently respectable citizens,'[165] had been willing to participate in (unplanned)[166] violent crowd behaviour. Equally noteworthy is that this single night of (by comparison to Cleveland, mild) rioting was the high-water mark of the violent phase of the London strike. The week-long presence of the soldiers, the arrest of a score of unruly citizens and, most important of all, the continued operation of Everett's non-union labour force, had diminished willingness to contest the strike in the streets. On the evening of 8 July, the limits of physical resistance to Everett's policies were not clear. By the morning of 9 July, they were.

The Cleveland strike, in contrast, was violent from the outset, and became more intensely violent as union supporters began to grasp two bleak facts: Everett was prepared both to absorb large losses of revenue[167] and to protect a large force of replacement labour. On the third day of the strike, Everett contended that he had received a 'quarter bushel' of applications from men all over the east and mid-west.[168] It was said that of those hired on, many were of the kind who 'made a regular business of "strike-smashing."'[169] These were men familiar with street railway strikes[170] and the violence associated with them. (One replacement motorman cheerfully admitted that he once had had a streetcar dynamited from under him.)[171] To their detractors, the strike-breakers were a 'moral cesspool horde of Pinkerton thugs, jail-birds, penitentiary toughs.'[172] This they may or may not have been. As the *Cleveland Press* observed, however, the most significant thing about Everett's replacement workers was that they were 'stayers.'[173]

On 16 June, after a week of near ceaseless confrontation between crowds of angry Clevelanders and the forces protecting the Big Con's replacement men and property,[174] union and company officials and their lawyers were back at the negotiating table. A committee of municipal politicians acted as mediators. It was clear to all that the strike had come to a pivotal juncture. 'This is probably the worst street railway strike that I have ever known,' AASRE President W. D. Mahon remarked. 'If it is not settled now ... it will develop into a long and bitter struggle.'[175]

As the mediation wore on, Everett continued to run cars staffed by non-union labour. Clevelanders, as many as eight thousand in a single crowd,[176] continued to make concerted attacks on the cars. On 20 June alone, ten streetcars were completely demolished. Against this backdrop, the union executive made a surprising offer, one which exposed the inherent weakness of its position. In exchange for reinstatement, an agreement to dismiss only after a fair hearing on cause, and company agreement to refer scheduling and wage disputes to a joint committee, the men would drop their demand for formal union recognition, binding arbitration of dismissals, and a closed shop. In response, Everett agreed to the union's proposals on dismissals and scheduling[177] but would take back only 'such of its former employees as its business demands, aggregating at 80% of its former employees.'[178] Remaining men would be placed on a substitute list. Non-union men who wanted to keep jobs would not be fired. Everett's counter offer would leave 175 union members out of jobs.

The union's chief negotiators, attorneys Carpenter and Reynolds, adopted a perplexing position on the company's offer. Refusing to concede that the offer was 'fair,' they nonetheless put it to the men as 'a solution to the difficulties.'[179] At a general meeting of the union on 22 June, the offer was discussed, voted on, and rejected. (Carpenter and Reynolds were then accused by Everett of bad faith for having reneged on a promise to recommend the deal to the men.)[180] Everett reaffirmed his threat to restore full service with permanent non-union labour. The union executive quickly convened another general meeting. This time Reynolds and Carpenter advised the membership that the company was unlikely to budge. While admitting that the offer meant 'hardship, temporarily' for some men, the two lawyers now 'heartily recommended' that it be accepted.[181] AASRE President Mahon presided over a heated debate. Many men expressed disgust with a deal that not only did not include union recognition, but left scabs in the jobs of union men. When put to a vote, however, all but four men stood up in assent to the agreement.[182]

The resentment felt by many citizens persisted. Ignoring the entreaties of union leaders, crowds of Clevelanders continued to attack streetcars driven by non-union men. Some 'imported' drivers were pulled from cars and beaten.[183] On at least two occasions, panicked motormen fired shots into the crowd.[184] Tension intensified when it became clear, within a few days of the return to work, that the Big Con was not prepared to forgive and forget. The company refused to explain why a number of union men with seniority had not been rehired.[185] To protect its imported men, the company began to require union employees to ride on the same cars. When ten union men refused, they were fired.[186] On 16 July, the union men met and, by 4:00 that afternoon, 'every line of the company was tied up tight.'[187] The men solemnly resolved not to return to work until 'every man' was reinstated.[188] The Cleveland strike was about to enter its most critical and violent phase.

JULY–SEPTEMBER 1899: 'THE SOCIAL VOLCANO'

The failure of the June agreement caused Clevelanders to confront the plain fact that Everett was prepared to defy the strike, even at great risk and cost. His official stance was that the union men quit and had been replaced. There was no longer a strike to be settled.[189] The union could do little but hope that escalating street violence might cause Everett to relent.

But Everett himself had an equally sobering reality to confront: Cleveland had become a disordered city, in one observer's words, a virtual 'social volcano' of discord.[190]

In 1889 Cleveland's police force numbered some 355 individuals. This relatively small[191] force was notorious for political corruption and for the miserable state of its training, equipment, and morale.[192] Many constables, perhaps a majority, were sympathetic to the streetcar union and its supporters.[193] Whatever was true of other industrial cities,[194] Cleveland's police department was not an effective strike-breaking agency, most particularly in the context of a mass-supported 'great' strike. By late June, in fact, its hopeless inadequacy in this regard had become a subject of urgent discussion, especially among Cleveland's business elite.[195] It was widely feared that the mobs would scare the replacement men from Big Con cars, forcing Everett to accede to union demands. In a letter written in July 1899, prominent Cleveland businessman R.H. Harman summed up the situation: '[T]he war is still on between union and non-union men. I suppose it cannot last long. The non-unionists will be apt to leave for a more healthy location.'[196]

The glaring weakness of local law enforcement did not move Everett to change course. His aim was still to break the strike. When in mid-July 1899 this aim seemed in jeopardy, Everett pressed local officials to call troops into the city.[197] On 21 July, after four days of near continuous 'anarchistic' violence against Big Con men and machines, and amidst still more riots, Mayor Farley met with the state's Assistant Adjutant-General Kingsley to discuss the possibility of calling in the military.[198]

Just as these discussions concluded, a new and desperate dimension was introduced to the terror being orchestrated against the Big Con's scabs and patrons. On 20 July unidentified men used dynamite to blow up a street railway switching terminal. Then, in the early morning of 21 July, two more sticks were thrown onto the roof of a Big Con car barn full of sleeping strike-breakers. The explosion ripped through the roof, destroying equipment but no men.[199] Later the same day, in a dozen areas of the city, crowds engaged in what the *Plain Dealer* called 'systematic guerrilla warfare' with Big Con streetcars and drivers.[200] There were more explosions, more trolley power lines cut. That evening, a 'NIGHT OF WILD LAWLESSNESS AND RIOTING,' the *Plain Dealer* blared in banner headlines, a Big Con car carrying two male and thirteen female passengers from a wealthy neighbourhood was blown off the tracks with an 'explosive cartridge.'[201] (Once again, no one was seriously hurt.) Yet another explosion occurred only three hundred feet from Everett's private residence. Street fighting between rioters, Big Con employees, and police, continued unabated until midnight.

The rioting and dynamite blasts of 21 July were, in fact, the beginning of the end of pro-union street violence in Cleveland. At 2:00 p.m. on 22 July, some 500 troops from various units of local militia (armed with carbines and gatling guns) joined 350 police in the protection of Big Con cars and car-barns.[202] Mayor Farley announced that the troops would support the Big Con's return to full service. Everett publicly declared his 'satisfaction'[203] with this development and reaffirmed his vow that striking union men would never regain jobs 'in a body.' (Only threats and intimidation, Everett further alleged, prevented large numbers of his former employees from resuming their work on the old terms.)[204] It was Everett's turn confidently to predict a decisive victory in the conflict.

The presence of local militia had little immediate effect on street violence. Large crowds continued to confront Big Con cars, police constables, and now soldiers, on virtually every major thoroughfare in the city. The night of 22 July, the *Plain Dealer* proclaimed, was one of ceaseless 'rioting and bloodshed.'[205] Tracks were obstructed, wires cut. More dramatically, on successive days (24 and 25 July) Big Con cars moving from wealthy neighbourhoods were blown off their tracks by nitroglycerin. A number of passengers were hurt, some seriously.[206] Then another violent incident further elevated tensions. On the afternoon of 25 July, a replacement driver (a man from Buffalo) left his car, then pursued, shot, and killed a fifteen-year-old name caller.[207]

As the street violence escalated, the subject of labour injunction was revived for the first time since the strike commenced in June. On 21 July, Everett had a long meeting with his lawyers. It was rumoured that the Big Con president had instructed them to move on the injunction.[208] This proved unfounded. One of Everett's lawyers offered this explanation: 'There is no intention of beginning injunction proceedings against the strikers. The street railroad company has won the strike. We have 160 cars in operation, and there is no possible way the strikers can win their point.'[209]

In London, meanwhile, the most violent phase of the street railway strike had been over for more than two weeks. Mob violence had not been commonplace in London before the events of 8 July; it was even rarer afterward. Many observers were scathingly critical of Mayor Wilson's decision to call in troops.[210] After twelve days of expensive,[211] pointless, and increasingly embarrassed parading, the military was ordered back to barracks. Once again London's humble police force was left to kept the peace.[212] By 21 July, the brief and semi-comic military occupation of London was over. But the strike, and the social and political divisions it had generated, was not.

By the end of July, the street railway strike had exposed deep divisions within the political and judicial power structure of London. An 'invertebrate' city council[213] seemed unable to take any effective steps to mediate, support, or oppose the strike. The mayor's personal prestige, never exalted, had been badly damaged by his decision to call (and then not promptly withdraw) the military. One of his sternest critics was the city's police magistrate, Edward Parke,[214] himself under fire for his alleged leniency toward men charged with strike-related offences.[215] The local County Court Judge, Edward Elliott, was also under attack for having published an open letter critical of unionism and its corrosive effects on the liberty of contract.[216] Even the police supervisory body, the police commission,[217] was openly divided over the failures of the force to maintain order, the advisability of resuming night service on the street railway, and the resignation of Sgt William Jenkins, a senior constable.[218] (Jenkins claimed that Chief of Police Williams had attempted to cover up an incident of alleged police brutality.)[219]

After mid-July, physical opposition to the LSR's operations all but ceased. The streetcar boycott was now the sole means of applying pressure. It shrunk the LSR's business to a tiny fraction of its former volume.[220] 'During the last three months,' an *Advertiser* editorial remarked on 12 August, 'there have not been enough bona fide passengers to pay for the grease on the wheels.'[221] '[A] vigorous boycott is still maintained,' a report of the Toronto *Globe* stated on 20 August, and '[t]here are no signs of resignation or reconciliation.'[222] One visitor to the city 'counted over twenty cars in which there was not over a dozen passengers.'[223]

Though his financial losses mounted, Everett refused to relent. The 'Cleveland Kaiser' and the people of London were at an impasse. In late August Mayor Wilson attempted to negotiate a municipal buy-back of the street railway franchise. This overture was 'flatly refused.'[224] 'Here,' the *Advertiser* observed, 'is the extraordinary spectacle of a company determined to conquer the public, and of the great mass out of 40,000 people determined not to ride, and not to be conquered.'[225] The London street railway strike had become a costly war of attrition.

'Cleveland today,' the *Plain Dealer* observed on 26 July 1899, 'is practically in a wartime condition.' Twelve hundred state troops, many of them Spanish war veterans and all sworn in as special police,[226] now patrolled the city's main streets. Just as the Big Con's attorney had predicted, the military's presence on the main streets foreclosed any serious prospect of Everett being defeated by the mob. The collective power of the crowd had been replaced by the selective power of the explosive. Neither were enough to stop Everett from running his cars.

By August 1899, the most violent phase of the strike was over (the occasional dynamite explosion notwithstanding). The leaders of the Cleveland union, ostensibly opposed to crowd violence,[227] shifted from passive support of active resistance to active support of passive resistance. Just as in London, by August the union's fate depended on the boycott. 'Mayor Farley may use the police and militia to aid plutocracy,' the pro-labour *Cleveland Citizen* stated on 5 August, 'but he cannot make people ride on Big Con Cars!'

When military intervention shifted the balance of power on Cleveland's streets from the strikers to Henry Everett, the streetcar boycott took on a desperate importance. On 28 July, union leaders credibly contended that it had organized the 'biggest boycott in labour's history.'[228] Union men and their families had stopped riding the Big Con, a primary boycott.[229] Clevelanders had been asked to stay off Big Con cars, a secondary boycott. Then pro-union forces also declared a boycott against any person or business that had social or commercial contact with boycott-breakers.[230] As matters stood at the end of July, the Big Con system was boycotted. Anyone who offered services or wares to Big Con scabs, security men, or patrons was boycotted. Anyone who had commerce with soldiers was boycotted.[231] Scores of union-loyal 'spotters' reported boycott violations.[232] The names of transgressors were posted in public places.

In early August the Cleveland boycott was described as 'general in its operations and complete in its enforcement.'[233] Only a handful of 'aristocrats and snobs' in the city's affluent east end continued to ride Big Con cars.[234] 'No amount of talk,' the *Cleveland World* wrote on 4 August, 'can change the fact that the refusal of many thousands of citizens to patronise the Big Con's cars is due to sympathy with the cause of the strikers.'[235] The *Citizen* called the boycott 'the greatest exhibition of class consciousness that has ever been seen in this state.'[236] Out of sympathy or fear, few Clevelanders were prepared openly to defy the ban.[237] Transgressors faced what the *Plain Dealer* decried as a 'social death' of condemnation and ostracism.[238] So dire were these consequences that the street railway union executive began to hear 'appeals' from individuals and tradesmen unlucky enough to have been named on the blacklist.[239]

Big Con officials regularly forecasted the demise of the boycott. Cleveland's business elite did not take such a sanguine view. On 4 August the

Chamber of Commerce held the first of a series of anti-boycott meetings.[240] Hundreds of Cleveland's 'leading' businessmen and professionals publicly resolved not to respect the boycott.[241] They also resolved to solicit a legal opinion on the legality of the secondary boycott.[242] Scores of Cleveland retailers, grocers, and barbers continued to refuse persons 'spotted' on Big Con railway cars.

In London, the boycott held until late autumn. By mid-November even the staunchly pro-strike *Advertiser* acknowledged that 'a larger number of persons' were riding streetcars.[243] Thousands of Londoners had respected the streetcar boycott for a full six months. Time, cold rain, and strike fatigue finally had eroded pro-union resolve in the city. Two more strikers broke ranks and returned to work.[244] The arrival of the autumn assizes added to the gloom. The main business of the presiding judge, Chief Justice Armour, was to charge a grand jury on twenty-seven strike-related criminal cases.

The chief justice's charge (to a jury composed mainly of substantial farmers)[245] might have been made by the most rabidly anti-union American judge. 'Under the common law,' the chief justice generalized, 'it was an indictable offence for anyone to interfere with commerce or trade.' The law 'was the same with regard to boycotting, combining to interfere with trade, that it is illegal under common law.' The chief justice's central contention was that '[a]ny employer might employ whom he chose and discharge whom he chose.' Warming to his subject the chief justice condemned strikes as 'deplorable,' and boycotts as 'mean and cowardly.' He urged the farmer-jurors to consider whether they would like unions to tell *them* who to hire and fire, and exhorted them to 'encourage the investment of capital' by defending the traditional privileges of property. 'It appeared,' the chief justice concluded, 'that the persons who went on strike were guilty of assembling in a disorderly manner and that acts of violence were committed.' That itself was enough to justify indictment. In the result, the grand jury returned 'true bills' against all of the accused.

The autumn did not bring better news for the Cleveland strikers. Pastor W.B. Pickard's early September sermon on the 'Logic of Dynamite' summed up the situation. Reflecting on two months of street violence, Pickard spoke of the 'insanity' of the 'mob method of securing the rights of labor.' The recent spate of explosions was seen in the same light. The 'logic of dynamite,' he asserted, was the logic of the defeated.[246] Pickard's oration was ponderous, overwrought and, in its central thesis, absolutely correct. As early as 5 August, Everett confidently boasted that the old schedules were being met with a completely new body of workmen. The door was no longer open to the old men. The strike, Everett stated, was 'a closed incident.'[247]

Neither the sporadic violence of August nor the massive Labor Day demonstration of 4 September did anything to undermine Everett's smug confidence. Although the boycott of the Big Con and its patrons continued to be widespread and extremely costly to the company, it was the last stand of desperate people. On the Sunday of Pickard's sermon, the great Cleveland strike of 1899 was over in all but name. By mid-September there had been a noticeable increase in public patronage of Big Con cars.[248] Upwards of ninety-five strikers had returned to their old jobs.[249] Although in October 1899 the strike had still not been officially declared over, even Cleveland's labour newspaper now spoke of it in the past tense.[250] So sure was Everett that the strike was broken that he cut the wages of 'high-priced scabs' still working the line. Quitters were replaced with 'country-boy' labour.[251]

By the end of November 1899, the London strike and boycott also were all but dead. The LSR had returned to full service. Its ridership, still greatly diminished, was on the increase. The union's flagging morale was further eroded by a series of strike-related criminal trials before County Court Judge Elliott. Although not every case ended with a conviction, the prosecution of union men[252] and their supporters[253] was a grim reminder both of the futility of street violence and of the basic commitments of the legal system. 'Every man in this country,' the judge's charge invariably concluded, 'whether he belonged to a union or not, should be just as free to labor as the air which he breathes.'[254]

In both London and Cleveland, the unions remained publicly resolute and defiant throughout the fall of 1899 and into the winter of 1900.[255] But while the unions continued to affirm the justice and viability of their strikes, Everett continued to offer full streetcar services to larger numbers of patrons. True to his word, the scabs had become permanent employees,[256] their numbers supplemented by a few contrite union men.[257] As the new century commenced, only the most self-deluded observer could have failed to grasp that streetcar unionism, in London and Cleveland equally, had been abjectly defeated.

CONSERVATIVE INSURRECTION: GREAT STRIKES AND DEEP LAW

Contemporary descriptions of the London and Cleveland street railway conflicts of 1899 as 'great' strikes can be safely endorsed. The conflicts attracted the active, sometimes violent, participation of large segments of their respective populations. They paralysed the business of a prominent corporate employer. They seriously impaired the social and commercial life of both cities. In London briefly, in Cleveland protractedly, the strikes finally overwhelmed the ability of local authorities to keep the peace. Widespread public disorder ended only with the intervention of soldiers. These events have a magnitude and gravity that mark them out for close historical investigation and explanation.

That the London and Cleveland strikes were important historical events is one thing, that they were 'typical' ones, another. Acknowledging that the generalization of case studies is a perilous business, two interpretive approaches are available. The first is historiographical. To what degree does existing scholarship on the relationship of law and labour relations in this period account for the features of these strikes? The second involves the tendering of new hypotheses where current scholarship provides no helpful explanation. What might explain what the extant historiography does not?

Legal historians, naturally enough, are interested in the work of judges. Recent American scholarship on the relationship of law and labour in the Gilded Age has focused primarily on judicial responses to the growth of labour organization and militancy in the period 1866–1914.[258] This literature describes the development and aggressive implementation of labour injunctions and criminal conspiracy prosecutions.[259] Judicial attacks on pro-labour legislation, and the effects of such attacks on the strategies and politics of organized labour, have also been closely examined.[260] While 'court-centred' interpretation has obvious explanatory value with regard to many strikes of the period,[261] it does not explain the contours of the Cleveland and London strikes of 1899.[262]

The work of leading historians of Canadian law and labour in the period 1880–1914 has a different emphasis. Eric Tucker,[263] and Eric Tucker and Judy Fudge,[264] have shown that the labour injunction developed later, and was used far less frequently and potently in Canada than in the United States.[265] (Federal legislation passed in the 1870s largely immunized Canadian unionists from criminal conspiracy indictments.)[266] Tucker and Fudge pointedly contend that 'direct' coercion by judges was not the only or even the most important factor in the defeat of striking unionists.[267] In most conflicts, the 'superior economic power' of employers, buttressed by the 'private' law of contract and property, were the decisive pivots.[268] This line of interpretation is conspicuously relevant to both strikes under study here – which raises a point concerning the insularity of North American labour historiography. Most scholars in this field have focused either on Canada *or* the United States. Comparative analyses, when they have been undertaken at all, have issued mainly from Canadian scholars, and in the absence of parallel source materials.[269] The study at hand is thus an experiment in the reconstruction and analysis of a cross-national and interwoven body of evidence. The London and Cleveland strikes against Everett's companies provide the historian (at least hypothetically) with a direct 'contrast of contexts.'[270] They present an opportunity to re-examine what we think we know about the role of American or Canadian law in strikes of this period, to discern, for instance, what legal interventions are, and are not, in evidence.[271]

Glaringly not in evidence in the great London and Cleveland street railway strikes of 1899 is direct intervention by union-busting judges. Given the alleged propensities of American employers and judges, the marginality of the courts during the Cleveland strike is especially noteworthy. As we have seen, Everett's Cleveland operation faced large-scale, damaging, and prolonged violence in the streets. These were precisely the circumstances, the American labour historiography suggests, which routinely generated (successful) applications for injunctive relief. And yet no such application was made.[272] This deserves some explanation.

On at least two occasions Everett and his Cleveland lawyers discussed, but did not pursue, the injunction option. There were three reasons for this decision. At the outset of the strike, first of all, Everett neither planned for nor relied on quick intervention by the state. His policy was one of self-help, to be achieved through replacement labour and private security forces. Second, when the question of judicial intervention was eventually discussed, Cleveland's federal attorney and state judges did not act according to the form sheet. The 'feelers' sent out by Everett's lawyers were frostily rebuffed. The federal attorney signalled serious doubt both about the necessity and justice of 'blanket' injunctive relief. As time passed, moreover, there was a third reason not to go to court. By mid-July, it was widely believed that troops would be called into the city without the aid of an injunction. Going to court simply became unnecessary.

This brings us to a point of divergence between the Cleveland and London strikes. Clevelanders were more violent, and were violent sooner and longer than Londoners. (Whether this was a manifestation of national traits or merely of the different size, demographics, and labour histories of the two cities it is impossible to tell.) But differences in the duration and intensity of the strike violence should not obscure another point of similarity: the local state's response to the strikes, and to strike-related violence, was essentially the same in both cities.[273] In both cities, mayors and city councilmen either permitted or could not stop angry citizens from bringing Everett's operations to a virtual standstill. Local officials were ambivalent, internally divided, and indecisive. They had neither the political will nor the coercive resources to crush the strike in its early phases. In both cities too, only the introduction of soldiers on the streets prevented crowds of irate citizens from destroying Everett's capacity to provide a street railway service.

The implementation of criminal law against strike supporters was also ineffective. In both cities police intervention was inept, sometimes half-hearted. Arrests and prosecutions were haphazard.[274] The petty criminal courts simply were not much feared by the thousands of men and women who resolved to fight Everett on the streets. In London, the local police court magistrate was notoriously lenient with strike-related crimes. And while both the county court and high court judges who heard strike cases were as hostile toward the collectivist aims of unions as any American judge, their role in the strike was confined to 'mopping up.' By the time that a handful of strikers and their supporters were sent to jail in the autumn of 1899, the main drama had been finished for some weeks. These sentences had no bearing either on the shape or outcome of the conflict. The situation was not much different in Cleveland. While over the course of the summer police made scores of strike-related arrests[275] (virtually none of strikers themselves), they had only a negligible impact on the behaviour of strike supporters. Street violence, even the use of dynamite, continued to escalate in the face of intensified policing. Soldiers, not police or judges, ended the long period of strike-related violence.

The feebleness of the local state as a strike-breaking agency in London and Cleveland of 1899 did not take Henry Everett by surprise. When it came to the investment of capital, or the implementation and defence of his chosen manner of business, he made no concession to the fact that London and Cleveland were located in different countries. Nor did he much care that in London he was widely reviled as a greedy Yankee monopolist, in Cleveland only as a greedy monopolist. Nor was it of great moment that some American judges were readier than their Canadian counterparts to grant labour injunctions. To Everett, what mattered most was that in both jurisdictions the state, when pressed hard enough, would exert military force to defend the fundamental legal moorings – the deep law – of his capitalism.

The 'deep' law was the set of *grundnorms* of private property and free contract that formed the ideological core of the Canadian and American states; the deep law was the legal substrata of late-nineteenth-century bourgeois economy. Labour injunctions and conspiracy lawsuits were expressions, sometimes potent expressions, of these primary commitments. But the survival of Everett's business empire did not depend on court orders. It rested on a bedrock of more fundamental legal commitments backed by military force.

In 1898–9, Everett moved boldly and confidently – in both Cleveland and London – to introduce new workplace rules, timetables, and work schedules and new teams of spotters and supervisors to enforce them. Pressed by the exigencies of rapid growth, persuaded of the need for 'scientific' labour organization, Everett swiftly imposed a 'new ethos of work' on all his streetcar men.[276] His aim was to reconstruct streetcar employment as a kind of factory labour.[277] Everett confronted, perhaps provoked, the strikes of 1899 in order to consolidate this shift. His policies had another, unintended, side effect: they connected the private apprehension of his employees to the collective anxiety of their larger working-class communities.

Just as Everett's syndicate was a cross-national concern, more or less indifferent to the international border, so too was the street railway union. The AASRE was a complementary outcome of the rise of international capitalism in the street railway sector. While their propaganda was moulded to fit the cultural reference points of particular communities, AASRE officials saw no need to adjust fundamental goals or tactics. In London and Cleveland, the AASRE organized streetcar workers into unions without interference from courts, police, or legislatures. In both places equally, union executives went unmolested as they planned and orchestrated strikes.

In both countries the pro-union cause was distinctly of a defensive character.[278] Pro-union rhetoric was not about remaking the deep law of capitalist commerce, property, or society.[279] In London and Cleveland, AFL labour unions were supported not as an intrinsic good but as a practical means of resisting unilateral changes in long-standing patterns of work. Collective bargaining became a popular cause not because it was consonant with a socialist vision of work, but as an antidote to corporate concentration and aggressive managerialism. Instead of rejecting the bourgeois language of contract, AFL unions adopted it. This stance struck many contemporaries, working and even middle class, as entirely reasonable and just.

For waged Londoners the purchase – then rapid transformation – of the LSR was an alarming first encounter with American monopoly capitalism, with the 'immense cultural force'[280] embodied in the combination of foreign corporation, scientific management, and nakedly nonpaternalistic pursuit of profit. '[T]he alien Everett and his trust,' the *Industrial Banner* repeatedly warned, 'has descended to crush down Canadian labour in London.'[281] Unions of skilled (and now unskilled)[282] workers were seen as a natural counterpoint to the threat posed by big business. Canadian workingmen, the *Advertiser* contended, 'have as much right to combine for mutual protection as the capitalists of the U.S. have the right to exploit the public franchises of Canada.'[283] It was widely perceived that Everett was interested in the London strike only with respect to its implications for his larger empire. 'London,' the editor of the *Advertiser* declared, 'is a cog in the Everett machine.'[284]

Labouring Clevelanders could not claim the same innocence of the ways and means of large-scale corporate capitalism. A number of violent and popularly supported strikes had been fought in preceding years.[285] As the city emerged from the Depression of the mid-1890s, Cleveland's working-class communities became emboldened to stand against the corrosive influences of big business and scientific management. The plight of the streetcar men was familiar and visible; it quickly became a lightning rod of widely felt fear and resentment.

Everett and his co-investors had their own fears as 1899 commenced. Their bid to create an empire of street and interurban railways in the mid-west had generated enormous financial strain.[286] The long-term viability of the corporation now seemed more dependent on a highly efficient (and compliant) labour force. The strikes of 1899 were anticipated, probably deliberately fomented, as wars of union extermination. 'Everett,' the *Cleveland Press* alleged in June 1899, 'is purposely fighting unionism in Cleveland.'[287] He was fighting (possibly in league with 'street railway magnates of different sections of the country')[288] to deal a death blow to the AASRE.

Everett's intransigence in the weeks prior to the walkout reflected unshakeable confidence in the rightness and defensibility of his policies. Of greatest consequence was the legal accessibility (and rapid mobility) of the vast 'industrial reserve army'[289] of workers in both states. Most crucially, however, Everett trusted that local officials, if resistance proved stubborn enough, would clear the streets with soldiers. He confidently predicted that his deep contractual and property rights would be vindicated by the force of arms.[290] At this most fundamental level, the law both of Ontario and Ohio was the pivotal factor in the era's labour struggles.

In late July 1899, the *Cleveland Leader* reported: 'Military officers are generally of the opinion that [the city], in the meaning of the law, is in a state of insurrection.'[291] Under the title 'THE LAW OF STEEL,' the *Leader* described how on 24 July, as pro-union rioting continued to overwhelm local militia units in neighbourhoods across the city, Everett and his lawyers met Mayor Farley in the mayor's office. The *Leader* editorialized against 'the sullen mobs and cowardly individuals committing the most flagrant crimes against law and order.' It also reported that the mayor summoned state troops to Cleveland immediately following his meeting with the Big Con boss.[292] Everett may or may not have directly influenced this decision, or Mayor John Wilson's like decision in London. The germane point is that troops were summoned and their presence all but ensured that the strikes would fail.

Everett had banked on the assumption that in Ontario and Ohio the state (at the expense of general taxpayers)[293] would crush popular resistance to his labour policies. His syndicate confronted the strikes prepared to absorb large financial losses. Everett further assumed that the losses associated with the strike would be more than repaid in subsequent, union-free, years of operation. In London, 1898 had been a profitable year for the LSR. In the strike and boycott year of 1899, the company lost money.[294] By 1900, however, revenues and profits had rebounded beyond 1898 levels. By 1901, the LSR profits had increased nearly 20 per cent over its previous best year.[295] The precise magnitude of the Big Con's losses from the 1899 strike is less easy to determine. But what is known is illuminating. In 1899 the Big Con made a profit in the face of a prolonged strike and boycott. In 1900, a year free of (potent) strikes or boycotts, the company's net earnings nearly doubled.[296] In Cleveland as in London, Everett's decision to accept sizeable short-term losses in order to stave off long-term unionization was vindicated by balance sheets.

Among the first to share in the spoils of victory were Everett's lawyers. In London and Cleveland his attorneys were handsomely rewarded for hard work well done.[297] Almost none of their toil, significantly, had taken place in courtrooms. They had overseen the logistical and political imperatives of a labour war of attrition, a war in which military forces were the decisive reserve corps. Replacement labour had been mustered and protected, ambivalent municipal officials badgered and cajoled. The conservative insurrections of two striking communities had been defeated by the combined power of money and the military, and by the solemn obligation of officials to exonerate the deep legal commitments of the state to private property and freedom of contract. In June 1899, a Methodist minister had warned his Cleveland congregation: 'All the great strikes of recent years have failed, and have caused unmeasured loss and sorrow to the labourers themselves.'[298]

NOTES

I am grateful to my colleague Robert Martin for having suggested (some years ago) that I undertake research on the London street railway strike. I am also grateful to Robert Hawkins, John McLaren, DeLloyd Guth, and especially Daniel Ernst, for their comments on drafts of this paper. The Law Foundation of Ontario and the Canada–U.S. Law Institute contributed financial support to the project.

1 Soon after the conflict commenced, the *Cleveland Plain Dealer* began to call it a 'Great Strike.' (11 June 1899).

2 The son of a wealthy physician and street railway entrepreneur, Henry Azariah Everett (1856–1917) took over and greatly expanded his father's business enterprises. In 1891, Everett and Cleveland financier E.W. Moore formed the Everett-Moore syndicate. By 1899, the syndicate controlled electric traction and telephone companies (in Ohio, Michigan and Canada) with a paper worth of tens of millions of dollars. See the *Cleveland Plain Dealer*, special limited edition, 1918, 484–5; and the *National Encyclopaedia of American Biography*, 28:180.

3 'All that is required of an applicant,' a labour arbitrator once stated of streetcar work, 'is an ordinary physique and a public school education.' Quoted in Emerson P. Schmidt, *Industrial Relations in Urban Transportation* (Minneapolis 1937), 82. An official of the London Street Railway remarked in 1899 that 'a street railway motorman or conductor cannot be looked upon as a skilled mechanic, as a few days training will make any intelligent working man efficient [at either job].' *London Advertiser*, 1 June 1899.

4 By 1899, three men, Wm C. Whitney of New York, P.A.B. Widener, and Wm L. Elkins of Philadelphia, had pooled their vast street railway and gas company holdings. Together they 'controlled 1,500 miles of street railways, on which 25,000 men are employed and 10,000 cars operated.' See 'America's Street Railway Kings,' *Cleveland Leader*, 6 August 1899. Contemporary observers repeatedly alleged that America's street railway magnates were colluding to crush organized labour.

5 Much to his later regret, in 1896 Everett had inherited a union contract when he consolidated competing Detroit streetcar lines into the Detroit United Railway. This contract, with Division 26 of the AASRE, was renegotiated every year between 1895–1899. During the strikes of 1899, Everett denounced the Detroit contract as anomalous and 'absolutely on the side of the employees.' *Cleveland Press*, 14 June 1899. Everett told reporters that 'he would not again sign a contract of like character.' *Cleveland Plain Dealer*, 14 June 1899.

6 *London Free Press*, 7 November 1898.

7 William Forbath has written plausibly of the law's 'central place in the historical experience of American labour.' Forbath, *Law and the Shaping of the American Labor Movement* (Cambridge, Mass. 1991), 6. The eminent labour historian David Montgomery has also recently commented on the centrality of law to the history of labour in America. See Montgomery, *Citizen Worker* (Cambridge 1993), 9–10. For an introduction to this historiographical trend, see Wythe Holt, 'The New American Labor Law History,' *Labor History* 30 (1989), 275–93 and the introduction to *Labor Law in America: Historical and Critical Essays*, ed. Christopher L. Tomlins and Andrew J. King (Baltimore 1992).

8 See Christopher L. Tomlins, *The State and the Unions: Labor Relations, Law, and the Organized Labor Movement In America, 1880–1960* (Cambridge, Mass. 1985); Dianne Avery, 'Images of Violence in Labor Jurisprudence: The Regulation and Picketing of Boycotts, 1894–1921,' *Buffalo Law Review* 37 (1988–89), 1–117; and Daniel R. Ernst, *Lawyers Against Labor* (Urbana 1995). For a contrary viewpoint, see Sylvester Petro, 'Injunctions and Labor Disputes, 1880–1932,' *Wake Forest Law Review* 14 (1978), 341–476. For an examination of labour decisions under the Sherman Act, see Herbert Hovencamp, 'Labor Conspiracies in American Law, 1880–1930,' *Texas Law Review* 66 (1988), 919–51. For Canadian legal-labour history, see Eric Tucker, '"That Indefinite Area of Toleration": Criminal Conspiracy and Trade Unions in Ontario, 1837–77,' *Labour/Le travail* 20 (1987), 14–51; Tucker, 'The Faces of Coercion: The Legal Regulation of Labor Conflict in Ontario, 1880–1889,' *Law and History Review* 12 (1994), 277–339; Tucker and Judy Fudge, 'Forging Responsible Unions: Metal Workers and the Rise of the Labour Injunction in Canada,' *Labour/Le travail* 37 (1996), 81–119.

9 See Haggai Hurvitz, 'American Labor Law and the Doctrine of Entrepreneurial Property Rights: Boycotts, Courts, and the Juridical Reorientation of 1886–1895,' *Industrial Relations Law Journal* 8 (1986), 307–61; William Forbath, *Law and the Shaping of the American Labor Movement* (Cambridge 1991); and Daniel Ernst, 'Free Labor, the Consumer Interest, and the Law of Industrial Disputes, 1885–1900,' *American Journal of Legal History* 36 (1992), 19–37.

10 This commensurateness existed in many other areas of law. See R.C.B. Risk, 'Law and Economy in Mid-Nineteenth Century Ontario,' *University of Toronto Law Journal* 27 (1977), 433–9.

11 For a trove of authoritative information concerning the economy and society of nineteenth-century Cleveland, see the *Encyclopaedia of Cleveland History*, David Van Tassel and John Grabowski, eds. (Cleveland 1987). For an overview of Cleveland economic history after 1860, see Weiner, 'The New Industrial Metropolis,' in ibid., xxix–xxxiv.

12 See Dennis Harrison, 'Labor,' in the *Encyclopedia of Cleveland History*, 604–6. See also James B. Whipple, 'Cleveland in Conflict: A Study In Urban Adolescence, 1876–1900' (PhD thesis, Case Western Reserve University 1951); Leslie Hough, 'The Turbulent Spirit: Violence and Coaction among Cleveland Workers, 1877–1899' (PhD thesis, University of Virginia 1977), 9–15, 102–17. See also *Cleveland Press*, 14 June 1899.

13 Hough, 'Turbulent Spirit,' 11.

14 For an overview of the social and economic structure of turn-of-the-century London, see Bryan D. Palmer, '"Give Us the Road and We Will Run It": The Social and Cultural Matrix of an Emerging Labour Movement,' in Gregory S. Kealey and Peter Warrian, eds., *Essays in Canadian Working Class History* (Toronto 1976), 106–18. See also F.H. Armstrong and Daniel Brock, 'The Rise of London: A Study in Urban Evolution in Nineteenth Century Ontario,' in F.H. Armstrong et al., *Aspects of Nineteenth Century Ontario* (Toronto 1974), 80–98.

15 Reported by Prof. S.M. Wickett, University of Toronto political economist, to *The Globe*, 21 July 1899.

16 Prof. Wickett alleged that the total sum of criminal fines and fees for a year 'do not amount to the salary of an ordinary official.' Ibid.

17 See Palmer, *Give Us the Road*, 117–18; and Gregory S. Kealey and Bryan D. Palmer, *Dreaming of What Might Be: The Knights of Labour in Ontario, 1880–1900* (Toronto 1987), 61–77.

18 *Industrial Banner*, November 1899. See also W.L. Davis, 'A History of the Early Labour Movement in London, Ontario' (MA thesis, University of Western Ontario 1930), chap. ii; and Palmer, *Give Us the Road*, 111–18.

19 'The company,' the *Industrial Banner* remarked in May 1899, 'cannot be entirely ignorant of the fact that the fraternal societies are honeycombed with members of labour organizations. To invite conflict now is to paralyse their traffic.' See also Palmer, *Give Us the Road*, 111.

20 By 1897, Cleveland had two independent electrified street railway systems (the Big Consolidated and Little Consolidated) operating over 170 miles of track in different sectors of the city. With 130 miles of track, the Big Con was by far the largest of the two operations. For the development of the Cleveland electric traction system, see 'Cleveland Electric Railway Company,' in *Encyclopedia of Cleveland History*, 230–1. For the general development of electric traction in America, see George W. Hilton and John F. Due, *The Electric Interurban Railways in America* (Stanford 1960).

21 'Cleveland Electric Railway Company,' *Encyclopedia of Cleveland History*, 230–1.

22 In 1898 the Everett-Moore syndicate had purchased a large block of Big Con

stock from street railway entrepreneur and Progressive politician, Tom L. Johnson. Orth, *History of Cleveland*, 205.

23 See Gerald A. Onn, 'The History of the London Street Railway Company' (MA thesis, University of Western Ontario, 1958). An account of the negotiations can be found in the *London Advertiser*, 27 July 1899.

24 The cities of Toronto and Montreal had already made electrification deals with the Everett-Moore syndicate prior to 1895. See 'Henry Everett,' *National Encyclopaedia*, 180.

25 This account in the *London Advertiser*, 17 July 1899.

26 The higher number in the summer season. *London Advertiser*, 29 June 1899.

27 For a description of the financial aspects of turn-of-the-century street railway capitalism, see Hilton and Due, *Interurban Railways*, 10; and Schmidt, *Urban Transportation*, 33–7.

28 Hilton and Due 19; Schmidt, 32.

29 Born in 1864, Edward W. Moore was a self-made Ohio millionaire who had made his fortune in banking. With Henry Everett, Moore developed a vast syndicate of telephone and electric traction companies. Moore was a brilliant financier, and these skills were a major factor in the expansion of the Everett-Moore empire. See Samuel P. Orth, *A History of Cleveland Ohio* (Cleveland 1910), 2:203–5.

30 See 'Henry Everett,' *The National Encyclopaedia*, 180.

31 Hilton and Due, *Interurban Railways*, 11.

32 The streetcar properties of the Everett-Moore syndicate 'were said to be capitalised at $47 million and to have netted $5.5 million in 1900.' Ibid., 11. This was considered a very high rate of return in an industry notorious for its corruption, overcapitalization, and inefficiency. See Schmidt, *Urban Transportation*, 33–4.

33 As the strikes of 1899 unfolded, the Everett-Moore syndicate was building two additional interurban railway lines, one in Michigan and one in Ohio. These expensive projects placed the syndicate under severe financial strain. Hilton and Due, *Interurban Railways*, 27–8.

34 Ibid. The Everett-Moore syndicate experienced a nearly catastrophic liquidity crisis in 1901.

35 The best general description of street railway labour, and the changes wrought by electrification in this period, is Schmidt, *Urban Transportation*, 71–85.

36 The *Detroit News* summarized the point thus: 'The maximum rate of fare is fixed, and the profits therefore are entirely dependent upon the volume of traffic and the cost of operation. The chief operating cost is wages.' Quoted in *London Advertiser*, 27 July 1899.

37 Ibid. See also Schmidt, *Urban Transportation*, 74–5. Although there is no evidence that he was directly influenced by Taylorism, the operational innovations introduced by Everett in the late 1890s were consonant with 'scientific management.' For historical background, see David Montgomery, *The Fall of the House of Labor* (New York 1987), 214–56; and Sarah Lyons Watts, *Business Culture and Labor Ideology in America* (New York 1991), 87–90.

38 For a review of these changes, see Sarah M. Henry, 'The Strikers and their Sympathisers: Brooklyn in the Trolley Strike of 1895,' *Labor History* 32 (1991), 334–53.

39 The split or swing shift involved scheduling the employee's day in a series of work periods broken up by unpaid 'down' time. The men would be asked to work two to four-hour periods in the early morning, at mid-day, and in the late afternoon. This scheduling technique, bitterly resented by streetcar men, was an important cost-saving device to streetcar companies. Schmidt, *Urban Transportation*, 74–5. For an account of the objections of Big Con men to the swing shift, see *Cleveland Press*, 14 June 1899.

40 Some rule books contained as many as 167 provisions and were 100 pages long. See Schmidt, *Urban Transportation*, 89–93.

41 The local Trade Unions Council had, on at least two previous occasions, organized meetings to encourage the unionization of the streetcar men. These meetings were not well attended. *Industrial Banner*, December 1898.

42 Ibid.

43 An employees' 'association' had been sustained by an unknown number of streetcar men since October 1896. *London Advertiser*, 4 November 1898.

44 A London by-law required that all street railway employees had to be 'residents.' *Industrial Banner*, December 1898.

45 The names of the eight men were published in the March 1899 issue of the *Industrial Banner*.

46 The last clause of the agreement stated: 'This agreement to be in force for six months, or for such further period as the employees remain in the service of the company.' The LSR contended that it bound the men indefinitely. The union contended that the agreement was to last only as long as the company respected its terms. *London Advertiser*, 1 June 1898.

47 See *London Free Press*, 12 November 1898; *London Advertiser*, 11 November 1898.

48 Ibid.

49 The board of directors of Everett's new acquisition was not unanimous in its approach to labour. At least some members were prepared to recognize a union in order to avert a costly strike. See *Cleveland World*, 11 June 1899.

50 Speech of congregationalist minister, Rev. A.B. Christy, 19 June 1899.

51 Chicago Tribune editorial, quoted in the *London Advertiser*, 13 October 1899. For a similar assessment of what Everett's changes meant to the men working on the Big Con, see Rev. Christy's speech, ibid.

52 *Cleveland Press*, 7 June 1899. See also speech of Rev. Christy, *Cleveland Plain Dealer*, 19 June 1899.

53 The precise number is unclear. Big Con motorman M.C. Welker was charged with manslaughter after an inquest found that he had been speeding when his streetcar struck and killed a pedestrian on 25 May. Big Con lawyers posted a $10,000 bond for Welker. *Cleveland Press*, 8 June 1899.

54 Sermon of Rev. Christy, *Cleveland Plain Dealer*, 19 June 1899.

55 'Now, six months ago, or even four months ago,' Rev. A.B. Christy alleged in July 1899, 'if anyone had suggested a union the men would not have listened a moment.' *Cleveland Plain Dealer*, 19 July 1899.

56 Ibid.

57 *Cleveland Press*, 8 June 1899.

58 Whatever the precise percentage of men, the union clearly enjoyed overwhelming majority support (at least 800 of 900 employees) by June 1899. *Cleveland Press*, 5 June 1899.

59 In Canada, the federal Trade Union Act and Criminal Law Amendment Acts of the 1870s rendered trade unions immune to the common law of conspiracy to restrain trade. Working men were free to form unions for the purpose of achieving collective bargaining and agreements and were free to strike. However, the means generally chosen to pursue these options – pickets and boycotts, for instance – remained legally vulnerable. See Claude D'Aoust and Françoise Delorme, 'The Origin of the Freedom of Association and the Right to Strike in Canada: An Historical Perspective,' *Relations industrielles* 36 (1981), 895–921; Mark Chartrand, 'The First Canadian Trade Union Legislation: An Historical Perspective,' *Ottawa Law Review* 16 (1984), 267–96; and Tucker, 'Faces of Coercion,' 281–4.

60 Neither judge-made nor statutory law prevented Ohio workers from forming combinations for the improvement of their wages or working conditions. As in Ontario, however, the means by which union goals were pursued were subject to a number of possible legal constraints, including conspiracy prosecutions and labour injunctions. See *Ohio Jurisprudence*, vol. 39, c. 411–13. See also Hovencamp, 'Labor Conspiracies.'

61 *Cleveland Press*, 2 June 1899.

62 Sermon of Rev. A.B. Christy, *Cleveland Plain Dealer*, 19 June 1899.

63 All of these allegations were reported in the *Industrial Banner*, May 1899.

64 Ibid.

65 Ibid. The precise number of dissenting votes was not reported.

66 Even Henry Everett claimed that Bryan and Pratt were too 'inexperienced' to handle the negotiations between union and company. *Cleveland Leader*, 14 June 1899.

67 '[T]he whole trouble,' E.W. Moore stated of the London dispute, 'has been caused by two men who came here from Detroit as labour agitators ... this work nets them $100–25 per month.' *London Advertiser*, 7 November 1898.

68 Although most of our information about the alleged 'agitators' came from the mouths of company officials, it is known with certainty that Jordan Pickell and Michael Delsile were from Detroit, were long-time members of the AASRE, and had come to London in 1898 'ostensibly as ... [motormen] in training.' Pickell began organizing the London men soon after his arrival. See the *London Advertiser*, 7 November 1898.

69 It was the strict policy of the AASRE that strikes were subject to the sanction and discipline of the union's central executive. This was the price of the AASRE's financial and logistical support, and of its (purported) expertise, in directing strikes. Schmidt, *Urban Transportation*, 137–8.

70 Both Carpenter and Reynolds were deeply involved in the strike, and clearly spent scores of hours on strike-related work. Although it is not clear how much they were paid, they did not work for free. In mid-June 1899, the union executive disclosed that it had paid $450 in 'indemnity fees, lawyers' hire and general expenses.' *Cleveland Leader*, 29 June 1899.

71 Given that only one AASRE union member was arrested during the first two months of the strike, Carpenter and Reynolds only rarely attended court on the union's behalf. They were hired for their knowledge of negotiation, contracts, and of the operation of municipal government.

72 In London, the LSR retained law partners C.H. Ivey and Isidore Hellmuth. Both men were well-connected and experienced business lawyers. In Cleveland, Everett retained the city's leading corporate law firm, Kline, Carr, Tolles, & Goff. William. F. Carr was past president of the Cleveland bar and a director of a number of local corporations. See *'The World's' History of Cleveland* (Cleveland, 1896), 424.

73 *London Advertiser*, 15 August 1899. Since the 1880s, the term 'people's strike' had been used to describe 'mass strikes that crippled whole industries or polarised entire communities.' See Bryan D. Palmer, *Working Class Experience: Rethinking the History of Canadian Labour, 1880–1991* (Toronto 1992), 144–5.

74 *Cleveland Citizen*, 12 August 1899. The *Citizen* was edited by Max Hayes (1866–1945), a leading socialist and labour activist. See 'Max S. Hayes,' *Encyclopedia of Cleveland History*, 494.

75 *London Advertiser*, 23 May 1899.

76 While he offered no proof, Rev. A.C. Ludlow, a Presbyterian pastor, once

publicly claimed that 'thousands of dollars of [street] railway stock' had been paid to city politicians when the Big Con's franchises had been secured. See 'The Strike and the Church,' *Cleveland Plain Dealer*, 30 July 1899. 'Whole Councils have been bought,' or so claimed the *Cleveland Press*, 29 June 1899. See also Henry, 'Brooklyn Trolley Strike,' 347.

77 For a blistering attack on the LSR's safety record, see editorial, *London Advertiser*, 23 May 1899.

78 See Hough, 'Turbulent Spirit,' 184–7, 190–3.

79 'At every street corner along the line of march crowds of sympathisers were gathered and more than one cheer was given for the strikers.' *London Free Press*, 26 May 1899.

80 Ibid.

81 The slogan 'No Surrender' was drawn from the heritage of London's large population of Ulster Orangemen.

82 *Cleveland Leader*, 8 June 1899.

83 Big Con men were often scheduled to 4–7 and 10–12 a.m., and then again at 4–10 or 12 p.m. *Cleveland Leader*, 14 June 1899.

84 *Cleveland Plain Dealer*, 7 June 1899.

85 *Cleveland Press*, 8 June 1899.

86 As Rev. Christy summarized, 'The men were put between two rocks – either to keep within the law and be discharged ... or be arrested by police.' Many men not previously committed to the union now agreed to 'act together.' *Cleveland Plain Dealer*, 19 June 1899.

87 '[Here] is an indictment against the Big Consolidated,' Rev. Christy stated later in June, 'in which we are all interested.' *Cleveland Plain Dealer*, 19 June 1899.

88 *Cleveland World*, 9 June 1899.

89 *Cleveland Press*, 9 June 1899.

90 Big Con officials had been busy signing up replacement labour at least a week before the strike actually began. *Cleveland Press*, 8 June 1899. By 13 June, Everett admitted that he had 'in concealment' about 300 'imported men' to run his cars. *Cleveland Leader*, 13 June 1899. Rev. Christy, a man in the confidence of many of the strikers, later alleged that the Big Con had begun to prepare to 'hire, house, feed replacement men' as early as Apr. 1899. *Cleveland Plain Dealer*, 19 June 1899. Forward planning by streetcar companies facing strikes was not uncommon. See Henry, 'Brooklyn Trolley Strike,' 336.

91 This was the estimate of Rev. Thomas Wilson, quoted in *London Advertiser*, 12 June 1899.

92 *London Free Press*, 29 May 1899.

93 27 May 1899.

94 This was the essential passage of a resolution passed by London's Trades and Labour Council. Quoted in *London Free Press*, 2 November 1898.

95 *London Advertiser*, 26 May 1899. Essery was referring to the fact that Everett had recognized a union in Detroit.

96 Joseph T. Marks (1858–1932) was a London socialist, labour organizer, and journalist. Once prominent in the Knights of Labour, Marks helped rebuild London's labour movement in the years after the economic slump of the mid-1890s. During the period of this study, Marks was chief editor of the *Industrial Banner*, a staunch supporter of the streetcar unionists. See David R. Spencer, 'London's Forgotten Visionary: The Life and Times of Joseph T. Marks,' *London and Middlesex Historical Society* 19 (1992), 23–33.

97 *London Free Press*, 29 May 1899; *Industrial Banner*, September 1899.

98 *Industrial Banner*, September 1899.

99 Ibid.

100 *London Advertiser*, 23 May 1899.

101 *Industrial Banner*, November 1899.

102 *London Advertiser*, 17 June 1899. The editorial also noted that Henry Everett's complaints about 'imported labour agitators ... comes with bad grace from a corporation the controlling shareholder of which is not a citizen of Canada.'

103 See 'London Strike,' by University of Toronto political economist Prof. S.M. Wickett, *Globe*, 21 July 1899.

104 When the London Board of Trade met to discuss the strike in early July 1899, many members expressed sympathy with the union demand for arbitration of dismissals, opposition to Everett's evident determination 'to employ more detectives and starve the strikers.' *London Free Press*, 6 July 1899.

105 *London Advertiser*, 26 May 1899.

106 Public rallies in support of the streetcar men were not unknown in Cleveland (thousands of people attended a rally in Cleveland's downtown on 19 June for example), but they appear to have been a far less important means of cultivating support than in London.

107 *Cleveland Plain Dealer*, 26 July 1899. An editorial in the Democratic paper, the *Cleveland Press* concisely summarized this point: 'What is the Big Consolidated? A union. Public opinion that endures the organization of trusts in every commodity, from nursing bottles to coffins, will be very apt to be on the side of human organizations that struggle for recognition of their existence.' *Cleveland Press*, 13 June 1899.

108 *Harper's Weekly*, 4 August 1899.

109 Rev. Jackson, *Cleveland Press*, 17 June 1899.

110 *Cleveland Press*, 10 June 1899.

111 See, for example, the anti-unionist *Plain Dealer*'s account of the 'thousands'

who turned out for a union demonstration on 19 June 'People were packed
so tightly [on the streets],' the paper reported, 'that locomotion was seriously impaired.' *Cleveland Plain Dealer*, 29 June 1899.

112 *Cleveland Leader*, 29 July 1899.

113 Letter of labour activist Tom Moore to the *Cleveland Citizen*, 1 July 1899.

114 This according to the report on the Cleveland strike by a reporter from
London, Ontario. *London Advertiser*, 14 June 1899.

115 *Cleveland Press*, 12 June 1899.

116 In mid-June, forty Cleveland women, most of whom were not wives of
strikers, formed an league to coordinate fund-raising and relief for the
families of union men. *Cleveland Plain Dealer*, 17 June 1899.

117 A woman named Bertha Carr is alleged to have 'met every car that arrived
at the Public Square.' Although pro-union men were held back, police
permitted Carr to board Big Con cars in order to 'berate' replacement men
into joining the strike. *Cleveland Leader*, 13 June 1899.

118 *Cleveland Plain Dealer*, 17 June 1899.

119 Ibid.

120 'Moral suasion' was another phrase used to describe the peaceful entreaties
of London's strike sympathizers. See *London Advertiser*, 14 June 1899.

121 One man sheepishly admitted that he had 'scabbed' for a couple of days, but
only 'to pay for [his] wife's operation.' *Cleveland World*, 11 June 1899. In the
same days, a large group of men marched in a union parade under the
banner, 'Here from Buffalo by false representation, but we won't scab.'
Cleveland Plain Dealer, 11 June 1899.

122 Big Con cars were bombarded with bottles, rocks, and 'filth,' their drivers
menaced and roughed up. The Big Con also claimed that the union employed teams of bully-boys ('walking delegates') to terrorize any Cleveland
men tempted to cross the union picket line. *Cleveland Plain Dealer*, 11 June
1899.

123 See 'Eight Thousand people attack Holmden Avenue Barns,' *Cleveland Plain
Dealer*, 21 June 1899.

124 *Cleveland Plain Dealer*, 16 June 1899.

125 At one point, twelve employees of the Big Con were in the hospital as a
result of injuries inflicted by strike sympathizers. Big Con, Director's
Minutes, 17 January 1899.

126 See detailed daily accounts of the street violence in the *Cleveland Plain Dealer*,
15–20 June 1899.

127 It was reported that AASRE Treasurer Rezin Orr was prepared to give
'complete support, financial and moral' to the Cleveland strikers. Due to the
newness of the Cleveland division of the AASRE, however, 'financial

support' probably did not involve the $5 per week per man strike pay that the central union had paid striking members of other locals. See 'Money – Plenty in Sight for Strikers,' *Cleveland Plain Dealer*, 12 June 1899; Schmidt, *Urban Transportation*, 136–7.

128 See report in the *Cleveland Plain Dealer*, 9 June 1899.
129 See Everett's public statements, *London Free Press*, 7 November 1898; *Cleveland Plain Dealer*, 17 June 1899.
130 *London Free Press*, 7 November 1898.
131 *London Advertiser*, 17 June 1899.
132 *Cleveland Plain Dealer*, 14 June 1899.
133 *Cleveland Plain Dealer*, 8 June 1899.
134 Ibid.; *Cleveland Plain Dealer*, 11 June 1899. It was suggested by one newspaper that Everett was able to recruit new men so quickly because he was party to a collusive agreement of mutual support with other street railway barons. *Cleveland Press*, 13 June 1899.
135 See 'Pinks: They Are Said to be On Duty,' *Cleveland Press*, 14 June 1899. See also report in *Cleveland Press*, 27 July 1899.
136 Although Big Con officials routinely denied having Pinkerton men on the payroll, there is evidence to the contrary. At least two Big Con replacement men, Jacob Newman and Ferdinand Luke, were later charged with firearms offences. They admitted under oath that they had been sent from Chicago by the 'Pinkerton Detective Agency.' *Cleveland World*, 25 July 1899. For similar reports, see *Cleveland Leader*, 13 June and *Cleveland World*, 8 June 1899.
137 The Field Agency's detectives were reportedly less expensive than Pinkerton men. *Cleveland World*, 26 July 1899.
138 *Cleveland World*, 10 June 1899.
139 *Cleveland Press*, 8 June 1899. It was Everett's standard practice to send undercover detectives to 'mix' with strikers and their neighbours in order to gather intelligence. In November 1899, Londoners were reportedly 'astonished and indignant' to learn that the chief witnesses against a man accused of assaulting a non-union man were Cleveland-based plainclothes detectives in the employ of the Big Con. *London Advertiser*, 20 December 1899.
140 *Cleveland Plain Dealer*, 12 June 1899. The board, in existence since 1893, had no power to compel arbitration or settlement. A board report later blamed the Big Con for the failure of negotiations. Hough, 'Turbulent Spirit,' 187.
141 *Cleveland Plain Dealer*, 11 June 1899.
142 The question of comparative availability of injunctive relief will addressed in the final section.
143 *Cleveland Plain Dealer*, 9 June 1899.
144 *Cleveland Plain Dealer*, 10 June 1899.

145 Ibid.

146 *Cleveland Press*, 12 June 1899.

147 Ibid. Judge Dissette also pledged that the strikers would be given a full hearing before an injunction would issue.

148 *Cleveland Leader*, 12 June 1899. Although paid less than private detectives, replacement labour earned the ordinary wages of their predecessors plus premiums for food, lodging, and risk.

149 *Harper's Weekly*, 5 August 1899.

150 One replacement man told the *Cleveland Leader* that he was a 'professional strike-breaker. I do nothing else but go from one city to another wherever there is a strike. It is an exciting life, and it pays pretty well' (12 June 1899).

151 The private detectives who acted as streetcar men were said to be making over four dollars per day, or more than three times the wages of streetcar men. *Cleveland Leader*, 26 July 1899.

152 There was debate over the legality of the practice of carrying pistols. On 10 August, however, County Court Judge Fiedler ruled that it was not a crime for a Big Con man to carry a concealed weapon. *Cleveland World*, 10 August 1899.

153 *London Free Press*, 7 June 1899.

154 *London Advertiser*, 26 June 1899.

155 *London Free Press*, 4 July 1899.

156 Among those arrested: a warehouseman, a tinsmith, and a railway brakeman, all in regular employment. *London Advertiser*, 10 July 1899.

157 This narrative events was assembled from reports in the *London Advertiser*, and *London Free Press*, 10–12 July 1899.

158 See letter from Cameron to the Editor, *London Advertiser*, 12 July 1899.

159 It is a telling comment on Londoners' deeply rooted respect for authority that so many in the crowd might still be reasoned with, even in a moment of extreme excitement.

160 *London Advertiser*, 20 July 1899.

161 Ibid.

162 *London Free Press*, 10 July 1899.

163 Crown attorney Magee later claimed that seventeen of the LSR's eighteen cars in operation that day had been 'wrecked' in the 8 July riots. See *London Advertiser*, 21 July 1899.

164 Unlike Cleveland, a number of those arrested for unruly behaviour were strikers. See *London Advertiser*, 11 July 1899.

165 According to an eyewitness to the unrest of 8 July, the Rev. Dr. Johnston. *London Advertiser*, 14 July 1899.

166 See editorial opinion of *London Advertiser*, 11 July 1899, that the violence was spontaneous.

167 An estimated $5,000 per day in lost revenue. Reported in *Cleveland Leader*,
   14 June 1899 and *Harper's Weekly*, 5 August 1899.
168 *Cleveland Leader*, 11 and 14 June 1899. See also *Cleveland Leader*, 15 June 1899.
169 *Cleveland Press*, 14 June 1899.
170 Some replacement men had driven streetcars during the May 1899 strike in
   Wheeling, West Virginia. *Cleveland Press*, 14 June 1899.
171 Ibid.
172 See letter of W. Whitworth, *Cleveland Citizen*, 5 August 1899.
173 *Cleveland Press*, 14 June 1899.
174 *Cleveland Plain Dealer*, 17 June 1899.
175 *Cleveland Press*, 21 June 1899.
176 *Cleveland Plain Dealer*, 21 June 1899.
177 These positions the company already had conceded in the circular sent to
   the men before the strike started. *Cleveland Leader*, 23 June 1899.
178 Ibid.
179 Ibid.
180 The Big Con's press release alleged that the union attorneys were 'misleading the men, to undo all the negotiations which have taken place since the
   commencement of the strike.' Big Con, Directors' Minutes, 24 June 1899.
181 *Cleveland Plain Dealer*, 23 June 1899.
182 Members may not have been free to speak their minds or vote against
   popular resolutions during union meetings. The idea of a secret ballot had
   been rejected, leaving dissenters vulnerable to retaliation. Ibid.
183 See account of one beating, *Cleveland Leader*, 1 July 1899. At one point during
   the summer, the Big Con had twelve employees in hospital 'as a result of
   bodily injuries inflicted upon them while in the proper discharge of their
   duties.' Big Con, Annual Meeting, 17 January 1900.
184 *Cleveland Plain Dealer*, 21, 23 July 1899.
185 One reporter alleged that the Big Con had, in effect, 'discharged twenty-
   seven union men.' See Edwards, *Harper's Weekly*, 5 August 1899. See also
   Cleveland World, 2 July 1899.
186 See *Cleveland Press*, 17 July 1899.
187 *Harper's Weekly*, 5 August 1899.
188 *Cleveland Press*, 19 July 1899.
189 On 21 July, the Big Con's board of directors decided, 'after considerable
   informed discussion, ... that there was no strike in existence, and hence the
   question was not to be arbitrated.' Big Con Directors' Minutes, 21 July 1899.
190 See speech of Rev. Brotherton, *Cleveland Leader*, 27 July 1899.
191 In the course of the summer of 1899, complaints (issuing mainly from
   members of the city's wealthy business community) about the inadequacy of
   Cleveland's police force became commonplace. See, for example, *Cleveland*

Plain Dealer, 30 June 1899. The comparative statistics on the size of police forces in large American cities tend to support the view that Cleveland's force was undersized. Buffalo, a city of almost identical population, had 782 police officers (to Cleveland's 355) in 1899. Another Ohio city of similar size, Cincinnati, had 531 police officers, Detroit 513. See Report of the Dept. of Police, *Annual Reports of the City of Cleveland*, 1900, 696.

192 As Mayor John Farley stated in an 1899 report to city council: 'The incoming of my administration found the department in a very demoralised condition. The pandering to vice for political reasons ... had reduced the police service to a degree of utter disloyalty to duty.' Mayor's Report, *Annual Reports of the City of Cleveland*, 1900. The dubious implication of this statement is that the character of the force changed under Farley's administration.

193 During a streetcar strike in 1894, four constables were fired for 'sympathising with strikers.' See Whipple, 'Cleveland in Conflict,' 162. For complaints about the suspect loyalty of the police during the strike of 1899, see *Cleveland Plain Dealer*, 1 July 1899; *Cleveland Leader*, 31 August 1899. In July 1899, one patrolman was discharged from the force after having been overheard to state that he 'wouldn't eat with goddamned scabs.' *Cleveland World*, 10 July 1899. Later in July officers were transferred in from the suburbs in hope that they might 'enforce the law.' *Cleveland World*, 14 July 1899. In August, police were criticized by the *Plain Dealer*, for having 'fraternised with the mob and allowed their sympathies to overcome their obligations.' *Cleveland Plain Dealer*, 10 August 1899.

194 In *Policing a Class Society: The Experience of American Cities, 1865–1915* (New Jersey 1983), Sidney L. Harring argues that in at least two industrial cities of the era, Buffalo and Milwaukee, the police forces were willing and efficient instruments of repression during strikes. This interpretation does not square with the evidence concerning the Cleveland strike of 1899.

195 'It is quite doubtful,' the *Plain Dealer*, reported on 30 June, 'if there are many businessmen in Cleveland who do not believe the police force of the city is entirely inadequate to the city's needs.'

196 Letter to R.A. Harmon from R.H. Harmon, 28 June 1899, Case Western Reserve Historical Society (CWRHS).

197 *Cleveland World*, 17 July 1899.

198 Ibid., 20 July 1899.

199 *Cleveland Leader*, 21 July 1899.

200 *Cleveland Plain Dealer*, 21 July 1899.

201 Ibid.

202 The first troops to arrive were two divisions of the naval reserve. These were reinforced by two companies of Troop A, Company K, and Battery B,

reserve infantry and artillery of the Ohio National Guard. *Cleveland Leader,* 22, 23 July 1899.

203 '[I]f bombs are thrown into our property,' Everett stated, 'we are entitled to all available protection.' *Cleveland Plain Dealer,* 22 July 1899.

204 Ibid.

205 *Cleveland Plain Dealer,* 23 July 1899.

206 In late July and August, there was growing alarm among the city's business elite about the spectre of violent class warfare. Everett and other Big Con officials had received death threats. An elderly Mellon banker was assaulted. On 12 August, a streetcar was blown up in Cleveland's 'richest neighbour-hood,' doors away from the house of J.D. Rockefeller. *Cleveland Plain Dealer,* 12 August 1899. The city's 500 leading businessmen already had begun to organize a private army under the auspices of a 'Law and Order League.' *Cleveland Leader,* 6 August 1899; *Cleveland Plain Dealer,* 10 August 1899.

207 *Cleveland Plain Dealer,* 25 July 1899. The nineteen-year-old victim was the only fatality directly attributable to the strike. The driver was later charged with second degree murder. *Cleveland Leader,* 26 July 1899.

208 It was said that Carr was preparing to approach the U.S. district attorney about the commencement of the application. *Cleveland World,* 24 July 1899.

209 *Cleveland World,* 22 July 1899.

210 See, for example, the hostile editorials of *London Advertiser, Woodstock Sentinel, Stratford Herald,* reported in the *London Advertiser,* 11–14 July 1899.

211 The military intervention cost the city about $4,000. This was seen as an enormous waste of public funds. See the *London Advertiser,* 20 July 1899.

212 The police commission deputized private detectives because of the obvious inadequacy of the local police force in times of public unrest. After the July riots, the commission confidentially (but unsuccessfully) requested that the Toronto force lend them the 'services of an Inspector, two Sergeants, and 25 constables.' Police Commission Minutes, LRA, W7M34-F7, 18, 22 July 1899.

213 See the *London Advertiser,* 25 July 1899.

214 During a police commission meeting, Magistrate Parke allegedly accused the mayor of having been 'frightened' into calling out the militia. *London Advertiser,* 12 July 1899.

215 See, for example, criticism of Parke by local businessman J.H. Ginge, *London Free Press,* 6 July 1899, and by Crown Attorney Magee, 31 July 1899. Magee publicly lamented the fact that no 'examples' had been made of those convicted of public order offences. At that point in time, not one of the half-dozen union men charged with strike-related offences had been convicted. *London Advertiser,* 7 November 1899. See *London Free Press,*

16 October 1899 for an editorial critical of Parke's lenient treatment of public order offences.

216 Elliott wrote of the 'free right of every man to seek and obtain employment from whomever he chooses.' See letter to the editor, republished in *London Advertiser*, and the *London Free Press*, 18 July 1899. Elliott had expressed the same view in a charge to a grand jury in June. See the *London Free Press*, 14 June 1899.

217 The commission consisted of the mayor, chief of police, the crown attorney, police magistrate, and county court judge. The central point of contention was the advisability of acceding to the LSR's request for police protection of a resumed night service. *London Advertiser*, 12 July 1899.

218 Jenkins had been on the force for twenty-one years and was said to have compiled 'a splendid record as an upright, courteous, discreet and most efficient officer.' *London Free Press*, 14 July 1899.

219 Although the precise nature of the allegation was never made public, Jenkins appears to have accused Police Chief W.T. Williams of covering up a police beating. *London Advertiser*, 20, 24 July 1899. Having failed in attempt at reinstatement with the police, Jenkins became an alderman in 1900. He then attempted (unsuccessfully) to get Williams fired. *London Advertiser*, 6 February 1900.

220 The precise financial figures will be discussed in the final section of the essay.

221 *London Advertiser*, 12 August 1899.

222 See reprinted in *London Advertiser*, 21 August 1899.

223 See Rev. Ludlow's article, *London Advertiser*, 22 August 1899.

224 *London Advertiser*, 4 September 1899.

225 Ibid.

226 *Cleveland Leader*, 25 July 1899.

227 Strikers had frequently issued statements urging people to refrain from violence. See, for example, union executive C.O. Pratt's statement condemning the use of dynamite. *Cleveland Press*, 25 July 1899.

228 *Cleveland Plain Dealer*, 29 July 1899.

229 For this typology of boycotts, see Haggai Hurvitz, 'American Labor Law,' 310. See also Gregory R. Zieran, 'The Labor Boycott and Class Consciousness in Toledo, Ohio,' in Charles Stephenson and Robert Asher, eds., *Life and Labor: Dimensions of American Working-Class History* (New York 1986), 134.

230 Perhaps fearing the possibility of injunction, the same executives later denied that *they* had called for the boycott against city merchants who did business with boycott offenders. See *Cleveland World*, 5 August 1899.

231 Soldiers were also subjected to boycott. When grocers refused to sell to the

militia's quartermaster, an outraged General Axline threatened to feed his troops in restaurants and bill the retailers. *Cleveland Plain Dealer*, 30 July 1899.

232 *Cleveland Leader*, 1 August 1899.

233 *Harper's Weekly*, 4 August 1899.

234 *Cleveland Citizen*, 12 August 1899. In an open letter to the strikers, real estate broker M.M. Brown conceded that 'a large part of the people of Cleveland have stood by you [the strikers] ... and have willingly suffered great inconvenience and personal sacrifice for your cause.' Brown described how thousands of working people had lost time, wages, even jobs, rather than patronize cars driven by strike-breakers. See Brown, letter to the editor, *Cleveland Plain Dealer*, 16 August 1899.

235 *Cleveland World*, 4 August 1899.

236 11 August 1899.

237 'Working-men generally, and the retail merchants of all classes,' *Harper's Weekly* reported, 'joined the boycotting with little hesitancy.' 4 August 1899. 'Never in the history of Cleveland,' the *Citizen* stated on 12 August, 'have the unions and the working people stood behind the strikes more unitedly.'

238 *Cleveland Plain Dealer*, 4 August 1899. *Harper's* magazine described how Herbert Murray, a cashier in a downtown bank, had been unable to buy anything in his neighbourhood of residence for weeks after he had been seen riding a Big Con car (5 August 1899). In another incident, two women were arrested on 1 August for screaming 'Scab women!' and threatening the wife of a policeman known to ride Big Con cars. *Cleveland Plain Dealer*, 2 August 1899.

239 *Cleveland Press*, 31 July 1899.

240 *Cleveland Plain Dealer*, August 1899.

241 A fund was also raised to provide rewards for the arrest of dynamiters, and for the organization of a permanent 'Law and Order League.' *Cleveland Plain Dealer*, 10 August 1899.

242 Legal opinion appears to have been divided on the applicability of the civil rights statute to the boycott. Others argued over the vulnerability of boycotters to prosecution under conspiracy or antitrust law. No such prosecutions were attempted. See *Cleveland Leader*, 2–3 August 1899.

243 *London Advertiser*, 16 November 1899.

244 *London Advertiser*, 7 November 1899.

245 The thirteen grand jurors were empanelled from a list of county property owners. Only two were from the City of London, eleven from outlying farm districts. *London Free Press*, 15 November 1899; *London Advertiser*, 21 November 1899.

246 *Cleveland Plain Dealer*, 4 September 1899.

247 *Cleveland Plain Dealer*, 6 August 1899.

248 Even the socialist paper acknowledged this fact, while putting it down to a spate of 'cool weather.' *Cleveland Citizen*, 10 September 1899.

249 *Cleveland Plain Dealer*, 15 September 1899.

250 'The *Citizen* believes that the working people of this city, the strikers and boycotters, deserve to be congratulated for the splendid battle they put up against [the Big Con].' *Cleveland Citizen*, 14 October 1899.

251 *Cleveland Citizen*, 30 September 1899.

252 At least two union men, Fred Goodacre and John Dare, were prosecuted for throwing stones at streetcars. Both were convicted. *London Free Press*, 22 December 1899; *London Free Press*, 1 February 1900.

253 At least a dozen Londoners were convicted of strike-related offences, many for incidents occurring during the July riots. Most were jailed for one or two months and fined. At least two stone throwers (and one perjurer) received penitentiary sentences. Most of the accused were employed at the time of their offence and had no previous criminal convictions. See the *London Free Press*, 1 February 1900.

254 *London Free Press*, 16 December 1899.

255 The strike against the LSR appears to have continued throughout 1900. In November, the LSR's annual report noted that the strike had had 'no ill-effects' for many months. The Cleveland strike was called off on 8 May 1900, when 300 union men were offered their old jobs back.

256 In January 1900, the LSR's board of directors told shareholders: 'The men now running the cars are a superior staff ... to those formerly employed.' LSR, Annual Meeting, 24 January 1900.

257 In London, the LSR had steadfastly refused the applications of former employees 'until such time as the strike and the boycott were declared off.' LSR, Directors' Minutes, 14 October 1899. The LSR, with a workforce of only 100 men, appears neither to have wanted or needed union men to return to work. The labour needs of the Big Con were much larger and, in May 1900, some 300 (of more than 800 who had gone on strike) union men were reinstated. The men went back on the old terms of employment. See Hough, 'Turbulent Spirit,' 189.

258 See the works cited in notes 7–8 above. See also Karen Orren, *Belated Feudalism: Labor, the Law and Liberal Development in the United States* (Cambridge 1991) and Victoria C. Hattam, *Labor Visions and State Power: The Origins of Business Unionism in the United States* (Princeton 1993).

259 According to William Forbath, 'During the Gilded Age the labour injunction became the principal vehicle of judicial intervention in labour disputes.'

American Labor Movement, 59. For a recent historical account of the labour injunction in the early twentieth century, see Ernst, *Lawyers Against Labor*, 55–6.

260 In this view, by 1914 judicial intervention into labour conflicts had deflected organized labour away from political action and toward AFL-style 'business unionism.' See Victoria Hattam, 'Economic Visions and Political Strategies: American Labor and the State, 1865–1896,' in Karen Orren and Stephen Skowronek, eds., *Studies in American Political Development* (New Haven 1990), 4:103–5. See also Forbath, 'American Labor Movement,' 1205, and Naylor, 'Bringing the State back In?,' *Labour/Le travail* 36 (1995), 317–28.

261 See, e.g., William Forbath, 'The Shaping of the American Labor Movement,' *Harvard Law Review* 102 (1989), 1126–9.

262 This is not to suggest that the prevailing theses, *ipso facto*, are wrong, only that they are overgeneralized. An inexactness of chronology is part of the problem. The extant scholarship is imprecise as to when the direct coercion of courts became the decisive factor in American labour disputes. Was it as early as the 1890s, or in the years immediately prior to the First World War? A second problem pertains to the frequency and efficacy of judicial intervention. Just how routinely were court orders sought? Were they routinely effective in breaking strikes? (Forbath concedes that at the height of the period of 'government by injunction' in the 1920s, fewer than 25 per cent of strikes generated injunctions. *American Labor Movement*, 61.)

263 See Tucker, 'Faces of Coercion,' note 8.

264 Tucker and Fudge, 'Responsible Unions,' note 8.

265 Injunctions were issued against Canadian strikers only nineteen times in the 2,400 strikes that occurred between 1900 and 1914. Tucker and Fudge, 'Responsible Unions,' 115; Tucker, 'Faces of Coercion,' 335–6.

266 Tucker, '"That Indefinite Area of Toleration": Criminal Conspiracy and Trade Unions in Ontario, 1837–77,' *Labour/Le travail* 27 (1991), 14–51.

267 Tucker, 'Faces of Coercion,' 278.

268 Tucker, 'Faces of Coercion,' 278; Tucker and Fudge, 'Responsible Unions,' 87. By the 1890s, a great many urban Canadians had new American employers. The historical repercussions of this fact have not been much studied.

269 See, e.g., Tucker, 'Faces of Coercion,' 328–30; Tucker and Fudge, 'Responsible Unions,' 90–1.

270 For suggestions regarding comparative historical methodology I relied on Theda Skocpol and Margaret Somers, 'The Uses of Comparative History,' *Comparative Studies of Society and History* 22 (1980) 175–97, and particularly their 'contrast of contexts' model, 178–9.

271 As Peter Burke has noted, comparative approaches to history are worth-

while 'primarily because they enable us to see what is not there.' As quoted in Gregory S. Kealey and Greg Patmore, 'Comparative Labour History: Australia and Canada,' *Labour/Le travail* 38 (1996), 2–15.

272 Interestingly, street railway strikes of similar scale in Brooklyn (1895) and Houston (1898, 1900) were also untouched by labour injunctions. See Henry, 'Brooklyn Trolley Strike,' note 38 and Robert Ziegler, 'The Limits of Power: The AASRE in Houston, Texas, 1897–1905,' *Labor History* 18 (1977), 71.

273 Eric Tucker has observed that law was used against labour 'much more coercively in the United States than in Ontario' during the 1880s. 'Faces of Coercion,' 337. It is undoubtedly true that in some American places and with regard to some Gilded Age strikes, the state exerted more force against labour than ever was seen in Ontario. However, the London and Cleveland strikes demonstrate that this different capacity for coercion was not always utilized, even in the context of very large-scale and violent strikes.

274 The London strike did not generate an enormous increase in prosecuted public order offences. The total number increased by only seventy-seven cases (from 1,011 to 1,088) from the previous year. About sixty of the additional prosecutions were strike-related. More than half of these accused were acquitted. See London Police, Record of Offenses, 1898–1900, Talman Regional Collection, University of Western Ontario.

275 The total number of arrests for the period June through September 1899 was 6,164, compared to 5,566 for 1898. (The number of arrests ballooned to 7,405 in the same months of 1900.) There were 305 more arrests for disturbance and disorderly conduct in 1899 than 1898. Report of the Department of Police, *Annual Reports of the City of Cleveland*, 1898–1900.

276 For this phrase, and a comprehensive study of the 'scientific' reorganization of work in Gilded Age America, see Sarah Lyons Watts, *Order Against Chaos: Business Culture and Labor Ideology in America, 1880–1915* (New York 1991), ix–xii, 1–10.

277 For a general account of the 'scientific management' movement and the transformation of the Gilded Age workplace, see Richard Edwards, *Contested Terrain: The Transformation of the Workplace in the Twentieth Century* (New York 1979), 18–22, 37–60.

278 For a vigorous defence of the 'partial, essentially defensive character of most worker struggles' during the Gilded Age, see Lawrence T. McDonnell, '"You Are Too Sentimental": Problems and Suggestions for a New Labor History,' *Journal of Social History* (1984), 642–54.

279 In his 1977 article on the London strike of 1899, Bryan Palmer claims that 'collective working class management over the processes of work' emerged as a central theme of the union and its sympathizers. '"Give Us the Road,"'

122–3. Apart from occasional appeals to the idea that municipalities should operate street railways there is little evidence to support this contention. Pro-union rhetoric concentrated on the legitimacy of collective bargaining and on public frustration with American corporate control of a vital public service. Generalized attacks on the legitimacy of capitalist enterprise did not figure prominently in the mainstream of pro-union propaganda.

280 Lyons, *Order Against Chaos*, 1.

281 'It should be a proud boast of the citizens of London,' the *Banner's* editorialist added, 'that they are not the kind of material that a Yankee monopolist can crush.' *Industrial Banner*, September 1899.

282 According to one contemporary observer, the London streetcar men were that city's first 'non-skilled union outside of regional railways.' *Cleveland World*, 18 August 1899. This according to the account of Cleveland minister, Rev. Arthur Ludlow. Ludlow had been sent to London to compile a report on the strike.

283 17 June 1899.

284 14 June 1899.

285 See the account of the Brown Machine Company strike of 1896 in Hough, 'Turbulent Spirit,' 182–3. So intense was the street rioting during this strike that over 700 militia troops spent a month policing the streets.

286 By 1901, the spiralling cost of new interurban projects forced the Everett-Moore syndicate into receivership. Only a series of shrewd reorganizations saved it from financial collapse. See Hilton and Due, *Interurban Railways*, 27–8.

287 13 June 1899.

288 Ibid. No specific evidence was offered to substantiate the claim (one made frequently by the *Cleveland Press* and other papers during the summer of 1899) that Everett was actively colluding with other streetcar magnates to crush the labour movement within their industry. For a similar allegation, see *Cleveland Leader*, 6 August 1899.

289 *Cleveland Citizen*, 16 June 1899. As the *London Advertiser*, 21 August 1899, put the same point: 'The pressure of the unemployed ... gave the victory to the Company, and the places of the strikers have been filled ... the fact remains that there are men ready and eager to fill every vacancy.'

290 This prediction was based on past experience. The military had been called out to quell strike violence in Cleveland on numerous occasions in the 1890s. Troops had played a key role in ending the crowd violence associated with the 1894 strike against an Everett's street railway. See Hough, 'Turbulent Spirit,' 180–2. State troops had intervened in over 300 labour disputes in the period 1886–95. Montgomery, *Citizens Workers*, 95–7. Although the military

had not been called upon to deal with strike-related violence in London, Ontario prior to July 1899, troops had intervened in over a score of other Canadian strikes before 1900. See Desmond Morton, 'Aid to Civil Power: The Canadian Militia in Support of Social Order, 1867–1914,' *Canadian Historical Review* 51 (1970) 406–25.

291 *Cleveland Leader*, 25 July 1899.

292 Ibid. Farley reportedly requested that Adjutant General Axline prepare to send an additional 1,000 state troops.

293 The cost of military intervention – $4,000 in London, over $28,000 in Cleveland – was footed by the ratepayers of London and the taxpayers of the State of Ohio respectively. See the *London Advertiser*, 20 July 1899; Annual Report of Adjutant-General, Executive Documents of Ohio, 1899, 558.

294 The LSR had net earnings of $48,000 on $113,000 of gross revenues. The boycott slashed revenues to $59,950 in 1899, generating an operating loss of nearly $7,000. See Onn, 'London Street Railway,' Chart D.

295 Ibid.

296 The projected gross earnings for 1899, based on five successive years of increases, was $1,850,000. The strike cost the Big Con at least $300,000.

297 Everett's Cleveland firm, Kline, Tolles et al., was to be paid a $6,000 retainer for 1900, $1,000 more than in 1899. Big Con, Directors' Minutes, 25 January 1900. In September 1899, the London firm of Hellmuth and Ivey received an additional $2,000 'for extra services consequent upon the strike.' LSR, Directors' Minutes, 1 September 1899.

298 Rev. L. Banks, *Cleveland Leader*, 19 June 1899.

10

Gooderham & Worts: A Case Study in Business Organization in Nineteenth-Century Ontario

C. IAN KYER

INTRODUCTION: INCORPORATION AND BUSINESS FORM IN NINETEENTH-CENTURY ONTARIO

Gooderham & Worts was one of Canada's most important nineteenth-century businesses. It operated a very profitable, vertically integrated milling, distilling, shipping, and cattle operation. For fifty years, from its inception in 1832 until its incorporation in 1882, the business was run as a partnership (initially of William Gooderham and James Gooderham Worts and later of W. Gooderham, J.G. Worts, and George Gooderham). The partners consistently rejected incorporation of their business, although they did invest their profits in a series of incorporated businesses, including the Toronto and Nipissing and the Toronto, Grey and Bruce railroads as well as the Bank of Toronto and the Canada Permanent Building and Savings Society.[1]

Why did the partners chose to operate other than as a corporation for so long, and why did they chose to incorporate when they did? In analyzing these questions I have drawn on the seminal work of Dick Risk on the interplay between the law and the economy in nineteenth-century Ontario, particularly his article on the evolution of incorporation law.[2] I have tried to build on the foundations laid down by Risk and others,[3] for while we know a good deal about the formal development of the law, we know little about how businessmen viewed and used that law, particularly about the choices they made when given the option to incorporate.

The corporate legislation of nineteenth-century Ontario was of three kinds.[4] Some statutes created individual corporations. Between 1841 and 1867 approximately two hundred corporations were founded by such special acts of the legislature. Public utilities such as gas, light, and water services, harbours; canals; bridges; roads; and railroads were incorporated in this way in the 1840s and the 1850s, and in the latter decade they were joined by financial institutions like banks and insurance and loan corporations. After 1855 some manufacturing and mining corporations were created. As we shall see, William Gooderham and his partner James Gooderham Worts invested in and controlled a number of these special act corporations. A second kind of legislation was the general incorporation statute, twelve of which were enacted between 1836 and 1864. These statutes 'established terms that authorized the creation of corporations by private individuals or by public authorities.' The early ones permitted the creation of mutual insurance corporations, building societies, and toll roads. The categories for incorporation without legislative intervention were significantly broadened in 1850 to permit banks, manufacturing, and mining businesses to incorporate. A third type of corporate legislation is described by Risk as 'statutes that established terms that governed all corporations or all corporations of a specified kind.' The earliest, dating from the 1830s, provided 'a few simple terms for all corporations.' By 1851, it was thought that more comprehensive terms should be specified for all railroad corporations. In 1861, the provisions of the 1860 general incorporation statute for manufacturing and mining corporations were extended to most future business corporations, other than railroads.

Risk makes two arguments about this legislation that I will consider in my analysis of Gooderham & Worts. First, he notes that the principal method of carrying on business was partnership, which had been 'adopted in Ontario without significant modification' of English law. That is, despite its increasing availability 'the corporation was ... not the ubiquitous form of business organization it has become.' While it was used quite extensively for transportation and financial businesses, 'none of the retailing and wholesaling businesses and only a few of the significant manufacturing businesses were corporations.' Partnership was used 'far more extensively than the corporation,' even 'for relatively large and complex businesses.' As I will demonstrate below, the history of Gooderham & Worts supports this assertion.

Risk's second argument concerns the origins of incorporation legislation and the factors that went into a particular business's decisions to take advantage of it. He suggests that the legislation was in part the product of businessmen seeing the investment advantages of limiting the liability of shareholders for the debts of corporations,[5] and in part the result of the attraction of the corporate form as an administratively convenient form of organization. 'The corporation,' he argues, 'offered an impersonal and enduring form for litigation, ownership of property and other rights, and commercial transactions, and offered a form that enabled a comparatively simple accommodation of unified management of a business and limited investments, by the managers or by strangers.' In addition, 'the corporation became an easily used standard form for usual allocations of functions and powers in business.' At the same time, while incorporation did bring with it some lessening of businessmen's freedom of action, the state 'imposed only a small degree of regulation on corporations.' The history of Gooderham & Worts suggests that we should modify some of these conclusions. First, although by modern standards the regulation may seem minimal, it did discourage incorporation for these men. There was concern about the fact that limited liability gave rise to greater restrictions on corporations than on partnerships. Second, while incorporation may have been attractive to some businesses for the reasons Risk suggests, Gooderham & Worts was eventually incorporated for a quite different reason.

GOODERHAM & WORTS AND THE BUSINESS FORM IN NINETEENTH-CENTURY ONTARIO

The story of the Gooderham and the Worts families is entwined to such an extent that it is common practice to treat them as one.[6] Few families in nineteenth-century Toronto were as influential in the business community, and few were so close-knit. They not only carried on business together, they lived and prayed together. The families occupied large adjoining estates on Front Street just north of the distillery and just south of the evangelical Anglican Little Trinity Church, of whose congregation they were ardent members. Both William Gooderham and James Gooderham Worts served as church wardens for over thirty years, and during that time 'the parish functioned rather like a proprietary chapel, with Gooderham, his nephew and partner James Gooderham Worts, and some other captains of industry and commerce of St. Lawrence ward as the benevolent proprietors.'[7]

Their story begins in 1831, when James Worts, a miller from Great Yarmouth, England came to Toronto (then called York) with his thirteen-year-old son, James Gooderham Worts, to establish a milling business.[8] They were sent ahead to prepare the way for other members of their extended family, who were to follow with William Gooderham, James's brother-in-law. Father and son constructed a windmill at the mouth of the Don River, to the southeast of the town. The next year William Gooderham arrived with fifty-four people (including servants and eleven children who had been orphaned on the journey) and £3,000, a substantial fortune at that time.

James Worts and William Gooderham chose to organize their business as a partnership under the name Worts and Gooderham. The choice of a partnership in 1832 was natural. Incorporation was not then common or perhaps even possible for a milling business – sole proprietorships and partnerships were the order of the day. In law, a partnership is defined as two or more persons carrying on a business in common with a view to profit.[9] The Worts and Gooderham partnership could carry on any lawful business. It had the powers of the natural persons who were its constituent partners; unlike a corporation, it was not a separate legal entity. The partners were the business and the debts of the partnership were their debts. Unless otherwise agreed all partners were equal and each could bind the partnership.[10] At the time of this first partnership and throughout the periods that the Gooderhams and the Worts were in partnership, there was no partnership legislation, although from at least 1870 there was a requirement to file a notice of the formation and dissolution of a partnership.[11]

The Worts and Gooderham partnership was dissolved in 1834, when, following his wife's death in childbirth, James Worts committed suicide by throwing himself down the family well. Worts's interest in the partnership assets passed to his son, a minor. William Gooderham in essence adopted his nephew, James Gooderham Worts, and assumed sole control of the milling operation. He carried on business as a sole proprietor under the name 'William Gooderham Company.' In 1837 William took the step that would create the family fortune. He expanded the business to include a distillery to use surplus grain. Four years later he started a cattle operation to use by-products of the distillery. In 1845, William Gooderham and his nephew James, now twenty-seven, went into partnership under the name Gooderham & Worts. Again, this was a common practice; it was neither usual to incorporate nor entirely clear that businesses of this sort could do so at this time.

In 1846 the partnership, faced with the need to bring grain from the United States for its distillery and to ship finished product to other parts of the United Canadas and the United States, expanded its operations to shipping and built its own schooners for use on the Great Lakes. Seeking control over the factors contributing to the success of this operation, Worts took an active role at the first meeting of the Canadian Ship Owners' Association, held in June 1857, and served on the board of the Toronto Harbour Commission from 1856 to 1863 and as its chairman from 1865 to 1882.[12]

It was in the 1850s that Gooderham and Worts began to become significantly involved in corporations. They did so, however, solely where the business was of a sort that was only carried on through a corporation – savings banks, saving societies, and railroads – and in each case what they sought and ultimately achieved was family control of the corporate business in which they invested. Both Gooderham and Worts played key roles in the Toronto Exchange, which was incorporated by special act in 1854 at the request of the Association of Merchants, Millers, and Businessmen to provide grain merchants with office space and a forum for buying and selling grain and other produce.[13] Although neither William Gooderham nor James Gooderham Worts are listed as incorporators of the Exchange, both were directors by 1856 and their partnership moved its offices into the Exchange Building.[14]

Both partners also became quite knowledgeable about and active in a series of corporations in which the families invested their profits, including the Bank of Toronto and the Canada Permanent Building and Savings Society, both of which were incorporated in 1855 by special act. Their partnership, with other members of the Association of Merchants, Millers, and Businessmen, was among the original incorporators of the Bank of Toronto and they made a substantial investment in it. Worts served on its board from 1858 to 1882, and from 1863 he was the bank's second largest stockholder. In 1864, Gooderham became president of the bank and Worts its vice-president, positions they would hold until their deaths.[15] Worts was also on the board of Canada Permanent and his son-in-law, William Henry Beatty, became first its vice-president and later its president.

Given their need for railroad services, the partners considered railway companies a natural extension of their operations.[16] In the 1850s Worts made a short-lived and costly investment in the Ontario, Simcoe and Huron Railroad Union. His unsuccessful experience with this railroad may have influenced the decision of the partners to invest in two narrow gauge lines promoted by George Laidlaw, a former employee. Both the Toronto and Nipissing Railway and the Toronto, Grey and Bruce Railway were incorporated in 1868, with William Gooderham one of the directors named upon the incorporation of the former.[17] In 1870, the partners made substantial loans to both railways to help give their bonds market value.

Gradually, their control over the operations of these railways increased, and they were especially influential in the operation of the Toronto and Nipissing, whose Toronto terminus was located next to their distillery. Gooderham & Worts was, in fact, the main customer of the railroad. In 1873 Gooderham's oldest son, William Gooderham Jr, became its president, a post he would hold until 1882. As Dianne Newell has noted, '[a]lthough family control of a railway built with much public funding did not escape criticism, defenders of the line pointed to the need for Gooderham's capital to launch the enterprise and to finance its chief activity, which involved buying cordwood in the north and storing it to season before transporting it for sale in the city.'[18]

Their significant role in this series of special act corporations shows that the partners had no aversion to incorporation as such and no lack of acumen in achieving control of such organizations. Assessing why they did not use the corporate form for their principal businesses tells us a good deal about the nineteenth-century businessman and the nature of incorporation in that era. One important reason was the inherent conservatism of these two men. C.M. Blackstock, in a recently published book based on an extensive collection of family letters, characterizes the Gooderhams as having 'many laudable virtues: integrity, generosity, and a strong social conscience,' but she also argues that '[f]or all their wealth, they were modest and shunned publicity' and that they were 'exceedingly conventional.'[19] William Gooderham in particular 'epitomized conservatism.' An adherent of an evangelical Anglican sect, 'he practised its precepts in daily living, held family prayers twice daily, and observed a strict Sabbath.' These were not the sort of men who sought out novel ways of carrying on business.

Social and religious conservatism, however, does not tell the whole story. The Gooderhams were a tightly knit family who liked to keep all their dealings under close personal control. The 'Gooderham network' was 'closely bound by blood and trade, ... a Family Compact in itself.' William's advice to his sons is said to have been 'Stick together boys.' In 1872 T.N. Gibbs, a member of Parliament soliciting funds to finance the Pacific Railway, approached James Gooderham Worts, but was rebuffed. As he told Sir John A. Macdonald: 'If assured half a million as the result he would not enter into it. His ideas are and his partner's the same, that wealth is only of service so long as it can be made to minister to the comfort and ease of its possessor. Any other obligation than those of self & family are ignored. They seem to have a natural aversion to have anything to do with matters not under their own immediate control.'[20]

Family businesses were common in nineteenth-century Canada, and many families looked to other family members for their business associates as well as their legal and other professional needs.[21] The Gooderham and Worts families perhaps took 'clanship' further than most. In any event, their conservatism, their desire to keep things in the family, and their consequent desire to control the enterprises in which they invested, are themes that run throughout the Gooderham and Worts business history and help to explain why they favoured the more traditional and more flexible and unregulated vehicle of partnership over the more novel and somewhat regulated corporate form.

Nineteenth-century incorporation law ran counter, to some extent, to the families' instincts. For example, the general incorporation statute for mining, manufacturing, mechanical, or chemical concerns enacted in 1850 was likely of little interest to them. For one thing, the objects for which a corporation could be created under this statute were limited and it may well have been that a diversified business like Gooderhams & Worts did not qualify. There was no mention in the list of permitted businesses, for example, of milling, distilling, or cattle raising.[22] In 1850 corporations could only carry on businesses within their statutory objects, and to do otherwise was to act *ultra vires*, or beyond their powers.[23] This does not mean that they could not have incorporated; given the flexibility of special incorporation laws they could have sought and would likely have received special incorporation legislation.

But the limited nature of corporate objects under the 1850 statute was not the only problem. The statute may have been 'a milestone in Canadian corporate law,'[24] but the process it created must have seemed awkward and unnecessary to Gooderham and Worts. To initiate the incorporation of a manufacturing, shipbuilding, mining, mechanical, or chemical business, five or more persons had to sign a declaration, acknowledged in duplicate before the registrar or register (or either's deputy) of the county in which operations were to be conducted. The result was 'a body politic and corporate,' a separate legal entity that would 'have succession' (it would not be dissolved by the death of a principal as was the case with a partnership). The new entity was capable of suing, being sued, and buying and selling real or personal property for the purposes of its operations. It was, however, prohibited from mortgaging its property and it had a limited life (not to exceed fifty years). A corporation created in this way was to be managed by between three and nine 'trustees,' who had to be shareholders, British subjects, and elected annually by the shareholders, each of whom had one vote per share. The trustees were to elect from their number a chairman or president.[25] The shareholders enjoyed limited liability, but only after all the capital provided for in the incorporating declaration had been paid in, either when the shares were first acquired or after subsequent calls by the trustees and a certificate to that effect had been provided. The 1850 statute also required that a sign with the name of the company and the amount of its capital was to be posted in some conspicuous place in every building where the business was carried on, and this information was also to appear on every promissory note, draft, cheque, order, bond, contract, and bill of lading. Failure to do this made the trustees personally liable for the note, bond, or agreement. As well, each year an annual report was to be published in a local paper listing the capital of the company together with the amount of its debts; again, failure to do so led to personal liability for the trustees.

All of these measures, enacted 'for greater certainty of persons dealing with any such Company,' would likely have seemed intrusive to Gooderham and Worts, who were unaccustomed to such rules or restrictions. There was no financial disclosure for a partnership. No one but Gooderham and Worts knew what their capital or debts were, and one assumes they had no wish for the public disclosure of either. In addition, incorporation would also bring with it an unneeded structure. What did the partners want 'trustees' for? The two of them adequately managed the business by and for themselves. As for shareholders, why would the partners want to share their business with others? Family members were already adequately provided for by the two patriarchs.[26] Perhaps most importantly, they likely saw no countervailing benefits from incorporation. They had a highly profitable business.[27] They did not need to sell shares to strangers to raise capital. Nor is it likely that they thought that they needed limited liability. William Gooderham had been in a wide variety of businesses for eighteen years, and adroit management had avoided serious problems.[28] In addition, being bankers and mortgage lenders,[29] they were likely of the view that people should pay their debts.

The partners do not seem to have changed their opinion at all in August 1856 when George Gooderham, William's third son,[30] became a partner in Gooderham & Worts.[31] Although George brought energy and a clarity of vision that contributed to a major expansion of the business, he seems to have shared the views of his father and cousin on the advantages of partnership.

Two further general incorporation statutes were passed in 1860 and 1864.[32] The first permitted incorporation by judicial decree, but seems to have been little used. The second, which built upon the 1850 general statute, provided for incorporation on application to the governor-in-council for the issuance of letters patent of incorporation. Once the letters patent were issued the new company was governed by general provisions somewhat improved from the 1850 act. The prohibition on mortgaging of the company's property had been removed, the company no longer needed to be of limited duration, and 'trustees' were now called directors. In addition, more flexibility was allowed in internal structure through an expanded power to vary the statutory scheme through the corporation's by-laws, and the limitation of liability provisions were significantly more favourable to shareholders. For the three partners, however, nothing had changed by 1864 to make incorporation necessary or more desirable. The advantages still did not, in their minds, outweigh the disadvantages.

THE INCORPORATION OF 1882

The decision to incorporate in 1882 resulted from the deaths of the two original partners. William Gooderham died in August 1881. This was certainly not unexpected, for he was ninety-one years old and in poor health. On his death the partnership was dissolved, and, after William's interest was distributed in accordance with his will, Worts and George Gooderham formed a new partnership, on 11 February 1882.[33] Then on 20 June 1882, only four months later, James Gooderham Worts died, at the age of sixty-four, of malaria.[34] Worts's death was unexpected and created serious problems. For the first time in the fifty-year history of the business, partnership law presented a difficulty. Under that law the death of a partner dissolved the partnership. The interest of Worts was to be distributed in accordance with his will and that will did not contemplate the continuation of the existing business for more than one year.

James Gooderham Worts's will, which included a series of codicils,[35] made some specific bequests and then left the residue of his estate to his sons, James Gooderham Worts Jr and Frederick Worts, and sons-in-law, W.H. Beatty (the lawyer who drafted the will and codicils), Alfred Morgan Cosby, David Smart, Edward Strachan Cox, and Robert Myles, in trust for his children. The will authorized the executors 'to continue any business in which I may be engaged at the time of my decease for one year after my decease if they see fit.' That is, the will appeared to require his business interests to be sold in no more than a year after death. He further provided that 'the residue of the income arising from my said estate [was] to increase and accumulate for [a] period of ten years ... At the end of the said period of ten years [the trustees were] to pay over to each of my said sons, if then alive, the seventh part or share of my estate as such share then exists ... [and] to pay over quarterly [thereafter] without power of alienation or anticipation to each of my daughters, if then alive, the income arising from the one-seventh part or share of my said estate as such share then exists for the period of the natural life of each of my daughters.' Worts's will also authorized the trustees 'to invest the moneys of my estate in such securities as they shall think proper,' with power to retain any investment existing at his death that they thought appropriate.

The provision that seemed to require the sale of Worts's interest within a year must have created great concern for George Gooderham. He faced the prospect of having to raise a very substantial amount of money to acquire Worts's share of the business, having a third party acquire the interest, or winding up the business and selling off the assets. None of these prospects would have been very appealing. But W.H. Beatty and his partners suggested a way to avoid these options, of preserving the status quo and yet complying with the terms of the will and trust. On 1 August 1882, just a few months after Worts's death, Thomas Gibbs Blackstock, a member of Beatty's firm, prepared an agreement between George Gooderham and the trustees and the beneficiaries of the trust created by Worts's will to incorporate a company to be known as Gooderham & Worts Limited.[36] The Worts's interest in the partnership was to be valued and those funds invested in the capital stock of the new corporation. The remaining shares were to be held by George Gooderham and his sons, William George Gooderham and Albert Edward Gooderham.[37] The agreement dealt with a number of management and ownership matters. To ensure adequate cash for any contingencies it stipulated that up to one-third of the profits of the company were to be retained in a reserve fund and not paid to the shareholders as dividends. To facilitate the provision in the will calling for a ten-year investment period, it provided for the eventual purchase by George Gooderham of the trust's interest in the new corporation.

As noted, not only the trustees but also the beneficiaries signed the agreement. This was probably done because of the conflict of interest the Beatty firm had; they were counsel to James Gooderham Worts, George Gooderham, and the other members of the Gooderham and Worts families. The firm had prepared the will that created the trust, and Beatty himself was a trustee and a beneficiary under the will, being 'bequeathed' Worts's seat on the board of the Bank of Toronto. Despite these seemingly conflicting interests it was a member of the firm, Tom Blackstock, who prepared the agreement between George Gooderham and Beatty and the other trustees and Blackstock was anything but a disinterested legal counsel. He had joined the Beatty firm in 1879 through the intervention of his uncle, James Gooderham, the second son of William Gooderham, who, like Blackstock's father, had married into the prominent Gibbs family. Shortly thereafter Blackstock became engaged to Harriet Victoria Gooderham, one of George Gooderham's daughters, and they were married early in 1880. Blackstock would later play an important role assisting George Gooderham in operating the distillery and other family businesses.[38]

The incorporation permitted the Worts family to maintain their interest in the business and saved George Gooderham the expense and uncertainty of the other options. But did it comply with the trust? Seven years later in an action seeking interpretation of the will brought by the executors and trustees, their legal counsel would argue that the will provided 'very unlimited powers of investment' and that 'no new moneys were invested in this business.' Referring to the power of the trustees to retain existing investments as well as their power to invest the money from the then current business, he would state that the trustees 'here retained the investment, but did not continue the business; they retained the investment and formed a joint stock company to which they turned over the whole business.' 'In one sense they retained the money in the business, in another they invested the money in the business. We say both the retention and the investment were authorized. We say there is here no breach of trust.'[39] In essence the argument was that James Gooderham Worts had stipulated that the trustees were to continue his current business for only one year. That business was a partnership, and it had not been continued beyond the stipulated one year. The will had then provided that on discontinuance of the business the money was to be invested in 'securities.' The incorporation of 'Gooderhams and Worts Limited' had created securities – shares of the incorporated business.

This was result-oriented legal analysis at its best, and arguably corrrect. One cannot help but wonder, however, if it was consistent with the intention of James Gooderham Worts. W.H. Beatty gave evidence under oath in the subsequent legal action that what had been done was in fact consistent with Worts's intent, but the court was not impressed.[40] Chancellor Boyd held that '[t]echnically there was a breach of trust,' and that the use of the money was an 'improper investment.' The clause in the will that authorized the trustees 'to invest in such securities as they shall think proper ... with power to retain any investments existing at his death as long as they shall see fit' did not mean that they could effectively continue 'the prosecution of the business he was engaged in,' because 'at the longest that was to end in a year.' Nor did it 'justify any change of form such as made here, whereby a partnership was superseded by a company of limited liability.' For Boyd this 'was not *retaining* the moneys in the shape left by the testator; nor was it retaining any *investment* existing at the time of his death. For *investment* is not a proper term as to moneys in trade, and the testator has not used it in any popular sense, because he speaks of investing in connection with securities and does not regard his business as an investment ... The direction to invest in such securities as the trustees shall think proper – that does not justify the putting of the estate into personal security much less into a trading concern.'[41]

This decision, however, was years in the future. In 1882 the immediate question was where to incorporate. At that time companies could be incorporated under the 1874 Ontario Joint Stock Companies' Letters Patent Act,[42] or federally under the 1869 Companies Act.[43] The issue of whether to incorporate federally or provincially was then much on lawyers' minds. The case of *Citizens Insurance Co. of Canada v. Parsons*[44] had recently found that there was a valid federal power to incorporate companies. The choice between a federal and provincial incorporation hinged on the words 'companies with provincial objects' in the British North America Act and the words 'objects to which the legislative authority of the Parliament of Canada extends' in section 3 of the federal Companies Act. Beatty and his firm chose to incorporate federally, probably because of the territorial scope of the company's operations. It was then commonly thought that an Ontario corporation could not carry on business outside the province.[45] The objects of the newly incorporated business specifically stated that the business could be carried on in and be extended 'to any or all of the Provinces of the Dominion of Canada.'

Whether incorporating federally or provincially, the procedure was to petition the government. At least five persons who were to be shareholders in the company were required to complete the petition. The petition had to be advertised in the appropriate *Gazette* one month before the petition was made, and like the petition itself the advertisement had to set out the full names, addresses, and occupation of the petitioners, as well as the name of the proposed company, its objects, place of business, amount of capital stock, share structure, names of the three or more shareholders who would be directors, the stock to be taken by the petitioners and how it had been paid for (cash, services, transfer of property, etc.) The petition was to be signed by all petitioners and their signatures confirmed by statutory declaration of witnesses. The name of the company could not be the name of any existing company. Statutory declarations were required to prove compliance with these regulations.

It was suggested above that one of the reasons for not incorporating was that partnership enabled the firm to maximize the diversity of its operations. Small surprise, then, that the objects of the new corporation were drafted both to include all existing operations and to ensure as much flexibility as possible. The objects were:

(a) To carry on the business at one time carried on by the late James Gooderham Worts and George Gooderham as distillers, maltsters, etc., at the City of Toronto;

(b) To carry on the said business in and to extend the same to any or all of the Provinces of the Dominion of Canada, and generally to carry on in all or any of the Provinces of the Dominion of Canada, manufacturing, distilling, rectifying, aging, buying and selling and dealing in all kinds of spirituous or alcoholic liquor and malting and any business which may be appropriately or conveniently carried on in connection with such business;

(c) To carry on the business of warehousing, elevating and forwarding;

(d) To do all such things as are conducive to the above objects;

(e) To carry on any business which may be necessary or expedient for the consumption or economic use of the refuse of any such manufacturers;

(f) To construct, maintain and alter any buildings or works necessary or convenient for the purposes of the company; and

(g) For the purposes of such business to acquire by grant, lease or otherwise real estate and buildings and to sell and otherwise dispose thereof.

The letters patent for the new corporation were issued on 24 November 1882.[46] They provided that George Gooderham and the trustees of the estate of the late James Gooderham Worts, together with William Henry Beatty, William George Gooderham, James Gooderham Worts, Albert Edward Gooderham, and Thomas Frederick Worts were 'created, a Body Corporate and Politic, under the name of "GOODERHAM AND WORTS (LIMITED)".' The capital of the company consisted of twenty thousand shares of $100 each. Of this two million dollar share value, $1.6 million was paid in and deposited in the Bank of Toronto. Some 12,202 of the shares, 61.1 per cent of the total, were owned by George Gooderham, with the trustees owning most of the rest – 7,748 shares, or 38.74 per cent. The remaining fifty shares were held, ten each, by W.H. Beatty and four of the Gooderham and Worts children – W.G. Gooderham, J.G. Worts, E.A. Gooderham, and T.F. Worts. The small size of these holdings suggests that these shares were what would later be called qualifying shares. That is, they gave the corporation more than the minimum number of shareholders it required under the act and qualified these individuals to be directors. It also suggests that it was thought that the shares held by several of these individuals as trustees did not qualify them as shareholders and directors. The name of the corporation, with 'Gooderham and Worts's in quotation marks and 'limited' in brackets, strongly suggests that while the family was seeking an 'enduring form' it did not wish the 'impersonal form' of which Risk speaks. The intent seems clearly to have been to emphasize the family connections and the link with the past partnership. The letters patent ensured that control remained with the families by stating that none of George Gooderham's shares could 'be transferred to a stranger so long as any Shareholder [was] willing to purchase the same at the prescribed price' (essentially equal to the amount paid up on the shares.) There was an exception for transfers by his executors or administrators to any of his sons or daughters or sons-in-law or grandchildren. These restrictions did not apply to the trust shares or the qualifying shares.

Gooderham and Worts was obviously not created for the reasons Risk suggested – limited liability, investment by strangers, and administrative utility. But that does not mean that other corporations were not. The incorporation of Gooderham and Worts can be contrasted with another incorporation carried out by the Beatty firm in 1883.[47] In that year the firm incorporated and organized the Fergus Brewing & Malting Company under the Ontario Joint Stock Companies' Letters Patent Act. As in the case of Gooderham and Worts, this was a situation involving an existing business, the small brewing and malting business of Holland & Co., commenced twelve years before. Here, however, a number of individuals were seeking to acquire and finance the business. They chose to incorporate because they needed to raise capital. It is likely that their potential investors would have wanted the protection that a limited liability company would provide. The number of shareholders and provisional board members was similar to Gooderham and Worts, although the amount they paid for their shares was not. In this case, seven persons, five from Fergus, one from Orangeville, and one from Guelph, agreed to pay $100 for each share in the company to be incorporated and to act as provisional directors. Three of the petitioners were to receive a hundred shares each, representing an investment of $10,000. The other shareholders received between five and twenty shares.

Unlike 'Gooderham and Worts' (Limited), this new corporation needed to raise additional capital – $50,000. Beatty's firm put together a prospectus to assist in these efforts. Unlike the modern prospectus, which is essentially a disclosure document, this one was a sales pitch. After setting out the seven provisional directors, the bankers of the company, and their 'secretary pro tem,' it stated that the company was being formed to acquire and carry on, on an enlarged scale, the brewing and malting business of Holland & Co. It noted that the business had expanded 'upon the excellent reputation which its products have always enjoyed, to about 5,000 barrels per year.' Potential investors were assured that 'this output can readily be increased with the aid of additional capital for the necessary building and plant ... A business of 10,000 barrels per annum can be reckoned on, which would result in a very handsome profit upon the investment being contemplated.' The prospectus went on to talk of the 'remarkably fine water' in Fergus and of 'barley of the best quality' being grown in the vicinity. It touted the fact that '[t]axes are light, wages low and fuel cheap,' and insisted that the 'profits of brewing are large' and that, given all the conditions, 'it is reasonable to expect the maximum return from this enterprise.'

Although the incorporation procedure was similar in each case, the respective motivation could not have been more different. In each case an existing business was incorporated, but one did so to overcome problems of succession and the other to raise capital from outside investors. One adapted its structure to fit within the corporate requirements without changing the family nature of the business, using qualifying shares held by family members, restrictions on share ownership, and a shareholders' agreement, while the other took advantage of the corporate statute to structure its operations and to assure potential investors that this was a good investment.

CONCLUSION

In a number of respects the history of Gooderham & Worts shows that Risk's arguments about nineteenth-century incorporation, made a quarter of a century ago, can stand the test of time. Like most significant manufacturing businesses, the firm favoured the more flexible and less regulated partnership structure to incorporation and the problems that would cause. Limited liability was less important to William Gooderham and James Gooderham Worts than the simplicity and control that partnership gave them. That history also demonstrates that transportation corporations, like the two narrow gauge railroads they invested in, and financial institutions like the Bank of Toronto and Canada Permanent, did use the new legal structures available to them. Had the two original partners not died within a few months of each other in 1881–2, Gooderham and Worts would most likely have continued as a partnership for some time. In assessing Gooderham and Worts' choice of partnership rather than corporation it is important to recognize the legal and economic environment in which they were operating. There was much less flexibility in incorporation law in the nineteenth century than there is today. Corporations were primarily used to facilitate investment by strangers to the management of the company, and limited liability was a necessary evil to induce these strangers to put their money into someone else's operation – in the nineteenth century it was not needed to shield businessmen from personal tax liability or the kind of costly litigation associated with products liability laws or created by environmental and other forms of regulation. For Gooderham and Worts partnership offered a flexible and largely unregulated way of carrying on business. The way that they protected their investment was to ensure that they had control of the corporations in which they invested. They trusted to their own business acumen and business ethics and those of the people with whom they dealt. Gooderham and Worts neither needed nor wanted the shield of limited liability that incorporation provided.

This story also reveals that Risk's general analysis does not fit all cases. When 'Gooderham and Worts' (Limited) was incorporated it was for reasons not discussed by Risk. Their story is, I suspect, a relatively unusual one, although just how unusual it is not possible to say. While we can draw general conclusions about the reasons why particular types of legal action may be taken, such action is always shaped to fit the particular circumstances. Despite their business acumen, the one problem the partners could not avoid was that partnerships are dissolved in death and death comes to all of us. The legal manoeuvering resorted to deal with the Worts will demonstrates how lawyers fashion solutions to fit unique conditions.

NOTES

1 Information on Gooderham & Worts is culled from a variety of sources. For published material see my work on the history of Fasken Campbell Godfrey, the successor law firm to Beatty Blackstock their nineteenth-century legal advisers: 'New Light on an Old Firm,' *Law Society of Upper Canada Gazette* 18 (1984), 205–9, and 'The Transformation of an Establishment Firm: From Beatty Blackstock to Faskens 1902–1915,' in C. Wilton, ed., *Inside the Law: Canadian Law Firms in Historical Perspective* (Toronto: University of Toronto

Press for The Osgoode Society for Canadian Legal History 1996). See also my
biographical sketches, 'William Henry Beatty,' 'Edward Marion Chadwick,'
and 'David Fasken' in *Dictionary of Canadian Biography* (Toronto: University of
Toronto Press 1966–), 14:42–3 and 15, forthcoming [hereafter *DCB*]. William
Henry Beatty was the son-in-law of James Gooderham Worts and the
confidant and chief adviser of George Gooderham. Under Beatty, the firm
was in many respects the Gooderham & Worts family firm, serving the legal
needs of both the Gooderham and the Worts families and their businesses.
There are two very detailed contemporary accounts of the Gooderham &
Worts businesses: 'Annual Review of the Trade of Toronto for 1861,' *The
Globe*, 7 February 1862, and 'Canadian Manufactures No. IV, One of the
Largest Distilleries in the World, Gooderham & Worts, Toronto,' *The Mail*,
23 April 1872. I have also drawn on the correspondence of Gooderham &
Worts in the Baldwin Room at Toronto Public Library. One of those letters
complete with engravings showing some of the partnership's buildings,
describes Gooderham & Worts as 'Distillers, Maltsters & Millers,' while
another describes them as 'Distillers, Millers, Maltsters & Linen Manufacturers.' For an overview of nineteenth-century Canadian business history see M.
Bliss, *Northern Enterprise: Five Centuries of Canadian Business* (Toronto:
McClelland & Stewart 1987). For other case studies see P. Baskerville, ed., *The
Bank of Upper Canada: A Collection of Documents* (Toronto: Champlain Society
1987) and M. Denison, *The Barley and the Stream: The Molson Story* (Toronto:
McClelland & Stewart 1955).
2 R.C.B. Risk, 'The Nineteenth-Century Foundations of the Business Corpora-
tion' *University of Toronto Law Journal* 23 (1973), 272–301. This was one of a
series of essays on law and the economy, which are summarized in R.C.B.
Risk, 'The Law and the Economy in mid-Nineteenth-Century Ontario: A
Perspective,' in D. Flaherty, ed., *Essays in the History of Canadian Law: Volume
One* (Toronto: University of Toronto Press for The Osgoode Society for
Canadian Legal History 1981). On the importance of these articles see D.
Flaherty, 'Writing Canadian Legal History: An Introduction,' in ibid., 8–9.
3 Other work on incorporation in nineteenth-century Canada includes F.E.
LaBrie and E.E. Palmer, 'The Pre-Confederation History of Corporations in
Canada,' in J.S. Ziegel, ed., *Studies in Canadian Company Law: Volume 1*
(Toronto: Butterworths 1967) 33; B. Patton, 'From State Action to Private
Profit: The Emergence of the Business Corporation in Nova Scotia,' *Nova
Scotia Historical Review* 16 (1996), 21–60, and J.-M. Fecteau, 'Les petites
republiques: les compagnies et la mise en place du droit corporatif moderne
au Québec a milieu du 19e siècle,' *Histoire sociale/Social History* 25 (1992), 35–
56. Also of interest on the incorporation of public utilities in the nineteenth

century is C. Armstrong and H.V. Nelles, *Monopoly's Moment: The Organization and Regulation of Canadian Utilities, 1830–1930* (Philadelphia: Temple University Press 1986).

4 This summary of nineteenth-century incorporation law is drawn principally from Risk, 'Nineteenth-Century Foundations.' The quotations that follow are from 272, 281, 298, 300, and 301.

5 In Ontario public debate about the extent of the liability of shareholders for debts of corporations were less frequent and less passionate than in England and the United States, and limited liability seems to have been more easily accepted: see ibid., 298.

6 See, for example, 'Messrs. Gooderham and Worts' in *The Canadian Biographical Dictionary and Portrait Gallery of Eminent and Self-Made Men* (Toronto: American Biographical Publishing Company, 1880–1), 62–70. See also the statement that 'Worts' career was so closely linked to the business interests of his uncle that ... their joint achievements cannot easily be separated': D. Newell, 'James Gooderham Worts,' *DCB* 11:937. The family history information in this paragraph is culled from the biographical entries cited above and from D. Newell, 'William Gooderham,' *DCB* 11:358–60; J.M.S. Careless, *Toronto to 1918: An Illustrated History* (Toronto: Lorimer 1983); and J. Ross Robertson, *Robertson's Landmarks of Toronto: Volume Two* (Toronto: Robertson 1896), 812–13.

7 A.L. Hayes, *Holding Forth the Word of Life: Little Trinity Church 1843–1992* (Toronto: Corporation of Little Trinity Church 1991), 11.

8 The following material on the Gooderham & Worts businesses is drawn in part from sources in the archives of the Toronto Dominion Bank and those of Fasken Campbell Godfrey, as well as newspaper accounts and other materials. For a listing of these materials see S.A. Otto, 'Gooderham and Worts Heritage Plan, Report No. 4, Inventory of Archival Sources, March 1994.' I have also used the following secondary sources: D. Newell and R. Greenhill, *Survivals: Aspects of Industrial Archeology in Ontario* (Erin, Ont.: The Boston Mills Press 1989), 85; Newell, 'James Gooderham Worts'; and J. Schull, *100 Years of Banking in Canada: The Toronto-Dominion Bank* (Toronto: Copp Clark Publishing 1958), 39–42.

9 This is the current definition, as it appears in the Partnership Act, RSO 1990, c. P5, s. 2. The first Ontario act on the subject was passed in 1920 and based on the English Partnership Act of 1890 (53 & 54 Vict., c. 39), which represented a codification of the common law. See *Lindley on the Law of Partnerships*, 15th ed. (London: Sweet & Maxwell 1984), 4. The definition of partnership in the first half of the nineteenth century was essentially the same. Although the second, 1867, edition of *Lindley on the Law of Partnership* refused to define partnership, it did say that '[a]greement that something shall be attempted with a view to

gain, and that the gain shall be shared by the parties to the agreement, is the grand characteristic of every partnership': vol. 1, p. 1. And by 1884 F. Pollock, *Digest of the Law of Partnership*, 3rd ed. (London: Stevens 1884), 1, gave a substantially similar definition to the modern one. This summary of partnership law is based principally on the 1867 edition of *Lindley on the Law of Partnership*.

10 This presumption of equality could be overcome by a written agreement or by clear and unequivocal evidence of conduct or the manner of keeping of the books of the partnership. There is no evidence that there ever was a written partnership agreement for Gooderham & Worts or other evidence of inequality of shares.

11 The registration of the 1856 change in the partnership, adding George Gooderham, was registered 5 April 1870 in the York County Copartnership Registry as doc. no. 59 (Archives of Ontario (AO)).

12 Worts and his son-in-law, William Henry Beatty, were also very active in the Toronto Board of Trade. Worts served as president from 1865 to 1869, and a portrait of him donated to the board by Beatty hangs in the board offices in downtown Toronto. See also *Souvenir: A History of the Queen City and her Board of Trade* (Toronto: Toronto Board of Trade 1893).

13 An Act to Incorporate The Toronto Exchange, *SC*, 18 Vict., c. 54 (1854).

14 *Toronto City Directory*, 1856; W. Dendy, *Lost Toronto: Images of the City's Past*, rev. ed. (Toronto: McClelland & Stewart 1993), 45; E. Arthur, *Toronto: No Mean City*, 3rd ed. (Toronto: University of Toronto Press 1986), 116–18. The *Directory* lists Gooderham & Worts as both distillers and commission merchants, suggesting that they also bought and sold grain.

15 In the 1882 *Annual Report* of the Bank of Toronto, the one that followed the deaths of the two men, George Gooderham gave the following assessment of their contribution to the success of the bank: 'During the year we have to regret the loss by death of two of the Bank's Presidents, Mr. Wm. Gooderham and Mr. J. G. Worts. The former was President of the Bank for 17 years, the latter Vice-President for 23 years, and succeeded to the Presidency on the decease of Mr. Gooderham. Let me briefly review the affairs of the institution during the regime of these two gentlemen. When Mr. Worts became Vice-President in July 1858, the Bank's Capital was $427,200; Rest, $20,000 – 5 per cent. of Capital; Circulation, $252,873; Deposits, $139,698; Discounts, $643,085. When Mr. Gooderham was elected President in July, 1864, the Capital was $800,000; Rest, $100,000 – 12 1/2 per cent. of Capital; Circulation, $460,855; Deposits, $863,660; Discounts, $1,661,227. Both worked hand-in-hand in the interest of the Bank from the time they became connected with it, and now on their decease, and at the close of the year's business, the position

of the Institution as is stated in the report, namely: Capital, $2,000,000; Rest, $1,000,000 – 50 per cent. of the Capital; Circulation, $1,194,367; Deposits, $3,730,470; Discounts, $6,937,863. Since the commencement of business 26 years ago, the Bank has paid 15 Dividends at 8 per cent., 3 at 10 per cent., 4 at 12 per cent., 4 at 7 per cent. Being an average of 8.69 per annum during the whole period, and in addition adding nearly $40,000 yearly to the Rest, likewise the Capital was increased $1,200,000, and allotted to the Stockholders at 5 per cent. premium, at a time when the Rest averaged 50 per cent. of the Capital, thereby giving them a clear Bonus of 45 per cent. or $540,000; but supposing the Stockholders instead sold their new Stock at the market value when the allotment was made, they would have profited to the extent of 40 per cent. on $200,000, 80 per cent. on $500,000, 94 per cent. on $500,000 – in all $950,000. I therefore venture to state there is not a Bank in the Dominion that has in this respect so largely contributed to the profits of its Stockholders as the Bank of Toronto.'

16 In 1877 the *Montreal Gazette* stated that 'they employ railroads and steam to bring 700,000 bushels of cereals to their vats every year': quoted in *The Canadian Biographical Dictionary*, 65.

17 An Act to Incorporate the Toronto, Grey and Bruce Railway Company, and An Act to Incorporate The Toronto and Nipissing Railway Company, *SC*, 31 Vict., cc. 40 and 41 (1868). For Laidlaw's role see Newell, 'James Gooderham Worts,' 938. There is a brief description of these railroads in R. Brown, *Ghost Railways of Ontario* (Toronto: Broadview Press 1994), 33–9 and 66–75.

18 Newell, 'William Gooderham,' 359.

19 C.M. Blackstock, *All the Journey Through* (Toronto: University of Toronto Press 1997), 16–18.

20 Ibid.

21 See D. McCalla, *The Upper Canada Trade, 1834–1872: A Study of the Buchanan's Business* (Toronto: University of Toronto Press 1979); L. Deschenes, 'Les enterprises de William Price,' *Histoire sociale/Social History* 1 (1968), 16–52; G.B. Baker, 'Law Practice and Statecraft in Mid-Nineteenth-Century Montreal: The Torrance-Morris Firm 1848–1868,' in C. Wilton, ed., *Beyond the Law: Lawyers and Business in Canada 1830–1930* (Toronto: University of Toronto Press for The Osgoode Society for Canadian Legal History 1990), 45–91; M. McCallum, 'Law and the Problems of Succession at Ganong Bros' and B. Austin, 'Structural Adaptation in a Family Firm: Hamilton Cotton, 1832–1891,' both in P. Baskerville, ed., *Canadian Papers in Business History: Volume II* (Victoria: Public History Group, University of Victoria 1993).

22 The limited nature of the permitted objects is seen in the fact that year after

year additional objects were added by legislation: see the statutes in Risk,
'Nineteenth-Century Foundations,' notes 18–27.

23 On pre-Confederation corporate law see F.W. Wegenest, *The Law of Canadian
Companies* (Toronto: Burroughs 1931), 20–7. The law is different today; federal
and Ontario corporations have all of the powers of a natural person.

24 T. Hadden et al., *Canadian Business Organizations Law* (Toronto: Butterworths
1984), 26.

25 In the nineteenth century the president of a corporation acted as chairman of
the board and was generally not in an operational position.

26 The two patriarchs personally controlled most of the family assets including
many houses of their children. For example, James Gooderham Worts
(together with George Gooderham) were the owners (in trust) of the home of
William Henry Beatty, Worts' son-in-law. The house was in the area known
as University Park (between present day College Street on the south, Bloor
Street on the north, Bay Street on the east, and St George on the west).
Beatty's house, The Oakes, was built in 1875 for more than $14,000, a fortune
at that time, on lots 12 and 13 on the south-west side of Queen's Park Cres-
cent, almost immediately south of where the legislative buildings would be
built about fifteen years later. It was an immense corner property with an
effective frontage of 400 feet. Even though the house was large and there was
a stable at the rear of the property the lot dwarfed the buildings, leaving a
large expanse of lawn and room for a sizable pond. There are extensive
materials on the plans for and the building of the house in the University of
Toronto Archives: see A73-0008/010. For a description of the role that The
Oakes played in the social life of Toronto in the late 1800s and early 1900s see
'Mrs. W.H. Beatty Saw 75 Years of Toronto Life,' in the Toronto *Telegram*,
21 May 1928.

27 Gooderham and Worts were among the wealthiest men in Toronto. In 1877
the *Montreal Gazette* stated: 'To sum up their business briefly – they have the
largest distillery in the world; they feed more cattle, directly and indirectly,
than are fed by any one establishment outside of Texas; they run a railway to
the great benefit of Toronto and the northern country, and they own a bank
which there is none in this country ranking higher in public confidence':
quoted in *The Canadian Biographical Dictionary*, 65. They each died leaving
estates in the millions of dollars even after giving substantial amounts to
Toronto General Hospital and other institutions: see the obituaries of William
Gooderham and James Gooderham Worts, both in *The Globe*, 22 August 1881
and 21 June 1882.

28 One gets some insight into their views in the yearly commentaries in the

Annual Reports of the Bank of Toronto of James Gooderham Worts in 1864 and William Gooderham from 1865 to 1881, copies of which are in the Archives of the Toronto Dominion Bank. They show them to have been men of vigilance and caution, carefully monitoring the economic performance of the country, guarding against downturns and business failures and stressing sound banking principles. For example, in 1872, at a time of 'remarkable prosperity,' Gooderham, based on 'the experience of former years,' warned against 'undue expansion in view of the reaction which must in time supervene.'

29 For their mortgage-lending activities see *Beaty v. Gooderham* (1867), 13 Grant's Chancery Reports 317 and *Gooderham v. The Traders Bank* (1888), 16 OR 438.

30 William Gooderham's first and second sons, William Jr and James, both became Methodists and preached against the consumption of alcohol, and for that reason did not wish to be partners in a business so heavily involved in liquor: see Blackstock, *All the Journey Through* and L. Johnson, 'William Gooderham,' *DCB*, 9:360–1.

31 See Dean Beeby, 'George Gooderham,' *DCB*, 13:387–90. The documents for the dissolution of the partnership of William Gooderham and James Gooderham Worts and the formation of the new partnership are in the Ontario Archives, see note 11, supra.

32 See Risk, '19th Century Foundations,' 276–7.

33 Affidavits of J.G. Worts and G. Gooderham attesting to the change in the partnership were registered in the Registry office for the City of Toronto, Copartnership register, Book 2, doc. 2567 CP (AO). See also AO, 2565–6 CP, the file cards showing the new partnership was effective 11 February 1882. The new partnership, of J.G. Worts and George Gooderham, had the same name as the old.

34 See his obituary in *The Globe*, 21 June 1882.

35 The will was made on 11 January 1878 and the codicils on 27 September 1880, 14 November 1881, and 4 and 22 May 1882: see *Worts v. Worts* (1889), 18 OR 332.

36 A partial copy of the agreement showing that it was prepared by Blackstock is in the Archives of the Toronto Dominion Bank. A summary of the agreement is in Otto, 'Gooderham and Worts Heritage Plan.' It is also summarized in *Worts v Worts*, 337.

37 For these men see 'Albert Edward Gooderham' and 'William George Gooderham' in *A Standard Dictionary of Canadian Biography 1875–1933*, 2 vols. (Toronto: Trans Canada Press 1934), 2:174–6.

38 On the Blackstock family see Blackstock, *All the Journey Through*; for the marriage see *Toronto City Directory*, 1881. Thomas Gibbs Blackstock was named after his grandfather, Senator Thomas Gibbs, who had joined William

Henry Beatty and William Gooderham Jr as promoters of the Confederation Life Association in 1870.

39 *Worts v. Worts*, 337.

40 Chancellor Boyd said this of Beatty's evidence: 'I may mention that evidence was tendered as to the wishes of the testator respecting the business of Gooderham and Worts, which I considered not material (even if admissible), having regard to the opinion.' *Worts v. Worts*, 343.

41 *Worts v. Worts*, 340; emphasis in original.

42 RSO 1877, c. 150.

43 An Act Respecting Joint Stock Companies Incorporated by Letters Patent, SC 1869, c. 13.

44 (1879–80), 4 SCR 215; affirmed (1881–2), 7 AC 96 (PC).

45 See Wegenest, *The Law of Canadian Companies*, 30. The company registered in Ontario as an extraprovincial corporation in 1900. A copy of the extra-provincial charter as well as a typescript of the original federal letters patent can be found in the Ontario Archives: Licences – Extra Prov. Corp. Lib. 3, p. 44 (R6 53-41).

46 AO, TC 1312 (43-28-25-2-12). Copies of the letters patent are also in the files of the Companies Branch of Consumer & Corporate Affairs, Ottawa.

47 The following is taken from a file in the archives of Fasken Campbell Godfrey.

11

The Sacred Rights of Property: Title, Entitlement, and the Land Question in Nineteenth-Century Prince Edward Island

MARGARET E. McCALLUM

'To cultivate land is one thing, to own it is another, and these two things must not be confused.' So commented the monk Bulloch on observing a murder in *Penguin Island*, Anatole France's satirical account of the development of civil society among a flock of penguins transformed into humans after being baptized by a near-sighted Christian abbot. The abbot is appalled at the violence, but Bulloch applauds it, because thereby the murderer establishes ownership of the fields of the victim and lays the foundations for law, property, and social order.[1] E.P. Thompson taught us to think of class as a relationship and of law as imbricated in that relationship, as in all relationships. Property is also a relationship, or, more accurately, a multiplicity of relationships.[2] Any relationship requires ongoing negotiations over how power will be exercised within the relationship: by whom, on what terms, and for what purposes. The possibility for renegotiating the exercise of power imports some fluidity into the property relationship. Thus, the meaning of property is not immutable in all times and places, but can be redefined as individuals and the state redefine the relationships encompassed by property rights. Such redefinitions have occurred at many points in the history of the common law world: in 1833, when slaves were freed in the British Empire; in 1870, with passage of Gladstone's Irish Land Act; in the First World War in Canada, when most jurisdictions prohibited the manufacture or sale of alchoholic beverages without compensation to owners of breweries, distilleries, or taverns; and in Prince Edward Island in 1875, when large landlords were compelled to sell their estates to the government for resale to tenants and squatters.

This chapter examines the meaning of property and property ownership as they were debated and defined in the struggle to end landlordism
on Prince Edward Island. Historical studies of how property comes to be
redefined provide a useful corrective to current hegemonic assertions of
the sacred rights of private property and the efficacy of market relations.
As Gregory Alexander argues, '[h]istorical "tradition" provides no shortcut
to any political end concerning the role of private property. There is no
single past to which we can return.'[3] To provide the context for the
particular debate about property that is the focus of this chapter, I begin by
introducing the history of the land question from its colonial beginnings
until 1875, when compulsory sale legislation forced the proprietors to part
with their estates. I then examine the arguments about property that were
articulated in Island newspapers and at public hearings into the land
question in the 1860s and 1870s.[4] Early historians of Prince Edward Island,
like many of the Islanders they write about, viewed Island history as the
struggle of stalwart tenant farmers against tyrannous absentee landlords.
There was some attention to parallels with the struggle of the Highland
Scots and Irish against their landlords, but little attempt to place Island
history in this broader context. Recent scholarship offers more complex
and nuanced accounts of land ownership, political allegiance, and class
relations on the Island, although much remains to be done in documenting
changes in land ownership, describing the social and economic relations of
landlords and tenants, and analysing investment opportunities and capital accumulation.[5] Historians have yet to examine the impact of the leasehold system on Island law, particularly methods of assessing liability for
land taxes and valuing land for taxation purposes, procedures for obtaining and enforcing judgments for debt, attempts to compel local registration of land titles, changes to the law to require landlords to compensate
tenants for their improvements, and public rights of access to the shore.
These subjects were addressed repeatedly in both houses of the colonial
legislature, although legislation that was perceived as inimical to the
proprietors was often turned back by the Legislative Council or the imperial government.[6] This chapter, then, provides a glimpse of the intellectual
history of a time and place in which the legal, political, and economic
context made questions about the meaning of property central in both
private and public discourse.

Historians who write about ideas face troubling methodological and
epistemological questions.[7] Did the purveyors of the arguments that the
historian reconstructs make those arguments from a commitment to their
truth or because the arguments were expedient? How representative were
the arguments that, by happenstance and circumstance, are preserved in

the documents available to the historian? What were the intellectual debts of the proponents of the arguments? How persuasive and influential were they? Often, the limitations of the sources deny the historian the means to answer these questions, but reconstructing the political ideas prevalent in a particular time and place is a worthwhile exercise, even though such reconstruction is inherently anachronistic: the historian organizes, categorizes, and imposes order and coherence on a debate in which the participants may have cared more about results than intellectual consistency or rigour. As J.G.A. Pocock reminds us, ideas are historical artifacts, and even 'historical events: ... things happening in a context which defines the kinds of events they were.' The study of ideas in their context is part of the historical project of describing in as much detail as possible the social institutions of other times, so as to understand the actions and thoughts of those who lived then and to reveal the continuities and changes that the historian seeks to explain.[8]

THE LAND QUESTION

Britain acquired sovereignty over Prince Edward Island by the Treaty of Paris, 1763. Formerly part of France's North American empire, Ile St-Jean, as it was called by the French, was a small island in the Gulf of St Lawrence, heavily wooded and sparsely populated by Acadians and Micmac. Considered valuable for its forests, fisheries, and potential as farmland, the new possession nonetheless posed a development problem for the cash-strapped British government. After reviewing several proposals for private development of the colony, the imperial government decided to grant the island in large lots to proprietors whose payment of quit rents would provide the funds necessary to administer the new colony and whose tenants would turn the island into tidy farms.[9] Accordingly, the island was surveyed and divided into sixty-seven lots of about 20,000 acres each. One lot was reserved as demesne lands of the Crown, and the remaining sixty-six were distributed in a single day to applicants selected by lottery. Three lots were given to the officers of the 78th Regiment of Fraser Highlanders, and the rest allocated among ninety-eight individuals, including high-ranking colonial administrators and military officers, members of Parliament, intimates of the establishment, merchants, and entrepreneurs. The Crown reserved to itself certain quantities of land within each lot for supporting religion and education, and construction of roads and defences. As well, the grants contained a variety of provisions intended to guarantee public access to the shore for fishing and building of stages and other structures necessary thereto. Grantees were required to settle their lands within ten years with one Protestant settler for every two hundred acres, and to pay quit rents to the Crown, of two, four, or six shillings per one hundred acres, depending on the quality of land in the township lot, as reported in the survey.[10]

The decision to dispose of the entire Island in large lots in a single day provided critics of the proprietorial system with an easy target, but proprietorial colonies were not an innovation in imperial policy. Many of the colonies on the Atlantic seaboard were founded as proprietorial colonies, but the frontier context provided an ideological justification for resistance to the proprietorial system: demands for rent could be characterized as attempts to recreate feudal institutions in the New World. Both private proprietors and the Crown had difficulty collecting rents and quit rents, and the vestiges of the proprietorial system that remained in the American colonies by the late eighteenth century were swept away during and after the American Revolution.[11] Nonetheless, the imperial government persisted with proprietorial grants in British North America. In Nova Scotia and New Brunswick, the colonies closest to Prince Edward Island, when proprietors failed to fulfil the settlement and quit rent conditions in their grant, their lands were reclaimed by the Crown and distributed in smaller parcels to those wanting to settle on them.[12]

On the Island, in contrast, the proprietorial system remained in place for over a century. Not everyone who came to the Island became a tenant farmer on a short-term lease paying rent to an absentee landlord. A few proprietors lived on the Island, while some immigrants were able to buy freehold properties, and others occupied land without signing a lease or recognizing any proprietorial claim. By the 1830s, small freeholders were about one-third of the Island population and owned about one-fifth of its land. Resident proprietors remained the exception, particularly among those with the largest holdings; more than three-quarters of the twenty proprietors who owned one or more townships lived in the United Kingdom. The six largest proprietors owned four or more townships each, that is, more than 80,000 acres, an amount that one proprietor described as 'a respectable family estate.' Leasehold terms varied widely, from a few to a thousand years. The rents specified bore no direct relationship to the quality or productivity of the land, with the exception of a provision in some leases for lower payments at the beginning of the tenancy, when land would have to be cleared – a long, arduous, and expensive endeavour – before it could be planted. Some proprietors considered their estates only as long-term speculations, while others spent time, money, and attention on immediate development. But none of the proprietors complied with the conditions for settlement in their original grants, either as stated initially or as modified from time to time in response to proprietorial pleas of hardship. Given the proprietors' default, there was both popular and elite support for an escheat, or reversion to the Crown, of estates of proprietors who had failed to meet the conditions of their grants. Some escheat proponents assumed that when the Crown reclaimed the estates of defaulting proprietors, the land would be regranted without charge to the occupiers, while others hoped that escheat would open up Crown lands for purchase.[13]

In the 1830s escheat became the rallying cry of a movement of agrarian protest which, from 1838 to 1842, held a majority of seats in the Island's House of Assembly. But opposition to the escheat program in the Legislative Council and the colonial office stymied efforts to turn political success into escheat legislation.[14] Nonetheless, the subsequent disintegration of escheat as an organized political force did not quell demands for the escheat of proprietorial lands and the conversion of leaseholds to freeholds. As successive Island governments struggled to diminish the power of the proprietors, the rhetoric became ritualized. Proprietors complained frequently, bitterly, and usually successfully about attacks on the sacred rights of property, while Island politicians blamed the proprietors, particularly the absentees, and their supporters in the colonial office, for the Island's economic woes.

Even after the implementation of responsible government in 1851, attempts to end the proprietorial system were constrained by the limited autonomy of the Island legislature, as well as by a lack of consensus on the best way to proceed. Legislation affecting property rights had to be referred for assent to the imperial government, which continued to reject requests for a general or partial escheat of proprietorial grants as well as other legislation that the proprietors opposed.[15] In 1853, passage of the Land Purchase Act gave the Island government authority to purchase proprietorial lands for resale to tenant occupiers, if the proprietors could be persuaded to sell. The first such purchase, of the 70,000-acre Worrell estate, was arranged by middle men who secured a large profit at the expense of both the government and the absentee proprietor. The ensuing scandal, along with a lack of funds, discouraged the government from making more purchases under the legislation.[16] In June 1860, in response to continued pressure for a comprehensive solution to the land question, the imperial government agreed to pay for a commission of inquiry, with a representative of both landlords and tenants and a third person to serve as chair. The commissioners held public hearings and hired an investigator to collect information secretly. Their report, which was unanimous, condemned the initial lottery and the proprietorial system that it had engendered and recommended an imperial guarantee of a loan of 100,000 pounds sterling to permit the government to purchase more proprietors' estates under the 1853 Land Purchase Act. Knowing that the imperial government had rejected a similar request from the Island government in 1858, the commissioners also recommended an alternative – that the landlords be compelled to sell out to their tenants at a price to be negotiated by the parties or, failing agreement, to be set by arbitration.[17] Compulsory sale legislation would not come into effect for another decade and a half, but the commission report was an important element in the growing acceptance of so significant an intrusion into established property rights.

The proprietors were surprised and appalled by the commission's recommendations, and, in face of their opposition, the imperial government refused to implement them. Instead, a group of five non-resident and seven resident proprietors agreed to give up all claims to arrears of rent up to 1 May 1858, except for those for which they had already obtained judgment, and to accept, for the next ten years, any offers from tenants to purchase the lands they occupied. The price stipulated was payment of all outstanding arrears since 1 May 1858 plus a sum equal to fifteen years of rental payments at the highest rental rate provided for in the tenant's lease.[18] The following year, the government enacted legislation, commonly referred to as the Loan Act, authorizing it to borrow on the security of government debentures up to £50,000 to assist tenants in purchasing freehold title to the land they farmed, providing they were able to pay one-third of the purchase price up front. The Loan Act capped the purchase price per acre at more than twice the maximum permitted under the Land Purchase Act, but landlords complained that this price was still too low. Thus, neither of these measures could resolve the land question. Without landlords willing to sell at a price that government or tenants were able to pay, there was no occasion for either act to operate.[19]

In 1860, while awaiting the report of the Land Commission, the government acquired 62,000 acres from the Earl of Selkirk.[20] The hopes raised by the sale of more to follow proved vain, and, with the rejection of the Land Commission recommendations, tenants turned, as they had during the years of the escheat movement, to rent resistance and political organization. At the best of times, rent collection on the Island was not easy: landlords complained that the Island legislature placed barriers in the way of using the legal process to collect rent and arrears,[21] and most tenants were behind in their rent some or all of the time. Sometimes tenants fell into arrears because they could not pay; at other times, particularly in the 1830s and 1860s, they resisted paying as part of an organized effort to force the landlords to negotiate or accept a different relationship.

Between 1864 and 1867, a short-lived Tenant League organized mass meetings calling for rent resistance to force rent reductions and for legislative action on measures for converting leasehold to freehold tenure. The organizers forwarded petitions to the newspapers and the legislature, and Tenant Leaguers vowed to withhold their rent until the land question was resolved. They also vowed to act together to prevent the sheriff or his officers from serving writs or other legal documents on tenants, to protect tenants from having personal property seized for arrears, and to ensure that no one would take possession of a farm made vacant by eviction of a tenant or squatter.[22] Given the common concerns and personal connections among landlords in Prince Edward Island and landlords in Ireland, the likelihood that tenant activism would foster 'outrages' was as apparent to landlords as to tenants. After several skirmishes between sheriff's officers and tenant supporters, including an attempt to secure, by force, release of a tenant who had been arrested for throwing a stone at a sheriff's deputy, the Island Cabinet called for military aid to the civil power.[23]

Troops arrived from Halifax in August 1865. Although deployed only three times in assisting sheriff's officers in carrying out their duties, troops remained in Charlottetown until June 1867. The military presence, and the severe sentences meted out to Tenant League activists in the Island's Supreme Court, were factors in the waning popular support for direct action.[24] So too were the voluntary sales of several small estates from 1864 through 1866, culminating in the sale to the government of the Cunard estate in 1866. Comprising over 200,000 acres, it was the largest estate on the Island, close to one-seventh of total Island land. In February 1866, the death of another great proprietor, Laurence Sulivan, prompted speculation that his daughter, Charlotte Sulivan, might sell the estate that she would inherit. She did not, but in the context of ongoing Confederation discussions, Islanders had reason to hope that the persuasive power and financial resources of the united colonies might lead to more sales.[25]

Initially, Prince Edward Island remained aloof from the new state created in 1867 with the union of four of Britain's North American colonies. Mounting debts for railway construction and a better offer brought it into the union in 1873.[26] Freed from the direct supervision of the British government, and provided with a loan from the Dominion government to buy out the proprietors,[27] the legislature moved quickly to dismantle the proprietory system. The Land Purchase Act, passed in 1874, required owners of large estates to sell their land to the government, at prices to be determined by a tri-partite commission. All estates of 500 or more acres were subject to the legislation, but owners could retain up to 1,000 acres if they occupied the land themselves.[28]

Robert Hodgson, who as chief justice served as the Island administrator in the absence of the lieutenant-governor, reserved the Land Purchase Act, 1874 for the assent of the Dominion government, in accordance with the practice before Confederation of referring all land legislation to the colonial office.[29] The Governor-General, Lord Dufferin, an Irish landlord, found the legislation 'monstrous' and, without even consulting with the federal Cabinet, rejected it. The following year, after some clarification of the distinction between the role of the governor-general and the governor-general in council, Lord Dufferin gave royal assent to the Land Purchase Act, 1875. Shorn of a somewhat contentious preamble, the second bill differed little in substance from the first, apart from a face-saving change on a point of significance to Lord Dufferin. As negotiated with him, the person to chair the Land Commission that would determine the proprietors' compensation would be chosen by the governor-general in council, rather than by agreement of the parties.[30]

The Land Commission began its hearings in Charlottetown in August 1875. Lord Dufferin's friend, Hugh Culling Eardley Childers, formerly First Lord of the Admiralty in Gladstone's government, was appointed as chair. Among his credentials was the fact that he was not a Canadian, as, in Dufferin's view, 'it could not have been expected' that the large number of proprietors resident in England would find a Canadian satisfactory.[31] When other business required his attention, Childers was replaced by Lemuel A. Wilmot, recently the lieutenant-governor of New Brunswick. Most of the proprietors chose Robert Haliburton as their nominee. A Nova Scotia lawyer, and one of the founders of the Canada First movement, Haliburton had been counsel for the proprietors at the 1860 Land Commission.[32] The provincial Cabinet had pledged to the legislature that it would choose its nominee from a list approved by the legislature; it chose Conservative MLA Dr John Jenkins.[33]

Jenkins's appointment must have confirmed the proprietors' fears. In debate on the Land Purchase Act, 1874, Jenkins had said that arbitrators appointed to determine the proprietors' compensation should remember that the proprietors had been forgiven much and held their land only by clemency of the Crown; their interest in the land was, at most, the value of the rent.[34] Three members of the Legislative Assembly were retained to represent the provincial government at the commission hearings. All three had participated actively in the debates on the Land Purchase Act, which passed unanimously. L.H. Davies was leader of the Liberal opposition, Frederick Brecken was attorney general, and William Sullivan was solicitor general, the post Davies had held prior to the change of government in 1873. Senior counsel for the government was Samuel Thomson, QC, from Saint John, New Brunswick, who had represented the Island government at the 1860 Land Commission hearings.[35]

After a fortnight of public hearings in Charlottetown beginning in mid-September, 1875, the commission, with Childers as chair, set prices for ten estates, including those of the four largest proprietors. Robert Bruce Stewart, by far the largest of the resident proprietors, owned over 60,000 acres. Charlotte Sulivan, Lady Georgiana Fane, and Lord Melville lived in the United Kingdom, and owned 66,000, 14,500, and 12,000 acres respectively.[36] Several proprietors, including the three largest, challenged the amounts awarded in the provincial Supreme Court. The three judges were unanimous in setting aside the awards, despite a strongly worded privative clause in the legislation.[37] The provincial government then appealed the decisions to the newly created Supreme Court of Canada, which, in its first reported judgment, ruled that the legislation was constitutional and that the impugned awards were valid exercises of the authority given to the Land Commission.[38] In his reasons for decision, Chief Justice William Buell Richards echoed some of the arguments that had been made by those who campaigned for an end to the proprietary system:

We may, without going beyond what is considered the legal province of a Judge, be supposed to know that there had been difficulties in the Island existing for many years in relation to the collection of rents ...; that there had been legislation on the subject, and that further legislation was deemed necessary. The recital in the [Land Purchase Act] that it was desirable to convert the leasehold tenures into freehold estates, indicates that it was a matter affecting the public interests. This Statute ought, therefore, to be viewed not as ordinary legislation but as the settling of an important question of great moment to the community, and in principle like the abolition of the Seigniorial tenure in Lower Canada, and the settling of the land question in Ireland. In carrying out such measures as these, there may be cases where the law works harshly, where important rights may seem to be disregarded, and private interests are made to yield to the public good without sufficient compensation being given ... The great object of the Statute seems to have been to convert the leasehold tenures into freehold estates, a matter of very great importance, and one which, if not settled, would be likely to affect the peace as well as the prosperity of the province.[39]

We now turn to the arguments that received this imprimatur of the final authority of the Supreme Court of Canada.

FOUR APPROACHES TO THINKING ABOUT PROPERTY

In their struggle to end landlordism in Prince Edward Island, opponents of the proprietorial system invoked different ways of thinking about property and the rights and obligations of property ownership. Those engaged in the debate may not have described their thinking in quite the way that I will, but for convenience, and without undue distortion, I will group their arguments under four major themes. The first is the thaumaturgic power of property ownership:[40] a mere leaseholder cannot attain the material prosperity and civic virtue that come from acquiring and maintaining a freehold property, and a colony without freeholders cannot prosper. The second is summarized by the label of producer ideology:[41] those who invest the capital and labour necessary to transform the wilderness into well-ordered communities are entitled to keep the product of their investment; conversely, those who do nothing with their property lose their rights as property owners.[42] The third is a denial that there are inherent, immutable rights attached to property ownership, and emphasizes instead the extent to which property is contingent historically and constructed socially: property has value and property rights have meaning only when owners of property are able to invoke the coercive power of the state to enforce the rights they claim. The fourth theme challenges the bright line distinction between public power and private property: questions about land distribution and the rights and obligations of land ownership are public questions, involving a delegation of power from the state to the person whose private property rights the state will enforce.[43]

THE THAUMATURGIC POWER OF PROPERTY OWNERSHIP

In nineteenth-century, liberal democratic societies, property ownership made a person a citizen, by enabling him to develop individual autonomy while making him dependent on the state to protect the conditions of autonomy.[44] In the New World, the thaumaturgic power of property ownership became a freehold ideology, idealizing the yeoman farmer, the self-sufficient, independent defender of liberty. American political rhetoric and popular thought linked liberty and land ownership inextricably, so that payment of rent was viewed as an imposition and a betrayal. Every white male, it was asserted widely, had the right to own a farm large enough to support himself and his family, unencumbered by ruinous or usurious economic burdens.[45] Such views, also prevalent among those who emigrated to British North America, whether they came from Europe or America, received support from the highest levels in government. In a speech in Halifax in 1875 reported in the Island *Patriot*, Liberal Prime Minister Alexander Mackenzie expressed his vision of a country of yeomen, not peasants, in which tillers of the soil owned the land they worked. It was the policy of his government, he averred, to extinguish anything resembling landlordism, because upon land-owning depended the independence of the country.[46] An Islander who farmed both freehold and leasehold property told the 1875 Land Commission: 'People will make sacrifices to get clear of the hateful name of paying rent. The very name of paying rent stings so badly that a person would not buy a leased farm, but would run away to another that is free.'[47] Hence, a writer to the *Patriot* could state confidently, without need of supporting argument, that '[e]very man in America should own the soil he cultivates, so long as he is willing to pay a fair price for it.'[48]

The commissioners appointed in 1860 to inquire into the Island land question would not have challenged the letter writer's assumption that he spoke only what everyone knew in asserting the superiority of freehold over leasehold tenure. In their report, the commissioners explained the hostility to leasehold tenure that they encountered by drawing a contrast between the Old World and the New:

It is difficult for an European to understand why almost every man in America considers it a personal degradation to pay rent. In the British Islands ... [a] wealthy man pays rent with no more sense of inferiority than he feels when he pays his taxes ... On this side of the Atlantic a very different sentiment grew out of the discovery and settlement of a boundless continent where ... even now, after two centuries of occupation, land is so easily obtained, at prices so low that almost every industrious man may own a freehold; if he does not, in the agricultural districts, something discreditable to his character or his capacity is assumed; and even in the towns a man prefers to own the house he lives in, though the amount of interest he would pay upon a mortgage may be quite equal to his rent ... The tenantry of Prince Edward Island share the common sentiment of the continent which surrounds them. The prejudice in favour of a freehold tenure, if it is one, is beyond the power of reason. The proprietors cannot change the sentiment, the local Government have no power to resist it.[49]

Witnesses before the commission had provided ample evidence to justify these conclusions, denouncing the proprietorial system as a scourge on the Island that stifled initiative, undermined a man's ability to provide for his family, and reduced Islanders to servility. Counsel for the Island government and witness after witness argued that the leasehold system turned industrious men into serfs, deprived British subjects of the 'rights, privileges and independence of freeholders,' retarded the Island's development, and kept the people in poverty. Tenants had no incentive to improve their holdings, or to produce much beyond the mere means of subsistence, when all surplus went to pay rent, and their farms ultimately would revert to the landlord.[50]

Without security of tenure, tenants had no assurance that they could provide for their children by leaving them a well-maintained farm. No matter how much labour and money a tenant put into clearing and fencing land, fertilizing with seaweed and mussel mud, erecting buildings, or planting orchards, the tenant could not compel the landlord to pay for the improvements if the tenant was evicted for falling into arrears on rent payments or if the landlord refused to renew the lease.[51] Tenants' children, recognizing the blight on their prospects, left the colony in search of better opportunities and land of their own, taking with them ability and energy that could have made Prince Edward Island grow and prosper. A representative of tenants from the west end of the Island, on part of the Cunard estate, told the 1860 Land Commission that the leasehold system 'may do very well for old bachelors who never expect to be any benefit to their country ... but ... [it] has sown the seeds of discontent in many families. Young men have seen and felt the difficulties under which their fathers have toiled ... and our sons have become wanderers from home, tossed hither and thither over the surface of the earth like the thistle down in autumn.'[52]

The economic insecurity created by the leasehold system also had a pernicious effect on the Island's political life. An important element in the idea of the yeoman farmer as the ideal citizen is the connection between ownership of property and the right to vote. Defenders of a property qualification for electors argue that only those who own property have sufficient stake in the stability of the state to exercise their franchise responsibly; furthermore, only those who have sufficient property that they are not dependent on others for their material security can determine their political allegiances free of the coercion of another.[53] In Prince Edward Island in the colonial period, despite frequent tinkering with the franchise qualifications, the important element in determining eligibility to vote was residence, not ownership of a freehold estate; adult white male leaseholders as well as freeholders who met a relatively modest property qualification could vote, if they were British subjects and Island residents for the previous year. After Roman Catholics were granted the right to vote in 1830, the franchise was denied only to squatters, labourers, and transients, and those whose property was not worth forty shillings per year. The Franchise Act of 1853 retained the forty shillings requirement, but permitted those who could not show clear title to establish their right to vote based on possession and extended the franchise to those who did not meet the property qualification but were liable to perform statute labour or pay a rate in lieu thereof.[54]

Even with a partial severing of the connection between property ownership and voting rights, opponents of the proprietory system used justifications for a property franchise to demonstrate that the proprietory system contributed to the demoralization of the Island's political culture as well as the retardation of its economic development. Pointing to the insecurity of leasehold tenure, they argued that leaseholders lacked the independence necessary to exercise the franchise according to their own judgment and will. Tenants who were liable to eviction at the termination of their leases, or when they fell into arrears, were vulnerable to pressure from landlords or their agents to vote according to the landlords' or agents' instructions. In a letter to the *Examiner* in January 1864, 'A Tenant,' and, judging by the content of his letter, a Tenant League supporter, attributed the excessive number of writs issued against the tenantry of Lot 61, one of the townships owned by Laurence Sulivan, to the landlords' desire to reduce tenants to 'the conditions of serfs, who will obey their slightest wish and vote for their friends, our oppressors.' But the writer proclaimed the tenants' defiance, asserting that even though they might be turned out of their homes to starve, tenants would not be 'coerced to sell our privilege to do with our votes as we please.'[55] In the opinion of William S. McNeill, Liberal MLA for North Rustico, the franchise could never be properly exercised, no matter how determined the tenants, while rents were collected at the point of the bayonet and politicians delivered writs of eviction before elections.[56]

Describing tenants as serfs invoked resentment of the power that the landlords could wield because of their position and privilege. Tenant supporters also drew on antislavery sympathy in the United Kingdom and the United States by describing tenants as slaves as well as serfs. Editorials on the land question in the *Examiner* frequently made the analogy between the tenants of Prince Edward Island and the slaves in the West Indies, arguing that the appropriate relief for the Islanders held in bondage would be a grant from the imperial government to emancipate them from the proprietors. When slaves were freed in the British Empire by an act of the Parliament of the United Kingdom, Parliament had voted a fund to compensate the former slave-owners, and Parliament had the same obligation to emancipate the leaseholders of Prince Edward Island. The leasehold system kept in bondage those who should be respectable and independent agriculturalists; it was mockery of freedom to expect them to purchase their farms from their landlords, just as it was to expect slaves to buy their freedom from their masters.[57] 'Free land for a free people' became one of the antilandlord slogans.[58]

LAND BELONGS TO THOSE WHO MAKE IT PRODUCTIVE

That idea that a free people should own the land that they cultivate is related closely to the second theme articulated repeatedly by opponents of the leasehold system – that land belongs to those who make it productive. Potentially the most radical of the arguments employed against the leasehold system, the idea that one acquired property rights through one's work, had an equally radical corollary: the proprietors, by doing nothing, had forfeited whatever rights they acquired in the original grants. Producer ideology, which in other places might unite urban labourers and farmers against bankers, manufacturers, and politicians, was used in Prince Edward Island to assert the rights of tenants, squatters, and small freeholders against the landed proprietors, particularly the non-residents. Rooted in a partial but widely accepted reading of Island history, producer ideology provided those who opposed the leasehold system with the unity and moral power to withstand the proprietors' invocation of the sacred rights of property and contract. In Prince Edward Island, producer ideology relied both on technical legal arguments and an assertion of a moral economy in which entitlement, determined by contribution, defeated mere title.

That the proprietors were in default on the obligations contained in their grants was acknowledged in the popular press, the Legislative Assembly, and even in imperial despatches. That failure provided legal justification for the demands for an escheat that were repeated through to 1875. Proprietors argued for strict enforcement of the obligations that tenants had undertaken when signing their leases, but the opponents of the leasehold system met these arguments with a question: why should tenants be held liable on their leases when proprietors had neither paid their quit rents nor fulfilled their settlement conditions?[59] Belief that they were asking for no more than British justice sustained the escheat movement and the Tenant

League, and kept opposition to the leasehold system alive even when the situation was not volatile in the countryside. The cry was not only 'free land for free people' but 'free land by constitutional means.'[60]

Tenants and squatters derived their belief in the justice of their claims in part from pride in what they had achieved with their own resources, contrasting their industry with the indolence of the proprietors and their indifference to the welfare of the Island and its residents. Landlords, especially the non-residents, were easily characterized as undeserving and vain, refusing to sell their Island properties merely to give themselves occasions to boast of their vast holdings in what was 'the garden of America.'[61] With progress celebrated as a great good of the nineteenth century, those who created farms and the infrastructure of commerce and industry from waste and wilderness deserved the highest honours and rewards that the New World could offer. The proprietors, in contrast, were 'drones' who wanted to 'lie on gilded couches,' living off the work of others.[62] In a metaphor that invoked both the honest work of the tiller of the soil and the dishonesty of the landlords, proprietors were condemned for 'reap[ing] where they had not sown.'[63] They wanted to claim the benefits of ownership without undertaking any of its obligations, either legal or moral: the true owners, therefore, were the tenants.

The argument that labour, not title, gave ownership rights was used in an editorial in the *Examiner* to dispel any misapprehensions about the effect of an escheat created by escheat's opponents or by the denunciation of escheat in the *Report* of the 1860 Land Commission. The editorial referred to claims that escheat would hurt those who demanded it, because resident tenants, squatters, and small freeholders, along with the proprietors, would be dispossessed of their land; all title in escheated estates would revert to the Crown, with no guarantee to occupiers that the lands would be regranted to them. But such an outcome was impossible, the editorial argued, for where lands have been improved and cultivated, they belonged to those who by their labour have 'reclaimed them from their forest or wilderness state.' In support of the assertion that cultivated land belongs to those who cultivate it, the editorial quoted from John Locke's *Two Treatises of Government*, first published in 1690.[64]

A labour theory of property entitlement might have some claim to respectability when supported by quotations from an eminent English moral and political philosopher, but it had quite a different ring in the writings of Karl Marx, or even the radical escheat leader, William Cooper.[65] Proprietors made free with words such as spoliation, confiscation, undisguised robbery, socialism, and communism to condemn compulsory sale legislation and the sentiments that lay behind it.[66] Some proponents of compulsory sale shared the proprietors' fears about loosing the forces of radicalism, recognizing that general acceptance of arguments that property entitlements should be based on labour rather than title had potential for destablizing the legal structure that supported capitalist relations of production. Attorney General Frederick Brecken, who piloted the 1874 compulsory sale bill through the Legislative Assembly, admitted that compulsion was an invasion of property rights that members of the Legislative Assembly would resist 'in our private capacity as owners of property.' But Brecken invoked necessity as his justification in the present circumstances: 'Necessitas non habet legem.'[67]

The *Patriot* supported the Land Purchase Act, 1875, but only because proprietors had already forfeited their title by failing to comply with the terms of the original grants. An editorial commenting on the official despatch denying royal assent to the 1874 compulsory sale bill said that the result was not surprising, when the act had not set forth facts to demonstrate that the people of Prince Edward Island would not disturb any person in the possession of what he rightfully owned. But, the editorial continued, the proprietors were not rightful owners of the lands that they claimed. 'The people of this Island have noticed that the proprietors have trusted rather to the forbearance and the indulgence of the Imperial Government to maintain them in the occupancy of the lands they hold than in the soundness of their titles to those lands ... When, therefore, the proprietors assume the airs of injured men and women – of persons whose sacred rights are invaded – they must, to convince the people of this Island, at any rate, that they have a real ground of complaint, prove that they possess those rights.' Even so, the people of the Island were prepared to give proprietors some compensation because, through passage of time and the protection of the imperial government, they had acquired something for which they could make a claim. To admit the validity of the landlords' title, however, while proceeding to take their property, would be an act consistent with advocacy of socialist or communistic principles, and earn the Island a reputation it did not deserve as a place where property rights were not protected.[68]

Those who were willing to acknowledge the validity of the landlords' title, or who had given up any hope for an escheat, still argued against compensating the landlords for more than they rightfully owned. Newspaper editorials, letters to the editor, and resolutions passed at public meetings asserted that tenants had an inherent right to the products of their labour; they had already paid dearly for the freehold of their farms through the work of clearing and fencing and their payment of rents and taxes.[69] Politicians made the same arguments in debate on compulsory purchase: if landlords received compensation, it should not exceed the value of their land as it had been granted to them, before improvements had been made by the tenants or the government.[70]

Counsel for the Island government at the 1860 Land Commission organized most of their argument around the contrast between hard-working settlers who had earned the right to ownership of their holdings and landlords who had forfeited their rights. In opening remarks, Joseph Hensley urged the commissioners to consider setting a price at which the proprietors should be required to sell their estates to their tenants. The price, he said, should be low, for the land had been made valuable solely 'by the industry and exertions of the tenantry.' If the commissioners visited 'some of the wild and distant settlements of the Island ... they could not but return with the conviction on their minds that he who fells the trees and clears the forests should be the freeholder, and not the far-distant proprietor.'[71]

When the 1875 Land Commission convened its hearings to determine the compensation to be paid to proprietors, counsel for the Island government and witnesses for tenants invoked these familiar images in support of their argument that the proprietors, if their lands were not to be escheated, should be awarded no more than the value of their estates as wilderness land. Frederick Brecken reminded the commissioners that it was tenants' hard work and sacrifice that had transformed the Island from wilderness into a 'smiling garden'; proprietors deserved no compensation for what had already been purchased with 'the life blood of the inhabitants.'[72] L.H. Davies cautioned the commissioners against allowing the present appearance of the country to influence them in the price they allowed the proprietors. The fertile fields and comfortable homesteads were all the work of the tenants, many of whom had received no help from the proprietors.[73] Samuel Thomson argued that tenants had already paid for their land by their labour, making it into something quite different from what they had leased; they should not be required to purchase it again.[74]

Proprietors offered a straightforward argument to the 1875 Land Commission: we have title and we should be compensated for loss of our title and the rights we have under our leases. Counsel for the government countered with witnesses who testified to the length of time and prodigious effort required to clear land, and to the continuing expenditure of money and labour to make the cleared land productive. Any increase in the value of the proprietor's estates belonged, therefore, not to the proprietors, who had done nothing except harass the occupants to pay rent, but to the tenants whose investment of labour and capital had created the increase. Nor, argued Davies and Brecken, should proprietors receive compensation for increases in land value due to construction of roads, railroads, and harbour improvements. Those things had been paid for by Island residents with their taxes, and the people, through the government, should not have to pay for them again.[75]

Squatters, too, relying on the doctrine of adverse possession, asserted that their claim, based on capital and labour expended to make the land productive, was superior to the claim of absentee landlords. The doctrine of adverse possession, whereby one can acquire ownershiplike rights in land by occupying it without the permission of the owner, had particular appeal in a sparsely settled colony, where unimproved land was seen as an impediment to progress. A legal system that enforces rights to land based on possession, even against the paper title holder, allows people to establish claims to land by using it. Generally, claimants by adverse possession can acquire rights to wilderness land only after they have cleared or fenced it. Such actions give notice to the whole world, and particularly to the person who claims title to the land, of the presence of the adverse possessor.[76] On Prince Edward Island, actual possession of only part of a plot of land, demonstrated by the changes necessary to make a farm out of the wilderness, could give the claimant rights to the whole plot, not just to the land actually cleared or fenced. When witnesses before the Land Commission spoke of what they owned by possession, they included land that they had marked off as theirs, and intended to clear when they were able. Once squatters settled on a piece a land and established boundaries that were not challenged by their nearest neighbours, they would blaze a few trees to show the boundary, and claim all that lay within the lines. There was enough confidence that such possession gave legal rights that men would 'buy another man's possession,' even if he had neither deed nor lease. Proprietors, witnesses told the 1875 Land Commission, hesitated to bring trespass actions against squatters because juries would confirm the squatters' claims.[77] The legislature also showed some partiality for the rights of the person in possession of land over those of an absentee landlord. Statutes of limitation, setting out the period after which the paper title holder will lose the right to bring an action to evict the adverse possessor, usually extend the limitation period for people who are unable, because of some incapacity, to assert their rights against the adverse possessor. In Prince Edward Island, absence from the Island did not extend the limitation period for bringing an action against an adverse possessor.[78]

PROPERTY IS HISTORICALLY CONTINGENT AND
SOCIALLY CONSTRUCTED

In complaining of their inability to evict squatters because they could not get verdicts against them, the proprietors were acknowledging, by implication, that their rights as owners were dependent on recognition and enforcement of those rights in the particular time and place in which they claimed them. Defining property rights requires an answer to three separate questions: what is property, what are the rights and obligations of property ownership, and who is able to claim the rights of ownership? Whenever legislators or judges decide controversial claims based on property ownership, they must first determine whether the particular resource, tangible or intangible, can be 'propertised,' that is, whether individuals can establish private ownership of the resource, and, based on that ownership, exclude others from access to the benefits of the resource except on the owners' terms. To answer affirmatively that a particular resource is property is to accept that it will not remain in the commons, available equally to all, but can be appropriated by individuals for their exclusive use.[79] This basic question of whether a resource can be 'propertised' is often answered without articulating either question or conclusion. Politicians, policy makers, and the public take for granted that the resource in question is capable of being owned and move immediately to the second and third questions: what are the rights and obligations of ownership in this context, and how have they been divided among the competing claimants?

All of the disputants in the struggle against leasehold tenure appear to have accepted that land is a resource that can be allocated to private ownership.[80] At issue throughout the century of struggle against landlordism was the extent of the proprietors' obligations, and whether their default deprived them of their rights, or, indeed, resulted in transfer of some of those rights to tenants and squatters. But even where landlords asserted rights to which they had clear legal entitlement, their rights would be of little value if there were insufficient social support for their enforcement. Through rent resistance and controlled use of violence to protect tenants from legal sanctions for non-payment of rent, the escheat movement in the 1830s and the Tenant League in the 1860s mobilized antilandlord sentiment and forced some proprietors to consider selling on terms their tenants would accept. Possibilities of significant achievements for either movement were curtailed when the government demonstrated its willingness to use force against activists, including heavy sentences for those charged with criminal offences and the deployment of armed civilians or troops to maintain order in the countryside.[81] But if landlords could not rely on the availability of imperial force to back their demands for rent, what could they say that they owned? The report of the 1860 Land Commission recognized that title unsupported by widespread acceptance of its legitimacy is of little value. In recommending that the imperial government assist the Island government in converting leasehold estates to freehold, by compulsory purchase if necessary, the commissioners noted that the imperial government, 'having become weary of collecting rents and supporting evictions in Ireland, can hardly be expected to do for the landlords in Prince Edward Island what has ceased to be popular or practicable at home.'[82] The commissioners' prediction was realized during the Confederation negotiations, as the imperial government made it clear to the Island government that it would provide neither money for buying out the landlords nor troops to help the government keep order.[83]

An editorial in the *Examiner* in the midst of the Tenant League agitation presented the same argument. While urging the Tenant League to stay within constitutional bounds, it warned the proprietors that there were limits on the power of the state to control tenants' actions, and costs for exercising that power: 'Let not the Tenantry be cowed or frightened in the least degree by the silly threat of a military force being sent into the Colony. When the brave soldiers come here – if ever they do come – to collect rents for the proprietors at the point of the bayonet – the people will respect their mission, sanguinary as the intent of it may be, and they will be glad to see British troops here, spending British gold amongst us ...'[84] Troops did come to deal with the Tenant League, but when the imperial government declared that it would no longer maintain a military establishment on Prince Edward Island, the *Examiner* urged the proprietors to sell, before their intransigence fostered another Tenant League organization that would defy them to collect their rents.[85]

The belief that proprietors no longer had rights under their grants, given the widespread questioning of the legitimacy both of their title and their entitlement, shaped much of the argument put forward by counsel for the government before the 1875 Land Commission. Proprietors demanded indemnification for the loss of their estates, arguing that the Land Purchase Act provided that they should be put, as nearly as possible, in the position they would have been in but for the act. They demanded, therefore, as a minimum, the capitalized value of the rents that they were entitled to collect under their leases. In support of their claim, the proprietors pointed to section 27 of the act, which stated that every proprietor should receive a fair indemnity or equivalent for the value of his interest.[86] Neither 'value' nor 'interest' was defined in the act, although section 28 listed a number of factors for the commission to consider in estimating the compensation due to any proprietor, including the price other proprietors received from the government for the sale of their lands; the quality of the land, the quantities of land that were vacant, occupied by squatters; or leased; the terms of the leases; the actual annual rentals paid for the previous six years; the costs of collecting these rents; the total outstanding arrears; and the likelihood of collecting the arrears.

In light of what the legislation directed the commissioners to consider in awarding compensation, lawyers for the government argued that to give the proprietors the capitalized value of their annual rent would put them in a better position than they would be in without the act. All the estates subject to sale under the Land Purchase Act carried substantial arrears, averaging four to six times the annual rentals, with the proprietors having no assurance that they could ever collect the arrears or even the annual rents when they came due. Witnesses for the proprietors testified that the arrears had accumulated because of the proprietors' forbearance, or because the legislature had made it difficult for landlords to collect their rents. They argued, too, that tenants were unwilling to pay when politicians and agitators encouraged expectations that rent arrears would be remitted and that tenants and squatters would receive freehold title to the land they farmed.[87] Resident proprietor Robert Bruce Stewart denied that tenants were too poor to pay, protesting that arrears could be collected under an honest government, that is, a government that did not pass 'class legislation ... levelled against the interests of property.'[88] William Cundall, another resident proprietor, and one of the group who had agreed to be bound by the Fifteen Years' Purchase Act, testified that arrears owing by his tenants 'would have been paid long ago but for the agitation which political demagogues stir up about every three years.'[89] Francis L. Haszard, who for the previous two years had collected rents for Lord Melville, said that arrears prior to that time were due to Lord Melville's leniency, and to the fact that many squatters refused to pay. In the past two years, it had been difficult to collect anything, 'as the tenants expected to get their farms for nothing.'[90] The agent for Charlotte Sulivan agreed, testifying that he could not collect rents because 'the tenants have been told by politicians and others to hold back, and they have done so.' He added that if he used harsh measures to collect, he would be abused by everyone, and the way the law stood, attempting to seize a tenant's personal property was almost useless.[91] In language that accurately captured, if not the history of the land question, at least the popular understanding of it, Robert P. Haythorne, a former proprietor and former premier of the Island, put the problem as starkly as possible: 'The rents have been collected more than once at the point of the bayonet.'[92]

L.H. Davies, summing up for the government, repeated and amplified Haythorne's statement of the problem: what compensation could the proprietors claim for property rights that could not be enforced using the ordinary legal process available on the Island? The leases were not worth the capitalized value of the rent if tenants and squatters refused to pay, or paid only when compelled to by the use of extraordinary force. Resort to such means of enforcement was expensive, unreliable, and often neither practical nor possible. Davies reminded the landlords of their own litany of complaints about the obstacles put in the way of collecting arrears. If landlords resorted to evicting tenants who were in arrears, whom could they find to take over the properties? 'Public opinion is against [wholesale evictions], and in the face of that opinion no man can exercise what may be his strict legal right. The system which has been practised in Ireland, and to a certain extent in Scotland, cannot be practised in free America. I deny the power of the proprietors to evict large numbers of their tenants.' How, then, could landlords claim that their leases were as good a security as a mortgage, when they were unable to collect what they claimed they were owed?[93]

When the proprietors demanded recognition of their rights as owners, Islanders responded that the ownership rights rested on recognition of the legitimacy of the owners' claims, and, when that recognition was lacking, on coercion. But where most adult males could vote, and large landowners, especially absentees, were regarded with resentment, proprietors could not count on being able to invoke the coercive power of the state when consent failed. Without social recognition of the legitimacy of the proprietors' claims to collect rent from those who occupied and improved Island land, proprietors were forced to submit to a redefinition of the sacred rights of property.

PROPERTY IS NEVER TRULY PRIVATE

The necessity of state power to enforce the rights that one claims as an owner is one illustration of the idea that property is never truly private: as

Kevin Gray argues, in every attempt to assert property rights against another, there is 'a third actor,' the state, 'expressing its collective judgment through the voice of the courts ... The state itself becomes a vital factor in the "property" equation: all "property" therefore has a public law character ... Behind the "owner" of "private property" stands the guardian "of public property" and the "commons"; and behind this guardian lie centuries of social thought about the ways in which the earth's resources should be shared and distributed.'[94] Opponents of the leasehold system in Prince Edward Island rebutted the proprietors' complaints that compulsory sale legislation was an invasion of their property rights with another illustration of the way in which property rights are public as well as private: when private rights impede the public good, the private rights must give way.[95]

The question whether the 1875 Land Commission had been created to deal with public wrongs or private rights provoked considerable acrimonious debate among counsel for the opposing parties, especially when they disagreed on matters of procedure and proof, such as whose witnesses would testify first, what documents parties were required to produce, who could be cross-examined by whom, who had the burden of proof, and what matters the commission could consider.[96] Davies argued that the Land Commission was a political tribunal, dealing with questions that had been the 'whole politics of the Island' for over a century.[97] Thomson added that the commission's purpose was to quiet long-standing troubles on terms that were just both to landlords and tenants. Edward J. Hodgson, a former proprietor who had sold his estate to the government in 1871, and the lawyer retained by many of the proprietors, argued that the commissioners' task was much simpler: to determine the price that the Commissioner of Public Lands would pay to private individuals who had the misfortune to be proprietors in Prince Edward Island, where it had become a crime to own property.[98] Brecken responded by asking why it had been necessary to bring a commissioner from England if he were merely required to make calculations within the competence of a clerk. The commissioners were not clerks doing sums, but men of stature and judgment who had been appointed to resolve a great public question – the terms on which the people of Prince Edward Island would regain lands wrongfully granted away.[99]

Those who demanded that the proprietors' lands should be reclaimed by the state for the benefit of Island residents sometimes referred to such a taking as an exercise of the state's right of eminent domain.[100] But the proprietors were correct in complaining that the Land Purchase Act went well beyond the expropriation of property for some public purpose, such as road or railway construction, because it compelled them to relinquish their rights so that those rights could be transferred to another private individual.[101] To opponents of the leasehold system, however, the wrong done to the Island by the original grants and by the proprietors' failure to fulfil their obligations was a great public wrong, to be remedied only by public action. As the *Examiner* argued in a series of editorials on the land question, when the government of Great Britain acquired sovereignty over Prince Edward Island, the power that it acquired to dispose of the con-quered territory was that of a 'trustee,' whose rights to control and manage the property could be exercised only for the benefit of the public who settled the Island. Instead, in an unconstitutional and unjust lottery, lands that should have remained in the public domain were alienated to indi-viduals who failed to carry out the public responsibilities that were im-posed on them as conditions of their grants.[102] In making the initial grants, therefore, the imperial government was breaching a trust in the same way that trustees of a public institution would be breaching their trust if they disposed of the institution's property for purposes other than those for which the institution was created.[103] Nor could the proprietors be excused of the conditions, when these had been imposed to ensure the progress and well-being of the colony and the welfare of the people of Prince Edward Island.[104] This 'monster grievance' it was now the obligation of the imperial government to remedy, in accordance with British law and constitutional principles. Blackstone's *Commentaries* were quoted as the authority for the argument that the original grants and concessions were void. Because the Crown can do no wrong, and because it would be wrong to grant to an individual a right or privilege prejudicial to the Common-wealth, any grants with that effect must have been induced by fraud or deception, and were therefore void. This being the case with the 1767 grants, they should all be escheated, not to the imperial government, but to the Crown for the benefit of the people of Prince Edward Island, to make good the original breach of trust.[105]

When the proprietors, in defiance of these constitutional arguments, asserted the sacred rights of property owners, opponents of the leasehold system drew on the popular appeal of producer ideology and the wide-spread belief in the illegitimacy of the proprietors' claims to characterize their determination to hold onto their title as 'whims' that should not be permitted to keep Islanders in bondage.[106] Precedent existed for legislative action that, at the stroke of a pen, would deprive the proprietors of the rights of property owners, in the commutation of seigniorial tenures in

Quebec, and – the example most frequently cited – in the decision of the imperial government to abolish slavery.[107] The proprietors who appeared before the 1875 commission complaining of being dragged into court to defend themselves against the charge of owning property[108] might have drawn their own parallel with the decision to abolish property rights in human beings, and claimed the same recompense as was given to the former owners of slaves. But doing so would have conceded the conclusion that they resisted so strenuously: when consensus develops that particular property rights are immoral, unjust, or an impediment to the welfare of the public, the public can rescind those rights.

CONCLUSION

The decision to compel the landlords to give up title to their property and to set a maximum limit of a thousand acres on the real property that any person could own was not the beginning of a revolution in Prince Edward Island. Supporters of legislation that was condemned by the proprietors as an attack on all property rights were very careful to distinguish the dishonest demands of the landlords from the claims of mechanics and merchants whose right to their property was unquestioned.[109] And, relying on the special regard that the common law has always accorded to land, they also argued that 'title to land is different from that of personal property ... when once [a person] acquires the land upon which we walk everyone is interested in that.'[110]

In marshalling their various arguments against the proprietors and in support of giving Island residents freehold title to the land they occupied, opponents of landlordism adapted and developed from ideas already in circulation among their intended audiences. As they devised and clarified strategies that they hoped would achieve their end, it is not surprising that at times their arguments were inconsistent or contradictory. They spoke and wrote as actors engaged in a political struggle, attempting to persuade others to their views by appeals to passion and prejudice as well as to reason. In common with activists elsewhere, they spoke and wrote so that others would come to understand the world in a way that made the end they sought seem just, natural, and inevitable. Ultimately, the opponents of the proprietory system were successful in using and inventing arguments that 'uniquely resonate[d] at that place and time with their intended audience, resolving the contradictions of the surrounding world in ways that other words and arguments simply [could not].[111] And their arguments continue to resonate today in Island law and culture, as those who want to buy a bit of the Island soon discover. Continuing antipathy to absentee ownership and to an individual or corporation acquiring control over extensive tracts of land is expressed in legislation placing severe restrictions on land transfers on the Island.[112]

The arguments about property examined here were tools in the campaign against the power of the proprietors. Many factors contributed to the proprietors' final defeat, as manifested in passage of the Land Purchase Act and judicial confirmation by the Supreme Court of Canada of the validity of awards made by the 1875 Land Commission. Because the proprietors as a group could be stigmatized as non-residents, and because their claims could be challenged on technical legal grounds, it was possible to deny to them rights that would normally go with title to property without inviting a general questioning of the rights of property ownership. And by 1875, as the proprietors recognized, they were particularly vulnerable. The decision of the imperial government to transfer responsibility for the land question to the Dominion government left the proprietors at the mercy of a people who had persuaded themselves and their elected representatives that proprietors had no rights worthy of recognition.[113] The arguments and ideas that proved so persuasive both with the politicians of Prince Edward Island and the judges of the Supreme Court of Canada were 'things happening' in a particular context, but they were more than that – they were also things that helped make other things happen. With the withdrawal of popular support for, and state enforcement of, their claims, the proprietors' title became, like any belief that property has an objective, immutable reality, 'mere illusion.'[114]

NOTES

Six people in particular have been instrumental in the writing of this paper. Philip Girard invited me to present a paper at the Atlantic Canada Legal History Workshop at Dalhousie in March 1995. Rusty Bittermann persuaded me to do a paper with him for that workshop on the Prince Edward Island land question, and I have been filling binders with research notes on the subject ever since. Conversations with Rusty and with David Bell, my colleague at UNB, always provide insight, focus, and sources. In particular, their comments on a draft of this paper improved the final version, as did comments from Jim Phillips and Blaine Baker, who have my gratitude and admiration for organizing this volume. Above all, I acknowledge the inspiration and encouragement of Dick Risk. A thoughtful, demanding, and supportive law teacher, and, later, field supervisor for a legal history field in my PhD program in Canadian history, he helped me recognize that ideas can be tools for social change. And when jobs were scarce in history departments, he advised me to apply to law faculties. It was good advice.

1 Anatole France, *Penguin Island*, trans. Belle Notkin Burke (1908; New York, 1968), 52.
2 See particularly E.P. Thompson, *The Making of the English Working Class* (London 1964), *Whigs and Hunters: The Origin of the Black Act* (London 1975), and *Customs in Common* (New York 1991). For an elaboration of the idea that property is a relationship, see K.J. Gray and P.D. Symes, *Real Property and Real People* (London 1981), 8–9 and Jeremy Waldron, *The Right to Private Property* (Oxford 1998), 26–7.
3 Gregory S. Alexander, *Commodity and Propriety: Competing Visions of Property in American Legal Thought* (Chicago 1997), 17.
4 For primary sources, I rely principally on the Reports of the Land Commissions of 1860 and 1875, on documents regarding the land question that were published in the Appendices to the *Journals* of the Prince Edward Island Legislative Assembly (JLA), and on discussion of the land question in two Island newspapers, the *Examiner* and the *Patriot*. The *Examiner*, founded in 1847 by Liberal politician Edward Whelan, changed editors frequently in the 1860s. In May 1873, when W.L. Cotton assumed the editorship, the paper switched political allegiance from Liberal to Conservative, although it maintained its opposition to the leasehold system. The *Patriot* was edited by Liberal politician David Laird from 1864 to 1872 and by Henry Lawson from 1876 to 1882. Lawson had been editor of the *Examiner* for a brief period in the 1860s. See Heather Boylan, *Checklist and Historical Directory of PEI Newspapers, 1787–1896* (Charlottetown 1987). See also an editorial in the *Patriot*, 25 November 1876, 'About the "Patriot,"' denying a rumour that L.H. Davies was proprietor and editor of the paper, and asserting that Henry Lawson is. Cairns, 'Louis Davies,' identifies Davies as the publisher in 1871 of a short-lived paper called the *Broad Axe* but does not link him with the *Patriot*.
5 On the historiography of the Island, see J.M. Bumsted, '"The Only Island There Is": The Writing of Prince Edward Island History,' in S. Dasgupta, D. Milne, and V. Smitheram, *The Garden Transformed: Prince Edward Island, 1945–1980* (Charlottetown 1982), 11–38 and M. Hatvany, 'Tenant, Landlord and Historian: A Thematic Review of the "Polarization" Process in the Writing of 19th-Century Prince Edward Island History,' *Acadiensis* 27 (1997), 109–32. On the trans-Atlantic parallels, see Ian Ross Robertson, 'Highlanders, Irishmen and the Land Question in Nineteenth-Century Prince Edward Island,' in L.M. Cullen and T.C. Smout, eds., *Comparative Aspects of Scottish*

and *Irish Economic and Social History, 1660–1900* (Edinburgh 1977), 227–40 and Rusty Bittermann, 'Agrarian Protest and Cultural Transfer: Irish Emigrants and the Escheat Movement on Prince Edward Island,' in Tom Power, ed., *The Irish in Atlantic Canada* (Fredericton 1991), 96–106. Errol Sharpe, *A People's History of Prince Edward Island* (Toronto 1976) is a fast-paced popular history that covers both the pre- and post-Confederation periods. Rusty Bittermann, 'Escheat! Rural Protest on Prince Edward Island, 1832–42' (PhD thesis, University of New Brunswick 1991), places the PEI land question in the context of agrarian protest in the North Atlantic world. Another unpublished thesis that draws on Bittermann's work, Matthew Hatvany's 'Tenant, Landlord, and the New Middle Class: Mercantile-Capitalist Development in the Proprietary System of Prince Edward Island, 1798–1848' (PhD thesis, University of Maine 1996), attempts an assessment of the impact of the proprietorial system on class formation and economic development.

6 For an introduction to the Island's legal history see David Bell, 'Maritime Legal Institutions under the *Ancien Regime, 1710–1850*,' and Philip Girard, 'The Maritime Provinces, 1850–1939: Lawyers and Legal Institutions,' *Manitoba Law Journal* 23 (1996), 103–31 and 379–405, respectively; see also H.T. Holman, 'The Bar of Prince Edward Island, 1769–1852,' *University of New Brunswick Law Journal* 41 (1992), 197–212.

7 See, for example, Michael Bliss's justification of his study of the ideas of Canadian businessmen in *A Living Profit* (Toronto 1974), 134–7. For a survey of current methodologies in intellectual history and their application to legal history, using recent work in American legal history as the examples, see William W. Fisher III, 'Texts and Contexts: The Application to American Legal History of the Methodologies of Intellectual History,' *Stanford Law Review* 49 (1997), 1065.

8 J.G.A. Pocock, 'Languages and Their Implications: The Transformation of the Study of Political Thought,' in Pocock, *Politics, Language and Time: Essays on Political Thought and History* (New York 1971), 11; Pocock, *The Ancient Constitution and the Feudal Law* (Cambridge 1957), 1–8.

9 J.M. Bumsted, *Land, Settlement, and Politics on Eighteenth-Century Prince Edward Island* (Montreal and Kingston 1987), chap. 1.

10 Calculation of number of grantees based on *Minute of his Majesty's Commis-sioners for Trade and Plantations*, 23 July 1767, cited in F.W.P. Bolger, 'The Beginnings of Independence,' in F.W.P. Bolger, ed., *Canada's Smallest Province: A History of Prince Edward Island* (Halifax 1991, originally published 1973), 39–41.

11 Beverley Bond, *The Quit-Rent System in the American Colonies* (New Haven 1919); for thoughtful studies of land riots and organized movements against

landed proprietors, land speculators, and heavy taxation in the pre-Revolutionary and Revolutionary periods, see Richard Maxwell Brown, 'Back Country Rebellions and the Homestead Ethic in America, 1740–1799,' in R.M. Brown and D.E. Fehrenbacher, eds., *Tradition, Conflict, and Modernization: Perspectives on the American Revolution* (New York 1977), 73–99 and Edward Countryman, '"Out of the Bounds of the Law": Northern Land Rioters in the Eighteenth Century,' in Alfred F. Young, ed., *The American Revolution: Explorations in the History of American Radicalism* (DeKalb 1976), 37–69. Alan Taylor, *Liberty Men and Great Proprietors: The Revolutionary Settlement on the Maine Frontier, 1760–1820* (Chapel Hill 1990) decribes the process of creating property through labour and resistance to landlordism on the Maine frontier. Landlordism continued well into the nineteenth century in upstate New York. Sung Bok Kim, *Landlord and Tenant in Colonial New York: Manorial Society, 1664–1775* (Chapel Hill 1978) describes pre-Revolutionary economic and social conditions on the four largest manorial estates. Kim's meticulously detailed study is avowedly revisionist: to counter the 'ingrained ideological animus against landlordism ... [and the] corollary ... worship of yeomanry' (x). Two theses have examined challenges to the leasehold system in New York through parliamentary agitation and direct action. See Eldridge H. Pendleton, 'The New York Anti-Rent Controversy, 1830–1860' (PhD thesis, University of Virginia 1974) and Thomas Summerhill, 'The Farmers' Republic: Agrarian Protest and the Capitalist Transformation of Upstate New York, 1840–1900' (PhD thesis, University of California, San Diego 1993) relying on Pendleton and some contemporary accounts, including the writings of novelist James Fenimore Cooper.

12 Bumsted, *Land, Settlement, and Politics*, 26; R.G. Riddell, 'A Study of the Land Policy of the Colonial Office, 1763–1855,' *Canadian Historical Review* 18 (1937), 385–405.

13 Bittermann, 'Escheat!' 41–8, 75–81, 93–5, 156, quotation from letter from David Stewart to Lt Col Sorell, 9 January 1832, cited at 146; Hatvany, 'Middle Class,' 78–92. For a sympathetic account of the proprietors' intentions and difficulties in the eighteenth century, see Bumsted, *Land, Settlement and Politics*, 45–51.

14 Bittermann, 'Escheat!' 328–83.

15 Frank MacKinnon, *The Government of Prince Edward Island* (Toronto 1951), 94, 95–6, 111–12, 115–16; W.R. Livingston, *Responsible Government in Prince Edward Island* (Iowa City 1931); Philip Buckner, *The Transition to Responsible Government: British Policy in British North America, 1815–1850* (Westport, Conn. 1985), 317–21. The requirement that legislation affecting property rights be reserved for the assent of the imperial government was not unique

to Prince Edward Island, at least in the pre–responsible government period. See, for example, 'Royal Instructions to Thomas Carleton, Governor of New Brunswick, 18 August 1874,' reproduced in *Collections of the New Brunswick Historical Society* No. 6 (Saint John 1905), 411.

16 Ian Ross Robertson, 'George Coles,' *Dictionary of Canadian Biography (DCB)*, 10:182–8; 'William Henry Pope,' ibid., 10:593–4; M. Brook Taylor, 'Charles Worrell,' ibid., 8:954.

17 For an edited version of the commission's *Proceedings and Report*, see Ian Ross Robertson, *The Prince Edward Island Land Commission of 1869* (Fredericton: Acadiensis Press 1988); the full *Report* without the *Proceedings* is reproduced in Prince Edward Island, *Journals of the Legislative Assembly* (JLA) 1875, Appendix E, 'Prince Edward Island Land Question.' For a critique of the activities of the secret investigator, see the *Examiner*, 25 August 1862, 'The Spy's Report.'

18 The agreement was enacted as An Act for settling differences between Landlord and Tenant, and to enable Tenants on Certain Townships to purchase the fee simple of their Farms, SPEI 1864, 27 Vict., c. 2, commonly referred to as the Fifteen Years' Purchase Act. For critiques of the bill and the process of negotiation with the landlords that led to it, see the *Examiner*, 29 February 1864, 'The Proprietors' Bill – End of the Delegation Humbug'; 14 March 1864, 'Correspondence. The Proprietors' New Bill'; 16 May 1864, 'The Government 15 Years Purchase Bill'; for the government's perspective, see Ian Ross Robertson, *The Tenant League of Prince Edward Island, 1864–1867* (Toronto 1996), 37–9, Ian Ross Robertson, 'Edward Palmer,' *DCB*, 11:664–9 and William H. Pope, *DCB*, 10:593–9.

19 SPEI 1865, 28 Vict., c. 5, An Act to Assist Leaseholders in the purchase of the Fee-Simple of their Farms; for the legislative debate on the bill, see the *Examiner* 3 April 1865, 'Summary of the Proceedings of the House of Assembly, 27 March 1865'; for editorial comment, see the *Examiner*, 8 May 1865, 'The Government Loan Bill'; on its efficacy, see *JLA*, 1877, Appendix K. In the ten years after passage of the Loan Act the government, on behalf of tenants, purchased less than 7,000 acres. See JLA 1875, Appendix E, 'Statement, showing the number of Acres of Land purchased by the Government of Prince Edward Island, under the Act, 28th Vict., Cap. 5 ...,' [8].

20 JLA 1875, Appendix E, 'Statement, showing the number of Acres of Land Purchased by the Government of the Province of P. E. Island, where situate, price paid per acre, ...' [6].

21 For comments about the difficulties of rent collection, see Robertson, ed., *Land Commission of 1860*, 79, 138, 142–5, 148.

22 Robertson, *Tenant League*, provides a detailed description of the activities of

the Tenant League. On organized rent resistance in the 1830s, and a description of other tactics used again by the Tenant League, see Bittermann, 'Escheat!,' 99–101, 104–5, 296–302.

23 Robertson, *Tenant League*, 155–7, 161.
24 Ibid., 166, 228–30, 232, 245–57, 258.
25 JLA 1875, Appendix E, [6]; *Tenant League*, 259; Map 9, 260 shows the location of the Cunard properties and those of five small proprietors who also sold their estates to the government or to the occupiers during the period 1864 to 1866.
26 F.W.P. Bolger, *Canada's Smallest Province: A History of Prince Edward Island*, chaps. 6–9, (Charlottetown 1973); Phil Buckner, 'The 1870s: Political Integration,' in E.R. Forbes and D.A. Muise, eds., *The Atlantic Provinces in Confederation* (Toronto 1993).
27 Buckner, 'Political Integration,' 57, notes that the Island government was still repaying the loan into the 1950s.
28 SPEI 1874, c. 3.
29 This procedure is provided for in the Constitution Act, 1867, s. 90, which makes applicable to the provinces the provisions of s. 55 regarding reservation by the governor-general of bills for the signification of the Queen's pleasure, with the necessary substitution of the lieutenant-governor of the province for the governor general and of the governor general for the Queen, and with a one-year period of grace for the reserved bill instead of the two in s. 55. For an account of the occasions on which bills have been reserved under these sections, see G.V. La Forest, *Disallowance and Reservation of Provincial Legislation* (Ottawa 1955).
30 John S. Cairns, 'Louis Davies and Prince Edward Island Politics, 1869–1879,' (MA, Dalhousie University, 1981), provides a detailed account of the Dufferin incident. The quotation is from a letter from Dufferin to Mackenzie, 19 November 1874, reproduced in note 34, 70. Some of the documents generated by the controversy over the legislation are reproduced in W.E. Hodgins, ed., *Correspondence, Reports of the Ministers of Justice, and Orders in Council Upon the Subject of Provincial Legislation, 1867–1884* (Ottawa 1886), 838–47. See also Garth Stevenson, *Ex Uno Plures: Federal-Provincial Relations in Canada, 1867–1896* (Montreal and Kingston 1993), 135–7, 273–4; Gwen Neuendorff, *Studies in the Evolution of Dominion Status* (London 1942), 161 and La Forest, *Disallowance and Reservation of Provincial Legislation*, 51, 108.
31 JLA 1876, Appendix E, 'Copies of Correspondence relative to the Land Tenure Question in Prince Edward Island,' Dufferin to Carnarvon, 14 May 1875, [77–9].
32 Philippe Sylvain, 'Lemuel Allan Wilmot,' *DCB*, 10:709–15; Bonnie Huskins, 'Robert Grant Haliburton,' *DCB*, 13:429–31;.

33 *Patriot*, 17 July 1875, 'The Tenants' Commissioner.'

34 *Patriot*, 28 March 1874, 'Parliamentary: Friday March 20'; 16 April 1874, 'House of Assembly Debates: The Land Purchase Bill Continued.'

35 R.S. MacGowan, *Report of Proceedings Before the Commissioners Appointed Under the Provisions of the 'Land Purchase Act, 1875'* (Charlottetown 1875), 4; John S. Cairns, 'Louis Davies and Prince Edward Island Politics,' at 9, 38, 57; H.T. Holman, 'Frederick de St. Croix Brecken,' *DCB*, 13:110–11.

36 JLA 1876, Appendix E, 'Copies of Correspondence relative to the Land Tenure Question in Prince Edward Island,' Haly to Carnarvon, [85]; JLA 1875, Appendix E, 'Prince Edward Island Land Question,' 'Tabular Statement, of Township Lands remaining in the hands of the Proprietors ...,' [7].

37 *Kelly v. Sulivan, Stewart and Fane* (1876), 2 PEIR 34. Section 45 of the Land Purchase Act, 1875 stated that no award made by the commissioners 'shall be held or deemed to be invalid or void for any reason, defect or informality whatsoever,' but that the Supreme Court could remit an award to which objection was taken to the commissioners for correction.

38 *Kelly v. Sulivan* (1877), 1 SCR 3.

39 Ibid., 34–5; Chief Justice Richards was appointed to the Court of Common Pleas of Canada West in 1853, the year before passage of *An Act for the Abolition of feudal rights and duties in Lower Canada*, 18 Vict. c. 3 (1854). He would have been familiar with the issue and the legislation, having sat as a Reformer in the legislature of the united Canadas since 1848. See Ian MacPherson, 'Sir William Buell Richards,' *DCB*, 11:730–1. Both Chief Justice Richards and the 1860 Land Commission compared the Prince Edward Island land question to Canada East as well as to Ireland. Island politicians and editorialists, at least in the 1860s and 1870s, preferred to embellish their arguments with comparisons to Ireland and Scotland, or to the precedent of the abolition of slavery in the British Empire. For a thoughtful reconstruction of the use of arguments about property and liberty in the debate over abolition of seignorial tenure in Canada East, see Tom Johnson, 'Perceptions of Property: The Social and Historical Imagination of Quebec's Legal Elite, 1836–1856' (SJD thesis, University of Wisconsin 1989), and 'In a manner of speaking: towards a reconstitution of property in mid-19th c. Quebec,' *McGill Law Journal* 32 (1987), 636–72. Brian Young, *In Its Corporate Capacity: The Seminary of Montreal as Business Institution, 1816–1876* (Montreal 1986), chap. 4, describes the process of voluntary commutation of seignorial tenure in the early 1840s on lands held by the Sulpician Order of Montreal.

40 The phrase comes from Paolo Grossi, *An Alternative to Private Property: Collective Property in the Juridical Consciousness of the Nineteenth Century*, trans. Lydia G. Cochrane (Chicago 1981). Grossi argues that societies based on

possessive individualism believe in 'the thaumaturgic virtues of *having* and in the progress won under the banner of an economic individualism blind to the problem of the distribution of goods.'

41 I have borrowed the term 'producer ideology' from labour and business historians. Sometimes it is used to bridge the gap between labour and capital, by describing both as engaged in the joint project of production. Other times, it is used to assert the workers' right to a greater share in the management and proceeds of the joint production. Ramsay Cook, '"Tillers and Toilers": The Rise and Fall of Populism in Canada in the 1890s,' *Canadian Historical Association Papers* (1984), 1–20, explores the origins of producer ideology and the unsuccessful efforts of organized labour and organized farmers to form a lasting political alliance based on shared perceptions that they were both exploited producers.

42 The same kind of arguments were among the many justifications offered for European appropriation of land occupied by indigenous peoples. See Anthony Pagden, *Lords of All the World: Ideologies of Empire in Spain, Britain and France, c. 1500 – c. 1800* (New Haven 1995), chap. 3.

43 Critiquing the public/private distinction by demonstrating the permeability and mobility of the boundary between public and private has been an important critical legal studies and legal realist project. See Elizabeth Mensch, 'The History of Mainstream Legal Thought,' in D. Kairys, ed., *The Politics of Law* (New York 1982), 18–39; Alan Freeman and Elizabeth Mensch, 'The Public-Private Distinction in American Law and Life,' *Buffalo Law Review* 36 (1987), 237–57; Morris Cohen, 'Property and Sovereignty,' *Cornell Law Quarterly* 13 (1927), 8–30.

44 C.B. MacPherson, *The Political Theory of Possessive Individualism, Hobbes to Locke* (Oxford 1962).

45 On the myth of the yeoman farmer in early American thought, see Chester K. Eisinger, 'The Freehold Concept in Eighteenth-Century American Letters,' *William and Mary Quarterly* 4 (1947), 42–59. For a brief discussion of its significance in the Maritimes, see Gregory Marquis, 'In Defence of Liberty: 17th Century England and 19th Century Maritime Political Culture,' *University of New Brunswick Law Journal* 42 (1993), 69–94 at 89–90. Brown, 'Back Country Rebellions,' describes the same concept as 'the homestead ethic,' and it is his characterization of its main elements that is relied on in the text. Brown points out that, despite the vastness of the American continent, land hunger was a major factor in the social crisis that preceded the American Revolution, with the fastest growing population in the Western world restricted to a relatively narrow strip of land along the Atlantic coast.

46 *Patriot*, 6 November 1875, 'Sound editorial on Speech given by PM Mackenzie

at Halifax'; the *Examiner* subsequently accused the *Patriot* of being Communistic for highlighting the parts of Mackenzie's speech in which he denounced landlordism. See *Patriot*, 18 November 1875, 'Communistic.'

47 MacGowan, *Report of Proceedings*, George Mallett, Lot 20, 28.

48 *Patriot*, 24 January 1874, 'Correspondence – The Land Question,' letter dated Queen's County, 6 January 1874, signed 'Colo.'

49 JLA 1875, Appendix E, 'Report of the Commissioners Appointed by the Queen to Inquire into the differences prevailing in Prince Edward Island relative to the rights of landowners and tenants, with a view to a settlement of the same on fair and equitable principles, 1861,' [27].

50 Quotation from the *Examiner*, 22 February 1864, 'The Land Question No. 8'; Robertson, ed., *Land Commission of 1860*, Samuel Thomson, Counsel for the Island government, 36, 44; Evidence William McNeill, Township 23, 43–4; Resolutions passed at meetings held on Lots 12 and 13, 77; R. Gordon, Lot 4, 88; John Clark, Township 5, 89; James Howatt, 94; Donald Montgomery, MLA, William Cousins, John McKie and Sutherland, Lots 20 and 21, 97; John Haggarty, Lot 36, 118; Heath Haviland, MLA and Land Agent, 156. Arguments such as these, iterated frequently by Island politicians, had a long history. Lord Durham had offered similar observations in his *Report on the Affairs of British North America*. See the passage quoted in MacKinnon, *The Government of Prince Edward Island*, 117.

51 Various efforts to secure compensation to tenants for their improvements were rejected by the imperial government; in 1874, the provincial legislature finally secured royal assent to a tenants' compensation bill. Modelled after the Irish Land Bill (1871) pushed through the imperial Parliament by Gladstone's government, the legislation gave the landlord the choice of renewing a tenant's lease or paying the tenant for any improvements, including clearing land and fertilizing the soil, constructing farm buildings and residences, and putting up fences. The value of the improvements, in case of dispute, would be determined by an arbitrator or arbitrators chosen by the parties. See SPEI 1872, c. 10; SPEI 1873, c. 24; JLA 1875, Appendix K; on the Irish legislation, see John E. Pomfret, *The Struggle for Land in Ireland, 1800–1923* (New York 1930), 80–96.

52 Robertson, ed., *Land Commission of 1860*, R. Gordon, Delegate from Lots 4 and 5, 88. For similar comments, see 53, 94, 97, 102, and 105.

53 For an exploration of the link between property ownership and the right to vote in American history, see Robert J. Steinfeld, 'Property and Suffrage in the Early American Republic,' *Stanford Law Review* 41 (1989), 335–76; Jacob Katz Cogan, 'The Look Within: Property, Capacity, and Suffrage in Nineteenth-Century America,' *Yale Law Journal* 107 (1997), 473–98.

54 John Garner, *The Franchise and Politics in British North America 1755–1867* (Toronto 1969), 3, 4, 41–53; Garner, 217, note 2, estimates that in 1850, 11.2 per cent of the total Island population was eligible to vote and that in 1870 the percentage was 22.3. The latter figure is close to Garner's estimate of the percentage of the population that would be entitled to vote in modern Canada if women were still denied the franchise. SPEI 1853, c. 9 defined the property qualifications for voters as ownership of a freehold estate or 'actual possession or use and occupation, however derived or acquired' of a town lot or of any other land of the clear yearly value of forty shillings. Mortgagors or holders of beneficial title to land could vote if they were in actual possession of real estate of the yearly value of forty shillings, as could the husband of a woman who was in possession of land of the clear yearly value of forty shillings to which she was entitled because of her dower interest in lands held by a deceased husband. See also Ian Ross Robertson, 'Edward Palmer,' *DCB*, 11:664–9; MacKinnon, *The Government of Prince Edward Island*, 51, 53.

55 *Examiner*, 25 January 1864, 'To the Editor of the Examiner.'

56 *Examiner*, 6 April 1868, 'Colonial Parliament House of Assembly 10 March'; Henry J. Morgan, ed., *The Canadian Parliamentary Companion*.

57 *Examiner*, 11 January 1864, 'The Land Question'; 22 February 1864, 'The Land Question, No. 8,' 14 March 1864, 'The Land Question, No. 11'; on the fund to compensate the slave-holders, see An Act for the Abolition of Slavery, 3 & 4 Wm. IV, c. 73 (1833).

58 *Examiner*, 19 January 1874, 'The Land Question.'

59 MacGowan, *Report on Proceedings*, Brecken, 233.

60 *Examiner*, 19 January 1874, 'The Land Question.' See Bittermann, 'Escheat!,' 103, 247, 250–1; Robertson, *Tenant League*, 61–2; Marquis, 'In Defence of Liberty,' 83, states, without citing any sources, that 'Proponents of land reform in P.E.I. demanded nothing less than the full implementation of constitutional principles.'

61 *Patriot*, 16 April 1874, 'House of Assembly Debates. The Land Purchase Bill Continued,' particularly the speech of Jenkins.

62 MacGowan, *Report of Proceedings*, Davies, 356.

63 Ibid., *Patriot*, 1 July 1875, 'The Land Purchase Act, 1875.'

64 *Examiner*, 8 February 1864, 'The Land Question, No. 6.' The editorial quotes Locke's famous passage arguing that a man owns what he creates by his labour, as follows: 'The labor of a man's body, and the work of his hands, we may say are properly his. Whatever then he removes out of the state that nature hath provided and left it in, he has mixed his labor with, and joined to it something that is his own, and thereby makes it his property.'

65 For examples of Cooper's use of the argument that it is labour that creates

entitlement to property during the escheat agitation, see Bittermann, 'Escheat!' 80–1; 396–7. For an example of Cooper's iteration of the arguments in the 1860s, see the *Examiner*, 6 March 1865, 'The Union of the Provinces to Settle the Land Question.' On Cooper, see Harry Baglole, 'William Cooper,' *DCB*, 9:155–8.

66 For examples, see James F. Montgomery, *An Experiment in Communism and Its Results: A Letter to the Right Honourable The Earl of Carnarvon, Secretary of State for the Colonies, on the Prince Edward Island Land Commission* (Charlottetown 1875) and JLA 1875, Appendix E, Fane to Dufferin, 19 June 1874, [19–21], Fane to Carnarvon, 25 November 1874, [27–30]; and Melville and others to Carnarvon, [June 1874], [15–17].

67 *Patriot*, 25 April 1874, 'Debates,' reporting on Committee of Whole on *Land Purchase Act*, 14 April 1874.

68 *Patriot*, 3 April 1875, 'The Land Bill Correspondence.'

69 *Examiner*, 22 February 1864, 'The Land Question No. 8'; *Patriot*, 24 Jan 1874, letter to editor from John Kenneth McInnis, Winsloe Road (North) dated 14 January 1874, reporting on meeting of Winsloe Road Debating Club.

70 *Patriot*, 28 March 1874, 'Parliamentary Friday, March 20,' speeches of Liberal MLAs William D. Stewart and Henry Callbeck.

71 Robertson, ed., *Land Commission of 1860*, 34; see also comments of William McNeill, 43; D. Douglass, 51; James Warburton, 63; James Howatt, 94; on Hensley, see G. Edward MacDonald, 'Joseph Hensley,' *DCB*, 12:425–7. Hensley was appointed to the Island Supreme Court in 1869; he concurred without written reasons in the decision in favour of the proprietors in their challenges to the awards made by the 1875 Land Commission.

72 MacGowan, *Report of Proceedings*, 231, 242–3.

73 Ibid., 9.

74 Ibid., 66–7.

75 Ibid., 155, 351.

76 Carol Rose, 'Possession as the Root of Property,' *University of Chicago Law Review* 52 (1985), 73–88, discusses possession as a clear act, whereby all the world understands that one intends to appropriate a particular resource to one's own use, and points out, using the example of indigenous peoples' claims to Aboriginal title in the United States, the difficulties of effectively communicating this intention if the use of the person who claims possession is not regarded as a suitable use by the person disputing the claim.

77 MacGowan, *Report of Proceedings*, Thomson, 65–6, asserting that juries find for squatters; Edward J. Hodgson, counsel for Charlotte Sulivan, proprietor, 134, asserting the strict application of the doctrine of adverse possession; John Longworth, counsel for Lady Fane, 50, to same effect; Robert Bruce Stewart,

166, explaining that he was unwilling to go to court because juries always brought in verdicts against the proprietors; John G. Scrimgeour, formerly MLA for Cardigan District, 263, asserting that most of inhabitants held by adverse possession, and, although they had been served with writs contesting their possession, they had employed counsel to represent them and the proprietor had not proceeded with the action; Donald Stewart and William P. Lewis, residents in Cardigan, 264–5, describing settlers buying another man's possession. Proprietors may have hesitated to test the limits of the adverse possession doctrine, too, because their own titles were insecure. See the exchange between Davies and Robert Bruce Stewart on this question at 162–4. I have not found any reported cases dealing with adverse possession in this period. Robertson, *Tenant League*, 188, states, without citing any sources: 'It was widely accepted that jurors on the Island tended to favour tenants over landlords whenever they had room for any discretion.'

78 See SPEI 1856, c. 8, An Act to Explain and amend the Statute of Limitations of Actions Concerning Real Estate.

79 For the terminology and argument relied on here, see Kevin Gray, 'Property in Thin Air,' *Cambridge Law Journal* 50 (1991), 252–307, in which he coins the verb, to 'propertise,' and another word that he calls 'ugly but effective,' excludable, to describe those resources that are capable of being owned. Gray argues at p. 268 that a resource is excludable 'only if it is feasible for a legal person to exercise regulatory control over the access of strangers to the various benefits inherent in the resource.'

80 I have not found evidence yet in the documentary sources of any one who raised objections to the assertion of private property rights in land. The related argument that the initial distribution of property rights was a breach of the imperial Crowns's obligations to the people of Prince Edward Island is explored in the next section.

81 Troops were not used 'in aid of the civil power' in the 1830s in Prince Edward Island, but an armed force of civilians was organized by the sheriff, and several Escheators convicted of criminal charges. As well, the imperial government made sure that Islanders were informed of the harsh punishments meted out to participants in the Rebellions in Upper and Lower Canada, including hanging and transportation to Australia. See Bittermann, 'Escheat!,' 305–6, 363–8. The use of the military and of the courts against the Tenant League is described briefly above. See Robertson, *Tenant League*, 228–30, 232, 245–57.

82 JLA 1875, Appendix E, Report of the Commissioners Appointed by the Queen to Inquire into ... The Rights of Landowners and Tenants, [58].

83 On the imperial government's determination to withdraw from military

commitments in British North America in general, see J.M. Hitsman, *Safeguarding Canada 1763–1871* (Toronto 1968), chap. 10. For some of the acrimonious correspondence over who would pay for the troops sent to P.E.I. 'in aid of the civil power' during the Tenant League agitation, see JLA 1866, Appendix G and JLA 1867, Appendix K; on their refusal to hold out any hope of a loan, see JLA 1875, Appendix E, Granville to Administrator, PEI, 13 March 1869, [123].

84 *Examiner*, 16 May 1864, 'The Government 15 Years Purchase Bill.'
85 *Examiner*, 9 September 1867, untitled editorial.
86 The main purpose of s. 27 was to prohibit the granting of any sum as compensation for 'the fact that the purchase or sale of the lands of any proprietor [was] compulsory and not voluntary.' The section was included to ensure that the Land Commission did not follow the precedent of compensation awards for land expropriated for building railways, which many of the speakers in the legislative debate considered to be exorbitant. See L.H. Davies, on motion to go into committee on the Land Purchase Act, 1874, 31 March 1874, reported in *Patriot*, 2 April 1874, 'Parliamentary, The Land Bill' and Brecken in Committee on Whole, 14 April 1874, reported in *Patriot*, 25 April 1874, 'Debates.' The proprietors ignored the opening lines of the section, however, pointing instead to its concluding clause, which stated that the object of the act was 'to pay every proprietor a fair indemnity or equivalent for the value of his interest *and no more*' (emphasis added).
87 MacGowan, *Report of Proceedings*, William Cousins, Lot 20, 13; DeBlois, agent for Charlotte Sulivan, 92–3; Donald McPhee, Lot 9, 103–4; James Montgomery, 283; Thomas Murphy, bookkeeper for James Yeo, 637; Archibald McDougald, Lot 13, 642; for a similar range of opinions from the 1860 Land Commission see Robertson, *Land Commission of 1860*, 91, 139, 141, 142, 148, and 159.
88 MacGowan, *Report of Proceedings*, 162, 166.
89 Ibid., 38.
90 Ibid., 271–2.
91 Ibid., G.W. DeBlois, 79–81, 96.
92 MacGowan, *Report of Proceedings*, 337; Robertson, *Tenant League*, 169, refers to use of this phrase as a metaphor, probably drawn from the Irish experience, suggesting the full range of tenant rent resistance strategies, up to the arrival of the sheriff. In both Ireland and Prince Edward Island, the phrase also has a literal application.
93 MacGowan, *Report of Proceedings*, 351–3; as this was the first case heard by the commission with Lemuel Wilmot as chair, Davies prefaced the government's closing argument with an impassioned review of the history of the land question.

94 Gray, 'Property in Thin Air,' 304.

95 For examples of such expressions from across the political spectrum, see the *Examiner*, 20 October 1862, 'The Land Question,' dated Campbellton, 6 October 1862, signed S.S. Hart, who moved one of the motions condemning the Fifteen Years' Purchase Act at a tenant meeting reported in the *Examiner*, 2 May 1864; *Patriot*, 3 January 1874, 'To the Editor of the Herald,' dated 30 December 1873, signed Robert Shaw; *Examiner*, 6 April 1868, 'Colonial Parliament. House of Assembly, Tuesday, March 10 A.M.,' speech of Joseph Hensley.

96 MacGowan, *Report of Proceedings*, 3–4, 22–3, 26, 31–5, 41–3, and 47.

97 Ibid., 57.

98 MacGowan, *Report of Proceedings*, 69; JLA 1875, Appendix E, Statement Showing the Number of Acres of Land Purchased by the Government ...' [6].

99 MacGowan, *Report of Proceedings*, 230, 242.

100 MacGowan, *Report of Proceedings*, Thomson, 63.

101 *Examiner*, 13 April 1874, 'Correspondence. The Land Question,' letter dated Queen's County, 10 April 1874, signed 'A Landlord'; Justice Peters in his reasons for decision in *Kelly v. Sulivan* (1876), PEIR 34 at 87–92, observes that the Land Purchase Act would exceed the powers of eminent domain recognized in the United States of America, but was within the constitutional authority of a legislature whose powers over property and civil rights were equivalent to those of the British Parliament itself.

102 *Examiner*, 11 January, 8 February, 22 February, 14 March, series entitled 'The Land Question'; 7 November 1864, 'The Land Question with Reference to the Projected Union of the Colonies'; 30 September 1867, 'A Compulsory Purchase of Township Lands – Who First Proposed It?'

103 *Examiner*, 1 February 1864, 'The Land Question No. 6.'

104 Ibid., 29 February 1864, 'The Land Question No. 9.'

105 Ibid., 25 January 1864, 'The Land Question No. 4.'

106 *Patriot*, 16 April 1874, 'House of Assembly Debates. The Land Purchase Bill Continued,' Jenkins.

107 JLA 1875, Appendix E, Report of the Commissioners Appointed by the Queen to Inquire into ... The Rights of Landowners and Tenants, [54–5]; *Examiner*, 30 September 1867, 'A Compulsory Purchase of Township Lands – Who First Proposed It?'; MacGowan, *Report of Proceedings*, Thomson, 65.

108 MacGowan, *Report of Proceedings*, Edward J. Hodgson, 22; William Cundall, 37; Robert Bruce Stewart, 160.

109 *Examiner*, 31 July 1865, quoted in Robertson, *Tenant League*, 160–1; *Examiner*, 27 April 1868, editorial.

110 MacGowan, *Report of Proceedings*, Thomson, 62.

111 Cogan, 'The Look Within,' 475.
112 Prince Edward Island Lands Protection Act, SPEI 1982, c. 16, sets an upper
    limit of 1,000 acres on aggregate land holdings for an individual, and 3,000
    acres for a corporation, and prohibits non-residents and corporations (apart
    from incorporated farming operations owned by resident farmers) from
    acquiring more than ten acres in total or shore frontage of more than five
    chains without a permit. This legislation, and its predecessor, have with-
    stood constitutional challenges on both division of powers and Charter
    grounds. See *Morgan v. Attorney General for Prince Edward Island* (1975), 55
    DLR (3d) 527 (SCC) and *Reference Re Lands Protection Act (PEI)* (1987), 64
    Nfld & PEIR 249 (PEI SC). See also Milton Acorn, *The Island Means Minago*
    (Toronto 1975), particularly the historical poems in Part I.
113 The proprietors felt betrayed and abandoned by the imperial government.
    See Montgomery, *Experiment in Communism*. See also letters written by the
    proprietors or by others on their behalf to the London *Times*, 29 July 1875; 28
    September 1875; 5 October 1875, 23 October 1875, and an account of a
    question raised in the House of Lords on behalf of the Prince Edward Island
    proprietors in the *Times*, 27 July 1875, 'Parliamentary Intelligence. House of
    Lords.'
114 Gray, 'Property in Thin Air,' 1.

12

Race and the Criminal Justice System in British Columbia, 1892–1920: Constructing Chinese Crimes

JOHN McLAREN

Dick Risk, in his path-breaking and inspirational article, 'A Prospectus for Canadian Legal History,' recognized 'unity and diversity' as one of the historical themes ripe for investigation by scholars. More particularly, after discussing the co-existence of the civil and common law systems and their legal cultures in Canada, he referred to '[t]he continuing existence of other religious, national or ethnic groups [as] an element of diversity in Canadian life.'[1] Professor Risk added that the legal record of this diversity was 'difficult to assess,' and doubted whether, apart from protection afforded to them for freedom of association, freedom of worship, and ownership of property, the law had contributed much 'to the existence and nature of these groups.'[2]

In the intervening years, several Canadian scholars have risen to the challenge of exploring the experience of various minority religious, national, and ethnic groups with Canadian law and legal culture. Assisted by an expanding literature generated by social and cultural historians and geographers,[3] these scholars have demonstrated the impact of the law, legal institutions, and legal ideology of the majority on these groups. This scholarship exposes the use of law by the dominant community in defining and evaluating minorities and their place within the community, the extent to which minorities invoked the dominant legal system to secure protection for themselves, and their success or failure in doing so.[4] Law *was* implicated in determining the political, economic, and social status of some minority groups and the treatment they received at the hands of Euro-Canadian government and society. It was also an instrument to which some of those groups appealed in order to protect themselves from discrimination and to facilitate their economic activities.

CONSTRUCTING RACE

In her important book on Vancouver's Chinatown, Kay Anderson examines the ways in which dominant cultural communities use spatial identity to construct understandings of the culture and values of minority racial and ethnic populations in their midst. They do this in ways that stress 'otherness,' irreducible difference, and the need for vigilance and control of the 'outsiders.'[5] Anderson proceeds from an ideological position which, while accepting that racism has been associated with and sharpened by materialist factors in colonial, capitalist societies, also recognizes that the concept of the 'other' is rooted in cultural biases and judgments. These, she suggests, are the product of complex forces with long gestation periods and often defy purely materialist explanations.[6]

Against the backdrop of the racist history of British Columbia, Anderson shows how the development of Chinese business and residential enclaves – Chinatowns – was viewed among the European population. She argues that these areas, which were the product of both the exclusionary policies of the majority and strong impulses among the immigrants to settle and live together for self-protection and mutual support, served a dual purpose in the mindset of the dominant settler community. Segregation, it was felt, both secured the control and regulation of 'alien hordes' and, at the same time, gave definition to what it meant to be members of a 'superior' community and culture.[7] 'With more or less force in different colonial settings, racial ideology was adopted by white communities, whose members from all classes indulged it (often in contradictory ways) for the definition and privilege it afforded them as insiders. The race paradigm gave white groups the power of definition in cultural and ideological terms, as well as more instrumental power in the hands of politicians, bureaucrats, owners of capital, labour unions, judges, police, and other influential members of the "ruling" sector.'[8] The state, Anderson notes, played a central role in the process of differentiating the characteristics that marked off outsiders from those considered to be 'legitimate citizens.' In the case of the Chinese the agents of the state 'sanctioned a concept behind which lay the most divisive world-view of "us" and "them."'[9] By defining China and the Chinese in contradistinction to all that 'white' Canada supposedly stood for, state representatives sought to 'build a dominant "Anglo" community' that enjoyed 'popular legitimacy.' There is little doubt from the historical record that they succeeded. As social and political historians of British Columbia have amply proven, in a jurisdiction noted for its political and social divisiveness the 'Oriental' issue by and large created an identity of purpose and action across the political, social, and economic spectrum.[10]

Despite Anderson's stress upon the power of racism within colonial societies, she is also quick to recognize that the 'process of racialization' did not take 'a fixed course' everywhere. It was 'a contradictory process with different levels of the state sometimes taking quite different postures toward the "Chinese."'[11] Research on the attitude of the earliest members of the Supreme Court of British Columbia to the race issue lends support to this thesis. Chief Justice Begbie and Justices Crease and Gray acted from mixed motives, including their antipathy to the excesses of popular democracy and support for the employment of cheap labour by risk-taking capitalists in a fragile economy, as well as a commitment to the 'rule of law.' For a variety of reasons, they reacted unfavourably and explicitly to the more egregious and public attempts at legislative discrimination against the Chinese, striking down discriminatory provincial statutes and municipal by-laws in the process.[12]

Anderson also notes that the process of racialization was productive of resistance not only within the dominant community, but also within the Chinese community. Chinese resistance manifested itself in public rejection of the stereotypes applied to the minority population and in attempts to demonstrate willingness to accommodate European values.[13] Again, existing work on Chinese immigrants in British Columbia's courts shows that some were not shy about appealing to the law to protect them against discrimination, and that they found support among both the well-heeled members of their own community and Chinese diplomats accredited to Great Britain or Canada.[14]

In this chapter I seek to test Anderson's thesis against the experience of the Chinese with the criminal justice system in British Columbia between 1892 and 1920. This period begins with the passage of the Criminal Code;[15] it ends just before the first Chinese exclusion legislation in Canada[16] and major amendments to narcotics legislation designed to increase penalties and vest special and wideranging powers in investigating suspected drug offences in the Royal Canadian Mounted Police.[17]

LAW, GEOGRAPHY, AND RACE

Law, like space, as Nick Blomley has argued, is an object of human construction.[18] It can be treated as an attribute of personality, of group or institutional affinity, of territorial location, or as a combination of these identifiers. In European legal and diplomatic practice there was a long tradition, existing well into this century, embodied in 'capitulations' with non-Christian states, of the latter granting voluntarily or under duress extraterritorial treatment for Europeans resident in those countries.[19] In other words, they were to be treated according to their 'personal' and not the host territorial or religious law. Within independent states a plurality of legal systems often obtained, in recognition of or as a concession to diverse cultural and religious traditions. Acceptance of personal law in matters of religion, succession, and family relations in the Iberian Caliphates, the Ottoman Empire, and Mughal India provide examples.[20] Even in the legalistic and culturally less pliable West the nationalization of law was a lengthy process. The law actually experienced by people was variously territorial or personal, centralized or localized into the modern era. This was true even in England, with its much vaunted 'common law,' as E.P. Thompson and Harry Arthurs have reminded us.[21]

The pattern of legal identity in colonial societies was similarly diverse. In large and populous territories – for example, British India and the Dutch East Indies – which were viewed as 'civilized,' significant elements of the traditional legal system/s were retained and applied to the local population either by existing institutions or colonial courts applying customary law.[22] For other purposes the domestic community was considered as subject to imported colonial law.

In colonies in which European settlers intruded on existing cultures that were viewed as 'uncivilized' and 'primitive,' there was a greater tendency to deny legitimacy to the existing system of 'custom,' and to treat the indigenous population as subject to European law.[23] This was only partially true, however. Indigenous populations were also subject to tribal or special courts administering elements of customary law,[24] or special legal regimes constructed to 'protect' them as uncivilized folk. Under the latter they were either segregated for good (apartheid),[25] or groomed for future entry into the mainstream of life in the colony.[26] Policies of isolation or reculturation of indigenous peoples were secured by the establishment of 'homelands,' reserves or reservations.

In colonial jurisdictions immigrants from non-European backgrounds were the objects of various regimes constructed to control them, to protect European settlers from them and their deviant ways, and, to a limited degree, to cater to their customs. These geo-legal systems were various. They included formal designation of 'special quarters,' as in the case of Manila in the Philippines and the camps established for the Chinese in the Australian gold fields in the 1850s.[27] In these areas a combination of traditional custom and European law applied, administered by special tribunals or immigrant leaders. Also embraced were informal systems of ghettoization produced by both external social and legal pressures and by the immigrants' desire to settle in common areas. In these instances the inhabitants were assumed to be subject to the general law and only followed their own customs unofficially, where they could. The latter was effectively the system operating in British Columbia's Chinatowns.[28]

Tina Loo, in her study of the establishment of British law and institutions in colonial British Columbia, has demonstrated that there was a strong impulse among European settlers, predominantly of British stock, toward a legal system that was centralized, predictable, consistent, and sensitive to the pervasive demands of economic liberalism.[29] However, she also notes that tensions developed within the dominant legal culture between the demands of centralization and uniformity on the one hand and localism on the other.[30] Situations arose in which the common law or statutory regimes were felt to work hardship on specific communities. As a result resistance occurred. The experience of the Chinese does not feature in this particular equation in Loo's account. However, there are distinct parallels between their experience of the law and that of their European neighbours. If this was not evident in the ideological meanings attributed to law in the two communities, it held true in the stresses born of application of the generalized legal system on the one hand and a desire to preserve elements of community autonomy and traditional normative systems on the other. What made the experience of Asian immigrants unique, however, was that they were working within an imposed system of law, one that varied in the extent to which the fact of 'Chineseness' was seen as relevant to its operation and outcomes. The picture is therefore necessarily complex.

LAW AND THE CHINESE IN BRITISH COLUMBIA

Law for the Chinese of British Columbia was contested terrain. Despite the widespread belief in the white community that British conceptions of law and government were alien to and unassimilable by the immigrants, the record suggests that the Chinese were well aware of the value of appealing to the general law. To a degree they had to be. Denied access to political, social, and economic status by disenfranchisement by the provincial legislature,[31] their only resort was to the courts and the hazy concept of 'the rule of law' to protect themselves against the discrimination to which they were subject.

The Chinese feature frequently in the early decades of British Columbia's existence as a province as challengers on constitutional grounds of legislation designed to make life more unbearable for them. These statutes sought to burden them with special imposts or denied them access to the few economic opportunities not already closed to them.[32] The Chinese also appear later in *habeas corpus* actions, directed against attempts to deport or deny them entry under immigration legislation.[33] Although the law as administered by the courts provided much-needed protection at an abstract level to the Chinese, it is important to recognize that the administration of justice in this context was racialized. European immigrants were not subjected to discriminatory legislation and administration of this type. During most of the period under review, white settlers were not forced to use the law to protect civil and economic rights only grudgingly afforded, or to fight a specially constructed and highly discriminatory immigration regime.[34] Furthermore, the necessity of appealing to the courts because they were denied other civil and political rights meant that the Chinese were subject to another form of European hegemony, that of judicial paternalism. Statements of Begbie, Crease, and Gray in particular, during litigation and in other public forums, leave little doubt that these men saw themselves as the protectors of a despised minority.[35] The Chinese operated in a world of limited opportunity made possible by a legal regime partially constructed by the judiciary.

But it was not only appeal to the law for protective purposes that impelled the Chinese to use the courts. Case lists and bench books indicate that they were often in court bringing or defending civil actions on commercial transactions in which they were involved.[36] Like white business people in the province they recognized the advantages of a system of commercial law that was uniform and predictable, and which placed value on opportunity and competition in the market place. Wholesale and retail business was one of the few areas of economic activity in which the Chinese were still free to operate. Although they may well have used their own informal resolution systems for some disputes, access to the court system was relatively quick and efficient, and it was available as a resort if other methods failed. Furthermore, they undoubtedly felt that going to court and subjecting themselves to the law legitimated their activities within the economic system.

Preliminary work on the civil record suggests that the law at this level operated by and large without racial discrimination. Indeed, several statements of the earliest Supreme Court bench suggests that judges felt that the Chinese were scrupulous in their business dealings, trustworthy and well aware of what the law demanded of them.[37] In one later case a 'Chinese practice' that was roundly deplored in the white community, but at that time not illegal, was treated by the judge as a totally neutral factor in assessing the relative rights and obligations of the parties to a commercial transaction. In *Lai Hop v. Jackson* (1895) Justice Drake declared void the transfer of property to his spouse by the defendant (a white) who was not then indebted. He was entering into an agreement to help bankroll the smuggling of opium into the United States on behalf of the plaintiff (a Chinese resident).[38] The judge in determining the defendant's motives seems to have been particularly impressed by the fact that this was a 'dangerous trade.' However, in his opinion, rather than weakening any legal obligation to pay up that Jackson might have, that reality strengthened it.[39]

When we move to the place of the Chinese within the criminal justice system the pattern of racialization described by Kay Anderson is much clearer. To a significant degree the Chinese were objects of the criminal justice system. They occasionally appeared as complainants and informants, and the system could operate to protect their interest in the safety of property and person, as it did with whites. Much more often, however, the Chinese were on the receiving end of investigation, arrest, charges and conviction.

The assumptions made about Chinese deviancy and its formalization in the construction of criminality and law enforcement were to a significant extent propelled by racist sentiment. A series of stereotypes, the product of a long period of writing, reports, and tales by western observers of the cultural peculiarities of the 'celestial Empire' and promoted uncritically by the press, embodied Eurocentric understanding of Chinese vices.[40] In terms of their general lifestyle they were considered to be unsanitary, a product of a lack of concern with personal cleanliness and a penchant for living cheek by jowl in cramped, substandard quarters where filth and vermin collected.[41] Worse still, there was assumed to be a direct link between their living practices and diseases that were or were imagined to be contagious. Any evidence of an outbreak of yellow fever, smallpox, or leprosy, especially if it happened to afflict a Chinese resident, invariably lent weight to the contention that this immigrant group was a source of contagion.[42] A particularly virulent form of medico-moral discourse surrounded the construction of the immigrants as the actual or potential harbourers of disease – terms such as 'leprous,' 'virulent,' 'verminous,' and 'cancerous' were bandied about in newspapers and journals, public speeches, and informal conversation. Such highly emotive descriptors helped to embed notions about 'unclean' immigrants firmly in the minds of many members of Euro-Canadian society as self-evident truths.[43]

Beyond their 'unsanitary' habits the Chinese were reviled for a series of vices to which they were seen as particularly prone. These activities, all of which were practised to one degree or another in white society, had or were to become the objects of high anxiety in western countries, increasingly governed by middle-class moral values during the period under review. As such they were part of a litany of supposedly perverse and socially corrosive forms of conduct that threatened to corrupt European society and required resolute political, social, and, not least, legal action to suppress them. The thought that these practises might be controlled by the representatives of a 'vicious,' 'substandard' and all too numerous alien race was too much for many white citizens of British Columbia to stomach. The level of anxiety was enhanced by the fact that these practices tended to take place within the mysterious confines of Chinatowns, areas to which most white folk did not resort by choice or, if they did, did not leave the streets.[44] Information about life in these enclaves was a product of the highly biased reports of the press and the associated fantasies of the white population about what must be going on behind closed doors.[45] The occasional, notorious case of mayhem and exploitation or serious criminality involving residents of Chinatown confirmed and sharpened what the white population already knew and feared about this 'debased community.'

CRIMINAL JUSTICE AND THE 'CHINESE VICES'

The triad of vicious practices that were thought to be either distinctively Chinese or particularly dangerous when organized by the Chinese were gambling, opium smoking, and prostitution.[46] Europeans had long noted the penchant of the Chinese at all levels of society for gambling,[47] a penchant that they carried with them wherever they migrated. In British Columbia, where playing the odds or indulging in games of chance was condemned by middle-class opinion formers as idle, unproductive, and addictive behaviour, gambling was identified as one area in which the

Chinese showed themselves as incapable of virtue. In their love of gambling they ran against the tide of European morality and posed a potential threat to the well-being of the young and impressionable in the white community. These concerns were enough to provide support, especially in moral reform circles, for using the general criminal law on gambling to suppress it in Chinese quarters.[48]

Opium smoking was also classified in the racist mindset of most white British Columbians as a distinctively Chinese activity. Few were prepared to recognize that the opium trade and the consumer demand that was supposed to fuel it had been forced upon the Chinese empire by Great Britain.[49] Historical sensitivity and accuracy were not marks of settler societies. The practice gave rise to exactly the same set of anxieties associated with gambling – about idleness, thriftlessness, and addiction – with the added worry that opium apparently besotted the mind of its users. However, it was sufficiently exotic and outside the experience of most white British Columbians to have remained for a time an irreducible point of cultural difference between white and Chinese society rather than a focus for vigorous legal action.[50] Ironically too, an economic barrier existed to the proscription of narcotic use. The European population contentedly consumed a wide array of beverages and patent medicines that contained agents such as opium, cocaine, and morphine to quench their thirst and relieve their ailments.

The impulse to criminalization of narcotics manufacture, distribution, and use in Canada was accidental in its timing at least. It was the happenstance of the Vancouver anti-Asian riots of September 1907, which produced extensive property damage and loss of business in Chinatown and Japantown, that provided the stimulus to action. William Lyon MacKenzie King, the deputy minister of labour in Ottawa, was dispatched by the government of Sir Wilfrid Laurier to Vancouver to consider compensation claims from those who had suffered property damage and loss.[51] During the course of his inquiry it emerged that there was a lucrative opium industry in British Columbia, and that whites used the narcotic as well as Chinese.[52] This revelation was to excite King's moral fervour and induce him to advocate immediate federal legislation outlawing the manufacture, distribution, and sale of opium in Canada. The result was the Opium Act of 1908 that proscribed the importation, manufacture, sale, or possession for sale of crude or powdered opium or of opium prepared for smoking.[53] The publicizing of the issue of opium smoking as a corrosive form of vice encouraged an expansion of concern about narcotics use more generally, outside the Chinese population. The use of other narcotics, such as cocaine, was being targeted in several Canadian cities by law enforcers as productive of crime among young people.[54] By 1911 Parliament was ready to enact broader narcotics suppression legislation.[55] The statute extended the proscription on the importation, manufacture, and sale of opium to other drugs, including cocaine, morphine, and eucaine.[56] To possess, transport, or export such drugs also became offences.[57] The act further made it an offence to deal in those drugs, except for legitimate medical purposes,[58] as it did smoking or possessing opium for purposes of smoking or being found in an opium den.[59] In 1909 Ottawa had already amended the Criminal Code to add 'opium joint' to the definition of 'disorderly house.'[60]

Prostitution was another concern. While prostitution was clearly not classified as a distinctively Chinese activity, it was viewed as widespread in Chinese society – a result again of ethnocentric reports by European observers shocked by the sale or pledge of women, polygyny, and what was seen as a brothel culture in China.[61] Moreover, by the turn of the nineteenth century moral reformers in western countries increasingly believed that an international, white slave traffic had extended its tentacles around the world, reaching into Europe, North America, and white societies elsewhere.[62] East Europeans and Jews featured largely in the factual or fictional descriptions of who was involved. The most sinister and vicious, however, were believed to be Orientals, especially the Chinese.

This form of stereotyping resonated strongly in white British Columbia. In a minority community that was overwhelmingly male and in which women were regularly bought and sold, it was assumed by their detractors that, with limited exceptions, any Chinese girl or woman who came to Canada must already be a prostitute or destined for that role.[63] Exposure of actual contracts of sale in a number of cases merely confirmed the suspicion. There were not many who, like Chief Justice Begbie, found definite parallels between Chinese marriage 'sales' and the matrimonial contract or dowry in western societies.[64] It was also believed in the white community that the multitude of unattached Chinese males would seek outlets for their sexual impulses, and, as the small number of Chinese women in the province could not meet their needs, they would naturally look to white women. The supposedly voracious sexual appetite of the Chinese meant that not only prostitutes but also virtuous white women were at risk.[65] These sentiments fed into the rhetoric and lobbying strategies of a reform coalition opposed to 'white slavery' during the first ten or so years of the present century.[66] They were assisted by amendments to the Criminal Code of 1913 and several years thereafter, designed to expose and punish harshly the exploiters of prostitution.[67] The campaign was also responsible for some provincial legislatures passing legislation outlawing the employment of white women by Chinese restauranteurs.[68] Rare but notorious incidents in which white girls or women were found with or imagined to be prostituting themselves under the control of Chinese men gave substance to the rhetoric and were played for all they were worth in the press.[69]

LAW ENFORCEMENT AND RACIALIZING CRIMES IN BRITISH COLUMBIA

Police records in both Victoria and Vancouver leave little doubt that the province's law enforcers subscribed to the view that some crimes were racially specific. A glaring and public example is the format by which the annual statistics for charges and convictions were reported by Victoria's police chief. The crime figures were organized under the rubrics of offences committed by 'all others but Indians and Chinese' or 'Whites,' those committed 'by Indians,' and those committed 'by Chinese.'[70] Nancy Parker, in her study of law and society in late-nineteenth-century Victoria, noted this practice and its reflection of the racialization of crime by the police.[71] The tradition continued into and through the period under review. When the crimes and figures are examined it is apparent that this mode of reporting was not purely the result of administrative convenience. Patterns emerge that indicate that the police associated certain types of crime with racial minorities. There were status offences in a racial as well as in a gender sense.

The range of offences committed by whites is significantly longer.[72] In terms of numbers the highest figures in that list were consistently registered for being drunk and disorderly. Among other frequent offences are the infringement of city by-laws; property offences, most notably larceny and stealing; vagrancy; and assault. From approximately 1910 increasing numbers of automobile offences are recorded. In the Chinese statistics the list of crimes was much shorter (a third to a half of the above). The consistently high figure before 1911 was by-law infractions, with 'stealing' reaching double figures and gambling appearing in a minority of recorded years as a significant percentage. After 1911 the relative importance of by-law infractions declined, theft barely reaching double figures, with significant increases in gambling prosecutions and consistently high figures for narcotics offences. The listing for Indians was shortest with the vast majority of offences involving liquor.

The Dominion crime statistics confirm the importance of gambling and drug offences as Chinese crimes, especially in the period after 1911. In Vancouver in several years between 1911 and 1920 well over a thousand charges were laid for gambling offences.[73] In the case of indictable offences some information is provided on natal origin. A large majority of those convicted of indictable gambling offences were foreign born, which almost certainly means China was their place of birth. The conviction rates are naturally more modest for Victoria, but again foreign born (i.e., Chinese) offenders predominate.[74] In the narrative reports on the Dominion crime statistics, there is a consistent message from 1912 to 1918 that British Columbia led the nation convincingly in terms of gambling convictions.[75] Again one can be reasonably confident that the explanation was the high number of prosecutions of Chinese in that province.

'UNSANITARY IMMIGRANTS'

The reports of the medical health officer and sanitary inspector in Victoria, especially in the 1890s, provide the clue to the high number of by-law convictions in the Chinese community.[76] Chinatown was recorded as a constant source of worry because of unsanitary conditions and overcrowding. In his 1893 report Dr George Dunn, the health officer, made note of cases of smallpox in the Chinese community. He pronounced it a miracle that disease did not spread, referring to the dangers of typhoid posed by the immigrants' use of sewage matter as fertilizer. He strongly recommended that sewers be laid in Chinatown and residents forced to instal the necessary equipment and pipes and hook up to the system.[77] In the same year Sanitary Officer Alexander Murray reported that the conditions in Chinatown required more energy on his part than the rest of the city put together.[78] In his 1894 report Dr Dunn stressed how important an extended sewage system was if Chinese residents were to be deterred from using human waste to 'enrich' their market gardens. The health officer, who had in the meantime visited China, Japan, and Hong Kong, also stressed the need to put pressure on the Dominion immigration authorities to fumigate the luggage and effects of Asian passengers.[79] Reference was made in the 1895 report of the board of health to the cubic feet of space by-law aimed at reducing overcrowding in Chinatown, and how prosecutions under this by-law in 1892–3 had assisted in relieving the problem.[80] Although the problems of Chinatown faded from the medical reports in the later 1890s, as those of what to do with Chinese lepers assumed crisis proportions, prosecutions for breach of sanitary and health by-laws by Chinese continued.[81] The Magistrate's Record Book for 1901, for instance, reveals sundry convictions for the by-law offence of sprinkling clothes by water sprayed from the mouth by Chinese laundry workers, not to mention infractions of provisions relating to the transportation of night soil and other human waste products used for fertilization.[82] Bureaucratic concern over the potential of the enclave as a source of contagion and as an example of the unsanitary practices of Asians was to re-emerge in 1906. The sanitary inspector's report referred to Chinese piggeries and gardens needing attention.[83] In 1907 the medical health officer referred to an outbreak of bubonic plague in Seattle. In taking steps to protect Victoria from a spread of this contagion Chinatown had, he said, been the primary focus of attention.[84]

The public health authorities in Vancouver were likewise determined to try and clean up the city's Chinatown and to use its unsanitary state to demonstrate the superiority of European lifestyles.[85] Despite the fact that, as in Victoria, there was no evidence brought to light that Chinatown was a source of any specific contagious disease, health authorities consistently labelled it a sanitary disaster area that warranted special by-law surveillance. Mention was never made in reports of formal and informal pressures to confine Chinese residents to a discrete area of the city, one with the very worst topography, nor of the resistance of the city to upgrading facilities and putting in sewers. As Kay Anderson notes, the leaders of the Chinese community were periodically active in seeking city support for 'neighbourhood improvement,' in at least one instance applying for a licence to do their own street cleaning.[86]

The 'hammer' of the Chinese in Vancouver was City Health Inspector Robert Marrion. From 1893 on when he was not conducting surveillance in Chinatown or piloting discriminatory by-laws directed at Chinese businesses, especially laundries, through the municipal process, he was regularly in court prosecuting by-law infractions by Chinese.[87] These included infractions of cubic footage, municipal tax, laundry sprinkling, and sanitation by-laws. Anderson suggests that 'Marrion's statement were entirely conformist for his day; he spoke not out of some irrational prejudice or unfortunate flaw in the human psyche, but rather in the accepted vocabulary for describing the district that housed these pioneers to Vancouver.'[88] Like other Europeans his pronouncements conflated identity and place. The result was that 'the process of racial classification was corroborated with every official expedition.'[89] Labelled as dirty and unsanitary by nature and inassimilable the Chinese were consigned to low-lying swampy land without the benefit of sanitary facilities. The pungent condition of the enclave was attributed by both public officials and the general European population to an inbred lack of concern by its residents for public health and basic civility.

There is little doubt that parts of Victoria's and Vancouver's Chinatowns were overcrowded and that the neighbourhoods were dirty and must have seemed unclean to outsiders. However, as Kay Anderson has pointed out in the case of Vancouver, other areas inhabited by Europeans, typically recent immigrants, ranked with Chinatown in squalor.[90] Moreover, there was no willingness on the part of the respective city halls to understand the causes of overcrowding and substandard housing in these enclaves. In most instances, indeed, municipal authorities and their electorates were responsible for or complicit in creating these conditions. The patterns by which Chinatowns emerged in Canada varied depending on location (urban or rural), chronology, economics, provincial and local politics, and relations within the Chinese communities themselves.[91] Although there were strong cultural and economic reasons why the immigrants from China and Hong Kong tended to congregate and live together, it is clear that as a group and as individuals they were not welcome in British Columbia communities, whether cities, towns, or mining camps. In Victoria, Chinese merchants were able early in 1859 to buy land to establish their businesses and dwellings, as well as to provide accommodation for labourers whose passage they sometimes helped to sponsor.[92] They had to settle, however, for the least desirable real estate close to the city core. Chinese labourers were not likely to find shelter from white landlords. Moreover, it was always possible to deter Chinese from residing or doing business in white neighbourhoods by the use of zoning, discriminatory by-laws, and restrictive covenants.[93] Where businesses run by Chinese were located outside Chinatown it was usually because they provided services required by white citizens, such as laundry facilities, that were not available from European entrepreneurs. In several communities in British Columbia active and violent steps were taken by local European populations to drive the Chinese out completely. The most notorious incident was the wholesale and forcible ejection of Chinese workers from Vancouver in 1887. Only intervention by the provincial government restored order and allowed the Chinese back.[94] When they returned it was evident that their presence would only be suffered if they settled in the area of low-lying, swampy land on the northern shore of False Creek. Later attempts to extend the boundaries of Chinatown to the north were vigorously resisted by both white residents and city hall.[95] Only businesses needed by Europeans were located outside the area.

Historically ghettos have become overcrowded because of the combined effects of lack of room to expand and the overall growth of population by births or further in-migration. The Chinatowns in Victoria and
Vancouver both exhibited overpopulation caused by geographic confinement and in-migration. Furthermore, as these areas were inhabited by
disenfranchised residents who had no political clout, they were the last to
be granted public facilities and services readily available to the dominant
community. The causes and effects of these constraints and limitations did
not enter the political or social calculus of the European community and its
political representatives. If Chinatowns were vile, it was simply because,
in the white mindset, their denizens were vile.

'CHINESE CRIMES'

The police record books from Vancouver for the period from 1898 to 1917
and the magistrate court records from Victoria from 1892 to 1920 provide
helpful insight into the extent to which much Chinese crime, other than
by-law infractions, was racially constructed in these cities.[96] The Vancouver records were designed to collect the records of those offenders who the
police felt should be photographed, presumably for future reference. They
are thus selective in their contents. However, the combination of a photo-
graph, information on age, occupation, date and place of arrest, nature of
the offence, the disposition of the case, and details of previous or later
brushes with the criminal law are helpful in divining motives of the law
enforcement authorities in relation to Chinese crime. As the statistics
already mentioned would suggest, the earliest mug shot records, for the
period 1898 to 1908, give the very distinct impression that for the police in
Vancouver the most serious examples of Chinese criminality were property offences, most notably theft. There are a series of charges and convictions for petty theft, involving stealing from retailers (from grocers to
jewellers),[97] hotels, private houses (clothing, cash, and chickens seem to
loom large),[98] and the CPR yards (scrap metal coveted by junk dealers and
coal, especially in the winter months).[99] Although the majority of the
victims were white individuals or European businesses, a minority was
from the Chinese community.[100] Charges and convictions also exist for a
small range of other types of offences, from vagrancy through to murder.
The penalties applied to the Chinese for petty theft are not, overall, different from those meted out to European offenders. As one might expect in a
maritime, frontier community there was a large shifting and shiftless
population of single males, some of who stole out of impulse or privation.

For both racial groups the normal penalty range for theft was three to six months in jail. There were, however, repeat offenders who received much longer sentences.[101] The lack of differentiation in sentencing was most likely the product of the machinelike and often formulaic process of sentence giving noted in studies of police magistrate courts in other Canadian cities.[102] Driven by stereotypes which, as Paul Craven has suggested, were reflective of notions of class superiority, traditional Canadian police magistrates were not disposed to reflect upon the social and economic inspirations to crime of those that came before them.[103] Expeditious justice, designed to teach offenders a lesson and control the masses, seems to have been the basic impulse. However, it is quite possible that some magistrates recognized the importance of even-handed justice, and were constrained from giving effect to racist sentiment by a formal commitment to the 'rule of law.' In the case of prosecution for crimes that both the Chinese and whites committed, the formal espousal of equality before the law and circumspection were undoubtedly important for those who administered the law in the courts.[104] Where discrimination is more open and blatant is in records generated by the police. Gratuitous descriptors such as 'Chink,' 'Opium Fiend,' and 'hophead' in the books that they generated indicate clearly that the police saw the Chinese as both strange and inferior and were not shy about saying so.[105]

The Victoria records, which were penned by the clerk of the police magistrate's court and included everyone formally charged, are more matter-of-fact but also more comprehensive than the Vancouver collection. There is little recorded apart from name, date of disposition, offence, and penalty, although in the case of mass arrests the address of the establishment (be it gambling house, opium joint, or brothel) is often included. The latter reference provides geographic specificity. These court books constitute a complete record of petty criminality in the city courts, including by-law infractions. The number of convictions for municipal offences prior to 1911 is high. As in Vancouver, stealing (theft) seems to have been the most constant crime recorded for the Chinese and it was handled in a similar way with similar results to those observed for the other city.[106]

Gambling

Listings of convictions for gambling offences emerge in the ledgers in Vancouver from 1905 on, although there were almost certainly individuals charged and convicted of these crimes much earlier. Entries for keeping common gaming houses, 'gambling,' 'dealing,' or 'playing' in unlawful games are the single most numerous record group for the period 1905 to 1907.[107] In the Police Record Book covering 1911 to 1917 convictions for gambling are only overshadowed by narcotics offences in the two sample years of 1913 and 1916.[108] Both the crimes statistics mentioned earlier and these records leave one confident that for the police gambling in Vancouver was essentially a Chinese offence.[109] The addresses of the gaming houses identified were all located in Chinatown, and there is a noticeable absence of non-Chinese charged with gambling. One would suppose that if Europeans running gambling dens had been picked up by the police and charged those events would have warranted photographs in the police ledger book. Certainly, that was true of many white keepers of houses of ill-fame. None exist for gambling joints for the sample period considered, even though gambling, including poker and dice, was commonplace in white working-class society, catered to formally in bars and clubs and informally in homes, apartments, and rooms.[110] Marquis notes that off-course betting on the horses was also widespread in the European community, and that the press hinted that some wealthy whites indulged in gambling and betting.[111] Even more significant in terms of the discriminatory application of the law in Vancouver is that the police sometimes found white gamblers in their raids on Chinese gambling haunts. Despite the fact that the games played were indigenous, such as mah-jong, pai-gow, chuckaluck, and fan-tan, and language must have been a barrier, whites found the games and environment compelling enough to be drawn to them. There are, however, few instances in Vancouver of whites being formally arrested and charged, let alone convicted in these situations. The informal evidence suggests that when caught they were cautioned rather than charged.[112]

While common gaming houses came under the rubric of 'disorderly houses' and keeping them was an indictable offence subject to up to one year's imprisonment, the standard penalty exacted during the sample years reviewed was three months' hard labour.[113] Police raids on Chinese gambling joints were episodic, rather than continual, prior to 1913. One may conclude that the objective of the law enforcement authorities, unlike that of moral and social reformers, was control, containment, and revenue generation rather than suppression.[114] Undoubtedly the police were of the view that the pervasiveness of gambling among the Chinese and its characterization as a status offence gave them power over a far greater segment of the inhabitants of Chinatown than more conventional offences such as theft, which required a victim. It was not a power, however, which they could or wanted to exercise consistently. Given other demands on their time and efforts the constant threat of arrest and prosecution at any time together with episodic raids were considered sufficient to make the point of who was in charge and the extent to which the Chinese community was subject to police power.

Police policy seems to have undergone something of change with the appointment of Police Chief Mulherne in 1912. Mulherne professed to be committed to the suppression of Chinese gambling. An antigambling unit was formed in 1913 to conduct more concerted and regular raids on 'gambling dens' in Chinatown.[115] This resulted in a dramatic increase in arrests, prosecutions, and convictions for the years 1913 to 1915, as well as widespread destruction of gambling paraphernalia. The campaign seems to have been successful only at a superficial level. This is evident in press reports of new 'dodges' developed by the Chinese to shroud gambling activities in the event of raids. Also, earnest discussion took place within the board of police commissioners over how to prevent the Chinese securing licences for social clubs, which were fronts for gambling activities.[116] The pressure on Chinese gambling relented only slowly, the number of convictions increasing dramatically in 1919 and in several years in the 1920s. By the late 1920s and 1930s, however, even within police ranks the sentiment was heard that gambling may have performed a useful social function in Chinatown, as it provided a relatively harmless recreational outlet for the large numbers of unattached males resident there.[117]

A similar pattern of increase in the volume of convictions of Chinese for gambling is evident in the Victoria police court records. Prior to 1910 prosecution for gambling was fitful. In two years in which the number of convictions was extraordinarily high, 1901 and 1906, the figures reflect mass arrests in police raids on particular gambling establishments. All thirty-nine men convicted of 'looking on' in 1901 were arrested in the one raid on 39 Fisgard Street in the heart of Chinatown.[118] In 1906 thirty-eight of the fifty-three persons convicted of playing or looking on in an unlawful gaming house were arrested in three locations on Fisgard and Cormorant Streets.[119] Mass arrests intensified after 1910, although the numbers of arrests and convictions fluctuated wildly. While there were occasional convictions for keeping gaming houses, playing or looking on were the offences most often charged. The Victoria records do reveal that Caucasians were being charged with and convicted of gambling offences, but invariably on Chinese premises, proof once again that the target of police activity in antigambling raids was Chinatown. Ten Caucasians were convicted on 4 June 1912 of looking on at 551 Cormorant Street and fined ten dollars each,[120] while on 7 June of the same year eleven were fined twenty dollars for playing at 550 Cormorant, a house run by Wing Sing and Ah Sam. The latter were fined forty dollars each for keeping, and their equipment ordered destroyed.[121]

Whatever the racial identity of the accused, from twenty to twenty-five dollars seems to have been the range of fines for playing, with ten dollars the norm for looking on. As in Vancouver, the stimulus to police action seems to have been the desire to harass the Chinese and to manifest their power over this despised population rather than any strategy of suppression. For their part the Chinese sought to shroud their operations by seeking licences as social clubs and incorporating inner doors and exits that would allow for early warning and fast escape, respectively.[122] For whites, except for those unlucky enough to be caught in a Chinese gambling house, the enforcement of the gambling laws was a nonissue.

The evidence is that many members of the Chinese community engaged in games of chance, often for money. Although there are no available figures for relative numbers of gamblers as compared with the white population, it is likely that a higher proportion of the Asian immigrants engaged in this pastime than the European community. In that sense one might expect the Chinese to have been a more frequent target for police activity directed against illegal gambling. However, it is not at all self-evident that a comparison between the Chinese labouring population, by far the largest segment of the Chinese community,[123] and European working-class communities would have rendered a significant disparity in gambling activity between them. Gambling and gaming had been and were deeply entrenched in British culture.[124] Although social and moral reformers, largely drawn from those already in or aspiring to the middle class, liked to preach otherwise and had success in outlawing these practices, it went on under their noses in both British and colonial society.[125] By and large, in British Columbia the police chose to go after illegal gambling sporadically. They pursued it in the main as and when it suited their need to indicate to the Chinese that they were in control. They were more active when a reformist police chief, such as Mulherne, was in charge, and during periods when reformers, municipal politicians, or middle-class communities were up in arms about gambling.[126] During the period under review, it was the 1910s when the police in both cities were under the greatest pressure from reformers to fight vice, including gambling, most vigorously.

Just as social and moral reformers and municipal politicians were, or chose to be, oblivious to the reasons for overcrowding and unsanitary conditions in Chinatown, so most of them failed to recognize the importance of gambling as a form of recreation for Chinese residents. Denied or granted limited access to a wide range of diversions open to whites, even those from the working-class, and increasingly a bachelor community, gambling was one of the few pastimes open to them that they could organize and control.[127] As a familiar part of their culture, it is understandable that the Chinese would resort to playing games of chance wherever they came together for relaxation.

It is possible that the police in both Vancouver and Victoria were prompted by a further consideration in pursuing Chinese for gambling. The practice was encouraged and sponsored in Chinatown by fraternal societies to which many Chinese immigrants belonged.[128] These were organized in some instances on a clan or language basis, reflecting old country connections, or as self-help or mutual benefit organizations in the host society.[129] Some were extensions of secret societies or 'tongs' organized much earlier in the Chinese empire to elude the gaze and attentions of imperial officials.[130] Gambling and gaming organized by the fraternal organizations operated at a higher level of commercial sophistication than pick up games in cafés or rooms. The police, who were in some respects just as capable of fantasizing about what went on in Chinatowns as the European public at large, may have worried about the potential power and capacity for subversion of these organizations. The fact that members of tongs did from time to time engage in violence toward each other and with Chinese political organizations may have strengthened this sentiment.[131] It is important, however, to recognize that the records examined reveal little hint of this thinking and discourse among the police in the two cities. Furthermore, neither police force had much in the way of a capacity for fighting what may have been seen as embryonic 'organized crime' during most of the period under review. The Vancouver police did set up an antigambling squad in 1913, which seems to have been responsible for a burst of prosecutions until 1915.[132] In 1918 a vice squad was established in the same city. The evidence examined by Greg Marquis suggests that it was not until the 1920s that the police and justice authorities began to focus seriously on gambling as a form of organized crime. This was largely a result of concerns about police corruption involving pay-offs by figures such as Shue Moy, a gambling kingpin, and Joe Yem, an illegal lottery organizer.[133] Even then, several of the detectives involved in vice work gave evidence to the effect that they did not view gambling by individual Chinese as a serious problem.[134]

The conclusion is irresistible that gambling was constructed as a Chinese crime in both cities. Chinese represented the vast majority of those arrested, charged, and convicted. White illegal gambling, which was widespread, was largely ignored. The police, who shared most of the negative stereotypes of the Chinese held by the European population at large, were interested in establishing control over this alien and 'inferior' community, largely to placate the white population, by showing periodically that the police had the measure of 'Oriental vice.' Police policy may also have reflected an incipient concern with organized crime. Finally, raids netted significant income through the multiple fines exacted. As the Chinese were much less prone to crimes of violence or property offences than their white neighbours, the two constabularies fastened on forms of deviance, such as gambling, which had no victim, were practised in known locations, and could be expected to produce multiple offenders when raids were conducted. Enforcement was highly discretionary, leaving the target community in doubt as to when the next raid would occur.

Narcotics

There was a significant increase in drug convictions of Chinese in the 1910s in both Vancouver and Victoria. The Dominion statistics for narcotics convictions in the former indicates that after records began to be kept for drug offences in 1912 there was a sharp rise for each of the next four years. The numbers then reduced to the low hundreds for the remainder of the decade, possibly a reflection of the demands made on the police force by another experiment in social control, this time along class lines: liquor prohibition. In 1916 there were actually more convictions for summary conviction drug offences than for summary conviction gambling offences. The sample years in the Police Record Books of 1913 and 1916 reveal a growing litany of charges and convictions for keeping opium joints and smoking or being in possession of narcotics.[135] With rare exceptions the accused were Chinese. In the single instance of a non-Chinese being convicted of keeping an opium den in the 1913 book, the scribe obviously wanted it to be known that the accused was not white and recorded him as a 'Negro.'[136] Several Europeans (typically transients or sailors) were convicted of being in possession of cocaine or morphine. On occasion the police could be equally judgmental about working-class whites who had slipped down into the depraved netherworld of narcotics. An Irish-Canadian miner, an amputee, was caught in possession of morphine. Notwithstanding that morphine addiction in his case may have originated in an attempt to alleviate the effects of his disablement, he was characterized dismissively as a 'morphine fiend.'[137]

The police now had available to them a new racially defined series of offences. These status offences, in common with gambling, allowed them much freer rein in harassing the inhabitants of Chinatown who were addicted to the practice and could be easily found and rounded up in known locations. It was only after 1920, with the stiffening of the drug laws and the penalties that attached to them, that the police declared war on the trade.[138] However, in the 1910s Vancouver police had established a law enforcement framework for using narcotics prosecutions to identify and exercise surveillance over that part of the Chinese population that ran opium joints and used narcotics. The control established undoubtedly assisted them when their powers were later extended. As with theft and gambling offences conventional penalties were attached to convictions. In the 1913 records the common sentence for smoking or being in possession of opium was a fifty dollar fine or three months in jail. This rose to between fifty and three hundred dollars or a three-month jail sentence in 1916 (the higher end was usually reserved for possession). Strangely, the sentences for keeping an opium joint were more modest, ranging from fifty to two hundred dollars or from two to three months in jail for 1916, even though this was an indictable offence. The results are explained by the fact that the Crown was able to proceed by summary process against keepers of disorderly houses.[139]

Victoria shared with Vancouver an increasing incidence of narcotics prosecutions after 1911, although in the capital the figures climbed steadily to a high in 1919. A survey of the magistrate's court records for six-month periods in 1912, 1914, 1917 and 1919 demonstrates an interesting, change in police charging strategy during the 1910s.[140] Being a 'found-in' replaced possession of opium for the purposes of smoking as the offence most frequently prosecuted. While the level of fines tended to fluctuate, a range of fifteen to twenty-five dollars, or one month in jail, was exacted from both found-ins and those convicted of possession of opium or cocaine. The attraction of the found-in offence, as with its counterpart of being found in a brothel or house of ill fame, was that the standard of proof was minimal – establishing that the accused was present in an opium joint was enough to secure a conviction. As with gambling, the impetus for action by the police was not suppression, but a desire to harass and impress upon the Chinese that they were subject to police power and discretion.[141] This charge of being a found-in was the easiest way to achieve that end. At the same time, by hauling in significant numbers of drug offenders in episodic raids the constabulary impressed on white, middle-class opinion that they were being both resolute and active in the pursuit of Asian criminals.

Drug use, like unsanitary practices and gambling, was constructed as a Chinese problem in British Columbia. However, during the 1910s this practice generated a fear about its possible corrosive effects that was more intense and enduring than worries about sanitation and gambling. Whites, especially the wealthy and eccentric, had been using and experimenting with narcotics over a long period, in most instances as a matter of personal choice. However, the drug trade was increasingly held up in white propaganda and by leading opinion makers – for example, Judge Emily Murphy – as the social practice most likely to 'emasculate' western society by luring young whites, male and female, of all classes, into its vortex, against their will.[142] The most troubling feature of this vice was the association of drug addiction with white slavery and the debasement of European female virtue, a theme underlined in both cartoons and staged photographs of drug-bemused 'beauties' lying with or in the clutches of an Asian or black male.[143] Even if the exploiter himself was white, the inevitable assumption was that the drug was manufactured and supplied by a Chinese. Lurking in the background was a set of anxieties surrounding miscegenation and the deterioration of the 'British race' that was bound to flow from racial intermixing.[144] The fact that members of the Chinese merchant class in Vancouver, not least those who had converted to Christianity, deprecated the distribution and use of opium, actually forming their own anti-opium league at one point, got lost in the alarmist rhetoric that invariably painted Chinatown as rotten to the core.[145]

Unlike gambling and prostitution, which were clearly not peculiarly Chinese obsessions, opium use was almost certainly much more widespread in the Chinese community than in the white community in general or in any particular segment of it. Moreover, opium had a market. This had led in British Columbia first to proliferation and then consolidation of opium production in factories in Vancouver and Victoria that supplied both the domestic and American markets for the product[146] – as Mackenzie King would find, to his horror. For social and moral reformers working busily to outlaw liquor use in European working-class communities, the thought that opium use might also be widespread in the white population was troubling in the extreme. European observers, with very few exceptions, conveniently forgot that the opium trade, and thus opium use, had been created by the British.[147] This result had been achieved by treaties, as Justice Henry Pellew Crease noted in *R v. Wing Chong*, secured by the British 'at the point of a bayonet.'[148] If opium was a Chinese vice, then it was so largely as a result of British economic and strategic calculations. The hypocrisy involved in labelling opium use as an inveterate sign of

Chinese deviance and moral weakness is further strengthened by more recent events. Attempts by Britain and other western nations, including Canada, to reduce drastically the growing of poppies and the production of opium by international accord was as much related to a decline in the western share of the market in the face of increased Chinese production as it was to high moral principle.[149]

Prostitution

Alongside the actual records of Chinese prosecuted for and convicted of exploitative offences involving prostitution – brothel keeping, procuring, and living off the avails – the fears and propaganda about their involvement in the sex trade seem overblown. The Police Record Books in Vancouver do list Chinese men convicted for these offences. Further work is needed to plot the location of addresses where bawdy-house offenders more generally were arrested to determine whether there might have been a less obvious Chinese connection. However, the records do not suggest that the numbers of arrests and convictions were out of proportion to Chinese representation in the general population.[150] If Chinatown was so riddled with dens of vice, as the moral reformers were fond of claiming, one would expect to see much more in the way of evidence of them, especially given the willingness of the Vancouver police to go into the quarter and arrest everyone in sight in gambling and opium joints. The records demonstrate that there were brothel keepers in the Chinese community, such as Hung Lee, who was given a three-year sentence for procuring in October 1911, and Charlie Quong, an apartment house janitor sent up for one year for the same offence in April 1913. However, it was the splash made by these infrequent, individual cases in the media, not evidence of an epidemic of Chinese brothel keeping, that seared in white consciousness that the Chinese were vice-mongers. In both instances the men were arrested in the company of white women.[151] Hung Lee was also an associate of the notorious Dr Lew of Victoria, who was convicted for procuring white girls in Vancouver for a brothel in Prince Rupert. That case in particular tied into a long-standing myth about the fate of young white women lured into brothels: that they were denied exit by their clothes being confiscated. Dr Lew was found to have the clothes of two white women in his luggage![152]

Some members of the Chinese community, especially among its leaders, sought to challenge the branding of their community as sexually vicious. In 1906, when the sex trade in Vancouver's east end moved close to and into Chinatown and city officialdom suggested that this was the place for it, the Chinese Board of Trade protested in the strongest possible terms, emphasizing the desire of the community to protect its children from 'the worst phases' of western civilization.[153]

In Victoria both the Magistrate's Record Book and the Annual Report of the Chief of Police indicate that during much of the period from 1892 to 1920, prostitution-related offences in the Chinese community were non-events. Apart from the occasional conviction for keeping a disorderly house, which probably meant a brothel, and the occasional dribble of men sentenced as found-ins, Chinese sexual vice does not appear to have been a police concern or priority. Again, one is left with serious doubts about the supposedly alarming dimensions of Chinese involvement in the sex trade.

As with narcotics, the label of criminality attached to the Chinese in the context of prostitution hearkened back to the long-standing myth of the 'other,' or alien, as the potential defiler of local, virtuous women.[154] The international anti–white slavery movement, which had in fact uncovered evidence of a trade in poor girls and women from unstable communities across borders and oceans, strengthened these fears.[155] Now every woman was in peril from the shadowy and vicious figures who controlled the sex trade, many of whom were claimed to be foreigners and, worse still, non-Christians and racially inferior. If their activities were not checked the result was certain race suicide.

STEREOTYPING OF THE CHINESE AND OTHER CRIMES

The newspapers' penchant for racializing offences was not confined to those labelled as peculiarly Chinese. It was also true with crimes such as murder, which ostensibly knew no bounds of colour. It does not seem to have mattered, moreover, whether the Chinese subject was the victim or the killer. Take the case of the notorious and bizarre murder of a Chinese house boy, Mah Lin, by eight-year-old Ernest Chenoweth in 1900 in Rossland, British Columbia. The local press, on hearing of the discovery of the victim's body, jumped immediately to the conclusion that he was on a tong hit list, the target of internecine killing within the Chinese community.[156] The same capacity to jump to conclusions was apparent in 1914, when Jack Kong, another house boy, was arrested for the murder of Mrs Millard, the wife of a prominent railway man and Kong's employer. This event was proof positive to both the media and city council of the innate criminality of Chinese youth. The reaction included attempts to have

Chinese children banned from white schools because of their potentially corrupting influence on European children.[157] This initiative, which failed, did not escape the notice of the Chinese consul, Lin Shih-Yuan. In Anderson's words the consul denounced the council's attempts as a vindictive response to a single alleged crime and reminded council, as reported by the *Sun*, that, 'next to "native-born Canadians," the percentage of criminals among Chinese in British Columbia was the lowest.'[158]

Both these cases are also interesting because they demonstrate that the construction of Chinese identity, normally associated with a defined geographic area, was carried with the individual into the wider society and could not be shaken off. Moreover, white reading of these events legitimated the process of racialization in spatial terms. In the white psyche the episodes proved that there were dangers in allowing members of this degraded and perverse minority outside their enclave, lest they infect the dominant population, and the wisdom of confining them within Chinatown.

THE CHINESE AND THE SUPERIOR COURTS

Apart from the obvious fact that some crimes were viewed and treated as racially specific (an issue that most British Columbia judges would not touch), there is little, if any, direct evidence that racial background played a role in the disposition of individual cases.

If the construction and enforcement of the criminal law in the case of the Chinese was openly racialized, their treatment in the superior courts of the province was not. Because the Chinese were charged overwhelmingly with summary conviction offences during the period examined (including both gambling and narcotics offences) there were relatively few appeals to the county or supreme court. On the surface at least lack of access to legal assistance does not appear to have been a problem. Where appeals were taken and the decisions reported the evidence is clear that Chinese accused had access to sound legal representation. Indeed, some of the contemporary leaders of the bar, including Theodore Davie, H. Dallas Helmcken, Sir Charles Tupper, J.A. Russell, and John De B. Farris, took cases on behalf of Chinese appellants. How these legal services were paid for deserves enquiry. In some instances money was put up in the Chinese merchant community.[159] It is also possible that the consul general in Vancouver helped out in certain circumstances. The extent to which some lawyers may have felt an obligation to provide representation on a *pro bono* basis has also to be looked into. Sympathy by lawyers for the Chinese only went so far, however. With several notable exceptions at the bar – freer-thinking members such as J.A. Russell and J. Edward Bird, for example – its leaders were unalterably opposed to allowing the Chinese into the ranks of the legal profession.[160] Service out of a sense of *noblesse oblige* was one thing: permitting the Chinese to become social and economic equals and competitors was quite another.

The swearing of the oath by non-Christians in forms that reflected their culture had been accepted early in the history of the colony of British Columbia by Matthew Baillie Begbie.[161] The court of appeal reaffirmed this precedent in 1904 in *R. v. Lai Ping*.[162] As long as a form of swearing was undertaken with the understanding that it bound the taker to tell the truth, said the court, it was acceptable. If the testimony were consciously untrue a perjury charge would lie. Interpreters were also available to translate the testimony for the benefit of the parties and witnesses; how reliable the translations provided were is perhaps another matter. That was something a judge could not control in terms of content, although from time to time convictions were quashed where an appeal court found that the process had been handled in a way that increased the chance that misunderstanding had occurred. Certainly, where there were serious doubts that an accused or witness understood English and no or inadequate attempts at interpretation had been made, appellate courts reacted unfavourably.[163]

Episodic concern of appellate courts with fairness of the process because of cultural difficulties with communication does not end there, however. In the first place, the trial of petty offences was not known for its deliberative character. Nor was there scrupulous concern for whether the accused understood what he had been charged with, let alone what evidential or procedural rights he may have had. These problems, which were endemic to the system of police court justice, must have become magnified in the case of poor Chinese with little or no English, in the absence of counsel. In the vast majority of cases that did not go on appeal there was no cure for this serious weakness in the process. Secondly, some judges, even in the ranks of the superior court bench, entertained the view that the Chinese were untruthful or deceitful as a race. Justice John Hamilton Gray of the earliest Supreme Court bench definitely harboured these views, as he made clear in his report as commissioner in the 1885 Royal Commission on Chinese Immigration.[164] To the extent that this stereotype existed and was not or only partially neutralized by 'rule of law' notions held by most judges, it likely played out in the way in which evidence and credibility was assessed. Moreover, it may have been allowed to shroud what other judges, such as Begbie and Crease, *were* prepared to recognize, that difficulties in securing reliable evidence from Chinese witnesses had more to do with problems of communication and comprehension than a devious desire to mislead.[165]

At a more abstract level of procedure and evidence the reported cases involving Chinese accused suggest that 'rule of law' thinking was front and foremost in the minds of appellate judges. Convictions were quashed, new trials ordered, or evidence declared inadmissible. These were the results where costs awarded on a conviction for selling liquor to Indians were retained by the magistrate convicting;[166] where a judge in a murder case omitted to instruct the jury on manslaughter as a possible alternative verdict;[167] where an accused charged with murder made a incriminating statement to the police after being cautioned, but only after making an earlier and similar statement without a caution;[168] and where the trial judge in the case of a charge of causing grievous bodily harm commented on the failure of the accused to testify in the preliminary hearing in his instruction to the jury.[169]

Even in the case of race-specific crimes, such as gambling and narcotics, judges proved themselves to be protective of the common law principles and values of the criminal process, despite statutory attempts to erode them. Thus in *R. v. Ah Jim* in 1905 County Court Judge Bole quashed a conviction for 'looking on' a gambling game that relied upon the uncorroborated evidence of an accomplice who was shown to have been given money to testify.[170] In *R. v. Chow Chin* in 1920 Chief Justice Hunter granted an application for *habeas corpus* with *certiorari* in a case in which the judge, rehearing a conviction for possession of narcotics, refused to issue bench warrants for the attendance of two witnesses at the request of the defence.[171] The decision is instructive because Hunter obviously thought that the evidence in the case was conclusive to convict 'the Chinaman.'[172] However, he cautioned that under the principles of English justice although a man was ever so guilty the conviction must be 'according to law.' There had, the chief justice added, been a departure in this case from 'fundamental principles – which is to hear the whole case and allow a full defence.'

A similar pattern of thinking and resistance to eroding the rule of law is evident in the way in which appellate judges in British Columbia construed the meaning of offences. The tendency was to construe narrowly even in the case of crimes or infractions that were essentially Chinese or in which Chinese involvement incensed public opinion. Municipal by-laws that were discriminatory in their content or application were struck down from time to time as *ultra vires*. These included by-laws or practices treating Chinese differentially as health risks and those barring them from setting up businesses in defined areas.[173] During the period under examination the process of constitutional interpretation became noticeably sanitized as the Privy Council decisions in *Union Colliery v. Bryden*[174] and *Cunningham v. Tomey Homma*[175] took hold. After the turn of the century the B.C. judges evinced a very strong tendency to confine themselves to determining whether the legislative matter fell into sections 91 or 92 of the British North America Act or within powers delegated to municipalities by provincial statutes. They eschewed comment on whether the legislation or action was reasonable or not. Justice MacDonald made the point in *In Re Glover and Sam Kee* in 1914. In response to the argument that a municipal by-law confining laundries to a restricted area was unreasonable and oppressive and intended to create a monopoly in restraint of trade, he opined that this was not a subject for judicial comment or interference.[176]

In the case of gambling, while the judges were clear that gaming houses fell within the more generic term 'disorderly house,'[177] they were at the same time ready to put the prosecution to the test in terms of satisfying the relaxed requirements of proof for some of these offences. So in *R. v. Hong Guey* in 1907 the police chief of New Westminster was not allowed to get away with seizing lottery paraphernalia under a warrant for seizing gaming equipment and having the accused charged with selling lottery tickets.[178] In rendering his judgment Justice Bole referred to the need to give cautious application of statutory inroads into the presumption of innocence at common law. Judges did give short shrift to appellants' arguments that clubs established by Chinese for 'social purposes' were not disorderly houses when games such as fan tan were being played and the club was taking a rake-off.[179] However, lack of evidence that a game of chance or of mixed skill and chance was being played for money was found to be fatal to a conviction for keeping a common gaming house.[180] Again, in *R. v. Sit Quin* a conviction for liquor being found on leased premises was quashed because, while the accused did rent out space to tenants, the liquor was found in storage space occupied by his son and was thus within the accused's private premises.[181]

Perhaps most revealing with respect to the apparent reticence of the judges to allow race to intrude into their characterization of offences is the 1914 decision of the court of appeal in *R. v. Sam Jon*.[182] In this case the court quashed a conviction of a Chinese householder for allowing a girl to be on the premises to have illicit intercourse 'with any man.' The evidence at trial was that it was the householder himself who had sexual relations with the girl. The appellate court, following an earlier decision of the Ontario Court of Appeal in a case also involving a Chinese householder, interpreted the phrase 'with any man' narrowly and excluded the householder from its reach.[183] This was of course the sort of incident that was capable of touching off strong and histrionic emotions within the press and among the white public. The judges proved themselves impervious to this sort of pressure. While the prior Ontario decision provided a convenient safety hatch for them, their general record suggests that their conclusion would have been the same had this been a case of first instance.

CONCLUSION

Although much more work needs to be done on the issue of the racialization of criminal justice in British Columbia and elsewhere in Canada, the pattern that has so far emerged fits neatly into the theoretical framework suggested by Kay Anderson. Indeed, the data examined suggest that the law was viewed by whites in the province as an important instrument in constructing a distinctive Chinese identity and in regulating their conduct. Legal definitions and characterizations of 'otherness' assisted significantly in the construction of spatial identification of immigrants within Chinatowns. The law was used consciously by legislators, administrators, and the police to establish and maintain the deviant character of these enclaves and so to control their inhabitants, at the same time providing a cultural model that constituted the antithesis of how whites saw themselves and their achievements. The law was also deployed in a way that ensured that those Chinese who did live and work outside Chinatown were subject to the same stereotypes as those within and understood that they were only out on sufferance for the convenience of their white masters and mistresses. If contrasts were to fade at times – as they must have done when Europeans considered the large numbers of Caucasians charged with liquor or prostitution offences, particularly drunkenness – 'respectable' white opinion makers were dexterous enough to find a class or gender explanation for white vice.

This examination of the legal construction of Chinese deviance proves that the law played an important role in the transmission and reproduction of racist stereotypes, a process that was amplified by a racist press. If Anderson is to be faulted it is perhaps for paying too little attention to the pivotal role of newspapers and magazines in opinion formulation in settler societies. As Raymond Evans, Kay Saunders, and Kathryn Cronin have pointed out in their extensive examination of racism in colonial

Queensland, in such communities, where time for reading was at a premium, information and opinion were often derived from the columns of the local press.[184] In newspapers and magazines identification with exclusionist sentiment was strong and buttressed by a totally uncritical acceptance of external news communications and opinion on race and ethnicity. There is clear evidence in British Columbia that the labelling of certain crimes as 'Chinese' was assisted by the sensationalist treatment of notorious cases in which immigrants were involved as victim, accused, or both. Where direct evidence of Chinese involvement was lacking, fantasy easily took over.

This initial study also tends to confirm Anderson's thesis that, within state institutions – in this case the law – there were tensions as to what constituted appropriate policy in dealing with the Chinese. The law appears as Janus-faced, with superior courts justices accepting that the legal system had a pervasive obligation to see that justice was done in a formal sense to all those, whether British subjects or not, who claimed the protection of the Crown. Meanwhile, the legislature, municipalities, and the police were using it to deny or limit the few rights that the Chinese continued to enjoy. The judicial branch of the legal system was to some extent responsive to the need of the Chinese for protection from discrimination, as well as the facilitation of their economic transactions, not as the result of any great admiration or respect for this minority, but from a belief that as judges they were obliged to uphold certain fundamental principles of law and justice. In this they were assisted by forensic pressure from the Chinese community, which was able in certain circumstances to harness the financial and moral resources of its wealthier members and diplomatic representatives first of the Chinese empire and later the Republic of China.

The balance was no means even between the law as discriminator and protector, affected as it was over time by developing constitutional constraints and narrowing of the vision of judges as to their role within the constitutional and governmental order. As the Chinese were subject to a particular form of hegemony, that exercised by the judges, they were always in danger of becoming victims of changing judicial agendas and biases. Moreover, there was, as we have seen, an important lower tier of court-administered criminal justice that lacked the more abstract values and sensitivities evident in the superior courts. The processes of these lower courts constituted the way in which justice was experienced and viewed by most Chinese in their daily lives and the basis for how most viewed the system to which they were subject. It was a system that by and large accepted the racist premises underlying the criminal law as it applied to visible minorities.

Sadly, the worst was yet to come, as the vestiges of judicial protection eroded further in the 1920s with the toughening of the narcotics laws, increases in police powers in arresting drug offenders, and exclusionary immigration legislation. Ironically, as Chinatowns, with their aging bachelor populations and no significant opportunity for regeneration, began to slip into decline, the paranoia and meanness in white society and among its politicians toward the Chinese increased in intensity.[185] Ultra-racism was fed by propagandist tracts such as Judge Emily Murphy's *Black Candle*, which laid the responsibility for the drug trade on the Chinese and blacks.[186] The newspapers, and even 'penny dreadfuls,' like *The Writing on the Wall* by Hilda Glynn Ward, furthered the cause by spreading the idea that both Chinese and Japanese were poised to take over the province economically. Chinese involvement in small retail businesses and services, such as grocery stores and laundries, and in market gardening was touted as the death knell for European competition in these areas of the economy.[187] All of these written sources of racism spouted on the one hand the gospel of social Darwinism and the innate mental inferiority of the 'Chinese Race,' and on the other emphasized their cunning and duplicity, which could fool even the brightest Caucasian. The campaign to marginalize and control Chinatowns continued relentlessly for the better part of twenty more years, despite evidence that some sections of the white community were beginning to have second thoughts about the justice of this form of racial segregation.[188] A combination of highly discriminatory law reform and a judiciary increasingly institutionalized to hear their legislative master's voice meant the further erosion of the law as the protector and facilitator of visible minorities. The 'racist state' in Canada reached its apogee in the inter-war years, and nowhere more so than in British Columbia.

It was only after the Second World War, with its dreadful legacy of state racism and racial cleansing in Nazi Germany and overt racial discrimination against people of Japanese birth in several allied countries, that racist structures and the law that supported them were dismantled in Canada. Between 1947 and 1949 Chinese Canadians acquired full rights of citizenship through the extension of the franchise at the provincial, federal, and municipal levels.[189] In turn legal barriers to their entry to the professions, trades, and various industries were lifted. Not until the late 1960s, however, with the adoption of more liberal immigration policies in Canada, would the Chinese population start to grow again.[190] In the 1990s the largest single ethnic group among new immigrants to Canada is Chinese, from Hong Kong, Taiwan, and mainland China. Although the structure of racist laws that form the background to the story told here has happily been demolished, the stereotypes that supported it have the capacity to live on. Chinese live and work in Canada in formal equality with white Canadians, but some are still subject to racist slurs and attacks by members of the majority European community. Moreover, as a group they are not entirely free from the judgmental stereotypes of officialdom, especially the police, who are still sometimes inclined to label particular ethnic groups as more criminogenic than others, and to relate particular crimes to particular ethnicities, as if that is somehow preordained.[191]

Part of the value of the seminal agenda constructed by Dick Risk twenty-five years ago has been its capacity to open up new areas of research and speculation, as the records of the major themes set out there – including the theme of the legal experience in Canada of minority religious, national, and ethnic groups – are exposed and analysed. Hopefully this work and that of other scholars on the Chinese experience will lead to further exploration in this field. The legal experiences in Canada of groups as diverse as Jews, Hutterites, Mennonites, Doukhobors, Ukrainians, Italians, Germans, Poles, Japanese, South Asians, various Caribbean and African communities, and Afro-Americans, to name just some, warrant extensive investigation in the future.[192]

NOTES

My thanks are due to Jeff Locke for assisting with the background research for this chapter and to Jim Phillips and Blaine Baker for their sage suggestions for its improvement.

1 Dick Risk, 'A Prospectus for Canadian Legal History,' *Dalhousie Law Journal* 1 (1973), 227, 230.

2 Ibid.

3 See W. Peter Ward, *White Canada Forever: Popular Attitudes and Public Policy Toward Orientals in British Columbia*, 2nd ed. (Montreal and Kingston: McGill-Queen's University Press 1990); Patricia Roy, *A White Man's Province: British Columbia Politicians and Chinese and Japanese Immigrants, 1858–1914* (Vancouver: UBC Press 1989); Hugh Johnston, *The Voyage of the Komagatu Maru: The Sikh Challenge to Canada's Colour Bar* (Vancouver: UBC Press 1989); Kay J. Anderson, *Vancouver's Chinatown: Racial Discourse in Canada, 1875–1960* (Montreal and Kingston: McGill-Queen's University Press 1991).

4 See Constance Backhouse, 'White Female Help and Chinese-Canadian Employers: Race, Class, Gender and Law in the Case of Yee Clun, 1924,' *Canadian Ethnic Studies* 26 (1994), 37; Constance Backhouse, 'White Women's

Labour Laws: Anti-Chinese Racism in Early Twentieth-Century Canada,' *Law and History Review* 14 (1996), 315; Alan Grove and Ross Lambertson, 'Pawns of the Powerful: The Politics of Litigation in the Union Colliery Case,' *B.C. Studies*, 103 (1994), 3; Ross Lambertson, 'After *Union Colliery:* Law, Race and Class in the Coalmines of British Columbia,' in Hamar Foster and John McLaren, eds., *Essays in the History of Canadian Law, Vol. 6, British Columbia and the Yukon* (Toronto: The Osgoode Society for Canadian Legal History 1995), 386; John McLaren, 'The Burdens of Empire and the Legalization of White Supremacy in Canada,' in W. Gordon and T. Fergus, ed., *Legal History in the Making* (London: Hambledon Press 1990), 187; John McLaren, 'The Early British Columbia Supreme Court and the "Chinese Question": Echoes of the Rule of Law,' in Wesley Pue and Dale Gibson, *Glimpses of Canadian Legal History* (Winnipeg: Legal Research Institute, University of Manitoba 1991), 111; J. McLaren, 'The Early B.C. Judges, the Rule of Law and the "Chinese Question": The California and Oregon Connections,' in John McLaren, Hamar Foster, and Chet Orloff, eds., *Law for the Elephant, Law for the Beaver: Essays in the Legal History of the North American West* (Regina and Pasadena, Cal.: Canadian Plains Research Centre and Ninth Judicial Circuit Historical Society 1992), 237; Bruce Ryder, 'Racism and the Constitution: The Constitutional Fate of British Columbia Anti-Asian Immigration Legislation, 1884–1909,' *Osgoode Hall Law Journal* 29 (1991), 638. For the most extensive theoretical and historical analysis to date, see James W. St. G. Walker, *'Race,' Rights and the Law in the Supreme Court of Canada: Historical Case Studies* (Toronto: The Osgoode Society for Canadian Legal History 1997).

5 Anderson, *Vancouver's Chinatown*.
6 Ibid., 20–3.
7 Ibid., 23–8. As Carolyn Strange and Tina Loo have demonstrated in *Making Good: Law and Moral Regulation in Canada 1867–1939* (Toronto: University of Toronto Press 1997) the period under review was one in which the deployment of the law in the cause of moral regulation, and the construction of a 'virtuous Canada' was in full swing. The vision was one of a 'white Canada.'
8 Ibid., 25.
9 Ibid., 25–6.
10 See note 3, supra.
11 Anderson, *Vancouver's Chinatown*, 6–7.
12 McLaren, 'The Earliest British Columbia Supreme Court and the "Chinese Question".'
13 Anderson, *Vancouver's Chinatown*, 27–8.
14 McLaren, 'The Early B.C. Judges,' 237, 237–42.
15 55–6 Vict., c. 29 (1892).

16 Chinese Immigration Act, SC 1923, c. 38.

17 Narcotics Control Amendment Act, SC 1921, c. 42; SC 1922, c. 36; SC 1923, c. 20.

18 Nicholas K. Blomley, *Law, Space, and the Geographies of Power* (New York: Guildford Press 1994).

19 Arthur Nussbaum, *A Concise History of the Law of Nations* (New York: Macmillan Co. 1961), 55–7, 64–5, 194–5.

20 René David and John E.C. Brierley, *Major Legal Systems in the World Today*, 3rd ed. (London: Stevens & Sons 1985), 455, 501–2. See also Bernard Lewis, *The Middle East: 2000 Years of History* (London: Weidenfeld and Nicholson 1995), 269–70 and Stanley Wolpert, *A New History of India* (New York: Oxford University Press 1993), 127.

21 Edward P. Thompson, *Customs in Common* (New York: New Press 1991); H.W. Arthurs, *'Without the Law': Administrative Justice and Legal Pluralism in Nineteenth Century England* (Toronto: University of Toronto Press 1985).

22 David and Brierley, *Major Legal Systems*, 491–6, 479–80.

23 Ibid., 555–6, 560–3. See also Robert Williams Jr, *The American Indian in Western Legal Thought* (New York: Oxford University Press 1991), and Bruce Kercher, *An Unruly Child: A History of Law in Australia* (Sydney: Allen & Unwin 1995), 3–21.

24 See, e.g., Max Gluckman, *Judicial Process among the Barotse of Northern Rhodesia*, 2nd ed. (Manchester: Manchester University Press 1967).

25 Leonard Thompson, *A History of South Africa* (New Haven: Yale University Press 1990), 154–220.

26 J.R. Miller, *Skyscrapers Hide the Heavens: A History of Indian-White Relations in Canada* (Toronto: University of Toronto Press 1989), 85–207.

27 On the regime in Manila, see Royal Commission on Chinese Immigration, *Report and Minutes of Evidence* (Ottawa: Queen's Printer 1885), report of Justice John Hamilton Gray, lxii–lxiii. For the Victorian gold fields, see Kathryn Cronin, *Colonial Casualties: Chinese in Early Victoria* (Melbourne: Melbourne University Press 1982), 80–102.

28 David Chuenyan Lai, *Chinatowns: Towns within Cities in Canada* (Vancouver: UBC Press 1988); Anderson, *Vancouver's Chinatown*, 34–105.

29 Tina Loo, *Making Law, Order and Authority in British Columbia, 1821–1871* (Toronto: University of Toronto Press 1994).

30 Ibid., 113–33.

31 Act to Make Better Provisions for the Qualification of Voters, SBC 1874, c. 12, s. 3. The denial of the franchise was extended to municipal elections by SBC 1876, c. 1, s. 1. As inclusion on the federal voters' list depended on provincial enfranchisement, Chinese were also absent from the Dominion voters' list.

32 McLaren, 'The Earliest British Columbia Supreme Court and the "Chinese Question,"' 107–25. The law was also deployed to deny Chinese access to Crown lands, to the professions, and to employment on public works projects.

33 See, e.g., *In Re Lee Sam* (1904), 10 BCLR 270 (SC); *In Re Chin Chee* (1905), 11 BCLR 102 (SC); and *In Re Lee Him* (1910), 15 BCLR 163 (SC).

34 On the evolution of the immigration regimes for Asian populations seeking to migrate to Canada, see McLaren, 'The Burdens of Empire.'

35 McLaren, 'The Early British Columbia Supreme Court and the "Chinese Question,"' 125–44.

36 Ibid., 136. Based on an analysis of Asian persons before the British Columbia Supreme Court (Civil), January 1885 to November 1895, using British Columbia Archives and Record Services (BCARS), GR 1863 (GR 1590 microfilm). During this period there were no less than 99 suits listed with Chinese plaintiffs and 118 with Chinese defendants.

37 See Royal Commission on Chinese Immigration, 1885, *Report and Minutes of Evidence*, vii–viii (Justice Gray); 72 (Chief Justice Begbie); and 141 (Justice Crease) for attitudes of the earliest three judges on the British Columbia Supreme Court on Chinese business practices.

38 (1895), 4 BCLR 168 (SC).

39 Ibid., 170, per Drake J.

40 See M. Zaffroni, 'The Great Chain of Being: Racism and Imperialism in Colonial Victoria, 1858–1871' (MA thesis, History, University of Victoria 1987). For accounts of the American experience, see S. Miller, *The Unwelcome Immigrant: The American Image of the Chinese, 1785–1882* (Berkeley: University of California Press 1969); A. Saxton, *The Indispensable Enemy: Labour and the Anti-Chinese Movement in California* (Berkeley: University of California Press 1971). The important role of the colonial press in disseminating racism is treated in Raymond Evans, Kay Saunders, and Katherine Cronyn, *Race Relations in Colonial Queensland*, 2nd ed. (St Lucia: University of Queensland Press 1988), 15–16.

41 Ward, *White Canada Forever*, 7, 49–51.

42 Ibid., 7–8, 51–2.

43 Evans, Saunders, and Cronyn, *Race Relations*, 289–340; Roy, *A White Man's Province*, 30–1. Roy notes that despite medical evidence before the 1885 Royal Commission on Chinese Immigration that indicated that the Chinese presented no public health threat, continued press reports mentioned the reputation of Chinatowns as unsanitary and Chinese immigrants as carriers of contagion. She also notes that 'no serious epidemic of disease was ever actually traced to a Chinatown in British Columbia' (p. 33).

44 Roy, *White Man's Province*, 29–30.
45 Ibid., 14–15.
46 Greg Marquis, 'Vancouver Vice: The Police and the Negotiation of Morality,' in Hamar Foster and John McLaren, *Essays in the History of Canadian Law, Vol. 6 British Columbia and the Yukon* (Toronto: The Osgoode Society for Canadian Legal History 1995), 242; Anderson, *Vancouver's Chinatown*, 92–104; Roy, *White Man's Province*, 15–18.
47 Miller, *Skyscrapers*, chap. 2.
48 The Criminal Code 1892, 55 & 56 Vict., c. 29 contained a series of provisions directed against gambling in various forms. Keeping or appearing to keep either a common gaming house or a common betting house, both described as 'disorderly houses,' was an indictable offence subject to a maximum of one year's imprisonment (ss. 198, 196, and 197). Moreover, by s. 199 playing or looking on in a common gaming house was a summary conviction offence subject to a maximum fine of $100 and a minimum of $20, or two months' imprisonment. It was also a summary conviction offence to prevent or obstruct the entry of a constable or other duly authorized officer to a disorderly house, on pain of a fine of $100 or six months in jail with or without hard labour. Under the vagrancy provisions (ss. 207, 208) it was possible to charge keepers and inmates of and those habitually frequenting disorderly houses with that summary conviction offence. The penalty was $50 or six months with or without hard labour.
        This basic pattern was preserved. However, in 1913 several amendments were made to these provisions. Criminal Code Amendment Act, 3 & 4 Geo. V, ss. 11, 12 (1913). The offence of keeping a disorderly house was extended to catch those knowingly permitting the use of premises as a disorderly house, i.e., landlords. At the same time a new summary conviction offence of being found in a disorderly house was added to catch anyone on the premises when a raid took place, whatever his or her reason for being there. The penalty prescribed was a fine of $100 or two months' imprisonment. In due course the vagrancy offences of keeping or being an inmate or habitual frequenter of a disorderly house were repealed. Criminal Code Amendment Act, 4–5 Geo. V, c. 12, s. 7 (1915).
49 See note 147, infra.
50 British Columbia had in fact tried to ban the use of opium in 1884 by statute – the Act to Regulate the Chinese Population of British Columbia, SBC 1884, c. 4, s. 18 – legislation designed more generally to induce the Chinese to leave the province. The courts neutralized the act by striking down several of its clauses.
51 On the riot and its consequences, see Roy, *White Man's Province*, 187–226. The

Canadian government of Wilfrid Laurier was initially inclined to consider only Japanese claims for damage caused during the riot, in order to placate Japan as the 'rising star' in Asia. China, seen as being in decline, attracted little or no respect. However, pressure from a variety of quarters, including King himself and the British government, induced Ottawa to extend King's mandate to consider claims by Chinese property owners.

52 W. MacKenzie King, *Losses Sustained by the Chinese Population of Vancouver B.C. on the Occasion of the Riots in that City in September, 1907* (Ottawa: King's Printer 1908), 15–16.

53 7–8 Edward VII, c. 50 (1908). The offences were described as indictable and subject to a maximum of three years' imprisonment, a fine between $50 and $1,000, or to both. S. 1.

On various interpretations of the impulses to this legislation, see Elizabeth Comack, '"We Will Get Some Good Out of This Riot Yet": The Canadian State, Drug Legislation and Class Conflict,' in Stephen Brickey and Elizabeth Comack, eds., *The Social Basis of Law: Critical Readings in the Sociology of Law* (Toronto: Garamond Press 1986), 70; M. Green, 'A History of Narcotics Control: The Formative Years,' *University of Toronto Faculty of Law Review*, 37 (1979), 42; Neil Boyd, 'The Origins of Canadian Narcotics Legislation: The Process of Criminalization in Historical Context,' in R.C. Macleod, ed., *Lawful Authority: Readings on the History of Criminal Justice in Canada* (Toronto: Copp Clark Pitman 1988), 192. The role of MacKenzie King as solo crusader and catalyst for drug law reform in Canada may be contrasted with the coalition of political concern that led to the introduction of anti-narcotics legislation in Australia, at roughly the same time. See Desmond Manderson, *From Mr. Sin to Mr. Big: A History of Australian Drug Laws* (Melbourne: Oxford University Press 1993), 39–58.

54 Glen Murray, 'Cocaine Use in the Era of Social Reform: The Natural History of a Social Problem in Canada, 1890–1911,' *Canadian Journal of Law and Society* 2 (1987), 29.

55 The Opium and Drug Act, 1 & 2 Geo. V, c. 17 (1911).

56 Ibid., s. 3. The offence was described as summary conviction and subject to a maximum fine of $500, or one year in jail, or both.

57 Ibid., s. 3, for possession and transporting. Section 6 proscribed exportation, with a maximum fine of $500 or six months in jail, or both. All the offences under s. 3 were subject to a reverse onus provision on proof (s. 10). Moreover, a magistrate could order that one-half of the amount of the fine exacted for an offence under the act go to the informant (s. 11).

58 Ibid., s. 5. The penalty for this summary conviction offence was a maximum fine of $200 or three months in jail or both.

59 Ibid., s. 4. For the summary conviction offence of smoking or possession a maximum fine of $50 was set or one month's imprisonment or both. Looking on was visited with the higher fine of $100, one month's imprisonment, or both.

60 Criminal Law Amendment Act, 8 & 9 Edw. VII, c. 9 (1909), Schedule, adding s. 227A. For the provisions relating to disorderly houses see note 48 above.

61 Anderson, *Vancouver's Chinatown*, 97–8. For a modern history of prostitution in China, see Sue Gronewold, *Beautiful Merchandise: Prostitution in China, 1860–1936, Women and History, No. 1* (New York: Haworth Press 1982).

62 Edward Bristow, *Vice and Vigilance: Purity Movements in Britain since 1700* (Dublin: Gill & MacMillan Ltd. 1977), 175–94; David Langum, *Crossing Over the Line: Legislating Morality and the Mann Act* (Chicago: University of Chicago Press 1994), 15–47; John McLaren, '"White Slavers": The Reform of Canada's Prostitution Laws and Patterns of Enforcement, 1900–1920,' *Criminal Justice History* 8 (1987), 53.

63 Roy, *White Man's Province*, 17–18.

64 David R. Williams, '… *The Man for a New Country' Sir Matthew Baillie Begbie* (Sidney, B.C.: Gray's Publishing Co. 1977), 127–8; Royal Commission on Chinese Immigration 1885, *Minutes of Evidence*, 81.

65 Anderson, *Vancouver's Chinatown*, 97–8.

66 McLaren, '"White Slavers."'

67 Criminal Code Amendment Act, 3 & 4 Geo. V, c. 13, ss. 9–12 (1913); Criminal Code Amendment Act, 5 Geo. V, c. 12, ss. 5, 7 (1915); Criminal Code Amendment Act, 7 & 8 Geo. V, c. 14, s. 3 (1917).

68 See An Act to Prevent the Employment of Female Labour in Certain Capacities, SS 1912, c. 17; An Act to prevent the employment of Female Labour in certain capacities, SM 1913, c. 19; Factory, Shop and Office Building Amendment Act, SO 1914, c. 40, s. 2(1); Women's and Girls Protection Act, SBC 1923, c. 76. This legislation and the reasons for it are dealt with at length in the context of the notorious Supreme Court of Canada decision in *Quong Wing v. The King* by Walker, *'Race,' Rights and the Law*, 51–121.

69 McLaren, '"White Slavers,"' 73.

70 Victoria City Archives, *Municipal Reports* (Reports of Police Chiefs), see, e.g., 1894, 75–8, from report of Chief Henry W. Sheppard.

71 Nancy Parker, 'The Capillary Level of Power: Methods and Hypotheses of the Study of Law and Society in Late-Nineteenth Century Victoria' (MA thesis, History, University of Victoria 1983), 136–7.

72 Based on analysis of Reports of Chiefs of Police from 1892 to 1919 (from 1902 to 1907 and in 1911 and 1912 no such reports appear in the municipal records).

73 Extracted from Parliament of Canada, *Session Papers*, for 1905–19. The statistics for Vancouver before 1904 were included in those for New Westminster. The statistics cover both indictable and summary conviction offences.

74 These records cover the period 1892–1919, and similarly relate to both indictable and summary conviction offences.

75 See especially the years 1912 to 1915.

76 These are also contained in the annual, printed *Municipal Reports*, held by the Victoria City Archives.

77 Report of the Health Officer, *Reports*, 1893, 67–9.

78 Report of the Sanitary Inspector, *Reports*, 1893, 35–6.

79 Report of the Health Officer, *Reports*, 1894, 38–41.

80 Report of the Board of Health, *Reports*, 1895, 115–16.

81 On the history of Victoria's contorted attempts to deal with leprosy see Laura Ford, 'Out of Sight, Out of Mind: Sixty-five Years of Leper Colonies in British Columbia,' 48 *The Advocate* (1990), 68. From 1891 to 1905 lepers were quarantined under city auspices on Darcy Island, on the east coast of Vancouver Island, just north of Victoria.

82 See Victoria City Archives, *Magistrate's Record Books* Series 116–17, 1901–4, 16 C5, especially records for November and December 1901.

83 Report of Health Officer, *Reports*, 1906, 95.

84 Report of Health Officer, *Reports*, 1907, 89–91.

85 Anderson, *Vancouver's Chinatown*, 82–92.

86 Ibid., 86–8.

87 Ibid., 85.

88 Ibid.

89 Ibid.

90 Ibid., 89–90.

91 Chuenyan Lai, *Chinatowns*, 34–5.

92 Ibid., 183–7.

93 Walker, '*Race,' Rights and the Law*, 71–2.

94 Patricia Roy, 'The Preservation of the Peace in Vancouver: The Aftermath of the Anti-Chinese Riot of 1887,' B.C. *Studies* 31 (Autumn 1976), 44–59; Anderson, *Vancouver's Chinatown*, 61–8; Chuenyan Lai, *Chinatowns*, 80–1.

95 Chuenyan Lai, *Chinatowns*, 83.

96 See Vancouver City Archives, *Prisoner Record Books*, Series 202-37-C-8 (1898–1900), 9 (1902–5); 202-76-C-2 (1905–7); 202-116-E-1 (1912–17); Victoria City Archives, *Magistrate's Record Books*, 116–17, especially 1901–4, 16 C5; 1904–7, 16 C10; 1911–13, 16 D4; 1913–15, 16 C9; 1915–18, 16 D6; 1919–22, 16 D9.

97 See, e.g., Al Lew, convicted 27 February 1900 for stealing meat from Marsden's Grocery, Hasting Street.

98 See, e.g., Ying, convicted 14 June 1901 of theft of money from the Secord Hotel.
99 See, e.g., Ah Hoo, convicted 26 March 1900 for stealing scrap iron from CP yard.
100 See, e.g., Nick Lee, convicted 13 November 1902 for theft of bottles from Lowe Lee.
101 See, e.g., Lui, alias Ling Sing, sentenced 6 May 1899 to three years, six months for one burglary, together with an attempted burglary carried out while charged with previous offence.
102 For discussion of this phenomenon in police court justice see, e.g., Gene Homel, 'Denison's Law: Criminal Justice and the Police Court in Toronto, 1877–1921,' *Ontario History* 73 (1981), 171.
103 Paul Craven, 'Law and Ideology: The Toronto Police Court,' in David Flaherty, ed., *Essays in the History of Canadian Law, Vol. 2* (Toronto: The Osgoode Society for Canadian Legal History 1983), 248.
104 In an interesting analysis of the treatment of drug offenders from various ethnic communities, including the Chinese, by various police courts in Ontario between 1908 and 1920, the authors find that there was tendency by the magistrates to hand out lighter sentences to the Chinese. This they attribute to two factors: first, concern over police arrest practices, particularly the indiscriminate character of police raids of opium dens and their indiscretion in the use of informants. The second was a measure of paternalism toward an ethnic group whom some magistrates considered as quiet, inoffensive, and unable to control their addiction. The first of these considerations is certainly one in which 'rule of law' thinking is evident. The study also suggests that regional and local justice contexts may well work against extrapolating the experience of the Chinese, or indeed, that of other visible minorities in one region or locality to others. See Clayton Mosher and John Hagan, 'Constituting Class and Crime in Upper Canada: The Sentencing of Narcotics Offenders, circa 1908–1953,' *Social Forces* 72 (1994), 613 at 622–6.
105 See reference to Lee On Yun who in company with Yew Yar Yick, 'another chink' burglarized stores in different parts of the city. Lee was convicted for burglary, 8 January 1899. Lee Won described as an 'opium fiend' was arrested on an indeterminate date in 1903.
106 See in particular *Magistrate's Record Book, 1901–4,* 16 C 5; 1904–7, 16 C 10.
107 Vancouver City Archives, *Prisoner Record Books,* 202-76-C-2.
108 *Prisoner Record Books,* 202-116-E-1.
109 See also Marquis, 'Vancouver Vice,' 246–52.
110 Anderson, *Vancouver's Chinatown,* 101–2, quoting from a letter to the editor of the *Vancouver Province,* 30 January 1900; Marquis, 'Vancouver Vice,' 245.

111 Marquis, 'Vancouver Vice,' 245.

112 Anderson, *Vancouver's Chinatown*, 101. See also evidence of Won Alexander Cumyow to the Royal Commission on Chinese Immigration, *Report*, 1902.

113 Criminal Code, 55 & 56 Vict., c. 29, ss. 196, 198 (1892).

114 Marquis, 'Vancouver Vice,' 248–9.

115 See report in *Vancouver Province*, 16 July 1913, 8.

116 Vancouver City Archives, Police Commission Minutes, 1912–20 Series 190-75-A-1 #3, Minutes, 14 April 1914; Minutes, 14 August 1914; Minutes 6 October 1914.

117 Marquis, 'Vancouver Vice,' 248–9.

118 Victoria City Archives, *Magistrate's Record Book*, Series 116–17, 1901–4, 16-C-5, convicted 9 December 1901.

119 *Magistrate's Record Book*, Series 116–17, 1904–7, 16 C 10, convictions on 6 October, 29 October, and 9 November 1906.

120 Ibid., Case #1412.

121 Ibid.

122 Chuenyan Lai, *Chinatowns*, 229–30.

123 Full 82.9 per cent of the Chinese population in Victoria in 1901 were labourers of one sort or another. See ibid., 202, table compiled from Report of the Royal Commission on Chinese and Japanese Immigration (Ottawa 1902).

124 See David Miers, 'A Social and Legal History of Gaming: From the Restoration to the Gaming Act of 1845' (unpublished Paper, Faculty of Law, University of Cardiff 1989).

125 For a revealing Australian piece on this phenomenon, see Charlie Fox, 'In Search of a Good Bet,' in Verity Burgman and Jenny Lee, *Constructing a Culture: A People's History of Australia* (Ringwood, Victoria: Penguin Books 1988), 77.

126 Marquis, 'Vancouver Vice,' 246–52.

127 For examples of barring of Chinese from various recreational pastimes, see Chuenyan Lai, *Chinatowns*, 216.

128 Harry Con, Ronald J. Con, Graham Johnson, Edgar Wickberg, and William Willmott, *From China to Canada: A History of Chinese Communities in Canada* (Toronto: McClelland & Stewart 1982), 69, 113–14.

129 On the various types of associations in the Chinese community, see Gunter Baureiss, 'Discrimination and Response: The Chinese in Canada,' in Rita M. Bienvenue and Jay E. Goldstein, *Ethnicity and Ethnic Relations in Canada: A Book of Readings*, 2nd ed. (Toronto: Butterworths 1985), 241, 254–5.

130 On the secret societies and their role in Victoria's Chinatown, see Chuenyan Lai, *Chinatowns*, 192–3 (on Chee Kung Tong founded in 1877), 205–6 (on Hip Sing Tong, the 'Hongmen'). The latter organization was set up in opposition

to the former. Both, it seems, ran brothels, opium dens, and gambling houses. Chee Kung Tong and the Hongmen merged in the late 1880s.

131 Ibid., 205–6, 210–11.

132 See footnote 112 and accompanying text.

133 Marquis, 'Vancouver Vice,' 251–2.

134 Ibid., 251. Marquis reports that Detective Joseph Ricci viewed gambling as a less than serious offence and admitted that revenue raising was one of the aims of morality work. Inspector of Detectives John Jackson told the Lennie Inquiry in 1928 that gambling patrons were not 'serious crooks.'

135 Vancouver City Archives, *Prisoner Record Books*, 202-116-E-1.

136 See ibid., L744, Thornton Robinson, convicted for vagrancy, 15 September 1913.

137 See ibid., L1816, Thomas Doyle arrested and charged with morphine possession, 20 March 1916. Although this charge was withdrawn, he later received imprisonment or fines for several other drug offences, including selling cocaine, and imprisonment for attempted suicide.

138 R. Solomon and M. Green, 'The First Century: The History of Non-medical Opiate use and Control of Policies in Canada, 1870–1970,' *University of Western Ontario Law Review* 20 (1982) 307; Boyd, 'Origins of Canadian Narcotics Legislation,' 102, 125–34.

139 Criminal Code, RSC 1906, c. 146, s. 773.

140 Victoria City Archives, MRB Series 116–17, 1911–13, 16D4; 1913–15, 16 C9; 1915–18, 16 D6; 1919–22, 16 D9.

141 As with gambling, the involvement of fraternal and secret societies in running opium dens, may have strengthened the desire of the police to keep tabs on Chinatown.

142 Judge Emily Murphy, *The Black Candle* (1922; Toronto: Coles Publishing Co. 1972). This book followed on from a series of newspaper articles the judge had written.

143 Ibid., photographs between 130 and 131. See Anderson, *Vancouver's Chinatown*, 98 for an example of a cartoon of white female virtue in danger.

144 Walker, *'Race,' Rights and the Law*, 82–3; Roy, *White Man's Province*, 18. On the broader implications of fears about racial debasement, see Angus McLaren, *Our Own Master Race: Eugenics in Canada, 1885–1945* (Toronto: McClelland & Stewart 1990), chap. 3.

145 Anderson, *Vancouver's Chinatown*, 99–101.

146 Chuenyan Lai, *Chinatowns*, 189–90, 219–21 (opium factories in Victoria's Chinatown, with map of their distribution, 1870s to 1900s).

147 This historical context was noted by Justice John Hamilton Gray in his section of the Report of the Royal Commission on Chinese Immigration,

1885. See *Report and Minutes of Evidence*, lvi. The Chinese, Gray said, had been bludgeoned militarily into taking and using the product by the British seeking a sure market for opium exported from India.

148 *R. v. Wing Chong* (1885), 1 BCR Pt. II, 150 at 161 (SC).

149 Boyd, 'Origins of Canadian Narcotics Legislation,' 194–5.

150 McLaren, 'White Slavers,' 85–101; Marquis, 'Vancouver Vice,' 254. Even the racist press were sometimes willing to concede this point, see editorial in *Vancouver Daily News Advertiser*, 7 April 1914, 4.

151 Charlie Quong was the janitor at the 'Jackson Apartments' and had two white girls in the establishment as prostitutes. He was convicted and sentenced to one year in jail for procuring, plus $1,000 or a further year in jail for keeping a disorderly house. Vancouver City Archives, *Prisoner Record Books*, 202-116-E-1, L403.

152 See *R. v. Lew* (1912), 17 BCLR 77 (CA).

153 Anderson, *Vancouver's Chinatown*, 99.

154 McLaren, 'White Slavers,' 57–8.

155 Ibid., 58–77. For interesting insights into the ideology of race in the white dominions see Sean Brawley, *The White Peril: Foreign Relations and Asian Immigration to Australasia and North America 1919–1978* (Sydney: University of New South Wales Press 1995).

156 David R. Williams, *With Malice Aforethought: Six Spectacular Canadian Trials* (Victoria, B.C.: Sono Nis Press 1993), 81–3.

157 Anderson, *Vancouver's Chinatown*, 90.

158 Ibid., 91. See editorial opposed to school segregation in *Vancouver Daily News Advertiser*, 7 April 1914, 4. For the trial at the Vancouver Spring Assizes, see *R. v. Kong* (1914), 20 BCLR 71 (SC).

159 See Roy, *White Man's Province* at 25, 115.

160 Joan Brockman, 'Exclusionary Tactics: The History of Women and Visible Minorities in the Legal Profession in British Columbia,' in Hamar Foster and John McLaren, ed., *Essays in the History of Canadian Law*, 508, 519–25.

161 Williams, 'The Man for a New Country,' 109. See also 122–3 for description of the 'chicken oath,' taken by the Chinese.

162 (1904), 11 BCLR 102 (CA).

163 See *In re Ah Gway* (1887–93), 2 BCLR 343 (SC), per Begbie CJ.

164 Royal Commission on Chinese Immigration, *Report*, lxi–lxii.

165 Royal Commission on Chinese Immigration, 1885, *Minutes of Evidence*, 82 (Begbie); 146 (Crease).

166 *Re Sing Kee* (1900–1), 8 BCLR 76 (SC).

167 *R. v. Wong On and Wong Gow* (1904), 10 BCLR 555 (SC).

168 *R. v. Hong* (1914), 20 BCLR 71 (SC).

442   JOHN McLAREN

R. v. Mah Hong (1920), 33 CCC 195 (BCCA).
(1905), 10 CCC 126 (BC Co. Ct).
(1920), 34 CCC 228 (BCCA).
Ibid., 231.
R. v. On Hing (1867–89), 1 BCLR Pt. 2 148 (SC); *Re Wing Kee* (1887–93), 2 BCLR 321 (BCSC); *Wong Hoy Woon v. Duncan* (1893–95), 3 BCLR 318 (SC); *R. v. Jim Sing* (1891–96), 4 BCLR 338 (SC); *R. v. Sung Chong* (1909), 14 BCLR (CA).
[1899] AC 580 (PC).
[1903] AC 151 (PC).
(1914), 20 BCLR 219 at 221 (SC).
See, e.g., *R. v. Ah Sam* (1907), 12 CCC 538 (BCSC).
R. v. Hong Guey (1907), 12 CCC 366 (BC Co. Ct).
R. v. Ham (1918), 29 CCC 431 (BC Co. Ct); *R. v. Hong Lee* (1918), 31 CCC 217 (BC Co. Ct).
R. v. See Woo (1910), 16 CCC 274 (BC Co. Ct).
(1918), 25 BCLR. 269 (BCCA).
(1914), 24 CCC 334 (CA).
R. v. Sam Sing (1910), 17 CCC 361 (Ont. CA).
Evans et al., *Race Relations*.
Anderson, *Vancouver's Chinatown*, 108–43.
Murphy, *The Black Candle*.
H. Glynn-Ward, *The Writing on the Wall* (Vancouver: Sun Publishing Co. 1921).
Anderson, *Vancouver's Chinatown*, 151–5, on the changing attitudes of the labour movement and support for greater tolerance from the CCF
Ibid., 172–3.
Ibid., 179–86.
Stanley Barrett, *Is God a Racist? The Right Wing in Canada* (Toronto: University of Toronto Press 1987), 297–9, 321–2.
Walker, *'Race,' Rights and the Law,* has made a significant contribution in this regard in analysing the Supreme Court of Canada's treatment of discrimination against Chinese, Afro-Canadians, Jews, and South Asians from the Caribbean.

13

Power, Politics, and the Law: The Place of the Judiciary in the Historiography of Upper Canada

PETER OLIVER

As its title suggests, this chapter is an exercise in historiography and is not based primarily on my own research. It probes the significance of a powerful body of recent legal/historical scholarship to argue that this new work has successfully challenged the long-standing interpretation of Upper Canada's political culture offered by such scholars as Dunham, Craig, and Wise, rejecting their primarily conservative approach and elevating legal conflict to pride of place in a generally persuasive revisionist synthesis. But in its sweeping condemnation of the elite's manipulation of Upper Canadian legal-judicial structures, recent scholarship raises but does not resolve several critical issues concerning the colonial judiciary. Until such issues are satisfactorily addressed, the new synthesis must itself remain on somewhat shaky and uncertain foundations.

In early nineteenth-century Upper Canada, more than in Britain, and perhaps more than in other British North American colonies, including Lower Canada, the judiciary was aggressively Baconian in nature. Sir Francis Bacon, attorney general under James I, had insisted that judges must act as 'lions under the throne, being circumspect that they do not check or oppose any points of sovereignty.' The notion stemmed from the early reality that high court judges were royal functionaries and members of the king's council, yet even in the seventeenth century this conception was forcefully challenged. For example, Chief Justice Sir Edward Coke insisted on impartial interpretation even if it ran contrary to the royal interest.[1] Coke's advocacy of an independent judiciary was signally advanced by the Revolutionary settlement of 1688–9 and the parliamentary enactment of 1701, which confirmed that judicial tenure was during good behaviour rather than the pleasure of monarch or executive. In Britain, a long road had still to be travelled before a truly independent judiciary was securely achieved but most of the necessary elements were put in place or emerged over the course of the eighteenth century. As Murray Greenwood has so cogently reminded us, 'the Bench in England was at least as Cokean as Baconian during the reign of George III.' Greenwood points to the fact that judges, with the notable exception of the Lord Chancellor, rarely sat in the House of Lords; from the seventeenth century they were excluded from the Commons; and from the Glorious Revolution, with the exception of the Lord Chancellor, only two judges ever sat in Cabinet.[2]

By contrast, Greenwood argues, in Lower Canada the judges remained 'thoroughly Baconian' well into the early nineteenth century. Yet even in that colony, possessed of what Greenwood describes as a 'garrison mentality,' which for a time made judicial independence seem a dangerous indulgence, the judiciary's political role was severely truncated by a relatively early date. After 1811 judges were not eligible to sit in the legislature. Perhaps more significantly, they were also excluded from the Executive Council in which they had formerly been 'a major and active presence,' constituting, by Greenwood's calculation, about a third of the total membership.[3]

In Upper Canada, the pattern was distinctly different and there is a large literature on the partisan involvement of King's Bench judges in the Executive and Legislative Councils into the 1820s and 1830s and on their questionable role in a number of notorious cases, including sedition, treason, and murder trials, in which they allegedly distorted the ends of justice to serve either self-interest or the wishes of the ruling oligarchy. Analysis of the judicial role has been central to the emergence of a rich new Upper Canadian historiography. This work has had the somewhat astounding effect of moving legal history from the periphery of Upper Canadian historical scholarship to the very centre.[4] To understand the significance of this historiographical sea change it should be recalled that from the publication in 1927 of Aileen Dunham's study of political unrest in Upper Canada to the outstanding work of Craig and Wise in the 1960s and 70s, an essentially conservative analysis dominated the literature.[5] The approach taken by these scholars is too well known to bear repetition here, other than to note that Gerald Craig regarded the ruling Tory elite, the so-called Family Compact, as an entirely natural and rather loose coalition of local power groups, one that effectively expressed the political values and material needs of an emerging political society. Craig dismissed many of the most prominent reformers, radicals such as Joseph Willcocks, Robert Gourlay, W.L. Mackenzie, and Francis Collins, as little more than self-interested demagogues and Thorpe and Willis, the dismissed judges, faired little better at his hands. His judgment of Willis, for example, was that Upper Canada was 'well rid' of him.[6] These men, not coincidentally, played leading roles in most of the prominent cases that the new legal historiography has deployed to reassess the colony's politics and political culture. S.F. Wise's widely acclaimed and brilliant essays complemented and extended Craig's analysis. Wise emphasized that the Tory elite, seeing itself as surrounded by enemies, compensated with a powerful sense of providential mission and primeval survival instincts that shaped the colony's identity into the late nineteenth century and beyond.[7]

It was Paul Romney, in his 1986 book, *Mr Attorney*, who first challenged the prevailing synthesis.[8] Focusing on the courts and the legal system, Romney revisited many of the discontents leading to the Rebellion, including the prosecution of Gourlay, the types riot of 1826, and the conviction of Francis Collins for libelling Attorney General Robinson. These and similar occurrences had been regarded by Craig as 'a number of rather petty instances of the exercise of executive authority which were blown up ... until they appeared as cruel and heartless "outrages."'[9] For Romney, however, the same incidents spoke to the scandalous maladministration of justice by Crown law officers and the judiciary. Romney concluded that 'of all the injustices perceived in the Upper Canadian political system, none aroused louder complaint than the inequitable administration of justice itself.'[10]

Robert Fraser has made a similarly large contribution to the revisionist account of Upper Canadian political culture in his numerous *Dictionary of Canadian Biography* articles and in his extended introduction to the 1992 publication, *Provincial Justice*. Commanding respect because of his unrivalled knowledge of the sources of Upper Canadian history, Fraser concludes that at no other point in Ontario's past had 'the judicial system been so embattled, so mired in controversy, so liable to the charges of partiality and maladministration, and so lacking in broad public legitimacy.'[11] For Fraser, as for Romney, the colony's Tory leadership, through its blatant manipulation of the legal and judicial structures, had engaged in a shameful effort to subvert the civil rights and political liberties of the subject. Focusing on the activities of the Crown law officers and the judges and referring to many of the same 'outrages' as Romney, Fraser concluded that they represented 'a stunning array of unjust practices which violated civil liberty and civil law, threatened and even took life in ways considered tantamount to judicial murder ...'[12]

To this story of judicial and legal outrage related by Romney and Fraser, involving incidents too complex and numerous to bear repeating here, must be added several publications of Barry Wright, which analyse the use and misuse of treason, libel, and sedition law, and also publications by Leo Johnson dealing with the notorious tar and feathers outrage and its judicial aftermath in the Gore District and the scandalous mistreatment of the reform judge John Walpole Willis by the Tory oligarchy. Johnson's conclusions echo those of Romney and Fraser. He writes of 'the manipulation of the judicial process by judges, magistrates, and court officials to enrich themselves' and of 'the failure of the courts and crown officers to bring justice to, and enforce the "King's peace" upon society.'[13] Several other contributions, including those by Blaine Baker and Carol Wilton, do not fit so easily into the historiography of political malfeasance and judicial outrage but contribute substantially to our comprehension of related themes.[14] My purpose is not to retrace or reinterpret these well-documented discussions of what Romney describes as 'outrages' but rather to attempt to use the insights the authors provide in order to stand back a little and assess the role the judiciary played in these developments. Recognizing that there has been some spirited debate about the attitude of the Tory oligarchy to the rule of law, it seems important to look again at the colony's Baconian judiciary to determine whether judicial subservience to a different ideal than justice in individual cases necessarily implicated the judges of King's Bench in a conspiracy to subvert the very laws and constitution they were sworn to uphold. In short, what evidence exists to support the argument that the King's Bench judges were part of a corrupt legal regime that threw the administration of justice into disrepute and by their misdeeds contributed to political discontent and ultimately to the outbreak of rebellion?

These questions piqued my interest because my own research into the role of the judges in the administration of criminal law, a by-product of investigation into colonial crime patterns and penal systems, was utterly at odds with notions of judicial corruption and malfeasance. In his condemnation of how the judicial system handled criminal cases, Robert Fraser focused on two murder trials. In the case of Michael Vincent, executed in 1828 for murdering his wife but who maintained his innocence until the end, Fraser directs attention to Justice Christopher Hagerman's charge to the jury, in which the judge expressed his own sense of Vincent's guilt. Describing this charge as an 'apparently stunning judicial novelty,' Fraser points to criticism of the judge in two Reform newspapers and to Francis Collins' claim three years later that Hagerman had behaved outrageously.[15] Similarly Fraser showed considerable sympathy for the nineteenth-century account written by Charles Lindsey of the case of Charles French, a young man condemned to death in 1828 by Justice Levius Peters Sherwood for killing a man in a street brawl. French had worked as a printer for William Lyon Mackenzie and had testified for Mackenzie in the successful civil action arising out of the types riot. According to Fraser, Lindsey went so far as to argue that the execution was somehow the Family Compact's revenge against French for his testimony in this action. According to Fraser, 'There was a measurable element of popular support for the allegations of partiality. Over 1,100 people, for example, signed the petition on behalf of Charles French.'[16]

In fact Lindsey's broad hint at impropriety strains the evidence. Lindsey, the son-in-law of Mackenzie, was highly partisan and it is notorious that his work on the period is laden with errors.[17] As for the Vincent execution, John Weaver, who has considered the case in his work on criminal justice in the Gore District, argues that there was 'nothing unusual about Hagerman's charge' to the jury, that the jury 'had good cause to arrive at a guilty verdict,' and that there is no evidence that the jurors felt that the judge had 'influenced them unduly.'[18] Weaver might have added that there is also little evidence to suggest that the case in the mind of the public ever became a *cause célèbre*.

More revealing than two individual cases would be the broader pattern of criminal trials, yet no one has yet essayed a systematic study of assize records for the Upper Canadian period, even though those records are reasonably complete.[19] My own preliminary incursion into those records, together with the study of scores of circuit reports and of a certain amount of routine correspondence and newspaper research reveals nothing at all conspiratorial or even political about judicial decision making in the mass of routine cases. The evidence suggests only a hard-working, humane, and merciful judiciary carrying out its assize responsibilities under trying conditions of pioneer hardship.

In numerous charges to grand juries Chief Justice Robinson, for example, put into words his own deeply held commitment to the fairness and integrity of the legal structure: 'it must never be forgotten for a moment,' he insisted, 'that the security of *all that is worth enjoying* depends not *partly* but *wholly* upon supremacy of the Laws ... There can exist no liberty ... except under the protection of law.' Upper Canada, he continued in another charge, was 'emphatically a government of the law' and there was 'no country whose laws are more *just* in principle or more *mild* in their actual administration.'[20]

The chief justice in an 1833 charge to the Home District jury, later published as a pamphlet, offered some evidence to substantiate these grandiose claims. Although the old criminal code contained about 150 capital offences, 'the law in Upper Canada,' said Robinson, 'was characterized by such lenity that even those found guilty have not actually paid the dreadful forfeit of life.' There had been, he continued, large numbers of convictions for horse stealing and other capital offences. But the number 'actually executed has not exceeded forty' in the forty years since the colony was founded. Eight of those had been executed for treason in 1814 and with three exceptions all the others were for murder. 'And no one had been executed over the past twenty years for any crime but murder.'[21]

By the 1820s, however, the judges themselves were showing increasing frustration with the system of discretionary justice that required them to condemn to death individuals who knew perfectly well they would never be executed. Such a system, they had come to believe, was making a mockery of the courts. The judges, especially Robinson, led the struggle for law reform. It was Robinson, it seems, who drafted the critical statute of 1833 reducing the number of capital offences from about 150 to 12. The sentiments pronounced by Lieutenant-Governor Colborne in giving royal assent expressed the judicial rationale for this far-reaching reform: 'The enactment which you have just sanctioned,' said Colborne, '... must prevent ... that frequent recurrence of mitigation of punishment appointed by the Statutes, which has hitherto necessarily taken place through the intervention of the power of the Crown and which enervated the general authority of the law.'[22]

Judicial advocacy of legal reform was by no means limited to the law itself but encompassed every aspect of the criminal justice system. Chief Justice Robinson was the principal advocate of building a penitentiary in Upper Canada and he and his judicial colleagues, as I argue elsewhere, were the most prominent supporters of jail reform and prisoners' rights.[23] The commitment to both efficiency and humanitarianism implicit in these reform efforts was replicated by the broad pattern of decision making that shaped and informed scores of ordinary criminal cases. My sense from studying many of these cases is that the judges, as might be expected, were shrewd interpreters of human nature, too experienced by far to attribute individual criminality to original sin, inherent evil, human greed, the excessive use of alcohol, or any other over-arching theory of human behaviour. To be sure, some crimes were ascribed to lack of self-control, others to bad character, but the judges were quite prepared to recognize that sometimes economic circumstances forced individuals to steal and that often there were mitigating circumstances of youth, ignorance, mental illness, and simple human frailty. Uninfluenced by the oppressive biological determinism of a later period, the Upper Canadian judges were confident that God had endowed man with the power of choice and were rigorous, therefore, in their examination of the facts of each case. Persuaded generally that Upper Canada was blessed with a society relatively free of serious crime, they inclined to lenience and mercy when at all possible. My own analysis therefore supports the conclusion of Ann McEwen, who studied the Niagara District, that the courts worked effectively to protect the rights and persons of all citizens. People of all callings, McEwen concludes, 'participated in the workings of the judicial system': 'justice was being done and being seen to be done.'[24]

If such conclusions stand, and if ordinary criminal cases were indeed adjudicated honestly and impartially, this may give pause to the argument that the legal system was thoroughly corrupt and biased, but it does not discredit it entirely. There was no conceivable reason for the courts to be other than objective in the adjudication of ordinary criminal cases and, as E.P. Thompson has insisted in *Whigs and Hunters*, it was in the elite's self-interest to ensure that justice was done in order to encourage the widest possible belief in the legitimacy of the system.[25] At the same time, however, the essential integrity and fairness with which assize court judges administered the criminal law could not have been without effect in shaping public and popular attitudes to the machinery of justice. Elites on both sides of the political fence might joust and skirmish over the significance of a few notorious 'outrages,' but it was important that the law dealt fairly and humanely with those ordinary persons who supplied the courts with their regular business. The evidence to date, which suggests strongly that this was the case, must cause us to hesitate before giving credence to arguments, largely divorced from analysis of popular opinion, that the Upper Canadian judicial apparatus was thoroughly discredited and therefore a principal cause of popular discontent leading to rebellion.

Nonetheless it remains true that the really critical issues on the criminal side, the ultimate test of integrity, came, as Barry Wright argues, in a few celebrated trials for treason, sedition, and libel.[26] The cases of Joseph Willcocks in 1808, the Ancaster 'Bloody Assizes' of 1814, the trials of Robert Gourlay in 1818, and the treason cases following the Rebellions of 1837–8 are well known. So too are the famous or infamous circumstances surrounding the dismissal of two King's Bench judges, Robert Thorpe in 1807 and John Walpole Willis in 1828.[27] These dramatic events were as much political as legal in nature and the literature, which is large and insightful, highlights how a nervous oligarchy, reeling from foreign invasion and armed insurrection, threatened by the hordes of democracy and republicanism, thrust out at its enemies. For the oligarchy, the rule of law in those circumstances remained a formidable weapon and, as Romney in particular has graphically demonstrated, the brilliant young attorney general, John Beverley Robinson, used and manipulated the law for his own purposes.[28]

Without doubt, the King's Bench judges were deeply implicated both politically and judicially in this process, and equally serious, they were perceived to be so. It could not have been otherwise, given the strength and depth of the colony's Baconian traditions. Far more than in contemporary England, the colonial executive exercised a large measure of control over the legal system, including the organization of prosecutions and the appointment of politically sympathetic justices of the peace. At the highest levels in particular, the shortage in the little colony of individuals of education and talent made it incumbent to co-opt King's Bench judges to political service. From the Constitutional Act to the mid-1820s, the judges, next to the governor himself and sometimes to the attorney general, were the most powerful political figures in the province. The tradition began with the first chief justice, William Osgoode. Osgoode lived for a time in Governor Simcoe's home and was his closest friend and adviser. He drafted several of the colony's earliest statutes, including that creating the Court of King's Bench, and Simcoe appointed him to the Executive Council and made him speaker of the Legislative Council. Although there was no formal provision in the Constitutional Act for the chief justice to become speaker, this began the tradition by which subsequent chief justices also assumed both these posts, a situation that obtained almost until the end of the Upper Canadian period. After Osgoode, Elmsley, Allcock, Scott, Powell, Campbell, and Robinson were all speakers of the upper house and two puisne judges, Powell and Jonas Jones, also served on the Legislative Council, with Jones as speaker in 1838 during Chief Justice Robinson's absence in England.[29] In the little society of Upper Canada, whose capital of York had a population of roughly three thousand into the early 1830s, such status brought with it great political power. Osgoode served as a virtual prime minister under Simcoe. Elmsley chaired the committee of the Executive Council that ran the province during Governor Hunter's frequent absences in Lower Canada and was, according to his biographer, the most powerful man in the province. Powell was the leading adviser to Francis Gore. Other judges, including Justice Henry Allcock before his elevation to chief justice and puisne Justice Robert Thorpe, were elected to the Assembly, in which position Thorpe became virtual leader of the Opposition. According at least to Gerald Craig's account, Thorpe revelled in the role of demagogue, describing the members of the Executive Council as 'overbearing reptiles' and 'servile instruments.' After eliciting grand jury addresses denouncing the many sins of the government, he provoked Lieutenant-Governor Francis Gore into reporting to London that his efforts were dangerous to the safety and security of the province. His subsequent suspension from office, which provoked little popular protest, was a firm statement that Thorpe's type of political activism from the bench would not be tolerated.

A clear distinction had thus been drawn between judicial support for the broad objectives of colonial governance and partisan activity in support of the enemies of the administration. Despite the Thorpe episode, which was truly extraordinary, it continued to be understood that all the judges were available informally to offer advice to the governor on the full range of political issues and to prepare extrajudicial opinions on a wide assortment of matters.[30] At critical moments, too, they could be called to attend the Executive Council as a body, as they seem to have done when asked for advice on the trials and execution of prisoners captured during American military incursions into the province in 1838.[31]

Was it possible in these circumstances for the judges to maintain any sense of judicial independence or to be perceived as impartial? The best test of the extent to which judicial political commitments prejudiced their objectivity is to be found by re-examining their role in several celebrated cases that necessarily mixed politics and law.

In the case of Joseph Willcocks it is important to recall that it was a unanimous legislature that found him guilty of contempt for a libel after a prosecution for seditious libel was initiated but before he was acquitted by the courts. In the tense international situation of 1807 Willcocks, as editor of the *Upper Canada Guardian*, was regarded by a nervous government as part Jacobin, part Irish radical. The government proceeded to trial at York but Justice Powell granted a change of venue to Niagara where Willcocks had recently won a by-election and where he was eventually acquitted in September of 1808 despite the use of a special jury under an *ex officio* information. In the meantime, the government proceeded against Willcocks in the Assembly of which he was a member and that body, acting before the trial in Niagara, found him guilty and committed him to jail for the duration of the sitting of the House.[32]

In view of frequent charges of jury packing, it is interesting to keep in mind how frequently juries throughout the Upper Canadian period brought in verdicts contrary to the wishes of the government party. Either the sheriffs were remarkably unskilled in finding right-thinking jurors or the processes of justice remained far freer than some would have us believe. The several prosecutions of Robert Gourlay lend some weight to the argument that the oligarchy's control of the legal system was less than absolute and there is little evidence that the judiciary attempted to bully juries into compliance with any official political posture. The Gourlay affair is well known and must be placed in the context of immediate post-war concern over provincial security and the perceived need to move forcefully to defend the colony against a range of internal threats, many of which had been amply demonstrated during the war with the United States. Rightly or wrongly, the ruling circles viewed Gourlay's promotion of township meetings held to consider 'grievances' as a threat to consti-tuted authority. Attorney General Robinson considered Gourlay's pub-lished addresses to be 'grossly libellous' and 'entirely subversive of that respect ... which the government of every country should vindicate to itself.' Significantly, however, he hesitated to begin prosecution because, as he told the administrator, 'however unquestionable the law may be, the improper lenity or worse conduct of Jurors' in such cases 'frequently screens the offender from punishment.'[33] Before proceeding to trial Robinson took the precaution of seeking the opinion of the judges. Gourlay was arrested for libel and the government proceeded with two somewhat different charges and two separate trials, one at the Midland District assizes and the other in the Johnstown District. The judge in each case was William Campbell and Gourlay defended himself effectively and exposed the weakness in the Crown's case. He was acquitted by juries in both trials.[34]

Although the records reveal little about Justice Campbell's role, Chief Justice Powell was privately cynical about the entire proceeding. He told Francis Gore, then in Britain, that the policy of wisdom, as Gore himself had urged, would have been to let the Gourlay agitation run its course. And even though the judges of King's Bench had been formally asked for a judicial opinion on the applicability to Gourlay of the 1804 sedition statute, Powell privately believed that its use was harsh and vindictive. As he told Gore, '... the enactment subjects Earl Bathurst if he should pay a visit to this province ... to be ordered out of the province ... and upon disobedience to be imprisoned and tried' and if found guilty to be ban-ished upon pain of death should he remain or return.[35] Notwithstanding his apparent disapproval of this statute, Powell presided over Gourlay's third trial, this time under the Sedition Act. A finding of guilty followed and Gourlay was banished from the province. W.R. Riddell has concluded that the responsibility for Gourlay's conviction and exile was hardly Powell's, for he only performed his duty as a judge to interpret the statute. In his own careful examination of the case, however, Barry Wright reaches a different conclusion. Although he notes that the chief justice's charge to the jury 'appears to have narrowly followed the letter of the law,' Powell's 'repeated consultations with the Attorney General' 'calls his impartiality into question.'[36] Perhaps it would be more apt to suggest that Powell's somewhat ambiguous role in the Gourlay affair, as well as other aspects of his judicial career, serve to emphasize that, even apart from Thorpe and Willis, King's Bench judges were never monolithic in their political values and beliefs.

In the related case of Bartemas Ferguson, who had published Gourlay's efforts in the Niagara *Spectator* and was charged with seditious libel, the accused was proceeded against by *ex officio* information and special jury and the finding of guilty was followed by a truly brutal sentence.[37] Barry Wright's final assessment of the Gourlay and Ferguson trials, especially the close consultation that took place between Powell and the attorney general, is that they reflected a legal culture in which the judges were deeply implicated in the political process 'and where their compliance was ensured by their tenure according to royal pleasure rather than good behaviour.'[38]

There is in fact little to suggest that the judges acted as they did primarily because they feared reprimand or removal. So drastic a remedy was quite simply unnecessary. In the legal and political culture of Upper Canada the judiciary understood and readily accepted their prior obligation to support the safety and security of the state and Chief Justice Powell, correctly from his perspective, could never allow his private views to interfere with his more pressing obligation to uphold the public interest defined, as it usually was, by the local government. If most of the judges acted most of the time to uphold the values of the colonial executive, it was because they shared those values and expressed them forcefully in the councils as well as on the bench.

It is the much-written-about series of events in 1827–8, known to posterity as the Willis affair, that demonstrated more than anything else the full implications of the continuation of a Baconian judiciary. As an appointee from England sent to the colony to establish an equitable jurisdiction, Willis was seen as a dire threat by some of the local establishment. Governor Maitland was perturbed from the beginning by the high public profile the new judge demonstrated in some of his benevolent and charitable activities. And Maitland was even more upset by Willis's association with John Galt of the Canada Company, a man considered by Maitland to be politically unsafe.[39] What was most disturbing to Maitland seems to have been the prospect of this free-thinking and possibly uncontrollable judge being admitted to his inner circle of political advisers.

At this point, Maitland began a series of manoeuvres with the colonial office whose intent was to clip Willis's wings.[40] And he did so, it must be emphasized, well before Willis had engaged in his famous confrontation with Attorney General Robinson over the attorney's alleged failure to carry out his duty to uphold the law by initiating prosecutions of the types rioters and also before Willis outraged the government by calling into question the right of King's Bench to sit without its full complement of three judges.[41]

In December 1827 Maitland, evidently concerned that the tenure of judges would be changed from pleasure to good behaviour, as had recently been done in the Cape of Good Hope, warned William Huskisson, the colonial secretary, against such a move for Upper Canada. He did so by deploying two quite contradictory arguments. In the first place, he insisted, such a change was entirely unnecessary. 'No judge I am sure in this Colony, and I dare say none in any other within the last century has been removed or threatened to be removed, or even feared to be dismissed on account of any judgment pronounced by him.' Having established to his own satisfaction the independence of the colonial judiciary, Maitland then claimed that no successful English lawyer would ever accept a colonial appointment because it must necessarily lead to an enormous drop in his income. The colonies, Maitland suggested, were doomed to accept only the unknown and the mediocre for their highest judicial officers. And for that reason, as Leo Johnson has put it, 'they were almost certain to fall prey to ambition for popular acclaim, as Judge Robert Thorpe had done, and use their judicial reputation for disinterednedness to aid their dishonest and demagogic careers.'[42] In other words, Maitland's argument was that tenure during pleasure must remain precisely because it was a powerful instrument of control over a weak and ineffectual judiciary.

Maitland's suspicions of Willis deepened in the months ahead. When the House of Assembly dragged its feet on the establishment of a court of equity, Willis aspired to replace the ailing Campbell as chief justice. Trapped by the colony's deeply rooted Baconian structure, the governor desperately tried to persuade the colonial office of the political disaster lurking in such an appointment: 'As the Chief Justice is usually Speaker of the

Legislative Council and President of the [Executive] Council it is necessary you should know, that from the conduct which Mr. Willis has hitherto exhibited I could anticipate nothing else than that his influence ... be given to persons conspicuous for nothing but a violent and abusive opposition to the Government ...' Willis's appointment to the Executive Council, said Maitland, 'would absolutely disable me ... from communicating cordially and confidentially with the Council.'[43]

By the date of this letter, May 1828, Willis had already chastised both the attorney general and Solicitor General Boulton over their failure, in his opinion, to prosecute law breakers and uphold the rule of law. Having thereby infuriated the Tory leadership, Willis in June informed the colonial office that in his opinion King's Bench could not act in the absence in England of Chief Justice Campbell. The administration moved swiftly and Willis, on the recommendation of the Executive Council, was removed from office.

Although Willis's quarrel was with the Crown law officers and the governor, the circumstances of his dismissal raised again the issue of judicial independence in its relationship to local as opposed to imperial authority. Willis, the government argued, was dismissed not because of any of his judgments but because he had moved in a political way and not through regular and respectable channels to challenge the court's legitimacy. Willis himself reacted furiously against accusations that he had been working in company with the reformers. He claimed that he had seldom even spoken to Baldwin, John Rolph, Bidwell, or any other person opposed to the attorney general, and that he had rebuffed those who had urged him to run for the legislature against Robinson. He had declined, he claimed, specifically on the grounds that 'a Judge should never interfere in politics.' And he later added sarcastically, 'I have now found how unwise it was in me to make this declaration so absolutely, "A Judge," I ought to have said, 'should never interfere in politics *but when it suits the purposes of the Local Government.*'[44]

In his formal defence of his actions, Willis offered a more exalted argument, one that emphasized the York oligarchy's failure to live up to principles fundamental to the rule of law. 'I firmly believe,' proclaimed the judge, 'that there are no laws demanding a more religious observance, than those that limit and define the power of individuals forming the Government over their fellow creatures ...'[45] At a public meeting at York to protest Willis's dismissal, the reformers adopted a petition demanding that judges hold office during good behaviour and that they be excluded from the Executive and Legislative Councils.[46]

In some very basic ways, the Willis affair was the turning point in debates within the colony over the rule of law and the meaning of judicial independence and the pace of events swiftly accelerated. Within weeks of Willis's dismissal Maitland himself was dismissed from office, although he also received a new position as lieutenant-governor of Nova Scotia.[47] The reform-dominated Assembly's response to Willis's dismissal was to ask the colonial office to remove the chief justice from the Executive Council because such an office tended 'to embarrass him in his judicial functions, and [to] render the administration of justice less satisfactory if not less pure.'[48] That same year the Canada Committee of the British House of Commons recommended that judges as a rule not be appointed to the councils.[49]

When John Beverley Robinson became chief justice in 1829, he was not appointed to the Executive Council. When he assumed the office *ex officio*, he learned to his dismay that the colonial office disapproved of his membership. In another significant step, the colonial secretary, Lord Goderich, signalled in 1831 the intention of giving the judges tenure during good behaviour, conditional on the Upper Canadian government assuming their salaries. He also removed the chief justice from the Executive Council and warned that his activities as speaker of the Legislative Council must be curtailed: 'His Majesty will not fail to recommend even to that high officer a cautious abstention from all proceedings by which he might be involved in any political contentions of a party nature.'[50] Although Robinson resigned, reluctantly, from the Executive Council, the colonial office was not then inclined to force the issue of his continuing position as speaker of the Legislative Council. That body, to be sure, had become a focus of Reform criticism, but probably the chief justice's leadership, especially in the formulation of legislation and in the criticism of bills from the lower house, was regarded as so important as to preclude his removal at that time. Nonetheless, a statute that passed the Assembly in 1834 formally excluded all judges from the Executive Council and explicitly changed their tenure from pleasure to good behaviour and provided for their removal only by 'address of Legislative Council and Legislature.' By 1838, if not earlier, even Robinson had accepted the situation in general, if not all its implications. In 1838 he told Lieutenant-Governor George Arthur, 'I have no concern in the executive affairs of the Colony, and no claim or wish to be consulted in any of them.'[51]

Judicial independence was extended and confirmed by the events surrounding the Union of 1840. Following the Rebellion, the Durham report in 1839 recommended, superfluously of course, 'that the Independence of the judges shall be secured, by giving them the same tenure of office and security of income as exist in England.'[52] With the Union itself, the practice of judges sitting on the Legislative Council soon ceased. On his appointment to Queen's Bench in 1837, Jonas Jones was made speaker of the council and served until the Union, at which point the position was assumed by R.S. Jameson, the vice-chancellor. As W.R. Riddell notes, Jameson resigned in 1843 and subsequently no judge ever sat in either council. Statutes of 1843 and 1857 formally declared all judges ineligible to serve in either house of the legislature.[53]

The process of achieving judicial independence was gradual and had developed as part of the impassioned struggle for responsible government. With the gradual emergence of party politics and the concomitant of increasing colonial self-government, the Baconian practice was becoming an anachronism. Yet not even the clearest of messages from the imperial government had entirely succeeded in the early 1830s in removing the Upper Canadian judiciary from political activity. Chief Justice Robinson, for example, unhesitatingly published a tract in which he denounced the Durham report and the scheme to unite Upper and Lower Canada. And his colleague Jonas Jones, as speaker of the Legislative Council, was a leader in the campaign against union. Robinson also was deeply involved in framing the emergency legislation passed by the legislature in response to American incursions across the frontier in 1838. Lieutenant-Governor Sir George Arthur seemed quite aware that this level of judicial involvement in the legislative and executive processes was contrary to British wishes. He justified it by informing the colonial office that he personally had asked Robinson to attend Executive Council, because his 'high character and great experience' were 'likely to be eminently useful, both to the prisoners and to the Government.'[54] Once again, judicial political involvement in Upper Canada had created tension between the colony and the colonial office, emphasizing one last time the extent to which the imperial authority and some Upper Canadian Tories still held remarkably different conceptions of the real meaning of the rule of law.

It is remarkable that Robinson, a decade after the Willis affair and long after he had been grounded politically by the colonial office, should again risk imperial displeasure by playing a large role on the Executive Council and in formulating the 1838 emergency legislation. After the British insistence that the judges withdraw from politics and especially after the 1828 Upper Canadian election, in which reformers for the first time won a massive victory at the polls, there was no doubt at all that the price of judicial Baconianism had become politically prohibitive. As Aileen Dunham has pointed out, when the House met for the first time after the election, 'the address in opposition to the speech from the throne was carried by thirty-seven to one.'[55] It would be natural to conclude that in part at least this represented a popular protest against the excesses of the Baconian tradition.

Yet election results can be only a crude indicator of broader social realities. It is by no means clear that the election represented a condemnation of how the judges had carried out their functions over the years. Barry Wright has pointed out the difficulty in demonstrating empirically how effective elite manipulation has been in using the apparent objectivity of the law to legitimate the administration of criminal justice.[56] It bears emphasis here that the decline and fall of judicial Baconianism did not necessarily represent a popular conclusion that the judges had used or abused their trust. And it is particularly difficult to break the legal system down into its component parts in order to assess public attitudes to the judiciary as distinct from the Crown law officers and the lieutenant-governor, who justifiably bore the brunt of Reform criticism during the Willis affair.

Certainly the reason for the local administration's determination in the face of much adversity to lean on the judges for political support is not difficult to explain. For an embattled oligarchy, the judicial and legal structures were essentially elements of social and political control in political circumstances that they regarded as threatening to the colony's very existence. For many years the outstanding historians of Upper Canada, including Dunham, Craig, and Wise, have agreed that this was not a calm or normal society. Its Tory rulers, feeling themselves besieged on every side by the revolutionary doctrines of American and French republicanism and democracy and constantly facing either the threat or reality of invasion, reacted, perhaps understandably, with near paranoia. Undeniably their harsh and exclusive Toryism, their thrust to achieve ideological conformity, and their relentless pursuit of their enemies created an explosive political climate. Yet these same scholars have also argued that Tory providentialism coupled with a single-minded pursuit of their political objectives created survival instincts that largely shaped and defined nineteenth-century Ontario society and, not incidentally, may have ensured its existence independent of the United States. The judiciary had its part to play in this scenario.

In Upper Canada's overheated political climate, however, the legal structure, while critical, became increasingly problematic. The legal historiography of the last decade and a half has largely undermined the essentially conservative historiography advanced by Dunham, Craig, and Wise. The work of Romney, Wright, Baker, Johnson, and others has indisputably widened the earlier and largely constitutional focus to include a myriad of new legal concerns and it has demonstrated precisely how issues critical to the rule of law were central to both Tory and Reform discourses. Paul Romney's so-called outrages must henceforth figure prominently in the analysis of every scholar who attempts to assess and understand the political and legal cultures of Upper Canada. But the fact that these issues did emerge as 'outrages' demonstrates that law, courts, and legal traditions remained as effective barriers to the more blatant forms of elite manipulation.

Precisely what role did the judiciary play in these events? The extent to which the Tories succeeded in bending the judiciary to their partisan will remains uncertain, and it is especially unclear whether the judges ever became mere servile creatures of the prevailing Tory orthodoxy in any significant way. To some degree, the Romney-Baker debate over Tory attitudes to the rule of law engages these issues but it leaves then unresolved. The Romney thesis that the Tory leaders, like almost all Britons, accepted rule of law ideas deriving from the Revolutionary settlement of 1688–9 but saw fit to breach them when it served their purposes begs the question of the extent to which the judiciary was complicit in so illicit a project.[57] The government had an impressive array of legal weapons at its disposal, including *ex officio* informations, extrajudicial opinions, the advice of the chief justice on both councils, close relationships with sheriffs who put together jury panels, the use of special juries and changes of venue, and of course the right of the law officers to exercise their prosecutorial monopoly, to say nothing of more informal means of influence in the close-knit society of little York. Taking all this into consideration, together with the prevailing sense that society was under siege and that the judges should govern themselves accordingly, it becomes clear that the threat to judicial integrity was formidable.

There is no doubt at all that from time to time, and especially in some critical cases with political overtones, the judges' political roles and professional duties became all but indistinguishable. Baconianism led inexorably to forms of political activism that could readily be portrayed by a vigilant opposition as judicial misbehaviour. In these circumstances what is perhaps more remarkable is the extent to which the judges maintained a substantial degree of independence, as opposed to the extent to which they betrayed it. Looking entirely at ordinary and routine criminal as opposed to civil cases, there is no persuasive evidence that the judges ever did anything but administer the criminal law fearlessly, objectively, and mercifully; their place in the Upper Canadian community and in the public regard was hardly unaffected by the quality of their performance. And in those criminal cases with political overtones, the record, as indicated above, is both mixed and murky. What does seem indisputable is that the government in some of the most sensitive cases felt enormous insecurity about the outcome and furthermore, judicial decisions in several such cases justified that feeling. In Upper Canada under the Baconian regimen, the courts never became the servile instruments of Tory hegemony.

In an important article Carol Wilton has demonstrated that some Tories responded to this unwelcome situation by sharply escalating their resort to extralegal methods, what Wilton has called 'lawless law.' Referring to the increasing incidence of charivaris and riots and the propensity of a few magistrates to engage in common assault, she has determined that incidents of Tory violence increased from a mere three in the 1820s to twenty-five between 1831 and 1840.[58] Clearly a response to a weakening Tory hold on power, these incidents, according to Wilton, signified a growing recognition among supporters of the government party that traditional legal manipulation was no longer politically effective. For example, the Seditious Meetings Act of 1818 used to gag Gourlay had been repealed in 1820 and the Sedition Act itself, after numerous earlier Reform attempts, was repealed in 1829.[59] The loss of these coercive measures was not entirely lamented, because the government understood both the legal barriers to conviction and the political price that their deployment elicited. In these circumstances, the resort to violence and intimidation by some Tories determined to uphold the rule of what Robinson called 'the regularly bred' seemed to be a necessary if reckless alternative. It must have come as a shock then to some of the perpetrators that the King's Bench judges were likely to come down hard on their extralegal interventions. For example when W.J. Kerr, a magistrate, beat William Lyon Mackenzie within an inch of his life, Justice James B. Macaulay expressed outrage at Kerr's action and in his circuit report stated that the political motivation of the attack had caused him to assess a heavy penalty.[60] The same judge acted with unimpeachable objectivity in the trial of the Tory magistrates implicated in the notorious Gore District tar and feathers case.

In these and other cases it would have been difficult for anyone on the government side to predict in advance the likely outcome. Despite their own Tory predilections and their intimate political association with the administration, the judges appear to have taken seriously their commitment to judicial objectivity. In their own minds at least, membership on the councils and their advisory role to the lieutenant-governor represented not narrow partisanship but simply service to the state in ways that they deemed both appropriate and necessary. In an era when political parties were widely regarded by those of varying political hues as dangerous factions and the notion of a loyal opposition was anathema, the Baconian ideal, until the Willis affair at least, was in harmony with the spirit of colonial institutions and values. The judges regarded themselves as royal officers and, like the lieutenant-governor himself, they served the needs of the state, and not any political faction, a perspective driven home by the dismissal of Thorpe and Willcocks, who refused to conform.

The problem, of course, was that it became increasingly apparent that in Upper Canada the Tories had co-opted the lieutenant-governor and tied the majesty of the state to the demands of partisanship. In this situation, it was becoming increasingly difficult for the judiciary to maintain the essential distinction between statecraft and partisanship. The opposition leaders, and especially lawyers like Rolph, Bidwell, and the Baldwins, understood perfectly this point of weakness. Determined to bring down the outmoded constitution of 1791, they attacked a reactionary administration at its most vulnerable point, working assiduously to turn legitimate grievances into towering outrages. In these circumstances, and considering the judiciary's strong record of doing right in ordinary criminal cases, the success of the oppositionists in stirring up opinion was decidedly mixed and the extent of public discontent with the judicial system remains unclear. Nonetheless the executive and their judicial allies, pressed as they were by the colonial office authorities, beat a hasty retreat. Baconianism was dead.

To return briefly to the message so deliberately conveyed in the numerous grand jury addresses promulgated by Robinson and his colleagues, these are informed by the loftiest sentiments of an independent judiciary administering a law that treats all subjects with fairness and lenity, knowing no distinctions of class, wealth, or power. From their own perspective, the judges as royal officers were the personal embodiment of the majesty and justice of British law. To even hint at their partisanship was to be ignorant or treasonous. But then and now there were those who could not share this faith in judicial impartiality.

In *Whigs and Hunters* E.P. Thompson said that English judges 'were subject to political influence' and their 'sense of justice was humbug.'[61] There is little hard evidence that such an assessment is appropriate in the Upper Canadian context. Yet, regrettably, the Upper Canadian judges apparently failed to repeat in any private correspondence the high-minded sentiments that flowed so readily from their lips before grand juries, and the veil of history hangs heavily between us and any franker or more open expression of their thoughts and beliefs as to their political role. One revealing insight into the convictions of the greatest of Upper Canadian judges was offered by Robinson in 1838, when he helped Sir George Arthur frame the emergency laws put in place in response to armed incursions from the United States. 'Unusual emergencies,' said Robinson bluntly, 'require often unusual laws to meet them' and 'there must be ... an implicit discretion in the colonial government to protect the welfare and safety of the community.'[62] Even in 1838, and acting in the face of the clearest instructions from the colonial office, Chief Justice Robinson never doubted for a moment that he remained a leading officer of the government of Upper Canada; and he never believed for a moment that he was acting in an improper or partisan way.

But therein lay the rub. Implicit always in the beliefs and values of the King's Bench judges was their unshakeable sense that the law and the state were one, and that they were the final expression and embodiment of the rule of law and of everything that powerful phrase implied. There was no humbug in their unwavering determination to ensure that the values inherent in English law be administered in the colony by a judiciary full of political wisdom and imbued with the virtues of statecraft. This after all was the essence of Baconism, but by the 1830s polarization of politics and the rise of a powerful opposition rendered this position indefensible and exposed the judges to charges of partisanship. After Willis, the balance shifted with remarkable speed and with the 1834 statute the entire Baconian structure toppled, unlamented except by a few Tory diehards, most notably the chief justice himself. The extent of change and the emergence to legitimacy of party politics, including the reality of a loyal opposition, had rendered the concept of the Baconian judiciary utterly anachronistic. When John Beverley Robinson resumed his old political role in 1838, this was the last gasp of the old judicial system.

Almost forty years later, in 1876, another chief justice of Ontario, Robert Harrison, declined to attend a speech being given by Sir Alexander Galt even though Galt was not then active in politics. The talk was on Canada's commercial future but Harrison felt he could not attend, as he put it, because 'the lecturer had a political object.'[63] In reality, however, the judiciary in the Union period beginning in 1841 was becoming thoroughly politicized in another sense. In the Union period judicial appointments became the prerogative of local politicians and notoriously partisan in nature. Indeed, the issue of political involvement has never disappeared and in the post-Charter era in Canada there are some who argue that in still other ways Canadian judges are more involved in politics and in making policy than ever before. If that is the case, it seems unlikely that the modern judiciary will be able to avoid some of the shoals encountered by judges and politicians in the era of the Baconian judiciary in Upper Canada. In that case perhaps they would benefit by paying some attention to the earlier story and regarding it as a cautionary tale.

NOTES

I thank Paul Romney, Chris Raible, and Barry Wright for giving this paper a critical reading. And I thank the editors, Blaine Baker and Jim Phillips, for their constructive criticism. The views expressed herein are solely my own.

1 F. Murray Greenwood, *Legacies of Fear: Law and Politics in Quebec in the Era of the French Revolution* (Toronto: The Osgoode Society for Canadian Legal History 1993), 27–34.
2 Ibid., 28–30. For other relevant British developments see C.D. Bowen, *The Lion and the Throne: The Life and Times of Sir Edward Coke* (Boston: Little Brown 1957); G.R. Elton, *Studies in Tudor and Stuart Politics and Government* (New York: Cambridge University Press 1974); and E.G. Henderson, *Foundations of English Administrative Law: Certiorari and Mandamus in the Seventeenth Century* (Cambridge, Mass.: Harvard University Press 1963).
3 Greenwood, *Legacies of Fear*, 29–31. They continued nonetheless to offer political advice and this was the point of most of the impeachment charges brought against Chief Justices Sewell and Monk in 1814–15. Significantly, Colonial Secretary Lord Bathurst would give no consideration to the political heads because 'to admit that a Councillor was responsible for the acts of a Governor' was 'contrary to every principle' and the Privy Council acted accordingly. See Evelyn Kolish and James Lambert, 'The Attempted Impeach-ment of the Lower Canadian Chief Justices, 1814–15,' in F. Murray Green-wood and Barry Wright, eds., *Canadian State Trials: Law, Politics and Security Measures, 1608–1837* (Toronto: The Osgoode Society for Canadian Legal History 1996), 475–6.
4 The most important example of the new work is Paul Romney's *Mr Attorney, The Attorney General for Ontario in Court, Cabinet and Legislature 1791–1899* (Toronto: The Osgoode Society for Canadian Legal History 1986). A collection of Robert Fraser's *Dictionary of Canadian Biography* portraits, with an impor-

tant introductory essay, is found in Robert Fraser, ed., *Provincial Justice: Upper Canadian Legal Portraits* (Toronto: University of Toronto Press for The Osgoode Society for Canadian Legal History 1992).

5 Aileen Dunham, *Political Unrest In Upper Canada 1815–1836* (Carleton Library No. 10, 1963); Gerald Craig, *Upper Canada: The Formative Years* (Toronto: McClelland and Stewart 1963). S.F. Wise's essays are collected in A.B. McKillop and Paul Romney, eds., *God's Peculiar Peoples* (Ottawa: Carleton University Press 1993).

6 Craig, *Upper Canada*, 192.

7 See especially S.F. Wise, 'Sermon Literature and Canadian Intellectual History,' 'God's Peculiar People,' and 'Upper Canada and the Conservative Tradition,' in McKillop and Romney, eds., *God's Peculiar Peoples*.

8 Romney, *Mr Attorney*, chap. 3, the heart of the book.

9 Craig, *Upper Canada*, 191–2.

10 Romney, *Mr Attorney*, 64; a somewhat different set of values and priorities, however, seems to have prevailed in some civil cases that touched upon the personal and pecuniary interests of the judges. To date there is no comprehensive study of the work of the King's Bench on the civil side. William Wylie's thesis covers only the first two decades of its existence and he concludes that while there was some controversy over such issues as high costs, delays, and accessibility, 'it would not do to exaggerate' these early difficulties. 'Articulate protest,' he argues, was 'limited to a few individuals who were themselves selfishly motivated.' Paul Romney offers a different perspective, however, and much of his criticism of the judges focuses on civil rather than criminal matters. For Romney the principal fault of the judges appears to have been their willingness to take advantage of their positions to further their own pecuniary and family interests. For example, in a series of law suits in which powerful merchant interests endeavoured to wrest property from the embattled speculator Robert Randal, two of the judges, D'Arcy Boulton and Levius Peters Sherwood, were disqualified from acting because of personal interests, yet a third, William Dummer Powell, encouraged jurors to find against Randal by threatening them with a writ of attaint. For Wylie see William N.T. Wylie, 'Instruments of Commerce and Authority: The Civil Courts in Upper Canada 1789–1812,' in David H. Flaherty, ed., *Essays in the History of Canadian Law, Vol. II* (Toronto: The Osgoode Society for Canadian Legal History 1983), 40. For Romney see *Mr Attorney*, 65–82.

11 Fraser, *Provincial Justice*, xxv.

12 Ibid., ixviii.

13 Leo A. Johnson, 'John Walpole Willis's Judicial Career in Upper Canada, 1827–28: The Research Impact of Computerized Documentation on a Noncontroversial Theme,' *Ontario History* (June 1993), 150; see also Leo Johnson,

'The Gore District "Outrages," 1826–1829: A Case Study of Violence, Justice, and Political Propaganda,' *Ontario History* (June 1991).

14 Blaine Baker, '"So Elegant A Web": Providential Order and the Rule of Secular Law in Early Nineteenth Century Upper Canada,' *University of Toronto Law Journal* 38 (1988); G.B. Baker, 'The Juvenile Advocate Society, 1821–1826,' Canadian Historical Association, *Historical Papers* (1985); David Howes, 'Property, God and Nature in the Thought of Sir John Beverley Robinson,' *McGill Law Journal* 30, no. 3 (1985); Paul Romney, 'Very Late Loyalist Fantasies: Nostalgic Tory "History" and the Rule of Law in Upper Canada,' in W.W. Pue and Barry Wright, eds., *Canadian Perspectives on Law and Society* (Ottawa: Carleton University Press 1988); Paul Romney, 'From Constitutionalism to Legalism: Trial by Jury, Responsible Government, and the Rule of Law in the Canadian Political Culture,' *Law and History Review* 7, no. 1 (Spring 1989); Carol Wilton, '"Lawless Law": Conservative Political Violence in Upper Canada, 1818–41,' *Law and History Review* 13, no. 1, (Spring 1995).

15 Fraser, *Provincial Justice*, xxi–xxv.

16 Ibid., ixviii–ixix. But see too Fraser's earlier conclusion that in the trial and execution, 'Everything seems to have been proper and above-board' (395).

17 Charles Lindsey, *The Life and Times of William Lyon Mackenzie*, 2 vols. (Toronto: 1862).

18 John Weaver, *Crime, Constables, and Courts: Order and Transgression in a Canadian City, 1816–1970* (Montreal and Kingston: McGill-Queen's University Press 1995), chap. 1.

19 For preliminary work on assize records see Peter Oliver, *'Terror to Evil-Doers': Prisons and Punishments in Nineteenth Century Ontario* (Toronto: The Osgoode Society for Canadian Legal History and University of Toronto Press 1998).

20 For a useful analysis of Chief Justice Robinson's sense of the vital role played by law and the judiciary in British constitutional governance and statecraft see Donald J. McMahon, 'Law and Public Authority: Sir John Beverley Robinson and the Purposes of the Criminal Law,' *University of Toronto Faculty of Law Review* (Winter 1988).

21 J.B. Robinson, 'A Charge of Chief Justice Robinson To the Grand Jury of the Home District, April, 1833' (York, Upper Canada: Robert Stanton).

22 Upper Canada, Journals of the House of Assembly, 3rd Sess., 11th Parl., 1833, 112–13 and 140.

23 See Oliver, *'Terror to Evil-Doers,'* especially chaps. 2 and 3.

24 Ann Alexandra McEwen, 'Crime in the Niagara District, 1827–1850' (MA thesis, University of Guelph 1991) 38–40.

25 E.P. Thompson, *Whigs and Hunters: The Origins of the Black Act* (New York: Pantheon 1975), conclusion.

26 For detailed work on treason, sedition, and libel trials, see Barry Wright, 'The Ideological Dimensions of Law in Upper Canada: The Treason Proceedings of 1838,' in *Criminal Justice History* 10 (1989); Barry Wright, 'Sedition in Upper Canada: Contested Legality,' *Labour/Le travail* 29 (1992); Paul Romney and Barry Wright, 'State Trials and Security Proceedings in Upper Canada during the War of 1812,' in Greenwood and Wright, eds., *Canadian State Trials*; F. Murray Greenwood and Barry Wright, 'Parliamentary Privilege and the Repression of Dissent in the Canadas,' in ibid.; Barry Wright, 'The Gourlay Affair: Seditious Libel and the Sedition Act in Upper Canada, 1818–19,' in ibid.; and Barry Wright, '"Harshness and Forbearance": The Politics of Pardons and the Upper Canada Rebellion,' in Carolyn Strange, ed., *Qualities of Mercy: Justice, Punishment and Discretion* (Vancouver: UBC Press 1996).
27 For Thorpe see G.H. Patterson, 'Robert Thorpe,' in Fraser, ed., *Provincial Justice*, 188–91.
28 Although Romney makes it clear that Robinson carried out many of his duties as attorney general with skill and integrity, the index entry for Robinson in *Mr Attorney* makes it clear that Romney regarded him overall as highly partisan and a 'slippery zealot.'
29 There are useful portraits of all the above in the *DCB* collection edited by Fraser, *Provincial Justice*.
30 In the United States in 1793, the Supreme Court refused to supply an extrajudicial opinion to President Washington on the grounds that the U.S. constitution provided for the separation of executive and judicial powers. For a good general discussion of American practices, see Stewart Jay, *Most Humble Servants: The Advisory Role of Early Judges* (New Haven: 1997).
31 For this episode see Oliver, 'Terror to Evil-Doers.'
32 F. Murray Greenwood and Barry Wright, 'Parliamentary Privilege,' *State Trials*, 418–23.
33 E.A. Cruikshank, 'The Government of Upper Canada and Robert Gourlay,' Ontario Historical Society, '*Papers and Records*' 23 (1926), 83–4. This publication includes numerous documents.
34 Ibid., 28. According to Cruikshank, Gourlay was acquitted in Kingston 'in the face of what the trial judge reported to be the clearest evidence of guilt.'
35 Lois Milani, *Robert Gourlay, Gadfly* (Toronto: Ampersand 1971) 207–9.
36 Wright, 'Sedition in Upper Canada,' 41.
37 Ibid., 40–2.
38 Wright, 'The Gourlay Affair,' 496.
39 Johnson, 'John Walpole Willis's Judicial Career,' 143.
40 Ibid., 145.
41 See ibid., 154, for Willis's opinion on the composition of King's Bench.

42 Ibid., 145.

43 NA, Co 42, vol. 384, Maitland to William Huskisson, 14 May 1828, as cited in ibid., 148.

44 J.W. Willis, described in Leo Johnson as 'Narrative G' enclosed in Willis to the colonial secretary, apparently 5 December 1828, and printed in British Blue Book, Papers Relating to the Removal of the Honourable John Walpole Willis from the Office of One of His Majesty's Judges of the Court of King's Bench of Upper Canada, 1829, NA, Co 42, vol. 386, 483–90. See Johnson, notes 8, 160 and notes 60 and 61, 164.

45 Journals of Legislative Assembly of Upper Canada, 1829, Appendix, 'Report of the Select Committee on the case of Mr Justice Willis and the Administration of Justice,' 26, 'Copy of Reply to the Report of the Honourable Executive Council ...,' by J.W. Willis, 23 September 1828, as cited in Johnson, 'John Walpole Willis's Judicial Career,' notes 54, 164.

46 Dunham, Political Unrest, 114 and Romney, Mr Attorney, 145–6.

47 For circumstances of Maitland's removal, see Johnson, 'John Walpole Willis's Judicial Career,' 158.

48 JLAUC, 1828, 76 as cited in Patrick Brode, 'Of Courts and Politics: The Growth of An Independent Judiciary In Upper Canada,' The Law Society of Upper Canada Gazette (September 1978), 268.

49 The fullest discussion of the work of the Canada Committee is in Helen Taft Manning, The Revolt of French Canada 1800–1835 (Toronto: 1962).

50 Colonial Office Papers 47/43, Lord Goderich to Colborne, 8 February 1831, as cited in Brode, 'Of Courts and Politics,' 269. Brode states (268) that 'an impecunious Assembly' in Upper Canada was unable to accept the offer of Goderich to give judges tenure dependent upon good behaviour, if the colony paid their salaries. But Dunham (Political Unrest, 121–2) points out that in 1830 Goderich told Colborne that 'revenue from the duties established by the Act of 14 George III' would be turned over to the Assembly in return for a permanent civil list. The Assembly in 1831 agreed to provide a civil list totalling £6,500, including salaries of the judges of King's Bench. Dunham also points out (122) that at this time Colborne was 'instructed to propose a bill for changing the tenure of judicial office to good behaviour.' Dunham relates that the Legislative Council delayed this measure until 1834. See Appendix B.

51 Arthur Papers, Robinson to Sir George Arthur, 16 April 1838, as cited in Brode, 'Of Courts and Politics,' 270.

52 Gerald M. Craig, Lord Durham's Report (Carleton Library 1963), 170.

53 W.R. Riddell, The Bar and the Courts of the Province of Upper Canada or Ontario (Toronto: 1928).

54 Colonial Office 42/447/21, 29 Arthur to Lord Glenelg, 10 September 1838, as cited in Wright, 'The Politics of Pardons,' 92.
55 Dunham, *Political Unrest*, 116.
56 Wright, 'The Politics of Pardons,' 95.
57 See Romney, 'Very Late Loyalist Fantasies,' for a persuasive statement of this position on rule of law.
58 Wilton, 'Lawless Law,' 117–19.
59 Ibid., 132.
60 Archives of Ontario (AO), RG5, A1, Upper Canada Sundries, Circuit Report, James B. Macaulay, 1 October 1832.
61 Thompson, *Whigs and Hunters*, 265.
62 J.B. Robinson, as cited in Wright, 'The Ideological Dimensions of Law,' 158.
63 AO, Diaries of Robert A. Harrison, entry for 31 May 1876.

14

The Criminal Trial in Nova Scotia, 1749–1815

JIM PHILLIPS

INTRODUCTION: THE OLD FORM OF TRIAL

In the mid-eighteenth-century, when a new imperial order was introduced into Nova Scotia with the founding of Halifax and the establishment of government there, the colony received English criminal law and procedure, including what criminal justice historians have termed the 'old form' of trial.[1] Criminal trial proceedings in eighteenth-century England were largely conducted without lawyers and tended to be rapid affairs. Accusation was quickly followed by evidence and refutation, with judge and jurors able to interrupt and ask questions. The trial was largely dominated by the drama of a quick and direct confrontation between victim and accuser.

The old form of trial gave way, by the middle of the nineteenth century and through a process much more evolutionary than revolutionary, to the more 'modern' form. After 1836 lawyers were permitted to take part for both prosecution and defence, and rules about such matters as the admissibility of evidence and the presumption of innocence had been established. While in theory the trial changed substantially, with a much reduced scope for the direct participation of defendant and complainant, the frequency of appearances by counsel is unclear and the evidence we have suggests that the majority of trials continued to be conducted without lawyers. Whatever the extent of changes by the mid-nineteenth century, when Halifax was founded these developments were in their earliest stages and Nova Scotia consequently received a criminal trial process much closer to the old form of trial than to the more modern one.

While we now know a good deal about the operation of the trial in eighteenth-century England, our knowledge of the process once it was exported to Canada is very limited. Much excellent recent work has been done on trials for political offences in the eighteenth and early nineteenth centuries and there are some very good accounts of particular non-state trials in the nineteenth century, but the student of the premodern trial must rely largely on older, often antiquarian, studies, which again concentrate on particular cases rather than trial process in general.[2] This chapter attempts to begin to fill the gap in our knowledge by providing a systematic descriptive analysis of the conduct of the trial. It is therefore a response to Dick Risk's lament, sounded more than two decades ago, that Canadian legal history was so much in its infancy that '[w]e have not even accumulated and organized most of the major facts.'[3]

Throughout this period the Nova Scotia trial remained a short, simple process, unencumbered by concerns about rules of evidence or procedure and often a straightforward test of the respective credibility and character of victim and defendant. In only one respect did the Nova Scotian trial depart significantly from the English model – prosecution was fundamentally a state activity in the colony, not left entirely to the initiative of victims. Reliance on public prosecution was the principal way in which Nova Scotia trial process resembled that employed in other North American colonies at mid-century. But important as this development was, and despite the fact that Nova Scotia's demography and economy in the eighteenth century was derived from and reflected its close connections to New England, this study is fundamentally about the reception and adaptation of the imperial model of criminal process. The colony's criminal law and procedure, and many of the ideological presuppositions that informed them, were English, for officials believed the English system to be the best guarantee of legal and social order in a new colony.[4]

Three caveats should be stated at the outset. First, I am principally concerned here with the trial itself. Thus I do not discuss the processes of jury selection and decision or the make-up of grand and trial juries, nor do I examine the wider ideological uses of courts and law embedded in the trial – grand jury addresses, the ceremonies of sentencing and pardons, and so forth.[5] My second caveat concerns the scope of this study. I deal here with trials for felonies conducted in the General Court (1749–54) and the Supreme Court (from 1754) of Nova Scotia; for the most part the analysis is of the court sitting in Halifax, although some cases are drawn from other venues. Thus this study is largely about trials for the capital offences of murder, rape, burglary, robbery, and some larcenies, and for noncapital felonies – manslaughter, grand and petit larceny, and assault. Lack of sources prevents me from dealing with the trials for lesser offences conducted in the sessions courts presided over by justices of the peace (JPs). In Halifax the quarter sessions tried assaults, a few petit larcenies, and a variety of minor and regulatory offences, while outside the capital the general sessions also exercised some jurisdiction over grand larceny.[6] Throughout this period, however, it was the General or Supreme Court, sitting in Halifax or travelling on circuit (after 1775) or by special commission, which conducted trials for capital offences and the more serious noncapital felonies. Thus while rather more cases were heard at the sessions, the important ones were conducted in the Supreme Court.

Third, while the sources for a study of trial procedure in the Supreme Court are adequate, they are limited. There are no true 'minutes' for the court; instead I rely principally on three kinds of sources. Proceedings books for the General and Supreme Courts sitting in Halifax provide very brief summaries of cases,[7] while a collection of accounts of some two dozen trials, from Halifax and elsewhere, reveal much more information on the details of the process. These trials were almost all capital cases – the reports were produced for the pardon process – and thus do not capture the more run-of-the-mill cases. Some insight into the latter can be obtained from my third source, Supreme Court judge Isaac Deschamps' benchbook, which records a variety of cases tried in Halifax and Windsor between 1776 and 1778.[8] While one would ideally want more and better sources, it is possible to construct a general picture of the trial from these, although they do not allow me to say much about one important issue – the development of rules of evidence.

THE TRIALS OF PETER CARTCEL AND WALTER LEE

I begin with an account of two trials, one from the beginning and one from the end of my period, which illustrate many of the essential facets of the Nova Scotian criminal trial. The first of these, indeed the first trial to be held in Halifax, took place on 31 August 1749. Settler Peter Cartcel was tried in the General Court for the murder of Abraham Goodsides, a sailor off one of the transport ships.[9] Cartcel had stabbed Goodsides in a fight on 26 August. The empanelling of both juries, the indictment, arraignment, and the trial all took place on the same day. Cartcel, who was of French origin, knew little English and was assigned an interpreter, through whom he pleaded not guilty. The jury then heard four witnesses. Three of them testified to some conversation between the two men, following which 'the said Goodsides asked the prisoner if he would fight him and gave the prisoner a slap on the face with his open hand upon which the prisoner struck the said Goodsides into the breast with his knife as far as it would go.' The fourth witness, constable Roger Snowden, testified that the two men had argued earlier the same day. After the four witnesses had given their evidence, and presumably through his interpreter, Cartcel asked one witness, James Gordon, 'whether said Goodsides did not run upon the knife which he held in his hand.' Gordon was not, however, disposed to assist the accused and stated that Cartcel 'stepped a little aside and with a backstroke stabbed him.' Cartcel called no witnesses of his own and did not address the jury. The jury retired and after deliberating for half an hour returned with a guilty verdict. Cartcel was sentenced to death and executed on 2 September.

This proceeding matches very well what we know of mid-century English trials. It was a quick proceeding and like most English trials it involved no lawyers and heard no disputes about evidence or law. Procedure was simple – eyewitnesses telling the court what they believed they had seen rather than the elicitation of evidence in chief by Crown counsel through a series of carefully crafted questions. The defendant, unaided, made some attempt to refute the case against him, but in the brief account we are left with it seems a forlorn, rather pathetic effort. In one sense only was the case untypical of an assize court trial in an English county town: no legally trained individual sat as judge.[10] In short, Governor Cornwallis was correct to tell London that the court had followed 'as nearly as possible the English Laws and Customs.'[11]

My second trial comes from near the end of this period. In June 1812 Walter Lee was tried at Guysborough, in what was then Sydney County, for the murder of Nicholas Wright, cooper, committed at Canso in September 1811.[12] Lee spent nine months in jail because Sydney County was not (until 1816) part of the circuit system; the court had to be appointed by a special commission of oyer and terminer and general gaol delivery, presided over by Supreme Court judge George Henry Monk.[13] After he was arraigned and pleaded not guilty, Lee requested a delay, 'to procure the attendance of two Witnesses, & for the Assistance of Counsel.' His lawyer of choice, John George Marshall, was some eighty miles away in Pictou, but had been sent for.[14] Lee was given a one-day adjournment but Marshall could not make the journey. Instead, he sent the court some notes on the law, notes that 'he could avail himself of in the Prisoner's defence were he present at his trial.' Marshall knew something of the case because he had been at Guysborough the previous year, when Lee was committed, and the latter had consulted him at that time. The court gave Lee the notes and asked him if there was anybody he wanted to consult with about his defence, 'as there were no professional Gentlemen present nor in the County that could be assigned his Counsel in the stead of the one he had expected.' Lee chose Marshall's brother Joseph Henry Marshall, who was present in court in his capacity as clerk of the peace for the county, and received another one-day adjournment to prepare.[15]

When the trial got under way the deputy clerk of the Crown for the county, who conducted the prosecution,[16] brought forward five witnesses. Four residents of Canso gave much the same evidence – that Lee and Wright, his neighbour, had had a dispute over some barrels Lee had made for Wright and that Wright had taken a barrel from Lee's workshop on the fatal day and walked away. Lee had then got his gun and discharged it in the direction of the retreating Wright, and Wright had been hit. All four witnesses saw this happen, from different places. The final witness, Lee's servant Mary Goreham, filled in the context, testifying that a few months before the incident Lee had threatened to shoot Wright if he tried to steal any barrels from his premises.

Lee, conducting his own defence, asked questions of each prosecution witness. Although Lee did the asking, the questions were undoubtedly inspired by Marshall's notes, and one can see the lawyer's mind at work, setting up a defence of lack of intention to kill. Each prosecution witness in turn was asked questions to elicit the fact that no one had heard Lee threaten Wright, that there was a considerable distance between Lee and Wright when the fatal shot was fired, and that Lee did not 'stoop' when firing. When it came to Lee's turn to present his story, he had three points to make. First, he called two witnesses to show that while a dispute had subsisted between him and Wright for some time, Lee had wanted it settled. Second, one of the witnesses testified that after the shooting Lee was 'very much grieved and distressed' and made no attempt to decamp even though he could have; indeed he had asked to be taken to the JP. Third, and most importantly, Joseph Henry Marshall – the man assisting Lee – testified that he had found and then examined the dead body, and ascertained that the wounds went up from the point of entry.

The linchpin of Lee's defence was his speech to the jury, which was given 'at some length.' He argued that the evidence revealed that 'he had never shewn any Malice against the deceased,' but had rather 'repeatedly & earnestly endeavoured' to come to a settlement with him to resolve their dispute. Crucially, he told the jury that he had not intended to shoot Wright but merely to frighten him and show that he was determined to defend his property. Hence he had fired at the ground. Unfortunately, and here came the importance of the questions to prosecution witnesses about his 'stooping' down when he fired, the barrel of the gun had been bent slightly upwards in an accident without his knowing it, and although aimed downwards at the ground behind the distant Wright, it instead shot him, 'contrary to the prisoner's aim, intent or wish.' Lee also made an appeal based on character: 'as he was very generally known in the County, he hoped that his uniform peacable demeanor would prevail on them to believe what he offered & declared, with a very solemn appeal to Heaven for the truth of what he said, not from any timidity or dread of death, however he could not but be griev'd at what he had done, though his conscience was clear of any design or intent of killing Wright.'

Monk's summation for the jury was a clear incitement to convict. He first made it abundantly clear that the prosecution had established 'the Fact [of Lee firing the fatal shot] laid in the Indictment, without even an attempt on the part of the prisoner to contradict.' He reviewed John Marshall's notes on the distinction between murder and manslaughter (essentially whether or not there was an intention to kill), but substantially undercut Lee's defence by 'adverting also to the Rule of Law which requires of those who venture to use a deadly weapon without sufficient provocation, or just apprehention of personal harm or injury, that they use such deadly weapon with proper precaution, at the peril of the fatal consequences.' In short, he did his best to take away the defence of lack of intention to kill. It worked, for the jury, after retiring and deliberating 'for some time,' found Lee guilty as indicted although they also recommended mercy.

Mercy was not Monk's to bestow and on the following Monday Lee was again brought to court to hear the death sentence pronounced. Despite petitions for mercy from leading citizens of Canso and from the jurors at his trial, he was hanged.[17]

These two cases reveal some change and substantial continuity in the form and nature of the criminal trial over some sixty years. For example, an experienced judge presided in the Lee trial, even though Monk may not have been legally trained. In addition, there was a form of public prosecutor present, although again probably not a man qualified as a lawyer. The defendant had legal assistance, albeit of a limited nature, and that assistance enabled the accused to both test the prosecution case and mount an affirmative defence of his own, one that involved argument over law as well as fact. Lee's trial occupied the court for a whole day, not just the hour or two (at the most) that Cartcel's must have lasted.

Yet there is rather more evidence of continuity. Both trials were short, the one only a few hours longer than the other. We could also note the simplicity of the case for the prosecution: in both cases a small number of witnesses gave eyewitness testimony that was overwhelmingly persuasive about the *actus reus* of the offence. And in both cases the defendant was on his own in trying to avoid the gallows. Cartcel was, of course, more alone than Lee, who had the notes of one Marshall and the help of the other, but when the prosecution case was closed and the witnesses for the defence had finished, it was Lee who had to stand up and explain himself to the jury with his life on the line. While the trial report suggests he made a good argument on paper, it was not a task to which Lee was well-suited. Perhaps suffering the effects of a nine-month confinement through the winter in the local jail, and obviously deeply afraid of the consequences of losing, he was not an eloquent advocate for his cause. Throughout his speech to the jury Lee needed 'repeated pauses for recollection and to recover from the distress he appeared to be in.' When he was pronounced guilty he was, not surprisingly, 'very much agitated.'

In the remainder of this chapter I will essay a more general description of the criminal trial over the sixty or so years which separated these two cases. My analysis is divided into four closely related sections. The first two examine what might be termed issues relating to the form of trial – how long trials took and to what extent prosecution and defence counsel participated. The third and fourth sections, dealing in turn with the conduct of the prosecution and defence cases, explore what actually went on during the trial – the kinds of evidence given and the nature of the courtroom give and take. Despite some changes, the criminal trial during this period was in nature the 'old form of trial,' or what one historian of colonial American criminal procedure has recently called the 'accused speaks' trial: a short, simple proceeding largely unencumbered by technical legal rules and one that demanded the active participation of the defendant.[18]

THE PACE OF TRIAL

Establishing how long trials took is important, for it provides a context for much of what follows. Doing so is difficult, however, as the records do not give trial times. The following account draws inferences from a variety of sources. Table 14.1 summarizes information on the number of individuals

TABLE 14.1
Individuals tried per day, Halifax General and Supreme Courts, 1749–1803

Individuals tried per day	Number of days	Total trial days %	Individuals tried N	%
1	133	55.0	133	(25.1)
2	45	18.6	90	(17.0)
3	24	9.9	72	(13.6)
4	16	6.6	80	(15.1)
5	10	4.1	50	(9.5)
6	6	2.5	36	(6.8)
7–10	8	3.3	68	(12.9)
Total	242	100	529	(100)

tried per day, compiled from trial date information (available for many but not all cases) in the proceedings books for the General and Supreme Courts in Halifax. It shows that on slightly more than half of the days that the court sat for criminal business it heard only one case. Such trials, however, accounted for only a quarter of the individuals tried, and indeed almost 40 per cent of defendants were tried on days when the court heard four or more cases.

The figures in Table 14.1 certainly suggest that the trial process was not as cursory as it was in England, where the courts often got through a dozen or more felony cases a day.[19] On only two occasions were as many as ten defendants tried on the same day in Halifax. It is also likely that trials were quicker in the first decade or so after 1749 than they were later. All but one of eight trial days on which between seven and ten defendants were tried appear in this first decade, with the other being the trials of nine co-defendants in Michaelmas Term, 1782.

In order to determine how long a typical trial took, however, we need to know how much of a trial day was actually taken up with the proceeding, and that information is not generally available. Some evidence suggests that the courts would have been busy with criminal business for all or most of the day, and therefore one or two trials a day meant the whole day or half of it absorbed with the case.[20] In 1797, for example, Chief Justice Sampson Salter Blowers reported that on most days during Michaelmas Term 1797 'the court was diligently employed, often until 5 or 6 in the afternoon.'[21] Unfortunately this is the only such reference we have, and Blowers was discussing the whole of the session, in which the court dealt with both criminal and civil business. It was also the case that the Supreme Court in Halifax did not, as a rule, intersperse criminal and civil business on the same day,[22] suggesting that when the court dealt with criminal cases the whole of the time, if not necessarily the whole day, was taken up with them. Finally, reports of particular trials do indicate that some cases occupied the whole of the day. The murder trial of three merchant sailors in the first term of the Supreme Court took ten hours, much of which was spent on legal argument,[23] and the trial of John Young in 1756 took about as long.[24] Some murder trials outside of Halifax, like that of Walter Lee, probably also lasted an entire day.[25]

Despite this evidence, I do not think that we can simply divide the day by the number of trials in it and arrive at an estimate of trial time. To do so would be to overestimate the length of trials, a conclusion I draw from three factors. First, fully 41 of the 133 days on which there was only one trial (see Table 14.1) come from court sessions in which only one person was tried. Second, and to similar effect, a further 30 or so of the trial days on which only one individual was tried represent occasions when a defendant was not in jail awaiting trial when the session began, but was apprehended after it had started, brought in, indicted, and tried. Sometimes this was because the crime had been committed more or less contemporaneously with the court session, sometimes because evidence given in one trial provided the information on which an arrest was made. Whatever the reason, the point for present purposes is that the fact that that individual was not tried with others tells us nothing about how long trials took. Third, the cases recorded in the benchbook of Isaac Deschamps strongly suggest trials of an hour or two on average, sometimes less, sometimes more. The number of witnesses and the evidence given would not generally have taken longer than that. The 1776 murder trial of George Thompson in Windsor, for example, probably occupied about half of the day, and this was the longest case of those recorded.

On the basis of this evidence we can conclude that trials rarely lasted more than a day, that some did take that long, but that on average most occupied perhaps a couple of hours. This is hardly elaborate process, but it was certainly more process than was the case in late-eighteenth-century England. Nova Scotian trials seem to have taken about as long as their counterparts in the American colonies in this period.[26] The cause was probably the role played in almost every case by the attorney general, and to a lesser extent by defence counsel, and thus it is to the role of lawyers in the trial that I now turn.

LAWYERS IN THE COURTROOM

The English criminal trial introduced to Nova Scotia in the mid-eighteenth century was a proceeding in which lawyers played a relatively minor role.

Unusual events like major treason trials aside, it was not a legally trained prosecutor who conducted the case for the prosecution, but the victim, or the judge, or both. That is, if the victim was in court he or she would come forward and give an account of the case, prompted by the judge and interrupted with questions from him. There might then be other witnesses on the prosecution side, whose stories were subject to similar examination by the judge. If there were no victim present, for example in a murder charge, the judge alone would take the lead, examining and cross-examining the principal witnesses. In the first half of the eighteenth century this picture began to change as governments occasionally hired prosecuting lawyers to conduct cases, and some private prosecutors followed suit. But for most of the century lawyers represented the prosecution in only a very small minority of cases; while in the late eighteenth and early nineteenth century as many as 20 per cent of the trials in London had prosecuting counsel, they appeared less often after 1805, in under 10 per cent of cases.[27]

This is an area where Nova Scotian trial procedure was, from very early on, quite different from that of England. While there is almost no evidence of victims hiring lawyers to present the case against those they accused, this was because prosecution was not only professional, but public. That is, most criminal prosecutions were conducted by a public prosecutor, usually the attorney general although occasionally the solicitor general or a lawyer in private practice deputised for the attorney general.[28] We know that Attorney General William Nesbitt, for example, prosecuted three merchant seamen for killing two naval sailors and also took the lead in the counterfeiting trial of John Young in 1756, a case in which the principal issue was the applicability to Nova Scotia of English statutes making the counterfeiting of foreign coin a capital offence.[29] He also prosecuted in trials of much less significance through the 1750s, 1760s, and 1770s; in 1777, for example, we find him conducting the prosecution in three property cases and in a sodomy trial.[30] Nesbitt held the post of attorney general until 1779 and his successors – James Brenton (attorney general from 1779 until his appointment to the Supreme Court in 1781), Richard Gibbons Junior (1782–5), Sampson Salter Blowers (1785 until his elevation to the chief justiceship in 1797), and Richard John Uniacke (1797–1833) – were all consistently present in the Supreme Court, criminal side.[31]

I am not suggesting that a government law officer prosecuted in every case. Very occasionally victims hired counsel privately to prosecute,[32] and there are scattered indications that in some cases the victim took on the job. For example, on 17 October 1777, James Hill and John Thorne were tried for 'stealing from William Allen two boxes of soap and six calf skins' and

Henry and Mary Elsworthy were tried for receiving those goods from them. Hill was tried first, and immediately after his arraignment and plea Allan came forward and told the court about the theft. He was followed by other witnesses and, while it is not entirely clear, my impression from the notes in Deschamps' benchbook is that Allan and Deschamps elicited the evidence that convicted all four.[33] This may have been the result of one of Nesbitt's bouts of illness rendering him unable to participate, but there is other evidence, from the very end of our period, that the victim could be the principal player. When Henry Jebb was tried for highway robbery in 1815 his victim, Captain Clarke of the 60th Regiment, probably prosecuted.[34]

If public and private prosecution co-existed, what was the extent of the former? If we were to rely solely on references to his presence in the proceedings books and reports of trials, the attorney general appeared in perhaps 30 per cent of all cases heard in the Halifax Supreme Court. I believe, however, that such mentions greatly underestimate his participation, for the trial reports and case files refer to the presence of the official prosecutor in other cases. Indeed, other evidence suggests that the attorney general was present at most criminal trials. In 1755 Nesbitt stated that he had attended five Supreme Court sittings and eight meetings of the quarter sessions over the previous two years.[35] Chief Justice Jonathan Belcher adverted to 'his great usefulness and assistance to me in the court' and to 'his service at all times in both the courts [Supreme Court and quarter sessions].'[36] An account of expenses submitted by James Brenton for 1781 shows that he definitely took part in most, though not all, criminal trials that year, including many in which his presence is not noted in the proceedings book.[37] A document from 1791, a series of instructions to the clerk of the court, shows Blowers involved in a variety of cases,[38] as does an account submitted by Attorney General Uniacke in 1799 for his attendance 'on all Indictments, Informations or other Prosecutions in the King's name in the Supream Court.'[39] As noted, the attorney general prosecuted minor cases in quarter sessions as well as more serious ones in the Supreme Court.[40]

The government law officers also on occasion conducted prosecutions, for murder or on other charges, outside of Halifax.[41] Then Solicitor General Uniacke conducted the prosecution of Ezekiel Hooper for murder at Annapolis in 1783, for example, while Attorney General Gibbons prosecuted a series of Shelburne robberies in 1784.[42] Gibbons' successor Uniacke prosecuted in the murder trials of Patrick Holland at Liverpool in 1810 and Alexander McIntosh at Pictou the following year.[43] As the trial of Walter Lee demonstrates, the government law officers were not always present when the court travelled outside of Halifax on circuit or pursuant to a special commission of oyer and terminer. Presumably the press of other business and/or the difficulties of travel to more remote settlements meant that at times they could not, or would not, travel, and in consequence other lawyers were deputed to prosecute. In 1791 George and John Boutelier were prosecuted by James Stewart, a future solicitor general (1798) although he had only four years' seniority at the bar when he took on this task.[44] Lawyers in private practice were engaged to prosecute Nancy O'Neal at Liverpool in 1814, John Pomp and Amy Pomp at Annapolis in 1813, and 'two criminals ... at the Court in Sydney' [County] in 1815.[45] The 1811 murder trial of Alexander McIntosh at Pictou is instructive in this regard. When McIntosh was first arraigned, in the May circuit term 1811, 'neither the Attorney General nor Solicitor General being present, [the Court] requested Messrs [S.B.] Robie and [S.G.W.] Archibald to undertake the charge of the prosecution.' McIntosh was able to get an adjournment and was eventually tried in August on a special commission. By then Uniacke was available, and he conducted the prosecution.[46]

By the late 1820s the increase in prosecutions caused by expanded settlement was such that the Supreme Court judges on circuit were empowered to appoint prosecuting counsel and to order them paid; significantly, this was to be done to fill the gap 'in the absence of His Majesty's Attorney-General and Solicitor-General.'[47] The only regularly established exception to prosecution by the law officers where possible occurred in the Sessions Court of Shelburne District/County, where from the mid-1780s local lawyer Richard Combauld prosecuted most cases.[48]

'Public prosecution' requires qualification. This was not a system in which cases were routinely submitted to a 'prosecutor's office' well before trial and the evidence digested, witnesses organized, etc. by a state agency. Prosecution before trial – apprehension of suspects, gathering of evidence, arranging for witnesses – remained a process heavily dependent on private initiative. Those who felt themselves wronged could call on the assistance of constables, and it was the job of JPs to take depositions, question witnesses, commit those accused to jail to await trial, and issue recognizances to ensure that prosecution witnesses turned up to testify.[49] All of this, of course, meant that there was a substantial public role in the pretrial prosecution process, but it was not a system run by the attorney general. What the attorney general did was to work with the clerk of the court to draw up indictments just before the court term began[50] and then appear at the trials and present the evidence. He may also have occasionally attended at the pretrial examinations of some accuseds and have

interviewed Crown witnesses; there is some slight evidence of these practices, dating from the end of the century.[51] Thus the attorney general was
largely a prosecutor only before the grand jury and at trial; the victim/
prosecutor remained a vital player, and if he or she did not appear in court
as well, the case was dropped or adjourned.[52]

The authorities relied so heavily on public prosecution because they
believed, particularly in the early years, that the effective prosecution of
crime was vital to social and political stability. 'The office of an attorney-
general is of the highest importance to the court,' wrote Belcher in 1755,
and two years later he repeated his conviction that an active attorney
general was very much 'for the interest of this colony.' Indeed, such an
officer was of a 'use and importance ... beyond the rest of the colonies in
America.'[53] The reference to other colonies is instructive, for most of the
jurisdictions to the south also made more extensive use of public prosecutors than was the case in England.[54]

There is little direct evidence of similar sentiments after the first decade
of the colony's existence, although the practice of extensive public prosecution was introduced into other late British North American colonies –
Prince Edward Island, New Brunswick, and Upper Canada.[55] What evidence there is comes from nearer to the end of our period. It was still the
case by 1799 that some prosecutions were being carried on 'at the particular desire' of government,[56] demonstrating a continued interest in this
particular exercise of authority. In 1812 and again in 1813 Lieutenant-
Governor Sherbrooke made special mention of the need to fund criminal
prosecutions in his addresses to the Assembly, and many appropriation
statutes from the early nineteenth century contain line items for criminal
prosecutions.[57] The cause of this interest in prosecution was obviously no
longer a concern about stability in an infant colony, but it may have
reflected continuing worries about order in a naval and garrison town.

While government lawyers played a large role in criminal trials, defence
lawyers were much less prevalent. English law in the mid-eighteenth
century gave no general right to a person accused of felony to be represented by counsel, although such a right existed if the charge was a
misdemeanour or treason.[58] The right to be represented by counsel did not
become part of English law until 1836 and in Nova Scotia it was not
granted until 1840.[59] Defence counsel were, however, permitted to take
part in the trial with the consent of the court. This practice began in
England in the 1730s, likely as a result of the increased use of prosecuting
counsel from c. 1715, and by mid-century judges routinely granted requests for counsel. The increased use of defence counsel was probably the

most important development in English trial practice during the second half of the eighteenth century, with between a third and a quarter of all Old Bailey defendants represented by 1800.

As is evident from the account of the Cartcel trial, Nova Scotia courts operated in all kinds of cases, capital and otherwise, without defence counsel. Yet shortly after the Cartcel trial the council enacted rules of court, including the stipulation that 'every Person be allowed to speak for himself in his own Cause, or produce one to speak for him, or desire the Court to name one.'[60] This rule, probably borrowed from Virginia,[61] made no particular reference to defence lawyers in criminal cases but presumably included them. When the Supreme Court was established in 1754 the right to counsel was taken away and their use was made discretionary as it was in England. For Belcher, presiding in the first term of the Supreme Court, allowing counsel was an 'indulgence,' one that he claimed to regret when three represented defendants were convicted of manslaughter rather than murder.[62] The use of defence counsel remained formally at the discretion of the judge,[63] although they were always allowed to take part.

I do not know precisely how often defendants had counsel. The proceedings books record sixty-seven defendants in Halifax as represented between 1749 and 1803. This figure, however, somewhat underrepresents the presence of defence counsel, as other evidence reveals that they were present at the Halifax Supreme Court trials of a further eleven defendants during this period. It is possible to make some estimate of the frequency with which defendants had counsel from the fact that their presence was frequently referred to in the period between 1778 and 1790, but rarely before and only once thereafter. As other evidence shows that they did appear before and after these years, it seems reasonable to conclude that for this thirteen-year period only the clerks diligently recorded the presence of defence lawyers. Thus a reasonably accurate assessment of their prevalence can be obtained for this period – at least 51 of the 209 people arraigned had counsel. At 24 per cent, this is roughly the same proportion as in late-eighteenth-century London and, indeed, Maryland.[64] It is a little lower than for both comparative jurisdictions, which may be a product of inaccurate record keeping: alternatively, it may reflect the lack of lawyers in Halifax, a point discussed below.

It was probably somewhat more common for those accused of capital offences to be represented than those facing other felony charges. Thirty-seven, or 44 per cent, of the eighty-four individuals tried in Halifax between 1749 and 1815 who we know had counsel faced capital charges, while only about a third of all charges were for capital offences. Although at some point in the nineteenth century it became the practice for the court to assign counsel when a defendant was arraigned on a capital charge,[65] many men and women accused of capital offences faced their trial alone in the eighteenth and early nineteenth centuries. Murder defendants included William Reach in 1761, who only requested counsel after conviction in an attempt to impugn the trial procedure.[66] John McGragh successfully defended himself on a murder charge in 1788,[67] and of three people accused of the murder of Maria Ball in 1791 who were unrepresented, one (Margaret Murphy) was convicted while the other two were acquitted.[68] Others accused of capital offences, other than murder, also defended themselves, sometimes successfully, sometimes not.[69]

Three factors probably operated to limit the use of defence counsel. One was that, as discussed in more detail in the following section, defence lawyers' roles were circumscribed, and much of the responsibility for the presentation of an effective defence was left to the defendant. Defence counsel might not therefore have seemed that necessary. A second factor was that there were few lawyers available at any point during this period.[70] Probably only two lawyers, Daniel Wood Senior and George Suckling, were among those who initially established the town of Halifax, and by the early 1750s only nine men had been called to the Nova Scotia bar, including the attorney general and those who worked as court clerks. A few more joined in the 1760s, but for most of the time prior to the Loyalist influx of the early 1780s no more than half a dozen attorneys were actively practising in the city, for a number of those qualified worked as court clerks. The Loyalist immigration of the 1780s brought into the colony a more substantial legal community, mostly lawyers from Massachusetts, New Jersey, and New York, but not all of the Loyalist refugees were called to the bar in their new home and others who were chose not to stay in Halifax. Only eleven lawyers' names are recorded as practising in the Supreme Court on the civil side between 1786 and 1790, and only twelve during the 1790s. A few others joined in the first two decades of the new century, but the active bar at the end of our period was still very small. Outside Halifax the situation was worse. Prior to the American Revolution there were no lawyers at all practising outside the capital, and while some communities were subsequently well served,[71] most were not, for in the early nineteenth century there were still probably fewer than a dozen lawyers in the out-settlements. Many defendants outside the capital therefore could not rely on having a local lawyer, and employed instead a

Halifax-based attorney travelling with the court or, like Walter Lee, some-one from another settlement.[72]

Finally, cost would have been a substantial problem for most of the defendants – private soldiers and sailors, artisans, labourers, domestic servants, prostitutes – tried for felony. There was no general provision for public payment of defence counsel fees, and I have found no evidence of government paying for defence counsel or of pro bono representation by the bar in particular cases. At various times, and particularly after the arrival of the Loyalist lawyers, there was keen competition for legal work; demand is unlikely therefore to have exceeded supply.[73] Indeed, even the men whose names appear most frequently among those who defended – David Lloyd in the 1750s, Daniel Wood Senior in the late 1760s and early 1770s, Gerald Fitzgerald and George Thompson in the 1770s and 1780s – had extensive civil practices also.[74]

TRIAL PROCEDURE: THE CASE FOR THE PROSECUTION

When I turn to discuss procedure during the trial itself the limitations of my sources become more of a problem than hitherto. The proceedings books say practically nothing about the cut and thrust of the trial. The trial reports are useful for some aspects of trial process – how evidence was given, what defence counsel tried to do – but they are not representative, for the majority report trials in which the accused was found guilty. More than that, most are about defendants such as Cartcel and Lee, who were clearly guilty and went to court facing a conclusive case against them. If one relied on the trial reports for an analysis of evidence and defences one would invariably conclude that only the guilty, indeed the obviously guilty, ever got as far as the courtroom. As a result, here and in the following section on defences I rely heavily on the Deschamps benchbook, in which the cases do not suffer this sort of selection bias.

Despite this caveat, it is possible to reconstruct much of what happened in the hour or two that it took to get through a typical criminal trial. Following the arraignment of the accused, his or her plea (almost always a not guilty plea), and occasionally a challenge of some jurors, the prosecu-tion case came on. Three features of that case are notable. First, it was usually a relatively short one, presented through the testimony of rarely more than three or four witnesses. This was the number that typically gave evidence before the grand jury,[75] and the run-of-the-mill cases recorded by Deschamps show an average of just three prosecution witnesses per case for fifteen cases. The trial reports average about five prosecution witnesses per case – although there was a substantial range, between the one witness at the 1801 trial of Gad Sanders and the twelve produced by the prosecution to make out its circumstantial case in 1791 against the Boutelier brothers.[76] However, many of the trials for which we have reports were unusual and high-profile cases. The figure of three to four witnesses is probably more accurate. The fact that trials were so short also argues for a paucity of witnesses.

The second feature of the prosecution case that requires notice is that these witnesses seem simply to have told their stories in narrative form rather than being led through their evidence by questions from counsel. Neither the Deschamps benchbook nor the trial reports indicate much in the way of questions from prosecution counsel; what questions were asked were supplementary, following the giving of the bulk of the witness's evidence. Although other questions may have been omitted to keep the account brief, it seems strange that the judge would do that if such questions were an integral part of the process. This quicker mode of proceeding matches both the time trials took and the fact that the prosecution case was conducted by the attorney general without much in the way of preparation. That is, neither the attorney general nor anybody else interviewed and prepared witnesses before the trial. The attorney general would have reviewed the depositions given before the justice of the peace and would generally have attended the grand jury when it considered an indictment. As a result he would have known the case he was to present, but perhaps not in sufficient detail to lead the witnesses by minute questioning.

Deschamps' account of the evidence of the chief prosecution witness, John Taylor, at the 1776 trial for murder of George Thompson, illustrates this point:

John Taylor. 16 Septr. Prisoner came to dep-t's. [Taylor's] house with another, it was between 11 & 12, that on some conversation relating to the house of one Scot, dept. told prisoner that he had no good name for going to the house & that he had been great with women there, that prisoner asked who told him so. Dept. told him that he was told so by the Decd., the prisoner then went out in a great passion to the Decd. who was sitting opposite to dept's. house, they had words and Spoke together near 5 minutes. Dept's. wife call'd to him & told him she believed poor [Sutherland] was kill'd. Dept. went out & saw prisoner standing by the Decd. with a Rattan in his hand & Strike decd. several times on the breech, prisoner's wife call'd to him not to beat decd. any more, he holding up the Stick said if I was near you I would serve you the same way. Dept. took up Decd. & found the right side of his head much fractured, that he called to Mr. Carroll, constable to take prisoner on charges of murdering decd., who was then as he supposed dead. Dept. took decd. into the house – blood run out of his ear.[77]

The above appears as a continuous narrative in the benchbook. It is followed by two further notes, both I would suggest answers to supplementary questions by prosecuting counsel:[78] 'was afraid prisoner wd. Strike him & took Rattan from him,' and 'Scot advised prisoner to run away.' Thus we have evidence given substantially as a narrative, perhaps in answer to the simple question 'tell the court what happened,' with a couple of additional questions to supplement that narrative. The evidence of the other prosecution witnesses – John Taylor's wife, two men who had witnessed the same events as Taylor, and the doctor called to the scene – was a little less in the form of a narrative and contained more answers to questions. By then the prosecutor probably believed that he had established the main facts and was looking to fill out aspects of the story. The questions asked concerned exactly where the deceased was struck, how long he had lived following the assault, whether he ever got up again, and whether he spoke.

Other cases from the Deschamps benchbook reveal essentially the same procedure. For example, on 17 October 1777, James Hill and John Thorne were tried for 'stealing from William Allen two boxes of soap and six calf skins' and Henry and Mary Elsworthy were tried for receiving those goods from them. Hill was tried first; immediately after his arraignment and plea Allan came forward and told the court about the theft. John Connor, a marine, followed with a very damaging story: 'beginning of August Hill came to his tent with Miller & brought 2 skins & bargained about [them] ... Then shewed them more skins in a Chest. That Hill & Miller went into Mr. Allan's cellar & bring out 6 Skins. That he & Thorn were set to watch. That he carried the skins to Elsworthy's house, then returning to look after Hill & the others he saw Hill & Thorn with each a box of soap which they left also at Elsworthy's.' As in the Thompson case, there follows what appears to be notes of answers to supplementary questions: 'they [Hill and Thorne] told Ev[idence – Connor] they bro-t. the boxes from Mr Allan's,' and 'the boxes were laid in their bed chamber – & were next day buried in the garden – Mrs Elsworthy was present & kept watch.'[79]

One consequence of the way the prosecution case was presented in Nova Scotia, with the attorney general rather than the victim/prosecutor taking the lead, was that judges seem to have assumed a less active role in marshalling the case than they did in England. While Chief Justice Belcher intervened with questions for the witnesses in one of the trial reports we have for him,[80] Deschamps seems to have done so very infrequently, and the reports from later in the century suggest only a limited role for the judges. Since it was judges who wrote the reports they may, of course, have chosen to omit what they did, but there seems no reason for them to have done so. They were certainly not shy either about having opinions or expressing them to the jury – witness Monk's stressing of the way he charged the jury in the Lee case. The attorney general, therefore, likely substituted for the judge as well as for victims.

My third subject here is the substance of the prosecution case. A good number of prosecutions featured accomplice evidence or confessions. With very limited investigative resources at its disposal, the eighteenth-century state relied a good deal on incentives, such as rewards, and on offers of freedom from prosecution and/or pardons to accomplices.[81] John Young was convicted of treason in 1754 largely on the evidence of accomplice Joshua Frost.[82] When three soldiers were apprehended for street robbery in 1770, one of them, Michael Duffey, was found guilty on an accomplice's evidence, although a co-accused, Francis Hynson, was acquitted, presumably on the same evidence.[83] In the Hill et al case discussed above the central role was played by an accomplice to those charged – marine John Connor. He had taken part in the theft with which two others were charged and had assisted the receivers, who were also on trial. Connor then was able to bargain for immunity in return for giving evidence against the four people tried.[84] Numerous other cases could be cited, and although the evidence of accomplices was often very important it did not always secure a conviction.[85]

The best possible prosecution evidence was, of course, a confession. Confessions usually came in the form of the deposition taken by a JP on apprehension of a suspect. Following English practice such depositions were admissible at the trial and were presented to the court by the clerk reading them out.[86] Any inconsistencies between defendants' depositions and their *viva voce* evidence at trial could cause serious problems. But worse than an inconsistency was a confession made before the JP and written down. The ranks of those who went to court to find such confessions confronting them included Felix Cannew, convicted of grand larceny in 1761,[87] and Cornelius Driscoll, who pleaded guilty on two charges of murder in 1765 perhaps because he had confessed the crimes to the examining JP.[88] The jury did not need to retire to convict Ebenezer Wright, a black man, of petit larceny in 1789; he had confessed to JP James Gautier a few weeks previously.[89] Sarah Wilson's confession was easily enough to convict her of burglary in 1810, when the only other evidence against her was the victim, John Murphy, who testified to waking up in the night and finding a back window forced. Some clothes that his wife had taken in for washing were gone, and he suspected Wilson, who worked for his wife. He had her apprehended and took her to the JP for an examination. All this he told the court, and no more, but it did not matter, for the prosecution had Wilson's confession, and she was convicted.[90] Again, many similar cases could be cited, and there were also instances of confessions made to other people.[91]

If the prosecution had neither an accomplice nor a confession to aid it, the trial reports would suggest that its case consisted invariably of eyewitness testimony from people who had witnessed the events, as it was in both the Cartcel and Lee trials. I suspect that a good many cases were conducted on this basis, in part because the state had few mechanisms to help individuals to collect circumstantial evidence, in part because trials were short and involved few prosecution witnesses, and in part because the Deschamps benchbook contains a substantial number of cases based on this kind of prosecution evidence. In the most unusual of them a black man named simply 'Prince' and marine John Smith were tried for sodomy in July 1777.[92] The former was tried first and two men gave damning evidence against him. John Toe testified that 'the negro's yard was as he believes in John Smith's body' and that 'the negro's breeches were down and so were Smith's.' James Ramsey said that it appeared to him that the two men 'were in the act of copulation.'

It would, however, be wrong to conclude either that all prosecutions were conducted or this kind of evidentiary basis, or that those that were always involved overwhelming and conclusive evidence against the accused, as it was in the Cartcel and Lee trials. To take the second point first, the conviction rate, discussed below, would have been much higher if all cases were like this. And from other evidence it is clear that many cases came down to one person's assertions measured against another's. When John Wattington was tried in October 1777 for stealing some £60 worth of goods, mostly silk, from the shop of one John Barnard Johnson it was the victim who gave the crucial evidence, evidence that revealed that he had publicized the theft through the town crier and in the newspapers; pursued Wattington when his efforts brought information; taken from him some of the stolen silk, which he produced in court and identified as his own; and apparently extracted an admission from him. In this case the only other evidence for the prosecution was that of a constable, who merely recounted that 'Johnson called on him to assist to take the prisoner and the silks which are those produced.' Wattington's defence was not to deny that he had the silks, but to claim that he found them 'near one of the wharves.' He was convicted entirely on Johnson's evidence, which prevailed over his denials.[93]

Many cases built solely on circumstantial evidence must also have found their way to court, although in only two of the available trial reports was the case against the defendant circumstantial. Nobody saw John and George Boutelier kill Frederick Eminaud and his family near Lunenburg in 1791, but a parade of prosecution witnesses established that they had stayed at Eminaud's house before the murders took place on their way to visit their mother; that there was time unaccounted for on their return journey, time the prosecution said was spent murdering Eminaud and burning his house; that tracks led from Eminaud's house to where the Bouteliers had moored their boat, and those tracks were made by moccasins, rarely worn in Lunenburg County but preferred by the Bouteliers; that they had carried a tomahawk, and a tomahawk found in the ruins of Eminaud's burned-down house was the likely murder weapon; that Eminaud had probably recently received £50 but that the money was nowhere to be found; and that in their depositions they had lied about where they had been at certain times. Collectively this evidence damned the accuseds, who later confessed their crime on the gallows.[94]

In the other circumstantial case from the trial reports the evidence was much less clear. In 1813 two blacks, John and Amy Pomp, were tried at Annapolis for the murder of their fifteen-month-old son, Emerson.[95] Although six witnesses appeared for the prosecution, three of them testified only to the discovery of the body on a beach and to its condition. Elizabeth Wright, a twelve-year-old girl, and Tobias Vroom gave evidence about a dispute between the Pomps over who should take care of their son (they did not live together) but said little else that implicated either defendant. It all added up to the weakest of circumstantial evidence. Presiding judge Brenton Halliburton told the jury that they must acquit John Pomp because there was no evidence against him, and went almost as far with Amy Pomp. The latter was convicted nonetheless, a fact that Halliburton attributed to the jury's racial prejudice.

Prosecution cases based on circumstantial evidence were probably well represented among those trials in which the accused was acquitted because, in a typical phrase from the proceedings books, the evidence was in 'no way Sufficient to convict the prisoner.'[96] Perhaps circumstantial cases were also well represented among cases in which the jury did not need to retire before acquitting an accused.

TRIAL PROCEDURE: THE CASE FOR THE DEFENCE

Before we look at defences in detail, it is necessary to discuss four factors that shaped both the way in which they were conducted and their content. First, as already discussed, the majority of defendants were unrepresented. Unused to the forum and not well-educated, defending themselves was a task that few probably performed well. Prisoners like Peter Cartcel who did not speak English endured a procedure entirely foreign to them and were at a great disadvantage, although interpreters were used on more than one occasion – indeed as of 1761 an official interpreter was appointed for French and German.[97] But English-speaking defendants were often not much better off. There were probably many like Samuel Ives, a soldier, who expressed a fear of being at a 'great Disadvantage on Tryall'; this was partly because he 'unfortunately has a great Impediment in utterance,' but he also noted that he had never been in such a situation before.[98] In some cases pretrial confinement likely rendered defendants physically and morally debilitated. Prisoners were rarely detained for more than two to three months in Halifax jail, although even that could be a dreadful experience,[99] but in the out-settlements, which, even if they were on the circuit, were visited just once or twice a year,[100] they might be confined for the best part of a year. Walter Lee's long pretrial confinement perhaps caused the physical distress he was obviously in as he made his speech to the jury.[101]

Second, even when an accused had the assistance of a lawyer, there were significant limits on what counsel were permitted to do. English procedure left it to the judge to decide the lawyer's role.[102] He could always argue points of law; beyond this most judges allowed the cross-examination of prosecution witnesses and the questioning of those for the defence, although some only let lawyers suggest questions which the judge or the defendant might put. Lawyers were not permitted to make speeches to the jury, although this prohibition was sometimes ignored in practice. The same rules formally applied in Nova Scotia; thus John Young's 1756 request for counsel was granted only 'in matters of Law.'[103] This was the only occasion, however, that I have found on which this restriction was enforced; defence counsel were not generally restricted to arguments about law (although they did engage in them), but could perform the other forensic tasks often allowed by English judges. They did so in every case for which we have such information – although there are not many of them – and it seems that over time this came to be seen as more or less a right.[104] But in all the cases where we know who spoke to the jury, it was, as in Lee's case, the accused who did so. Not until 1840 was the restriction on lawyers' roles lifted for Nova Scotia, in the same legislation that gave felony defendants counsel as of right.[105]

Third, defendants faced significant obstacles in preparing for trial. They rarely knew much, if anything, about the precise nature of the evidence against them until they were in court that day, for not only had they been in jail since apprehension, they were not permitted to see documents such as their examinations before the JP or any evidence to be used by the prosecution before they got to court.[106] Represented defendants often fared little better, for counsel had no greater rights to see the prosecution's case. In addition, counsel were generally engaged immediately before the trial or even once it had started. This was always the case for those tried on circuit and represented by one of the Halifax-based lawyers travelling with the court; we saw that even if Walter Lee had obtained Marshall's help it would have been a last minute engagement. This frequently happened in Halifax also, so that defence counsel often went to court quite ignorant of the charges against their client.[107] Occasionally a day or two's delay might be granted for preparation, but rarely any more than that.

My fourth point also applies both to those with and those without counsel. For most of this period trial procedure required that the defendant actually put forward a defence. That is, he or she was not able to rely on legal rules that imposed a special burden of proof on the prosecution or which allowed the accused to effectively remain silent and simply argue that the Crown had not discharged its burden of proof. I am not suggesting that legal rules were never at play, for on occasion they were.[108] Nor am I suggesting that English criminal procedure's concern with the technicalities of indictment wording was not imported to the colony, for it was.[109] But in neither the English trial procedure of the eighteenth century inherited by Nova Scotia, nor in the procedural rules developed in the American colonies to the south[110] was there either a presumption of innocence in the modern sense or a notion that the accused had a right to remain silent. He or she could do so, of course, but that would suggest guilt, would show that the accused had no answer to the charge.

Thus the accused was effectively obliged to offer a defence, even though he or she could not give sworn testimony.[111] The best defence was simply 'the prisoner's ... own natural and unprepared response to the charges as they were asserted by the prosecution in court.' The prosecution, of course, had always to provide evidence of guilt, but 'if any assumption was made in court about the prisoner himself, it was not that he was innocent until the case against him was proved beyond a reasonable doubt, but that if he *were* innocent he ought to be able to demonstrate it for the jury by the quality and character of his reply to the prosecutor's evidence.'[112] By the later eighteenth century these assumptions were changing in England, but the notion that an accused was innocent until proven guilty was not established until well into the next century.[113]

There is no reason to think that in Nova Scotia the law was any different, and some, admittedly slight, indications that it was the same as in England. The prosecution had to produce a case to answer, and in a capital case in particular it needed to bring what Judge James Brenton called 'full and sufficient Evidence.'[114] But once the prosecution had presented a case the defendant was expected to answer, and to do so in a straightforward and unvarnished way. When the lawyer for Timothy Keith, arraigned in May 1765 for assault with intent to commit a rape, asked to see the examination taken by the JP and a copy of the indictment, the court refused both requests. All that was needed was that the indictment 'be distinctly read to the Attorney that he might observe the contents thereof,' and to accede to the request would be 'opening a path to the delay of Justice.'[115] The court did not want to hear anything other than Keith's response to the charges in a courtroom confrontation with his accuser.

Beyond such slight indications there is no evidence about the legal rules and presumptions that operated, except for one 1791 case, and that case deserves detailed consideration, for it suggests not only that the presumption of innocence and the reasonable doubt standard were not well-established features of criminal procedure, but also that, as in late-eighteenth-century England, such principles were at least beginning to be framed in a recognisably 'modern' way. The 1791 trials of brothers John and George Boutelier began with an opening speech by Crown counsel, James Stewart, which extensively laid out the Crown's theory linking the brothers to the murder, discussed the nature of different kinds of evidence, and made some reference to what he was required to prove.[116] The jury should convict, he said, only if they agreed with him that the evidence was strongly against the accused. But if they did not agree, 'they were equally bound to acquit.' While he went on to say that 'though counsel for the prosecution, he would be happy to remind them of an ancient maxim, well known to the humanity of the English law, that "it is better that ninety-nine guilty men should escape than one innocent man suffer",' the fact remains that all he talked about by way of the burden of proof was the notion that it was necessary for the evidence to be 'strongly' against the accused.

As importantly, the defendants had to take some responsibility for whether that evidence met the standard. According to Stewart the Bouteliers 'were ... left to shake off that heavy burden of suspicion' that the evidence would create; once the evidence was in 'the burden of presumption' would 'lay heavy' upon them. The impression of guilt in the minds of the jury would need to be 'effaced by testimony in support of their defence.' He also asserted that their conduct left 'something to be accounted for, something inconsistent with the plain path of truth and innocence.' In short, once the Crown's case was put defendants were obliged to establish their innocence, and if they failed in this endeavour the case for the prosecution was greatly strengthened.

The presiding judge, Chief Justice Thomas Strange, offered no correction to Stewart, so we must assume he approved of these sentiments. Strange also had something of his own to say on these issues when he addressed the jury, although the precise meaning of his remarks is difficult to discern. He warned the jury against convicting if they had only 'a mild presumption of guilt'; by implication, something more than a 'mild presumption' was required, but that something could fall a good deal short of certainty. Elsewhere in his speech he said that if the jury had 'the smallest doubt' about guilt the Bouteliers were entitled to be acquitted; this sounds closer to the notion of proof 'beyond a reasonable doubt.' But Strange's remarks must also be considered against his comments on the evidence. In his summary he was quick to point out that aspects of the Bouteliers' conduct – decamping rapidly from the area, lying in depositions before JPs – was 'not the course of innocence,' for innocence 'commonly trusts to itself.' That is, the defendants had not satisfied their burden of discharging the suspicion that lay upon them.

Strange's failure to either correct Stewart or offer a clear statement of the presumption of innocence and the beyond a reasonable doubt standard demonstrates that these ideas were not firmly implanted in the law. Yet his speech also indicates some awareness of special rules governing the jury's verdict, and it is surely significant that such comments were made by a chief justice recently arrived from England,[117] for it was at this time that the presumption of innocence was being formulated there. Thus we see here understandings in transition. Prior to the late eighteenth century no particular rules about burdens and presumptions existed to assist the accused. By c. 1790 in Nova Scotia some such idea was being expressed, but it was not yet solidified.

We witness what may have been a greater concern with the burden of proof and the presumption of innocence right at the end of our period, in the trials of John and Amy Pomp, discussed above.[118] Amy Pomp had given evidence that she had received the child from his father on the night he died, but '[h]ere she stopped and gave no further account of the child, though the court waited some time in expectation that she would proceed.' In his summation to the jury Brenton Halliburton stated that there was some circumstantial evidence against her, but it was not strong. Although he adverted to the fact that 'her conduct,' meaning her conduct in the witness box, 'could not but excite strong suspicions against her,' he nonetheless urged the jury to disregard it and to acquit her:

if the case were considered solely upon the evidence adduced by the prosecution, it did not bring home the fact against her, in that clear and satisfactory manner which is necessary in capital cases ... [I]t was always desirable that the testimony on the part of the crown should be sufficient to support the charge, when it was of so serious a nature – without resorting to the case, as it might appear, on the part of the prisoners. The jury [was] recommended to consider the case against the prisoner Amy upon the proof produced in support of it, without adverting to her conduct when put on her defence, which might have proceeded from agitation of mind.

In Halliburton's comments we again see a mix of 'old' and 'new' approaches to the presumption of innocence and the burden of proof. Halliburton urged the jurymen to be sure of themselves if they wanted to convict and came close to telling them that the prosecution had not proved its case. He did tell them that they should disregard what was effectively her silence. Yet we see the continued hold of an older understanding, for he did not employ terms familiar to us – 'beyond a reasonable doubt' and 'innocent until proven guilty' – in doing so. Moreover the jury was only 'recommended' not to draw an adverse inference from Amy's not giving her own story about the events of the evening in question, and the references to the prosecution's proof are always qualified by the fact that this was a capital case – suggesting perhaps that less strong proof was required in a noncapital trial. Ideas about onus and burden were still evolving in this period; they were not yet firmly established.

Often unprepared, invariably inexperienced, always needing to do something to refute the prosecution case – how did defendants go about their task? One tactic was to cross-examine prosecution witnesses after they had given their evidence in chief in an attempt to lessen its efficacy. We saw earlier Peter Cartcel's very limited intervention, when he asked a witness whether his victim might have run onto his knife rather than being stabbed by it. Unrepresented defendants like Cartcel tended to be unskilled in questioning and did not make a very good job of it; certainly the trial reports reveal no examples of an unrepresented defendant successfully undermining the case for the prosecution.

One would expect lawyers to do better here.[119] Counsel for George Thompson, for example, the man accused of murder at Windsor in 1776, asked two questions of the principal witness, John Taylor. Taylor had testified to seeing Thompson repeatedly hit his victim, Alexander Sutherland, with a cane in the head. Counsel asked Taylor how long he had known Thompson, and whether he knew of any enmity between Thompson and Sutherland. The answer to the first question was two months, to the second, no. Given that Taylor had just recounted in detail seeing Thompson beat Sutherland heavily with a stick, we must assume that the lawyer knew that he was unlikely to be able to shake that part of the prosecution case that established that Thompson had indeed attacked the dead man. But he did want to remove any impression that this was a planned attack and/or that it was carried out with an intent to kill Sutherland. When we see the lawyer asking another prosecution witness whether Sutherland had been drunk, it becomes clear that he wanted to establish that this was a spur-of-the-moment encounter, driven by sudden passion. Such evidence, I assume, was meant to negate any intention to kill and achieve the manslaughter verdict that resulted.[120]

Perhaps the best example of the lawyers' ability to test and diminish the persuasiveness of prosecution evidence was that put forward by James Buchanan, counsel for Nancy O'Neal when she stood trial in 1814 for the murder of her newborn child. Buchanan was able to get the prosecution's principal witness, her employer James Barss, to admit that he did not know that O'Neal was pregnant, did not know what night it was that he heard her groaning, and could not say that the blood he had found on the privy was not menstrual blood – indeed, 'he thought at the time it might be.' Barss was also drawn into agreeing that O'Neal 'was well enough the next morning to get the breakfast for the family, and he thinks the dinner too.' Buchanan enjoyed similar success in his cross-examination of other prosecution witnesses.[121] Unfortunately there is too little evidence of the use of such tactics to know how effective they were, largely because the trial reports are principally from cases that produced a guilty verdict.

Another tactic for the defence, whether conducted by counsel or offered by the defendants themselves, was to seek to put forward affirmative evidence refuting that of the prosecution. The proceedings books occasionally mention that defendants produced their own witnesses. In addition, there are frequent references to the fact that the prisoner 'put on his defence,' although it is difficult to know exactly what that means.[122] It must in some instances have involved defence witnesses. Henry Jebb used them to very good effect in his highway robbery trial in 1815. The principal evidence against him was that the stolen property had been found in his possession and he was able to rely on a defence of finding the stolen goods because he had apparently told people about the find at the time and in court 'produced witnesses who swore to that effect.'[123]

It is difficult to say how often affirmative defences were employed. Since trials were short there would not have been much time for the appearance of many defence witnesses in addition to the prosecution witnesses whom we know were present. The trial reports suggest that defendants made very little use of material witnesses, but, again, biased in favour of cases in which the prosecution evidence was strong and defences correspondingly weak, they are a poor source for this type of information. Probably the best evidence we have is the Deschamps benchbook; in only two of his cases in the mid-1770s did a defendant call witnesses other than character witnesses. One of those was Prince, the black man whose sodomy trial has already been discussed. His principal line of defence was 'that he was drunk [and] does not know what he did.' Two witnesses appeared to support the claim that he was very drunk on the night in question.[124] Thus it seems likely that, as in New York at mid-century, most defences did not involve witnesses.[125]

Questioning prosecution witnesses and offering evidence of their own took defendants only so far. At the end of the day the defendant was expected to tell his or her own story and then appeal to the jury. The trial reports, of course, suggest consistently pathetic defences,[126] but the Deschamps benchbook indicates that for many more run-of-the-mill cases they were little better. It is striking, for example, how little was said by the defendants in the Hill et al. case discussed above. Mary Elsworthy was the only one of the four who said anything, and her remarks were limited to a statement that 'of her own accord she went and kept watch while Connor and Elsworthy dug the hole to put the soap in.' John Wattington's defence, it will be remembered, was that he had found the stolen property discovered on him. Peter Shore, a black servant, said nothing himself but had apparently offered one prosecution witness an explanation of how a stolen watch had come into his possession: 'he found watch in his pocket, could not tell how he came by it, believed a soldier had put it into his pocket.'[127] It would have been surprising had such explanations carried much weight.

One type of defence consistently introduced into court was character evidence, something that in England was 'immensely important' because it 'encouraged the judge and jury to believe in ... [the defendant's] trust-worthiness.'[128] Halifax was a small community throughout this period, the out-settlements even less populous, and many of the combatants in court were known, personally or by reputation, to the jurors. Character evidence went to two issues in the minds of the jurors. First, in cases where the evidence was not conclusive or in which it was one person's word against the other's, it helped the jury to decide credibility. Second, and in many ways more importantly, character evidence could be used to decide whether, even if the defendant had committed the crime, he or she ought to be convicted and, in many cases, to hang. That is, juries exercised a broad discretion, going well beyond simple factual decision making. They were prepared to acquit or convict only for a less serious offence if they did not wish to see a defendant suffer capital punishment.

Character evidence, we have seen, was adduced by both Walter Lee and George Thompson in their murder trials, and may well have helped the latter to a verdict of manslaughter only. Character witnesses were employed by William Callahan and Samuel Neale, soldiers tried for grand larceny in 1778, whose lawyer does not seem to have done any more in their defence than have two sergeants give them 'a good character,' which turned out to be a successful defence.[129] Alexander McIntosh, tried for murder at Pictou in 1811, had the *custos rotulorum* for the district, the commanding colonel of the Pictou militia, and the local collector of customs testify to his 'fair character,' 'good conduct,' and 'peaceable quiet demeanour,' although he was convicted nonetheless.[130] A defence witness for John Pomp said nothing of consequence beyond the fact that Pomp was 'an industrious man' who took 'good care of his children.'[131] Lack of character, or more precisely lack of character witnesses, was a problem for William McLean, who was convicted of street robbery in 1782. According to presiding judge Brenton, MacLean was 'called upon to produce evidence to his Character' but 'he could not produce any.'[132]

The final act of the defence was the address to the jury. Walter Lee's address, though unsuccessful, is the best we have of those recorded – elaborate and well-reasoned, if not necessarily articulate. Others from the trial reports were much shorter,[133] and there is plenty of evidence that some defendants simply had nothing to say, a particularly damaging fact given the prevailing belief that the defendant should refute the prosecution case. Thomas Stevens said nothing in his defence in April 1777, as did four other defendants in the cases tried before Deschamps.[134] John Anderson, charged with grand larceny in 1786, 'had nothing to say in his defence' and was convicted.[135] Perhaps it was such reticence by the accused that enabled the jury to convict without retiring in a number of cases and to consistently render verdicts very quickly in others.[136]

THE RESULTS OF TRIALS

While space constraints prevent an examination of all aspects of the trial process (most notably I do not deal here with juries), and while the limitations of my sources preclude any discussion of such matters as the rules of evidence, the physical organization of the courtroom, and, to a large extent, the cut and thrust of the trial drama,[137] there is sufficient evidence to provide a sense of what the trial was generally like. The foregoing account has shown that throughout the second half of the eighteenth century it was a relatively rapid and simple proceeding. In no more than a couple of hours the state marshalled its case and the accused, usually unprepared and alone, did his or her best to refute it. Such a refutation was as likely to rely on asserting good character as on denying facts.

Rather than review in more detail the principal points already made, I think it more useful to conclude by asking how the trial process affected the aggregate results of trials. Between 1749 and 1803 65 per cent of defendants tried in Halifax were convicted, 51 per cent of them as charged and 14 per cent for a lesser offence than the one charged. Between 1811 and 1815, for which period we also have systematic results of trials, 56 per cent of defendants were convicted. Putting both periods together gives a conviction rate of 64 per cent. Thus about a third of defendants escaped conviction. This conviction rate was relatively high compared to other contemporary jurisdictions, and it is surely not unreasonable to suggest that public prosecution was, at least in part, responsible for driving up the conviction rates.[138]

Yet these figures also show that defendants could, despite all the obstacles they faced, mount effective defences. There is no evidence that defence counsel consistently made a difference in the results,[139] and while fear of capital punishment did influence juries it was not a significant factor in keeping the overall conviction rate down.[140] Thus we are forced to conclude that a significant minority of those charged were able to overcome the apparent high odds against them, to either directly refute the factual basis of the prosecution case or to convince the jury, through evidence or knowledge of character, that the defendant should be acquitted. In appropriate circumstances, and despite the imposing presence of the attorney general, the jury could measure the quality of the prosecution evidence against the defendant's demeanour and candour and find the former wanting.

NOTES

Financial support for the research for this paper was provided by the SSHRC, the Faculty of Law, University of Toronto, and the Centre of Criminology, University of Toronto. I thank Michael Boudreau, Rebecca Veinott, and James Muir for research assistance at different times. For their comments on an earlier version I am indebted to John Beattie, Barry Cahill, Rosemary Gartner, Allyson May, Peter Oliver, Carolyn Strange, and the reviewers for this volume. This paper was presented to the Early Canada History Group at the University of Toronto, and I am grateful to Alan Greer, organizer of the group, and to the members for their comments.

1 For the reception of English criminal law and procedure in Nova Scotia see J. Phillips, '"Securing Obedience to Necessary Laws": The Criminal Law in Eighteenth Century Nova Scotia,' *Nova Scotia Historical Review* 12 (1992), 92–106. For the English criminal trial in the eighteenth century see particularly J.M. Beattie, *Crime and the Courts in England, 1660–1800* (Princeton: Princeton University Press 1986), chap. 7; J.H. Langbein, 'The Criminal Trial Before the Lawyers,' *University of Chicago Law Review* 45 (1978), 263–316 and 'Shaping the Eighteenth-Century Criminal Trial: A View from the Ryder Sources,' *University of Chicago Law Review* 50 (1983), 1–136; S. Landsman, 'The Rise of the Contentious Spirit: Adversary Procedure in Eighteenth Century England,' *Cornell Law Review* 75 (1990), 497–609; and A.N. May, 'The Old Bailey Bar, 1783–1834' (PhD dissertation, University of Toronto 1997), chap. 3.
2 For state trials see especially F.M. Greenwood and J.B. Wright, eds., *Canadian State Trials Volume One: Law, Politics and Security Measures, 1608–1837* (Toronto: University of Toronto Press for The Osgoode Society for Canadian Legal History 1996). For a review of the literature generally see J. Phillips, 'Crime and Punishment in the Dominion of the North: Canada from New France to the Present,' in C. Emsley and L.A. Knafla, eds., *Crime History and Histories of Crime: Studies in the Historiography of Crime and Criminal Justice* (Greenwood, Conn.: Westview Press 1996).
3 R.C.B. Risk, 'A Prospectus for Canadian Legal History,' *Dalhousie Law Journal* 1 (1973), 227.
4 See generally Phillips, 'Criminal Law in Eighteenth-Century Nova Scotia.'

5 For some of these topics see J. Phillips, 'Halifax Juries in the Eighteenth Century,' in G. Smith et al., eds., *Criminal Justice in the Old World and the New: Essays in Honour of J.M. Beattie* (Toronto: University of Toronto Centre of Criminology 1998); 'Criminal Law in Eighteenth Century Nova Scotia'; and 'The Operation of the Royal Pardon in Nova Scotia, 1749–1815,' *University of Toronto Law Journal* 42 (1992), 401–49. Others are discussed in my monograph in progress, 'Crime and Criminal Justice in Early Canada: Nova Scotia, 1749–1815.'

6 For an account of the operation of the criminal court system see chapter 6 of 'Crime and Criminal Justice in Early Canada.'

7 These are at Nova Scotia Archives and Records Management (hereafter NSARM; formerly Public Archives of Nova Scotia), Record Group 39, Supreme Court Records, Halifax (hereafter RG 39), Series J, vols. 1, 2 and 117.

8 NSARM, Manuscript Group (hereafter MG) 20, vol. 221, file 91.5 (hereafter Deschamps Benchbook).

9 For this trial see 'Cartcel Trial Report, 1749,' NSARM, Colonial Office Series [hereafter CO] 217, vol. 9, 97–101; RG 39, Series C, vol. 1, no. 26; RG 39, Series J, vol. 117; NSARM, RG 1, vol. 342, nos. 1 and 2; J. Chisholm, 'Our First Trial For Murder: The King v. Peter Cartcel,' *Canadian Bar Review* 18 (1940), 385–9.

10 The trial in the General Court was presided over by Governor Cornwallis and his councillors. No legally trained judge officiated until the colony's first chief justice, Jonathan Belcher, arrived in October 1754, at which time the highest criminal court became known as the Supreme Court of Nova Scotia.

11 Cornwallis to Board of Trade, 11 September 1749, CO 217, vol. 9, 89.

12 Unless otherwise stated all information here is from 'Lee Trial Report, 1812,' RG 1, vol. 226, no. 16.

13 The commission of oyer and terminer, dated 20 May 1812, is at RG 1, vol. 173, 132. It named Monk to sit with either Thomas Cutler or Joseph Marshall, both local JPs and judges of the county's Inferior Court of Common Pleas. Monk was the son of James Monk, a Judge of the Court of Common Pleas, Massachusetts, and brother of James Monk, variously solicitor general of Nova Scotia and Chief Justice of Lower Canada. He served as clerk of the Crown in the Supreme Court at Halifax for a number of years. He was appointed a Supreme Court judge in 1801 and resigned in 1816. Although many sources describe him as a lawyer, it is unclear whether he was one: see J.B. Cahill, 'Henry Dundas' Plan for Reforming the Judicature of British North America,' *University of New Brunswick Law Journal* 39 (1990), 164.

14 Marshall is one of nineteenth-century Nova Scotia's best-known lawyers, largely because of his authorship of the province's first JP manual: *The Justice of the Peace and County and Township Officer in the Province of Nova Scotia*

(Halifax: Howe 1837). He joined the bar in 1808 and practised in Pictou and on circuit from then until 1816, when he moved to Halifax. He served as First Justice of the Court of Common Pleas and President of the Court of Sessions of Cape Breton Island from 1823 until the court reorganization of 1841. For his career see J.G. Marshall, *A Brief History of Public Proceedings and Events, Legal, Parliamentary, and Miscellaneous, in the Province of Nova Scotia, During the Earliest Years of the Present Century* (Halifax: privately published n.d.) and C.E. Thomas, 'John George Marshall,' *Dictionary of Canadian Biography* (Toronto: University of Toronto Press 1966–), (hereafter *DCB*), 10, 496–7.

15 Joseph Henry Marshall is described in some sources as a 'barrister,' but there is no record of his admission to practice.

16 The clerk of the Crown, or prothonotary, was responsible for organizing the criminal business of the Supreme Court in Halifax. He drew up indictments from depositions taken before JPs and presented them to the grand jury, and then ran the show – arraignment, pleading, etc. – at trial. He held his commission for the entire province until 1853, so all county clerks of the Crown, who were generally not lawyers, were his deputies.

17 Warrant to Christian Muller, Sheriff of Sydney County, 25 July 1812, 'for executing Walter Lee for murder.' Returned executed 15 August 1812. RG 1, vol. 251, 154. For the petitions in his favour see Statement of Thomas Cutler, JP, 29 June 1812; Petition of John McKeough, foreman, for himself with the concurrence and recommendation of all the other Jurors, n.d. and Petition of Walter Lee, n.d.: RG 1, vol. 226, nos. 8, 15, and 17.

18 The phrase is from E. Moglen, 'The Privilege in British North America: The Colonial Period to the Fifth Amendment,' in R.H. Helmholz et al. *The Privilege Against Self-Incrimination* (Chicago: University of Chicago Press 1997).

19 This figure is for the Surrey assizes at mid-century. At the Old Bailey it was common for twenty to thirty felons to be tried in a day: J.M. Beattie, 'Crime and the Courts in Surrey, 1736–1753,' in J. Cockburn, ed. *Crime in England, 1550–1800* (Princeton: Princeton University Press 1977), 165.

20 Note that I found only two instances where a trial lasted more than one day. These were the trial of John William Hoffman in 1754 for high crimes and misdemeanours, which 'lasted 26 hours,' and that of one Blackwell for rape in 1812, which took up two full days: Lawrence to Board of Trade, 1 June 1754, CO 217, vol. 15, 40, and Petition of J.W. Nutting, 24 February 1829, in NSARM, Assembly Papers, RG 5, Series P, vol. 41, no. 102.

21 Blowers to Thomas Strange, 25 October 1797, CO 217, vol. 69, 275.

22 I examined the civil proceedings books for sixty separate days on which criminal cases were heard between April 1768 and July 1796. On only three of

them did the court hear civil cases as well as criminal ones, and in each
instance just one civil case was dealt with: RG 39, Series J, vols. 5–10.

23 Belcher to Pownall, 16 January 1755, CO 217, vol. 15, 188.

24 'Young Trial Report, 1756,' CO 217, vol. 16, 134–7.

25 See *The Trials of George Frederick Boutelier and John Boutelier, for the Murder of
Frederick Eminaud, Before a Special Court of Oyer and Terminer and General Gaol
Delivery, Held at Lunenburg ... in the Province of Nova Scotia, ... 1791* (Halifax:
Stewart 1792), (hereafter *Boutelier Trials*). This is the only published trial
account for this period, and was put out by prosecuting counsel James
Stewart. See also 'McIntosh Trial Report, 1811,' RG 1, vol. 225, no 107.

26 See D. Spindel, *Crime and Society in North Carolina, 1663–1776* (Baton Rouge:
Louisiana State University Press 1989), 41–2; P.C. Hoffer and W.B. Scott, eds.
Criminal Trial Proceedings in Colonial Virginia (Athens, Ga.: University of
Georgia Press 1984).

27 This account of the way the prosecution was conducted is based on Beattie,
Crime and the Courts, 340–5 and 353–4. See also Langbein, 'The Criminal Trial
Before the Lawyers.' The figures for prosecuting lawyers are from J.M.
Beattie, 'Scales of Justice: Defense Counsel and the English Criminal Trial in
the Eighteenth and Nineteenth Centuries,' *Law and History Review* 9 (1991),
227, and May, 'The Old Bailey Bar,' 91.

28 The post of attorney general, until 1754 styled King's Attorney, was created
in 1750 and held by Otis Little, who had been sworn in as an attorney in
February 1750, the second man to be so. He is first described as 'King's
Attorney,' in October 1750: J.B. Cahill, 'The Origin and Evolution of the
Attorney and Solicitor in the Legal Profession of Nova Scotia,' *Dalhousie
Law Journal* 14 (1991), 278; NSARM, Council Minutes (hereafter Minutes),
11 October 1750, RG 1, vol. 209, 87. The office of solicitor general, initially
styled King's Solicitor, was created in 1760, with James Monk Senior its first
incumbent: see 'The Solicitor-General Redivivus,' *Nova Scotia Historical Review*
8 (1988), 102–4.

29 For these two cases see respectively 'Street Trial Report, 1754,' CO 217, vol.
15, 310–29, and Phillips, 'Criminal Law in Eighteenth-Century Nova Scotia,'
esp. at 98–104. Nesbitt was appointed attorney general in April 1753, replacing Little, who was dismissed for corruption. Hopson to Board of Trade,
22 October 1753, CO 217, vol. 14, 280.

30 RG 39, Series J, vol. 1, 277–9; Deschamps Benchbook. For the 1750s see the
minutes of proceedings for 1755 in RG 39, Series C, vol. 2, no. 2; Minutes,
26 May 1757, RG 1, vol. 187, 514–16; RG 39, Series J, vol. 117; RG 39, Series C,
vol. 2, no. 36. For the 1760s see RG 39, Series J, vol. 117, and vol. 1, 9–12. For
the 1770s see, in addition to the sources cited above, RG 39, Series J, vol. 1,
218–19, 232–3, 235–7, and 260.

31 See RG 39, Series J, vols. 1 and 2, *passim*. See also, *inter alia*, 'Wilson and Cornish Trial Report, 1810,' RG 1, vol. 225, no. 91; 'Fox Trial Report,' RG 1, vol. 227, no. 64.

32 I have found only two mentions of a privately hired prosecution lawyer: cases of John Murphy (forcible detainer, 1779) and Mark Ruth (assault, 1791): RG 39, Series C, vol. 20, no. 76, and vol. 63, no. 42. This probably happened more often, however; see the fee tariff laid down by the council in 1799, which includes an indication that the AG was to 'receive of [private] prosecutors if employed by them the same fees as other Counsel would be entitled to if employed': Minutes, 13 July 1799, RG 1, vol. 191, 8.

33 Deschamps Benchbook. See also in the same source the April 1778 trial of two soldiers accused of grand larceny, who seem to have been prosecuted by victim George Smith.

34 *Acadian Recorder*, 22 April 1815. In another case the report in the same issue of the newspaper suggests that Supreme Court judge Brenton Halliburton was the prosecutor in a fraud case.

35 Minutes, 2 June 1755, RG 1, vol. 187, 294.

36 Belcher to Pownall, 16 January 1755 and 20 January 1757, CO 217, vol. 15, 188, and vol. 16, 130. See also the fact that in September 1760 Nesbitt was voted an additional £100 by council as recompense for 'his extraordinary services as attorney-general for the current year': Minutes, 27 September 1760, RG 1, vol. 188, 156.

37 RG 1, vol. 221, no. 48. See also Brenton's expenses for 1770 and 1778 at RG 1, vols. 217 and 397.

38 RG 39, Series C, vol. 65, no. 45.

39 'Report of Council Committee, 13 July 1799,' RG 1, vol. 287, no. 70.

40 For the early period see the reference to Nesbitt's attendance at quarter sessions, text accompanying note 33 above. For a later period see NSARM, Records of Courts of General Sessions of the Peace, RG 34–312, Series P, vols. 1–4, which are minutes of proceedings for the Halifax Quarter Sessions in the 1790s and early nineteenth century. Attorney general (from 1797) Uniacke was consistently present as Crown prosecutor in petit larceny cases, and occasionally also prosecuted assault charges.

41 In 1762 Belcher noted that Solicitor General James Monk Senior's services were important 'for the administration of justice in the more remote settlements': Belcher to Pownall, 12 November 1762, CO 217, vol. 19, 288. His son was required by Governor Legge to attend at least one court session in the out-settlements: Monk to Legge, 28 April 1775, CO 217, vol. 51, 194.

42 James Brenton Benchbook, Acadia University Archives (microfilm at NSARM – hereafter Brenton Benchbook), 58–60; Bulkeley to Shelburne JPs, 24 September 1784, RG 1, vol. 136, 345.

43 'Holland Trial Report, 1810,' CO 217, vol. 87, 56–9; G. Patterson, 'Old Court Records of Pictou County, Nova Scotia,' *Canadian Bar Review* 13 (1935), 146–7.
44 *Boutelier Trials.*
45 'O'Neal Trial Report, 1814,' RG 1, vol. 343; 'Pomp Trial Report, 1813,' RG 1, vol. 226, no. 114; Appropriation Act, SNS 1816, c. 1. The prosecution of the Pomps was conducted by W.H.O. Halliburton and Thomas Ritchie. The prosecuting lawyer in the O'Neal case was Robert Bolman. Bolman, a resident of Liverpool, was also apparently 'induced by the repeated solicitations of Gentlemen residing at Liverpool' to conduct a murder prosecution in 1815, and he was paid by the Assembly for doing so (RG 5, Series P, vol. 41, no. 5, and Appropriation Act, SNS 1816, c. 1. The prosecutor at Sydney was John George Marshall, and he was paid £23 6s. 8d. for his services.
46 Patterson, 'Old Court Records,' 146.
47 Criminal Prosecutions Act, SNS 1828, c. 13.
48 Combauld, who went to the Americas from London in the 1770s and to Shelburne as a Loyalist exile in 1783, has his name on numerous indictments as appearing 'for Our Lord the King'. See NSARM, Sessions of the Peace Records, RG 60 [Shelburne], vols. 2 et seq, *passim*. A 1786 document describes him as 'one of the attorneys of His Majesty's Supreme Court ... who prosecutes the pleas for Our Lord the King ... for this County at Shelburne': RG 60 [Shelburne], vol. 20, no. 3.
49 For the pretrial process see Phillips, 'Crime and Criminal Justice in Early Canada,' chap. 5
50 The evidence of Blowers' and Brenton's involvement in this is respectively at RG 39, Series C, vol. 65, no. 45, and RG 1, vol. 221, no. 48.
51 See 'Report of Council Committee, 13 July 1799,' RG 1, vol. 287, no. 70. The report recommended a fee scale for the attorney general, one that included sums for attending examinations and interviewing witnesses. However, this is the only evidence that the attorney general did such things, and it comes from late in our period.
52 See examples of both in RG 39, Series J, vol. 1, 30, 254, 335, 339; vol. 2, 90, 189, 206; vol. 117.
53 Belcher to Pownall, 16 January 1755, CO 217, vol. 15, 187, and 20 Jan. 1757, CO 217, vol. 16, 130.
54 See J. Rice, 'The Criminal Trial Before and After the Lawyers: Authority, Law and Culture in Maryland Jury Trials, 1681–1837,' *American Journal of Legal History* 40 (1996), esp at 459–62; Hoffer and Scott, eds. *Criminal Proceedings in Colonial Virginia*, esp. 41–2; Moglen, 'The Privilege in British North America,' 113–14 and 122; D. Flaherty, 'A Well-Ordered Society: Crime and the Courts

in Massachusetts, 1692–1780,' (unpublished ms 1995), chap. 6. (I am grateful to Professor Flaherty for permission to quote from this manuscript.)

55 From the establishment of Upper Canada the attorney general claimed the right to conduct all criminal prosecutions: see P. Romney *Mr Attorney: The Attorney-General for Ontario in Court, Cabinet, and Legislature, 1791–1899* (Toronto: University of Toronto Press for The Osgoode Society for Canadian Legal History 1986), esp. 37–8. For Prince Edward Island see J. Hornby, *In the Shadow of the Gallows: Criminal Law and Capital Punishment in Prince Edward Island, 1769–1941* (Charlottetown: Institute of Island Studies 1998), chaps. 1 and 2. For New Brunswick the court book of Judge Ward Chipman for 1809–16, housed in the New Brunswick Museum, shows that at least the vast majority of prosecutions were conducted either by the attorney general or the clerk of the Crown on circuit. I am grateful to David Bell for this reference.

56 Minutes, 13 July 1799, RG 1, vol. 191, 8.

57 RG 1, vol. 298, no. 124, and vol. 304, no. 57.

58 This section on lawyers is based on Beattie, *Crime and the Courts*, 352 and 356–62, and 'Scales of Justice.' See also J.B. Post, 'The Admissibility of Defence Counsel in English Criminal Procedure,' *Journal of Legal History* 5 (1984), 23–32.

59 *Prisoner's Counsel Act*, 6 & 7 Wm. IV, c. 114 (1836); Defence Counsel Act, SNS 1840, c. 9. For the debate over the English Act see Beattie, 'Scales of Justice,' esp. 250–8, and A.N. May 'Reluctant Advocates: The Legal Profession and the Prisoner's Counsel Act,' in Smith et al., eds., *Criminal Justice in the Old World and the New*.

60 Minutes, 13 December 1749, RG 1, vol. 186, 34.

61 A Virginia statute of 1735 permitted defence counsel in felony cases: Moglen 'The Privilege in British North America,' 112–13. Although Moglen refers to the colonial American system as one based on the '[s]ystematic exclusion of counsel,' (113), lawyers were allowed as of right in colonies other than Virginia. Felony defendants could have counsel in Massachusetts throughout the eighteenth century, and in Rhode Island from 1669, albeit with restrictions on their roles: see D. Flaherty, 'Criminal Practice in Provincial Massachusetts,' in D.R. Coquilette, ed., *Law in Colonial Massachusetts, 1630–1800* (Boston: Massachusetts Historical Society 1984), 193–4, and 'A Well-Ordered Society,' 223–5; Moglen, 'The Privilege in British North America,' 113. New York, however, did not confer this right: see J. Goebel and T. Naughton, *Law Enforcement in Colonial New York: A Study in Criminal Procedure, 1664–1776* (New York: Commonwealth Fund 1944). For a general review see P.C. Hoffer, *Law and People in Colonial America* (Baltimore: Johns Hopkins University Press 1992), 86.

62 Sentencing speech, CO 217, vol. 15, 330.
63 At the 1791 trial of George and John Boutelier, for example, Voster Lombard was 'admitted Counsel' for the defendants: *Boutelier Trials*, 13.
64 For Maryland see Rice, 'The Criminal Trial Before and After the Lawyers,' 457.
65 It is not clear when this happened, although it was the practice by the 1830s: B. Murdoch, *Epitome of the Laws of Nova Scotia*, 4 vols. (Halifax: Howe 1832–33), 4:190. Massachusetts required a defence lawyer in all capital cases from before the Revolution; see A. Rogers, '"A Sacred Duty": Court Appointed Attorneys in Massachusetts Capital Cases, 1780–1980,' *American Journal of Legal History* 41 (1997), 440–65.
66 Belcher to Egremont, 31 March 1762, CO 217, vol. 43, 10–11.
67 RG 39, Series J, vol. 2, 77.
68 RG 39, Series J, vol. 2, 120. See also other cases at RG 39, Series J, vol. 1, 406–9; vol. 2, 152, 179, 191, 206, 213, 219, 228, 253 and 255.
69 RG 39, Series J, vol. 1, 357–9, 382, 390, 410; vol. 2, 29, 48–9, 62–3, 67, 89, 107, 111, 127, 142, 145–6, 195, 211–12, 227, 234, 246 and 248. This only covers examples of individuals defending themselves when I know, from references in the proceedings books or elsewhere, that they did indeed do so. That is, I have not assumed that the absence of information about counsel necessarily means that the defendant was unrepresented.
70 Much of this paragraph on the size of the legal profession is based on the work of J.B. Cahill: See 'The Judges' Affair: An Eighteenth Century Nova Scotian *Cause Célèbre*' (unpublished ms [I am grateful to Mr Cahill for allowing me to quote from this work]); 'James Monk's "Observations on the Courts of Law in Nova Scotia," 1775,' *University of New Brunswick Law Journal* 36 (1987), 9; 'Richard Gibbons' "Review of the Administration of Justice in Nova Scotia," 1774,' *University of New Brunswick Law Journal* 37 (1988), 35; 'Origin and Evolution.' See also RG 39, Series J, vols. 3–11; *Nova Scotia Magazine*, October 1791; *Nova Scotia Gazette*, 17 October 1797; List of Admissions to the Bar, RG 39, Series M, vol. 24A.
71 In the mid-1780s Shelburne had six lawyers: Cahill, 'Origin and Evolution,' 283.
72 See John Marshall's account of going from Pictou, where he practised at the time, to another settlement 'to attend to the defence of a cause which was to be tried there before one of the Judges of the Supreme Court, under a Special Commission': Marshall, 'Perils and Preservations' (unpublished ms), MG 1, vol. 1283.
73 Cahill, 'Origin and Evolution,' 283.
74 RG 39, Series J, vols. 3–11.
75 While the number of witnesses listed on indictments as giving evidence

before the grand jury ranged from only one to a high of eight, the average number was 3.1. This calculation is made from a sample of sixty property cases from all decades except the 1770s, and from six other cases. The grand jury heard only prosecution evidence, a proceeding justified in English law by the fact that its role was to decide only whether a case should go to trial, not to deliberate on guilt or innocence: Beattie, *Crime and the Courts*, 319; Belcher's notes on grand jury charges, MG 1, vol. 1738, no. 110.

76 'Sanders Trial Report,' CO 217, vol. 75, 8–9; *Boutelier Trials*.

77 Deschamps Benchbook, October 1776.

78 They were not answers to questions by Thompson's lawyer, for the next section in the benchbook begins 'Qu: by Prisoners Council.'

79 Deschamps Benchbook, October 1777. Rice argues that this was also how proceedings were conducted in Maryland before the nineteenth century: see 'The Criminal Trial Before and After the Lawyers,' 461.

80 'Street Trial Report, 1754,' CO 217, vol. 15, 310–29.

81 A detailed account of the system of investigation and pretrial prosecution is contained in chapter five of Phillips, 'Crime and Criminal Justice in Early Canada.'

82 'Young Trial Report, 1756,' CO 217, vol. 16, 136–7.

83 RG 39, Series J, vol. 1, 95–7.

84 At the end of the trials Connor was 'discharged by proclamation,' meaning that he too had been held in custody: Deschamps Benchbook, October 1777.

85 For an example of accomplice evidence failing to secure a conviction see the case of Thomas Wiseman and Rueben Hemsley, RG 39, Series C, vol. 1, nos. 43, 44, 51–3.

86 Petition of J.W. Nutting, 24 February 1829, RG 5, Series P, vol. 41, no. 102. For the rules on deposition evidence in England see Beattie, *Crime and the Courts*, 350.

87 RG 39, Series C, vol. 3, nos. 70 and 71.

88 RG 39, Series J, vol. 1, 11.

89 RG 39, Series J, vol. 2, 83, and Series C, vol. 56, no. 76.

90 'Wilson and Cornish Trial Report, Oct. 1810,' RG 1, vol. 225, no. 91.

91 See the case of Peter Shore, Deschamps Benchbook, October 1776.

92 Deschamps Benchbook, July 1777.

93 Deschamps Benchbook, October 1777. Other trials from the Deschamps benchbook in which it was more or less one man's word against another include those of James Stevens, convicted of grand larceny in April 1777, and soldiers William Callahan and Samuel Neale, tried for grand larceny the same term but acquitted when the only evidence against them was that of a labourer.

94 *Boutelier Trials, passim.* For their confessions see *Weekly Chronicle*, 14 May 1791.
95 The following account is largely taken from 'Pomp Trial Report, 1813,' RG 1, vol. 226, no. 114.
96 This phrase or some variant of it – 'the witnesses for the Crown not being sufficient to convict' or 'the Evidence not being sufficient' – appears, *inter alia*, at RG 39, Series J, vol. 2, 12–14 and 23.
97 Minutes, 15 May 1761, RG 1, vol. 188, 241.
98 Petition of Samuel Ives, n.d., RG 39, Series C, vol. 1, no. 56.
99 When more frequent sittings of the various county Courts of Sessions were introduced in 1785 the preamble to the enacting statute gave as one of the reasons for doing so the fact that prisoners 'frequently suffer from the severity of the weather, and length of confinement': Special Courts of Sessions Act, SNS 1785, c. 2.
100 The circuit system was inaugurated in 1774 and incorporated Annapolis, King's, and Cumberland counties. The circuit went to the first two counties semi-annually until 1799, and annually thereafter. Cumberland was switched to an annual sitting in 1783, when much of the county was made part of New Brunswick. Between 1802 and 1805 the circuit system was expanded with annual sittings in the Colchester and Pictou districts of Halifax County, and Lunenburg County. Shelburne, Queen's, and Sydney counties were added in 1816. See Supreme Court Circuit Act, SNS 1774, c. 6, and J. Phillips, '"The Majesty of the Law": Circuit Courts in Theory and Practice in Early Nova Scotia,' paper presented to the Canadian Legal History Conference, University of Toronto Faculty of Law, 1998.
101 For other examples of long confinement, drawn from Annapolis County, see Thomas Millidge, JP, at Granville, to H.H. Cogswell, 8 January 1813, RG 1, vol. 226, no. 46.
102 The following section on the English rules and practice is based on Beattie, *Crime and the Courts*, 359–61, and 'Scales of Justice.'
103 RG 39, Series C, vol. 2, no. 39.
104 See Blowers' report on the trial of Pierre Poulin in 1805, when he told London in a matter of fact way that the prosecution witnesses were 'cross-examined by the counsel for the prisoner ... as he suggested or desired': 'Poulin Trial Report, 1805,' CO 215, vol. 80, 32–3.
105 See Murdoch's comment written in the early 1830s that 'counsel can only examine witnesses, or address the court on questions of law ..., the prisoner being only allowed to state his defence himself to the jury': Murdoch, *Epitome*, vol. 4, 190. Here again Nova Scotia differed from Massachusetts, for lawyers there regularly made speeches to the jury: Flaherty, 'Criminal Practice in Provincial Massachusetts,' 241.

106 See the case of Timothy Keith, tried for an assault with intent to commit a rape in 1765. His lawyer's request to see the examination was refused. RG 39, Series J, vol. 1, 7. For the (same) English rules on this, see May, 'The Old Bailey Bar,' 113–17.

107 See 'Young Trial Report, 1756,' RG 39, Series C, vol. 2, no. 39, and 'Poulin Trial Report, 1805,' CO 215, vol. 80, 33.

108 See the cases of John Young, 1756 (was a particular English statute in force in Nova Scotia), Benjamin Street et al., 1754 (did the Supreme Court have jurisdiction to try the case rather than the Court of Vice-Admiralty, and did a naval officer have the authority to board a merchant ship), and John Hoffman, 1753 (charge reduced from high treason to high misdemeanour because of the English rule that treason prosecutions required two witnesses): Phillips, 'Criminal Law in Eighteenth-Century Nova Scotia'; Lawrence to Board of Trade, 1 June 1754, CO 217, vol. 15, 40.

109 See, for example, the 1790 prosecution of Jehu Midgley. The grand jury indicted him as 'John Mitcheller' and he was able to avoid a trial on the grounds that 'his name is Jehu Midgley and not John Mitcheller as indicted': RG 39, Series J, vol. 2, 97.

110 For the American colonies see Moglen, 'The Privilege in British North America.'

111 On the issue of the incompetency of the accused, which was not changed until the late nineteenth century, see C.W. Allen, *The Law of Evidence in Victorian England* (Oxford: Clarendon Press 1997).

112 Beattie, *Crime and the Courts*, 341 and 350.

113 The first edition of Archbold's *Criminal Procedure*, published in 1822, did not mention the presumption of innocence. However, the second edition did so, and cited as authority some cases decided in the first two decades of the nineteenth century. (I owe these references to Allyson May.) This change, like the introduction of rules of evidence, was likely a product of the increased participation in the trial of defence counsel.

114 Brenton made this comment when asked to advise the council as to whether William MacLean should hang following his 1782 conviction for street robbery: Minutes, 4 November 1782, RG 1, vol. 189, 492.

115 RG 39, Series J, vol. 1, 7.

116 This account is from *Boutelier Trials*.

117 Strange was appointed chief justice of Nova Scotia in 1789, and arrived there in the spring of 1790: *Nova Scotia Gazette*, 1 June 1790.

118 'Pomp Trial Report, 1813,' RG 1, vol. 226, no. 114.

119 John Beattie has argued that the most important contribution of defence lawyers lay in the fact that they did this much better than defendants. After

the introduction of lawyers, he suggests, prosecution evidence was tested more rigorously than it had been before. Counsel could 'force the prosecution onto the defensive,' questioning witnesses' recollections, credibility, and motives: Beattie, *Crime and the Courts*, 361–2 and 372–5.

120 Deschamps Benchbook, October 1777.

121 'O'Neal Trial Report, 1814,' RG 1, vol. 343.

122 The phrase 'the prisoner put on his defence' or some variation of it appears for a total of thirty-nine defendants tried between 1765 and 1783, and for 138 defendants tried between 1784 and 1804. See RG 39, Series J, vols. 1, 2, and 117, *passim*.

123 *Acadian Recorder*, 22 April 1815.

124 Deschamps Benchbook, July 1777.

125 For New York see Moglen, 'The Privilege in British North America,' 114.

126 Gad Sanders did 'not contradict' the testimony of the one witness against him: 'Sanders Trial Report, 1801,' CO 217, vol. 75, 8. Sarah Wilson, tried for burglary, produced no witnesses in her defence, but she had confessed to the JP: 'Wilson and Cornish Trial Report, 1810,' RG 1, vol. 225, no. 91.

127 All reference are to Deschamps Benchbook, October 1776.

128 Beattie, *Crime and the Courts*, 350. For the importance of character in Maryland trials see the excellent discussion in Rice, 'The Criminal Trial Before and After the Lawyers,' 470–3.

129 Deschamps Benchbook, April 1778.

130 'McIntosh Trial Report, 1811,' RG 1, vol. 225, no. 107. See also 'Hart Trial Report, 1813,' CO 217, vol. 91, 157–60.

131 'Pomp Trial Report, 1813,' RG 1, vol. 226, no. 114.

132 Minutes, 4 November 1782, RG 1, vol. 189, 492.

133 Pierre Poulin, who did have counsel to advise him, 'told the jury in his defence that he was provoked by the deceased ... but did not intend to kill him: 'Poulin Trial Report, 1805,' CO 215, vol. 80, 33. Nancy O'Neal, tried for murder at Liverpool, said nothing: 'O'Neal Trial Report, 1814,' RG 1, vol. 343.

134 Deschamps Benchbook, *passim*.

135 RG 39, Series J, vol. 2, 64.

136 RG 39, Series J, vols. 1 and 2, *passim*. The way the trial jury operated is discussed at more length in chapter 7 of Phillips, 'Crime and Criminal Justice in Early Canada.'

137 For example, the English historians have shown that in the old form of trial it was not uncommon for both the prosecution and the defence evidence to be interrupted by questions from jurors. Unfortunately I only have one instance of such an interruption occurring in a criminal trial in this period

('Holland Trial Report, 1810,' CO 217, vol. 87, 58–9), although there is another indication from a civil trial presided over by Deschamps. While these examples are sufficient to demonstrate that this was an accepted practice, the dearth of examples suggests that it was not common, owing perhaps to the public prosecutor's control of the proceedings.

138 Conviction rates in Halifax and elsewhere are discussed in detail in Phillips, 'Halifax Juries in the Eighteenth Century.' I argue in that paper that high conviction rates also in part resulted from the particular socio-economic composition and experience of trial jurors. These figures are for those cases in which the trial produced a definite result – guilty as charged, guilty of a lesser offence, or not guilty. They do not include cases where, for some reason, the proceeding was inconclusive. The 1811–15 figures are based on relatively small absolute numbers (ninety-four trials) and are artificially deflated by one multiple-defendant murder trial in 1815 which resulted in eight acquittals.

139 While there are suggestions in one or two cases that lawyers made a crucial difference, the statistics do not bear this out generally. Of the seventy-five individuals represented by defence lawyers in Halifax whose cases went to trial and produced a result, fully forty-eight of them, or 64 per cent, were found guilty of the offence charged and a further eleven (15 per cent) were found guilty on a partial verdict; only sixteen (21 per cent) were acquitted. The overall figure of 79 per cent convicted is higher than for unrepresented defendants, although partial verdicts in capital cases should probably count as 'wins' for the lawyers. To some extent the figures are skewed by the fact that for some cases we know about the presence of counsel from a trial report, and as already discussed the trial report cases were mostly ones in which the evidence was heavily against the accused. But against this we should note the fact that a disproportionate number of represented defendants were charged with a capital offence, and, as noted below, there was overall a lower conviction rate in capital cases. This finding about the effect of defence counsel is different to Rice's conclusions based on the evidence of Maryland proceedings in the nineteenth century. See 'The Criminal Trial Before and After the Lawyers,' 459. The explanation likely has much to do with the fact that it was not just the presence of lawyers that mattered, but the introduction and elaboration of rules of evidence and burdens of proof.

140 Only 39 per cent of those accused of capital offences were convicted as charged in the 1749–1803 period, and just 30 per cent between 1811 and 1815. These figures are much lower than the overall conviction rates in the two periods discussed above, and therefore lower than the conviction rate for noncapital offences, showing that capital punishment did influence juries.

15

'The Disquisitions of Learned Judges': Making Manitoba Lawyers, 1885–1931

W. WESLEY PUE

It behooves you not only to aspire to be the thorough lawyer, but to be the best Canadian, and to create a sentiment and ideals among the people with whom you come into contact which will place them upon a higher level and justify your influence. You should aim to be leaders in thought, promoters of the intellectual and moral development of our young nation, so that it may become a strong and forceful leader in the Empire.

James Aikins, Address on Opening of Manitoba Law School, 1914[1]

INTRODUCTION

When the history of lawyer's education in common law Canada comes to be written it will probably be noted that Manitoba has often marched to its own drummer: sometimes at the forefront of national developments, often not. Paradoxically, the home of one of common law Canada's first university-affiliated schools was also the last Canadian province to adopt a system of full time university legal education.[2]

This paper explores the rise and fall of Manitoban legal education from 1885 to 1931. For much of this period Manitoba, the 'keystone province,' held a central place in the aspirations and plans of English Canadian nationalism. As a new territory on which the virtues of 'British Canadianness' were yet to be inscribed, some influential lawyers thought it crucially important that the culture of English Canadian law be protected. Some, as the epigraph from James Aikins suggests, thought they could best do this by nurturing an appropriately educated, socialized, and structured legal profession. This cultural project of certain elite lawyers was one force propelling extraordinary changes in professional legal education during the second and third decades of the twentieth century.

It was not the only force, however. Though the story of Manitoban legal education is partly about forceful, visionary men and their work, it is also a tale of professional inertia, borrowing from abroad, happenstance, and an unstable accommodation between competing visions of professionalism and pedagogy. 'Visionaries' (to so describe is not to endorse their views) were almost certainly a minority within the legal profession at any given point in time. Most lawyers probably viewed their work prosaically, as being primarily about earning a living, serving their clients, and surviving another month, rather than as a public calling directed to the mission of implanting British law in a new land. For such individuals 'law' was their trade, something best learned by doing, and for which training by apprenticeship made both good business sense and good practical education.[3]

A third important factor was the dissatisfaction apprenticing lawyers felt with turn-of-the-century systems of professional qualification. In the nature of things the leadership of student organizations turns over rapidly and there were inevitably ebbs and flows in both the positions and energy of Manitoba's law students (the sparsity of the historical record makes it impossible to sketch this out in any detail). It is important too not to lose sight of the facts that apprenticing lawyers' views on legal education probably spanned the entire ambit of opinion held by their professional elders and that only outspoken student leaders produced the sort of record that leaves historical trace. Nonetheless, it was always the case that apprenticing lawyers more than anyone else benefited from or suffered under prevailing forms of professional qualification. For most of the period before 1914 apprenticing lawyers seem to have felt the need for some form of regular instruction in law. While it is admittedly less clear that they shared fully in the cultural vision of senior professional reformers, the overlap of interest was sufficient to make the two groups allies of sorts. Whatever potential there was for cleavage to develop between a 'cultural' vision of legal education and one directed more narrowly toward ensuring regularity of technical instruction would not have been fully apparent in a time and a place where neither was available.

LAW SOCIETY LECTURES, 1877–1914

Legal education in Manitoba has always been primarily about training aspiring lawyers for careers. The first rules of the Law Society of Manitoba, adopted in 1872, established a structure whereby aspiring lawyers earned professional qualification by examination and service of an extended apprenticeship as an 'articled clerk' or 'a student at law,[4]' without the benefit of any systematic instruction.[5] The quality of on-the-job training probably varied enormously from one law office to another.[6]

Though the University of Manitoba offered an LLB degree as early as 1885, the degree was not an important part of professional education in this period.[7] '[M]erely a question of reading the books and passing the examinations,'[8] the law degree provided no professional qualification or exemption other than entitling graduates to a slightly shortened period of apprenticeship – a benefit to which any university graduate was entitled. Not surprisingly, few aspiring lawyers took the university program until its transmogrification and effective merger with Law Society courses in 1914.

Before then there were repeated efforts to establish regular lectures under the auspices of the Law Society (often at the urging of apprenticing lawyers)[9] and less frequently, but nonetheless important, investigations or reports on the province's method of professional credentialling in law. Apprenticing lawyers actively sought out systematic legal education both to prepare them better for their chosen careers and, more immediately, to help them pass the Law Society's professional examinations. Their motivations may have been self-interested and pragmatic but in articulating their demands students both drew upon and contributed to evolving discourses of professionalism.[10] By 1908 a more or less regular series of lectures had been established under the auspices of the Law Society of Manitoba. In the winter of 1908–9, the Law Society organized and paid for lectures on five subjects in central Winnipeg on Tuesdays and Fridays. Scheduled to avoid conflict with office duties, attendance at these lectures was entirely voluntary. Though 'some students attended very regularly indeed, others never took the trouble to go to a single lecture.'[11] Despite these seeming inadequacies, the achievement of more-or-less regular lecture series was a genuinely significant accomplishment in their time and place. No script ordained this: the subsequent development of university-based professional education as the North American norm was not in any sense a necessary end toward which all turn-of-the-century developments inevitably pointed.

Such an arrangement was not, however, satisfactory to ardent professional reformers who sought the establishment of a full law school, either on the model of the Toronto profession's trade school at Osgoode Hall[12] or in affiliation with the provincial university.[13] Students, for their part, appreciated the lectures but felt they were still left to 'blind preparation' for their qualifying examinations. The 'general' lectures provided by interested practitioners were, they pointed out, not intended to address the texts upon which professional examinations were based.[14] Student pressure to create either a professional school of law or a university program suited to their needs was unrelenting. A scripted choreography developed involving repeated demands by law students,[15] supported or encouraged by elite lawyers, and cautious, usually minimal responses from the benchers. The influence of a few elite lawyers, including James Aikins, Isaac Pitblado,[16] and H.A. Robson, is usually discernible; they appear sometimes in highly visible roles, while on other occasions they are found behind the scenes. The omnipresent Aikins was a key figure in the Winnipeg Bar Association (founded in 1906), and founding father of both the Manitoba Bar Association (as the Winnipeg Bar Association renamed itself in 1911) and the Canadian Bar Association (effectively founded in 1914).[17] Not surprisingly, each of these professional organizations supported the cause of cultural training for lawyers championed by their creator.

The Manitoba Bar Association called for the creation of university legal education at its inaugural banquet in November of 1911,[18] passing a motion calling for the University of Manitoba to create 'either two chairs to the Faculty of law, or that provision be made for one professor to lecture in the department of law in connection with the university' in coordination with the Law Society of Manitoba.[19] The importance of individual agency in all of this is nowhere made more apparent than in the fact that one newspaper account of these events appeared under the heading 'Aikins Entertains Local Barristers.'

There are hints that this particular motion was part of an orchestrated campaign run by apprenticing lawyers in concert with elite lawyers. A 15 December 1910 newspaper article, for example, revealed that:

The law students of the city have been for some time considering some improvements which they think might be made in their course of study and examinations. A hint dropped at one of their moot courts by the attorney-general who was acting as judge, has given an encouragement to their purpose, and it is probable that they may petition the university regarding the holding of their examinations under its auspices ... It is hoped that some means may be devised for holding a course of lectures upon the authorized texts as well as upon the general subjects and the students feel that this could be done to more advantage under the tutelage of the university. Though nothing definite has been attempted so far, it is possible that some steps may be taken shortly towards securing the desired lectures, and having a university control of examinations.[20]

In addition to these pressures from apprenticing lawyers, individual members of the legal profession, and the Manitoba Bar Association, one official inquiry reported on legal education in this period. A provincial Royal Commission on Manitoba University Education (established in 1907) reported in 1909. The royal commission's work was not centred on legal education and the commissioners' widely divergent reports were largely ignored by the government on all issues. One of the commissioners was none other than James Aikins who, along with Rev. A.A. Chevrier, issued a report that touched on legal education. Building on the precedent provided by existing arrangements for university training in medicine and engineering[21] they called for the creation of a college of law affiliated with the university. They proposed a model of administration for the college of law analogous to that governing the constituent denominational colleges of the University of Manitoba:[22]

We believe it would not be difficult for the University to make an arrangement with the Law Society whereby a regular course of instruction would be given to those studying, the University establishing Chairs in some subjects such as Constitutional, Municipal, Commercial and Criminal Law, and the Law Society providing Lectures in the other subjects. If the University has the funds available to do so, we recommend such a course ...

If the University has not the funds to do so after providing for the teaching of those subjects which we have previously recommended as University subjects, then we recommend that State aid be granted so as to place the Students of these Professions on a somewhat equal footing in respect of a regular course of instruction in their intended vocations, and that when regular teaching in Law is undertaken by the Law Society with the aid of the State or of the University, then the Law Society should be affiliated with the University in respect of such teaching or of the School or College it may establish for such purpose.[23]

Aikins and Chevrier's report, like those of the other commissioners, was ignored by the government. Though it had no immediate practical consequence, the report did give voice to a developing notion of practical university education in law. Hindsight shows that it effectively became a blueprint for what developed only a half-decade later.

Force of logic or personality, imagination, coordination of efforts, and the power of persistence are not always sufficient to overcome the weight of inertia. Major reforms need all of these, but significant change rarely comes about unless there is a coincidence of such forces with a precipitating event that both draws attention to the need for reform and points to the inevitability of change. The precipitating event with respect to Manitoba legal education is found in a development which, though modest, illustrated clearly that the status quo could not persist indefinitely. Forces entirely beyond the control of the provincial law society were in play.

THE SPECTRE: LEGAL EDUCATION FOR PROFIT

Law societies and universities are not the only conceivable providers of structured legal education. Private 'crammers' of one sort or another had long been in existence in both England and the United States.[24] In March 1912, the Manitoba legislature gave consideration to a 'University Extension Bill,' which would have permitted a private business to grant degrees by correspondence or instruction in the fields of 'law and business.' The benchers immediately recorded their disapproval.[25] Speaking with his authority both as a member of the legislature and as a long-term bencher, Mr Coldwell[26] told the legislature that such an institution would infringe the provisions of the Law Society Act and he feared that it would 'cause many to shirk the more thorough training in law demanded under the terms of the Law Society Act.' He objected in any event to a correspondence school granting degrees. Interestingly, though the gender composition of the legal profession is nowhere mentioned in the body of the article, the Winnipeg Telegram's account of the matter was headed, 'Would Give Women Right to Practice Law in Province.'[27] On another occasion Coldwell expressed concern that a private law school would throw 'the province open to professional men without training.'[28]

It is not entirely clear why private education so disturbed the benchers and their supporters. Direct evidence is sparse. It seems unlikely that anyone could possibly have thought that *any* private system of education might have been less thorough or rigorous than the Law Society's amalgam of voluntary attendance at sporadically offered lectures, unregulated service in a law office, and undemanding examinations. On the other hand, the introduction of a proprietary law school would inevitably have challenged the Law Society's role as the sole authoritative voice and would certainly have diminished its cultural authority. Coldwell's comments also serve as a reminder that Canadian law societies at this time were relatively insecure in their monopoly. Graduates of a private law school would likely have assumed the right to practise law as they saw fit, with or without the blessing of the Law Society. Manitoba lawyers would have known that, despite opposition from the organized medical profession and lack of any formal recognition by qualifying associations, Dr Charlotte Ross had practised medicine in both Quebec and Manitoba for thirty-seven years after her graduation from the Women's Medical College of Pennsylvania in 1875.[29] There was no reason to assume that locally graduated lawyers would have proved any more amenable to regulation by the Law Society than Ross had been to Manitoba's College of Physicians and Surgeons.

Another factor also probably came into play, though this remains a matter of speculation. Experience in the United States had shown that private law schools provided access to legal careers for a broader and more diverse group of individuals than other means of qualification. The result, from one point of view, was to open a key social role to much larger numbers of inadequately socialized young men *and women* – particularly those of working-class or ethnic minority background – than was thought desirable. Such a prospect would not have appealed to Manitoba's Anglo legal elite, whose culture was 'British,' hierarchical, nativist, and sometimes even xenophobic.[30] Their professional counterparts in the United States had by this time reached a consensus about the dangers of 'proprietary' law schools. Julius Cohen's 1916 book on the legal profession drew heavily on a report prepared by University of Michigan Law Dean Henry M. Bates[31] to observe that, in the United States, 'there are still proprietary schools run for profit, which do not take into account "the larger interests of the State, the profession, and the requirements of justice" and which grant diplomas on low standards of admission and of work. "Unless this tendency is checked, much of the good that the better university schools are attempting to accomplish, at the expense of loss in students and money to themselves, will be offset by the schools run mainly for revenue only."'[32] Reflecting on such matters many years later, E.H. Coleman (then dean of the Manitoba Law School), asserted that U.S. commercial law schools took students ill-equipped 'by education, character or temperament' for legal practice, producing graduates with 'little conception of ethical standards and who enter on practice without any idea that the profession has any other end or duty than the making of money by the practitioner.'[33] The Manitoba dean celebrated the 'advantage' Manitoba enjoyed of 'having the control of legal education lodged in our official society.' In apparent reference to the 1912 University Extension Bill, he observed that 'Had the

Law School not been established, I think I may say quite safely that you would have in Winnipeg a commercial law school, probably a branch of one of the institutions in Chicago or Minneapolis, the only aim of which would be the profit of the owner with the result that there would be pumped out each year an army of graduates, whose chief qualifications, so far as the Law School would be concerned, would be the payment of fees.'[34]

Manitoba was spared both education-for-profit and the increasingly open legal profession it then promised. A university-affiliated law school soon emerged to occupy the field.[35]

CREATION OF THE MANITOBA LAW SCHOOL, 1911–1913

From 1911 to 1913 the Law Society organized lectures for students, much as it had in the past.[36] Robson continued his work to create a law school and prodded apprenticing lawyers to 'keep hammering at the question' of legal education.[37] Despite all efforts, however, a provincial law school seemed a distant prospect at best. As late as autumn, 1913, Robson told the University of Manitoba's new president, James Alexander MacLean:[38] 'The Law School idea is developing slowly but I think surely.' Encouraged by the fact that 'lectures are taking more formal shape this year'[39] Robson sought to have Law Society lectures held in a university building so as to 'bring us into the desirable atmosphere of higher education.' Dr MacLean himself sought the creation of a university law school and Robson told him that this would 'in a small way be a start in the direction you have in mind.'[40]

The opening of not one, but two new law schools in Saskatchewan in October 1913[41] provided another sort of incentive for Manitoba's Law Society to review the matter. Robson, assisted by recent Osgoode Hall graduate E.K. Williams, was authorized by the benchers to 'lay plans for the establishment ... of a permanent law school modelled after Osgoode Hall.'[42] Fearful of private crammers, pressured by law students and professional leaders alike, shamed by the example of other prairie legal professions, the Law Society finally acted.

What emerged was an innovative arrangement for a school of law run as a sort of joint enterprise of the university and the Law Society under the governance of a 'Board of Trustees'[43] – much as Aikins and Chevrier had recommended in their 1909 Report. In June 1914 the University of Manitoba approved a 'plan for legal institution.'[44] The form of the board of trustees suggested equal control and influence by the university and the

Law Society but in fact the university was careful to ensure that its appointees were acceptable to the Law Society. Winnipeg lawyer Edwin Loftus served with Rev. Dr G.B. Wilson as university appointees on the first board. With Robson as chair and two lawyers (I. Campbell and J.H. Munson) serving as Law Society appointees[45] the dominance of elite lawyers in structuring legal education was ensured. To underline the point, the early board took the view that even the academic decisions of the school should be subject to Law Society review[46] and the outcomes of their deliberations were routinely brought to the Law Society for approval. Moreover, the Law Society retained in full its power to make rules for admission to practice in the province.[47] Informally and behind the scenes, the influence of the benchers was no doubt greater still.

The law school's first classes were taught in the YMCA building on 5 October 1914. There was initially no developed pedagogy, no dean, and no teaching staff other than a 'recorder,' R.P. Hills, 'assisted by seven practising lawyers as part-time lecturers.'[48] The school offered two programs, an 'academic' bachelor of laws and a practice-oriented program of qualification for solicitor's practice. Carefully structured incentives made the academic program highly attractive and most students near Winnipeg in fact took both programs. The law school at first operated as a supplement to the pre-existing apprenticeship structure, its courses running concurrently with articles and taught outside of normal office hours. An early curriculum explained that the course would cover 'work necessary for Bachelor of Laws degree from the University or for admission as an Attorney at Law by the Law Society. It does not include the special reading for the Call to the Bar, but Call examinations will be conducted by the Law School ... Graduates in Arts must serve a period of four years as clerks and students in articles; non-graduates must serve five years. Those who complete Manitoba Law School will have this period reduced by one year.'[49] Limited though it seems in retrospect, this was a significant turning point. One historian has observed that '[t]he seeds of didactic legal education as a basic component of training had now been firmly sown ...'[50]

Not surprisingly, the years of the Great War produced few opportunities for further development. The law school survived, however. Apart from some change in personnel,[51] it entered the post-war period more or less as it had begun, as a three-year, part-time, program. Radical change was to come. Despite the disruptions of war, Manitoba lawyers and the Canadian Bar Association (within which Manitobans clearly constituted a hegemonic fraction) had been giving careful consideration to the reform of legal education. An early indicator that significant change was contemplated was the gradual increase in admission requirements. By 1919–20 admission to the law school was restricted to those who had completed 'First Year in Arts of the University of Manitoba or its equivalent,'[52] a requirement clearly signalling a conviction that lawyers should be both learned and cultured. More fundamental change followed with surprising speed.

PROFESSIONAL EDUCATION IN MANITOBA: THE EARLY VISION, 1914–1921

It is important to recognize that the changes that created the law school's 'Golden Age' (1921–7) had been anticipated and planned from the start. Probably influenced by progressive ideas about legal education in the United States,[53] the arrangements that came into being in the 1920s were more or less fully formed in the heads of James Aikins, H.A. Robson, and others ten or even twenty years before they were implemented. Despite the misfortune of being launched just as Canada was drawn into 'total' war, the law school's first six years provided a crucial testing ground for new ideas about training for lawyering. Lacking either the staff or facilities one might think necessary to implement any 'program' whatsoever, the early board of trustees nonetheless sought to create a program of legal education that would be a continental leader. They endorsed all that was considered 'state-of-the-art' at the time: the case method, the goal of making attendance at law school the necessary and sufficient method of qualification for the legal profession, an ambition to create a full-time staff of professional law teachers, and a pedagogical vision embracing both 'cultural' and 'practical' legal education. There was also, from the beginning, a desire to raise admission standards, perhaps even to the point of requiring that all law students be university graduates.

Although everything the board of trustees sought was to become established throughout common law Canada in the decades to come, these were radical ideas for their time and place.[54] Many Manitoba lawyers probably did not endorse these visions – if they thought about them at all – and there were probably differences of opinion on particulars even amongst the law school's lecturers and trustees. Nonetheless, the early Board moved consistently in these directions.

Displacing Apprenticeship

The clearest articulation of Manitoba legal educators' ambitions is found in the writings and correspondence of H.A. Robson. In 1914 he told the board of trustees '[t]he ultimate aim' was to establish 'attendance at the Law School and passing the examinations thereof' as 'the exclusive method of call to the bar or admission as a solicitor' and expressed his view that teaching should be done by professional, full-time instructors.[55] Manitoba's large geographic area and substantial rural population made it practically impossible to actually *require* attendance at a Winnipeg law school, but Robson proposed that the period of articles be shortened for those who did attend and that the lecturers should also serve as examiners for all student lawyers in the province. His intent clearly was to do indirectly that which could not be done directly: to create a system 'practically equivalent to making law school attendance compulsory.'[56] Robson hoped that formal legal education would, in time, displace apprenticeship altogether.[57] He told his fellow trustees: 'If we follow the pure Law School method there would be no office attendance requirement for students taking that method except in the "Barrister's year," and a substitute method of student enrollment would be adopted by the Law Society.'[58]

Although he quickly retreated from his objective of making 'University examination and degree the only means of obtaining admission as a Solicitor or Call to the Bar,'[59] Robson viewed this as only a temporary, strategic, concession in the battle to drag Manitoba 'out of the backward state in which it now is in respect of the important subject of legal education.'[60] Frustrated by the *real politick* surrounding professional innovation, he felt that the 'idea will ultimately come, but it is too big a step to take at once.'[61]

'Scientific' Legal Education: The Case Method

In early twentieth-century Canada 'science' and technocratic thought was looked to by many as providing the means to peaceful resolution of social and economic problems.[62] Not surprisingly, many thoughtful Canadian lawyers saw the creation of a 'scientific' legal education as their contribution to this larger project. Fortunately, a 'science' was readily available in the form of the 'case method' of legal instruction developed by the Harvard Law School's innovative dean, Christopher Columbus Langdell.[63] Langdell's 'case teaching' was considered state-of-the-art in these years. In 1914 the Carnegie Foundation released an influential report endorsing the approach.[64] By that time Langdell's method had already attained almost complete dominance at leading U.S. centres of legal instruction:[65] '[t]he spirit of scientific expertise inspired the generation of law teachers who spanned the Progressive era after the turn of the century.'[66] 'Scientific,' 'practical,' somewhat Darwinian, the case method resonated well with the dominant cultural ethos of early twentieth-century North America.[67] It also reflected and reinforced the political status quo.[68]

In the introduction to his ground-breaking 1891 *Cases on Contracts* Langdell explained that the science of law consisted of principles found in the decided cases:

To have such a mastery of these as to be able to apply them with constant facility and certainty to the ever-tangled skein of human affairs, is what constitutes a true lawyer; and hence to acquire that mastery should be the business of every earnest student of law ... [M]uch the shortest and best, if not the only way of mastering the doctrine effectively is by studying the cases in which it is embodied ... It seems to me, therefore, to be possible to take such a branch of the law as Contracts, for example, and without exceeding comparatively moderate limits, to select, classify, and arrange all the cases which had contributed in any important degree to the growth, development, or establishment of any of its essential doctrines; and that such a work could not fail to be of material service to all who desire to study that branch of law systematically and in its original sources.[69]

Law was a science, the library its laboratory, the case approach its method.

In practice, the study of appellate decisions 'became entangled with the question-and-answer technique, similar in purpose and form to the traditional law school "quiz".'[70] The 'method' sought to displace lectures delivered in podium-down fashion, to passive student note takers. Instead, instructor-interrogators would pepper students with questions, leading or bullying them to discover fundamental principles of law for themselves. It aimed not to convey information but to teach students to teach themselves, to 'think like lawyers.' 'The law teacher's task,' Kyer and Bickenbach argue, 'was changed from that of setting out the principles and practices of the law to the considerably more challenging one of selecting and presenting cases that embodied or exemplified legal principles and, through a process of careful questioning, drawing out these principles from the responses of his students.'[71] This task was enthusiastically taken up by a new breed of full-time U.S. law teachers who 'happily made the change from treatise-reading clerk to flamboyant actor in a drama.'[72]

The outstanding early Canadian master of the method was the University of Saskatchewan's Thaddeaus Hébert. He assigned

specific cases from the law reports for students to read and study with care. They had to be prepared to state in class the essential facts of a case, the precise decision made by the judges on the facts, and the legal reasoning given for the decision. The student (or perhaps I should say the victim) who reported on a particular case was then questioned by the instructor and by such of his fellow students as found some defect in his report. Did he think the decision right or wrong by law? Why? What facts had been decisive in the opinion of the judges? How did he distinguish this decision from that in other cases on similar facts where the decision had been different?

Then, if the distinction could not be made clearly other, often suppositious, cases would be put to the student – or to the class as a whole. What was the right answer in these cases? Could he reconcile his views on these hypothetical cases with the judgment in the principle case as he had reported it? If there were strong differences of view within the class as a whole, there might be a torrent of suppositious cases to be analysed.

The immediate purpose was to shake the student in the view he had adopted, entice him into adopting indefensible positions, and trap him into contradicting himself. Any other student who had expressed firm views would be given the same treatment. It was a great victory to get most of the class confused. The longer-run purpose, of course, was to rouse the student's critical faculties, sharpen his mind, compel him to think clearly and consistently, and make him wary of pitfalls. In short, the objective was to make him think, as a lawyer must, about all sides of the facts and to anticipate opposing legal arguments which would almost certainly be raised in a courtroom.[73]

Advocates of the 'Socratic' method considered it to be a significant advance over the formal lecture method 'inherited from English universities.' This older approach to teaching, developed in a period before books were readily available, did offer the advantage of clarity of exposition. It tended, however, as C.R. Smith noted in 1935, 'to degenerate into dictation of notes by the lecturer, written down at breakneck speed by the students.' Even at its best, 'the formal lecture ... does very little to develop the power of analysis and gives little practice in expression and argument.'[74] It was not always at its best: Cecil Wright said his student experience at Osgoode Hall involved entirely uninspired lectures, dogmatic presentation, furious note taking, and the assignment of a solitary textbook, slavishly followed by students and lecturer alike.[75] The Socratic method should not be confused with other teaching styles that attempt to draw students into discussion:[76] there is a world of difference between the sort of education students experienced at Hébert's hands and less combative classroom discussions. Few students exposed to 'discussional' teaching think of themselves as 'victims.' Non-Socratic teachers do not relish leaving a class confused, nor do they seek to generate 'perplexity, frustration, and anger.'[77]

Willis has observed that 'the case method is something more' than discussional teaching 'and more rigorous and more demanding both of teacher and of student.'[78] Because of the peculiar demands it imposed, the case method became associated both with the view that legal education should take place within a university setting (the appropriate place for study of a 'science' rather than a craft) and with an emphasis on the need for a full-time teaching staff, who alone would be able to take on the rigorous preparation that such teaching required.[79]

It is not surprising that the case method became the focus of pedagogical innovation in Manitoba. Although Dalhousie,[80] Saskatchewan,[81] and Osgoode Hall Law School[82] each claim the first Canadian adoption of the case method, the Manitoba Law School made the approach integral to its mission at least five years earlier. As early as 1914 Manitoba legal educators invested considerable effort in developing teaching materials and a curriculum that would Canadianize this leading-edge teaching strategy imported from south of the border. Although their efforts to emulate an approach none of them had experienced first-hand were probably imperfect, the earliest Manitoba Law School curriculum demonstrates their commitment to and enthusiasm for the task.

Two commercially published casebooks developed by Manitoba law teachers appeared in 1916. Both were compiled jointly by H.A. Robson and J.B. Hugg. Unfortunately the editors were parsimonious with introductory or prefatory material and the volumes consequently lack any clear statement of educational philosophy. The preface to *Leading Cases on Public Corporations* explains simply that their 'collection of cases' in the area of municipal law brought together numerous 'judicial discussions of important topics.' The editors provide little insight into the principles of selection that motivated them, promising only that the book offered an 'interesting ... opportunity' to examine 'side by side the considered work of the representative English and Canadian Judges.' Despite the volume's title, they declared their intent to present cases of educational value rather than 'leading' status as such: 'Clear expositions of principles have been sought for rather than cases in which the principles have been first laid down.'[83]

The preface to *Cases on Company Law* explained only that '[t]he desirability of placing actual cases on Company Law before law students was the motive for this collection.'[84] No doubt this points in part to a desire to provide students with miniature portable law libraries at a time when access to extensive legal materials could be difficult.[85] This was only part of what motivated their work, however. Robson and Hugg provided a somewhat fuller explanation of their jurisprudential assumptions in the volume's introduction. Despite variations in the statutory schemes governing companies from one place to another, the editors quite deliberately included cases from several jurisdictions. They justified this approach on the grounds that each statutory scheme was undergirded by 'the same solid body of general principles as expressed in a thoroughly matured jurisprudence ...' As in 'many other branches of our law' they thought '[t]he differences in the organic provisions and in the details of regulation' were 'easy to grasp.'[86]

The introduction concluded with a testimonial to the superiority of a legal education focused on reading judicial decisions over one organized around assigned textbooks. The editors explained that, though the cases were arranged under headings and subheadings, '... a perusal of the selected judgments will expose a view broader in comprehension than would be indicated merely by the topic under which the case is usually cited. The disquisitions of learned Judges are more illuminating than a text writer's epitomes.' The excerpted cases were said to 'faithfully state the principle and indicate its origin, that is to say, the leading case ... the student by means of the cases used will get the leading cases. It is not merely the selected cases that he is to learn, but the cases referred to in them, and which form their foundation.'[87]

Turning from the expressed 'philosophy' of these volumes (such as it is) to their substance, it is notable that the table of contents for *Leading Cases on Public Corporations* has only one substantive heading and that – 'Leading Cases' – is not very helpful. The editors expended little effort in creative taxonomy and, as the following excerpt illustrates, the cases are unadorned, explained only by a brief parenthetical note indicating the principle of law addressed.

Only one case is presented in support of each principle and the excerpts are brief. Much of what later came to be thought of as part-and-parcel of the case method is missing. There is, for example, no critical engagement of point and counterpoint, no seeking out of the difficult, confusing, or brilliantly misleading judicial analysis. There are no excerpts from secondary literature, no editorial notes, comments, critiques, or recommended further readings. The volume makes no attempt to encourage policy critique by exposing students to divergent streams of judicial opinion. The only user's guide is a lengthy 'Table of Cases' indexing cases cited in the volume ('Leading Cases' are italicized).

Cases on Company Law, which appeared several months later, is similar in form though somewhat more developed in arrangement. Cases are classified by subject and the volume is divided into twenty-five chapters, most of which reproduce portions of several cases. Chapter two is divided into two parts, as indicated in the following excerpt.

II. Obligation to Take Shares

A. *Company Incorporated by Registration*

B. *Company Incorporated by Letters Patent*

London Speaker Printing Co., In re The.
   (Assumed Subscription before Actual Incorporation) 20
Speight Mfg. Co., In re The.
   (Assumed Subscription before Actual Incorporation) 20

An editors' note in the volume (a single paragraph) provides further references on the 'Effect of Local Laws upon International Comity' in relation to recognition of foreign corporations. Though more sophisticated than its sister volume, *Cases on Company Law* remains a rudimentary first effort. From our post-realist vantage point it is easy to dismiss the work as a failure, the smallest possible deviation from the black-letter tradition, amounting at best to a crude and oversimplified digest. The editors, had they wished, might as easily have written a 'nutshell' pamphlet of ten or twenty pages listing a series of propositions, each supported by citation of a single case.

Like much western Canadian legal history these books have been overlooked. From one point of view the oversight may be insignificant, if indeed the volumes fail to qualify either as 'casebooks' properly understood or as a significant contribution to Canadian legal education. Kyer and Bickenbach's brilliant assessment of Toronto legal education, for example, defines 'a Langdellian casebook' as a volume 'intended to be not merely a compendium of current decisions, but a tool for leading students through a line of legal argument.' In such a volume, 'cases are selected more as examples of legal reasoning than as "leading cases" setting out current law.'[88] Their disqualification of two other early volumes seems to establish standards by which Robson and Hugg's efforts also fail. Cockle's *Cases on Evidence* does not qualify, they say, because 'selected cases, heavily edited, were set out with the aim of presenting the "textbook" rules.'[89] A.H.F. Lefroy's *Leading Cases in Canadian Constitutional Law*[90] is similarly dismissed as too 'English,' too 'black letter,' mechanically reproducing cases reflecting current law. Lefroy, 'instead of offering for discussion cases that might not state current law, but were there to show the evolution of leading principles ... collected cases that stated the law applicable at the date of publication.'[91] Robson and Hugg's work is clearly closer to Lefroy's effort than to the idealized 'Langdellian casebook' Kyer and Bickenbach prefer.

We need to be careful though not to overlook one historical achievement merely because it is not identical to another. In the history of legal thought and legal education it is important not to conflate either 'cultural' legal education or 'case method' with the forms of American legal realism and rule scepticism that subsequently affected Canadian academic law teaching. At a minimum the two Manitoba volumes demonstrate a conviction that law is to be found in the decisions of the courts and that a study of the primary sources of law provided the best possible education in both substantive legal knowledge *and* desirable habits of legal thought. The editors clearly thought their work marked a significant departure from the more traditional study of 'text writer's epitomes.' They certainly had good reason to think that their materials contributed to establishing a new method of legal education in Canada. The significance of a new Canadian approach to legal education premised on the notions that '[t]he common law was a set of internally consistent and coherent general rules, which expressed important moral and social standards, but which were autonomous or independent from their immediate context'[92] should not be overlooked merely because it is the opposite of later approaches. Moreover, Robson had frequently expressed his desire to push Manitoba into compliance with the 'modern ideas of law teaching' of U.S. University law schools.[93] The two co-editors would have endorsed J.T. Hébert's classic argument that the case method provided an altogether superior training in legal reasoning: 'it makes him study the opinions of the great lawyers of the past, and it compels him to reach his own conclusions on the same or similar legal problems. It teaches him the law as it is, in a manner which, interesting if not easy, indelibly fixes it in his mind, and gives him a just appreciation of its application to the specific questions which are going to come before him as a practising lawyer, and where the law is uncertain or unsatisfactory, it offers him the opportunity and the means to find out what it ought to be.'[94] Manitoba's earliest casebooks exposed students to 'the opinions of great lawyers,' forcing them to seek out principles for themselves in order to discern the 'law as it is' *and* to absorb the method by which uncertainty can be approached. Near in both space and time to Hébert, it is reasonable to infer that Robson and Hugg inhabited a similar discursive universe and shared something of his educational vision. All told, these books marked a significant departure from past practice and their achievement should not now be underestimated. Given the leadership – indeed, dominance – of the Manitoba legal profession in the work of the early Canadian Bar Association, this prairie experiment provides something of a benchmark in the history of Canadian legal education.[95]

Commitment to the case method at the early Manitoba Law School is also manifest in other ways. In 1914 the board of trustees had established a committee (Robson and Hugg) to consider the utility of the 'case system'[96] and Robson wrote to Pitblado early in 1915 indicating that his draft curriculum incorporated 'a number of "Case Books".' This, he said, was to be 'a growing feature but I think we are going as far as possible just now in that direction.'[97] One early draft curriculum emphasized an intended reliance on teaching through the cases:

First Year.
Contracts: Caporn's *Leading Cases on Contracts*
English Constitutional Law and History: *Thomas Leading Cases*

Second Year.
Evidence: *Cockles' Leading Cases*
Canadian Constitutional Law: *Lefroy's Leading Cases*

Third Year.
Equity: *Randall's Leading Cases*
Torts: *Radcliffe and Miles Cases illustrating the Law of Torts*

Fourth Year (barrister's examinations).
International Law: *Bentwick Leading Cases and Statutes*[98]

Ultimately, the curriculum adopted for the 1914–15 academic year was more conventional than this suggested.[99] The case method was however in the air and certainly would have been implemented to some extent in the teaching of Robson, Hugg, and other members of the early faculty (another Manitoba law teacher of the same period, R.F. McWilliams, edited the second edition of Lefroy's *Leading Cases in Canadian Constitutional Law*).[100] In addition to assigning treatises and 'casebooks,' the school also produced pamphlets listing cases that were recommended reading in various courses.

Speeches delivered at the opening ceremonies for the new school also underlined its founders' intentions. The ubiquitous James Aikins (by now founding president of the Canadian Bar Association) delivered an 'Inaugural Address' emphasizing the expectation that the case method would make students 'enthusiastic lawyers, interested and absorbed in their profession':[101]

It is not the purpose of the school simply to instruct in text books, but rather in cases which decide principles and which system has to some extent changed the teaching of law in some parts of Canada and in the United States, and is being adopted in England ... There is an advantage in teaching case law for when once the student has vividly before him a concrete instance he will remember the principle decided much more readily than by reading the principle alone. The tendency will be for the students to examine with greater accuracy any question submitted, having studied decided cases, than they will from simply reading a text book which states only general principles.

.....

In the study of case law, the student is really teaching himself and will become more thoroughly conversant with the law in that way than if he was simply a docile listener to a dry lecture. The purpose of this school is to make the students know the law not superficially, but to take them to the very fundamentals of what they seek to know, and thus create in them an inextinguishable desire to become perfect as students, ambitious to know thoroughly the law.[102]

For Aikins the case method was central to the law school's educational mission. It would make its students superior lawyers, more competent advisers, more learned professionals and – importantly – better 'men.'

Unfortunately, little evidence survives to tell us how the case method was embodied in its teachers, lived by its students. We cannot know precisely in what form the method flourished in the early Manitoba law school, nor even whether its teachers were competent in 'Socratic' instruction. Such matters will unfortunately remain mysteries unless student notebooks, teacher's lecture notes, diaries, or reminiscences speaking to these matters turn up.

'Scientific' Legal Education: Curriculum

More evidence is available with respect to another educational innovation of the early Manitoba Law School. This was the attempt to create an education that would simultaneously provide 'guild training' in law practice and the 'professional education'[103] required of a new breed of cultured gentleman[104] lawyers. The school's curriculum from 1914 to 1920 incorporated relatively heavy doses of 'cultural' education.

In order to appreciate the significance of these developments it must be remembered that 'the really distinctive characteristic' of Dalhousie's celebrated law school (founded three decades earlier) had been its focus on the '"cultural" or "public law" subjects of Constitutional History, International Law, and Conflict of Laws.' Courses such as these were lacking at Harvard, for example, where legal education was limited 'to subjects which would be of immediate use to the hard-shell practitioner.'[105] These were still highly controversial components of professional education when Manitoba's law school was launched. Well into the twentieth century such offerings stood beyond the pale of 'practitioners''' training. When W.P.M. Kennedy founded an academic program in law at the University of Toronto in 1926, its commitment to 'law as a science' and distancing from practical training was marked out by a singularly unpractical curriculum 'focused on Roman law, the history of English law, English and Canadian constitutional law, jurisprudence, international law, and – rare in Canada – Canadian administrative and municipal law.' Such courses 'were viewed by lawyers as being of limited practical importance, and indeed as having little to do with the law.'[106] Kennedy's program brought its students no qualification recognized by Ontario's Law Society. This unlawyerly 'scientific' legal education of the 1920s, however, reproduced to a large extent courses that Manitoba lawyers had been forced to study *as part of qualification for practice* throughout the proceeding decade. The Manitoba Law Society's embrace of the 'intellectual' or 'cultural' agenda was, then, remarkable.

The following list excludes readings required for the barrister's examinations, which were set by the Law Society and not part of the Law School curriculum as such. It includes courses that were part of the basic professional curriculum as well as those required of students taking the LLB degree. The imposition of a 'cultural curriculum' on non-degree students speaks powerfully to the educational vision of Manitoba's early legal educators.[107]

Constitutional History of Canada with special reference to BNA Act (Bourinot's Manual) [first year, 1914–1915]
Canadian Constitutional Law [second year, 1915–16, 1916–17, 1917–18, 1918–19]
Canadian Constitutional Law and History [second year, 1919–20]
English Constitution Law and History [first year, 1915–16]
History of English Law [third year, 1915–16, 1916–17, 1917–18, 1918–19, 1919–20, 1920–1]
Roman Law [second year, 1915–16, 1916–17, 1917–18, 1918–19, 1919–20, 1920–21]
Jurisprudence [first year, 1918–19, 1919–20, 1920–1]
International Law [third year, 1915–16, 1916–17, 1917–18, 1918–19, 1919–20, 1920–1]
Dicey's Conflict of Laws [second year, 1914–15]

Municipal Law [third year, 1915–16, 1916–17, 1917–18, 1918–19, 1919–20, 1920–1]

One reason why the Manitoba Law School went so far so fast may simply have been the practical necessity of justifying itself to the university. The curriculum was jointly negotiated and involved nominally distinct programs for professional qualification and the LLB degree. Furthermore, university president Dr J.A. MacLean, a classicist by training,[108] took an early active interest in the business of the law school and opposed the development of a narrowly practical curriculum.[109] The Law Society of Upper Canada's proprietary law school at Osgoode Hall, by comparison, suffered no such constraint.

One must be careful, however, of making too much of institutional structures. The structures in Manitoba were not imposed on a reluctant Law Society by politicians or university administrators but had been actively sought out by leading legal practitioners themselves. Influential working lawyers subscribed to a vision of professional education every bit as 'intellectual' or 'cultural' or 'scholarly' as that of any academic of the period. There is no evidence of conflict in Manitoba between 'the profession' and legal educators that is even remotely similar to that which characterized the story of legal education in twentieth-century Ontario. On the contrary, Manitoba's leading lawyers believed changing legal education from a merely mechanical to a scholarly undertaking would transform the profession for the good, making it useful to the state, and preserving Canada from the centrifugal forces that threatened it.[110]

MANITOBA'S GOLDEN AGE, 1921–1927

Manitoba's law school consolidated its past achievements and advanced rapidly during a brief golden age, quickly responding to recommendations of the Canadian Bar Association's Committee on Legal Education.[111] The system of concurrent articles was virtually abolished in 1921 and replaced with an arrangement whereby 'students were required to serve only one year in law offices; simultaneously with the Law School program in the case of university graduates, and after completion of the program in the case of nongraduates.'[112] In a bold move that unequivocally established the full-time character of the new program, teaching hours were extended 'throughout the business day' daily except for Saturday and holidays.[113] Manitoba also became the first Canadian law school to adopt the new model curriculum of the Canadian Bar Association[114] (see

TABLE 15.1

Comparison of Manitoba Law School Curriculum, 1922–1923,[116] and Canadian Bar Association, 'Standard Curriculum,' 1920

Manitoba Law School	*'Standard Curriculum'*
First Year	
Contracts	Contracts
Torts	Torts
Real Property	Property (Real and Personal) 1
Personal Property	
English Constitutional Law and History	Constitutional History
Criminal Law	Criminal Law
Civil Procedure	Practice and Procedure (Civil and Criminal)
Criminal Procedure	Elementary
History of English Law	History of English Law
Roman Law	Jurisprudence*
Second Year	
Equity	Equity 1
Wills	Wills and Administration
Evidence	Evidence 1
Sale of Goods	Sale of Goods
Bills and Notes	Bills and Notes
Agency	Agency
Corporations	Corporations and Partnership
Partnerships	
	Insurance
	Practice and Procedure
	(including instructions as to the use of
	law reports, digests, and textbooks)
Real Property	Property (Real and Personal) 2
Personal Property	
Landlord and Tenant Law	Landlord and Tenant
Ancient Law	
Third Year	
Constitutional Law and History (Canadian)	Constitutional Law
Equity – Trusts and Trustees	Equity 2
	Evidence
Practice and Procedure (Civil and Criminal)	Practice and Procedure (including
	criminal procedure)
Conflict of Laws	Conflict of Laws
Mortgages	Mortgages
Suretyship	Suretyship
Practical Statutes	Practical Statutes
Rules of Interpretation and Drafting	Rules of Interpretation and Drafting
	Shipping and/or Railway Law
Domestic Relations	Domestic Relations
Public International Law	Public International Law†
Jurisprudence	Jurisprudence† ‡
Legal Ethics	Legal Ethics†

*if not taken in the third year
† recommended if in accordance with the needs of the province or school
‡ if not taken in first year

Table 15.1) and to increase entrance requirements to 'second year Arts standing commencing in the 1921–1922 session.'[115]

Manitoba's curriculum was more 'cultural' than either Dalhousie's or the CBA's model. Advances were quick in other respects, too. J.T. Thorson,[117] a graduate of Manitoba College, Rhodes Scholar, and Manitoba lawyer, was appointed the faculty's first dean in May 1921. Two further full-time law professors were hired (H.W.H. Knott and Frederick Read) in 1922, bringing the school's staff up to the level attained by Dalhousie Law School at the beginning of its own 'golden age'[118] – and well surpassing the Law Society of Upper Canada's single full-time instructor at Osgoode Hall.[119] When Knott was sacked by the board of trustees in 1925 he was replaced by the formidable C. Rhodes Smith.

Anyone familiar with Canadian scholarship on the history of legal education will be puzzled by how it came about that Manitoba's profession-dominated school went further in scholarly directions than even the Canadian Bar Association Committee on Legal Education had recommended. This question, however, reverses the order of things. Historians have not generally realized that the most influential and creative force propelling 'cultural' legal education *for the profession* in this period was in fact Manitoba's working profession. Both the Canadian Bar Association and its Committee on Legal Education were very largely Manitoba creations: Sir James Aikins was founding father, eminence-grise, and president of the Canadian Bar Association: H.A. Robson headed the first CBA committee on legal education, laying the foundation on which the 1918 'Lee' committee report was built.[120] The related committee on legal ethics was chaired by Manitoba's Chief Justice Mathers.[121] When the education sub-committee ultimately recommended a curriculum similar to that of Dalhousie, Isaac Pitblado, a powerful Manitoba lawyer, spoke in its defence at the association's annual meeting.[122] Pitblado spoke with both authority and commitment: then in his seventeenth year as a bencher, third year as president of the Law Society, *and* chair of the University of Manitoba's first board of governors, he had consistently worked for the establishment of a Manitoba Law School.[123]

Both the active involvement of Manitobans in the development of the 'Lee Report' and their immediate embrace of its program make it clear that the leaders of the Manitoba profession were philosophically at one with the CBA committee. Lee, fortunately, was an articulate spokesperson for the arrangement who left a more substantial written record of his assumptions than his practitioner or judicial allies. It was, he thought, absurd to confine legal education to cramming students' heads with rules or, more narrowly still, teaching students how to practise law. These were not the purposes of the classroom. He considered the project of legal education to be primarily about developing and imparting a 'science' of law for the good of the larger political community.[124] In endorsing a wide vision of the purposes and functions of legal education, Lee's committee tapped a deep cultural current among elite Canadian lawyers of the day,[125] one which had professional antecedents both in mid-nineteenth century England[126] and in early Ontario (Upper Canada). There are distinct continuities of thought linking the proposals of Aikins, Lee, Robson, and others in the early twentieth century and Toronto's Arch Deacon John Strachan's oft-cited observations of 1826:

Lawyers must, from the very nature of our political institutions – from there being no great landed proprietors – no privileged orders – become the most powerful profession and must in time possess more influence and authority than any other ... [they should] acquire similar views and modes of thinking, and be taught by precept and example to love and venerate our parent state. It is surely of great consequence that a class of intelligent men belonging to a profession which offers the highest inducements of reputation, wealth, influence, and authority, should be actuated by sentiments and feelings of attachment to the British Empire.[127]

Not surprisingly, the newly structured law school quickly gained a reputation for excellence. It was hailed as a model for the rest of Canada by the chair of the Canadian Bar Association's committee on legal education in 1923,[128] and, in both 1926 and 1927, was found by the Carnegie Foundation to be the best law school in Canada.[129]

DECLINE, 1927–1931

The glory was, however, short-lived. Dean Thorson was elected to Parliament and departed to take his seat in the House of Commons in September 1926.[130] H.A. Robson (assisted by Edwin Loftus) assumed duties as acting dean without pay and on a part-time basis. Though it was probably not immediately apparent, the changes that were to follow were momentous. No full-time dean was again appointed for over a decade. Within two months of Thorson's departure the board of trustees approved a resolution requiring students to serve a full year in actual service under articles in the case of graduates, or a full two years for nongraduates.[131] This resolution never took effect, however, for it was supplanted by another that effectively sounded the death knell for academic legal education. Dale and Lee Gibson have reported a 'decision in 1927 to lengthen the Law

School course to four years, and to re-institute concurrent articling in the third and fourth years.'[132] Under the new rules all students were required to provide service in a law office during the last two years of their law school course. An additional year of apprenticeship was required of students who held no prior university degree.[133] Surprisingly, Robson, who had struggled so long and effectively to create full-time academic legal education, presided over its denouement. It has been suggested that there may have been a perception that the full-time program was 'too theoretical in nature'[134] but it is unclear what precisely this connotes.

DEMISE OF PROFESSIONAL EDUCATION, 1931

In July 1929 E.H. Coleman assumed duties as dean under a part-time arrangement that left him free to practise law in the afternoons.[135] Although he had been secretary to James Aikins in an unusually close and sustained relationship,[136] Coleman apparently shared little of his mentor's vision for the legal profession or legal education. Trained exclusively within Manitoba and uncontaminated by exposure to the leading educational institutions of the world, Coleman's tenure saw the last vestiges of a full-time program abolished. In 1931 the benchers established a requirement that 'all students should serve under articles for the entire four year period (5 years in the case of non-graduates) except for the time they were actually required to be in the classroom.'[137]

In barely a decade the school had come full circle. Its most daring innovations expunged entirely by 1931, the Manitoba Law School turned decisively away from full-time legal education for the next three decades. It was only in 1965, then well behind the rest of Canada, that Manitoba again launched full-time university legal education.[138]

It is curious that a small province with a tiny legal elite should have witnessed such rapid and contradictory changes in so short a period. What these changes may have symbolized to the key players in cultural or ideological terms is unclear and it is hard to determine why Manitoba turned so decisively away from full-time academic legal education after so short an experiment. The Canadian Bar Association's Committee on Legal Education explained:

In Manitoba a modification of the concurrent system was tried whereby the student was required to serve in an office only during the last two years of his four years' course – the course there having been extended from three to four years. But this system proved unsatisfactory, apparently because the student was not required to be articled before being admitted to the Law School. The result was that many students found, at the end of their first two years in the Law School, that they could not get into offices, and so were blocked in the midst of their course. To remedy this situation, Manitoba reverted to the old system.[139]

Writing twenty years after the last vestiges of a full-time program had been expunged, E.K. Williams explained:

We found that the students who passed through the school during the 1921–1931 period almost without exception felt that they had lost something by not having had any office training during their academic years. Although they had passed all the examinations entitling them to be called and admitted, they realized that they were not yet ready to practise law. They found, too, that the members of the profession generally preferred students who combined their academic work with practical experience in an office. There was, too, a very practical matter that entered into their consideration, and that was the salary they could earn as law students in an office.[140]

Jack London has asserted that Williams' reasoning in this regard is unpersuasive, noting that 'one of the inarticulate premises of the opposition of the lawyers to a full-time study programme might have been the deprivation of low-paid legal assistants for the practising law offices of the period.'[141]

Both Williams' account and London's 'market-control' explanation seem inadequate. Disentangling the various threads of principle, interest, ideology, and bluster surrounding legal education is, as anyone who has ever been near a law faculty knows, a virtually hopeless task. The explanation for the decline and fall of Manitoba's Law School is likely found in some combination of economic circumstances, the 'practical' demands of the profession, and competing visions of what it meant to be a lawyer. The mental image one holds of 'the good lawyer' profoundly affects the forms of legal education deemed necessary, the limits of acceptable compromise, and how excellence itself is defined and understood. The ascendancy of a vision that portrayed lawyering as a noble public calling was marked by the creation of the Canadian Bar Association and its initial flurry of activity. The notion that the legal profession had important obligations to community and state motivated professional reformers of this period. Their vision took institutional form in Thorson's School of Law.

A counter vision always persisted, however. Its more workaday view saw law as a business, legal work as capitalist enterprise, the lawyer as white-collar worker, and the law student as drudge. It is difficult to discern where virtue lies or which of these alternative professional visions is more clearly antisocial in its tendency. The broad tradition encompassing Strachan, Aikins, and, more recently, the Arthurs' Committee[142] has emphasized learning, scholarship, and the need for socially located understandings of the legal profession and its duties. Opponents of such visions have often seemed inarticulate, short-sighted, unthinking – sometimes incapable of thought. Paradoxically, however, the better articulated professional visions have often worked so as to create class, gender, and racial or ethnic barriers to admission to the legal profession.[143] 'Liberal advocacy' and all its contributions to democracy and human freedom[144] has often emerged from lawyers whose practices lay outside the pale of 'respectable' professionalism. In short, though the intellectual ambition, public spiritedness, and integrity of the Aikins tradition seems admirable, its social exclusivity, narrow definition of the public good, and elitism are not endearing features.

The question remains: why did Manitoba lawyers allow their state-of-the-art law school to die? It is a fair guess that Thorson's resignation from the deanship and James Aikin's death were significant factors. The more interesting question is not whether the force of their personalities was important in creating and sustaining a leading law school. Undeniably it was. What is puzzling, rather, is why the vision of powerful and influential professional reformers failed to take root within the leadership of the profession at large. Surviving accounts suggest only four possible reasons. These relate to cost, the public interest, lawyers' interests, and law students' interests. A fifth possible reason relates to the cultural projects of elite lawyers.

The possibility that the cost of providing a quality legal education was simply too great for the Law Society to bear should be taken seriously. Law Society finances in this period have not yet been researched by historians and the direct effect of financial considerations on legal education remains a matter of speculation. It is indeed possible that Manitoba simply could not afford state-of-the-art legal education during the Depression years.[145] There are, however, two reasons for thinking that finances were not the decisive consideration in the decline of Manitoba legal education. First and most directly, this is not the reason cited by those few Manitoba lawyers of the era who explained or commented upon the decision to downgrade their law school.

Second, even in difficult financial times available funds are allocated according to perceptions of relative priorities. Except in the most extreme circumstances – which apparently was not the situation of the Manitoba Law Society in this period[146] – an economic rationale can provide only partial explanation for cultural and institutional changes. Everything about how one perceives or understands legal education is coloured by personal inclinations with respect to the two competing and very different visions of lawyering. In the midst of the Great Depression, for example, members of the Canadian Bar Association Committee on Legal Education were surveyed on the question: 'In your opinion wherein does the lawyer, when admitted, fall short?' One member responded that 'times have so altered that the lawyer must lay less stress on the purely academical and become a practical everyday business adviser of his client.' Another responded in quite different vein: 'I must say that what I think it lacks most is scholarly interest in law. The lawyer seems to me to acquire quickly enough the technical tricks of his trade, and a knowledge of those business methods which are really tending to destroy the liberal character of the profession. Law is far too much regarded by law students as an avenue to eminence in big business. Where I think our legal education breaks down worst is in its failure to inculcate a love of law and the lawyer's work as a liberal mode of life.' The intellectual and professional orientation of these two unidentified gentlemen are clearly worlds apart.[147] The fact that their perceptions with regard to the desirable structure of legal education diverged so markedly even given a particular social, economic, and political context serves as a useful reminder that economic constraint rarely in fact dictates educational policy: budget concerns are themselves articulated against a backdrop of cultural and ideological assumptions.

The only 'public interest' that has been tied to the return to qualification by apprenticeship is E.K. Williams' assertion, quoted above, that law school graduates who had not served law office apprenticeships 'were not yet ready to practise law.' Exactly what he meant by this is unclear. It does seem likely that graduates of the full-time program would have known little about law office procedures, solicitor's form-filling, or the procedural niceties of barrister's practice. Even a very good graduate might have had little or none of the local 'recipe knowledge' that makes effective legal work possible.[148] Though defects such as these might have been met (as they are now) by a relatively brief stint of supervised work in a law office, law school graduates seeking their first professional employment found themselves in competition with less educated but nonetheless fully qualified new lawyers who had accumulated as much as five years of law office experience: the law school of the 1920s had never entirely displaced qualification by apprenticeship.

In such circumstances it is possible that the market may have spoken rather directly. Understandably, lawyers who employed newly qualified lawyers were more concerned with their own immediate profit maximization than any 'public interest' attached to mentoring a degreed profession. The market does not typically reward time invested in mentoring – at least, not in circumstances in which there is an available pool of lowly paid workers who, though not 'learned gentlemen,' are familiar with the mechanical side of law office work and immediately able to generate profit. The 'public interest' in having lawyers who could actually *do* law jobs overlapped with the 'private interest' of established lawyers. London's point that apprenticeship provided established lawyers with a pool of useful, inexpensive labour is certainly valid and need not be cynically understood. Sir George Stephen observed of the English profession in 1846 that, by performing repeated mundane tasks, articled clerks 'pick up a great deal of practical knowledge, more especially a great deal of familiarity with the peculiar business and papers of the clients of their employer; ... and they become of extreme value to him.' They were kept by their employers 'upon a very moderate salary,' Stephen said, 'probably with a view to ultimately making them partners, to take off the burthen of his business ...'[149] In short, the business and personal reasons why established lawyers would approve of the apprenticeship system are simple: the system worked to their personal pecuniary advantage. Only the wealthiest lawyers and the most saintly would feel no attraction to such a system.

The law students' interests in matters of professional education are reasonably clear, too. The intangible though not inconsiderable benefit of 'gentlemanly education' lay in the conferral of status on those who did not inherit it. For most people, most of the time, however, the pursuit of status is secondary to the search for food, shelter, and material comfort. Some law students voted with their feet, preferring office work, a modest salary, and the development of personal connections to three years off the job market in pursuit of a degree. Students in Manitoba as elsewhere sought out systematic legal education, regularity of instruction, and predictability in examination. An ambitious full-time program of 'cultural' legal education was unnecessary in relation to their most basic needs.[150]

A 'cultural' education of the sort Aikins, Robson, Lee, and Thorson sought to establish was clearly propelled by a transformative vision of professionalism subscribed to by an elite fraction of the early twentieth-century Canadian legal professions. Aimed explicitly at securing Anglo ascendancy and at inculcating values of 'Britishness' in lawyers regardless of their ethnic background, it was patently elitist. It is not clear, however, that opposition to structured legal education necessarily arose from any levelling instinct. Whereas apprenticeship systems of professional qualification can sustain illegitimate hierarchy by hiding its operation in the interstices of the 'private sphere,' the university's meritocratic warrants hold forth the promise of opening professions to talented individuals from discriminated-against groups. Articling certainly can serve as 'a kind of social screening device; undesirables – women, racial minorities, and Jews – knew that they would have to struggle to find and keep suitable articling employment.'[151] It remains possible, then, that Manitoba's cutting-edge law school may have caused offence in some quarters precisely because it provided a route to upward social mobility and legal influence for 'undesirables' in Canada's most multi-ethnic, polyglot province.

CONCLUSIONS

The failure of Manitoba's bold experiment in legal education was certainly noticed and talked about by lawyers in other provinces. The word that full-time academic education in law was undesirable went out, communicated privately, by word of mouth. Professional culture was (and is) formed less in formal correspondence and earnest publication than in conversation at gentlemen's clubs, Bar Association dinners, meals and drinks, golf games, and railway cars.[152] One result is that most of what lawyers told each other about these matters is shielded from the prying gaze of the historian. We can to some extent infer what they chattered about from two traces left behind.

When the Ontario Law Society's 'Special Committee' on legal education reported to Convocation in early 1935 it followed Manitoba's most recent lead, recommending lower admission standards, emphasizing office training over law school work, and criticizing the 'case method.'[153] A decade later, when the University of British Columbia's Faculty of Law was being created, Canada's westernmost province also felt ripple effects of Manitoba's earlier battles. Memory of Manitoba's experience haunted the new initiative and, apparently, caused some influential lawyers to resist it. C.H. Locke, 'treasurer' (i.e., president) of the Law Society of British Columbia, told Dean George Curtis in 1945 that he had opposed the creation of university legal education because he had 'been through all this in Manitoba' and was aware of 'the controversy there.'[154]

The Manitoba Law School's brief moment of glory was not unimportant in its day and not without consequences in the rest of Canada. The story is worthy of study for its own sake. It also stands as a reminder that historical significance cannot be geographically ascribed or 'read back' from the present. Metropolitan legal history is partial legal history.[155] Failed institutions can tell us as much, or more, about cultural evolution as accounts of institutional survivors. The curious question is perhaps not why the Manitoba Law School 'failed.' The greater mystery, rather, relates to why and how the sort of university law faculty we now take for granted could ever have become successfully established as the exclusive route to professional qualification in common law Canada. Although the outline history of events that produced this result is reasonably well known,[156] the shifting cultural terrain that made possible so remarkable a transformation only three decades after Manitoba's failed experiment has yet to be explored.

The hope remains, as Dick Risk observed a quarter-century ago, that the study of our legal past will 'give understanding and perspective'[157] as we confront the future. Many puzzles remain to be solved in pursuit of that mission. Canada's 'peripheral' places need to be part of the mix.

NOTES

1 Sir J. Aikins, 'Formal Opening of the Manitoba Law School. Inaugural Address to the Students by Sir James Aikins, K.C., M.P.' *Canadian Law Times* 34 (1914), 1183–90 at 1189.

2 D. Gibson and L. Gibson, *Substantial Justice: Law and Lawyers in Manitoba, 1670–1970* (Winnipeg: Peguis Publishers 1972), 302–4.

3 This diversity of opinion as to the purposes and functions of a legal education has a long lineage and was reflected in debates in mid-nineteenth century England which, like early twentieth-century Manitoba, also produced an innovative educational program that failed. See W. Pue, 'Guild Training versus Professional Education: The Department of Law at Queen's College, Birmingham in the 1850's,' *American Journal of Legal History* 22 (1989), 241–87 and writings cited therein.

4 Manitoba lawyers at this time were well attuned to the different histories and functions of solicitors and barristers and the use of different terms for individuals intent on work as barristers or solicitors characterized Law Society discussions in this period. See, for example, Law Society of Manitoba Minutes, 6 May 1910, varying the educational requirements of 'any student at law or articled clerk' (hereafter 'LSMM').

5 Gibson and Gibson, *Substantial Justice*, 128.

6 Cf. W. Pue, *Law School: The Story of Legal Education in British Columbia* (Van-

couver: Faculty of Law, University of British Columbia and Continuing Legal Education Society of British Columbia 1995), chap. 2, 'Indentured Labour,' 1–29. [also published at: http://www.law.ubc.ca/handbook/history/school.html].

7 J.R. London, 'The Admissions and Education Committee: A Perspective on Legal Education and Admission to Practice in the Province of Manitoba – Past, Present and Future,' in C. Harvey, ed., *The Law Society of Manitoba, 1877–1977* (Winnipeg: Peguis Publishers 1977), 74–120 at 77. The attempt to create law degrees as part of a 'liberal' education rather than as part of professional training has antecedents in nineteenth-century Ontario. See R.D. Gidney and W.P.J. Millar, *Professional Gentlemen: The Professions in Nineteenth-Century Ontario* (Toronto: University of Toronto Press 1994), 172–3; C. Moore, *The Law Society of Upper Canada and Ontario's Lawyers 1797–1997* (Toronto: University of Toronto Press 1997), 114–18.

8 Letter to L.G. McPhillips of Vancouver, author unknown, 29 May 1909 (Archive of Manitoba Legal-Judicial History, Public Archives of Manitoba – hereafter 'AMLJH' – file A225).

9 See Gibson and Gibson, *Substantial Justice*, 129 (Chief Justice Wood's 1877 lectures and subsequent Law Society lectures). See also AMLJH file A225; LSMM, 12 January 1903 (Report of Law Society of Manitoba Examining Committee, establishing a course of lectures pursuant to student petition), 7 February 1905 (complaint by D.R. White, 'Secretary of the Law Students' Society,' resulted in appointment of James Aikins and Isaac Pitblado 'to discuss with the University of Manitoba a course of lectures in connection with the LL.B. course'), 7 December 1906 (petition from the Law Students' Society asking for a course of lectures, referred to a special committee of the president, Mr Wilson, and Mr Cameron), 7 January 1907, 9 October 1907, 14 October 1907; 28 October 1907, 11 November 1908, 28 October 1909.

10 The mixture of interests and discursive strategies is well reflected in 'Quill,' 'Correspondence,' Vancouver Law Students' Annual (1911) 17–18 (and see discussion of this piece in Pue, *Law School*, 36–8.

11 See note 8, supra.

12 The LSMM 29 September 1908 record, for example, that 'in response to a letter from Mr. W.H. Trueman, secretary to write and say no idea of establishing a Law School at the present time.' Trueman was a frequent lecturer in the early courses of lectures and in 1915 was briefly named head of the teaching staff of the new Manitoba Law School. LSMM, 19 February 1915. Gibson and Gibson, *Substantial Justice*, 216, argue (mistakenly I believe) that Toronto's Osgoode Hall Law School provided the blueprint from which the Manitoba Law School was developed.

13 The *Report by J.A.M. Aikins and Rev. A.A. Chevrier on the University and professional training. Commission appointed 26 Sept. 1907. Report delivered in the fall of 1909* (University of Manitoba Archives [hereafter UMA] 20, Box 7, Folder 5, P378.7127 W B MS) records a petition received from apprenticing lawyers: 'That it is the desire of many of the Manitoba Students-at-Law, owing to the obvious disadvantages under which we as a student body are labouring in our study of the principles of law, that a law school be established in connection with the University of Manitoba.'

A similar recommendation was made by Ontario's 1906 Royal Commission on the University of Toronto, chaired by J. Flavelle, 'that a Faculty of Law should be established in the University' under arrangements agreed between the university and the provincial Law Society. Ontario's Law Society rejected this notion altogether: see C.I. Kyer and J.E. Bickenbach, *The Fiercest Debate: Cecil A. Wright, the Benchers and Legal Education in Ontario 1923–1957* (Toronto: The Osgoode Society for Canadian Legal History 1987), 36.

14 15 December 1910. 'Desire University Control' (AMLJH, Law Society of Manitoba Newspaper Clipping Scrapbooks, unidentified 1910 newspaper clipping).

15 For example, LSMM, 17 December 1909, record that three law students (identified as 'Adamson, Baker and Martin') sought the benchers' permission to count time in attendance in a law school in another jurisdiction as part of their apprenticeship. Though their request was initially denied on the grounds that the Law Society Act did not permit it, the benchers agreed to seek the necessary changes in their governing statute. A few months later they agreed to allow up to a year's leave of absence to non-graduate apprenticing lawyers (and up to six months for university graduates) for a student wishing to study law at a law school in Canada, the United States, or England. (LSMM, 6 May 1910, and the account provided in a newspaper clipping of 6 June 1910, 'Rules for Law Students'; AMLJH, Law Society of Manitoba Newspaper Clipping Scrapbooks, unidentified newspaper clipping. These events are discussed by L. Gibson, 'A Brief History of the Law Society of Manitoba,' in Harvey, ed., *The Law Society of Manitoba*, 28–53 at 33 and by Gibson and Gibson, *Substantial Justice*, 216, who point to this as the first explicit acknowledgment by the benchers that systematic legal instruction was of value in training for the legal profession. In fact, during the next four years at least a dozen students attended law schools outside of the province with the approval of the Law Society. LSMM record their approvals as follows: 14 June 1910 (E.G.P. Balser, W. Martin, A.E. Dilts); 27 September 1910 ('four students ... to attend Osgoode Hall Law School'); 7 June 1912 (G.C. Lindsay 'to attend the Law School at the University of Chicago'); 14 May 1913

(L.P. Napier credited with 'two terms at the Inner Temple'); 10 June 1913 (William Nasore – illegible – to attend Oriel College, Oxford, for six months); 30 September 1913 (C.D. Roblin to attend Osgoode Hall; F.C.S. Davision to attend law lectures at England's University of London). Other indicators of student calls to create a law school include: Letter to the benchers from Mr E.D. Honeyman, 20 February 20 1911 (AMLJH file, A225); LSMM, 21 February 1911 (recording receipt of a letter from 'the Law Students' Association'); LSMM, 28 November 1911 (response to request from the 'Winnipeg Law Students' Society').

16 See LSMM, 7 February 1905 (Aikins and Pitblado formed a committee to discuss with the University of Manitoba a course of lectures in connection with the LL.B. course); 15 February 1910 (Pitblado's notice of motion re establishment of a law school either by the Law Society or in connection with the University of Manitoba); *Tribune*, 16 May 1914 (Pitblado reported as saying that 'the Law society was determined to establish a law school, and that it would be a great mistake if the university did not take it under its wing.' UMA 20, Box 8, Folder 2).

17 Gibson and Gibson, *Substantial Justice*, 219–20.

18 'Manitoba Bar Association Born at Banquet,' *Winnipeg Telegram*, 10 November 1911 (AMLJH, Law Society of Manitoba Newspaper Clipping Scrapbooks).

19 'Aikins Entertains Local Barristers,' 1911 (AMLJH, Law Society of Manitoba Newspaper Clipping Scrapbooks, unidentified newspaper clipping).

20 'Desire University Control,' 15 December 1910 (AMLJH, Law Society of Manitoba Newspaper Clipping Scrapbooks, unidentified 1910 newspaper clipping). The attorney general at this time was Colin Campbell.

21 *Report by J.A.M. Aikins and Rev. A.A. Chevrier on the University and professional training*, 73 (UMA 20, Box 7, Folder 5, P378.7127 W B MS).

22 W.L. Morton, *One University: A History of the University of Manitoba, 1877–1952* (Toronto: McClelland & Stewart 1957), 65 describes Aikins and Chevrier as 'traditionalists' who 'accepted the original organization of the university with its denominational control through the constituent colleges supported by the churches and private benefactors, but coupled with a modicum of state aid for the maintenance of an examining body and a teaching faculty limited to the natural sciences.'

23 See note 21, supra.

24 See R.H. Kersley, *Gibson's 1876–1962: A Chapter in Legal Education* (London: Law Notes Lending Library 1973); W.R. Johnson, *Schooled Lawyers: A Study in the Clash of Professional Cultures* (New York: New York University Press 1978); R. Stevens, *Law School: Legal Education in America from the 1850s to the 1980s* (Chapel Hill: University of North Carolina Press 1983).

25 LSMM, 8 March 1912.

26 Brandon's G.R. Coldwell was a bencher of the Law Society of Manitoba from 1898 to 1916. Harvey, ed., *The Law Society of Manitoba*, 278. Coldwell is an important figure in C. Backhouse's 'The Legal Prohibition of Aboriginal Dance on the Canadian Prairies: The 1902 Trial of Wanduta' (paper presented at Canadian Legal History Conference, 'Exploring Canada's Legal Past,' University of Toronto, 7–9 May 1998): I am grateful to Professor Backhouse for sharing her information about Coldwell with me. There are notes on Coldwell in the Index Cards of the AMLJH citing M. Baker, *Manitoba's Third Legislative Building, Symbol in Stone, The Art and Politics of a Public Building* (Winnipeg: Hyperion Press 1986) as a principle source. Coldwell is also discussed in G.F. Barker, *Brandon: A City 1881–1961* (Altona: G.F. Barker 1977); 'Coldwell, Hon. Geo. Robson, K.C.,' in Major E.J. Chambers, ed., *The Canadian Parliamentary Guide 1915* (Ottawa: Gazette Printing 1915), at 428; W. Leland Clark, *Brandon's Politics and Politicians* (Altona: D. W. Friesen & Sons 1981), at 51–5, 71–5, 85; C.W. Parker, ed., *Who's Who and Why: A Biographical Dictionary of Men & Women of Canada and Newfoundland* (Vancouver: International Press 1914) 5:220; and 'Brandon,' *Western Sun* 15 January 1903.

27 'Would Give Women Right To Practice Law in Province,' *Winnipeg Telegram*, 7 March 1912.

28 Unidentified newspaper clipping, 1912 (AMLJH, Law Society of Manitoba Newspaper Clipping Scrapbooks, Clip 83–69, 21).

29 F. Edge, *The Iron Rose – The Extraordinary Life of Charlotte Ross, M.D.* (Winnipeg: University of Manitoba Press 1992). (James Aikins had been Ross's lawyer in some of her struggles with the Manitoba medical profession.) Gidney and Millar, *Professional Gentlemen*, 39, point to the lack of conceptual clarity around the idea of 'irregular practice' that characterized nineteenth-century thought and their point applies equally to law and medicine. Effective policing of professional monopoly only became established during the middle half of the twentieth century.

30 See J.W. Hamilton, 'Metaphors of Lawyers' Professionalism,' *Alberta Law Review* 33 (1995), 833–58; W. Pue, 'Becoming "Ethical": Lawyers' Professional Ethics in Early Twentieth Century Canada,' *Manitoba Law Journal* 20 (1991), 227–61 [also published in D. Gibson and W. Pue, eds., *Glimpses of Canadian Legal History* (Legal Research Institute, University of Manitoba, Fall 1991), 237–77]; W. Pue, 'Common Law Legal Education in Canada's Age of Light, Soap and Water,' *Canada's Legal Inheritances*, symposium issue, *Manitoba Law Review* 23 (1996) (edited by Pue and Guth), 654–88; W. Pue, 'Revolution by Legal Means,' in P. Glenn, ed., *Contemporary Law 1994 Droit contemporain* (Montreal: Editions Yvons Blais 1994), 1–30.

31 H.M. Bates, Dean of the Law School, University of Michigan, 'Recent Progress in Legal Education' *U.S. Bureau of Education Report,* Chapter 10 (1914), 227.

32 J.H. Cohen, *The Law: Business or Profession?* (New York: Banks Law Publishing 1916), 138–9. Cohen concludes the observation: 'Education for the Bar must include moral training – if it is to be education for the Bar' (141). Though couched in the language of public interest and objective standards, the attempts of the 'better university schools' to raise their standards may itself have been the result of discriminatory and exclusionary motivations. See J.S. Auerbach, *Unequal Justice: Lawyers and Social Change in Modern America* (New York: Oxford 1976), chap. 4, 102–29. This interpretation is strongly corroborated by H.A. Robson's impressions of Columbia University's law program. Robson reported, favourably, that Columbia University's project of raising educational standards was a 'pious fraud.' See notes enclosed in a memo, H.A. Robson to President MacLean, 22 April 1914, UMA, 20, Box 10, Folder 5.

33 E.H. Coleman, 'Legal Education,' *Manitoba Bar News* (1933), 1–3, 5–6 at 2.

34 Ibid.

35 LSMM, 26 April 1912, indicates that the University Extension Society Bill was withdrawn.

36 Gibson, 'Brief History,' 33.

37 'Annual Banquet of Law Students,' 23 November 1912 (unidentified newspaper clipping, AMLJH, Law Society of Manitoba Newspaper Clipping Scrapbooks, 71).

38 Dr J.A. MacLean, a University of Toronto–trained classicist, came to Winnipeg from the presidency of the University of Idaho as the first president of the University of Manitoba (which had earlier been governed by a different administrative structure). Morton, *One University,* 93.

39 Letter to J.A. MacLean from H.A. Robson, 19 September 1913 (UMA 20, Box 10, Folder 5). The shape things were taking at this time are reflected in a letter from H.A. Robson to W.A. Taylor, 26 September 1913, discussing the arrangements for a course of lectures for law students for the coming year. There were to be two or three lecturers and they would cover almost all aspects of common law. A room was to be provided at the university at cost. The proposed lecturers asked that the lectures commence at 8:00 p.m. and that they be compulsory for the students (AMLJH, A925).

40 See Robson to MacLean, 19 September 1913. It is possible that the university's new president may have been an important behind-the-scenes player in initiating structured legal education in the province.

41 See Notice of the Law Society of Saskatchewan, 10 September 1913 (AMLJH, A931) regarding the Law Society of Saskatchewan's law school (later named 'Wetmore Hall') in Regina. The University of Saskatchewan's College of Law

started in Saskatoon at the same time. On legal education in Saskatchewan
see W.H. McConnell, *Prairie Justice* (Calgary: Burroughs and Co. 1980); B.
Bilson, '"Prudence Rather than Valor": Legal Education in Saskatchewan
1908–1923,' *Saskatchewan Law Review* 61, no. 2 (1998), 341–75. Professor
Bilson's account shows that the University of Saskatchewan's President
Murray played central roles. On Walter Murray's role see also D.R. Murray
and R.A. Murray, *The Prairie Builder: Walter Murray of Saskatchewan* (Edmonton: NeWest Publishers 1984).

42 *Robson Hall: Faculty of Law, University of Manitoba* (Winnipeg: Faculty of Law,
University of Manitoba 1969) (pamphlet published on official opening of
Robson Hall, 15 September 1969) 6; Gibson and Gibson, *Substantial Justice*,
216. A prominent Winnipeg lawyer, Isaac Pitblado, was quoted in a local
newspaper in May 1914 as saying that 'the Law Society was determined to
establish a law school, and that it would be a great mistake if the university
did not take it under its wing.' The arrangement would, he said, be similar to
that between the university and the school of medicine (UMA 20, Box 8,
Folder 2).

43 Gibson, 'Brief History,' 33–4; Gibson and Gibson, *Substantial Justice*, at 216.

44 Letter from W.J. Spence, Registrar of University of Manitoba to Benchers, Law
Society, 25 June 1914 (AMLJH, A440) (on 14 June, moved by President
McLean, seconded by C.K. Newcombe).

45 LSMM, 17 July 1914 (recording letter from registrar of the University of
Manitoba).

46 AMLJH, A440 (1914).

47 Gibson, 'Brief History,' 34.

48 Ibid. The recorder was 'R. P. Hills, LL.D.' *Robson Hall*, 6.

49 Curriculum of the Manitoba Law School under the University of Manitoba
and The Manitoba Law Society, Winnipeg, June 1915 (AMLJH, A100), 1–2.

50 London, 'Admissions and Education,' 77–8. In 1915, the Law Society Act was
amended to retroactively authorize the benchers to make arrangements with
the university regarding education.

51 Hills resigned as recorder in 1918, he was succeeded by a non-lawyer
administrator, R.J. Russell, overseen in 'the administration of academic
matters' by 'a three-man "Board of Supervisors," consisting of D.H. Laird,
J.B. Hugg and A.T. Hawley' Gibson and Gibson, *Substantial Justice*, 247;
Robson Hall, 7–8.

52 From Curriculum of the Manitoba Law School, Session 1919–20 (AMLJH, A100).

53 Discussed in passing in Auerbach, *Unequal Justice*, 76–80 and in W.P. LaPiana,
Logic & Experience: The Origin of Modern American Legal Education (New York:
Oxford University Press 1994), 152–3.

54 Concurrent apprenticeship, for example, did not cede to full-time formal
instruction in British Columbia until 1945 or in Ontario until 1957. See Pue,
Law School, chap. 5; Moore, *Law Society of Upper Canada*, 258–64.

55 UMA 20, Box 10, Folder 5 (also appears in Board of Trustees Minutes,
AMLJH, A440. See also a memo of 1914 recording discussions on the proposed law school (AMLJH, A205/2).

D. Bell, *Legal Education in New Brunswick: A History* (Fredericton: University of
New Brunswick 1992), 110–11 notes that the development of the type writer
and the concomitant shift from male clerks to female typists and secretaries
coincided with a developing view amongst Canadian lawyers that apprenticeship should be replaced with education as a means of qualifying for the
legal profession (quoting J.B.M. Baxter, *Proceedings of the Third Annual Meeting
of the Canadian Bar Association* (1918), 48–9). To similar effect, A.M. Whiteside
told a University of British Columbia Committee in 1923 that lawyers
considered 'articled men ... as of doubtful value since more and more of the
work is being done by clerical assistants' (*Senate Committee on Establishment of
a Faculty of Law*, UBC Special Collections, President's Office, Microfilm Roll
#5, file 40: 'Law School' 1916–23). See also Stevens, *Law School: Legal Education
in America*, 75.

The movement in favour of full-time legal education antedates the typewriter, however, originating in longer-standing cultural projects. The modern
typewriter appeared only in the 1890s. See M.H. Adler, *The Writing Machine*
(London: George Allen & Unwin 1973), R. Dale and R. Weaver, *Machines in
the Office* (Oxford: Oxford University Press 1993). The move to formalize legal
education in British universities goes back at least to the mid-nineteenth
century, however (see Pue, 'Guild Training').

56 UMA 20, Box 10, Folder 5; also appears in 'Trustees Minutes.'

57 This result had not been attained anywhere in common law Canada.
Dalhousie's law school contributed to professional qualification by means of a
system that 'interpolated' apprenticeship and classroom attendance even after
law school examinations were accepted by the Barrister's Society in lieu of
their own. See J. Willis, *A History of Dalhousie Law School* (Toronto: University
of Toronto Press 1979), 42, 131–2.

58 UMA 20, Box 10, Folder 5; also appears in 'Trustees Minutes.' This idea was
also pursued in a letter from H.A. Robson to Isaac Pitblado, 18 May 1915,
indicating that three years of attendance at the law school should make 'a
person an LLB or an Attorney.' However, it would take six to twelve months
more to be called as a barrister. AMLJH, A369.

59 Letter from H.A. Robson to J.A. MacLean, 3 April 1914 (UMA 20, Box 10,
Folder 5).

60 Ibid.

61 Ibid.

62 For a discussion of the effects of science and technology on western Canadian thought see D. Laycock's extraordinary *Populism and Democratic Thought in the Canadian Prairies 1910–1945* (Toronto: University of Toronto Press 1990).

63 Langdell is generally credited for the development of the case method, though, as Kyer and Bickenbach, *Fiercest Debate*, 15, observe, there is reason to suspect Harvard President Charles W. Elliot's hand in this. Elliot had, they say, earlier argued for a 'case method' in science education that 'involved the replacement of lectures by an "inductive" analysis of concrete cases with the aim of identifying general principles.' Stevens, *Law School*, 53, argues that Langdell was extraordinarily confused as between 'science as an empirical and as a rational activity.' See also A.E. Sutherland, *The Law at Harvard: A History of Ideas and Men, 1817–1967* (Cambridge, Mass.: Belknap Press 1967); A. Chase, 'Birth of the Modern Law School,' *American Journal of Legal History* 23 (1979), 329; Auerbach, *Unequal Justice*, chap. 3, 74–101; LaPiana, *Logic*; R.W. Gordon, 'The Case For (and Against) Harvard,' *Michigan Law Review* 93 (1995), 1231–60.

64 Josef Redlich, *The Common Law and the Case Method in American University Law Schools* (New York: Carnegie Foundation for the Advancement of Teaching 1914).

65 Kyer and Bickenbach, *Fiercest Debate*, 84–5; the Redlich report was evaluated in J.H. Beale, 'The Law School as Professor Redlich Sees It,' *Harvard Graduates' Magazine* 23 (1915), 617; Albert Kocourek, 'The Redlich Report and the Case Method,' *Illinois Law Review* 10 (1915), 321–33; Cohen, *The Law*, 137, 140–1.

66 Auerbach, *Unequal Justice*, 76.

67 Stevens, *Law School*, 55. In a passage ripe with implications for the study of legal education in twentieth-century Canada, Auerbach, *Unequal Justice*, at 79, observes: 'Without the particular rhythms characteristic of early twentieth-century life, law teachers might have remained merely the 'expounders, systematizers, and historians' described by Eliot ... Such, indeed, was the experience in England ... The delayed birth of university legal education in the United States, and its coincidence with national reform, was fortuitously decisive. Had it emerged before 1890, or after 1915, the profession of law teaching probably would have been conspicuously different.'

68 Gordon, 'The Case For (and Against) Harvard.' For a trans-Atlantic comparison see D. Sugarman, '"A Hatred of Disorder": Legal Science, Liberalism, and Imperialism,' in P. Fitzpatrick, ed., *Dangerous Supplements* (London: Pluto 1991), 34–67.

69 C.C. Langdell, *Record of the Commemoration, November Fifth to Eighth, 1886, on*

the *Two Hundred and Fiftieth Anniversary of the Founding of Harvard College* (1887), 97, 98, as quoted in Sutherland, *Law at Harvard*, 174–5.

70 Stevens, *Law School*, 53.

71 Kyer and Bickenbach, *Fiercest Debate*, at 15.

72 Stevens, *Law School*, 63.

73 J.A. Corry, *My Life and Work: A Happy Partnership (Memoirs of J. A. Corry)* (Kingston: Queen's University 1981). Corry's own contributions to Canadian legal thought are discussed in R.C.B. Risk, 'Lawyers, Courts, and the Rise of the Regulatory State,' *Dalhousie Law Journal* 9 (1984), 31–54.

   The process of education Corry describes is remarkably similar to the 'endless class of competitive evaluation' by means of 'verbal clashes' that characterized the core of male youth culture in young men's societies. E.A. Rotundo *American Manhood: Transformations in Masculinity from the Revolution to the Modern Era* (New York: BasicBooks 1993), 68.

74 C.R. Smith, 'Legal Education: A Manitoba View,' *Canadian Bar Review* (1935), 404–13 at 408. Smith was, at the time, a lecturer at the Manitoba Law School.

75 'Memorandum by Cecil A. Wright Concerning Matters Discussed at the Legal Education Committee, Law Society of Upper Canada Meeting Dec. 1 1933,' cited in Kyer and Bickenbach, *Fiercest Debate*, 82. More recently, a senior legal academic with whom I once worked consistently presented lectures that were thoughtful, well organized, informative, and erudite: an effect achieved by reading word-for-word the text which, selected on the advice of other professors, he had assigned to his students!

   For a discussion of Cecil Wright's jurisprudence see R.C.B. Risk, 'Volume 1 of the Journal: A Tribute and Belated Review,' *University of Toronto Law Journal* 37 (1987), 193–211. See also J.E. Bickenbach and C.I. Kyer, 'The Harvardization of Caesar Wright,' *University of Toronto Law Journal* 33 (1983), 162–83.

76 The antebellum Harvard Law School itself had been characterized by both 'interactive discussion and lectures.' Gordon, 'The Case for (and Against) Harvard,' 1233.

77 Willis, *History of Dalhousie*, 83.

78 Ibid.

79 Stevens, *Law School*, esp. chap. 4, 'Harvard Sets the Style,' 51–72; Kyer and Bickenbach, *Fiercest Debate*, 16, summarize Langdell's subsequent celebration of the case method thus: 'Since the law is a science, and since cases are the experimental data of the science, legal education must be limited to the university; he boldly rejected the notion that law was "a species of handicraft ... best learned by serving an apprenticeship to one who practices it."'

80 Willis, *History of Dalhousie*, at 82, asserts that in 1920 'no teacher' at any Canadian law school had yet used the case method and thus accords pride of

place to either Sidney Earle Smith (who 'sprang' the case method on the Dalhousie graduating class in contracts and trusts in 1921–2 (84, 97)) or to John Read (who used it in his conflict of laws class in the same year and who was 'in 1924 or 1925 the author of the first case book ever compiled in Canada, a mimeographed one on Constitutional Law' (97)). In support of this latter assessment Willis cites C. Morse, 'The Teaching of Law,' *Canadian Bar Review* 4 (1926), 483–8 at 487.

81 Kyer and Bickenbach, *Fiercest Debate*, at 76 suggest that J.T. Hébert (who resigned from the University of Saskatchewan Law Faculty in 1924) 'may have been the first legal educator in Canada to adopt the casebook method in his teaching.' The case method in Saskatchewan is briefly discussed in Bilson, *Prudence*,' 344.

82 Kyer and Bickenbach, *Fiercest Debate*, suggest that Falconbridge's 1924 mimeographed casebook on the sale of goods (subsequently published as J.D. Falconbridge, *A Selection of Cases on the Sale of Goods* (Toronto: Canada Law Book 1927)) 'may be counted as the first Harvard-inspired casebook compiled and published in Canada' (43). The Falconbridge volume was reviewed by V.C. MacDonald, *Canadian Bar Review* 6 (1928), 173.

83 H.A. Robson, KC. and J.B. Hugg, *Leading Cases on Public Corporations* (Toronto: The Carswell Co. 1916), Preface.

84 H.A. Robson and J.B. Hugg, *Cases on Company Law* (Toronto: The Carswell Co. 1916), Preface.

85 Casebooks continued to serve as a valuable source of basic legal information for lawyers even many years later, as in British Columbia thirty years later (Pue, *Law School*, 261–3).

86 Robson and Hugg, *Company Law*, 'Introduction,' 8.

87 Ibid. at 9.

88 Kyer and Bickenbach, *Fiercest Debate*, 52.

89 Ibid.

90 (Carswell 1914). Lefroy's juristic thought is ably described in R.C.B. Risk, 'A.H.F. Lefroy: Common Law Thought in Late Nineteenth-Century Canada: On Burying One's Grandfather,' *University of Toronto Law Journal* 41 (1991), 307–31; R. Risk, 'The Scholars and the Constitution: P.O.G.G. and the Privy Council,' in Canada's Legal Inheritances, *Manitoba Law Review* 23 (1996) (symposium issue edited by Pue and Guth), 496–523 at 497–500.

91 Kyer and Bickenbach, *Fiercest Debate*, 43.

92 Risk, 'A.H.F. Lefroy,' 312.

93 Letter from H.A. Robson to Isaac Pitblado, 30 April 1915 (AMLJH, A369); Letter from H.A. Robson to Pitblado, 20 April 1915 (AMLJH, A369).

94 J.T. Hébert, 'An Unsolicited Report on Legal Education in Canada,' *Canadian Law Times* 41 (1921), 593 at 611.

95 Western leadership has been consistently overlooked in the developing histories of legal professionalism in Canada. Kyer and Bickenbach, argue, for example, that 'Falconbridge's initial steps ... count not as the beginning but as the climax of the first important country-wide campaign to bring legal education in Canada into line with the standard advocated by legal academics in the United States in the first two decades of the twentieth century. The Canadian movement was led by Falconbridge, MacRae, R.W. Lee, and H.A. Smith, the last two of whom were English scholars sojourning in Canada at McGill University Law School' (at 51). 'Leaders' of the movement whose contributions are overlooked in this assessment include J.A.M. Aikins, founder of the Canadian Bar Association and president from 1914 to 1927; H.A. Robson, founder of Manitoba legal education and early chair of the CBA committee on legal education; Manitoba's Thorson, a member of the committee on legal education and first Canadian law dean to implement the CBA's curriculum proposals; Saskatchewan's Hébert, likely the first whole-heartedly 'Socratic' teacher in Canada, and others. I have sketched out Prairie contributions in this period in Pue, 'Common Law Legal Education,' while British Columbia's role in the development of Canadian legal education is recorded in Pue, *Law School*.

96 E.K. Williams, 'Legal Education in Manitoba: 1913–1950,' *Canadian Bar Review* 28 (1950), 759–79 at 771–2.

97 Letter from H.A. Robson to Isaac Pitblado, 18 May 1915 (AMLJH, A369).

98 Second Draft of Proposed Curriculum, Manitoba Law School (AMLJH, A369); The emphasis on a case-book approach stands in contrast to the curriculum at Osgoode Hall in 1923, where the first-year curriculum emphasized assigned treatises, statutes, or forms, with a lesser emphasis on direct exposure to case law: Contracts: C.S. Kenny, *A Selection of Cases Illustrative of the Law of Contracts* (published in England in 1922), and *Anson on Contracts*; Real property: E.D. Armour, *A Treatise on the Law of Real Property*; Jurisprudence: Thomas Erskind Holland, *The Elements of Jurisprudence*; Common Law: John Indermaur, *Principles of the Common Law*; Constitutional law and history: Sir J.G. Bourinot, *A Manual of the Constitutional History of Canada*, and A.H.F. Lefroy, *Leading Cases in Canadian Constitutional Law* (1914). The remainder of the 'first year curriculum – criminal law, practice, and procedure and statute law – concentrated on statutory material and forms.' Kyer and Bickenbach, *Fiercest Debate*, 42–3, 43.

99 'Trustees Minutes,' 14 September 1914, indicate acceptance of the following curriculum for 1914–15 (only the first two years were taught in law school in the initial period):
First Year: *Williams on Real Property*, *Snell's Equity* (Part I and Part II, to

Making Manitoba Lawyers, 1885–1931   555

end of Cap. XIX), *Smith's Common Law, Anson on Contracts*. Statutes: Manitoba Wills, Devolution of Estates, Bills of Exchange, Constitutional History of Canada with special reference to BNA Act (*Bourinot's Manual*).

Second Year: *Armour on Titles* (L.S.) and *Challis on Real Property* (U.), *Stephen's Digest of Evidence* (L.S.) and *Best on Evidence* (U.), *Underhill on Torts* (L.S.) and *Radcliffe on Torts* (U.), *Snell's Equity* (L.S.), and *Strachan's Leading Cases in Equity* (U.). Possible offerings were *William's Personal Property* (L.S.) and Dicey's Conflict of Laws (U.).

100 Gibson and Gibson, *Substantial Justice*, 251. McWilliams was selected as a teacher by the board of trustees at the law school at its 9 June 1915 meeting ('Trustees Minutes').

101 Aikins, 'Inaugural,' 1188.

102 Aikins, 'Inaugural,' 1188–9.

103 An early English attempt to found 'professional education' for lawyers in Birmingham floundered. Pue, 'Guild Training.'

104 Despite the presence of women lawyers in Manitoba at this time, professional leaders persisted of thinking of their profession as 'manly' work and aspired to create a profession of gentlemen. Cf. Gidney and Millar, *Professional Gentlemen*; Moore, *Law Society of Upper Canada*. On women lawyers in Manitoba, see M. Kinnear, *In Subordination: Professional Women, 1870–1970* (Montreal and Kingston: McGill-Queen's University Press 1995), chap. 4, 78–97.

105 Willis, *History of Dalhousie*, 31. On Harvard's late-nineteenth-century law program see, among many others, Sutherland, *Law at Harvard*; LaPiana, *Logic*; Gordon, 'The Case for (and Against) Harvard.'

106 Kyer and Bickenbach, *Fiercest Debate*, 58. The program imitated 'the general outlines of BA courses in jurisprudence offered at Oxford, Cambridge, and Dublin' (58). A useful general description of Kennedy's program and the jurisprudential school that informed it is to be found in R.C.B. Risk, 'The Many Minds of W.P.M. Kennedy,' *University of Toronto Law Journal* 48 (1998), 353–86; R.C.B. Risk, 'W.P.M. Kennedy and Canadian Constitutional Thought' (paper presented at Canadian Legal History Conference, 'Exploring Canada's Legal Past,' University of Toronto, 7–9 May 1998); and Risk, 'Volume 1 of the Journal. See also Risk, 'The Scholars and the Constitution' at 497–500; R.C.B. Risk, 'Lawyers, Courts, and the Rise of the Regulatory State,' *Dalhousie Law Journal* 9 (1984), 31–54.

The University of Toronto's curriculum under W.P.M. Kennedy in fact covered territory that overlapped considerably with general arts education at the University of British Columbia in this period. Pue, *Law School*, chap. 3, 65–94.

107 Compiled from the following sources: 'Trustees Minutes,' 14 September
    1914; *Curriculum of the Manitoba Law School under the University of Manitoba
    and The Manitoba Law Society*, Winnipeg, June 1915) (AMLJH, A100);
    'Trustees Minutes,' 15 September 1916, 'Trustees Minutes,' 25 September
    1918 (AMLJH, A440); *Curriculum of the Manitoba Law School*, June 1917,
    *Curriculum of the Manitoba Law School, Session 1919–20, Curriculum of the
    Manitoba Law School, Session 1920–2* (AMLJH, A100).

108 Morton, *One University*.

109 See Letter, H.A. Robson to J.A. MacLean, 30 April 1915 (enclosing a draft
    curriculum and indicating that the Law Society had broadened its own
    curriculum to match the university's more closely); Letter, H.A. Robson to
    J.A. MacLean, 31 December 1915 (explaining that the university lectures on
    international law and the history of English law are considered 'unprofit-
    able'); Letter, J.A. MacLean to H.A. Robson, 7 January 1916, indicating that,
    while the selection of courses is completely within the purview of the board
    of trustees, he would be sorry to see the courses in international law and
    history of English law disappear from the curriculum or the course of
    instruction permanently. MacLean made the strength of his commitment to
    'cultural' education in law clear, indicating: 'it would be a mistake to confine
    the lectures of the School to the subjects which the lawyer needs in his daily
    practice. I suppose it is not necessary to enlarge on this point because I think
    I know that you and the members of the Board are doing everything in your
    power to make the course broader as well as more intensive, and am writing
    this only because I wanted you to know that I am regarding the discontinu-
    ance of the lectures in International Law and the History of English Law as a
    temporary and not a permanent disposition in respect of these subjects'
    (UA20, Box 10, Folder 5).

110 This is not the place to develop these themes at length. See however Pue,
    'Common Law Legal Education.'
    Though Ontario's path to legal education seems to be very different,
    Manitoba's early twentieth-century path to law school is similar to that of
    British Columbia. See B.D. Bucknall, T.C.H. Baldwin, and J.D. Lakin,
    'Pedants, Practitioners and Prophets: Legal Education at Osgoode Hall to
    1957,' *Osgoode Hall Law Journal* 6 (1968), 137–229; cf. Pue, *Law School*.

111 See discussion in Kyer and Bickenbach, *Fiercest Debate*, 64–70.

112 Gibson and Gibson, *Substantial Justice*, 248; *Robson Hall*, 8.

113 *Curriculum of the Manitoba Law School, Session 1921–22* (AMLJH, A100/6).

114 'Trustees Minutes,' 28 February 1921, 123, motion to move curriculum as
    close as possible to that proposed by the Canadian Bar Association, motion
    for a permanent teaching staff of two.

115 H. Buchwald, 'The Manitoba Law School – 40 Years,' *Manitoba Bar News* 26

(1954), 77 at 80; Gibson and Gibson, *Substantial Justice*, 248; *Robson Hall*, 8; *Curriculum of the Manitoba Law School, Session 1921–22* (AMLJH, A100/6).

116 *Curriculum Book for 1921–22* (AMLJH, A100) and 'Trustees Minutes,' 31 May 1922.

117 Thornson (although not his role as a legal educator) is discussed in I. Bushnell, *The Federal Court of Canada: A History, 1875–1992* (Toronto: The Osgoode Society for Canadian Legal History 1997), chap. 12, 124–37 and in Gibson and Gibson, *Substantial Justice*, 247–8, 274, 299, 314.

118 Willis, *History of Dalhousie*, 81.

119 Kyer and Bickenbach, *Fiercest Debate*, 42.

120 When the CBA Committee on legal education struck a subcommittee to consider curriculum Robson was appointed alongside McGill's Dean R.W. Lee, Dalhousie's Dean MacRae, the University of Saskatchewan's Dean T.D. Brown, and the Law Society of Upper Canada's W.F. Kerr. When Robson found himself unable to participate, Brown represented both the Saskatchewan and Manitoba law societies. Brown consulted 'with Judge Robson, with the head of the Manitoba Law School, and with some of the benchers of the Law Society ...' 'Committee on Legal Education, Standard Curriculum,' *Proceedings of the Canadian Bar Association* (1920), 250 at 252.
The committee's 'first draft report was printed in Canadian Law Times 38 (1918) 257, and the final report in the Canadian Bar Association Year Book for 1918. Changes were made and adopted at the 1919 CBA meeting ...' Williams, 'Legal Education in Manitoba, 762.
See R.W. Lee, 'Legal Education: A Symposium,' *Canadian Law Times* 39 (1919), 13. Lee's report on legal education also appeared in *Proceedings of the 4th Annual Meeting of the Canadian Bar Association, 1919* (published 1920), 150–2; 'Committee on Legal Education – Standard Curriculum' – Report and Notes on Report,' *Proceedings of 5th Annual Meeting of the Canadian Bar Association, 1920,* 250–7.

121 See Pue, 'Becoming "Ethical"'; 'Legal Ethics: An Address by Chief Justice Mathers,' *Proceedings of the 5th Annual Meeting of the Canadian Bar Association, 1920* (published 1920), 268–301.

122 Minutes of the *Proceedings of the Canadian Bar Association* (1919), 150, as cited in Kyer and Bickenbach, *Fiercest Debate*, 66.

123 C. Harvey, 'Some Benchers and Secretaries, Benchers 1877–1920's, Isaac Pitblado,' in Harvey, ed., *The Law Society of Manitoba*, 222–72 at 231–4.

124 R.W. Lee, 'Legal Education Old and New (Part III),' *Canadian Law Times* 36 (1916), 109–15; Lee, 'Legal Education.' See Roderick Macdonald, 'The National Law Programme at McGill: Origins, Evolution, Prospects,' *Dalhousie Law Journal* 13 (1990) 211–363.

125 See, for example, *Canada Law Journal* 51 (1915), 161–204; report on the

proceedings of the CBA, including speeches of Sir J. Aikins, KC, president of the CBA on 'The Advancement of the Science of Jurisprudence in Canada.' For discussions of the cultural ethos surrounding legal education at this time see Pue, 'Common Law Legal Education' and 'Revolution by Legal Means.'

126 For a discussion of the 'gentlemanly' aspirations and cultural objectives of Victorian English professional reformers see Sugarman, 'A Hatred of Disorder'; Pue, 'Guild Training.'

127 J.G. Hodgins, comp., *Documentary History of Education in Upper Canada*, 28 vols. (Toronto: Warwick Bros. and Rutter 1894–1910), 1:213. The passage is cited in Moore, *Law Society of Upper Canada* at 78 and in G.B. Baker, 'Legal Education in Upper Canada 1785–1889: The Law Society as Educator,' in D.H. Flaherty, ed., *Essays in the History of Canadian Law, vol. 2* (Toronto: The Osgoode Society for Canadian Legal History 1983).

128 *Proceedings of the Canadian Bar Association* 8 (1923), 387; quoted in Gibson and Gibson, *Substantial Justice*, 248; *Robson Hall*, 9.

129 Gibson and Gibson, *Substantial Justice*, 249; *Robson Hall*, 9; Carnegie Foundation, Annual Review of Legal Education, 1926, 1927.

130 Gibson and Gibson, *Substantial Justice*, 249.

131 12 November 1926, 'Trustees Minutes' (AMLJH A440, 187).

132 Gibson and Gibson, *Substantial Justice*, 249; *Robson Hall*, 9–12; 'Trustees Minutes' 7 July 1927, 195, approved the proposal for a four-year course of study with lectures during the third and fourth year outside of office hours, recommended non-graduates three years' articles, graduates two years' articles, to be completed after first two years of law school.

133 Gibson and Gibson, *Substantial Justice*, 249; *Robson Hall*, 12.

134 Ibid.; London, 'Admissions and Education,' at 79.

135 Gibson and Gibson, *Substantial Justice*, 249; *Robson Hall*, 12.

136 The unconventional living arrangements of James Aikins, his de facto separation from his wife, and his apparent intimacy with Coleman are described briefly in L. Gibson and D. Gibson, 'Sir James Aikins' Seamless Web: Finding Fortune and Fame as a Lawyer in the Adolescent Canadian West,' *Manitoba Law Journal* 21 (1992), 161–212.

137 *Robson Hall*, 12; see also Gibson and Gibson, *Substantial Justice*, 250–1.

138 Gibson and Gibson, *Substantial Justice*, 303, 304.

139 Committee on Legal Education, *Proceedings of the Canadian Bar Association* (1931), 206–7.

140 Williams, 'Legal Education in Manitoba, 779. (A bencher by 1931, Williams had earlier assisted Robson in creating the 1914 law school.)

141 London, 'Admissions and Education,' 80.

142 Consultative Group on Legal Education, Law and Learning, *Report to the*

Social Sciences & Humanities Research Council of Canada by the Consultative Group on Research and Education in Law (Ottawa: SSHRCC 1983) ('Arthurs Report'). See also Ron Saunders' book review: 'Law and Learning: Report of the Social Sciences and Humanities Research Council of Canada,' *Ottawa Law Review* 23 (1984), 218.

143 See J. Brockman, 'Exclusionary Tactics: The History of Women and Minorities in the Legal Profession in British Columbia,' in H. Foster and J. McLaren, eds. *Essays in the History of Canadian Law, Vol. VI, British Columbia and the Yukon* (Toronto: The Osgoode Society for Canadian Legal History 1995), 508–61); D. Tong, 'Gatekeeping in Canadian Law Schools: a History of Exclusion, the Rule of 'Merit,' and a Challenge to Contemporary Practices' (LL.M. thesis, University of British Columbia 1996); D. Tong 'A History of Exclusion: The Treatment of Racial and Ethnic Minorities by the Law Society of British Columbia in Admissions to the Legal Profession,' *The Advocate* 56; no. 2 (March 1998), 197–208; M. Thornton, *Dissonance and Distrust: Women in the Legal Profession* (Melbourne: Oxford University Press 1996); S. Ramshaw and W.W. Pue, 'Feminism Unqualified,' *Law in Context* 15, no. 1 (1997) 166–78; Auerbach, *Unequal Justice*; Gordon, 'The Case for (and Against) Harvard'; M.J. Powell, *From Patrician to Professional Elite: The Transformation of the New York City Bar Association* (New York: Russell Sage Foundation 1988).

144 See L. Karpik and T. Halliday, eds., *Legal Professions and Political Liberalism* (Oxford University Press 1997).

145 See Gibson and Gibson, *Substantial Justice*, 256, 267.

146 Ibid., 256 (indicating that even in 1931 the Law Society was reasonably well-off).

147 Letter to H.A. Robson from Cronkite at University of Saskatchewan in relation to the Canadian Bar Association Committee on Legal Education, 5 February 1934 (AMLJH, A224).

148 On the notion of 'recipe knowledge' see R. Ericson and P. Baranek, *The Ordering of Justice: a Study of Accused Persons as Dependents in the Criminal Process* (Toronto: University of Toronto Press 1982)

149 Evidence of Sir George Stephen, solicitor, *Report of the Select Committee on Legal Education*, 25 August 1846, 144, para. 1965.

150 There are striking similarities in these respects to the meteoric rise and fall of a cutting-edge program of legal education at Queen's College, Birmingham, in the previous century. See Pue, 'Guild Training.'

151 Kyer and Bickenbach, *Fiercest Debate*, 75. M. Kinnear, *In Subordination*, 85, makes a similar point in her observation that, once a full-time law faculty was re-established in Manitoba in the 1960s, 'when training switched to an academic system, it was "a door opener for women. You didn't need to find

an office at the start." Even then, the reluctance of firms to take on women for their subsequent articling persisted.'
152 Rotundo, *American Manhood*, reminds us that much important business was concluded in 'informal talks' that 'happened within the context of male sociability. They took place in train cars, on station platforms, in hotel lobbies; often they happened at formal social occasions' (199).
153 Kyer and Bickenbach, *Fiercest Debate*, 125–33; the committee report was published *Canadian Bar Review* 13 (1935), 347.
154 As quoted in Pue, *Law School*, 148.
155 Risk pointed to the need for a geographically informed legal history a quarter-century ago in R.C.B. Risk, 'A Prospectus for Canadian Legal History,' *Dalhousie Law Journal* 1 (1973), 227–45 at 230–1.
   See also G. Parker, 'Canadian Legal Culture,' in L. Knafla, ed., *Law and Justice in a New Land: Essays in Western Canadian Legal History* (Toronto: Carswell 1986), 3–29; I. Duncanson, 'Close Your Eyes and Think of England,' *Canberra Law Review* 3, no. 2 (1997), 123–38; I. Duncanson, 'Finding a History for the Common Law,' *Australian Journal of Legal History* (1996) 1–30; Ian Duncanson, 'The Politics of Common Law in History and Theory,' *Osgoode Hall Law Journal* 27 (1989), 687–707.
156 Bucknall, et al., 'Pedants'; Kyer and Bickenbach, *Fiercest Debate*; Gibson and Gibson, *Substantial Justice*; J.P.S. McLaren, 'The History of Legal Education in Common Law Canada,' in R.J. Matas and D. McCawley, eds., *Legal Education in Canada* (Montreal: Federation of Law Societies of Canada 1987), 111–45; J.P.S. McLaren, 'Book Review: Kyer and Bickenbach, *The Fiercest Debate: Cecil A. Wright, the Benchers and Legal Education in Ontario 1923–1957*,' *Canadian Bar Review* 68 (1989), 193–202; Moore, *Law Society of Upper Canada*; Pue, *Law School*.
157 Risk, 'A Prospectus for Canadian Legal History,' 245.

16

The Law of Evolution and the Evolution of the Law: Mills, Darwin, and Late-Nineteenth-Century Legal Thought

ROBERT VIPOND AND GEORGINA FELDBERG

'The tendency, of late, has been to extend the domain of science into regions which lie wholly beyond its own domain,' the lawyer and politician David Mills wrote in 1894. 'But such regions science cannot expect to hold.'[1] Mills's reservations about 'science,' or more aptly Darwinian science, were common to his time. By 1894, when he published his no-holds-barred attack on Darwinism in The Canadian Monthly, under the title, 'The Missing Link In The Hypothesis of Evolution, or Derivative Creation' the debate over Darwinian science had been raging in Canada for over three decades. The main lines of Mills's argument resonate powerfully with, and were probably derived from, earlier attacks. Yet his attack on Darwinism was unusually uncompromising – especially for the mid-1890s. Most Ontarians who had some stake in the debate over Darwinism had by this time made their peace with Darwin.[2] Mills, however, found no merit in Darwin's work, and he dismissed not merely Darwin's account of humanity but the whole evolutionary enterprise.

Despite his strong views about the errors and failings of Darwinian science, scarcely one year later, Mills employed the very Darwinian language that, in 'The Missing Link,' he had unequivocally rejected. Again in The Canadian Magazine in April 1895, Mills published an article bluntly entitled 'Saxon or Slav: England or Russia?,' in which he argued that 'it is not always the best that survives, but the fittest,' and without 'moral stamina, without public virtue, without a spirit of self-sacrifice, it is impossible to maintain the front rank ...'[3] Darwinian principles, barred from the front door of natural science, thus entered through the back door of social theory.

The purpose of this essay is to understand David Mills's complex reaction to Darwinism and to place it in the context of late-nineteenth-century Canadian legal thought. The sceptical reader may wonder how an essay on Darwinism fits in a volume about legal history celebrating the career of Dick Risk. Actually, there are two complementary justifications. First, we want to argue that the non-legal life of a major legal, political, and constitutional figure like David Mills is worth knowing about. There is now an immense literature on the reception of Darwinism in Canada, some of the most important contributions to which centre on figures who were not themselves scientists.[4] Yet this literature is almost silent on the part played by lawyers even though some, like Mills, took Darwin's theory of natural selection as seriously as they took developments in the law. Our goal here is to understand why Mills was preoccupied with Darwin and how his ways of thinking about law connected with, indeed informed, his scientific and religious thought. The 'legal' and 'scientific' were not hermetically sealed compartments in Mills's mind. It seems worthwhile, therefore, to tease out how his intellectual commitments as a lawyer may have informed Mills's understanding of Darwinian science.

The apparent connection between law and science suggests a second justification for lingering over David Mills's anti-Darwinism. If it was informed by the way he thought about law, we want to suggest equally that this anti-Darwinism refracts in a way that illuminates Mills's legal and political thought. David Mills is usually taken as one of the best and purest exemplars of nineteenth-century rule of law thought in Canada. This is nowhere truer than in his approach to the constitutional division of powers between federal and provincial governments. Yet Mills was also deeply worried, as a public figure and politician, about the various threats posed at century's end to liberal imperialism, a whole set of standards that he associated, alongside the rule of law, with the British way of life. Stated baldly, our argument here is that Mills's anti-Darwinist tracts expose the deep tension between these basic legal and political commitments in a way that his other, more conventionally legal and political writings do not.

In so doing, Mills's anti-Darwinism becomes a perch from which to view and appreciate Dick Risk's contribution to Canadian legal history. Over the years, David Mills has been one of Dick's favourite subjects of analysis. And Dick stands out as one who is committed to an integrated view of legal history in which considerations of science and religion form part of the legal historian's apparatus. But more than this, Dick has always resisted the temptation to reduce late-nineteenth-century legal thought to a caricature of legal formalism. This chapter is intended ultimately to reinforce and pay tribute to this aspect of Dick Risk's intellectual project. The chapter is divided into three parts. In the first, we reconstruct in detail Mills's anti-Darwinism and show how his deepest objections to Darwin follow from a perceived threat to his legal universe. In the second, we show, conversely, how and where Mills departed from other anti-Darwinists on scientific and religious questions. In the third and final section we propose a way to understand this apparent contradiction that highlights Mills's basic legal and political commitments.

I

David Mills (1831–1903) is one of the more remarkable and most underestimated figures of late-nineteenth-century Ontario liberalism.[5] He was born in Orford Township, Kent County, in 1831, his father having emigrated from Nova Scotia and his mother from Ireland slightly more than a decade earlier. Mills received his early education at the local common school and through private tuition thereafter. He acted as a school inspector in Kent County for ten years, then, in 1865, left to attend law school at the University of Michigan. In 1867 he returned to the family farm, secured the Reform nomination for the federal constituency of Bothwell, and narrowly won a seat in the first Parliament.

Mills held Bothwell almost continuously from 1867 to 1896 and established himself over the course of his career as a fixture in national politics. He served as minister of the interior in Alexander Mackenzie's Cabinet from 1876 to 1878; argued the Ontario boundary case before the Judicial Committee of the Privy Council in 1884; was one of Edward Blake's closest friends and advisers; became one of the principal theorists and propagandists of the provincial rights movement; spoke out eloquently in defence of minority language rights in the North West; and broke with his own party on the Manitoba schools question by arguing that the federal government had a constitutional obligation to restore separate schools in the province. In part because of his heterodox position on the Manitoba question, Mills lost the election of 1896 but the following year Laurier appointed him to the Senate and made him minister of justice. Five years later in 1902, Mills unapologetically recommended his own appointment to the Supreme Court of Canada. He died a little more than a year later, in May 1903.

Mills had also created a second career for himself – as an editorialist for the London *Advertiser*, as a public lecturer on a wide variety of moral and religious subjects, and as a frequent contributor to semipopular magazines. To a considerable extent, he justified this role on political grounds. Parliament, he liked to say, was 'a great national university' to which 'the public look for light and guidance' and 'from which is given to the nation daily instruction.'[6] But Mills was equally fond of pointing out that, in the absence of self-regulating institutional checks and balances, the British constitution is especially dependent for its good operation upon popular control and a vigilant public opinion. 'The British Constitution,' in contrast to the American, 'is entrusted to the guardianship of the nation. Its defence is the strength of custom, and the wisdom, moderation, and fairness embodied in the public spirit of the nation.'[7] The conscientious public servant, he believed, had a responsibility to ensure that the 'moral sense' of the people was 'kept sensitive,' for 'when the moral stamina (of the electorate) is gone, real life will have departed, from the political organism, and no element of strength or of stability will remain.'[8]

In short, Mills assumed the persona of public moralist, and it was in this guise that he first undertook his critique of Darwin. Though Mills used various forums to set out his objections to Darwinism, *The Canadian Magazine* seems to have been his periodical of choice. Here, in a half-dozen or so articles published in the 1880s and 1890s, he took it upon himself to attack directly the sources of 'decay' that sapped 'the moral stamina' of the nation.

Mills identified moral threats on several fronts, but none was as important or as insidious as Darwin's 'hypothesis' of evolution by natural selection. As Mills appreciated, Darwin's theory of evolution by natural selection had issued a profound challenge to the orthodox scientific, religious, and philosophic beliefs of late-nineteenth-century Ontarians. Ambiguous to its core, Darwin's *Origin of the Specie* (1859) - and later his *Descent of Man* (1871) - stood at once as the last statement of natural theology and the first of secular humanism. His methodologic and substantive contributions had forced Canadians to reassess their traditional assumptions about God's place in the universe and 'Man's' place in the natural world; it required them as well to redefine divine and human relations in the social order. The uneasy tension between Darwinism and evangelical Christianity that this redefinition engendered preoccupied scientists, philosophers, and theologians. Thanks to the renaissance of religious history and the history of science in Canada, the contributions of John Watson, George Monro Grant, Daniel Wilson, Nathaniel Burwash, and other notables in the academy are well known.[9]

In a way, however, this focus on the academic debate over Darwinism has obscured the extent to which Darwinism exercised others who were neither professional scientists nor professional theologians, but who were nonetheless deeply worried about the implications of Darwinism. Mills belongs in this category. Undeterred by his lack of formal scientific training, Mills plunged headlong into the debate, working his way through Darwin's theory of natural selection to expose its inadequacies. He began, as many critics of Darwin began, by setting out the methodological principles in light of which Darwin's work had to be judged. 'All science,' he pronounced, 'consists of two elements, facts and inferences – observation and reasoning on the facts observed.' When 'large classes of facts are wholly at variance with a hypothesis, it would be a departure from scientific methods to adopt such a hypothesis.' The difficulty, from Mills's perspective, was that the facts did not vindicate Darwin's hypothesis of natural selection. Like Daniel Wilson, Mills argued that there were simply too many gaps in the evidence, too many 'missing links' in the evolutionary chain, to make the Darwinian hypothesis persuasive. From Mills's vantage, Darwin simply could not provide the evidence that would 'bridge over the immense chasm, which divides the human race, from all the animal kingdom below them.'[10]

This attack on the alleged 'missing links' in the evolutionary chain is a useful place to start in unpacking Mills's thought because it shows the ways in which his objections to Darwinian science linked formal and substantive criticism. Mills found Darwin's argument weak from an evidentiary perspective; it also offended the fundamental moral and religious principles that he held dear. Like many of his contemporaries, Mills feared more deeply than anything else the insidious theological and moral implications of Darwinism. A confirmed Protestant, he based his faith on two central tenets: divine creation and the fundamental difference between animals and humans. The notion that change occurs through some form of 'evolution' produced more or less randomly by a 'struggle for existence'[11] directly contradicted his faith that God had intervened in 'the successive creation of new species of a higher and more complicated organism.'[12] Moreover, if one believed that new species appeared through natural selection rather than divine creation, it required but one further step to say that all life originated with a single protoplasm of unknown origin. Mills well understood Darwin's own ambivalence on this question of divine creation, and he carefully acknowledged that Darwin himself claimed to be an agnostic on the question. Still, Darwin's work represented the proverbial thin end of the wedge, for it was easy for other evolutionists to draw inferences that effectively removed 'the Creator from the universe'[13] – a conclusion that was both utterly implausible on the evidence and deeply disturbing.

Darwin's work seemed also to challenge the special moral status of humans. Alternating between critique and accusation, Mills charged that the evolutionists' refusal to admit that there exist essential differences between animals and humans demonstrated the 'failure' of the theory, for it left them unable to account for the 'moral constitution of the universe.'[14] The very attempt to trace 'the descent of man' from animals, he maintained, demonstrated that the evolutionists' goal was to 'eliminate the soul from man"[15] and to reduce morality to 'a modified form of selfishness based on experience.'[16] By this analysis, the evolutionists were not merely obtuse, they were deeply threatening, for they challenged the 'moral capacity to distinguish between right and wrong'[17] that is uniquely human. It is not altogether clear which vice, obtuseness or amoralism, was worse from Mills's perspective.

Familiar as these arguments would have been to anyone following the Darwinian debate in Ontario, Mills's legal training gave them a distinctive spin and connected them to a different intellectual context. If the attack on evidence was pure Baconianism and a standard arrow in the anti-Darwinian quiver, it was also a position that came quite naturally to someone like Mills, who was deeply versed in the inductive method of the common law. Mills dissected Darwin in the manner that he might a legal case. 'I purpose to say why,' he began, 'I think the conclusions drawn are not warranted by the facts.'[18]

The structure of Darwin's argument deeply offended Mills's legal mind. In launching his critique of Darwin, Mills summarized 'the doctrine of evolution' this way: '[Mr Darwin] maintains ... the derivation of species. He holds that variations in the forms of life have been produced by environing influences, operating for thousands of years, causing slow and imperceptible departures from the original type. According to this view the physical forces which operate upon successive generations, through long periods of time, must produce numerous divergences which become grouped into sub-kingdoms, and life in one case becomes a mollusc, in another a reptile, in another a bird, and in another a mammal.'[19] While Mills (and most others) were willing to admit that important variations and changes occurred over time, he could not admit, nor did he believe, the evidence demonstrated that this process of natural selection culminated in the 'evolution of higher forms of life from those that are below them"[20] in which humanity "is the natural produce of the faculties and instincts of brutes.'[21]The origins of right and wrong were not academic or even purely moral questions but ones which had profound bearing on the ability to sustain a legal system based on individual moral responsibility. The evolutionists' inclination to 'define' remorse 'to be the sense of regret which one feels from not having followed a persistent instinct' deeply perturbed him. If this held true, he asked, 'Whence has come the regard for truth and the detestation of falsehood? ... How, then, could such an origin invest truth with sanctity? How could it induce men to value truth for its own sake and to practise it regardless of consequences? Unless we admit there is a Judge of all the earth, who does right, and who has in the original constitution of man implanted a moral capacity to distinguish between right and wrong, we have no intelligible explanation.'[22]

What really sets Mills's attack on Darwin apart from others, however, is his highly distinctive concentration on the questions of variation and classification. The observation that there exists a considerable degree of variation among members of the same species was, for Mills, one of the crucial conditions of Darwin's theory of evolution by natural selection. For if one could assume that some variations are better suited to survival in a particular environment than others; if one could further assume that, in conditions of scarcity, these favourable variations give some individuals a competitive edge over others in 'the struggle for existence'; and if, finally, one could assume that the 'successful' variations would, therefore, be reproduced while those that were unsuccessful would disappear, then one could account for the sort of biological change or evolution that Darwin was concerned to explain.

One of the great problems with this emphasis on variation, however, is that it threw into question the traditional or 'essentialist' way of ordering and classifying the forms of life. If wide variations exist among individuals within species, what, if anything, binds them together? If varieties of the same species have more in common with other species than with each other, is the conventional classification system of any real value? And if through the process of natural selection quite different forms of life are produced over time, are new species created thereby, or are the most recent evolutionary forms merely variations on the old? Darwin himself drew out the implications of his theory for the species question frankly and explicitly: 'From these remarks it will be seen that I look at the term species, as one arbitrarily given for the sake of convenience to a set of individuals closely resembling each other, and that it does not essentially differ from the term variety, which is given to less distinct and more fluctuating forms.'[23]

Mills was deeply exercised, almost obsessed, by Darwin's cheerful admission that the definition of species was essentially arbitrary, and he returned again and again in 'The Missing Link' to the question of variability. Mills was prepared to admit that 'there are certain environing influences which develop variations in structural growth'[24] over time, just as he admitted that, absent the conditions that maintain domestication, 'there is a tendency in animals to return to an original type.'[25] He allowed to pass the observation that there was considerable variation among humans and, conversely, agreed that it was 'very true, that the anatomical structure of man and the Anthropoids is much the same.'[26] But these were limited concessions. Mills continued to insist that the variations that did exist were 'confined within certain fixed limits,' and he continued to maintain with confidence that 'there are no fewer than one hundred and twenty thousand species of animals in the world' created 'after four distinct types.'[27]

This was the nub of the issue for Mills. The theory of evolution denied the fundamental proposition that there exist in the world 'certain archetypes, or Divine forms ... around which the various species of animals found in the world, group themselves,'[28] and that 'life, under the creative energies of God, moves, so to speak along certain lines' that are clearly established and 'extremely few'[29] in number. According to Mills, in other words, the theory of evolution denied the existence of a clearly discernible and divinely created order to the world in which each living thing has its appointed place. To embrace evolutionary theory was thus to admit that 'there could be neither sub-kingdoms, nor species, nor genera, but a mob of animals differing from each other by scarcely perceptible degrees, and reaching from the protoplasm up to man.'[30]

The species question was deeply interesting to professional scientists, and Darwin's approach to it spawned an important debate in the history of biology. His views on the malleability of species elicited comment as well from theologians who believed, quite rightly, that the Darwinian approach challenged the faith that there was a divinely created, intelligible, and purposeful order to the world. But Mills was not a professional scientist, and he remained concerned with the Darwinian view of variation long after most theologians and religious critics had turned their attention to other, what must have been considered more threatening, aspects of Darwinism. What, then, explains Mills's preoccupation with the species question?

The answer, in part, is that the Darwinian attack on species classification offended Mills not only as a believer but as a lawyer. Mills the lawyer was an almost textbook product of the dominant mode of Anglo-American legal thought in the late nineteenth century, often called rule of law thought and typically associated with the likes of A.V. Dicey and James Bryce (in England) and Langdell and Ames (in the United States).[31]

The rule of law paradigm developed as one part of a larger strategy of professional legitimation that was linked to the introduction of academic legal training in England and North America in the latter part of the nineteenth century. Stated baldly, the rule of law thinkers wanted to show that the legal universe, far from being a confused mob of precedents, categories, and facts, was actually a systematic, coherent, and ordered world whose meaning could be reduced to a number of fundamental principles – with the proper study. For the rule of law reformers, 'the law was ultimately governed by principles akin to the laws of natural sciences and was, thus, a subject worthy of a place in the university firmament.'[32] The leading rule of law theorist in Britain, A.V. Dicey, encapsulated this understanding in his inaugural lecture at Oxford in 1883 when he predicted that 'a school of lawyers imbued with this turn of mind would gradually reduce the whole chaotic mass of legal principles to a clear, logical and symmetrical form.'[33] Even a lawyer as iconoclastic as Oliver Wendell Holmes Jr embraced the basic goal of scientific legal reform. Indeed, Holmes stated the project behind his classic study *The Common Law*, first published in 1881, in the form of an analogy to natural science: 'to make known the content of the law; that is, to work upon it from within, or logically, arranging or distributing it, in order, from its *summum genus* to its *infirma species*, so far as practicable.'[34]

Holmes's statement is especially suggestive because it reflects the extent to which the new legal science, like pre-Darwinian natural science, was concerned centrally with proper classification and order. Law and natural science were alike as well in assuming that this order was not imposed or humanly created but sprang from nature itself. Law could be objective, neutral, and classified systematically because the categories employed by the common lawyer corresponded to some objective reality – be it nature or some other standard external to the judge's will. Judges did not 'make' law. They did not 'balance' competing 'interests,' much less read their own 'policy' preferences into their decisions. Rather, they attempted to discern the 'natural meaning of words' and to judge accordingly. Judicial decision making thus was not a subjective, idiosyncratic, or arbitrary exercise because both the legal categories and the subject matter with which they worked were, like nature itself, intelligible, clearly defined, and stable.

The Canadian legal community contributed little to the general or theoretical elaboration of the rule of law paradigm, but many Canadian lawyers, including Mills, were deeply influenced by it.[35] Mills came by his faith in the rule of law honestly. He trained at the University of Michigan law school under Thomas Cooley, one of the great systematizers of nineteenth-century American law, and he had the opportunity to inculcate his own systematic approach to the law when he taught at the University of Toronto from 1888 to 1896. But Mills really belonged in Parliament, not in the classroom, and it is there, in the course of defending his provincialist understanding of Canadian constitutional federalism, that he was called on to spell out the implications of the rule of law most clearly.

Mills's understanding of constitutional federalism turned on the basic premise that the British North America (BNA) Act had divided governmental powers into two mutually exclusive 'spheres' – one federal, the other provincial. Within its sphere, each government was legally free to act as it pleased; each was in this sense sovereign or supreme within the limits of its jurisdiction, but powerless to act beyond these limits. There was no large overlap in powers, and with the express exception of immigration and agriculture, there was no sharing of powers between governments. Rather, legislative subjects fell either under section 91 or section 92 of the BNA Act, but not both, and they were separated by well-lit, clearly discernible 'boundaries.' As long as the provincial governments stayed within their jurisdictional sphere, indeed, 'the Federal Government has no more authority than it has over the affairs of the State of New York.'[36] Or as he put it on another occasion: 'The Provinces for Provincial purposes are not in the Union. For all these exclusive purposes, they are as much out of the Union as if no Union existed.'[37] The legal categories of the BNA Act in this sense were like the hermetic categories of pre-Darwinian natural science. They described the many, but distinct and clearly definable, 'species' of legislative power.

This understanding of the legal structure of Canadian federalism became a live political issue for Mills because he believed that the Conservatives in general, and John A. Macdonald in particular, were attempting to destroy the constitutional order rather as Darwin had subverted the prevailing order of natural science. In Mills's view, the Macdonald administration behaved as if the provinces were not 'separate' political organizations, as if provincial functions were not 'distinct' from Ottawa's, and as if the lines separating federal from provincial jurisdiction were merely 'imaginary.'[38]

In response, Mills devoted considerable energy to constructing an elaborate constitutional taxonomy both to demonstrate Macdonald's errors and to defend the constitutional order from the Tory government's reckless assault. Mills argued, for instance, that the federal government had no right to disallow or veto provincial acts at will because there were certain matters that were 'in their nature local' and subject therefore to absolute local control. When the Macdonald government attempted to use its jurisdiction over trade and commerce to pass legislation regulating the adulteration of food, Mills responded that the legislation was clearly unconstitutional because 'the subject of trade and commerce has nothing to do with manufactures.'[39] And when the government introduced legislation to regulate factory working conditions by imposing criminal penalties on violators, Mills reminded the House that the criminal law extended only to those offences against society that are 'in themselves bad,' leaving to the provinces the broad 'police' powers to promote the 'morality, decency and good health' of the community.[40]

When pressed, Mills had to admit that this classification of the legal world had a few rough edges, and he equally allowed that the law, like nature, could evolve and vary within limits. Still, what is striking about Mills is the unshakeable conviction that even in the wilful and politicized world of Canadian constitutional federalism there exists an objective and intelligible legal order, 'spheres' of jurisdiction separated by well-marked boundaries. 'The line which separated the powers of the Local Legislatures from those of the Parliament of Canada,' he liked to say, 'was as distinct as if it was a geographical boundary marked out by the surveyor;'[41] it was a 'line of division ... traced by landmarks visible to the eye.'[42]

The metaphor is an evocative statement of Mills's legal science. It is also exceptionally revealing for its identification of constitutional federalism and the 'geographical' or 'mechanical' tradition of pre-Darwinian Victorian science[43] with which Mills was most comfortable. For Mills, natural science and legal science were equally grounded in the fundamental assumption that the world is an intelligible and ordered place. As Macdonald's politics challenged the constitutional order, so Darwin's hypothesis of evolution by natural selection challenged the natural order. In that one important respect they were crucially similar. Preoccupied with Macdonald's attempt to undermine the constitutional order, Mills was especially and keenly sensitive to the subversive implications of Darwinism for the natural order.

II

Mills's critique of Darwinism differed from those of his contemporaries for reasons that follow from his political and legal beliefs. His reactions to Darwinism also provide a variant model. Though troubled by the implications of Darwin's work, few Ontarians dismissed it as entirely as Mills. Instead, they endeavoured to reconcile the new biological theories with conventional belief by attempting to select what was useful or simply irrefutable from the new biology while preserving the core of traditional belief – or in other words to have it both ways. Many had found some 'escape' from the full implications of Darwinism – often by distinguishing between Darwin's materialistic account of the 'descent of man' (which was deeply problematic for most believers) and his theory of evolution in the natural world (which won much quicker acceptance). Mills attempted no such reconciliation. Staunchly antimaterialist, he opposed both the descent of man and natural selection. In effect, Mills sided with the likes of J.W. Dawson, geologist and principal of McGill, against those who believed that some accommodation with Darwinian principles was possible.

The irony is, however, that Mills was more willing than most to appropriate or transpose some Darwinian arguments. Three examples stand out. The first is drawn from Mills's article on 'The Missing Link.' In it Mills launched an utterly uncompromising antimaterialist attack on Darwin, some of which we have outlined above. Yet paradoxically, what makes "The Missing Link" remarkable is the way in which Mills quietly but explicitly embraces the materialist argument he wants elsewhere to refute. Nowhere is this tension more patent than in Mills's discussion of evolution and the "science" of craniometry.

To make his case against Darwin's theory that humans were descended from inferior animals, Mills found it necessary to both point to the various gaps and mistakes in Darwin's method, analysis, and conclusions – hence the emphasis on the 'missing link.' He deemed it necessary, as well, to furnish his own counter-evidence that catalogued the qualitative and essential differences between animals and humans, thus rendering implausible Darwin's hypothesis concerning their ultimate kinship. In this effort, Mills turned to the material bases of craniometry. If animals and humans were part of the same evolutionary continuum, he argued, one would expect to find an incremental progression in brain size from the 'smallest anthropoid' up to the most 'civilized' human beings (whom Mills, predictably, identified as Europeans). In fact, however, there existed no such continuum. Between the most advanced animal – the gorilla – and even the most primitive 'savages' and 'idiots' there was an enormous difference in cranial capacity. Where the gorilla, according to Mills, had a cranial capacity of some 34.5 cubic inches, the Bushman had been measured at 77 inches and cranial capacity of 'the Australian savage' weighed in at 80.9 inches.

The implications of this craniometric gap were, for Mills, perfectly clear: 'If from the lowest form of animal life up to the gorilla, you have one hundred and twenty thousand species, that is from zero up to 34.5, how many ought there to be between that and the man with one hundred cubic inches of brain? A wide space no doubt separates a man of culture from the Bushman; but it is small indeed compared to the chasm which lies between the Bushman and the gorilla.'[44] Conversely, the relatively large skulls of even the most 'primitive' of humans convinced Mills that there must be some 'latent powers,' peculiar to human beings, which 'seem to anticipate a future condition, far higher, and more complex, than that in which they are found.' Continued Mills: 'The Australian savage who floats upon his log, fishes with his hands, and sleeps in a tree, does not require a much higher degree of intellect than the ourang. How did he get this excess of brain beyond his actual requirements upon any theory of development, he has not used it?' Since Darwinism was built upon materialist premises, it could admit 'neither latent forces, nor latent powers.' Yet such forces clearly existed, and Darwin's inability to account for them was both 'the conclusive argument' against him and a solid clue pointing towards a divine presence and purpose in the world. 'If we admit the existence of an Omniscient Creator, looking into the future of our race, we have an intelligible explanation'[45] for the discrepancy between the actual needs of 'primitives' on the one hand and their potential capacity on the other.

The craniometric argument for latent powers is strikingly curious coming from a thoroughgoing antimaterialist like Mills, for by resting his case on the evidence of craniometry Mills was obliged to derive the existence of nonmaterial qualities ('latent powers') from materialistic evidence (skull size). Moreover, since Mills tended to equate materialism and Darwinism, the argument from latent powers was actually an anti-Darwinian argument based on premises that Mills himself identified as Darwinian. And if that were not troubling enough, this willingness to infer moral differences from variable skull sizes violated his own advice, offered elsewhere in the same article, not to equate 'progressive development' with 'increased cranial capacity.'[46]

Here again, however, Mills's political beliefs provide an explanation. As Stephen J. Gould has shown in detail,[47] scientific racism based in craniometry was enormously popular in North America at the time Mills wrote because it offered the powerful moral satisfaction of reinforcing or legitimating a social hierarchy in which European civilization occupied the highest position. Mills, in his persona of public moralist, had championed this cause. He took as his task the disclosure of threats to a British way of life; he offered, as well, a series of moral pep talks that would reassure Canadians of the superiority of English law, the British empire, and the Anglo-Saxon way of life at a time when those things were under attack. Knowing the importance Mills attributed to the moral order, it is perhaps not hard to understand why he would have been impressed by the evidence of skull size. Darwin's evidence confirmed that which Mills believed to be divinely ordained and historically demonstrable.

Mills similarly adopted the reconciliationist strategy of 'higher criticism' to his own ends. At the most general level, the scientific (or 'higher') biblical criticism that swept through Protestant theology in the late nineteenth century marked an attempt to reconcile religion with modern science, including (or perhaps especially) Darwinism. The critics' attempt to place the Bible, especially the Old Testament, in its historical context was connected to the difficulty of sustaining the older Biblical cosmology in light of modern scientific evidence. The higher critics' emphasis on the multiple human authorship of the Bible allowed them to avoid, or at least to downplay, the question of revelation. And their efforts to interpret Biblical texts as extended moral stories, rather than as providential commands, made it easier to interpret the Old Testament as part of a moral 'evolution' toward Christianity.

It is usually assumed, therefore, that those who championed scientific Biblical criticism were also disposed favourably towards evolutionary science – and vice versa. Thus on the one hand, a liberal theologian like Principal Nathaniel Burwash of Victoria College both supported the new Biblical criticism and made his peace with Darwin.[48] On the other, everyone's favourite anti-Darwinian, Principal Dawson of McGill, viewed evolutionary theory and the higher criticism as part and parcel of the same attack on evangelical Christianity.[49] Mills does not fit the pattern, however. While Mills was nothing if not a critic of Darwinian evolution, he supported the higher criticism just as vigorously and just as openly as he denounced Darwinism.

Mills's contribution to the debate over Biblical interpretation took two forms. The first, a general defence of the higher criticism, was a classic statement of liberal theology. Mills began by comparing the opponents of modern Biblical criticism to the Dutch divines who opposed Copernicus; he then deferred respectfully to the leading German intellectuals of the higher criticism movement, argued against 'the popular view' that every verse of the Bible 'is the direct utterance of God himself,' moved on to present a demystified and 'natural' account of how Moses produced water from a rock, and ended with a plea to remember the 'human element' in the Bible. Here, in short, was one believer's attempt to understand the Bible in a way that was consistent with the insights of modern science, to engage modern science without undermining 'the authority of the narrative as a guide to men in settling their relations with their Maker.'[50]

Yet, for Mills, the beauty of the higher criticism was that it also illuminated the 'divine element in human history' and allowed him, by means of a simple and direct analogy, to impute divine approval for the British empire and the British way of life. Mills exploited the political possibilities of the higher criticism in a series of lectures candidly entitled 'Abraham As A Leader of a Political Revolution,' in which Abraham's departure from Ur was likened to the Puritans' migration from England, and in which the history of Israel was taken as the model of the British empire. 'Who is there,' Mills asked rhetorically, 'that has studied the growth of the British Empire, and the extension over the world of our race, our language, and our literature, our free institutions, and the spirit which pervades them, can doubt this, – that it is no less under Divine direction, than the one begun at Ur nearly four thousand years ago? There is all along the pathway of human history, an unseen hand, that directs and guides human affairs, to accomplish its great design, in furthering human progress.'[51] This was the key. In an 'age of anxiety,' Abraham's story provided a deeply reassuring political message about the status of the empire and its 'conformity to the general law of evolution, disclosed in the history of human progress.'[52]

Faith in moral progress was one of the dominant themes of late Victorian social thought in Canada, and Mills could hold his own with even the most romantic defenders of the empire. Yet there was also a darker and more pessimistic side to Mills's view of history and of the empire. This dark mood did not usually predominate, but when it did surface it turned Mills away from a rhetoric of reassurance toward one of defiance. And the profound irony is that, in his defiant moods, Mills based his analysis of society on the very Darwinian concepts that he had said could not explain the natural world – which brings us to Mills's social Darwinism and to the third example of the way in which Mills was influenced by the very ideas he claimed to reject.

The best example of Mills's social Darwinism appears in an article published in *The Canadian Magazine* in April 1895 – that is, less than a year after the same periodical had published his refutation of Darwin. The purpose of the article, bluntly entitled 'Saxon or Slav: England or Russia?,' was to awaken Canadians to the military threat posed by imperial Russia. The body of the article consisted of an extended historical analysis of

Russian foreign policy, in which Mills made the case that the czars had long intended to conquer British India as a base from which it could then acquire an Asian empire. 'Can any one doubt,' he asked rhetorically, 'that Russia aims at the conquest of India, and that with the resources of India in her possession she would make herself master of the other portions of Asia?'

Mills realized, however, that Russian foreign policy was hardly a pressing concern to most Canadians. Indeed, he waxed almost Tocquevillian as he described the difficulties of persuading citizens in a democracy to treat distant events as serious political issues, even in those democracies, like England, that were global powers: 'It is easy to conceive that in a period of distress, when the English elector, who toils for his daily bread, finds it difficult to obtain constant employment, and to whom domestic reforms, which if obtained, will, in his opinion, improve his circumstances in life, probably would ask himself the question: "What interest have I in these struggles for Empire? What advantage is it to me that we of the United Kingdom should remain politically connected with our colonies?"'[53] If the English were likely to be unmoved by such ominous developments, Canadians were doubly vulnerable to complacency, for their domestic parochialism was reinforced by the view 'that they can better their position by controlling their external relations, when standing alone, than if they remain politically united to the British Empire.'[54]

While understandable, these sentiments were misguided, according to Mills, for what isolationists did not fully understand was that the likely battle over India was much more than a discrete episode in Anglo-Russian foreign policy. The struggle for India, rather, was the opening salvo in a much larger struggle for 'supremacy' and 'domination,' in which the whole future of British 'civilization' was at stake. In Mills's view, the complacent isolationist who remained indifferent to Russian designs on India was living in a fool's paradise: 'It is sometimes asked, what have we in Canada to do with a war between England and Russia in Central Asia? We have everything to do with it. Whenever that contest comes, it will involve the supremacy of the race to which we belong. It will be a contest to decide whether Russia shall dominate the world, or whether freedom of commerce shall remain in the ascendant, and political freedom be the heritage of any portion of mankind.'[55] The crucial question raised by Russian foreign policy was, therefore, simply put: 'Saxon or Slav – which shall, in the future that lies before us, lead humanity?'[56]

The Anglo-Russian quarrel in Asia, in sum, was likely to become a 'desperate struggle for supremacy.'[57] If Mills was right, the world of high diplomacy would thus come to be characterized by the very 'struggle for existence'[58] that he had earlier said misdescribed the animal world and debased the human. And the likely outcome of this 'struggle for supremacy'? Mills willingly drew out the Darwinian implications of his international relations theory. While it was perfectly clear to Mills that the British empire was morally superior to 'Asiatic despotism,'[59] he feared that those loyal to the British empire did not fully appreciate the political and military advantages enjoyed by unified and despotic states. Again complacency was the enemy, and again the very Darwinian language that he had rejected unequivocally in 'The Missing Link' proved useful as a way of awakening public opinion to the threat at hand. Moral superiority aside, Mills argued, the fact of the matter is that 'it is not always the *best* that survives, but the *fittest*,' and without 'moral stamina, without public virtue, without a spirit of self-sacrifice, it is impossible to maintain the front rank ...'[60]

On one level, Mills was intransigently anti-Darwinian in a way that the 'reconciliationists' were not. Darwinian science threatened the core both of his religious and legal world-view and he rejected it outright as an explanation of the natural world. Yet in crucial respects, Mills actually went further than the 'reconciliationists' in accepting Darwinian principles, for, when translated into social axioms, they helped to justify a form of imperial politics to which he was deeply committed. Where Darwinian science threatened one part of Mills's world, it provided crucial support for another part of his world that was itself under attack.

III

How can we best understand David Mills's curious double identity? One obvious possibility is simply to attribute the apparent contradiction in his anti-Darwinism to opportunism. Mills appropriated what suited his purposes and opposed what he disliked in a way that made him blind to the apparent contradiction between them. This is possible, but we want to argue, with the indirect help of Dick Risk, that there is another, intellectually more interesting explanation for David Mills's various apparently contradictory commitments.

Legal thought in late-nineteenth-century North America is often described as the apogee of 'classical' or 'rule of law' thought, in which lawyers and legal scholars went to great lengths to describe a rational, legal, and liberal universe in which the boundaries between right and wrong, law and politics, individual and state were clearly seen and cleanly enforced. Most legal historians, of course, recognize that this description is something of a caricature; legal thought was invariably more textured and nuanced than this generalization suggests. Still, the view that the late nineteenth century represents the high water mark of classical legal thought prevails.

Dick Risk has never been satisfied with this characterization and the case of David Mills helps to explain why. For Risk, the essence of legal thought in the late nineteenth century was not the strength and purity of its identification with classical legal thought. Rather, what distinguishes the period for Risk is the sense that this was a transitional moment in which lawyers and legal scholars were struggling to reconcile, live with, and sometimes to ignore the tension between two quite different intellectual worlds; the world they had inherited from their forbears and the modern world they had some hand in creating. In short, intellectual tension, not purity, characterizes legal thought in the late nineteenth century. This is the world David Mills inhabited. Caught between a legal world in which meaning was fixed, knowable, and ordered and one in which meaning was uncertain and contested, he struggled to make sense. Mills's attempt to live with the many meanings of Darwinism thus provides another example of Dick Risk's basic insight, and therefore another opportunity to appreciate his contribution to the Canadian intellectual community.

NOTES

1 D. Mills, 'The Missing Link in the Hypothesis of Evolution, or Derivative Creation,' *The Canadian Magazine* 3 (1894), 297–308, 298.
2 On the place of Darwinism, and more generally theories of evolution, in Canada see, for instance, C. Berger, *Science, God and Nature in Victorian Canada* (Toronto: University of Toronto Press 1983); M. Gauvreau, *The Evangelical Century* (Montreal and Kingston: McGill-Queen's University Press 1991); D. Marshall, *Secularizing the Faith* (Toronto: University of Toronto Press 1992); and R. Cook, *The Regenerators* (Toronto: University of Toronto Press 1985). As Cook points out, and as these citations suggest, most of the controversy surrounding Darwin's theories in Canada, 'at least in the non-scientific intellectual world, turned less on the validity of the evolution-by-natural selection hypothesis than on the theological implications which Darwinism appeared to bear for the biblical account of creation and man. It was more a debate about "evolution" than about Darwinism, more about religion than science.' Cook, *The Regenerators*, 9.

3 D. Mills, 'Saxon or Slav: England or Russia?' *The Canadian Magazine* 4 (1895), 518–530, 521.

4 Michael Gauvreau points out that 'there is no comprehensive study of the impact of evolutionary thought on Canadian culture.' That remains as true today as when he wrote in 1991 (see Gauvreau, *Evangelical Century*, 327). The absence of a comprehensive study notwithstanding, there have been some important contributions to our understanding of the impact of evolutionary thought on disciplines and thinkers outside the sciences. See, for instance, Cook, *The Regenerators*; A.B. McKillop, *A Disciplined Intelligence* (Montreal and Kingston: McGill-Queen's University Press 1979); and L. Armour and E. Trott, *The Faces of Reason* (Waterloo: Wilfrid Laurier University Press 1981). The volume by Armour and Trott is enormously helpful in showing the extent to which Canadian philosophy was informed by German Idealism and how these Idealists responded to the threats posed by Darwin (in natural science) and Spencer (in social theory). See, especially, chapter six.

   To the best of our knowledge, there has been virtually nothing written on Darwinism and lawyers in Canada. In the United States, however, there is considerable literature. See, for instance, J. Vetter, 'The Evolution of Holmes, Holmes and Evolution,' *California Law Review* 72 (1984), 343–68; H. Hovenkamp, 'Evolutionary Models in Jurisprudence,' *Texas Law Review* 64 (1985), 645–85. See also P. Stein, *Legal Evolution: The Story of an Idea* (Cambridge: Cambridge University Press 1980).

5 For a more complete biography, see 'David Mills,' *Dictionary of Canadian Biography* 13:707–12.

6 D. Mills, 'The British and American Constitution Compared,' 28 *David Mills Papers* University of Western Ontario, Regional Collection.

7 Ibid., 14.

8 Ibid., 31.

9 The scholarly controversy with this awakened interest in late-nineteenth-century Canadian intellectual history has kindled centres largely on the extent to which Protestant theologians and their parishioners were able to reconcile their religion with the principles of modern science, including evolution. This scholarly debate has recently been summarized in a wonderfully provocative review, written by Ramsay Cook, of Michael Gauvreau and Nancy Christie's *A Full-Orbed Christianity* (Montreal and Kingston: McGill-Queen's University Press 1996). The review, entitled 'Salvation, Sociology and Secularism,' appears in *The Literary Review of Canada* 6(1) (1997), 10–12.

10 D. Mills, 'Missing Link,' 298.

11 Ibid., 300.

12 Ibid., 302.

13 Ibid., 298.
14 Ibid., 308.
15 Ibid., 298.
16 Ibid., 304.
17 Ibid., 308.
18 Ibid., 297.
19 Ibid., 299–300.
20 Ibid., 302.
21 Ibid., 304.
22 Ibid., 308.
23 Cited in E. Mayr; *The Growth of Biological Thought* (Cambridge, Mass.: Harvard University Press 1982), 267. The quotation is from *The Origin of Species*.
24 D. Mills, 'Missing Link,' 302.
25 Ibid., 304. Italics in original.
26 Ibid.
27 Ibid., 301.
28 Ibid.
29 Ibid., 302.
30 Ibid., 305. Emphasis added.
31 On rule of law or classical legal thought, see T. Grey, 'Langdell's Orthodoxy,' *University of Pittsburgh Law Review* 45 (1983), 1–53; D. Kennedy, 'Toward an Historical Understanding of Legal Consciousness: The Case of Classical Legal Thought in America, 1850–1940,' *Research in Law and Sociology* 3 (1980), 3–24; and R. Gordon, 'Legal Thought and Legal Practice in the Age of American Enterprise, 1870–1920,' in G. Geison, ed., *Professions and Professional Ideologies in America, 1730–1940* (Chapel Hill: University of North Carolina Press 1983).
32 D. Sugarman, 'Legal Theory, the Common Law Mind, and the Making of the Textbook Tradition,' in William Twining, ed., *Legal Theory and the Common Law* (Oxford: Basil Blackwell 1986), 30.
33 Ibid.
34 O.W. Holmes, *The Common Law* (M. Howe ed. 1963). On Holmes, see also R. Gordon, 'Holmes' *Common Law* as Legal and Social Science,' *Hofstra Law Review* 10 (1982), 719–46.
35 See R.C.B. Risk, 'A.H.F. Lefroy: Common Law in Late-Nineteenth-Century Canada: On Burying One's Grandfather,' *University of Toronto Law Journal* 41 (1991), 307–31.
36 London *Advertiser*, 7 February 1883.
37 London *Advertiser*, 13 October 1882. Mills's rule of law thought applied to Canadian federalism is developed at greater length in R. Vipond, *Liberty and*

Community: Canadian Federalism and the Failure of the Constitution (Albany: SUNY Press 1991).
38 Canada, Parliament, *House of Commons Debates*, 11 April 1877, 1369.
39 Canada, Parliament, *House of Commons Debates*, 1 April 1884, 1249.
40 Canada, Parliament, *House of Commons Debates*, 1 April 1885, 883.
41 Canada, Parliament, *House of Commons Debates*, 1875, 576.
42 London *Advertiser*, 14 March 1883.
43 S. Zeller, *Inventing Canada: Early Victorian Science and the Idea of a Transcontinental Nation* (Toronto: University of Toronto Press 1987).
44 D. Mills, 'Missing Link,' 306.
45 Ibid.
46 Ibid., 302–3.
47 S. Gould, *The Mismeasure of Man* (New York: Norton 1981).
48 M. Van Die, *An Evangelical Mind: Nathaniel Burwash and the Methodist Tradition in Canada, 1839–1918* (Montreal and Kingston: McGill-Queen's University Press 1989).
49 See Cook, *Regenerators*, 8–14.
50 D. Mills, 'The Higher Criticism,' *Mills Papers*, University of Western Ontario, Regional Collection.
51 D. Mills, 'Abraham as a Leader of a Political Revolution,' *Mills Papers*, 5–6.
52 Ibid., 17.
53 D. Mills, 'Saxon or Slav,' 528.
54 Ibid., 529.
55 Ibid., 528.
56 Ibid., 518.
57 Ibid., 522.
58 D. Mills, 'Missing Link,' 300.
59 D. Mills, 'Saxon or Slav,' 529.
60 Ibid., 521 (emphasis added).

R.C.B. Risk Bibliography

Billings v. Riden. *University of Toronto Faculty of Law Review* 16 (1958), 126–8.

Recent Developments in Contracts. In Law Society of Upper Canada, ed. *Special Lectures of the Law Society of Upper Canada.* Toronto: Richard de Boo Publishers 1966, 207–57.

Condominiums and Canada. *University of Toronto Law Journal* 18 (1968), 1–72.

Current Practices and Possibilities for Improving Systems of Land Titles and Records in Canada and the United States: A Comparative Analysis. *Conference Proceedings.* Indianapolis: Indiana Law School 1968, 163–82.

The Computer and the Title to Land. *Canadian Surveyor* 23 (1969), 89–93.

The Records of Title to Land: A Plea for Reform. *University of Toronto Law Journal* 21 (1971), 465–97.

The Legal Concept of the Condominium and the Legislative Response, with Particular Reference to Ontario. In H.N. Janisch, ed., *The Law and Condominium Development.* Halifax: Dalhousie University Faculty of Law 1973), 2–11.

A Prospectus for Canadian Legal History. *Dalhousie Law Journal* 1 (1973), 227–45.

The Nineteenth-Century Foundations of the Business Corporation in Ontario. *University of Toronto Law Journal* 23 (1973), 270–306.

The Golden Age: The Law About the Market in Nineteenth-Century Ontario. *University of Toronto Law Journal* 26 (1976), 307–46.

The Last Golden Age: Property and the Allocation of Losses in Ontario in the Nineteenth Century. *University of Toronto Law Journal* 27 (1977), 199–239.

The Law and the Economy in Mid-Nineteenth Century Ontario: A Perspective. *University of Toronto Law Journal* 27 (1977), 403–38.

With B.J. Reiter, *Real Estate Law*. Toronto: Emond, Montgomery 1979.
With J.M. Evans, H.N. Janisch, and D.J. Mullan. *Administrative Law: Cases, Text, and Materials*. Toronto: Emond, Montgomery 1980.
The Law and the Economy in Mid-Nineteenth-Century Ontario: The A Perspective. In D.H. Flaherty, ed., *Essays in the History of Canadian Law*. Volume 1. Toronto: The Osgoode Society for Canadian Legal History 1981, 88–131.
A Long, Sad Story: Siting Transmission Lines in Ontario. *University of Toronto Law Journal* 31 (1981), 27–71.
With B.N. McLellan and B.J. Reiter. *Real Estate Law*. 2nd ed. Toronto: Emond, Montgomery 1982.
This Nuisance of Litigation: The Origins of Workers' Compensation in Ontario. In D.H. Flaherty, ed., *Essays in the History of Canadian Law*. Volume 2. Toronto: The Osgoode Society for Canadian Legal History 1983, 418–91.
Sir William R. Meredith C.J.O.: The Search for Authority. *Dalhousie Law Journal* 7 (1983), 713–41.
The Beginnings of Regulation. In E.G. Baldwin, ed., *The Cambridge Lectures: Selected Papers Based upon Lectures Delivered at the Conference of the Canadian Institute for Advanced Legal Studies*. Toronto: Butterworths 1983, 252–5.
Lawyers, Courts, and the Rise of the Regulatory State. *Dalhousie Law Journal* 9 (1984), 31–54.
John Willis – A Tribute. *Dalhousie Law Journal* 9 (1984), 521–54.
With J.M. Evans, H.N. Janisch, and D.J. Mullan. *Administrative Law: Cases, Text, and Materials*. 2nd ed. Toronto: Emond, Montgomery 1984.
With B.N. McLellan and B.J. Reiter. *Real Estate Law* 3rd ed. Toronto: Emond, Montgomery 1986.
John Skirving Ewart: The Legal Thought. *University of Toronto Law Journal* 37 (1987), 335–57.
Volume 1 of the Journal: A Tribute and a Belated Review. *University of Toronto Law Journal* 37 (1987), 193–211.
New Directions for Legal History. In D. and R. Gagan, eds., *New Directions for the Study of Ontario's Past*. Hamilton, Ont.: McMaster University 1988), 117–26.
With J.M. Evans, H.N. Janisch, and D.J. Mullan. *Administrative Law: Cases, Text, and Materials,* 3rd ed. Toronto: Emond, Montgomery 1989.
Canadian Courts Under the Influence. *University of Toronto Law Journal* 40 (1990), 687–737.
Constitutional Thought in the Late Nineteenth Century. *Manitoba Law Journal* 20 (1991), 196–203.
A.H.F. Lefroy: Common Law Thought in Late Nineteenth-Century Canada: On Burying One's Grandfather. *University of Toronto Law Journal* 41 (1991), 307–31.

Blake and Liberty. In J. Ajzenstat, ed., *Canadian Constitutionalism, 1791–1991*. Ottawa: Canadian Study of Parliament Group 1992, 195–211.

With B.N. McLellan and B.J. Reiter. *Real Estate Law*. 4th ed. Toronto: Emond, Montgomery 1992.

The Privy Council and Its Scholars: Canadian Constitutional Law. Winnipeg: University of Manitoba Faculty of Law 1992.

With P. Macklem, C.J. Rogerson, K.E. Swinton, L.E. Weinrib, and J.D. Whyte. *Canadian Constitutional Law*. 2 vols. Toronto: Emond, Montgomery 1994.

With J.M. Evans, H.N. Janisch, and D.J. Mullan. *Administrative Law: Cases, Text, and Materials*. 4th ed. Toronto: Emond, Montgomery 1995.

The Puzzle of Jurisdiction. *South Carolina Law Review* 46 (1995), 703–18.

With R.C. Vipond. 'Rights Talk in Canada in the Late Nineteenth Century: The Good Sense and Right Feeling of the People. *Law and History Review* 14 (1996), 1–32.

The Scholars and the Constitution: P.O.G.G. and the Privy Council. *Manitoba Law Journal* 23 (1996), 496–523.

Constitutional Scholarship in the Late-Nineteenth Century: Making Federalism Work. *University of Toronto Law Journal* 46 (1996), 427–57.

With P. Macklem, C.J. Rogerson, K.E. Swinton, L.E. Weinrib, and J.D. Whyte. *Canadian Constitutional Law*. 2 vols. 2nd ed. Toronto: Emond, Montgomery 1997.

In Memoriam: John Willis. *University of Toronto Law Journal* 47 (1997), 301–4.

The Many Minds of W.P.M. Kennedy. *University of Toronto Law Journal* 48 (1998), 353–86.

The Scholars and the Constitution: Models of Canadian Federalism. Unpublished ms.

W.P.M. Kennedy's Canadian Constitutional Thought. Unpublished ms.

1995 David Williams, *Just Lawyers: Seven Portraits*
Hamar Foster and John McLaren, eds., *Essays in the History of Canadian Law: Volume VI – British Columbia and the Yukon*
W.H. Morrow, ed., *Northern Justice: The Memoirs of Mr Justice William G. Morrow*
Beverley Boissery, *A Deep Sense of Wrong: The Treason Trials and Transportation to New South Wales of Lower Canadian Rebels after the 1838 Rebellion*
1996 Carol Wilton, ed., *Essays in the History of Canadian Law: Volume VII – Inside the Law: Canadian Law Firms in Historical Perspective*
William Kaplan, *Bad Judgment: The Case of Mr Justice Leo A. Landreville*
Murray Greenwood and Barry Wright, eds., *Canadian State Trials: Volume I – Law, Politics, and Security Measures, 1608–1837*
1997 James W. St.G. Walker, *'Race,' Rights, and the Law in the Supreme Court of Canada: Historical Case Studies*
Lori Chambers, *Married Women and Property Law in Victorian Ontario*
Patrick Brode, *Casual Slaughters and Accidental Judgments: Canadian War Crimes and Prosecutions, 1944–1948*
Ian Bushnell, *The Federal Court of Canada: A History, 1875–1992*
1998 Sidney Harring, *White Man's Law: Native People in Nineteenth-Century Canadian Jurisprudence*
Peter Oliver, *'Terror to Evil-Doers': Prisons and Punishments in Nineteenth-Century Ontario*
1999 Constance Backhouse, *Colour-Coded: A Legal History of Racism in Canada, 1900–1950*
G. Blaine Baker and Jim Phillips, eds., *Essays in the History of Canadian Law: Volume VIII – In Honour of R.C.B. Risk*
Richard W. Pound, *Chief Justice W.R. Jackett: By the Law of the Land*
David Vanek, *Fulfilment: Memoirs of a Criminal Court Judge*